THE LATIN AMERICAN COOKBOOK

THE

LATIN AMERICAN COOKBOOK

VIRGILIO MARTÍNEZ
WITH NICHOLAS GILL
AND MATER INICIATIVA

Introduction

Growing up in Peru's capital city, Lima, my perception of food from other Latin American countries, such as Argentina or Brazil, not to mention the furthest corners of Peru, was limited. Some of the more obscure ingredients would find their way to Lima, though I had a poor understanding of their possibilities. Traveling through the region, however, has given me the chance to discover firsthand how spectacular our food is, but also how much remains to be revealed.

One of the main objectives of our research center, Mater Iniciativa, is to investigate the food in Peru in its natural, social, and cultural context, and to shed light on and preserve the richness of our biodiversity. In this sense, it's relevant for us to keep a permanent record of everything we observe, to spread this new knowledge, and integrate it into our vision of cuisine as it applies to our restaurants. We have become aware of the opportunities in identifying new ways to address issues surrounding the recovery and conservation of native ingredients. With Mater, we traveled through our home territory, exploring different geographies, but over time, we couldn't find any justification for limiting our research to Peru only and so we decided to expand across Latin America.

Exploring a variety of ecosystems, altitudes, social dynamics, and culinary preparations, the ingredients and recipes that we have documented have their own origins and histories that predate us. Many recipes have not stopped evolving since the day they were created. Different cultures have changed their composition, and ingredients have been adapted to different landscapes and seasons. One person might prepare a dish in one way, while someone else will do it another way. A Peruvian ceviche, for example, is of Pre-Colombian origins, but modern recipes include limes and onions that were introduced by the Spanish and the treatment of the fish has been tweaked by Japanese immigrants in Lima. Each recipe is woven from complex layers that tell a story of their history. In collating the recipes for this book, we have chosen preparations we thought showcased the spirit of Latin American cuisine.

Through the process of creating this Latin American cookbook, we carefully observed what we Latin Americans have in common: the meals we serve at home, the foods made in the streets and in our markets, and what an emblematic neighborhood restaurant has served for decades. While the flavors may change from one place to another, these recipes are our shared identity. Our commitment to making delicious things to eat unites us all.

Potatoes, tomatoes, peppers, corn, and cocoa have become staple ingredients the world over. Wherever you are, you are eating Latin American on a daily basis, whether you realize it or not. We have a huge variety of nutrient-laden resources, with the wisdom to use them without disturbing the environment, and to adapt them easily to imminent changes. Our region serves as the world's food pantry. We do firmly believe that the world of food can encourage different sectors to achieve our region's social, economic, and cultural development.

For so many years, we viewed the sophistication of French and Italian food with admiration, feeling perhaps that the gap between European and Latin American cuisines was too great to overcome. But over time, we learned to appreciate the luxury in our own native foods and culinary traditions, and to appreciate the artisans who make them a reality. When we talk about a cuisine that represents us, we talk about hundreds of colors and shapes closely related to our culture, telling us about the things of which we are made.

Putting together a book that covers a geography this extensive with any sort of geographic and cultural balance is no small feat, so our approach in how we gathered and tested recipes included a wide variety of sources. Our primary method, and often the most efficient one, was simply to travel to a recipe's source to experience it in all its beauty, implanting the flavors in our minds. Like the *pirarucu com açaí* that was eaten in the Mercado Ver-o-Peso in Belém beside the hum of the Amazon River, or the steaming hot bowls of *caldo de costilla* that soothed our souls on a chilly, late night in Bogotá. Other recipes were recommended by our hundreds of colleagues around the region, while others were brought to our attention by studying old recipe books, many of them out of print or buried in the deepest corners of the internet. Regardless of how we found them, it was rare to come to a concrete conclusion about how a recipe should be prepared. For example, in trying to determine the proper way to "clap" roti from Guyana, every person we met or was in a YouTube video we watched, each did it a little bit differently. Even amongst the kitchen teams at Central, Kjolle, Mil, and Mayo, coming from every part of the region and tasked with recreating many of the recipes, it would be illogical to expect any single recipe could satisfy the memories of their grandmother's cooking. Our aim was simply to come up with recipes that wouldn't be out of place in their place of origin, that if someone from that place tastes the dish, even if it isn't exactly like how their family would make it, they would find the ingredients and the preparation fitting.

We like to think of our cookbook as a snapshot of Latin American food. We aimed to be faithful to the roots of the dishes researched, though that doesn't necessarily mean they should be prepared in the same way as the first time they were created, or that they will taste exactly like they do in their place of origin. They might not even taste exactly the way we made them. Even if you could source every single ingredient in the same condition from a particular place where that recipe comes from, the very air you are cooking in will have some effect.

It isn't just acceptable to substitute ingredients, it is expected. The glossary in this book (pages 413–416) will help you understand exactly what each ingredient is, as some regional names might sound strange, but are actually something that's familiar. In some recipes we also mention easy substitutions, but you don't have to use them. Use what's seasonal around you. Find the best ingredients you can and see what you can make with them.

The truth is that Latin Americans often don't follow strict recipes. We like to improvise while cooking and be spontaneous, all the while thinking how a dish can change slightly when we are missing an ingredient, or get creative when we feel the impulse to use something

completely new in our cooking. I wonder if this is because we have gone through tough times and have had to make do with whatever we had at hand. We have never felt that the lack of an ingredient limits us from bringing a dish to the table. We have never come up with a standardized recipe for a mother sauce, like the French Hollandaise, which is entirely replicable, with exactly the same results, anywhere in the world. Imagine if a Oaxacan *mole* tasted the same wherever you were? How much would be lost? In Peru, some insist that you cannot make ceviche without *ají limo*, a native chile pepper, while others are certain that without the limes from the north of the country, your *leche de tigre* will never be quite right. Grandmothers cooking for their families, the heads of local restaurants big and small, passionate self-taught cooks, and young culinary students finding their way will make their own versions of a recipe, adding the flavors and ingredients around them, adapting for their own use. This is the way we understand our cooking. It also explains why our cuisine is so versatile and, at the same time, can be both traditional and contemporary.

From the Rio Grande to Cape Horn, this territory is tremendously vast and diverse, and extremely complex. There are glaciers and wetlands, cloud forests and deserts, savannahs and coral reefs. Within these rich biomes are roughly half of the world's biodiversity, giving us an almost endless assortment of flavors and textures to use in the kitchen. Many of the species found in Latin America are found only here and will probably never be able to adapt or be replicated elsewhere. We also recognize that our cuisine was born from a variety of geographical roots: by cultures that built ancient cities, left faint traces, were brought forcibly to the region, displaced by war and a changing climate, and came from the furthest reaches of the globe in search of a better life. The variety of recipes that have arisen and continue to come to life in this biological and cultural masterwork that we call home is seemingly endless. By cooking many of these recipes, we are encouraging

that they are preserved, while appreciating the diversity of ingredients that make them unique and the culinary heritage of the people who created them.

Food talks, sometimes a lot. The recipes described here express our enormous appreciation for the unceasing grandeur and promise of the cuisines of Latin America, which, for the purposes of this book, extends from Mexico in North America across the entirety of South and Central America, including English, French, Dutch, and German speaking countries and regions and countless indigenous territories, among others. While the names in English are generic in most cases, just enough for a reader to understand what it is, below each recipe title you will find names listed from a recipe's place of origin. Sometimes they have multiple names reflecting how they are used in different regions or by different cultural groups. For example, corn masa steamed in a corn husk might be called a *humita* in Peru, but in Brazil a very similar recipe is called a *pamonha* and in Mexico an *uchepo*. Whenever we could, through names, headnotes, and the choice of preparations and ingredients, we were careful to respect to a recipe's roots and the cultures that made it possible.

While there are likely many recipes you have heard of, we hope you will find a few surprises too. We hope to have succeeded in selecting dishes that can be prepared easily enough, that will transport our readers to each destination, and encourage them to learn more about the remarkable stories behind them. Don't take every direction so seriously. Adapt each recipe to your own personal time and place. There's no right or wrong here. The very act of cooking helps keep the richness of Latin American food present, visible, and relevant. For those who are reviving the flavors, textures, and scents embedded in their hearts, or those making a recipe for the first time, share them with your friends and loved ones. The true spirit of our cuisine is how it can bring us all closer.

Gluten-free	
Dairy-free	
Vegetarian	
Vegan	
5 ingredients or fewer	
30 minutes or less	

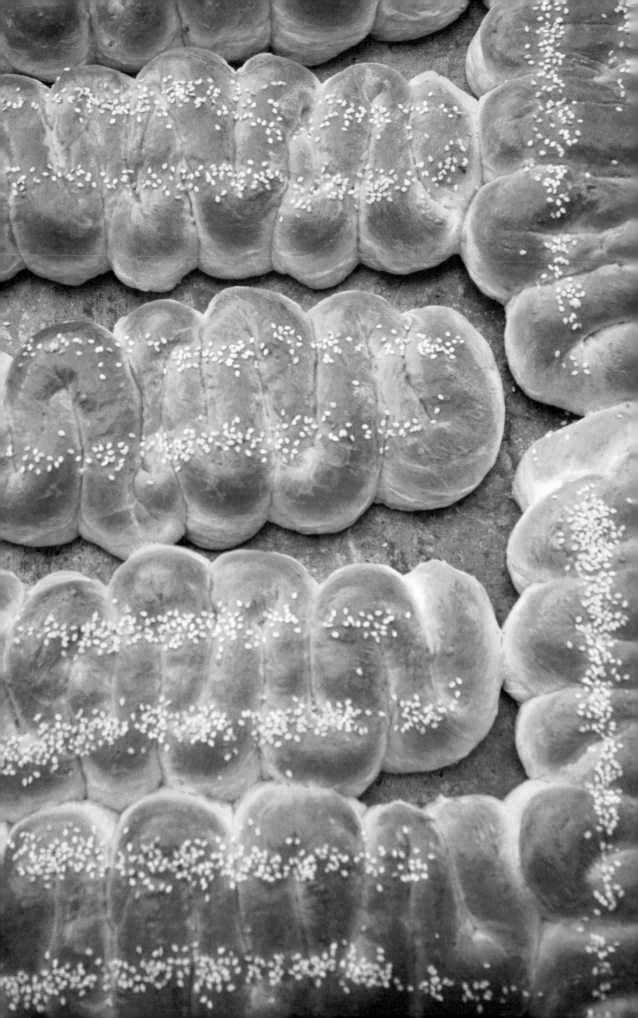

Breads and Baked Goods

Prior to the arrival of wheat, fluffy white breads were nowhere to be found in Latin America, though there were other forms of bread. Besides tortillas in all their wonderful forms, there were also dense, unleavened flatbreads and cakes made from corn in Mesoamerica. Throughout the Amazon and other tropical regions, breads were often—and still are—made from coarse manioc flour. Elsewhere, dough was wrapped around sticks and baked over coals or cooked in clay ovens. Still, the introduction of wheat into native diets wasn't exactly a given.

While Spanish and Portuguese settlers and convent kitchens established their own breadmaking traditions throughout the region, in many places they took on a life of their own. Communities from Ambato, Ecuador to Minas Gerais, Brazil created breads with unique shapes, using the ingredients they had on hand, and developed their own techniques for making dough. In the tropical regions of Brazil, Paraguay, and northeastern Argentina, indigenous yuca breads were adapted to the milk, eggs, and cheese that became available. In the Andes, every town developed their own styles of bread, often baked in communal wood-burning ovens. There are *t'anta wawas*, sweet breads shaped like babies wrapped in blankets, and sourdoughs made from the dregs of *chicha*, a corn beer. In Afro-Antillean communities along Central America's Caribbean coast, breads are often infused with coconut milk, while in Guyana, roti, brought from India, gets clapped in the air to release air pockets in the dough. There are flours from quinoa, potatoes, chickpeas, and coca leaves. There are breads for celebrations, and others for sandwiches. There are breads baked in clay ovens and others cooked in the sun. While gas ovens and industrial flours have found a place in Latin American society, the craft of artisan breadmaking refuses to be displaced.

Johnny Cakes

Belize, Honduras

Preparation time: 20 minutes
Cooking time: 15 minutes
Makes: 15

Johnny Cakes are a breakfast staple in Belize and are eaten in numerous Afro-Latin American communities along Central America's Atlantic coast. Related to the cornmeal flatbread of the same name, eaten by indigenous North Americans, and still commonly made in New England, they are thought to have traveled south in the sixteenth century during the Atlantic slave trade—they are occasionally called "journey cakes," as these rolls have been known to last for weeks on long sea voyages. In the Caribbean, the cornmeal is replaced by wheat flour, and the cakes are eaten with butter and marmalade, or used to make breakfast sandwiches filled with ham and cheese.

    2½ cups/12 oz (340 g) all-purpose (plain) flour
    2 teaspoons baking powder
    1 teaspoon salt
    1 teaspoon sugar
    ½ cup/4 oz (115 g) butter
    2 cups/16 fl oz (475 ml) coconut milk

Preheat the oven to 400°F/200°C/Gas Mark 6.
    Sift the flour, baking powder, and salt into a large bowl. Stir in the sugar, and add the butter, cut into small cubes. Using your fingertips, rub the butter into the flour until it has a crumbly texture. Add half the coconut milk to the mixture and continue working the dough with your hands. Add the remaining coconut milk a few table-spoons at a time, just until the dough comes together. You may not need all of it. Do not overmix the dough.
    Roll the dough into a log about 12–15 inches (30–38 cm) long, then cut the log into 15 equal pieces. Form each piece into a ball and place on an ungreased baking sheet. Slightly flatten the balls with your palm and mark them with a fork, as you would with cookies or pie dough.
    Bake for 10–15 minutes until nicely browned. If you have a broiler (grill), use it during the last 2 minutes of baking to ensure a fully browned crust; if not, increase the oven temperature for the last few minutes to 425°F/220°C/Gas Mark 7. Serve hot.

Belizean Fry Jacks

Belize

Preparation time: 20 minutes,
plus 20 minutes resting
Cooking time: 15 minutes
Makes: 8–10

These fried pieces of dough, usually shaped into discs, frequently appear on breakfast tables in Belize. They are often served alongside, or stuffed with, refried beans and eggs.

    2 cups/9 oz (260 g) flour, plus extra for dusting
    3 teaspoons baking powder
    1 teaspoon salt
    2 tablespoons (30 g) butter
    ¾ cup/6 fl oz (175 ml) coconut milk
    vegetable oil, for deep-frying

Sift the flour, baking powder, and salt into a large bowl. Add the butter, cut into small cubes. Using your fingertips, rub the butter into the flour, until it has a crumbly texture.
    Add the coconut milk a few tablespoons at a time. The dough should be soft, but not sticky. Divide the dough in 8–10 equal parts. Set aside and let the dough rest for 15–20 minutes.
    Lightly flour your work surface and roll each piece of dough into a disc, cut in half and then make a small cut in the middle of each piece.
    Pour enough vegetable oil for deep-frying into a large, heavy pan, making sure it is no more than two-thirds full, and heat to 350°F/177°C.
    Deep-fry in small batches, between 3–5 minutes, or until golden brown. Remove with a skimmer and place on a plate lined with paper towels, to absorb excess oil. Serve warm.

Brazilian Cheese Rolls

Pão de queijo 🖻
Brazil

Preparation time: 20 minutes
Cooking time: 20 minutes
Makes: 12

An unleavened, naturally gluten-free cheese roll with a thin shell and elastic center that is ubiquitous in snack bars and bakeries, *pão de queijo* has become one of Brazil's most common national recipes only in the last half a century. Its exact origins are murky, though it is believed that slaves in the state of Minas Gerais made a simple bread from leftover yuca starch, or tapioca, on farms where wheat didn't grow well. Later, probably in the late nineteenth century when the dairy industry in Minas began to develop, milk and cheese were added. Around the 1950s, the recipe voyaged beyond Minas and bakeries such as Casa do Pão de Queijo, which began in 1967 as a single location and now counts hundreds of locations, brought it to every corner of the country. In the 1990s, Minas Gerais-born president Itamar Franco insisted that *pão de queijo* be served at government meetings, earning his administration the name "república do pão de queijo."
    Queijo mineiro, or Minas cheese, is a salty, semi-soft cow's milk cheese that can be *frescal* (fresh), *meia-cura* (half-matured), and *curado* (matured), which is most common for *pão de queijo*. *Polvilho azedo*, or fermented tapioca flour, is generally preferred and gives the bread a slight tang, though *polvilho doce*, sweet tapioca flour, can also be used.

    1 egg
    1½ cups/6 oz (175 g) tapioca flour
    ⅓ cup/2½ fl oz (80 ml) olive oil
    ⅔ cup/5 fl oz (160 ml) milk
    ¼ cup/2¼ oz (65 g) Minas cheese, or any semi-soft aged cheese, shredded

Preheat the oven to 400°F/200°C/Gas Mark 6.
    Place all the ingredients in the bowl of a mixer, or knead them by hand until you have smooth dough.
    Divide the dough into 12 equal-sized balls. Place them on an oven tray lined with parchment paper.
    Bake for 15–20 minutes, until golden brown.

Breads and Baked Goods

Brazilian Cheese Rolls

Mapuche Wheat Bread

Catuto, mültrün 🍳
Chile

Preparation time: 20 minutes
Cooking time: 1 hour 15 minutes   Makes: 15–20

Also called *mültrün* in Mapudungun, catuto is an oblong bread made from ground *trigo mote*, or wheat berries, which are wheat that has been boiled and removed from its husk. While wheat was introduced by the Spanish, the Mapuche adapted their process of removing the husk as they did with corn, as Chilean soldier Francisco Núñez de Pineda y Bascuñán noted when he was held prisoner in the 1620s. Traditionally, it is mashed with a stone called *kudi*, then mixed with lard and cooked over hot coals, a process known as *rescoldo*.

2 lb 3 oz (1 kg) wheat berries
1/8 teaspoon salt
1 tablespoon butter (or lard)
vegetable oil (if frying)

Cover the wheat berries with water and bring to a boil, then reduce to a simmer and let cook for about 1 hour, or until soft. Strain. In a mortar, grind the wheat until it becomes a paste. Place it in a bowl and incorporate the salt and butter with your fingertips.

Once the dough is dense, form into 15–20 long, relatively flat pieces with pointed ends.

You can either bake them in an oven heated to 400°F/200°C/Gas Mark 6 or fry them in 2–3 tablespoons of oil. In either case, they should take about 4 minutes to get slightly golden brown.

Serve with honey or preserve (jam). In Chile, they are often served as a savory snack too, with a garlic and herb sauce, or *ají pebre*.

Colombian Cheese Rolls

Almojábanas
Colombia

Preparation time: 25 minutes
Cooking time: 40 minutes   Makes: 8

Similar to *pandebono* or Brazilian *pão de queijo* but made with precooked corn flour, though unlike the cheese fritters of the same name from Puerto Rico, *almojábanas* are found in cafés and bakeries and served alongside coffee all over Colombia. They are especially prevalent in the administrative departments of Boyacá and Cundinamarca. While cottage cheese or any generic *queso fresco* can be substituted, the signature flavor comes from *cuajada*, a watery fresh white cheese made from pressing curds of whole pasteurized milk together.

1 cup/4 oz (120 g) masarepa (precooked corn flour/maize flour) or corn (maize) flour
2 cups/1 lb (450 g) *cuajada* cheese (or use shredded *queso fresco*)
1 tablespoon melted butter
1/2 tablespoon baking powder
1/4 tablespoon salt
2 eggs
2 tablespoons milk

Preheat the oven to 400°F/200°C/Gas Mark 6.

In a blender, mix the *masarepa* with the cheese to form a paste/dough.

Transfer to a bowl and add the melted butter, baking powder, salt, eggs, and milk. Slowly knead the dough. If the dough seems especially sticky, add extra *masarepa*. Once you get a soft dough, divide it into 8 equal parts.

Shape into small balls and place on an oven tray. Bake for 30–40 minutes until golden brown. Serve hot.

Roti

Paratha Roti
French Guiana, Guyana, Suriname

Preparation time: 10 minutes,
plus 1 hour resting
Cooking time: 40 minutes   Makes: 6

More than one-third of Guyanese people have heritage from the Indian subcontinent, though the custom of making roti has expanded to nearly all parts of the population, including indigenous groups far from the coast. This common flatbread is also made elsewhere in the southern Caribbean, though the Guyanese have added their own special touch, which they call clapping. The method involves tossing the hot dough up into the air right after cooking and clapping it with both hands. The process releases air pockets and gives the bread a flakier texture. In the Guyanas, roti is cooked on a *tawa*, a flat metal pan used specifically for roti, though a cast-iron frying pan works just as well.

3 1/2 cups/1 lb (460 g) all-purpose (plain) flour
1 1/2 teaspoons baking powder
1/4 teaspoon salt
1 teaspoon butter
1 1/2 cups/12 fl oz (350 ml) water
1/4 cup/2 fl oz (60 ml) vegetable oil (or ghee or melted butter)

Sift the flour, baking powder, and salt into a large bowl. Add the butter and mix with your fingertips until incorporated. Add the water and knead until you get a smooth dough.

Place a clean, damp tea towel on the surface of the dough to prevent a crust from forming, then let rest for 45 minutes.

Divide the dough into 6 equal parts. Using a rolling pin, roll out each of the pieces into a large disc, about 1/8 inch (3 mm) thick. Roll up each dough disc from one end to the other (like a cigar) and coil each into a spiral shape. Pinch the ends into the coil.

Place a damp tea towel over the dough spirals and let rest for about 15 minutes.

Heat a cast-iron frying pan over high heat.

Roll out one dough spiral into a thin round about 5 inches (13 cm) in diameter. Brush one side with oil (or ghee), place oil side down in the heated frying pan and cook until tiny bubbles begin to form, about 5 minutes.

Flip the roti and brush the top with more oil or ghee. Cook for a further 1 minute, or until brown flecks appear.

Remove the roti from the pan and, while it is still hot, toss it in the air and clap it between your hands to release the air pockets, using a tea towel if it is too hot to handle. As an alternative to clapping, you can place the roti in a deep bowl and cover with a plate before shaking it vigorously. Set the bread aside; you can keep it wrapped inside a clean tea towel to maintain the heat.

Repeat with the remaining dough rounds to make more roti. Serve warm.

Breads and Baked Goods

Mapuche Wheat Bread

Paraguayan Cornbread

Sopa Paraguaya
Paraguay

Preparation time: 25 minutes
Cooking time: 45 minutes
Serves: 10

Despite its name, which translates to Paraguayan soup, this isn't a soup at all, but rather a cheesy cornbread. Allegedly, Paraguay's first president Carlos Antonio López told his cook to make him a creamy soup with milk, fresh cheese, egg, and corn flour, though she added too much corn flour. Without time to make another, she placed it in a cast-iron frying pan and baked it in a *tatakua*, a clay and adobe oven, a method not so different from the way that Guaraní cooked a dough made from cornmeal in banana leaves over hot ashes. Jokingly, the president, who enjoyed it, called it soup.

2¼ cups/9 oz (250 g) chopped white onions
1½ cups plus 2 teaspoons/12 oz (350 g) butter
8 eggs
10½ oz (300 g) *queso Paraguay* (or any soft mild cheese), diced or shredded
3½ teaspoons salt
7 cups/2 lb 3 oz (1 kg) corn (maize) flour
4 cups/32 fl oz (1 liter) milk

Preheat the oven to 375°F/190°C/Gas Mark 5.

Stir-fry the onions in the butter over low heat until translucent, then set aside and let cool. In a bowl, mix the eggs with the cheese, then add the fried onions and salt. Add the corn (maize) flour a little at a time, alternating with milk to create a dough that is not too liquid, but not too solid either. Think of a cake batter.

Pour the mixture into a 13 x 9-inch (33 x 23-cm) oven dish greased with butter and bake for 40 minutes until golden brown at the edges and firm in the center. Let cool, before serving, cut into squares.

Three Point Bread

Pan de tres puntas
Peru

Preparation time: 15 minutes,
plus 1 hour 40 minutes rising
Cooking time: 10–20 minutes
(depending on type of oven)
Makes: 30

This triangular bread, traditionally baked in wood-fired clay ovens, is found on the tables of families in Arequipa, often accompanying rich, spicy stews like *Adobo Arequipeño* (Arequipa-Style Pork Stew, page 288), where it gets dipped in the broth.

2.4 oz (20 g) fresh yeast
1½ cups/12½ fl oz (370 ml) warm water
3 teaspoons sea salt
⅓ cup/1½ oz (40 g) sugar
5 cups/1 lb 6 oz (625 g) bread flour (strong white flour)
1 tablespoon (15 g) lard (or butter)
vegetable oil, for greasing

In a bowl, dissolve the yeast in the warm water with the salt, sugar, and 1 tablespoon of the flour. Let it rest for 1 hour in a warm place.

Place the remaining flour in a large bowl and mix with the lard. Create a small well in the middle and pour the yeast mixture in the well in the flour and knead with your hands until it becomes a soft dough. Cover with a tea towel and leave to rise for 40 minutes in a warm place.

Preheat the oven to 375°F/190°C/Gas Mark 5 or have a wood-fired oven heated to 440°F/226°C.

Pour a little vegetable oil on a paper towel and grease a clean work surface.

Place the dough on the surface and shape it into 30 balls, each 1½ oz (40 g). Slightly flatten each ball with the palm of your hand then take one side of the flat ball and fold it toward the middle. Repeat the process with two other sides to shape the dough into a triangle. Space at least 1 inch (2.5 cm) apart on a baking sheet lined with parchment paper and bake for 10 minutes in a wood-fired oven or 20 minutes in a conventional oven, or until golden brown.

Andean Bread Baby

T'anta wawa
Bolivia, Ecuador, Peru

Preparation time: 35 minutes
Cooking time: 30 minutes

Makes: 6

A combination of the Aymara and Quechua words for bread and baby, *t'anta* and *wawa*, these baby-shaped breads are eaten throughout the Andes in some form or another. They likely date to colonial times as an adaptation of the ritual of parading mummified humans, often decorated with paint and wigs for celebrations. Much like *pan de muerto* in Mexico, these painted, swaddled loaves are eaten mostly on or around All Saints' Day, and left as offerings at gravesites.

7½ cups/2 lb 3 oz (1 kg) all-purpose (plain) flour
½ cup minus 1 tablespoon/3 oz (80 g) sugar
1 oz (25 g) salt
1⅓ cups/10½ oz (300 g) cold butter
1¼ cups/10 fl oz (300 ml) milk
4 eggs, beaten
2 oz (50 g) fresh yeast

For the frosting (icing)
1 egg white
¾ cup/2½ oz (75 g) confectioner's (icing) sugar
food coloring in colors of your choice

Preheat the oven to 375°F/190°C/Gas Mark 5.

In a bowl, mix together the flour, sugar, and salt, then work the butter in with your fingertips.

In another bowl, combine the milk, eggs, and yeast.

Mix both preparations together until you get a soft, uniform dough.

Cut the dough into 6 equal parts. Shape each piece into the form of a doll. Every region seems to form the bread into a different shape. Some prefer the dolls to look a bit like a swaddled baby, while others form heads and occasionally arms and legs. There's no right or wrong. Place the loaves on two lined baking sheets.

Bake the breads for 30 minutes, or until golden brown. Take them out of the oven and let them cool down out of the oven trays.

For the frosting (icing), mix the egg white with the confectioner's (icing) sugar and use different coloring to decorate your *wawas* once they have cooled completely.

Venezuelan Ham Bread

Pan de jamón
Venezuela

Preparation time: 40 minutes,
plus 1 hour rising
Cooking time: 40 minutes   Serves: 8

This Venezuelan Christmas bread is thought to have been invented by a Caracas bakery owner in 1905, then stuffed only with ham. As more bakeries made it, other ingredients like nuts, dried fruits, and olives were added.

   1/5 oz (5.5 g) active dry yeast
   1 cup/8 fl oz (250 ml) warm water
   3¾ cups/1 lb 2 oz (500 g) all-purpose (plain) flour,
   plus extra for dusting
   1 oz (30 g) powdered milk
   3¼ tablespoons white sugar
   3 teaspoons/½ oz (15 g) salt
   2 eggs, beaten, plus an extra beaten egg to glaze
   ¼ cup/2 oz (60 g) butter, melted
   1 lb 2 oz (500 g) smoked sliced ham
   ½ cup/2½ oz (75 g) raisins
   1 cup/6 oz (180 g) green olives with pimentos, sliced
   1 tablespoon panela (or use light muscovado)

Tip the yeast into the warm water and let activate for 10 minutes. In a bowl, mix the flour with the powdered milk, white sugar, and salt, using a whisk. Make a well in the center of the flour and pour the eggs and water with yeast inside the well. Mix. Once the flour has absorbed the water, add the melted butter and knead the dough.
   Place the dough on a floured surface and continue kneading, adding small amounts of flour until you get a soft dough. Place the dough back in the floured bowl, put a damp tea towel on top, and let rise for 1 hour.
   Preheat the oven to 350°F/150°C/Gas Mark 2.
   Place the dough on a floured surface and stretch into a rectangular shape with a rolling pin. Cover the dough with the sliced ham, leaving a thin, free space around the edges of the dough. Spread the raisins and olives over the ham. Use your finger or a pastry brush to spread water on the edges of the dough, then roll from the long side. Fold inside the free edges of the bread to close it.
   Place the dough on a baking sheet lined with parchment paper. Prick the bread with a fork in different spots and bake for 20 minutes. Remove the bread from the oven, brush with beaten egg and sprinkle over the panela. Bake for a further 20 minutes until golden brown.
   Remove from the oven and let the bread cool on the tray. Cut into slices and serve while still warm or once the bread has cooled down.

Chilote Potato Bread

Chochoca
Chile

Preparation time: 30 minutes,
plus cooling
Cooking time: 50 minutes   Serves: 12

The dough of this unusual potato bread gets wrapped around a *chochoquero*, a large wooden stick, which is then rotated slowly over hot coals. It is traditional of the magical, misty Chiloé archipelago off the coast of southern Chile, where potatoes are plentiful, as well as with the Huilliche, or southern groups of Mapuche people, in the provinces of Osorno and Ranco, where it is called *trutruyeko*. It's primarily made at festivals or large gatherings. Two versions can be found: *blanca* (white) and *negra* (black). The black, for which you will find an adapted recipe below, is the traditional version, though it is not as common anymore. The white is less labor intensive, as it doesn't require grating, and is made from equal parts wheat flour and mashed cooked potatoes.

   6 lb 9 oz (3 kg) raw potatoes
   5 lb 8 oz (2.5 kg) cooked, mashed, and cooled potatoes
   2 tablespoons (28 g) salt
   1 tablespoon butter, melted
   ½ cup/3½ oz (95 g) lard
   3 lb (1.4 kg) *Chicharrón* (Pork Cracklings/crispy pork
   skin; page 276 for homemade or can be store-bought)

Peel and grate the raw potatoes and press them with a tea towel to remove excess water. Tip into a bowl, add the mashed potato, salt and melted butter, and knead until you get a soft dough.
   Wrap the dough around a *chochoquero* (see headnote; you can use a rolling pin). Place it over a charcoal grill (barbecue). Keep the fire low and keep turning the *chochoquero* to give a slow and even cook.
   When the *chochoca* is half brownish, about 30–40 minutes, spread the lard over the surface, and keep cooking for a further 10 minutes.
   Take the bread off of the grill. Cut it in half down its length to remove the *chochoquero*. Place the bread on a clean surface, fill with *Chicharrón*, and bring the halves together to close. Cut into 12 portions, and serve hot.

Chilean Country Bread

Pan amasado
Chile

Preparation time: 30 minutes,
plus 1 hour rising
Cooking time: 30 minutes   Makes: 12

Translating as "kneaded bread," *pan amasado* has a flaky crust with a soft center. Serve with *ají pebre* or mashed avocado.

   2 teaspoons (7 g) active dry yeast
   1 cup/8 fl oz (250 ml) warm water
   3 cups/15 oz (420 g) bread flour
   1 teaspoon salt
   2 tablespoons melted butter
   1 teaspoon sugar
   milk or beaten egg, to glaze

Activate the yeast in the warm water in a small bowl. Let it rest for 10 minutes.
   In another bowl, mix the flour with the salt and form a small well in the middle of the flour mix. Pour the melted butter into the well, along with the water and yeast mixture, and the sugar. Mix with your hands to bring into a ball, then knead for around 10 minutes, until smooth, adding more water if needed.
   Separate the dough into 12 equal pieces and shape each into a disc. Space apart on two lined baking sheets, cover with a damp tea towel and let rise for 1 hour. Preheat the oven to 350°F/180°C/Gas Mark 4.
   Brush the dough discs with a little bit of milk or beaten egg, then prick each in the middle with a fork and bake for 30 minutes until golden brown.
   Let cool a little on the tray and serve warm.

Charcoal-Baked Bread

Tortilla de rescoldo 🔲
Chile

Preparation time: 20 minutes
Cooking time: 20 minutes
Makes: 8

Baked in the hot ash and coals of a campfire, *tortillas de rescoldo* were traditionally made by travelers on long journeys. Ranging in size from a *pupusa* (a small cake) to an extra-large pizza, they are infused with the flavors of smoke and ash and are usually served with butter or *ají pebre*, though some variations will stuff them or serve them with shellfish or pork. Today they are sold on busy streets in towns like Antilhue and Laraquete by women known as *palomitas*, or little doves, because of their white clothes.

    4 cups/1 lb 4 oz (560 g) all-purpose (plain) flour
    1 teaspoon baking soda (bicarbonate of soda)
    1 cup/8 oz (225 g) butter, melted
    2 cups/16 fl oz (475 ml) warm water with
    1 tablespoon salt added to create a brine

On a work surface, mix the flour and baking soda (bicarbonate of soda) together and form into a heap. Form a small well in the middle and pour in the melted butter and some of the brine. Mix with your fingers, adding the salt water little by little until you get a soft and malleable dough.

Divide the dough into 8 equal parts and shape each into a disc at least 1 inch (3 cm) thick.

Prepare a grill or fire with hot ashes and charcoal. Place the tortillas directly on the ashes and cover with more ashes and some charcoal. Cook for about 15–20 minutes, depending on the heat.

Remove from the ash, and clean with a brush and a tea towel. Use a knife to cut out the burnt spots. Serve hot.

Crusty Chilean Rolls

Pan marraqueta, pan francés, pan batido
Chile

Preparation time: 10 minutes,
plus 2 hours 20 minutes rising
Cooking time: 25 minutes
Makes: 6

This French-style roll was popularized in the late nineteenth century by European immigrants at the port of Valparaíso, and quickly became the most common bread found in Chile; its reach has spread throughout the southern half of South America in one form or another. The bread is shaped as four small rolls that are joined together, like a "tear and share" bread, so ordering in a bakery is often confusing—there is no standard agreement as to whether each unit consists of four rolls or just one. They are picked up by the bag from a bakery and eaten while still warm, or used for sandwiches.

    3½ cups/1 lb (460 g) all-purpose (plain) flour,
    plus extra for dusting
    3½ cups/1 lb 1 oz (480 g) bread flour (strong
    white flour)
    2½ teaspoons salt
    1 teaspoon brown sugar
    1½ teaspoons (5.5 g) dry active yeast
    2⅔ cups/21 fl oz (625 ml) cold water
    oil, for spraying

Mix both flours in a bowl, then add the salt, sugar, and yeast. Add the water slowly and use your hands to bring the mixture into a ball.

Place the ball on a floured surface and knead vigorously for about 10 minutes until soft. Place it back in the bowl, cover with a damp tea towel and let rest for 30 minutes. Knead the dough one more time and place back in the covered bowl for a further 1 hour or until it doubles in size.

Divide the dough into 12 equal-sized balls, spray with a little bit of oil, and let sit for a further 30 minutes, without covering.

To shape the *marraquetas*, take 2 small balls and join them together at the sides, kneading them slightly to make them more elongated (but staying more or less round). Use a wooden spoon handle to press down lengthways into the joined breads, creating a cross with the join. Spray a little oil on top and place the breads on two lined baking sheets.

Let them rest, uncovered, for 20 minutes. Preheat the oven to 350°F/180°C/Gas Mark 4 and bake for 25 minutes until golden brown.

Chilean Biscuits

Hallullas
Chile

Preparation time: 20 minutes,
plus 1 hour rising
Cooking time: 20 minutes
Makes: 20

This round Chilean biscuit, often eaten with afternoon tea or as sandwiches, has the taste and texture of a scone, though it is larger.

    3 cups/15 oz (420 g) all-purpose (plain) flour,
    plus extra for dusting
    2 teaspoons (7 g) active dry yeast
    2 teaspoons salt
    1 teaspoon sugar
    1¼ cup/10 fl oz (300 ml) warm water
    3½ tablespoons/2 oz (50 g) butter, at room
    temperature
    1 egg, beaten with a little milk, to glaze

In a large bowl, mix the flour, yeast, salt, and sugar using your hands, and slowly add the water. Knead for about 10 minutes, then add the butter and continue kneading until the dough becomes smooth. Let it sit for 10 minutes, covered with a damp tea towel.

On a floured surface, roll the dough into a rectangular shape, about ½ inch (1 cm) thick, and fold it in half. Repeat the process 4 times, the last time stretching and rolling the dough to a ½-inch (1-cm) thickness. Using a 4-inch (10-cm) round cutter, stamp out 20 discs from the dough and place on a lined baking sheet.

Cover with a tea towel and let rise for 1 hour. Preheat the oven to 350°F/180°C/Gas Mark 4.

Brush the biscuits with the beaten egg mixture and prick each in the middle with a fork. Bake for 15–20 minutes or until brown.

Remove from the oven and let cool a little on a wire rack. Serve warm.

Breads and Baked Goods

Charcoal-Baked Bread

Christ's Knees

Rodillas de Cristo
Ecuador

Preparation time: 35 minutes,
plus 2 hours 30 minutes rising
Cooking time: 20 minutes

Makes: 10

The tradition of bread making in the colonial city of Cuenca, Ecuador, is defined by the uniquely designed ovens, which are fired with eucalyptus wood and made of local materials like adobe, cattle bones, rock salt, and broken glass. Many of the recipes came out of the city's convents, like this one, where the cheese is stained red from achiote, meant to resemble the blood dripping from Christ's knees.

3 tablespoons sugar
1¼ cups/10 fl oz (300 ml) water
2½ tablespoons butter
1 teaspoon (3.5 g) active dry yeast
3⅓ cups/1 lb 1 oz (480 g) all-purpose (plain) flour, plus extra for dusting
1 tablespoon salt
1 cup/4 oz (120 g) crumbled *queso fresco*
1 tablespoon achiote oil

Put the sugar, water, and butter in a small pan, place over low heat and let it slowly heat, stirring until the sugar completely dissolves. Let the mixture cool down and add the yeast while it's still just warm. Let sit until bubbly then whisk it.

In a large bowl, mix the flour and salt. Make a well in the middle and slowly add the yeast mixture. Mix until the ingredients are combined then place the dough on a floured work surface and continue kneading until you get a soft dough, about 10 minutes.

Place the dough back in the bowl, cover with a damp tea towel, and let it rise for 1 hour 30 minutes, or until it doubles in size. Place the dough on a floured surface, knead for about 3 minutes then shape it into an even log. Cut into 10 pieces and shape each piece into a small ball.

In a small bowl, mix the *queso fresco*, achiote oil, and 1 tablespoon warm water.

Place the rolls on a lined baking sheet and flatten them slightly with the palm of your hand. Make a small cut in the middle of each with scissors and place a spoonful of the cheese mixture in the cut, onto the middle of each bun. Cover with a tea towel and let them rise again for about 1 hour.

Preheat the oven to 400°F/200°C/Gas Mark 6 and place another baking pan in the bottom to heat up.

Place the rolls inside and reduce the heat to 350°F/175°C/Gas Mark 4. After 10 minutes, quickly pour a little water into the baking pan in the bottom of the oven to keep the oven moist. Bake the rolls for a further 10 minutes until golden brown, then remove to a wire rack to cool a little before serving warm.

Argentine Stuffed Cheese Pizza

Fugazzeta
Argentina

Preparation time: 30 minutes,
plus 1 hour 10 minutes resting
Cooking time: 30 minutes

Serves: 8

Immigrants from Genoa and Naples began opening pizzerias in Buenos Aires in the late 1800s and, over time, Argentine pizza began to mutate into its own version, often overflowing with cheese. The most common is *pizza de molde*, thick slices that are cooked in a pan and heavy on cheese, while the *fugazza*, also called the *fugazza con queso*, is a flatbread inspired by focaccia, topped with sweet onions, herbs, and cheese. Its wayward cousin, which uses more or less the same ingredients, is the *fugazzeta*, made by stuffing the cheese inside the crust and placing the onions on top, usually with more cheese.

¼ cup/2 fl oz (60 ml) warm milk
⅓ oz (9 g) fresh yeast
1 teaspoon sugar
3 cups/12¾ oz (360 g) bread flour, plus 1 tablespoon for dusting
1 teaspoon salt, plus extra for the onions
1 tablespoon olive oil
1 cup/8 fl oz (240 ml) warm water
1 tablespoon vegetable oil, plus extra for greasing
2 white onions, sliced into thin rings
1½ tablespoons dried oregano
1 teaspoon chile powder
2 cups/8 oz (230 g) shredded mozzarella

Add the warm milk, yeast, sugar, and the 1 tablespoon of flour to a small bowl, mix well with your hands and let it rest in a warm place for 10 minutes or until a slight foam starts to form.

Meanwhile, add the flour to a large bowl. Make a well in the middle and add the salt and olive oil. Mix slightly then slowly add the yeasted mixture. Add the warm water little by little, then knead with your hands until the dough is soft.

Place the dough on a floured surface and continue kneading for a further 7 minutes.

Return the dough back to the bowl, cover with a tea towel and let it rest for 1 hour.

Heat the vegetable oil in a frying pan on medium heat. Add the onions and sauté for 6 minutes or until soft, then add the oregano, chile, and a little salt. Remove from the heat and let cool.

Divide the dough into two unequal parts, one-third and two-thirds. Preheat the oven to 400°F/200°C/Gas Mark 6.

Grease a 12-inch (30-cm) pizza pan. Place the bigger part of the dough in the pan and stretch with your hands from the middle to the edges. Spread the cheese on top, saving some for later for scattering over the top. Stretch the remaining dough and use it to cover the first dough. Seal the edges with your fingers, pinching them together. With a fork, gently prick the top of the dough a few times.

Spread the cooked onions on top and sprinkle over the remaining cheese. Bake for 20 minutes until golden brown along the edges. Serve hot.

Chickpea Flatbread

Fainá
Argentina, Uruguay

Preparation time: 15 minutes
Cooking time: 20 minutes

Serves: 6

In Uruguay and Argentina, the nutty flatbread *fainá*, made from chickpea flour and related to the Italian *farinata*, is usually served as an accompaniment to pizza, either on the side or sometimes right on top of a slice, which is called *pizza a caballo* (pizza on horseback).

3/4 cup/3 1/4 oz (90 g) chickpea (gram) flour
2 1/2 cups/20 fl oz (600 ml) water
1 3/4 tablespoons olive oil, plus extra for greasing
salt and ground white pepper

Preheat the oven to 375°F/190°C/Gas Mark 5.
　　In a bowl, using your hands, mix together the flour, water, and olive oil. Add a little salt and white pepper, then taste a bit of the dough and adjust the seasoning as needed. Let the dough rest for 15 minutes.
　　Meanwhile, heat a little olive oil in a pan, then pour it into a round ovenproof pan or dish, 6 inches (15 cm) in diameter, to coat the base and sides.
　　Pour the dough into the prepared pan or dish, and pat it into an even thickness using a spatula. Bake for about 20 minutes, until the top is golden brown. Cool slightly before slicing in triangles, like pizza, and serve warm.

Chilean Squash Fritters

Sopaipilla
Chile

Preparation time: 20 minutes
Cooking time: 30 minutes

Makes: 30

Unlike the fried, sweet doughs made of wheat flour in *sopaipillas* from elsewhere in Latin America, the version found across central Chile adds squash. Eaten in either a sweet or savory form, the savory version is a spongy bread, eaten with *ají pebre* sauce, and used to replace the buns in sandwiches. In winter, the sweet version called *sopaipillas pasadas* is boiled in *chancaca*, or unrefined sugarcane syrup infused with orange peel and cinnamon.

3 cups/14 oz (400 g) all-purpose (plain) flour, plus extra for dusting
1 teaspoon baking powder
2 tablespoons melted butter
1 cup/8 oz (230 g) squash or pumpkin purée (strained)
vegetable oil, for deep-frying

In a bowl, mix the flour and baking powder. Create a well, pour in the melted butter and mix. Add the squash purée and a pinch of fine sea salt. Knead to a smooth dough.
　　Stretch the dough out on a floured surface using a rolling pin, to a 1/4-inch (5-mm) thickness. Using a round cutter, cut out 30 discs, 4 inches (10 cm) in diameter, and carefully prick them a few times using a fork.
　　Pour enough vegetable oil for deep-frying into a large, heavy pan, making sure it is no more than two-thirds full, and heat to 360°F/182°C. Deep-fry the *sopaipillas* in batches for 2 minutes each side, or until golden and crispy. Use a skimmer to remove to a plate lined with paper towels, to absorb excess oil. Serve hot.

Curried Chickpea Flatbread

Doubles
Guyana

Preparation time: 20 minutes, plus 1 hour 30 minutes rising
Cooking time: 40 minutes

Serves: 5

Created off of the coast of Venezuela on the island of Trinidad, doubles are the greatest vegan breakfast sandwich. They are adapted from the Punjabi dish *chole bhature*, brought by contract laborers from India who came to work on plantations in Trinidad and Guyana after the abolition of slavery. They are made from two pieces of fried, dense flatbread called *bara*, dyed yellow from turmeric, filled with spiced chickpea curry called *channa*.

4 1/2 cups/1 lb 5 oz (600 g) all-purpose (plain) flour
1 teaspoon fine sea salt, plus extra for seasoning
1 1/2 tablespoons sugar
1 1/2 teaspoons ground cumin
1 teaspoon ground turmeric
3 teaspoons (10 g) active dry yeast
2 cups/16 fl oz (475 ml) warm water
vegetable oil, for cooking, greasing, and deep-frying
1 white onion, diced
3 teaspoons minced garlic
3 teaspoons dried thyme
1 1/2 teaspoons ground cumin
1 1/2 teaspoons ground allspice
4 tablespoons curry powder
1 1/2 teaspoons ground nutmeg
2 teaspoons paprika
1 1/2 teaspoons ground pepper
3 cups/25 fl oz (750 ml) vegetable stock
2 1/2 cups/12 oz (350 g) drained canned chickpeas, blanched
1 tablespoon any Scotch bonnet-based chile sauce, optional
3 spring onions (salad onions), chopped
3 tablespoons chopped parsley

Combine the flour, 1 teaspoon salt, sugar, cumin, turmeric, and yeast in a medium bowl.
　　Slowly add the warm water to mix to a soft dough. Remove the dough, grease the bowl with oil, then add the dough back to the bowl. Cover with a tea towel and set it in a warm place for 1 hour 30 minutes, or until it doubles in size.
　　Meanwhile, to make the curry filling, heat a dash of oil in a large pan. Sauté the onion and garlic on medium heat for 5 minutes. Add the thyme and all the spices, and a pinch of salt, stirring continuously for 3 minutes. Add the stock and chickpeas with the chile sauce and spring onions.
　　Bring briefly to a boil, then lower the heat and let simmer for 15 minutes or until the sauce thickens. Finish by adding the parsley, and check the seasoning. Set aside and keep warm.
　　Once the dough is ready, divide it into 10 equal-sized balls. Flatten each piece with a rolling pin until you get a disc 1/2 inch (1 cm) thick.
　　Pour enough vegetable oil for deep-frying into a large, heavy pan, making sure it is no more than two-thirds full, and heat to 360°F/182°C.
　　Add the doubles one by one and deep-fry for 30 seconds on each side. Remove with a skimmer to a plate lined with paper towels, to absorb excess oil. Serve 2 per person while still warm, with the warm curry in a bowl alongside for scooping into the middle.

Corn, Cheese, and Rapadura Breads

Tustacas
Honduras, El Salvador

Preparation time: 10 minutes
Cooking time: 10 minutes   Makes: 12

Dry, sweet, and crunchy, tustacas are eaten with morning coffee throughout southern Honduras and parts of El Salvador.

    4 cups/32 fl oz (950 ml) water
    1 lb (450 g) *cuajada* cheese (or use
    cottage cheese or *queso fresco*)
    3 cups/15 oz (420 g) corn (maize) flour
    ½ cup/4 oz (115 g) butter, softened,
    plus extra for greasing
    3 tablespoons baking soda (bicarbonate of soda)
    2 eggs
    12 tablespoons rapadura (or use light muscovado)

Preheat the oven to 400°F/200°C/Gas Mark 6.
Boil the water in a pan and slowly add the *cuajada*, cut into slices. Whisk with a balloon whisk and then strain in a cheesecloth. Mix the *cuajada* with the corn flour and knead with the butter, baking soda (bicarbonate of soda), and eggs until you have a smooth dough. Divide equally into 12 pieces and roll each into a ball. Flatten into small tortillas, then fold up the edges to create a small ridge around the edge of each.
Place 1 tablespoon of sugar in the middle of each, then place them on a baking sheet lined with greased parchment paper.
Bake for 10 minutes until golden brown. Serve warm.

Panamanian Fried Bread

Hojaldres
Panama

Preparation time: 30 minutes,
plus 2 hours resting
Cooking time: 20 minutes   Makes: 20

The Panamanian *hojaldre* is eaten at any time of the day. For breakfast, it is often eaten with eggs or cheese. For lunch or dinner, it is served alongside steak and onions. For dessert, it might be sprinkled with sugar and cinnamon.

    5 cups/1 lb 7 oz (650 g) all-purpose (plain) flour
    3 teaspoons baking powder
    3 teaspoons salt
    2 eggs, beaten
    2 tablespoons oil
    1½ cups/12 fl oz (350 ml) water
    vegetable oil, for deep-frying

Sift the dry ingredients into a bowl and mix. Make a small well in the middle and add the eggs and oil to the well. Using your hands, knead the ingredients while slowly incorporating the water until you get a smooth dough. Cover with a tea towel and let it rest for 2 hours.
Divide the dough into 20 golf ball-sized pieces. Flatten each with your hand until you have discs that are ¼ inch (5 mm) thick.

Pour enough vegetable oil for deep-frying into a large, heavy pan, making sure it is no more than two-thirds full, and heat to 360°F/182°C.
When the oil is hot, add the *hojaldres* one by one and fry for 2 minutes each side, or until crisp and brown on both sides.
Remove with a skimmer to a plate lined with paper towels, to absorb excess oil, and serve warm.

Middle Eastern-Style Meat Flatbread

Esfiha
Argentina, Brazil

Preparation time: 30 minutes,   Makes: 20
plus 1 hour 15 minutes rising
Cooking time: 30 minutes

Lebanese and Syrian immigrants brought the recipe for this leavened flatbread with them when they started to arrive to cities like São Paulo and Buenos Aires in the late nineteenth century. In the Levant, where they're called *sfiha*, they are made with ground and seasoned lamb or beef, though in South America toppings are quite varied, ranging from the more traditional meats to chicken, cheese, *Carne-de-sol* (Sun-Dried Beef, page 264), and palm hearts. They are most commonly circular shaped, though square and triangular versions with folded edges can also be found.

    2 teaspoons/¼ oz (7 g) active dry yeast (or use
    ½ oz/14 g fresh yeast)
    2 teaspoons sugar
    1 cup/8 fl oz (250 ml) warm milk
    2 cups/9½ oz (260 g) all-purpose flour,
    plus extra for dusting
    2 teaspoons salt
    ½ cup/4 fl oz (120 ml) oil
    14 oz (400 g) ground (minced) beef
    1 tablespoon butter
    5 oz (140 g) onions, chopped
    6 oz (175 g) tomatoes, chopped
    4 garlic cloves, minced
    ¼ cup/½ oz (15 g) parsley, chopped
    salt and ground pepper
    lime wedges, to serve

Dissolve the yeast and sugar in the warm milk and let activate for 15–30 minutes.
In a bowl, mix together the flour, salt, oil, and yeast and milk mixture. Knead the dough on a floured surface until smooth, cover with a damp tea towel and let rise for 1 hour or until it has doubled in size.
Meanwhile, mix the ground (minced) beef, butter, onion, tomato, garlic, and parsley. Season with salt and pepper.
Place the dough on a floured surface. Cut into 4 and roll each piece into a thick log. Cut each log into 5 pieces and shape into balls. Cover and let rest for 15 minutes.
Preheat the oven to 375°F/190°C/Gas Mark 5.
Flatten the balls, starting from the center of the dough in circular motion, forming a disc with raised edges. Divide the filling between the centers, pressing it to flatten.
Bake for about 30 minutes until golden brown, then serve with lime wedges.
Note: For a cheese filling, use a mixture of 1 lb (450 g) ricotta cheese, 2½ oz (75 g) heavy (double) cream, and chopped parsley. Season with sea salt and fresh ground pepper. Proceed in the same way.

Breads and Baked Goods

Middle Eastern-Style Meat Flatbread

Surinamese Chicken Pot Pie

Pastei ⊡
Suriname

Preparation time: 45 minutes　　　　Serves: 8
Cooking time: 45 minutes

Suriname had a thriving population of Sephardic Jews for a time, who initially arrived in 1638 mostly from Spain and Portugal, fleeing the Inquisition. They owned sugarcane plantations, as well as slaves, and while most Surinamese Jews left the country after Independence in 1975 and the civil war that followed, they left behind dishes like *pastei* and *pom*, a chicken and grated tayer root casserole.

For the dough
¾ cup/6 oz (175 g) butter, plus extra for greasing
¾ cup/6 fl oz (175 ml) cold water
1¼ cups plus 1 tablespoon/7 oz (200 g) all-purpose (plain) flour
2 teaspoons baking powder
1 teaspoon sea salt

For the filling
½ cup/4 oz (115 g) butter
2 large onions, chopped
1 fresh chile, chopped
1 red bell pepper, cored, seeded, and chopped
3 large pieces of chicken
1 celery stalk, chopped
1 bay leaf
1 teaspoon ground allspice
1 cup/8 fl oz (250 ml) water
1 tablespoon oil
1 cup/4 oz (120 g) frozen peas
1 cup/4 oz (120 g) chopped carrots
2 large tomatoes, chopped
1 tablespoon piccalilli
2 tablespoons tomato ketchup
1 teaspoon Worcestershire sauce, optional
3 hard-boiled eggs, sliced
sea salt and ground pepper

To serve
cooked white rice

First make the filling. Place a pan over medium heat. Add the butter and, once melted, sauté half the chopped onion, the chile, and bell pepper for about 6 minutes until the onion starts to brown. Add the chicken, celery, bay leaf, and allspice and cook for a few minutes, then add the water. Season with salt and pepper and cook for about 30 minutes, until the chicken is cooked through. Remove the chicken and shred, reserving the cooking liquid and vegetables while discarding the bay leaf.

Heat the oil in a separate pan over medium heat. Add the remaining chopped onion and the shredded chicken. Sauté for 2 minutes, then add the peas, carrots, and tomatoes. After a further 2 minutes, add the reserved cooking liquid to the pan. Add the piccalilli, ketchup, and Worcestershire sauce, if using. Cook until the liquid is absorbed, then let cool. Preheat the oven to 400°F/200°C/Gas Mark 6 while making the dough.

Beat the butter using an electric mixer. Gradually beat in the water until the butter has absorbed it all.

Sift the flour, baking powder, and salt together. Gradually mix the dry ingredients into the butter mixture. The dough should be firm; if necessary, add more flour.

Divide the dough into 2 unequal pieces, one-third and two-thirds. With a rolling pin, roll out both pieces, to ¼ inch (5 mm) thick. Grease a baking pan, 10½ inches (27 cm) diameter, with butter then shape the larger dough piece into the pan, bringing it up the sides for form a pie case. Prick in a few places with a fork.

Spread the cooled filling evenly over the dough and add the hard-boiled eggs on top. Cover the pie with the reserved dough, pressing the edges to seal. Crimp with a fork and bake for 45 minutes or until golden brown.

Serve hot in slices, with white rice.

Belizean Meat Pie

Belize

Preparation time: 30 minutes　　　　Makes: 12
Cooking time: 20 minutes

The meat pie is believed to have been introduced to Belize during the British occupation, when the country was known as British Honduras. A distinctly Belizean version developed over time, where the ground beef filling is usually mixed with *recado rojo*, or hot chilies like habaneros. Made at home or sold at gas stations and bakeries, they're eaten at any time of the day.

8 oz (225 g) ground (minced) beef
½ teaspoon dried thyme
½ teaspoon ground allspice
½ teaspoon annatto paste
2 tablespoons vegetable oil
½ red onion, finely chopped
½ green bell pepper, cored, seeded, and finely chopped
2 teaspoons minced garlic
1 cup/8 fl oz (250 ml) water
1 tablespoon all-purpose (plain) flour
sea salt and ground pepper

For the dough
3 cups/14 oz (400 g) all-purpose (plain) flour, plus extra for dusting
1 tablespoon salt
½ cup/4 oz (115 g) butter, cut into small cubes
1 cup/8 fl oz (250 ml) water
¼ cup/2 fl oz (60 ml) whole milk

For the filling, season the ground (minced) meat to taste. Mix in the thyme, allspice, and annatto paste.

Heat the oil in a pan over medium heat and sauté the onion, bell pepper, and garlic for 5 minutes. Add the seasoned ground meat and water. Stir well and cook for 15 minutes. Mix the flour in 2 tablespoons of water, add to the pan and cook for a further 5 minutes, or until it thickens. Remove from the heat and set aside to cool.

Preheat the oven to 400°F/200°C/Gas Mark 6.

In a large bowl, mix the flour for the dough with the salt. Add the butter and rub into the flour with your fingertips, then start kneading with your hands. Add the water and continue mixing until a smooth dough is formed.

Divide the dough into 2 equal pieces. Stretch one piece of dough on a floured surface to ¼ inch (5 mm) thick. Using a 3-inch (7.5-cm) round cutter, stamp out 12 discs and line the cups of a muffin tin. Roll out remaining dough in the same way and stamp out 12 more discs.

Place 1 tablespoonful of the filling in each lined cup. Using your fingers, dampen the edges of the dough. Top with another disc of dough and press gently to seal the edges. Using a toothpick, gently prick the middle of each pie. Bake in the oven for 15–20 minutes, or until the crust turns golden brown. Let cool a little. Serve warm.

Surinamese Chicken Pot Pie

Easter Pie

Tarta pascualina
Argentina, Uruguay

Preparation time: 15 minutes
plus 30 minutes resting
Cooking time: 1 hour

Serves: 8

At first glance you could mistake the *tarta pascualina* for an *empanada gallega* (page 41), as they are both thick, double crusted pies, originating from immigrant populations, and often sit beside each other on bakery shelves. However, the *pascualina*, brought by the Genoese and traditionally served during Lent, is filled with spinach and/or Swiss chard with ricotta, instead of tuna.

For the dough
4½ cups/1 lb 5 oz (600 g) all-purpose (plain) flour, plus extra for dusting
1½ teaspoons salt
1¼ cup/10 oz (285 g) butter, chopped into small pieces, plus extra for greasing
½ cup/4 fl oz (120 ml) cold water
1 egg yolk, to glaze

For the filling
8 oz (225 g) fresh spinach
1½ tablespoons vegetable oil
1 white onion, finely chopped
½ red bell pepper, cored, seeded, and diced
1 teaspoon ground nutmeg
¼ teaspoon dried oregano
5 hard-boiled eggs, plus 2 beaten eggs
1 cup/4 oz (115 g) ricotta
½ cup/1¼ oz (35 g) shredded parmesan
confectioner's (icing) sugar, for dusting
salt and ground pepper

For the dough, mix the flour and salt together in a bowl. Add the butter and rub it into the flour with your fingertips, then knead to a crumbly dough. Slowly add the water, while kneading, until it easily comes away from the bowl. Divide the dough into 2 equal pieces and place on a floured surface. Roll out each piece into a disc to fit an 8-inch (20-cm) pie plate, allowing for overhang on one of the pieces. Cover both dough discs with plastic wrap (clingfilm) and place in the refrigerator for 30 minutes.

Preheat the oven to 350°F/180°C/Gas Mark 4 and lightly grease the pie plate with butter.

For the filling, bring a pan of salted water to a boil, add the spinach leaves and cook for 1 minute. Remove with a skimmer and plunge into a bowl of ice-cold water. Squeeze the excess water from the spinach and reserve.

In a frying pan, heat 1 tablespoon of the oil and sauté the onion and bell pepper on medium heat for 5 minutes, or until they become soft. Add the spinach and continue cooking for a further 5 minutes. Season with the nutmeg, oregano, and salt and pepper. Remove from the heat.

Combine the beaten egg with both cheeses, add to the spinach mixture and let cool.

Remove the dough from the refrigerator and use the slightly larger disc to line the greased pie plate, to leave about 1 inch (2.5 cm) dough hanging over the edges of the plate. Spread the vegetable mix over the base, cut the hard-boiled eggs in half and arrange over the top. Dampen the edge of the dough with water, place the second dough disc on top and seal the pie by pressing the dough together with your fingertips.

Brush with the egg yolk and carefully prick the dough in a few places with a fork. Dust the top with confectioner's (icing) sugar and bake for 40 minutes or until golden brown.

Let cool a little. Serve warm.

Paraguayan Cheese Flatbread

Mbejú
Paraguay

Preparation time: 15 minutes
Cooking time: 10 minutes

Makes: 6

Meaning "cake" in Guaraní, the high-calorie *mbejú* is a breakfast staple in Paraguay and is part of the *tyrá*, the foods meant to be eaten with *mate cocido*, a bitter herbal tea, along with *chipas* and *sopa Paraguaya*. There are eleven different variations, such as the *avevó*, using more of the fatty ingredients, and the *mbejú jopara* or *mestizo*, which uses both manioc and cornstarch.

⅓ cup/2½ fl oz (75 ml) water
⅔ cup/5 fl oz (150 ml) milk
4 cups/1 lb 5 oz (560 g) cassava flour
1 cup/5 oz (140 g) corn (maize) flour
1 teaspoon salt
½ cup/4 fl oz (120 ml) melted butter, plus 1 teaspoon for frying
1 egg, beaten
2 cups/10½ oz (300 g) crumbled *queso Paraguay* (or use havarti cheese)

Mix the water and milk together and set aside.

In a bowl, mix the cassava and corn flour with the salt. Make a small well in the middle and pour in the butter, egg, and water and milk mix. Knead with your hands.

When the ingredients are well mixed, and the dough becomes smooth, add the cheese and continue kneading. The dough must have a dry texture.

In a frying pan, melt the teaspoon of butter on medium–high heat.

Spread the dough in the frying pan to a ½-inch (1-cm) thickness, flattening it evenly to leave no gaps.

Cook for 3 minutes until golden then flip over and cook for a further 3 minutes.

Panes Dulces

When the Spanish introduced wheat breads in the 1500s, most did not take to them. Many considered them bland until an incident where a viceroy allegedly dipped it in a bowl of hot chocolate in Mexico, and was won over. As Mexico City became more cosmopolitan, Mexico's *pan dulce*, or sweet breads, became a tradition for breakfast or a mid-afternoon snack called *la merienda*. During the nineteenth century, when there were two wars between France and Mexico (one actually best known as the *Guerra de los Pasteles*, or the Pastry War, because it began over an unpaid bakery debt), the art of French breadmaking grew in influence in Mexico's *panaderías* and spread south. Bakers began using a dough similar to a French brioche for their breads, but also added local ingredients, such as corn (maize) flour and guava, and made them into playful shapes like *moños* (bow ties) and *puerquitos* (little pigs).

King Cake

Rosca de reyes
Mexico

Preparation time: 1 hour,
plus 7 hours resting and rising
Cooking time: 30 minutes

Makes: 2

Eaten twelve days after Christmas to celebrate the epiphany, oval-shaped *rosca de reyes* has Spanish origins though it is eaten throughout Latin America, most widely in Mexico, usually with hot chocolate. A tradition is to bake six to eight small, plastic babies, representing baby Jesus, inside of the cake. Those who find one of the babies in their slice of *rosca de reyes* are meant to host a party together on February 2nd, where each person must bring a dish, such as *tamales* or sweets.

For the "sponge"
$^1/_{16}$ oz (2 g) fresh yeast (or 3 teaspoons/10 g active dry yeast)
2 tablespoons warm water
$2^1/_4$ oz (65 g) sugar
$3^3/_4$ cups/1 lb 2 oz (500 g) all-purpose (plain) flour
$^1/_3$ teaspoon salt
3 eggs

For the dough
$3^3/_4$ cups/1 lb 2 oz (500 g) all-purpose (plain) flour
pinch of salt
8 eggs, beaten with 2 tablespoons water
1 cup plus 2 tablespoons/8 oz (225 g) sugar
2 tablespoons orange flower water (*agua de azahar*)
1 teaspoon finely grated orange zest
1 teaspoon finely grated lime zest
$^3/_4$ cup plus 2 tablespoons/7 oz (200 g) softened butter

For the coating
$^2/_3$ cup minus 1 tablespoon/3 oz (80 g) all-purpose (plain) flour
$3^1/_2$ teaspoons (20 g) salt
$3^1/_2$ tablespoons/2 oz (50 g) butter, softened
$^1/_3$ cup/$1^3/_4$ oz (50 g) confectioner's (icing) sugar, plus extra for dusting
1 egg

To shape and decorate
1 egg, beaten
confit fruit

For the "sponge," put the yeast, warm water, and 1 teaspoon of the sugar in a small bowl. Let it rest for 15 minutes. Mix the remaining sugar, flour, and salt in another bowl. Add the yeast mixture and eggs, and mix until it gets lumpy. Cover with a damp tea towel and let it sit for 2 hours.

For the dough, place the flour in a large bowl, add the salt and mix. Add the "sponge," the beaten egg mixture, orange flower water, and the orange and lime zest, and knead for 10 minutes until you get a smooth, uniform dough. Add the butter and knead for a further 10 minutes until the butter is completely incorporated; it must be shiny and elastic. Put back in the bowl, cover with plastic wrap (clingfilm) and let rise for 4 hours or until it doubles in size.

Cut the dough into two equal pieces. Stretch each piece into a roll 2 inches (5 cm) in diameter, join the two ends of each to form a ring, sealing the ends together with a little beaten egg. Put each ring on a lined baking sheet and cover each with a damp tea towel. Let rest for 1 hour.

Preheat the oven to 400°F/200°C/Gas Mark 6.
To make the coating, mix all the ingredients in a bowl to a uniform paste. Cover with plastic wrap (clingfilm) and keep in the refrigerator until needed.

Brush both rings with beaten egg. Take the coating mixture out of the refrigerator and form into 8 strips, about 3 inches (7.5 cm) long and $^1/_4$ inch (5 mm) thick. Drape one of them over the join in each ring to cover and place the remaining strips spaced out evenly around the rings to decorate. Brush with the beaten egg and dust with confectioner's (icing) sugar. Decorate the spaces between the coating with confit fruits, and dust again with confectioner's sugar.

Bake for 25–30 minutes, checking them after 20 minutes; if they're not cooked, but are already golden brown, cover them with foil and finish the cooking.

Remove from the oven and let cool on a wire rack.

Corn-Shaped Sweet Bread

Elotitos, elotes
Mexico

Preparation time: 40 minutes
Cooking time: 20 minutes

Makes: 15

While Mexico's *pan dulce* comes in hundreds of whimsical forms—ears, bow ties, ox eyes, and mice—*elotes*, resembling little ears of corn, are one of the few actually resembling something that is normally eaten.

For the dough
3 cups/14 oz (400 g) all-purpose (plain) flour
2 teaspoons/$^1/_4$ oz (7 g) active dry yeast
1 teaspoon salt
$^1/_2$ cup/$3^1/_2$ oz (100 g) sugar
1 egg
1 egg yolk
$^1/_2$ cup/4 fl oz (120 ml) water
pinch of ground cinnamon
$^3/_4$ cup/6 oz (170 g) butter

For the filling
$^3/_4$ cup/$3^1/_2$ oz (100 g) flour
$^1/_2$ cup/$2^1/_2$ oz (70 g) confectioner's (icing) sugar
$^1/_3$ cup/3 oz (75 g) butter
1 egg yolk

For the dough, place the flour on a work surface and create a well in the middle. Add the yeast, salt, and sugar. Mix all the ingredients with your hands. Make a well again and add the egg with the yolk. Mix with your hands until you get a gritty texture. Continue mixing, slowly adding the water until you have a rough dough. Add the cinnamon and the butter and knead for about 10–15 minutes until smooth. Cover with a tea towel and let it rest for 10 minutes.

Meanwhile, make the filling. Mix all of the ingredients by hand until soft and smooth.

Preheat the oven to 400°F/200°C/Gas Mark 6.
Roll the dough into a log and divide into 15 small but equal parts. Roll each into a ball and then flatten into a disc. Make a grid pattern on each disc, using a knife and without cutting through it completely. Turn onto the non-marked side and place about 1 tablespoon of the filling lengthways. Fold each side into the middle and seal by pressing the sides together. Form the ends into a roundish, corn-like shape.

Place the breads on a greased or lined baking sheet and bake for 20 minutes.

Remove from the oven and let cool before eating.

Shell-Shaped Sweet Bread

Concha
Guatemala, Mexico

Preparation time: 30 minutes,
plus 4 hours rising
Cooking time: 25–30 minutes

Makes: 18

One of the most famous of the thousands of types of *pan dulce* in Mexico, the concha has two parts: a sweet roll made from a brioche-like dough and a crumbly, sugar-based topping, which gets stamped onto the bread in a seashell pattern using a special mold (the topping can also be scored with a knife to mimic the pattern). Variations include the *chilandrina*, which has a crust made of brown sugar, and the *chorreada*, made with *piloncillo* (raw cane sugar), and a common style that has a bit of cocoa powder in the topping mixture. The concha enjoys cult status in Mexico, which has resulted in donut-like hybrids, cream-filled conchas, concha sandwiches, and exotic toppings that go far beyond the typical strawberry or chocolate.

For the dough
1/3 cup plus 1 tablespoon/3 1/2 fl oz (100 ml) milk
3 3/4 cups/1 lb 2 oz (500 g) all-purpose (plain) flour,
plus extra for dusting
3/4 cup/5 oz (140 g) sugar
3 1/2 teaspoons (12 g) active dry yeast
1/2 teaspoon salt
1 tablespoon powdered milk
1/2 cup/3 1/2 oz (100 g) butter, at room temperature
4 eggs, beaten

For the topping
1/2 cup/3 1/2 oz (100 g) butter, at room temperature
3/4 cup/3 1/2 oz (100 g) confectioner's (icing) sugar
3/4 cup/3 1/2 oz (100 g) all-purpose (plain) flour
2 tablespoons unsweetened cocoa powder, optional
1/2 cup/8 oz (225 g) butter, melted

To make the dough, boil the milk in a pan, then remove from the heat and let cool to room temperature.

In a bowl, mix 2 tablespoons of the flour with 1 1/2 teaspoons of the sugar, cooled milk, and yeast. Let it sit until it doubles in size, about 1 hour 30 minutes.

Sift the remaining flour with the salt into a mound on a surface. Add the remaining sugar and powdered milk, then make a well in the middle and add the butter, eggs, and yeast mixture. Knead until soft and slightly elastic. Form a ball and cover it with plastic wrap (clingfilm) or a damp tea towel until it doubles in size, about 1 hour.

Meanwhile, make the topping. Using an electric mixer or a wooden spoon, beat the butter with the sugar until you get a soft, creamy paste. Add the flour or flour-cocoa mixture and mix until it looks like a glazing dough.

Grease a baking sheet with melted butter. When the dough has risen, turn it onto a floured surface and divide into 18 equal pieces. Roll each piece into a ball and place on the baking sheet. Brush each roll with melted butter.

Divide the topping into 18 equal portions. Take a portion and roll it out into a disc roughly the diameter of the formed conchas. Place the flat topping on one of the rolls, then use a floured concha mold or a small knife to score the shell pattern into the topping. Repeat with the remaining topping, then let the breads prove uncovered until they are doubled in size, about 1 hour 30 minutes.

Preheat the oven to 375°F/190°C/Gas Mark 5.

Bake the breads for 25 minutes or until cooked (a knife inserted in the middle comes out clean). Transfer the breads to a wire rack. Serve warm or at room temperature.

Bread of the Dead

Pan de muerto
Mexico

Preparation time: 1 hour,
plus 4 hours resting and rising
Cooking time: 40 minutes

Serves: 3–4

The exact origins of *pan de muerto* aren't clear, though most signs point to it being created right after conquest. Human sacrifices, as tribute to the gods, were not unheard of in those days, and some have said sacrificial blood was mixed with ground and toasted amaranth seeds to make a bread. The Spanish, said to be horrified by the concept, created a wheat bread colored with red sugar. There are variations of *pan de muerto* found in every region of Mexico. Some are shaped like rabbits, or dolls to honor children. This recipe from central Mexico is the best known. It is a round, sweet roll decorated with a cross of *huesitos*, or bones, topped with a circular skull. Orange blossom is added for the remembrance of the deceased. Typically, it is eaten on *Día de Muertos*, or Day of the Dead, at an altar called an *ofrenda*, alongside visiting spirits and their favorite foods, though now it's commonly eaten throughout the month before.

For the dough
1 cup/8 fl oz (250 ml) milk
3 3/4 cups/1 lb 2oz (500 g) all-purpose (plain) flour,
plus extra for dusting
1/2 cup/3 1/2 oz (100 g) sugar
1 1/2 teaspoons (5.5 g) active dry yeast
4 eggs
1/2 teaspoon salt
1–2 tablespoons orange flower water (*agua de azahar*)
1 tablespoon finely grated orange zest
3/4 cup plus 2 tablespoons/7 oz (200 g) cold butter,
cut into cubes
a little melted butter, for greasing and brushing
confectioner's (icing) sugar, for dusting

To coat
1 egg, beaten
pinch each of salt and sugar
1 tablespoon water

Bring the milk to a boil in a pan, then cool to just warm.

Put the flour in a bowl and form a well in the center. Add the sugar, yeast, and warm milk to the well, cover the well with flour and rest for about 1 hour.

Add the eggs, salt, orange flower water, and zest to the ingredients in the bowl, bring together and shape into a ball. Place the dough on a floured surface and knead for 10 minutes. Add the cubed butter and knead for a further 10 minutes. Return to the bowl, cover with a damp tea towel, and rest for 2 hours or until doubled in size.

Grease two baking sheets with melted butter. Cut the dough into 3 equal parts. Form 2 pieces into tight balls and flatten them. Place on the baking sheet, cover and let rise for 1 hour. Set the remaining piece aside, covered.

Preheat the oven to 400°F/200°C/Gas Mark 6. From the reserved dough, shape 2 balls and 8 long, thin strips.

For the coating, combine all the ingredients and brush over the round breads. Place 4 strips of dough in an X shape on one bread, then add the ball to the middle of the X, pressing to make them stick. Repeat for the other bread. Glaze all over with a little of the egg mixture.

Bake for 40 minutes or until golden brown. Let cool completely on a wire rack, then brush with melted butter and dust with confectioner's (icing) sugar to serve.

Bread of the Dead

Chipas

In Paraguay, there are more than 70 varieties of *chipa*, which are, mostly, unleavened corn or yuca (cassava) flour breads of various shapes and sizes. Some, like the *chipa guazú*, are baked like a sheet cake and then cut into squares, while others are more like small rolls, or donut-shaped. They are often sold by roving vendors, called *chiperas*, from covered baskets or streetside stands, most often eaten alongside a cup of *mate*. Historically, in the Guaraní region (which straddles parts of Paraguay, northeastern Argentina, southeastern Bolivia, and southwestern Brazil), the most basic form of *chipa* is made of just yuca starch and water, though it evolved when colonists arrived with livestock milk, cheese, and eggs. Other variations of *chipas* are made with wheat flour, like the *chipa pirú*, or stuffed with ground beef, like the *chipa so'o*.

Paraguayan Corn Cakes

Chipa guazú
Paraguay

Preparation time: 25 minutes
Cooking time: 40 minutes
Makes: 16

The word *guazú*, or *guasu*, means "big" in Guaraní, hence, the *chipa guazú* is the biggest of the *chipas*. The cake is rather similar to *sopa Paraguaya* (page 24), though substitutes corn kernels for cornstarch.

½ cup minus 1 tablespoon/3½ oz (100 g) butter, plus extra for greasing
1 onion, thinly sliced
7 cups/2 lb 3 oz (1 kg) fresh corn kernels
6 eggs
1 cup/8 fl oz (250 ml) vegetable oil
a little milk, to thin the batter if needed
3 teaspoons/½ oz (15 g) salt
10½ oz (300 g) *queso Paraguay*, shredded (or use any fresh, salted cheese)

Preheat the oven to 375°F/190°C/Gas Mark 5. Butter a square ovenproof dish measuring 8 x 8 x 2 inches (20 x 20 x 5 cm).
　Melt the butter in a frying pan over medium heat. Add the onion and sauté until brown, about 10–15 minutes. (You can swap the butter for pork fat to make it more savory although, of course, no longer vegetarian.)
　In a blender, combine the corn, eggs, vegetable oil, and fried onions. Blend on high speed for about 2 minutes, or until uniform, adding a little bit of milk if it is too thick to blend. Add the salt and shredded cheese, and blend for a further 30 seconds.
　Pour the mix into the prepared dish and bake for 30–40 minutes, or until golden brown and cooked in the middle (test with a tip of a knife; if it comes out clean, it is ready).
　Remove from the oven and let cool slightly. Cut into squares and serve warm.

Stuffed Savory Corn Cakes

Chipa so'o
Argentina, Paraguay

Preparation time: 30 minutes
Cooking time: 40 minutes

Makes: 8

The *chipa so'o* is like a round, handheld version of the *sopa Paraguaya* (page 24). Dating to the Guaraní-Jesuit missions, it's made of eggs, cheese, and whipped pork fat mixed with corn flour, then stuffed with minced meat.

For the dough
7 cups/1 lb (450 g) corn (maize) flour
1 teaspoon cassava starch
1 teaspoon salt
5 oz (140 g) *queso Paraguay*, shredded (or use Muenster cheese)
3½ oz (100 g) lard
1 egg
1 cup/8 fl oz (250 ml) whole milk

For the filling
2 tablespoons vegetable oil
1 red onion, finely chopped
2 garlic cloves, minced
1 red bell pepper, cored, seeded, and chopped
1 lb (450 g) veal loin, finely chopped
4 hard-boiled eggs, coarsely chopped
1 teaspoon ground cumin
salt and ground pepper

Preheat the oven to 400°F/200°C/Gas Mark 6.
　To prepare the dough, mix the corn flour, cassava starch, salt, cheese, and lard in a large bowl. Knead until you have a crumbly dough. Make a well in the middle of the dough and crack in the egg with the milk. Continue kneading with your hands until the dough is smooth and uniform. Cover with plastic wrap (clingfilm) and set aside in the refrigerator.
　To make the filling, heat the oil in a frying pan and sauté the onion, garlic, and bell pepper over medium heat for 10 minutes or until the onions are translucent. Add the chopped meat, chopped eggs, and cumin, season with salt and pepper, and stir well. Turn off the heat and set aside.
　Shape the dough into 8 equal-sized balls. Using your thumb, create a small cavity in the middle of each ball and add a spoonful of filling. Seal the dough over the filling and place on a lined baking sheet. Gently press down to make a thick patty. Repeat with all the dough balls and filling, then bake for 30–40 minutes or until golden brown.

Paraguayan Corn Cakes

Stick-Roasted Lard and Cheese Bread

Chipa kavuré, chipa asador, chipá mbocá
Argentina, Paraguay

Preparation time: 15 minutes
Cooking time: 20 minutes   Serves: 4

Made of fat, cheese, and a mix of corn and yuca (cassava) flour, the *chipa kavuré*, which dates back to Jesuit-Guaraní missions in Paraguay's colonial period, is wrapped around a wooden stick and roasted over hot embers. The size may vary considerably, depending on the length of the stick and size of the heat source. Sometimes this *chipa* might be quite long, while other times it will just cover the end of the stick.

½ cup/4 oz (115 g) lard
4 eggs
1 cup/4 oz (115 g) shredded *queso Paraguay* (or use Muenster cheese)
1 teaspoon anise (green aniseed) seeds
1 cup/8 fl oz (250 ml) whole milk
⅓ teaspoon salt
1 cup/5 oz (140 g) cassava flour, plus extra for dusting

You will need a wooden stick, about ½ inch (1 cm) in diameter and 12 inches (30 cm long).

Preheat a grill (barbecue).
Place the lard in a bowl and whisk to soften. Add the eggs, stirring after each addition. Add the cheese, anise seeds, milk, and salt and continue stirring. Using a spatula, fold in the cassava flour until the dough is firm and uniform; if necessary, add more cassava flour.
Stretch the dough on a surface dusted with cassava flour into an 8-inch (20-cm) square, ½ inch (1 cm) thick. Wrap the dough evenly around the wooden stick, place on top of the grill and cook for 10 minutes each side, or until the dough starts cracking. Remove the *chipa* from the stick and serve warm.

Ring-Shaped Easter Cheese Bread

Chipa argolla
Paraguay

Preparation time: 15 minutes,
plus 20 minutes resting
Cooking time: 30 minutes   Makes: 4

Served during Holy Week in Paraguay, the *chipa argolla* is a dense, ring-shaped cheese bread flavored with anise seeds. It's often passed around and eaten at cemeteries during the holiday, in remembrance of those passed.

1 tablespoon butter
1 egg
3 oz (80 g) *queso Paraguay*, shredded (or use a mixture of parmesan and mozzarella)
½ teaspoon anise seeds
2 tablespoons whole milk
pinch of salt
½ cup/2½ oz (70 g) cassava flour
½ cup/2½ oz (70 g) corn (maize) flour

Preheat the oven to 400°F/200°C/Gas Mark 6.
In a bowl, vigorously mix the butter and egg, using a whisk, until smooth. Add the cheese and anise seeds. Add the milk and salt, and continue mixing. Using a spatula, fold in both the flours until the dough is soft and uniform. Divide into 4 equal pieces and place on a plate. Cover and chill in the refrigerator for 20 minutes.
Stretch the pieces of dough into 6-inch (15-cm) logs on a floured surface. Bring the ends together of each and press together gently to seal. Place on a lined baking sheet, as far apart as possible (they will double in size). Bake for 20–30 minutes, or until golden brown.

Empanadas

Empanadas are a form of hand pies or turnovers that are now found in nearly every part of Latin America. Their roots lie in the Middle East, from where they made their way to Europe to evolve, before the Spanish brought them to the Americas. During the colonial period in Latin America, they didn't look different from the ones in Galicia: large, baked, circular, or rectangular double-crust pies with yeasted dough and savory fillings like tuna or chicken, served by the slice. Some Latin American versions are still made in a similar form to this, such as the *empanada gallega* (page 41) or the *empadão de frango*.

Over time, empanadas were adapted in Latin America and took on a life of their own. The smaller, handheld version became standard. Yeast was forgotten, and the dough didn't necessarily need to be made from wheat flour either. It could be made from cornflour or tapioca flour, or cut with beef fat. The fillings ventured out into the terrain, adding in potatoes, chilies, mushrooms, and local spices.

Some of the best, like those in and around Salta, Argentina, are baked in a wood-fired, clay oven (*horno de barro)*, where leoparding, black burn spots and bubbles, just like on a Neapolitan pizza, are prized. Others are fried (*frito)*, like the potato- and peanut sauce-filled *empanada de pipián* from Popayán, Colombia.

The *repulgue*, or braided seam that seals the fillings inside the empanada, can be made by pressing down with a fork, being squeezed with your fingertips, or woven into a braid. It's usually on the side, though a Bolivian *salteña* places the *repulgue* right on top.

Empanadas can be eaten for breakfast, as an afternoon snack, or while preparing an *asado*. They are made at bakeries and restaurants or in home kitchens and sold in baskets on buses. For the most part, they are to be eaten with your hands. You want to eat them hot, almost right out of the oven or frying pan, though you must be careful as the contents can be quite hot, especially when there are stewed fillings.

We recommend making your own dough for the very best flavor. Dough discs, available at superstores, are a useful alternative if you don't have time to make your own dough for your empanadas. If you have some leftovers that can be used for a filling, these dough discs are useful for making an empanada at short notice.

Galician-Style Tuna Empanadas

Empanada gallega
Argentina, Uruguay

Preparation time: 30 minutes,
plus 1 hour resting
Cooking time: 45 minutes

Serves: 8–10

These empanadas are closest in form to the ones made by Galician immigrants who arrived in cities throughout the New World, such as Buenos Aires and Montevideo, in the 1800s. They are larger than the typical empanada, and more the size of a pie, and the dough is sometimes thicker. They're found at bakeries and pizzerias and can be filled with a wide range of fillings.

For the dough
2 cups/9 oz (260 g) all-purpose (plain) flour
2 tablespoons baking powder
½ teaspoon paprika
¼ teaspoon salt
½ cup/4 oz (115 g) butter, softened
2 eggs, plus an extra egg, beaten, to glaze

For the filling
1 tablespoon oil
2 cups/8 oz (225 g) chopped onions
1 red bell pepper, cored, seeded, and julienned
1 green bell pepper, cored, seeded, and julienned
2 garlic cloves, minced
1 teaspoon paprika
2 cups/1 lb (450 g) flaked tuna (canned is traditionally used)
2 tomatoes, chopped
½ cup/2 oz (50 g) pitted olives, chopped
1 tablespoon parsley, chopped
2 hard-boiled eggs, chopped
salt and ground pepper

Pile the flour onto a clean surface. Make a well in the center and add the baking powder, paprika, and salt. Add the butter and rub it in with your fingertips, then knead from the center to form a granulated mass. Mix in the eggs and add enough water to form a uniform but not sticky dough. Shape into a smooth ball, cover with a damp tea towel, and let rest for 1 hour. Preheat the oven to 400°F/200°C/Gas Mark 6.

Meanwhile, heat the oil for the filling in a large pan over medium heat. Sauté the onions, bell peppers, and garlic for 5 minutes, until translucent. Add the paprika, cover and let cook for 2 minutes, until slightly browned. Season with salt and pepper and set aside.

Put the tuna, tomatoes, olives, parsley, and hard-boiled eggs in a bowl, and mix.

Divide the rested dough into two equal pieces, then roll out one piece using a rolling pin until big enough to line an oiled, deep-sided pie pan, 10 inches (25 cm) in diameter. Prick the base a few times with a fork. Roll out the second piece until big enough to fit over the pan.

Spread half the cooked vegetables out over the dough, then spread the tuna mixture evenly on top, and cover with the rest of the vegetables. Cover with the dough lid, tightly sealing the edges. Prick the dough in a few places with a fork.

Brush with beaten egg and bake until golden brown, about 45 minutes.

Tucumán-Style Empanadas

Tucumana
Argentina

Preparation time: 1 hour
Cooking time: 20 minutes

Makes: 12

These empanadas, either baked in a clay oven or fried, hail from the northwest Argentine town of San Miguel de Tucumán, though they are commonly found elsewhere in Argentina. In Tucumán, *matambre* (rolled flank steak) is the most traditional filling, though *mondongo* (tripe), chicken, or cheese are also common. They are usually served with a lemon wedge to squirt inside after each bite. In Bolivia, *tucumanas* are widespread, however, they look quite different. They are always fried, for one, and the filling usually consists of ground beef, onions, potatoes, carrots, peas, hard-boiled eggs, and olives.

8 oz (225 g) flank steak
1 tablespoon vegetable oil
½ white onion, chopped
3 scallions (spring onions), chopped
1 teaspoon ground cumin
6 hard-boiled eggs, chopped
4 cups/19 oz (550 g) all-purpose (plain) flour
¾ cup/6 fl oz (175 ml) melted lard
salt and ground pepper

Boil the flank steak in plenty of salted water for 40 minutes. Remove with a skimmer and let cool, reserving the cooking water. Once cooled, cut the meat into small cubes and set aside.

In a medium pan, heat the oil over medium heat. Sauté the onion for 8 minutes, then add the scallions (spring onions) and cook for a further 5 minutes. Add 1 cup/8 fl oz (250 ml) of the reserved beef cooking water, and the cumin, and season with salt and pepper. Remove from the heat, mix in the chopped eggs, and set aside.

Preheat the oven to 350°F/180°C/Gas Mark 4.

To make the dough, heap the flour onto a clean surface. Slowly add the lard while mixing with a wooden spoon, then rub it into the flour with your fingertips. Add enough reserved beef cooking water (about 1 cup/8 fl oz/250 ml), then knead with your hands until a soft dough forms.

Divide the dough into 12 equal pieces, shape into balls, and roll each into a disc with a rolling pin, about 6 inches (15 cm) in diameter and ⅛ inch (3 mm) thick.

Place a tablespoon of the filling in the middle of each and bring the dough edges together, moistening them with a little water to seal.

Place on a lined baking sheet and bake for 20 minutes or until golden brown. Serve warm.

Bolivian-Style Turnovers

Salteña 🍲
Bolivia

Preparation time: 20 minutes   Makes: 12
Cooking time: 15 minutes

The flat-bottomed *salteña*, with its stewed interior, is like the soup dumpling of empanadas. Despite its name, which refers to the Argentine city of Salta, this baked empanada actually has its origins in Bolivia. During the dictatorship of Juan Manuel de Rosas in the nineteenth century, a writer named Juana Manuela Gorriti, from Salta, was exiled to Potosí just over the border in Bolivia, and came up with the recipe as a way to make a living. People in Potosí would often say go and pick up an empanada from "la Salteña", the woman from Salta. The nickname stuck and eventually the form left Potosí and spread around Bolivia, with many regions creating their own versions.

To add to the confusion, the city of Salta is also known for its empanadas, which in Argentina are generally referred to as *empanadas salteñas*. The fillings are more similar to the Bolivian version than they are to other empanadas in Argentina and it's served with a spicy sauce similar to the Bolivian hot sauce *llajua*, though the dough is quite different and the *repulgue* (seam) is usually on the side rather than the top like those in Bolivia.

For the dough
5 cups/1 lb 7 oz (650 g) all-purpose (plain) flour, plus extra for dusting
2 tablespoons sugar
1 cup/8 fl oz (250 ml) melted butter
2 egg yolks
½ cup/4 fl oz (120 ml) warm water with ½ tablespoon salt added
1 whole egg, beaten, to glaze

For the filling
½ cup/4 fl oz (120 ml) melted lard
2 white onions, chopped
1 fresh *ají amarillo*, chopped
1 lb (450 g) ground (minced) beef (or use shredded chicken)
5 cups/40 fl oz (1.2 liters) beef stock
1 gelatin leaf, soaked in ice-cold water
3 tablespoons parsley, chopped
6 peeled and boiled potatoes, cut in small cubes
1 cup/4½ oz (130 g) cooked peas
1 tablespoon *ají amarillo* paste
salt and ground pepper

Heat the lard for the filling in a large frying pan until very hot. Sauté the onions and fresh chile for 8 minutes or until soft and brown. Add the beef, cook for 4 minutes then pour in the stock with the squeezed-out gelatin and let it simmer for about 35 minutes. Add the parsley and season with salt and pepper, then remove from the heat. Add the potatoes and peas and place in the refrigerator until needed.

For the dough, mix the flour and sugar in a bowl. Add the melted butter and mix with a wooden spoon until the dough is broken. Add the egg yolks and slowly stir in the warm, salted water. Knead into a soft and uniform dough with your hands, then place on a floured surface and roll it out with a rolling pin to a thin sheet, about ⅛ inch (3 mm) thick.

Preheat the oven to 350°F/180°C/Gas Mark 4.

Using a 4½-inch (11-cm) round cutter, stamp out discs from the dough and place on a lined baking sheet. Place a full tablespoon of the filling in the middle of each disc. Using your finger, wet the edges of the disc with water, and fold the empanadas in half to seal.

Brush with beaten egg and bake for 15 minutes or until golden brown.

Belizean Empanadas

Panades
Belize

Preparation time: 25 minutes,   ※ ⊘
plus 15 minutes resting   Makes: 12
Cooking time: 40 minutes

Often made during communal events or sold as street food, these Belizean empanadas made of corn masa are usually filled with smoked fish, refried beans, or cheese. *Panades* are served with *curtido*, an acidic relish made from white vinegar, onions, salt and habanero chilies.

3 cups/15 oz (420 g) corn (maize) flour
1 teaspoon baking powder
3 tablespoons annatto paste
about ½ cup/4 fl oz (60 ml) warm water
3 cups/1 lb 8 oz (675 g) flaked fish (such as tuna)
vegetable oil, for deep-frying
salt

For the *curtido* garnish
1 white onion, finely diced
1 cup/2 oz (60 g) sliced white cabbage
1 tablespoon cilantro (coriander), chopped
juice of 2 limes
1 cup/8 fl oz (250 ml) white vinegar
1 habanero chile, seeded and coarsely chopped

In a medium bowl, sift together the corn (maize) flour and baking powder. Add a pinch of salt and start kneading with your hands while you slowly add the annatto paste and enough of the water to knead to a soft and uniform dough; you may not need all the water. Cover with a tea towel and let rest for 15 minutes.

Once the dough is ready, divide into 12 equal pieces and shape into balls. Using a tortilla press or a flat utensil, flatten each dough ball into a circular and medium-thick disc.

Place 1 tablespoon of fish in the middle of each disc and fold it in half. Seal the edges by pressing them together with your fingertips.

Pour enough vegetable oil for deep-frying into a large, heavy pan, making sure it is no more than two-thirds full, and heat to 360°F/182°C.

Fry the *panades* in small batches for 4 minutes each side or until golden brown and crispy on the outside. Remove with a skimmer and place on a plate lined with paper towels, to absorb excess oil.

For the *curtido* garnish, mix the onion, cabbage and cilantro (coriander), add the lime juice, vinegar and season with salt and the habanero.

To serve, spread the garnish on top of the *panades*.

Bolivian-Style Turnovers

Chilean Meat Empanadas

Empanadas de pino 🍲
Chile

Preparation time: 50 minutes,
plus 1 hour 10 minutes resting
Cooking time: 30 minutes

Makes: 10

In Chile, empanadas are a national pastime. Upon being elected President in 1970, Salvador Allende even spoke of a "revolution with the taste of red wine and empanadas." Best when made with lard and cooked in a wood-burning oven, they are everywhere, from roving street vendors to train station cafés to ski resorts. They come baked or fried and in a variety of shapes and endless number of fillings, though *empanadas de pino* are the most widespread Chilean empanada. "De pino" is a variation of the Mapuche word *pinu*, which just means cooked meat, though it has grown to signify a mixture of ground beef and onions, plus hard-boiled egg, olives, and raisins.

For the dough
4 cups/1 lb 3 oz (540 g) all-purpose (plain) flour, plus extra for dusting
1½ teaspoons salt
3 tablespoons sugar
2 tablespoons butter, chilled
12 tablespoons lard
2 egg yolks, whisked with ¾ cup/6 fl oz (175 ml) water

For the filling
2 tablespoons vegetable oil
2 tablespoons butter
3 white onions, chopped
2 garlic cloves, minced
1 lb (450 g) ground (minced) beef
2 teaspoons ground cumin
1 teaspoon chile powder
1 tablespoon paprika
½ cup/4 fl oz (120 ml) beef stock
2 tablespoons all-purpose (plain) flour
½ cup/2½ oz (70 g) raisins
½ cup/6 oz (170 g) pitted and chopped black olives
2 hard-boiled eggs, sliced
salt and ground pepper

To glaze
1 egg yolk, beaten with 2 tablespoons milk

Place the flour for the dough in a bowl, then the salt and sugar. Using your hands, mix the butter and lard and knead into the dry ingredients. Slowly add the beaten egg mixture to the flour, until the dough starts to become uniform and smooth. Cover with a tea towel and let rest in the refrigerator for 1 hour.

For the filling, heat the oil and butter in a medium pan over medium heat. Add the onions and garlic and sauté for 10 minutes or until soft. Add the beef, cumin, chile powder, and paprika. Continue stirring for a further 3 minutes before adding the beef stock. Season with salt and pepper and cook for about 10 minutes. Add the flour and continue cooking for a further 3 minutes. Remove from the heat and mix in the raisins and olives, without heating. Let cool.

Preheat the oven to 350°F/180°C/Gas Mark 4.

Divide the dough into 10 equal pieces, shape into balls, and let rest for 10 minutes. On a floured surface, stretch each ball into a 6-inch (15-cm) square, about ¼ inch (5 mm) thick.

Place 1 tablespoon of the beef filling in the middle of each square, and top with one slice of hard-boiled egg. Brush the edges of the dough with water and fold the square in half. Brush the sealed edge with water and press with your fingers to seal. Brush the empanadas with the egg yolk glaze and bake for 30 minutes or until golden brown.

Dogfish Empanadas

Empanadas de cazón
Venezuela

Preparation time: 30 minutes,
plus 10 minutes resting
Cooking time: 20 minutes

※ ∅
Makes: 8

On a trip to almost any beach in Venezuela you will likely encounter a vendor selling various types of empanadas, and *cazón*, most famously from Isla Margarita, is a favorite of many. They are made from the spiny dogfish (*Squalus acanthias*), a type of small shark found in shallow waters. It has conservation status, depending on where it is caught, so if you have any doubts use a substitute such as cod or swordfish.

¼ cup/2 fl oz (60 ml) corn oil
1 tablespoon achiote (annatto) seeds
1 onion, minced
2 garlic cloves, crushed
1 teaspoon ground cumin
1 red bell pepper, cored, seeded and diced
2 tomatoes, peeled and chopped
9 oz (250 g) dogfish (or cod or swordfish)
¼ cup/¾ oz (20 g) finely chopped scallion (spring onion)
¼ cup/¾ oz (20 g) chopped cilantro (coriander) leaves
corn oil, for deep-frying
salt and ground pepper

For the dough
2 cups/10 oz (280 g) corn (maize) flour
4 tablespoons sugar
1 teaspoon salt
2 cups/16 fl oz (475 ml) water

Place a pan over medium heat. Add the oil and achiote (annatto) seeds, and once the oil becomes colored, strain and return the oil to the pan. Add the onion, garlic, and cumin and cook for 2 minutes, then add the bell pepper and tomatoes. Add the fish and season with salt and pepper. Cook slowly, stirring occasionally, until the fish falls apart. Add the chopped scallion (spring onion) and cilantro (coriander). Adjust the seasoning to taste.

Place the corn flour in a bowl, then add the sugar and salt. Incorporate enough of the water to form a smooth dough. Knead for a few minutes, then let rest for 5–10 minutes.

Divide the dough into 8 balls. Roll into discs using a rolling pin (placing the dough between two layers of food wrap will help). Place a spoonful of filling in the center of each dough disc. Fold the dough in half to close the empanadas, pressing down around the edges to seal.

Pour enough corn oil for deep-frying into a large, heavy pan, making sure it is no more than two-thirds full, and heat to 350°F/177°C.

Fry the empanadas in batches, about 4 minutes each side until golden brown. Transfer to a plate lined with paper towels, to absorb excess oil. Serve hot.

Breads and Baked Goods

Chilean Meat Empanadas

Potato and Peanut Empanadas

Empanadas de pipián 🔲
Colombia

Preparation time: 40 minutes
Cooking time: 20 minutes

Makes: 10

These tiny fried empanadas come from the colonial town of Popayán, one of the hubs of Colombian gastronomy, and are common throughout the department of Cauca. They are filled with *pipián*, a mixture of *papas coloradas*, a local creole potato, with roasted and ground peanuts and other seasonings. The same filling can also be used to flavor *tamales*. They are usually served with *ají de maní*, a spicy, peanut-based sauce.

For the dough
1 cup/8 fl oz (250 ml) warm water
½ tablespoon panela sugar (or use light muscovado)
1 cup/4 oz (120 g) *masarepa* (precooked corn flour/maize flour) or corn (maize) flour
1 teaspoon baking powder
½ teaspoon annatto paste
½ teaspoon vegetable oil

For the filling
2 potatoes, peeled and diced
1 tablespoon olive oil
¼ cup/1 oz (30 g) chopped white onion
1 garlic clove, minced
2 tomatoes, chopped
¼ cup/1 oz (30 g) cored, seeded and chopped red bell pepper
1 scallion (spring onion), chopped
2 tablespoons cilantro (coriander), chopped
1 hard-boiled egg, chopped
½ cup/2 oz (50 g) finely chopped roasted peanuts
vegetable oil, for deep-frying
salt and ground pepper

Put the water for the dough in a large bowl, add the sugar, and stir until it dissolves. Slowly sift in the corn flour and baking powder while stirring with a whisk. Add the annatto paste and vegetable oil while kneading with your hands until it becomes a soft dough. Cover with a tea towel and let rest for 15 minutes.

Meanwhile, for the filling, simmer the potatoes in a pan of salted water for 10 minutes or until soft, then drain, and set aside.

Heat the olive oil in a large frying pan over medium heat. Add the white onion and garlic, and sauté for 5 minutes or until soft. Add the tomatoes, bell pepper, and scallion (spring onion), and continue cooking, stirring frequently, for a further 5 minutes or until the vegetables are soft. Add the cilantro (coriander), and season with salt and pepper. Add the cooked potatoes, hard-boiled egg, and peanuts, and stir until well mixed.

To shape the empanadas, divide the dough into 10 equal pieces and shape into balls. Flatten each ball with a tortilla press or place them between two layers of plastic wrap (clingfilm) and flatten them with the bottom of a pan.

Place 1 tablespoon of the filling in the middle of each disc. Fold the dough in half and gently press the edges together to seal, using a fork or your fingertips.

Pour enough vegetable oil for deep-frying into a large, heavy pan, making sure it is no more than two-thirds full, and heat to 360°F/182°C.

Fry the empanadas a few at a time for 3 minutes each side or until golden brown with a crispy exterior. Remove with a skimmer and place on a plate lined with paper towels, to absorb excess oil. Serve hot with *ají de maní*.

Wild Mushroom Empanadas

Empanadas de changles
Chile

Preparation time: 35 minutes
plus 10 minutes resting
Cooking time: 15 minutes

Makes: 10

Changles (*Ramaria flava*) are a type of edible, yellow coral mushroom that appear in forests with beech trees throughout southern Chile in April and May. On street corners and markets in towns like Osorno and Temuco you'll see them for sale in giant woven baskets. It is unlikely you'll find *changles* outside of Chile, though the more widespread lion's mane mushrooms (*Hericium erinaceus*) are a good substitute and you could really use any wild mushrooms available. The *changles* can be eaten fresh or pickled and preserved, though these empanadas, spiced with a smoked chile powder called *merkén*, are a special treat each autumn.

For the dough
1 cup/4½ oz (130 g) all-purpose (plain) flour
1 cup/4 oz (120 g) rye flour
1 tablespoon olive oil
1 tablespoon sunflower oil
1 teaspoon salt
1 cup/8 fl oz (250 ml) warm water

For the filling
2 tablespoons vegetable oil
½ white onion, chopped
1 lb 2 oz (500 g) *changles* (or any wild mushrooms available), chopped
1 teaspoon *merkén* (smoked chile powder)
1 teaspoon dried thyme
1 egg yolk, beaten
salt

To prepare the dough, sift both flours into a medium bowl and create a small well in the middle. Pour both oils into the well and add the salt. Knead with your hands and slowly add the water until you have a soft and uniform dough (use more water if necessary). Cover with a tea towel and let rest for 10 minutes.

Preheat the oven to 350°F/180°C/Gas Mark 4.

Meanwhile, make the filling. Heat the vegetable oil in a non-stick frying pan over high heat. Add the onion and sauté for 5 minutes, then lower the heat and add the mushrooms. Season with the *merkén*, thyme, and some salt. Cook the mushrooms until soft, then remove from the heat and set aside.

Divide the dough into 10 equal pieces and shape into balls. Stretch and flatten each ball into a disc 4½ inches (12 cm) in diameter.

Place 1 heaped tablespoon of the mushroom mixture in the middle of each disc. With your fingertips, moisten the edges of the dough with a little water, fold in half and press the edges together to seal. Carefully prick the dough twice with a fork, and brush with the beaten egg yolk.

Place the empanadas on a lined baking sheet and bake for 15 minutes or until golden brown. Serve warm.

Breads and Baked Goods

Potato and Peanut Empanadas

Sandwiches

There is a long and storied history of sandwiches throughout Latin America, and each country uses their own set of components. In Peru, slices of boiled sweet potatoes serve as a complement to fried pork between hunks of crusty bread. In northern Brazil, the palm fruit pulp dances with melted cheese amidst soft white rolls. In Mexico, sandwiches can get covered in sauce like an enchilada.

In Chile, *fuentes de soda*, the old-school sandwich spots, have their own lingo. Order a sandwich "italiano" and it will be topped with avocados, mayonnaise, and tomatoes (the colors of the Italian flag) and will be too big to hold and need to be eaten with a knife and fork. In some cases, the women and men who work the grill have been there for decades, and have loyal customers who insist on eating their *barros luco* or *lomito palta* only from them.

Bolivian Pork Sandwich

Sándwich de Chola
Bolivia

Preparation time: 30 minutes,   Serves: 8
plus 12 hours brining and 1 hour resting
Cooking time: 2 hours

You'll find these pork sandwiches sold at sidewalk vendors and market food stalls around Bolivia, most famously in La Paz's famed Parque de las Cholas, where a handful of women have been selling them for decades. The pork leg is brined overnight then roasted until the skin is as crisp as candy. It's typically made with *pan sarnita*, a smallish, soft, round roll made with milk and butter, then sprinkled with cheese before baking. Pickled carrots and onions act as slaw, and a slice of fresh tomato is often added too, as is a spoonful of *llajua*, a chile sauce made of *locoto* chile peppers ground in a mortar.

    1 cup/9½ oz (270 g) salt
    8½ cups/4¼ pints (2 liters) water
    1 lb 8 oz (675 g) pork leg
    2 tablespoons *ají colorado* paste (chile paste)
    1 onion, finely chopped
    2 heads of garlic, cloves peeled and finely chopped
    ½ teaspoon black pepper
    1 teaspoon ground cumin
    8 sandwich rolls
    1 tomato, sliced
    pickled carrots and onions

    For the *llajua*
    3 tomatoes
    2 *locoto* chiles (or 3 tablespoons rocoto paste)
    ½ cup/⅓ oz (10 g) fresh mint leaves, chopped
    ¼ cup/¼ oz (7 g) parsley leaves, chopped

First prepare the pork. Dissolve the salt in the water in a bowl, add the pork leg, making sure it is fully submerged, and let soak overnight at room temperature. The next morning, drain the brine.
    Rub the pork with the chile paste, onion, garlic, pepper, and cumin to coat all over, and marinate in the refrigerator for 1 hour.
    Preheat the oven to 400°F/200°C/Gas Mark 6.
    Bake the pork in an oven tray for about 2 hours, turning it over every 30 minutes or so. Cut it into slices as soon as it is done, and let cool to room temperature.
    For the *llajua*, grind the tomatoes in a mortar with the chiles and season with salt. Stir in the mint and parsley.
    Cut the rolls in half. Add slices of pork and tomato, then pickled carrots and onions. Serve with the *llajua* on the side.

Brazilian Roast Beef Sandwich

Bauru
Brazil

Preparation time: 30 minutes   Serves: 4

In the early 1930s, a law student named Casimiro Pinto Neto went into the São Paulo bar Ponto Chic and asked them to make a sandwich with roast beef, melted cheese, and slices of pickles and tomatoes. Someone in the restaurant saw his creation and asked for "*um lanche igual ao do Bauru*," or a snack like Bauru, referring to the town in São Paulo state where Pinto Neto was from. The name and sandwich stuck, and the Bauru quickly became the most popular item on the menu.

    6 oz (175 g) yellow cheese slices (a mixture of
      Edam, Gouda, and Swiss in equal proportions,
      or mozzarella)
    3 tomatoes, sliced
    1 teaspoon dried oregano
    4 small, crusty French rolls
    1 lb (450 g) roast beef, thinly sliced
    1 large dill pickle (pickled cucumber), thinly sliced
    salt

In a heatproof bowl set over a pan of simmering water, melt the slices of cheese, then remove from the heat. Season the tomatoes with salt and oregano.
    Slice the rolls in half and tear out the interior, leaving the crust. Add slices of roast beef, sliced tomato, dill pickle, and lastly, melted cheese.

Chilean Steak and Green Bean Sandwich

Chacarero 🔲
Chile

Preparation time: 20 minutes
Cooking time: 10 minutes   Serves: 4

Churrasco means something a little bit different everywhere you go in Latin America, all having something to do with beef. In Chile, it refers to a sandwich of grilled and thinly sliced beef tenderloin or sirloin, usually topped with tomato, mayo, and/or mashed avocado. One version of the *churrasco* stands out above all others: the *chacarero*. Its addition to the sandwich comes in the form of haricots verts (French beans), piled on the meat like slaw, with or without a touch of chile peppers or mayo. Instead of steak, roasted pork loin, just like in the *lomito* on page 52, may also be used.

    2 tablespoons olive oil
    1 garlic clove, minced
    1 lb 8 oz (675 g) beef sirloin, cut into 4 thin (1-inch/
      2.5-cm) steaks
    10 oz (275 g) haricots verts (French beans)
    1 tomato
    4 crusty French rolls
    2 tablespoons butter
    salt
    mayonnaise, to serve, optional

Warm 1 tablespoon of the olive oil in a frying pan over low heat, and add the garlic. Increase the heat to high, add the steaks and cook on each side for about 1½ minutes until medium rare. Let cool, then slice thinly.
    Meanwhile, cook the beans in boiling salted water for a few minutes, making sure they stay crisp, then drain and place in a bowl of iced water.
    Slice the tomato as thinly as possible and season with salt and the remaining olive oil.
    Cut the rolls in half and spread one side with butter. Add the meat, tomato, and finally the beans. Add some mayonnaise, if using. Serve at room temperature.

Chilean Steak and Green Bean Sandwich

Beef Tartare Toast

Crudo
Chile

Preparation time: 20 minutes

Serves: 6

Mettbrötchen, or *Mett*, is a German dish of raw, seasoned, minced pork that's spread on a slice of bread and often topped with onions. German colonists brought the recipe to southern Chile in the late 1800s, but it was adapted to the prevalence of cattle farming in the region. In Valdivia, where the German influence can be seen in the architecture and love of beer, *crudos* are a snack in taverns around town, most famously at Café Haussmann, where they are served with diced onions, lemon wedges, and tartar sauce.

  1 lb (450 g) beef round (topside or silverside)
  2 lemons, halved
  1 onion
  6 slices of bread (any bread, but not overly soft or sweet)
  fresh cilantro (coriander), chopped
  ½ cup/3¾ oz (110 g) mayonnaise
  salt and ground pepper

Pass the beef through a meat grinder or processor so that it becomes a paste (this might need to be done several times).

Add the juice of half a lemon, and a few shakes of salt and pepper, then mix. Cut the rest of the lemon halves into wedges.

Cut the onion into small chunks and submerge them in a bowl of ice-cold water for at least 10 minutes, then set aside.

Toast the slices of bread, then spread with the beef. Serve with the separate bowls of onion, cilantro (coriander), lemon wedges, and mayonnaise.

Chilean Steak and Melted Cheese Sandwich

Barros Luco
Chile

Preparation time: 5 minutes
Cooking time: 10 minutes

Serves: 4

Ramón Barros Luco, who was Chile's president from 1910 to 1915, was known to always order a grilled steak and melted cheese sandwich from Confitería Torres in Santiago. While Barros Luco isn't remembered for having a particularly great administration, he has been immortalized by this beloved sandwich. Barros Luco's cousin, the minister of foreign relations Ernesto Barros Jarpa, allegedly wasn't a fan of steak and would order it with ham instead, leading to that variation being called the Barros Jarpa.

There's not a specific bread used in either sandwich, though hamburger-style rolls called *pan frica* and French rolls called *pan marraqueta* are some of the most common. The Barros Jarpa is sometimes made with white bread.

  1 tablespoon olive oil
  2 garlic cloves, finely chopped
  1 lb (450 g) sirloin steak, cut into 4 equal pieces
  8 slices of *mantecoso* cheese (or use Muenster)
  4 crusty French rolls
  salt and ground pepper

Heat the oil in a large frying pan, and add the garlic. Let it brown then remove as much as possible and discard, leaving only the oil infused with garlic.

Season the steak pieces with salt and pepper, add to the pan with the garlic oil over medium heat and cook for 2 minutes on each side. Add 2 slices of cheese to the top of each steak piece, and let it melt, then remove from the pan.

Cut the rolls in half and place in the pan to heat briefly on both sides. Fill each with a steak and melted cheese, cut in half, and serve warm.

Pork Loin and Avocado Sandwich

Lomito palta
Chile

Preparation time: 30 minutes
Cooking time: 1 hour 30 minutes

Serves: 6

The *lomito*, made of slow-braised pork loin, is one of Chile's favorite sandwiches and found in sandwich shops throughout the country, but it's even better with a smear of mashed avocado on it.

  3 lb (1.4 kg) pork loin
  4 teaspoons olive oil, plus extra to season
  1 teaspoon dried oregano
  1 teaspoon yellow mustard
  1 onion, cut into wedges
  1 garlic clove, finely chopped
  2 cups/16 fl oz (475 ml) cold water
  2 avocados
  juice of 1 lemon
  3 tomatoes, sliced
  6 white rolls
  mayonnaise
  salt and ground pepper

Preheat the oven to 350°F/180°C/Gas Mark 4.

Season the pork shoulder with salt and pepper.

In a large frying pan, heat the olive oil over high heat. Add the pork shoulder and brown on all sides, to seal the juices, then place in a roasting pan and add the oregano, mustard, onion, and garlic to the pan. Tip in the water, cover the pan with foil and roast for 1 hour, or until completely cooked.

Place the pork on a cutting board and cut into slices. Strain the juices from the roasting pan and place in a pan. Reduce over high heat to a saucy consistency. Add the slices of meat to the sauce and set aside.

Peel, pit, and smash the avocados, season with lemon juice and salt. Season the tomato slices with salt and olive oil.

Cut the rolls in half and spread mayonnaise on one of the sides. Place the meat generously inside with a little bit of sauce, then layer in the slices of tomato and smashed avocado. Serve at room temperature.

Sandwiches

Salvadoran Turkey Sandwich

Pan con chumpe, Panes con pavo
El Salvador

Preparation time: 30 minutes   Serves: 6
Cooking time: 3 hours

Chumpe is slang for turkey in El Salvador and some say the country prepares it better than anywhere else on earth. Here, they are cooked in an *olla chompipera*, a Salvadoran Dutch oven (casserole), and livened up with *relajo*, a semi-spicy seasoning. This sandwich can also be made with chicken.

    2 large turkey drumsticks
    6 bay leaves
    1 tablespoon black peppercorns
    1 teaspoon cloves
    2 teaspoons sesame seeds
    ¼ cup/1 oz (30 g) peanuts, chopped
    1 dried chile (*ciruela* or *pasilla*), seeded
    1 teaspoon dried oregano
    1 teaspoon dried thyme
    1 tablespoon annatto paste
    10 tomatoes, chopped
    1 onion, finely chopped
    2 garlic cloves, peeled
    1 green bell pepper, cored, seeded, and chopped
    1 cup/8 fl oz (250 ml) water
    1 head of lettuce, leaves very thinly sliced
    juice of 1 lime
    4 tomatoes, thinly sliced
    2 cucumbers, thinly sliced
    1 tablespoon olive oil
    6 crusty French rolls (Portuguese rolls, Mexican *bolillos*, or hoagie buns also work)
    mayonnaise
    salt and ground pepper

Preheat the oven to 350°F/180°C/Gas Mark 4.
Rinse the turkey legs and pat dry; season all over with salt and pepper, and set aside.
Set a *comal* or frying pan over medium heat, add the bay leaves, peppercorns, and cloves and toast for a couple of minutes, then set them aside. Repeat the process with the sesame seeds and peanuts, moving them continuously so that they don't burn. Add everything to a mortar, along with the dried chile, oregano, thyme, and annatto paste. Grind to a paste. (This paste is *relajo salvadoreño*, which can also be store-bought).
Combine the paste and turkey legs in a Dutch oven (casserole) with ½ cup/4 fl oz (125 ml) of water; season with salt and pepper, bring to a boil on the stove, cover, reduce to low, and braise until the turkey is very tender, about 2 hours.
Remove the turkey from the cooking juices and let cool, then remove the skin and debone. Cut or tear the meat into strips, about 2 inches (5 cm) long. Keep the cooking juices in a pan.
In a blender, purée the tomatoes, onion, garlic, bell pepper, and water, until smooth. Add to the cooking juices and boil over medium-high heat, stirring continuously so it does not stick to the bottom, about 45 minutes, or until thick.
Add the turkey strips to the sauce, reduce the heat to medium and let cook for a further 5 minutes. Season with salt and pepper.

Season the lettuce with lime juice, and the tomatoes and cucumber with olive oil and salt.
Slice the rolls in half and spread mayonnaise on each side. Add the tomatoes, lettuce, cucumber and the turkey, then ladle on the sauce.

Pueblan-Style Sandwich

Cemita poblana
Mexico

Preparation time: 20 minutes
Cooking time: 10 minutes   Serves: 4

The *cemita*, named after the sesame seed-topped bun it is served in, is the signature *torta* (sandwich) from Puebla. There, some *cemita* operations, restaurants or market stalls, put the towering sandwiches together with assembly-line efficiency, where individuals dedicate themselves just to shredding the cheese or cutting avocados. Most vendors offer different variations of meat, though breaded and fried veal, beef, pork, or chicken cutlets called *milanesas* are the most common. *Papalo*, the strong, cilantro- (coriander-) like herb that isn't for everyone, helps cut through the layers of fat. Note: As there are a lot of toppings, removing some of the inside of the top of the bun helps achieve balance.

    ½ cup/2¼ oz (65 g) all-purpose (plain) flour
    2 eggs, beaten
    1 cup/3 oz (80 g) breadcrumbs
    4 pork cutlets
    2 tablespoons olive oil
    2 avocados
    juice of 1 lime
    3 tablespoons *papalo* or cilantro (coriander), chopped
    4 *cemita* buns (or a brioche bun topped with sesame seeds)
    ½ cup/4 oz (120 g) shredded *queso Oaxaca* (or use mozzarella)
    4 canned chipotle chiles in adobo, finely chopped with some of the sauce from the can
    salt and ground pepper

Place the flour, eggs, and breadcrumbs in three separate shallow dishes. Season the pork with salt and pepper, then coat with the flour. Set in the bowl of beaten eggs, and then dredge in the breadcrumbs. Repeat with the remaining cutlets.
Heat the oil in a medium frying pan over medium-high heat, and cook the pork cutlets for about 3 minutes each side, or until brown. Remove to a plate lined with paper towels.
Peel and pit the avocados, and mash with a fork. Season with the lime juice and some salt, and mix in the *papalo* or cilantro (coriander).
Cut the buns in half, then place on a grill (barbecue) or in the oven until golden brown. Add a pork cutlet to the bottom half of each bun and place a tablespoon of avocado on top. Garnish with cheese and the chipotles in sauce. Serve warm.

Drowned Sandwich

Torta ahogada ⬚
Mexico

Preparation time: 30 minutes,
plus 15 minutes soaking
Cooking time: 2 hours 30 minutes

Serves: 4

While the *Pambazo* (Mexican Potato and Chorizo Sandwich, page 56) is dipped and fried in extremely spicy chile sauce, the *torta ahogada* soaks in a pool of it. Hailing from Guadalajara and found throughout the state of Jalisco, it is said to have been created in the early 1900s by a street vendor who accidentally dropped the sandwich into a container full of salsa, which the customer loved. You can order it "*media ahogada*," which means the sandwich is only partially dipped in the sauce (a good option if you order from a street vendor and are eating with your hands), or "*bien ahogada*," meaning totally submerged in sauce. As an alternative to the very spicy *chile de árbol*-based sauce, a sweeter, tomato-based version is sometimes offered. We use a mixture of both in the recipe below, though you can adjust as you see fit. The *birote* is a long, salted, crusty roll that helps hold the sandwich together amidst the sauce and *carnitas*. A good substitute is a hunk of baguette.

1 lb 8 oz (675 g) pork shoulder
2 garlic cloves, chopped
1 bay leaf
1 cup/8 fl oz (250 ml) water
1 red onion, halved and thinly sliced into half-moons
juice of 1 lime
4 *birote* rolls (or hunks of baguette)
4 tablespoons cilantro (coriander) leaves, finely chopped
salt and ground pepper
lime wedges, to serve

For the spicy sauce
1/2 oz (15 g) dried *chiles de árbol*
1 cup/8 fl oz (250 ml) hot water
2 garlic cloves, chopped
2 tablespoons apple cider vinegar
1/4 cup/1 oz (30 g) toasted sesame seeds
1 teaspoon dried oregano
1 teaspoon ground cumin

For the tomato sauce
2 lb (900 g) tomatoes
1/4 teaspoon ground cumin
1/2 white onion, chopped
1 teaspoon dried oregano
1 garlic clove, chopped
1 tablespoon olive oil

Preheat the oven to 350°F/180°C/Gas Mark 4.
Season the pork with salt, pepper, and garlic, and place in a roasting pan. Add the bay leaf and water to the bottom of the pan and cook in the oven for 2 hours, turning the meat over after 1 hour; it is ready when a knife inserted in the middle comes out warm. Remove and let cool until warm, then shred the meat with your hands, and set aside.
For the spicy sauce, place the *chiles de árbol* and hot water in a bowl and leave to soak for 15 minutes. Drain, and place the chiles in a blender with the garlic, vinegar, sesame seeds, oregano, and cumin. Season

with salt and pepper and blend until smooth. Strain the mixture and keep the liquid sauce.
For the tomato sauce, boil the tomatoes in a pan of water for 10 minutes, then drain, and peel. Clean the blender and add the tomatoes, cumin, onion, oregano, and garlic, and blend to a paste. In a medium pan, heat the oil until hot, add the tomato mixture, and cook for 20 minutes, letting some of the liquid evaporate, stirring continuously so it doesn't stick.
Season the red onion with lime juice and some salt and leave for 5 minutes.
Cut open the bread and place some meat inside and then onions on the top. Pour some tomato sauce on the bread, add the spicy sauce and some cilantro (coriander). Serve warm with lime wedges.

Pork and Sweet Potato Sandwich

Pan con chicharrón
Peru

Preparation time: 30 minutes,
plus 30 minutes soaking
Cooking time: 2 hours

Serves: 4

In Peru, the term *chicharrón* refers to fried pork in general, and not just fried pork skin. This sandwich, with braised then fried pork, is served at all hours of the day, though there is a special fondness for having it for breakfast with a cup of coffee.

1 lb (450 g) pork ribs without bones
3 cups/25 fl oz (750 ml) water
1 teaspoon ground cumin
2 tablespoons salt
1 teaspoon ground pepper
2 tablespoons olive oil
2 sweet potatoes, peeled, and sliced into rounds about 1/4 inch (5 mm) thick
4 crusty French rolls

For the *salsa criolla*
1/2 red onion, thinly sliced into half-moons
1 fresh *ají amarillo*, finely chopped
1 tablespoon cilantro (coriander), finely chopped
juice of 1 lime
salt

Cut the meat into large chunks and place in a bowl. Add 2 cups/16 fl oz (475 ml) of the water, the cumin, salt, and pepper, leave for 30 minutes, then drain and set aside.
In a pan, heat 1 tablespoon of the oil over medium heat. Add the meat a little at a time, pour in the remaining water, cover, and cook for 45 minutes. Remove the lid and cook for 1 hour or until the water evaporates. Set aside.
Meanwhile, bring a small pan of water to a boil. Add the sweet potato and cook for 30 minutes or until soft. Drain and let cool.
Heat the remaining tablespoon of oil over medium heat in a medium pan. Add the pieces of pork and cook until brown on all sides. Set aside. (If you want, you can also fry the slices of sweet potato in this pan too.)
For the salsa, put the red onion slices in a bowl with iced water and leave for 20 minutes. Drain and place in a bowl with the chopped *ají amarillo* and cilantro (coriander). Season with lime juice and salt.
Cut open the rolls and place sweet potato on the bottom halves and add the meat on top. Garnish with the salsa and close. Serve at room temperature.

Drowned Sandwich

Mexican Potato and Chorizo Sandwich

Pambazo
Mexico

Preparation time: 30 minutes
plus 30 minutes soaking
Cooking time: 45 minutes

Serves: 4

During Mexico's Vice-Regal era, bakeries called *pambacerías* specialized in low-quality breads made with unrefined flour, called *pan basso*, or *pan bajo*. Yet that cheap, beloved bread of the masses represented opportunity, so it got dipped in earthy, red *guajillo* chile salsa and fried. The standard fillings are chorizo and potatoes, though there are regional variations around the country. In the state of Mexico, chicken and the aromatic herb *epazote* are added; in Puebla, *cemita* bread (see Pueblan-Style Sandwich, page 53) is used; and in Veracruz the fillings consist of refried black beans, chorizo, and chipotle sauce.

    4 potatoes, peeled and cut into ½-inch (1-cm) cubes
    2 cups/16 fl oz (475 ml) water
    1 white onion, halved
    3 *ancho* chiles
    2 *guajillo* chiles
    1 garlic clove, roughly chopped
    3 cups/25 fl oz (750 ml) vegetable oil, plus an extra 1 tablespoon
    3 chorizos, chopped
    1 teaspoon dried oregano
    4 *pambazo* rolls (kaiser or *telera* rolls or any white roll)
    ½ lettuce, shredded
    juice of 1 lime
    1 cup/8 fl oz (250 ml) heavy (double) cream
    salt and ground pepper

Par-boil the potatoes in boiling water with a pinch of salt for 7 minutes, then drain and set aside.

Meanwhile, bring the measured water to a boil in a pan. Dice one onion half and add to the pan, along with both chiles, and the garlic. Take off the heat and set aside to soak for 30 minutes.

Meanwhile, chop the other onion half as finely as possible, and fry in the 1 tablespoon of vegetable oil in a medium pan over medium heat, for 7 minutes or until soft. Add the chorizo and cook for 5 minutes, then add the drained potatoes. Season with salt and leave over low heat, stirring occasionally, for 10 minutes or until the potatoes are tender.

Drain the chiles, onion, and garlic, reserving 1 cup/8 fl oz (250 ml) of the soaking water. Put in a blender with the oregano and the reserved soaking water. Blend until smooth, then strain through a sifter (sieve) into a bowl.

Pour the vegetable oil into a heavy pan and heat it to 325°F/162°C. Cut a roll nearly all the way in half, leaving a piece so the halves do not separate, and soak in the blended sauce for about 10 seconds. Let any surplus sauce drip off, then add the roll to the hot oil, and fry for 1 minute per side. Remove, then repeat with all the rolls, adding more oil if necessary.

Season the lettuce with lime juice and salt. Set aside.

Put the cream into a bowl with some salt, pepper, and 1 teaspoon of lime juice. Whip until thickened to a spoonable consistency.

Fill the rolls with the potato and chorizo mixture, add lettuce and then spoon cream on top. Serve warm.

Fried Silverside Fish Sandwich

Pan con chimbombo, pan con pejerrey
Peru

Preparation time: 20 minutes
Cooking time: 10 minutes

Serves: 4

The classic breakfast of fishermen and dockworkers in Lima, and Peru's gritty port city of Callao, this sandwich is made from battered and fried *pejerrey*, the tiny neo-tropical silverside fish, often with a bowl of mussel broth on the side. A similar version, *pan con chimbombo*, uses bonito instead of *pejerrey*, and is equally beloved.

    1 cup/4½ oz (130 g) all-purpose (plain) flour
    2 eggs, lightly beaten
    12 silverside fish or smelt, cleaned
    3 cups/25 fl oz (750 ml) vegetable oil
    4 crusty French rolls
    mayonnaise
    lettuce leaves
    Salsa criolla (Creole Sauce, page 406), to serve

Place the flour in a bowl and the eggs in a second bowl.

Place the fish on a tray and season with salt, then place first in the beaten eggs, then in the flour, to coat.

Heat the oil in a deep frying pan over high heat. Once hot, add the fish and fry for about 2 minutes each side. Remove with a skimmer to a plate lined with paper towels to drain excess oil.

Cut the rolls in half and spread mayonnaise on both sides. Place a couple of lettuce leaves on the bottom half, add three fish, and top with some *Salsa criolla*.

Tucumã and Cheese Sandwich

Caboquinho
Brazil

Preparation time: 10 minutes
Cooking time: 10 minutes

Serves: 2

In Brazil's northern Amazon, there is a palm fruit for everything, even a sandwich. Prepared by street vendors or from cafés, the X-Caboquinho, made with orange pulp of the tucumã fruit (*Astrocaryum vulgare*), is the most typical sandwich in Manaus and eaten for breakfast or as a snack between meals. Another version is the Tapioca Caboquinho, which has the same fillings, but uses a tapioca pancake instead of bread. Slices of sweet, grilled bananas are sometimes added to the fillings. A good substitute for tucumã, at least in texture, is peach palm fruit, called *pejibaye* or *chontaduro*, which grows throughout South and Central America.

    2 white rolls
    1 tablespoon butter
    4 slices *queijo coalho* (or use halloumi)
    2 tucumã, cut into pieces

Heat a medium frying pan. Split the rolls open and butter the cut sides. Close up again and place in the pan to warm up, then remove. Place the cheese in the pan and allow to melt slightly, then put inside the rolls, along with the tucumã. Serve warm.

Uruguayan Steak Sandwich

Chivito
Uruguay

Preparation time: 10 minutes
Cooking time: 20 minutes   Serves: 4

In the 1940s, an Argentine woman from Córdoba walked into the seaside bar El Mejillón in Punta del Este, Uruguay, and asked for a sandwich with kid goat meat, or *chivito* as it is called in Córdoba. The chef, Antonio Carbonaro, didn't have goat, so he created a sandwich on toasted and buttered bread with *churrasco* (grilled steak) and ham instead. He called it a *chivito* when he handed it to her jokingly, and the name and sandwich stuck. It became so popular that rumors suggest that at its peak El Mejillón, which closed in the 1960s, kept two local butchers in business just with the sale of *chivitos*.

    4 slices of bacon
    4 tenderloin or sirloin steaks, 4 oz (125 g) each,
    ½ inch (1 cm) thick
    2 tablespoons oil
    4 eggs
    4 soft rolls
    4 tablespoons mayonnaise
    4 lettuce leaves
    4 slices of ham
    4 slices of *queso blanco* or mozzarella
    1 tomato, thinly sliced
    salt and ground pepper

Heat a frying pan over medium heat and add the bacon. Cook until crispy, then place on a plate lined with paper towels, to absorb excess fat. Clean and dry the pan.

Season all the steaks with salt and pepper. Heat 1 tablespoon of the oil in the pan over high heat. When hot, add the steaks and cook for 2 minutes each side. Place on a cutting board and let rest.

Clean the pan again and heat the remaining oil until it shimmers. Break in the eggs one at a time and cook until the whites are cooked with the yolks still runny.

Slice the steak.

Cut the rolls in half and spread mayonnaise on both sides. Place a lettuce leaf on the bottom half of each, then add a slice of bacon, and the steak. On top, place a slice of ham and the cheese, some tomato, and finally a fried egg. Serve warm.

Chorizo Sandwich

Choripán
Argentina, Chile, Uruguay

Preparation time: 15 minutes
Cooking time: 25 minutes   Serves: 2

Throughout the Southern Cone, chorizo is usually one of the first items to come off the *parrilla*, or grill (barbecue). You can cut it lengthways, called *mariposa*, or butterfly, or leave it intact. It gets set on a crusty roll and slathered with chimichurri and serves as an appetizer, holding you until the bigger cuts are ready. The sausages are usually a mixture of beef and pork, with ratios and seasonings depending on the butcher. Most are seasoned simply, with just salt, pepper, and maybe some garlic. It's not overly spicy like in Mexico, nor are they fermented and cured like in Spain.

The *choripán* is one of the pre-eminent snacks of sporting events and festivals throughout the region, plus the king of street foods in Buenos Aires. Regional variations include using *longaniza*-style sausages, especially in Chile, or skipping the chimichurri in favor of mayo and ketchup. The bread can vary from soft, industrial hot dog or burger buns, to a French baguette.

    2 Argentinian-style chorizos
    2 small, crusty French rolls

    For the chimichurri
    ½ cup/1 oz (30 g) finely chopped parsley
    2 tablespoons finely chopped fresh oregano
    4 garlic cloves, smashed
    ½ cup/¾ oz (20 g) finely chopped chives
    1 small fresh chile, finely chopped
    2 tablespoons vinegar
    1 tablespoon lime juice
    ½ cup/4 fl oz (120 ml) olive oil
    salt and ground pepper

For the chimichurri, mix all the ingredients in a bowl, with salt and pepper to taste. Set aside in the refrigerator.

On a grill (barbecue), cook the chorizos for 20 minutes, turning them every 5 minutes or so, ensuring each side becomes golden brown. Once they are completely cooked, cut them in half lengthways and grill for a further 2 minutes on the cut side.

Cut the rolls in half lengthways and place them on the grill for 3 minutes per side. Place one chorizo in each roll and cover them with 1–2 tablespoons of chimichurri.

Hot Hole

Buraco quente
Brazil

Preparation time: 20 minutes
Cooking time: 20 minutes   Serves: 8

This is essentially a Sloppy Joe where the ground beef fills a hole carved out of a crusty French roll (called *pão francês*, *pão de sal*, or *pão carioquinha* in different parts of Brazil). Its favored territories are luncheonettes, snack bars, and children's parties in São Paulo and Rio de Janeiro.

    2 tablespoons extra-virgin olive oil
    1 onion, finely chopped
    1 garlic clove, minced
    2 tomatoes, peeled and chopped
    1 lb 8 oz (675 g) ground (minced) beef
    1 tablespoon parsley leaves, chopped
    1 hard-boiled egg, finely chopped
    ½ cup/3½ oz (90 g) pitted green olives, chopped
    8 crusty French white rolls
    salt and ground pepper

Heat a pan over medium heat, add half the olive oil, then the onion and garlic, and cook for about 5 minutes, or until the onion is translucent. Add the tomatoes and continue to cook for a further 15 minutes, or until saucy.

Meanwhile, in another pan, heat the remaining olive oil over medium heat. Add the beef and cook, stirring, until evenly brown, about 7 minutes. Tip the beef into the tomato pan, along with the parsley. Stir and season with salt and pepper, then add the chopped egg and olives.

Cut one end off each roll and scoop out the insides. Spoon the beef mixture into the hole and serve warm.

Hot Dogs

Perros calientes, otherwise known as hot dogs, are sold under a number of names country to country: Venezuelan *perros*, Guatemalan *shucos*, Chilean *completos*. While each are unique, the one uniting factor amongst all of them is that they are usually so overloaded with toppings that it can be hard to find the meat. Unlike hot dogs in the United States, where a slick of ketchup and mustard, maybe even some chile or slaw top a dog, in Latin America the sauces and toppings are layered in mashed avocado, deluges of mayonnaise, and piles of crunchy shoestring potato fries.

Guatemalan Hot Dog

Shuco
Guatemala

Preparation time: 10 minutes
Cooking time: 15 minutes   Serves: 4

On the streets of Guatemala City, *shuco* carts linger outside of schools, hospitals, and other busy places. Like in Panama, Venezuela, and most other Latin American countries, these aren't just plain hot dogs, but messy, overloaded beasts where you try to fit on as many toppings as possible. You can order them *mixto*, with additional meats, like ham or chorizo. The hybrid *mixta* uses the same ingredients as a *shuco* but serves them on a tortilla instead of a bun.

    ½ cabbage, finely shredded
    4 hot dogs (frankfurters)
    2 avocados
    juice of 2 limes
    4 hot dog buns
    ketchup, mayonnaise, and mustard
    salt

Bring salted water to a boil in a pan. Add the cabbage and cook for about 7 minutes, or until softened. Drain and let cool. Season with salt and pepper.
     In a hot frying pan or on a grill (barbecue), cook the hot dogs (frankfurters) until seared and brown on each side, about 3 minutes each side.
     Peel and pit the avocados, scoop the flesh into a bowl and mash, using a fork. Add the lime juice and season with salt.
     Heat the buns on the grill or in the oven until golden brown. Add a tablespoon of avocado to one side and top with a hot dog, sliced lengthways. Add some cabbage to each bun along with ketchup, mayonnaise, and mustard. Serve warm.

Chilean Hot Dog

Completo ⌗
Chile

Preparation time: 20 minutes
Cooking time: 10 minutes   Serves: 4

In the early 1920s, Eduardo Bahamondes Muñoz, who had worked as a cook in the United States for a few years, brought with him the concept of the hot dog. From a small café off Santiago's Plaza de Armas, he began serving hot dogs, but loading them up with toppings such as the smear of mashed avocado that has become emblematic to the *completo*. You can order the *clásico*, the basic version, that tops a *vienesa*, a basic frankfurter, with thick layers of sauerkraut, tomatoes, and mayonnaise. Though the favorite for many, and the one our recipe is based on, is the *Italiano*, which will give you the green, white, and red of the Italian flag via avocados, mayonnaise, and chopped tomatoes. There's also *A lo Pobre*, with fried onions, French fries, and a fried egg. You can put anything you want on a *completo*, really, and many vendors offer a variety of additional toppings like salsa Americana (a slaw of pickled onions, carrots, and cucumbers), crunchy shoestring potato fries, and grilled onions.

    1 tablespoon olive oil, plus extra to season
    4 hot dogs (frankfurters)
    ½ onion, finely chopped
    4 hot dog buns
    2 tomatoes, finely diced
    2 avocados
    juice of 1 lime
    4 drizzles of mayonnaise
    salt

Heat the oil in a medium pan. Add the hot dogs (frankfurters) and cook, turning occasionally, for about 5 minutes or until cooked.
     Put the onion in a bowl of iced water for 5 minutes, then drain and reserve.
     Toast the buns until slightly brown.
     Season the tomato with olive oil and salt.
     Peel and pit the avocados, scoop the flesh into a bowl, season with lime juice and salt, then mash them using a fork.
     Add a hot dog to each bun while still hot, then add some tomato and onions, mashed avocado, and lastly a generous drizzle of mayonnaise.

Chilean Hot Dog

Grains, Quinoa, and Amaranth

In a remote village in the forested Andean foothills of the Araucanía region of southern Chile, a Mapuche woman dances on wheat grains with her bare feet. Her repeated stomps make a steady beat of thuds that echo out from the *batea*, a hollowed-out log that is about a meter wide and worn to a patina from years of use. Some say, the more Mapuche she is, the fewer blisters she gets. The elaborate act peels the wheat, which she then mashes with a *kudi* and *ñumkudi*, a stone mortar and pestle, to make flour. She will toast the flour to make *mürke*, which is then boiled in water to make a porridge called *ulpo*.

Growing more rapidly than traditional crops like maize, quinoa, and *madi*, wheat was rapidly assimilated into the Mapuche food system in the 1600s as they were being pushed by the Spanish into marginal landscapes. It became a staple in the Mapuche diet and often replaced corn in traditional recipes. Grains would be fermented to make *mudai*, harvested green to enrich *cazuelas* (stews), or made into a dough that gets cooked directly in the embers of a fire called *mültrün*, or *catuto*.

While the Mapuche took to it, wheat—along with rice and barley—was used forcibly to replace native pseudograins in other parts of the region. The Spanish burned fields of quinoa in the Andes and amaranth in Mexico. The Incas and the Aztecs saw them as divine crops, with both seeds and leaves that could be consumed in a myriad of ways. However, the Spanish saw the spiritual attachment to these plants as ungodly and their consumption sinful. It was a way of destroying culture, of erasing beliefs. In decades, they nearly wiped out centuries of crop diversification, which allowed pseudograins to expand their reach to other climates. Thankfully, it didn't work very well. In isolated regions like the Andean altiplano and highlands of Oaxaca, farmers preserved their seeds free from contaminants, working within the limits of their ecosystems. The people, and the crops, have proven resilient.

Chilean Dumpling Soup

Pantrucas
Chile

Preparation time: 20 minutes
Cooking time: 20 minutes
Serves: 4

You probably won't see these square, homemade dumplings in broth at any Chilean restaurant, though mention them to any Chilean and they will immediately feel at ease. This is comfort food that a mother might make, served warm to soothe your soul in the doldrums of winter. It can be quite humble, just noodles and broth, or quite lively, adding anything you might find in your pantry.

2 tablespoons olive oil
1 onion, minced
2 garlic cloves, minced
7 oz (200 g) ground (minced) beef
1 carrot, julienned
1/2 red bell pepper, cored, seeded, and julienned
1 teaspoon dried oregano
1/2 teaspoon ground cumin
1 teaspoon *mérken* or paprika
2 potatoes, peeled and diced
4 cups/32 fl oz (950 ml) beef stock
2 eggs, beaten
1/2 cup/3/4 oz (20 g) cilantro (coriander) or parsley, chopped
salt and ground pepper

For the dumplings
3/4 cup/3 1/2 oz (100 g) all-purpose (plain) flour
1 egg
1 tablespoon olive oil
1/4 cup/2 fl oz (60 ml) warm water

Heat the oil in a pan over medium heat. Add the onion and garlic and cook for about 3 minutes. Add the beef and cook for a further 2 minutes, stirring, then add the carrot and bell pepper, oregano, cumin, and *mérken* or paprika. Season with salt and pepper and stir. Add the potatoes and stock, then cover and continue cooking for 5 minutes.

Meanwhile, put all the dumpling ingredients in a bowl with a pinch of salt, mix, and knead to form a smooth and uniform dough, adding extra water if needed. Roll the dough out to 1/4-inch (5 mm) thick, then cut into 1-inch (2.5-cm) squares.

Add the dumplings to the broth and cook for about 10 minutes, then stir in the eggs and let them cook in the broth.

Serve sprinkled with the coriander (cilantro) or parsley.

Argentine Round Ravioli

Sorrentinos
Argentina

Preparation time: 25 minutes
Cooking time: 5 minutes
Serves: 4

Despite what the name might suggest, *sorrentinos* didn't come from a town in southern Italy. Nor was it brought by the Italian migrants who started to arrive by the hundreds of thousands in the second half of the nineteenth century. There isn't even a pasta in Italy with that name. It was invented in Argentina, supposedly by a grandmother from Mar del Plata in the early 1900s. Much like many other things in Argentina, *sorrentinos* seem very Italian, just more eccentric. They resemble ravioli and use the same fillings, but are round and puffed up, looking a bit like bowler hats. As they are commonly sold alongside other pastas in delis and restaurants, many Argentines just assume they are Italian.

1 1/2 cups/7 oz (200 g) all-purpose (plain) flour
1 tablespoon salt
2 eggs
4 tablespoons olive oil
2 tablespoons semolina, for dusting
1/2 cup/2 oz/50 g shredded parmesan, to serve

For the filling
1 cup/9 oz (250 g) ricotta
9 oz (250 g) ham, finely chopped
1 egg
1 teaspoon fresh oregano
salt and ground pepper

Add the flour to a bowl, and make a well in the center. Add the salt, eggs, and oil to the well, and gradually mix into the flour, to form a uniform dough, adding a little warm water if needed. Knead until smooth, then cover with a damp tea towel.

For the filling, mix the ricotta, ham, and egg together, then add the oregano and season with salt and pepper. Set aside.

Spread the semolina on a work surface, then roll the dough out to a sheet 1/4 inch (5 mm) thick. Place small mounds, about a teaspoon, of filling on half the dough, spacing them out evenly. Using water, dampen the edges around each mound of filling. Fold the remaining half of the dough over on top of the filling, then press around each *sorrentino*; each parcel should be tight, with no air inside. Using a 1 1/2-inch (4-cm) round cutter, cut around each filling, forming individual *sorrentinos*. Use a fork to press around the borders to seal.

Heat a large pan of water over high heat. When boiling, add the *sorrentinos*, bring back to a boil, and simmer for about 5 minutes, until they float.

Drain, and serve with shredded cheese. You can also serve these with cream, tomato sauce, or butter.

Coconut Rice

Arroz con coco
Belize, Brazil, Colombia, Costa Rica, Honduras,
Nicaragua, Panama, Venezuela

Preparation time: 5 minutes,
plus 10 minutes resting   Serves: 4
Cooking time: 25 minutes

Coconut rice is primarily found in regions with strong
African ancestry, such as along the Caribbean coast of
Central and South America, as well as northern Brazil,
and there are lots of different variations. In Panama, it's
sometimes sweet, cooked in coconut milk and shredded
coconut flesh, with sugar and occasionally even raisins.
Reduced and caramelized coconut milk, called *titoté*,
which can be store-bought, gives the dish a brownish
color in Colombia. In Garifuna settlements on the coast
of Honduras and Belize, coconut rice is savory, with
garlic, onions, and red or black beans often added.
Regardless of location, it's often an accompaniment
to seafood dishes.

2 cups/12½ oz (360 g) long-grain white rice
1 tablespoon butter
1 garlic clove, finely chopped
1 onion, finely chopped
1 cup/2½ oz (75 g) grated fresh coconut
1 cup/8 fl oz (250 ml) coconut milk
2 cups/16 fl oz (475 ml) water
1 tablespoon finely chopped scallion (spring onion)
salt

Rinse the rice in cold, running water until it runs clear.
    Melt the butter in a medium pan over medium heat,
add the garlic and onion, and cook for about 5 minutes,
until transparent. Stir in the rice and grated coconut,
then add the coconut milk, water, and salt to taste.
Bring to a boil, then reduce the heat, cover, and continue
cooking until there is no liquid and the rice is tender,
about 20 minutes.
    Remove from the heat and rest, with the lid on, for
about 10 minutes.
    To serve, use a fork to fluff the rice, and sprinkle over
the chopped scallion (spring onion).

Pequi Rice

Arroz de pequi
Brazil

Preparation time: 5 minutes,
plus 5 minutes resting   Serves: 6
Cooking time: 25 minutes

Pequi (*Caryocar brasiliense*), a pungent fruit found in
the immense tropical savanna called the *cerrado* that
dominates south-central Brazil, has a strange flavor
with hints of citrus and a really funky cheese. It has a
thin, green skin that covers, usually, one large pit (stone)
surrounded by a yellowish pulp. Great care must be
taken in eating the fruit, just scraping the layer of pulp
with your teeth, as the spiky pits are known to pierce a
tongue. Pequi is usually served in cooked preparations,
like this one, a typical dish from the state of Goiás.

3 cups/1 lb 4 oz (540 g) long-grain rice
1 cup/8 fl oz (250 ml) vegetable oil
6 pequi, fresh or preserved, skin removed
1 onion, chopped
2 garlic cloves, chopped
4 cups/32 fl oz (950 ml) boiling water
2 cups/16 fl oz (475 ml) hot chicken stock (or you can
use vegetable stock)
2 tablespoons chopped scallion (spring onion)
salt and ground pepper

Rinse the rice in cold, running water until it runs clear.
    In large pan, heat the oil over medium heat. Add the
pequi and fry. Add the onion and garlic and continue
cooking, stirring occasionally, until everything is lightly
browned. Add the rice and fry for a few minutes until
slightly transparent, then add the hot water and stock.
Season with salt and pepper, bring to a boil, then reduce
the heat to low and cover. Cook until all of the liquid is
absorbed, about 20 minutes.
    Remove from the heat and rest, covered, for 5 minutes.
Scatter over the scallion (spring onion) and serve hot.

Stewed Chicken and Rice

Galinhada
Brazil

Preparation time: 30 minutes,
plus 2 hours marinating   Serves: 6
Cooking time: 20 minutes

Eaten throughout Brazil, but especially in the states of
Minas Gerais and Goiás, the *galinhada* is a slow-cooked
chicken stewed with rice and flavored with saffron or
turmeric. Some add beans, okra, or *guariroba*, a type
of heart of palm, into the mix too. Known as a hangover
cure, it's often made at dawn after a night of partying.

½ cup/4 fl oz (120 ml) chicken stock
1 tablespoon finely chopped parsley
1 tablespoon finely chopped cilantro (coriander)
juice of 1 lime
1 whole chicken, divided into 10 pieces (legs, thighs,
drumsticks, wings, and breasts), fat trimmed
2 cups/12½ oz (360 g) long-grain white rice
2 tablespoons olive oil
2 onions, finely chopped
2 garlic cloves, crushed
½ teaspoon saffron threads
2 tomatoes, peeled, cored, and diced
1 green bell pepper, cored, seeded, and diced
4 tablespoons peas
3 cups/25 fl oz (750 ml) boiling water
salt and ground pepper

Put the stock, parsley, cilantro (coriander), and lime juice
in a medium bowl. Add the chicken pieces and marinate
for at least 2 hours.
    Rinse the rice in cold, running water until the water
runs clear.
    Heat the oil in a large pan over medium heat. Add
the onions and garlic and cook until fragrant. Add the
chicken pieces from their marinade, and cook for about
4–5 minutes per side, then add the saffron, tomatoes,
bell pepper, peas, and rice and sauté for a few minutes.
    Mix well and cover with the boiling water, season
with salt and pepper, stir well, and cook, covered, for
20 minutes over medium-low heat, stirring gently so that
the rice does not stick to the bottom of the pot. Remove
from the heat and let rest for 5 minutes before serving.

Campfire Rice

Arroz de carreteiro 🍲
Brazil

Preparation time: 15 minutes
Cooking time: 30 minutes,
plus 10 minutes resting

Serves: 6

This dish originated from the drivers of horse-pulled wagons in southern Brazil. On long voyages across the countryside, cooked rice with dried meat was an easy meal to prepare in a cast-iron pot over a fire. Today it's commonly made with leftovers from a barbecue, and is one of the most typical dishes of Rio Grande do Sul. Similar dishes can be found elsewhere in the country, like *arroz Maria Isabel* in the northeast, using lightly salted and dehydrated *carne de sol* instead of the drier *charque*, or *feijão tropeiro*, from Minas Gerais, adding beans and leafy greens.

   2 cups/12½ oz (360 g) long-grain white rice
   2 tablespoons oil
   3 oz (80 g) bacon, diced
   9 oz (3¼ oz) *linguiça calabresa* (spicy Calabrian-style cured sausage), cut into 3 sections
   ½ onion, thinly sliced
   2 garlic cloves, minced
   3½ oz (100 g) *charque* or beef jerky, shredded
   2 bay leaves
   1 tomato, peeled and chopped
   4 cups/32 fl oz (950 ml) hot beef stock, or water
   ½ cup/¾ oz (20 g) parsley, chopped
   salt and ground pepper

Rinse the rice in cold, running water until the water runs clear.
   Heat the oil in a large pan over medium heat. Add the bacon and sausage and cook for 5 minutes, stirring occasionally, until brown. Add the onion and garlic and sauté for 2 minutes. Add the *charque* or jerky and let brown. Add the rice and bay leaves, then the tomato, and sauté for a minute or so. Add salt to taste.
   Add the hot stock or water and scrape the bottom of the pan with a wooden spoon so the rice doesn't stick. Cover with a lid and cook for about 20 minutes or until the rice has absorbed the water.
   Remove from the heat and rest, with the lid on, for about 10 minutes.
   Serve scattered with parsley and some pepper.

Rice with Small Fish

Arroz con chaupiza
Colombia

Preparation time: 10 minutes
Cooking time: 50 minutes,
plus 10 minutes resting

Serves: 6–8

Chaupiza or *chautiza* are tiny fish, less than an inch in length, of the Sicydium genus that are native to fast-flowing streams and rivers in parts of Central and South America. On the Pacific coast of Colombia and Cauca Valley, fishermen catch them in nets, then dry them in the sun with a little salt, smoke them in banana leaves, and eat them on their own. They can also be used fresh to flavor stews and rice dishes. Small anchovies can be used as a replacement.

   4 lb (1.8 kg) *chaupiza*
   4 tablespoons coconut oil
   1 onion, chopped
   1 garlic clove, chopped
   1 tomato, chopped
   2 cups/12½ oz (360 g) long-grain white rice
   2 cups/16 fl oz (475 ml) coconut milk
   1 cup/8 fl oz (250 ml) water
   4 bananas, sliced
   1 cup/1½ oz (40 g) cilantro (coriander) leaves
   salt and ground pepper

Wash the fish in cold running water. Set aside.
   Melt 1 tablespoon of coconut oil in a frying pan over medium heat. Add the onion and garlic, and cook until transparent. Add the tomato and continue cooking until fully cooked, about 7–10 minutes. Season with salt and pepper, and tip into a bowl.
   In the same pan, heat 2 tablespoons of oil and fry the fish for about 2 minutes, then add the onions and tomatoes back to the pan and sauté for 10 minutes.
   Rinse the rice in cold, running water until the water runs clear.
   Heat 1 tablespoon of coconut oil in a medium pan over medium high heat, add the rice and fry for a few minutes, then add the coconut milk and water, and bring to a boil. Add the sliced bananas, cover, and reduce to a simmer. Cook until the rice has absorbed the water, about 25 minutes, then add the fish mixture.
   Remove from the heat and let stand, covered, for 10 minutes.
   Serve scattered with cilantro (coriander) leaves.

Campfire Rice

Nicaraguan Chicken and Rice Stew

Arroz aguado
Nicaragua

Preparation time: 15 minutes
Cooking time: 1 hour
Serves: 8

Some call *arroz aguado* Nicaraguan risotto. Translating as "watery rice," it's soul food for all walks of life, livened up with herbs and peppers, served for family lunches.

1 tablespoon vegetable oil
1 onion, finely chopped
3 celery stalks, thinly sliced
3 carrots, cut into ½-inch (1-cm) slices
2 tomatoes, sliced
4 garlic cloves, smashed
2 chicken breasts, cut in half
4 chicken thighs
4 cups/32 fl oz (950 ml) chicken stock
3 cups/25 fl oz (750 ml) water
1 cup/6 oz (180 g) long-grain white rice
10–12 stems fresh cilantro (coriander)
2 sprigs fresh *yerba buena* (or mint)
3 potatoes, diced
2 ripe bananas, sliced
1 zucchini (courgette), diced
juice of 1 bitter orange
½ teaspoon ground achiote (annatto)
salt and ground pepper

To garnish
1 cup/1½ oz (40 g) chopped fresh cilantro leaves
¼ cup/¼ oz (5 g) chopped fresh mint leaves
2 limes, cut into wedges
1 ripe avocado, sliced
½ cup/4 oz (125 g) pickled jalapeños

Heat the oil in a large pan over medium-high heat. Add the onion, celery, carrots, tomatoes, garlic, and some salt. Cook, stirring, until the onion is soft and translucent, about 5–7 minutes.

Season all the chicken with salt and pepper and add to the pan. Add the stock, water, rice, cilantro (coriander) and *yerba buena* (or mint). Bring to a boil over high heat, then reduce the heat and simmer, skimming the surface from time to time, until the chicken is cooked through, about 25 minutes. With tongs, remove the chicken and place in a bowl. Remove and discard the herbs.

Stir the potatoes, bananas, and zucchini (courgette) into the pan and cook until tender, about 15 minutes, then add the sour orange juice and achiote (annatto).

Meanwhile, carefully remove and discard the chicken skin and debone. Cut the chicken into bite-size pieces and return to the pan. Adjust the seasoning to taste.

Serve in bowls, garnished with cilantro and mint, with lime wedges, avocado, and jalapeños on the side.

Chocó Sausage Rice

Arroz clavado, arroz clava'o
Colombia

Preparation time: 5 minutes
Cooking time: 35 minutes
Serves: 8

There are almost as many variations of rice-based recipes as there are people in the Chocó, the wild and undeveloped Pacific coastal region of Colombia. Dozens of varieties were grown in the rich, swampy soil until cheaper, industrial rice arrived in the region. Some were used for the risotto-like *atollado*, others mixed with coconut milk or for *fututiao*, where they're toasted in a pot during the rainy season. *Arroz clavado* is a vehicle for serving *longaniza chocoana*, a regional pork sausage flavored with onions, peppers, achiote, and aromatic herbs, then dried in the sun and smoked.

3 cups/1 lb 4 oz (540 g) long-grain rice
2 tablespoons vegetable or palm oil
1 lb (450 g) *longaniza* sausages, sliced
2 onions, chopped
1 ripe tomato, peeled and chopped
2 garlic cloves, minced
½ teaspoon ground achiote (annatto)
6 cups/3 pints (1.5 liters) water
8 oz (225 g) *queso blanco*, or another semi-soft white cheese, diced
4 scallions (spring onions), chopped
salt and ground pepper

Rinse the rice in cold, running water until the water runs clear.

Heat the oil in a medium pan over medium heat, add the *longaniza* and cook until browned, then add the onions, tomato, garlic, and achiote (annatto). Season with salt and pepper, then add the rice and stir, coating the grains. Sauté for 2 minutes then add the water, cover, and cook for 20 minutes.

Remove the lid, stir in the cheese, cover and cook for a further 10 minutes, until the rice is cooked and has absorbed all the water.

Scatter over the scallions (spring onions) and serve.

Nicaraguan Chicken and Rice Stew

Spicy Flour Soup

Uchu jacu
Ecuador

Preparation time: 20 minutes   Serves: 6
Cooking time: 1 hour 30 minutes

Made primarily in the Pichincha province in northern Ecuador, *uchu jacu* is a nutritious flour blend made of dry and toasted grains that include wheat, barley, corn, peas, lentils, and field beans. In Kichwa, it means *harina picante*, or spicy flour, referring to the spices like cumin, garlic, and achiote that are usually added to the blend. Its sole purpose is as the base of this thick soup of the same name, for which other ingredients might be added, such as potatoes, maize, eggs, or guinea pig. While you will likely only find *uchu jacu* in Ecuador, you can substitute by mixing flours of the grains that are available wherever you are. You can add spices to your own version of this flour.

    1 lb (450 g) pork ribs
    8 cups/64 fl oz (1.9 liters) water
    1 bay leaf
    1 celery stalk
    2 tablespoons vegetable oil
    1 onion, finely diced
    1 tablespoon garlic paste
    10 oz (275 g) cooked or canned mote (or use Andean hominy)
    1 lb (450 g) potatoes, cut into medium dice
    7 oz (200 g) *uchu jacu* flour
    4 oz (125 g) *queso fresco*, shredded
    ¼ cup/⅓ oz (10 g) cilantro (coriander), finely chopped
    salt

    To serve
    avocado
    roasted corn

Place a large pan over medium heat. Add the pork ribs, water, bay leaf, and celery. Bring to a boil, turn down the heat and simmer for 1 hour, until the meat is tender. Remove the pork ribs from the broth, clean of the meat, and set aside. Decant half the broth and let cool; keep the remaining half in the pan.

Heat the oil in a medium pan over medium heat, then add the pork, onion, and garlic paste, and sauté. Add the still warm half of the broth, mote, and potatoes. Cook for 30 minutes, or until the potatoes are cooked through.

Use enough of the reserved cold broth to dissolve the flour, then add this mixture to the hot pan, season with salt, and stir until thick, similar to a potato soup.

Add the shredded cheese and cilantro (coriander) and serve hot, with avocado and roasted corn.

Cook-Up Rice

Guyana

Preparation time: 35 minutes,
plus overnight soaking   Serves: 6
Cooking time: 45 minutes,
plus 10 minutes resting

One of Guyana's national dishes, this one-pot recipe is found under a variety of names in the southern Caribbean. The exact ingredients can vary, though there's always rice, some form of protein, and fresh herbs cooked in coconut milk. Traditionally it was made on Saturdays, adding whatever leftover scraps from previous meals to a pot and cooking it up. The protein might be tripe, pigtail, oxtail, chicken, shrimp (prawns), or a combination of several, though beans, like pigeon peas or black-eyed peas, are common too. Some add *cassareep*, the sweetened and spiced cassava reduction used in pepperpot recipes, or scotch bonnet peppers.

    1 chicken, about 3 lb (1.3 kg), cut into large pieces
    2 teaspoons vegetable oil
    1 cup/4 oz (115 g) diced onions
    4 sprigs thyme
    2 cups/12½ oz (360 g) long-grain white rice
    1 cup/6 oz (165 g) dried black-eyed peas, soaked overnight
    1 cup/8 fl oz (235 ml) warm water
    4 cups/32 fl oz (950 ml) fresh coconut milk or 2 cups/16 fl oz (475 ml) canned coconut milk and 2 cups/16 fl oz (475 ml) water
    ½ cup/¾ oz (20 g) basil leaves
    ½ cup/3 oz (80 g) diced tomatoes
    2 scallions (spring onions), thinly sliced
    salt and ground pepper

Season the chicken lightly with salt and pepper. Heat the oil in a large pan over medium-high heat. Add the chicken and brown lightly. Remove and set aside, then sauté half the onions and half the thyme.

Rinse the rice in cold, running water until the water runs clear.

Drain the black-eyed peas, add to the pan, stir, and cook for 2 minutes. Add the warm water and cook until reduced, and the peas are three-quarters done, then mix in the coconut milk. Add the chicken back to the pan, along with the rice, the remaining onions and thyme, the basil, tomatoes, and scallions (spring onions).

Cover and bring to a boil, cook for 6–7 minutes, then reduce the heat and let cook for about 30 minutes, or until the liquid has mostly evaporated.

Let rest for 10 minutes, then serve.

Paraguayan Cheese Rice

Arroz kesú, arroz quesú
Paraguay

Preparation time: 10 minutes
Cooking time: 20 minutes,   Serves: 2
plus 5 minutes resting

One of the best uses of *queso Paraguay*, the slightly acidic, soft cow's milk cheese, *arroz kesú* is mostly served alongside grilled beef.

    1 teaspoon vegetable oil
    ½ white onion, chopped
    1 garlic clove, minced
    1 cup/6 oz (180 g) long-grain white rice
    1¾ cups/14 fl oz (410 ml) boiling water
    ¾ cup/2½ oz (75 g) shredded *queso Paraguay*
    salt

Heat the oil in a pan over medium heat. Add the onion and garlic and stir-fry for 5 minutes or until soft. Add the rice and fry for 1 minute, then add the boiling water. Season with salt and simmer for 12 minutes or until the rice is cooked and the water evaporated.

Sprinkle over the cheese, mix it in well and let rest for 5 minutes. Serve warm.

Grains, Quinoa, and Amaranth

Fried Dough Crumbles

Reviro
Argentina, Paraguay

Preparation time: 15 minutes
Cooking time: 25 minutes   Serves: 4

Within rumbling distance of Iguazú Falls in the Alto Paraná area of Paraguay, *reviro* is a simple recipe, using pantry staples, that's often used to replace bread. There are just three ingredients: flour, water, and salt, plus fat for frying. In the late nineteenth century, *mensús*, rural field hands on *yerba mate* plantations, would eat this day in and day out, sometimes for every meal. For breakfast, they might add a fried egg, while other times it might be sprinkled with sugar and joined by a cup of *Maté cocido* (Paraguayan Burnt Tea, page 388). It's commonly served with soups and there's a custom of taking a spoonful of *reviro* and dipping it in broth before eating.

    4 cups/1 lb 4 oz (560 g) all-purpose (plain) flour
    1 tablespoon salt
    1 cup/8 fl oz (250 ml) water
    2 tablespoons butter
    2 tablespoons lard

In a large bowl, mix the flour, salt and water together. Knead well until you have a soft dough.
    Heat the butter and lard in a flameproof clay (earthenware) pot over medium heat. When hot, add the dough in one piece, and let cook for about 5 minutes, or until golden brown. Turn the dough and use a wooden spoon to start gently separating the dough into small pieces. Continue cooking, stirring continuously, for a further 20 minutes, or until the dough is golden brown and crispy.
    Remove from the heat and serve warm.

Crispy Rice

Concolón
Panama

Preparation time: 5 minutes
Cooking time: 25 minutes   Serves: 4

Everyone loves the crispy rice that has formed on the bottom of the pan, so why not make a full dish out of it? That's what the Panamanians have done. You can use this technique with other rice dishes too, and the *concolón* becomes even more flavorful when fatty bits of meat or seafood are mixed in.

    4 tablespoons melted butter
    2 cups/12½ oz (360 g) long-grain white rice
    2 cups/16 fl oz (475 ml) water

Rinse the rice in cold, running water until the water runs clear.
    Heat half the butter in a cast-iron pan, add the rice and stir to coat the grains. Add the water, mix, and bring to a boil. Cover with a lid, reduce the heat and continue cooking, every once in a while scraping the bottom of the pan with a wooden spoon.
    When the rice is almost done, add the remaining melted butter and increase the heat, allowing the bottom part to brown.
    Serve immediately.

Surinamese Mixed Rice

Moksi-alesi
Suriname

Preparation time: 15 minutes
Cooking time: 25 minutes   Serves: 6

This creole rice dish likely started just by adding scraps and leftovers to rice. *Moksi-alesi* has morphed into a staple Surinamese dish with endless combinations of local proteins like fish, salted meat, smoked chicken, shrimp, or beans. Cooking in coconut milk or topping with cabbage are optional additions.

    2 cups/12½ oz (360 g) long-grain white rice
    1 teaspoon ground turmeric
    2 cups/16 fl oz (475 ml) chicken stock
    2 tablespoons vegetable oil
    1 white onion, chopped
    3 garlic cloves, minced
    1 tomato, diced
    1 scotch bonnet chile, seeded and chopped
    2 tablespoons dried shrimps, soaked
    5½ oz (150 g) smoked chicken breasts, cut into cubes
    1 cup/5 oz (145 g) cooked black-eyed peas
    ground black pepper
    1 banana leaf

Add the rice and turmeric to a medium pan. Mix well, and add the stock. Place over medium heat and cook for about 15 minutes, or until the rice is cooked and the stock absorbed. Remove from the heat and set aside.
    Meanwhile, heat the vegetable oil in a wok. Stir-fry the onion and garlic, then add the tomato and chile, and let cook for 8 minutes. Add the dried shrimps, chicken, and black-eyed peas. Cook, stirring, for 12 minutes or until the tomato is almost dissolved and the chicken is cooked through.
    Add the cooked rice to the wok, with ground pepper to taste, mix well, and serve warm, on a banana leaf with fried plantains and slices of cucumbers or tomatoes.

Toasted Rice

Arroz fututeado, arroz fututiao
Panama

Preparation time: 5 minutes
Cooking time: 30 minutes,   Serves: 4
plus 15 minutes resting

The Panamanian term *fututear* signifies the act of toasting freshly harvested rice before the husks have been removed. This method was a way for rice farmers to quickly use some of their crop, though now it is used to give store-bought rice a toasted, nutty flavor.

    1 tablespoon lard
    1 cup/6 oz (180 g) long-grain white rice
    2 cups/16 fl oz (475 ml) water

Heat the lard in a heavy-bottomed pan over medium heat. Add the rice and cook for about 5–7 minutes, or until golden brown. Add the water and stir. Bring to a boil, then cover with a lid and reduce the heat to low. Cook for about 20 minutes, or until the water is absorbed, then remove from the heat.
    Let rest, covered, for 10–15 minutes before serving.

Bijao Leaf-Wrapped Rice

Juane de arroz
Peru

Preparation time: 50 minutes
Cooking time: 1 hour   Serves: 4

The rice-based *juane* has become the most common form of this traditional recipe found throughout the Peruvian Amazon, far outnumbering more traditional cassava-based *juanes de yuca* (Jungle Tamales, page 98). However, few realize that it is in fact a fusion dish. It's not just the name, *juane*, given by the Spanish in the town of Moyobamba, in honor of San Juan Baptista (St. John the Baptist), the patron saint of the Amazon—some claim that it represents his head being served on a platter after his beheading—but the ingredients that are introduced too. The Spanish brought the olives to the region, while the Chinese brought the rice. Rice *juanes* are the food of choice during the Festival de San Juan, celebrated throughout the Peruvian Amazon.

2 tablespoons lard
1 whole chicken, cut into 4 pieces
1 white onion, chopped
2 garlic cloves, minced
1 teaspoon ground turmeric
3 tablespoons *ají amarillo* paste
6 cups/3 pints (1.5 liters) chicken stock
2 tablespoons sachaculantro or culantro (or use cilantro/coriander), chopped
2 cups/12½ oz (360 g) long-grain white rice
2 *ají dulce*, seeded and sliced (or use another small, round mild chile)
4 eggs, plus 4 halved hard-boiled eggs
1 tablespoon olive oil
8 *bijao* or banana leaves
8 black olives, pitted
salt and ground pepper

In a medium pan, heat the lard over medium heat, sear the chicken pieces for 4 minutes each side, and remove to a dish.

In the same pan, stir-fry the onion and garlic for 4 minutes. Add the turmeric and *ají amarillo* paste. Sear for 5 minutes and replace the chicken in the pan. Pour in the chicken stock and season with salt, pepper, and the sachaculantro. Simmer for 15 minutes over medium heat until the chicken is completely cooked, then remove the chicken from the pan.

Add the rice and chiles to the pan with the stock, and cook over low heat for 15 minutes.

Separately, in a large bowl, beat the 4 raw eggs. Once the rice is cooked, add the beaten eggs. Pour in the olive oil and check the seasoning. Divide the mixture into four portions.

Take 2 *bijao* or banana leaves and form them into a cross. In the middle of the cross, spoon one portion of the rice mixture, add 1 piece of chicken, a cooked egg half, and 2 olives. Close the leaves and tie with string at the top, then repeat with the remaining leaves and filling.

Heat enough water in a large pan to cover the *juanes*. Once the water starts boiling, add the *juanes*, cover, and cook over low heat for 30 minutes.

Remove from the pan and keep warm while you cook the remaining *juanes*.

Open them up and serve while still hot.

Trujillo-Style Wheat Soup

Shambar ⬚
Peru

Preparation time: 20 minutes, plus overnight salting and soaking
Cooking time: 1 hour 10 minutes   Serves: 4

Shambar originated in the village of Otuzco in the Andean foothills, in the department of La Libertad in northern Peru. It can be made with whatever types of legumes (pulses) you have around, plus three kinds of meat, such as chicken, sausages, smoked pork, pig ears or tails, or pork skin. Thick and nourishing, it is prepared every Monday in the city of Trujillo to help sustain residents for the week of work ahead.

1 lb (450 g) pork belly
8 oz (225 g) wheatberries
8 oz (225 g) dried chickpeas
8 oz (225 g) dried fava (broad) beans
1 lb (450 g) smoked pork chops
2 lb (900 g) chicken pieces
1 tablespoon vegetable oil
2 spring onions (salad onions), chopped
5 garlic cloves
2 *ají panca*, toasted and ground
2 *ají mirasol*, toasted and ground
½ teaspoon ground cumin
2 tablespoons cilantro (coriander), chopped
salt

To serve
Cancha serrana (Toasted Andean Corn Kernels, page 114)
lime wedges
chile sauce

Place the pork belly on a tray and rub and cover with 1 cup (270 g) of salt, then refrigerate overnight. Soak the wheatberries, chickpeas, and fava (broad) beans in plenty of cold water, in separate bowls, overnight.

The following day, rinse the meat with ice-cold water. Place in a large pot with the pork chops and chicken, and cover with water. Bring to a boil over high heat, then simmer for 30 minutes over medium heat or until the meats are tender.

Meanwhile, place the drained wheatberries in a pan and cover with plenty of fresh water. Cook for 30 minutes, halfway through adding the chickpeas and fava beans.

Heat the oil in a large pan, add the spring (salad) onions and garlic, and stir-fry for 4 minutes. Add the ground chiles and cumin. Add the drained wheatberries, chickpeas, and beans, along with the meat mix and its cooking liquid. Cook for 30 minutes over low heat. Remove the meat, and any bones, and cut the meat into chunks.

Serve the *shambar* hot, with the meat, and the cilantro (coriander) scattered on top. If preferred, serve any of the following alongside: *Cancha serrana*, lime wedges, and any chile sauce.

Grains, Quinoa, and Amaranth

Trujillo-Style Wheat Soup

Pig Tail Guacho

Guacho de rabito de puerco
Panama

Preparation time: 30 minutes
Cooking time: 1 hour 20 minutes   Serves: 8

Guacho is a soupy rice that is combined with another leading ingredient, such as *guandú* (pigeon peas), shellfish, *ñame* (yam) cassava, or culantro. Pig tails are one of the most common options. Some prefer to cook all of the ingredients together in a single pot, while others cook them separately and mix upon serving. In some places in Panama, such as La Guaira on the Caribbean coast, *guacho* is served in hollowed out gourds.

2 lb (900 g) pig tails (salted)
2½ cups/1 lb (450 g) dried black beans
2 tablespoons oyster sauce
1 tablespoon Worcestershire sauce
2 cups/16 fl oz (475 ml) chicken stock
3 white onions, chopped
5 garlic cloves, minced
1 red bell pepper, cored, seeded, and diced
3 tablespoons cilantro (coriander), chopped
2½ cups/1 lb (450 g) long-grain white rice
1 tablespoon vegetable oil
3 tomatoes, peeled and diced
4 tablespoons tomato paste (purée)
salt and ground pepper

Place the pig tails in a pan, cover them with water, and bring to a boil. Drain and repeat the process twice more.

Meanwhile, place the black beans in a medium pan and cover with water. Add salt, and simmer for 20 minutes or until the beans soften a little. Add the pig tails and the oyster sauce, Worcestershire sauce, and chicken stock. Mix well. Add half of the chopped onion and minced garlic, the bell pepper, and cilantro (coriander), lower the heat and simmer for 30 minutes. Meanwhile, rinse the rice. Add the rice to the pan, then add water to cover, and cook for a further 30 minutes.

Meanwhile, in a small frying pan, heat the oil and stir-fry the remaining onion and garlic for 5 minutes, then add the diced tomatoes and tomato paste (purée). Cook over medium heat for 15 minutes or until the tomatoes are soft.

Serve the *guacho* in deep plates with the tomato sauce spread on top.

Venezuelan Pasta Casserole

Macarronada 🔲
Venezuela

Preparation time: 20 minutes   Serves: 6
Cooking time: 1 hour 10 minutes

Pasta is beloved in Venezuela, and at one time the country ate more pasta per capita than anywhere else outside Italy. Numerous pasta dishes have been adopted into Venezuela's national cuisine, such as *pasticho*, a lasagna covered in béchamel sauce. *Macarronada* is typical in and around the city of Maracaibo in the northwest of the county, and is primarily eaten around Christmas time. There is no exact recipe, requiring only pasta and cheese, though each family adds their own additions; things like raisins, capers, olives, or ham.

1 lb (450 g) rigatoni pasta
2 chicken breasts, poached
4 eggs
1 cup/8 fl oz (250 ml) whole milk
1 lb (450 g) shredded *queso de año* (or use parmesan)
4 hard-boiled eggs, sliced
5 oz (150 g) sliced ham, cut into strips
4 oz (125 g) cured sausage, cut into thin slices
4 potatoes, boiled and sliced
1 teaspoon annatto oil, plus an extra drizzle
salt and ground pepper

For the tomato sauce
6 tomatoes, peeled
1 teaspoon vegetable oil, plus extra for greasing
1 white onion, chopped
2 garlic cloves, minced
1 red bell pepper, cored, seeded, and chopped
1 tablespoon parsley, chopped
1 tablespoon sugar
ground cumin, to taste

Start by making the tomato sauce. Blend the tomatoes in a mixer and set aside. Heat the vegetable oil in a frying pan, add the onion, garlic, and bell pepper and stir-fry for about 5 minutes. Sprinkle in the chopped parsley and cook for 8 minutes over medium heat. Add the blended tomatoes and season with salt, pepper, the sugar, and cumin. Add the drizzle of annatto oil and let simmer over low heat for 35 minutes.

Meanwhile, cook the pasta for about 12 minutes in boiling, salted water or until al dente. Drain and mix well with the teaspoon of annatto oil.

When the tomato sauce is ready, shred the chicken and mix it into the sauce.

Beat the eggs with the milk and preheat the oven to 350°F/180°C/Gas Mark 4.

Grease the bottom and sides of a 13 x 9 x 2-inch (33 x 23 x 5-cm) baking dish with oil. Add a layer of pasta on the bottom, spread half the tomato sauce with chicken over the top, sprinkle over the cheese, and place slices of the boiled eggs, ham, sausage, and potatoes on top. Pour half the egg and milk mixture over, and repeat the layering, finishing with a layer of rigatoni and cheese.

Cover the dish with foil and cook in the oven for 20 minutes, then remove the foil and cook for a further 7 minutes or until the cheese is brown.

Remove from the oven, let cool and serve warm with salad on the side.

Venezuelan Pasta Casserole

Rice and Beans

These two staple ingredients are found in nearly every corner of Latin America, and for some families it is eaten three times a day. Rice and beans doesn't have to be just a filling meal, however. It can be culinary innovation at its finest, turning the humblest of foods into the stars of a plate.

Central American Rice and Beans

Gallo pinto
Costa Rica, Nicaragua

Preparation time: 5 minutes, plus overnight soaking
Cooking time: 30 minutes, plus 5 minutes resting

 Serves: 6

Translating as "spotted rooster," so named because of the speckled appearance of the rice and beans, *gallo pinto* can be eaten as a side to any meal. It's claimed as the national dish of Costa Rica and Nicaragua and both say it originated on their soil, though the exact origins aren't clear. Its roots most likely trace back to coastal plantations during the time of slavery. There are countless regional preparations and customs surrounding *gallo pinto*. In Costa Rica, where they mostly use black beans, it's often made with *salsa lizano*, a light brown sauce similar to Worcestershire. In Nicaragua, using small red beans called *frijoles rojos de seda*, also called red silk beans or Central American beans, is more typical. Along much of the Caribbean coast in either country, coconut milk, and sometimes chiles, are added.

    3 cups/1 lb 2 oz (500 g) red silk beans, soaked
    overnight in plenty of cold water
    2 tablespoons oil
    1 onion, chopped
    4 garlic cloves, minced
    ½ red or yellow bell pepper, cored, seeded, and
    chopped
    3 cups/1 lb 4 oz (540 g) long-grain rice
    2 cups/16 fl oz (475 ml) reserved bean cooking water
    bunch of fresh thyme
    2 x 14-fl oz (400-ml) cans of coconut milk

Add the drained beans to a medium pan and cover with fresh cold water. Bring to a boil over medium-high heat, reduce to a simmer and cook until tender but firm. Remove from the heat and reserve the beans in the water until ready to use.

Heat the oil in a large pan over medium heat. Add the onion, garlic, and bell pepper, and sauté for about 6 minutes, or until the onions are translucent. Add the rice, stir to coat the grains, and toast for about 4 minutes, then add the beans and the cooking water, thyme, and coconut milk. Cook until the rice has absorbed the liquid.

Remove from the heat and let sit for 5 minutes, covered, before serving.

Rice and Black-Eyed Peas

Baião de dois
Brazil

Preparation time: 1 hour, plus overnight soaking
Cooking time: 1 hour, plus 5 minutes resting

Serves: 8

Named after a traditional folk dance of the Ceará region, *baião de dois*, or a "dance for two," pairs two of the most basic elements of Brazilian gastronomy: rice and beans (in this case *feijão fradinho*, or black-eye peas). It's common in the impoverished, rural areas of the region, and usually eaten at night. Every household has their own recipe and it might change from day to day based on what's around the house. If there is meat, it gets tossed in.

    1 lb 2 oz (500 g) *carne-de-sol* (or use beef jerky),
    cut into 2½-inch (6-cm) cubes
    1 cup/6 oz (165 g) black-eyed peas
    5 cups/40 fl oz (1.2 liters) water
    3 tablespoons butter
    3½ oz (100 g) slab bacon, diced
    3½ oz (100 g) *linguiça calabresa* (spicy
    Calabrian-style cured sausage), sliced
    1 onion, finely chopped
    3 garlic cloves, minced
    1 red bell pepper, cored, seeded, and chopped
    2 ripe tomatoes, peeled and chopped
    2 cups/12½ oz (360 g) long-grain white rice
    1 bay leaf
    12 oz (340 g) *queijo coalho*, cubed (or use
    mozzarella)
    ½ cup/1¼ oz (35 g) scallions (spring onions),
    finely chopped
    ½ cup/¾ oz (20 g) cilantro (coriander),
    finely chopped
    salt and ground pepper

Rinse the *carne-de-sol* under cold running water, then place in a bowl, cover with water and refrigerate overnight, changing the water at least once. Drain and finely chop.

In a separate bowl, soak the black-eyed peas in twice their amount of water overnight.

Add the drained black-eyed peas to a medium pan, add the measured water, and cook over medium heat for about 30 minutes or until tender, then drain, reserving 4 cups/32 fl oz (950 ml) of the cooking water.

Melt the butter in a medium pan over medium heat. Add the bacon and fry until golden brown. Add the *carne-de-sol* and cook for 5 minutes, then add the *linguiça*, onion, and garlic. Sauté for 3 minutes, then add the bell pepper, sauté for 5 minutes, then add the tomatoes. Meanwhile, rinse the rice. Finally, add the rice to the pan and cook for 2 minutes. Season with salt and pepper.

Drizzle the reserved bean cooking water over the rice. Add the bay leaf, and cook over medium heat, covered, for 15–20 minutes until the rice has absorbed all of the water, then take off the heat and let sit for 5 minutes. Add the beans and cheese, and mix.

Serve garnished with the scallions (spring onions) and cilantro (coriander).

Rice and Black-Eyed Peas

Venezuelan Shredded Beef, Rice, and Beans

Pabellón criollo
Venezuela

Preparation time: 30 minutes
Cooking time: 1 hour 15 minutes   Serves: 5–6

The most emblematic Venezuelan recipe after *arepas*, *pabellón criollo* is, in its basic form, a hearty plate of rice, black beans, and shredded beef, all served side by side on a plate. You can serve it *a caballo*, or on horseback, with a fried egg on top, or *con barandas*, with fried plantains. Regional variations replace shredded beef with shredded bushmeats like capybara, caiman, or fish.

For the beans
3 cups/12 oz (360 g) dried black beans
2 tablespoons olive oil
1 white onion, finely chopped
½ red bell pepper, cut into strips
10 cups/80 fl oz (2.3 liters) water
1 tablespoon panela sugar (or use light muscovado)
1 teaspoon ground cumin, optional
5 slices bacon, chopped
4 garlic cloves, chopped

2 lb (900 g) flank steak
4 garlic cloves
1½ white onions, chopped
2 *ají dulce*
2 cups/16 fl oz (475 ml) water
4 tablespoons vegetable oil
½ red bell pepper, cored, seeded, and chopped
5 oz (150 g) tomatoes, peeled, seeded and diced
2 tablespoons Worcestershire sauce
1 teaspoon ground cumin, to taste
1 tablespoon tomato paste (purée)
2 green plantains
salt and ground pepper
cooked white rice, to serve

Wash and drain the black beans. Heat the olive oil in a medium pan over medium heat. Add the onion and bell pepper and stir-fry for 3 minutes, then add the black beans, followed by the water. Simmer over low heat for 1 hour or until the beans become softened. Remove the bell pepper and season with salt, pepper, the panela, and the ground cumin, if using.

Cook the bacon without any fat added and stir-fry the garlic with it. Add this mix to the beans and let cook until they have the consistency of a thick stew (add more water if needed).

Meanwhile, add the steak to a medium pan with 1 of the garlic cloves, crushed, two-thirds of the chopped onion, 1 of the chiles, and the water to cover. Bring to a boil, then simmer for 1 hour, covered, stirring frequently. Remove from the heat and remove the meat. Strain the cooking stock and reserve. Once the steak has cooled, shred it as thinly as possible.

Heat 2 tablespoons of the vegetable oil in a frying pan over medium heat, and add the remaining 3 garlic cloves, chopped, remaining chopped onion, the bell pepper, and remaining chile. Stir-fry, without letting them color, for 3 minutes, then add the tomatoes, Worcestershire sauce, cumin, and tomato paste (purée). Cook for 3 minutes, before adding the shredded steak. Add ½ cup/4 fl oz (120 ml) of the reserved cooking stock

and cook for 15 minutes over low heat, or until the meat is tender and the liquid has reduced to half.

Peel the plantains and cut them into diagonal slices. In a frying pan, heat the remaining 2 tablespoons vegetable oil over medium heat. Once hot, add the plantains (if necessary, cook in batches) and cook for 3–5 minutes each side or until brown and soft. Remove to a plate lined with paper towels, to absorb excess oil.

Serve each portion of *pabellón* with 2 tablespoons of shredded meat, 2 tablespoons of beans, 3 slices of fried plantain, and some rice in the middle.

Peruvian Leftover Rice and Beans

Tacu tacu
Peru

Preparation time: 20 minutes
Cooking time: 40 minutes   Serves: 4

Derived from the Quechua word *takuy*, which means "to combine one thing with another," slaves working on coastal sugar and cotton plantations during Peru's colonial period created *tacu tacu*, seasoning and frying leftover rice and beans or lentils from the day before. It has become one of the ultimate *criollo* dishes, often stuffed with shellfish in a spicy sauce or partially hidden beneath *bistec apanado* (a pounded steak, breaded and fried) with fried bananas and a fried egg. *Tacu tacu* can be a circular mound when filling the entire pan, or it can be shaped like a teardrop with the spatula when only filling part of the pan. It's usually served with several accompaniments, such as some *Salsa criolla*, *ají amarillo* sauce, or a small carafe of olive oil to be drizzled on top.

2 tablespoons vegetable oil
2 white onions, roughly chopped
2 garlic cloves, roughly chopped
2½ cups/12 oz (350 g) cooked canary beans (or use cannellini beans)
5 tablespoons olive oil
1 tablespoon *ají amarillo* paste
2 cups/9 oz (250 g) cooked long-grain white rice
1 cup/8 fl oz (250 ml) vegetable stock
salt and ground pepper
Salsa criolla (Creole Sauce, page 406), to serve

Heat half the vegetable oil in a frying pan over medium heat. Add the onions and cook for 10 minutes until soft, stirring frequently, and not letting them turn golden. Tip into a blender to process to a purée; set aside. Repeat the process with the garlic and remaining oil.

Put 2 cups/10 oz (280 g) of the canary beans into the blender and process until smooth.

Heat 1 tablespoon of the olive oil in a frying pan until hot. Add 1 tablespoon of the onion purée, the *ají amarillo* paste, and 1 tablespoon of the garlic purée. Stir-fry for 2 minutes then add the blended beans, remaining whole cooked beans, and rice. Mix well and add the stock. Season with salt and pepper and simmer over low heat for 6–8 minutes, or until the rice and beans are well mixed. Remove from the heat and divide into 4 equal portions.

Heat 1 tablespoon of the olive oil in a frying pan until hot, then add one portion of the rice and beans and form into either a circle or teardrop shape using a spatula. Sear it well on each side for 3 minutes or until a crust forms on the outside.

Keep warm while you fry the remaining portions in the remaining oil. Serve hot with *Salsa criolla*.

Peruvian Leftover Rice and Beans

Quinoa and Amaranth

For thousands of years, quinoa seeds have been traded among farmers in the Andean altiplano, the arid, high-altitude plateau straddling the border of Peru and Bolivia. They often planted more than a dozen varieties at a time. While not all of the plants would thrive under this method, it ensured that at least some of the year's quinoa crop could withstand fluctuations in temperature and rainfall, and there would be food to eat.

The Incas called it *chisoya mama*, or the "mother of all grains," and legend has it that each year the Inca emperor would sow the ground with a golden spade and plant the first seeds of the season. More than 3,000 varieties have been developed in the Andes, suitable for a range of climates from southern Colombia to northern Chile. This agricultural biodiversity is not something that just happened. It required active participation among farmers throughout the region over centuries, adapting the plant to changes as they occur.

Nutritionally, quinoa has a better balance of amino acids than the protein in most true cereals. It is eaten in a myriad of ways in the region. The seeds are boiled like rice and added to soups, sweetened like a breakfast porridge, or roasted and turned into flour to make breads or pasta. It can be fermented to make *chicha* or turned into a plant-based milk alternative. Even the edible green leaves are comparable to spinach, of which quinoa is a botanical relative. A study by NASA once claimed: "While no single food can supply all the essential life-sustaining nutrients, quinoa comes as close as any other in the plant or animal kingdom."

In the altiplano, farmers still employ an organic system of stabilizing the soil by pasturing llamas on fallow fields, then rotating them to another. They still plant a variety of different quinoa seeds each season, which ensures something to harvest even when the increasingly unpredictable climate doesn't cooperate. While industrial quinoa grown at lower altitudes, and usually sprayed with pesticides, grows to greater quantities and is often cheaper, the quality and flavor of the seeds is far superior in the altiplano. When purchasing, look for Royal Quinoa (also called Quinoa Real) grown between the salt lakes of Uyuni and Coipasa in southern Bolivia, or quinoa grown by cooperatives in highland regions of Peru such as Ancash, Cusco, Apurimac, Huanuco, Huancavelica, Ayacucho, and Puno.

Quinoa comes in several different colors. Golden, or white, is the most common, with a mild nutty flavor and soft texture. Red quinoa, as well as less common purple and orange varieties, has an earthy flavor and a slight crunch to it, while black quinoa is rich in antioxidants, holds up in cold dishes, and has a sweet yet mild flavor. Cañihua or kaniwa, sometimes called baby quinoa for its small size, is dark red or brown, and quite crunchy.

Like quinoa, amaranth, the species of plants belonging to the genus Amaranthus, is grown primarily for its edible seeds. It was once as widely spread across the region as corn, though during the conquest of the region it was nearly wiped out. Rich in protein and amino acids, amaranth seeds and leaves have been an integral part of diets throughout the New World for thousands of years. The Aztecs prepared it much like corn by cooking it in water, popping it, grinding it into a flour to make tortillas, tamales, and *atole*, Today, it is found in breakfast cereals

or used to make a candy called *alegría*. In Peru, a native species of amaranth (*Amaranthus caudatus*), known as *kiwicha*, is used in much the same way.

Cooking these pseudograins is relatively straightforward. Much like rice, you use twice as much water as the quinoa or amaranth and cook uncovered with a little bit of salt until the liquid is absorbed. Remove from the heat and cover for 5 minutes and then fluff with a fork. They can be eaten plain, stir-fried like rice, or served in salads and cold dishes. When ground they can be turned into flour and used to make porridge, tortillas, or pasta.

Note: It is important to rinse the seeds to remove the saponin, quinoa's natural coating, which can make it taste bitter or soapy. Some boxed quinoa is pre-rinsed, though an extra rinse won't hurt.

Savory Quinoa Porridge

P'esque de quinua
Bolivia

Preparation time: 10 minutes
Cooking time: 20 minutes

Serves: 4

On chilly mornings in altiplano towns like El Alto, Oruro, and Potosí, this nourishing porridge is a favorite breakfast made from pantry staples. The most common version mixes milk and butter gradually into cooked quinoa as it heats, then adds shredded *quesillo*, a fresh, soft cheese from Cochabamba, or even crumbled *queso fresco* on the edges like a crown in the bowl. Some variations of *p'esque* leave out the milk, but add a sauce made from sautéed onions and *ají* peppers before covering with the cheese.

> 1 cup/6 oz (170 g) white quinoa
> 2 cups/16 fl oz (475 ml) water
> 2 tablespoons whole milk
> 2 tablespoons (30 g) butter
> ³⁄₄ cup/3 oz (80 g) shredded *quesillo* or *queso fresco*
> salt

Rinse the quinoa in a sifter (sieve) under cold running water until the water runs clear.
　　Bring the water to a boil in a medium pan, add the quinoa and simmer for 15 minutes. Place in a bowl. Using a spoon, coarsely mash the quinoa into a rough purée.
　　Put the milk and butter in a small pan, bring to a boil, and season with salt. Pour over the mashed quinoa and stir. Place the warm quinoa in bowls, add the shredded cheese around the edges, and serve.

Savory Quinoa Porridge

Steamed Quinoa Dumplings

Kispiña, quispiña
Bolivia, Peru

Preparation time: 5 minutes
Cooking time: 30 minutes
Serves: 4

These quinoa dumplings, eaten on their own or as a side to a larger plate, are hand formed and rarely uniform. They may be of different sizes and are sometimes circular or tubular, or shaped like animals, such as llamas or cows. They are steamed in rural kitchens by placing the dumplings on straw that is layered over a small amount of water in a deep clay pot placed directly over a wood-fired hearth. *Kispiña* is also used as a way to utilize pig blood, and some communities still use it instead of water to mix the dough.

2 cups/8 oz (235 g) quinoa flour
¼ cup/2 fl oz (60 ml) oil
1 teaspoon salt

In a large bowl, mix the quinoa flour with the oil and salt. Add enough cold water to form a uniform but somewhat dry dough.
Using your hands, shape the dough into smaller, flat pieces, about the size of the inner palm of your hand.
Place in a steamer over low heat and cook for about 30 minutes. They should still be moist and not overly dry or crumbly.

Quinoa Fritters

Bocados de quinoa 🍳
Bolivia

Preparation time: 5 minutes
Cooking time: 25–30 minutes
Serves: 4

These fried quinoa cakes are a staple in highland kitchens in Bolivia. Made by mixing quinoa with egg and a little bit of flour before frying, they are sometimes stuffed with canned tuna, chopped vegetables, leafy greens, or shredded cheese.

1 cup/6 oz (170 g) quinoa
2 cups/16 fl oz (475 ml) water
1 egg, beaten
1 tablespoon flour
2 tablespoons vegetable oil
salt

Rinse the quinoa in a sifter (sieve) under cold running water until the water runs clear. Tip into a pan.
Cover the quinoa with the water, bring it to a boil, and cook for 15 minutes. Drain and cool.
In a bowl, mix the quinoa with the beaten egg, and flour.
Heat the oil in a frying pan over medium heat. Using a spoon, scoop out 18–20 small balls of the quinoa mixture, a little bigger than a golf ball. Place in the hot oil in two batches. Cook for about 2–3 minutes on each side, until golden brown. Season with salt and serve.

Amaranth Porridge

Mazamorra de kiwicha, atole de amaranto
Bolivia, Ecuador, Mexico, Peru

Preparation time: 5 minutes
Cooking time: 25 minutes
Serves: 4

Various forms of amaranth porridge can be found throughout the Andes, usually as a hot breakfast treat. In Mexico, it's prepared much like an atole, with a consistency that can range from a drink to a porridge.

4 cups/32 fl oz (950 ml) water
1 cup/7 oz (195 g) amaranth seeds

To serve
dried cape gooseberries and dried bananas, to taste
agave syrup or panela sugar, to taste
ground cinnamon, to taste
coconut or almond milk, to taste

Heat the water in a medium pan over medium heat, then add the amaranth seeds. Bring to a boil, then set the heat to low and cook, stirring occasionally, for about 25 minutes or until the water is absorbed. Remove from the heat.
To serve, stir in cape gooseberries, dried bananas, agave or panela, cinnamon, and coconut or almond milk.

Grains, Quinoa, and Amaranth

Quinoa Fritters

Roots and Tubers

In an isolated field in Ecuador's Bolívar province, a Quechua farmer selects which potato seeds he will plant on a five-acre (two-hectare) plot of land. The sloping land has been resting for seven years, but he knows it's ready because it's now covered in *ichu*, a tall grass that will be dug up by hand and used for fertilizer. He'll pick several hundred varieties of potato for his mixed plot, all planted together because they'll help each other to grow. Some have pink skin and yellow flesh, others are blue or purple, or red and speckled. Some are round, some are long, some are twisted. Other plants like the *lupine tarwi* and *tuber mashua* will be planted alongside them, a natural way of keeping away pests, not to mention helping to diversify the community's diet. Not all of the potatoes will thrive this season, though. It has always been that way. Yet, even with patterns of rain, drought, and frost that are becoming more unpredictable every year, he knows that by planting so many varieties there will be potatoes to eat.

For more than 8,000 years, since the potato was domesticated near Lake Titicaca, this selection process has resulted in more than 4,000 varieties of potato. Once wild and bitter and the size of a coin, they have been bred to be larger, survive in different climates, and have greater intensity of color and nutrients, not to mention be more flavorful.

The potato has become a global commodity, a staple crop that has sustained a sizable chunk of the earth's population for the last 400 years. In the Andes, potatoes serve as the primary source of calories and have allowed civilization to thrive. Freeze-dried in the frigid night air, they could be stored for years at a time, allowing Inca armies to march across the continent.

Throughout Latin America, from the highlands of Guatemala to the Chiloé archipelago of Chile, potatoes, as well as other tubers like ocas, *ollucos*, and *arracacha*, are mashed, boiled, fried, baked, fermented, stewed, and ground into flour. Immigrant groups have adapted them to the recipes of their homelands, turning them into dumplings and pies. The story of the potato and other native tubers from this part of the world is still being told.

Peanut and Potato Chowder

Chupe de maní, sopa de maní 🔲
Bolivia, Ecuador

Preparation time: 10 minutes
Cooking time: 30 minutes
Serves: 2

Cultivated peanuts, a hybrid of two wild species, likely first appeared somewhere around southern Bolivia, Paraguay, southwestern Brazil, and northern Argentina, then spread throughout much of South America where countless landraces evolved before being spread throughout the world by European traders. This thick stew can be found in dozens of forms that alter the thickness and level of spice, as well as opting to add meat.

    1 tablespoon groundnut (peanut) oil
    1½ white onions, chopped
    2 potatoes, peeled and cut into 1-inch (2.5-cm)
    cubes
    4 dried chiles
    2 cups/16 fl oz (475 ml) vegetable stock
    8 tablespoons peanuts, toasted and ground
    2 tablespoons cilantro (coriander), chopped
    salt and ground pepper

Heat the oil in a deep frying pan over medium heat and sauté the onions for 7 minutes. Add the potatoes and chiles, followed by the stock. Bring to a boil, then lower the heat and simmer for 15 minutes or until the potatoes are cooked.

Transfer half the soup and the peanuts to a blender and blend well, then return to the pan. Add the chopped cilantro (coriander) and season with salt and pepper. Serve hot.

Chilean Potato Dumplings

Chapaleles, pan de papa
Chile

Preparation time: 15 minutes
Cooking time: 35 minutes
Makes: 6

These dumplings, made of boiled potatoes and flour, are prevalent in the Chiloé archipelago, which is home to several hundred distinct varieties of potatoes. Various versions are made throughout the island chain. Sometimes *chapaleles* are steamed under the earth with *curanto* (a seafood and meat dish), while others are pan-fried or baked. They can be served on their own with *ají pebre* or honey and a cup of tea, as well as served alongside heartier stews and meats.

    1 lb (450 g) potatoes, peeled and cut into 2-inch
    (5-cm) chunks
    1 cup/4½ oz (130 g) all-purpose (plain) flour,
    plus extra for dusting
    2 tablespoons butter, softened
    2 eggs
    1½ oz (40 g) *Chicharrón* (Pork Cracklings/crispy pork
    skin; page 276 for homemade or can be store-bought)
    salt
    melted butter, for brushing

Preheat the oven to 350°F/180°C/Gas Mark 4.

Put the potatoes in a medium pan with enough salted water to cover them. Bring to a boil and cook for 10 minutes, or until soft, then drain and place in a bowl. Mash them, then mix in the flour and knead until you get a soft and uniform dough. If the dough is too sticky, add a little extra flour.

Add the butter and continue kneading, followed by the eggs and, if the mixture is too sticky, more flour. Mix in the *Chicharron*, and salt to taste.

Place the dough on a floured surface and shape into 6 discs, about 4 inches (10 cm) in diameter and ½ inch (1 cm) thick.

Line an oven tray with parchment paper, place the dough discs on it, and brush with melted butter. Bake for 25 minutes or until golden brown. Serve warm.

Chilote Potato Dumplings

Milcao
Chile

Preparation time: 45 minutes
Cooking time: 30 minutes
Serves: 8

Heavy potato dumplings, *milcaos* are native to the Chiloé archipelago, however, the migration of Chilote families to Patagonia has made it a common dish there as well. On the islands, a variety of native potatoes—colored red, yellow, and purple; sometimes small and round, other times long and thin—are used to make *milcaos*. They are most commonly baked, though they can be fried or steamed within *curanto* (a seafood and meat dish) as well. Another form, *milcados pelados*, are boiled and eaten with sugar or honey.

    2 lb (900 g) raw potatoes, grated
    2 lb (900 g) potatoes peeled, cooked, mashed,
    and cooled
    1 teaspoon salt
    1 tablespoon lard
    3 oz (80 g) *Chicharrón* (Pork Cracklings/crispy pork
    skin; page 276 for homemade or can be store-bought),
    chopped into small pieces

Preheat the oven to 350°F/180°C/Gas Mark 4.

Place the grated potatoes on a clean tea towel and squeeze the water out. In a bowl, mix the mashed and raw potatoes together. Mix in the salt and lard.

Divide the dough into 8 equal pieces and shape into 4-inch (10-cm) discs, ½ inch (1 cm) thick. Crumble the *Chicharrón* and press some into the middle of each disc and cover over with the dough to seal.

Place the dumplings on an oven tray lined with parchment paper and bake for 30 minutes or until golden brown. Serve warm.

Peanut and Potato Chowder

Ecuadorian Potato Pancakes

Llapingachos
Ecuador

Preparation time: 10 minutes,
plus 1 hour 5 minutes resting
Cooking time: 40 minutes

Makes: 12

In the highlands of Ecuador, these bulky potato pancakes are ever present. They are believed to have originated in the Tungurahua province where large, red skinned potatoes with a yellow flesh called *papa chola* are used, though common varieties like Yukon Gold or Russet will also work. *Llapingachos* are usually served with roasted pork or chorizo, slices of avocado, and a fried egg.

5 potatoes, peeled and cut into 2-inch (5-cm) chunks
2 tablespoons vegetable oil
2 scallions (spring onions), finely chopped
1 teaspoon annatto paste
½ cup/2 oz (60 g) shredded cheese (mozzarella)
vegetable oil, for frying

Cook the potatoes in a pan of salted water for 15 minutes, or until soft. Drain and mash in a bowl.

In a frying pan, heat the vegetable oil and add the scallions (spring onions) and annatto paste. Cook, stirring, for 10 minutes, or until the onions are soft. Add the mixture to the mashed potato and use your hands to mix. Add salt to taste and rest in the refrigerator for 45 minutes.

Shape the cold potato dough into 12 small balls (about 1½ inches/4 cm in diameter), then make a cavity in the middle of each to add some cheese, seal, and form into patties. Let them rest in the refrigerator for a further 20 minutes, until cold.

Pour enough vegetable oil to cover the surface of the clean frying pan, and place over medium heat. Fry the *llapingachos* for 3 minutes on each side, or until golden brown. Serve warm.

Ecuadorian Potato Soup

Locro de papas
Ecuador

Preparation time: 15 minutes
Cooking time: 30 minutes

Serves: 5–6

This thick, cheesy stew with annatto is found in markets throughout the Ecuadorian Andes. Like *llapingachos*, *locro* is usually made with *papa chola*, though starchy, russet potatoes will work. A variation called *yahuarlocro* adds lamb entrails and lamb blood to the stew.

2 tablespoons lard
1 white onion, chopped
2 garlic cloves, minced
1 teaspoon annatto paste
10 potatoes, peeled and cut into cubes
2 teaspoons ground cumin
7 cups/56 fl oz (1.6 liters) water
1 cup/8 fl oz (250 ml) milk
1 cup/4 oz (125 g) shredded *queso fresco*
4 tablespoons cilantro (coriander), chopped
sliced avocado, to serve

Heat the lard in a pan over medium heat, add the onion, garlic, and annatto paste and sauté for 7 minutes or until brownish and soft.

Add the potatoes, stir well and season with salt and the cumin, and continue cooking for a further 5 minutes. Add the water, bring to a boil and cook for 10 minutes, until soft. Mash half the potatoes in the pan, adding the milk and cooking for a further 5 minutes.

Add the cheese and cilantro (coriander), and check the seasoning and consistency; the *locro* should be creamy. If needed, add more milk, or water.

Serve hot with avocado slices.

Potato Varenikes

Varenikes de papa
Argentina

Preparation time: 15 minutes
Cooking time: 1 hour 20 minutes

Serves: 6–8

The Jewish diaspora has resulted in *varenikes*, Eastern European potato dumplings, appearing in Argentina alongside cups of *mate*.

3 cups /14 oz (400 g) white type 00 flour, plus extra for dusting
2 eggs
1 cup/8 fl oz (250 ml) vegetable oil
2 lb 3 oz (1 kg) white potatoes, peeled and cut into 2-inch (5-cm) chunks
3 onions, thinly chopped
7 oz (200 g) *queso fresco*, shredded
1½ cups/10½ oz (300 g) sugar
1 cup/8 fl oz (250 ml) heavy (double) cream, optional
½ teaspoon salt
¼ teaspoon ground pepper

Add the flour, eggs, 3 tablespoons of the oil, and some salt to a mixer. Process briefly to a uniform dough, adding water if necessary to bring it together. Remove from the mixer and knead on a floured surface. Let rest for about 20 minutes.

Meanwhile, place the potatoes in a pan and cover with water. Add salt, bring to a boil, and cook for 15 minutes or until soft. Drain, peel, and purée with a wooden spoon or potato masher. Season with salt and pepper.

Heat 2 tablespoons of the oil in a frying pan over medium heat, and sauté one-third of the onions for about 5 minutes, until lightly browned. Mix in the puréed potatoes and *queso fresco*. Set aside.

Add the remaining chopped onion to a small pan, then add the sugar and the remaining ¾ cup/6 fl oz (175 ml) oil. Caramelize over very low heat for about 40 minutes, stirring every few minutes. If desired, add the cream at the end and let it reduce for a couple of minutes.

Using a rolling pin or pasta machine, roll out the dough and cut out 4–5-inch (10–13-cm) discs, ⅛-inch (3 mm) thick. Add a tablespoon of the potato mixture to the middle of each. Fold the dough over on itself and seal by pressing the edges together with a fork. Set aside.

Bring a large pot of water to a boil, add the *varenikes* and cook until they rise to the surface, then drain and serve hot with the caramelized onion.

Ecuadorian Potato Pancakes

Chilean Disco Fries

Chorrillana
Chile

Preparation time: 15 minutes
Cooking time: 20 minutes

Serves: 4

Chile's answer to American disco fries or Canadian poutine, *chorrillana* is considered by some as a "heart attack on a plate." This heaping pile of minced beef, grilled onions, and scrambled egg over greasy French fries is the typical snack of a Chilean *picada*, essentially a dive bar. It's believed to have been invented in the port city of Valparaíso at a *picada* called Casino Social J Cruz, tucked away in a graffiti-covered alleyway. It is essentially the pub version of *bistec a lo pobre*, a steak with a fried egg. J Cruz began serving it around 50 years ago to students who came in for a few beers and needed something in their stomachs. The origins of the name aren't clear. Some suggest it's in reference to the Battle of Chorrillos in Peru, or perhaps in relation to the chorizo sometimes used as the protein.

    vegetable oil, for deep-frying and sautéing
    2 lb (900 g) potatoes, peeled and cut into fries
    1 lb (450 g) beef (round lower cut), cut into 1½-inch
    (4-cm) chunks
    ½ teaspoon *merkén* (smoked chile powder)
    2 white onions, thinly sliced
    4 eggs, beaten

Pour enough oil for deep-frying into a large, heavy pan, making sure it is no more than two-thirds full, and heat to 360°F/182°C.

Fry the potatoes in batches for 8 minutes or until golden brown and crispy. Remove with a skimmer and place on a plate lined with paper towels, to absorb excess oil. Place on a baking sheet and set in the oven at a very low temperature to keep warm.

In a frying pan, heat 2 tablespoons of vegetable oil and add the beef, seasoning with salt and *merkén*. Cook over high heat, stirring, for 8 minutes, then remove from the pan, set aside, and keep warm.

Heat 1 tablespoon of vegetable oil in the same frying pan, over medium heat, and sauté the onions for 4 minutes. Once soft, add the beaten eggs. Stir continuously for 4 minutes or until the eggs are cooked.

To serve, place the fries on a large plate, then add the onions, eggs, and beef on top.

Green Stew

Caldo verde, yaku chupe
Peru

Preparation time: 20 minutes
Cooking time: 15 minutes

Serves: 4

This nutritious stew from the northern Andean city of Cajamarca get its green name and strong flavor from the aromatic herbs found within. For the best flavor, the herbs should be ground in a *batán*, or grinding stone. In Cajamarca, there is a strange form for beating the eggs, called *chicoteados*, where you make a small opening in the shell and then shake the liquid into the stew. *Caldo verde* is often eaten in the mornings, with a piece of bread, and believed to be good for stomach problems (and the soul).

    1 tablespoon olive oil
    1 white onion, sliced
    4 cups/32 fl oz (950 ml) vegetable stock
    2 lb (900 g) potatoes, peeled and cut into cubes
    2 cups/9 oz (250 g) crumbled *queso fresco*
    1 tablespoon parsley, chopped
    1 tablespoon cilantro (coriander), chopped
    8 fresh *paico* (epazote) leaves, chopped (or use
    2 teaspoons dried epazote)
    4 eggs, beaten
    salt and ground pepper

Heat the oil in a pan over medium heat, add the onion, and sauté for 4 minutes. Add the stock and bring to a boil, then add the potatoes and cook for 10 minutes or until soft.

Add half the cheese and season with salt and pepper. Add the parsley, cilantro (coriander), and *paico* and, while still boiling, add the beaten eggs and stir, then take off the heat.

Serve hot, sprinkled with the remaining cheese.

Peruvian Potato Casserole

Causa a la limeña
Peru

Preparation time: 20 minutes
Cooking time: 10 minutes

Serves: 6

Many restaurants have tried to turn *causa* into something it's not, making little sushi-size bites stacked with exotic toppings. At its heart, *causa* is a homey casserole eaten among family. Made with *papas amarillas* (yellow potatoes) in Peru, it is scooped out of a dish in squares like lasagna, though when served at restaurants it is often round, made in individual portions, using a mold.

    4 potatoes, peeled and cut into 2-inch (5-cm) chunks
    ½ cup (120 ml) *ají amarillo* paste
    juice of 2 limes
    ¼ cup/4 fl oz (120 ml) vegetable oil
    ½ cup/2 oz (60 g) finely chopped red onion
    ½ cup/4 oz (115 g) mayonnaise
    2 chicken breasts, cooked and shredded (or use tuna)
    1 avocado, sliced
    2 tomatoes, thinly sliced
    4 hard-boiled eggs, sliced
    salt and ground pepper

    To serve
    sliced avocado
    black olives
    hard-boiled eggs

Cook the potatoes in boiling, salted water for 10 minutes until tender. Drain and place in a bowl. Add the *ají amarillo paste*, lime juice, and vegetable oil. Mash together, seasoning with salt. Set aside.

In another bowl, place the red onion, mayonnaise, and chicken, mix well and season with salt and pepper.

In a square ovenproof dish, 6 x 6 x 1½ inches (15 x 15 x 4 cm), add half the potato mixture in an even layer. Spread a layer of the chicken filling over the top, then the sliced avocado, tomatoes, and hard-boiled eggs. Finally, cover with the remaining potato.

Cut into squares and serve with slices of avocado, black olives, and hard-boiled eggs.

Roots and Tubers

Guatemalan Potato Tamales

Paches
Guatemala

Preparation time: 20 minutes
Cooking time: 2 hours 15 minutes
Serves: 10

Usually prepared on Thursdays, a custom in Guatemala that also includes making tamales on Saturdays and *caldo de rés* on Mondays, these potato-based tamales originated in Quetzaltenango in the western highlands, where potatoes are grown in abundance.

6 lb (2.7 kg) potatoes, peeled and cut into 2-inch (5-cm) chunks
1 *guaque* chile
1 *pasa* chile
½ cup/2¼ oz (70 g) *pepitas* (squash seeds)
1 tablespoon vegetable oil
½ white onion, chopped
2 garlic cloves, chopped
8 oz (225 g) tomatillos
1 tablespoon annatto paste
1 lb (450 g) pork lard, melted
10 banana leaves, cut into 12 x 14-inch (30 x 35-cm) rectangles
1 lb 8 oz (675 g) pork loin, cut into 10 chunks, about 1 inch (2.5 cm)
cibaque (vegetable fiber) or string, to tie the *paches*
4 cups/32 fl oz (950 ml) water

Cook the potatoes in boiling, salted water for 15 minutes, or until soft. Drain, peel, add to a bowl, and let cool.

Meanwhile, heat a frying pan over medium heat, add the chiles and squash seeds, and toast for 5 minutes, stirring frequently. Tip into a blender.

Heat the oil in the same pan, add the onion, garlic, and tomatillos, and sauté over medium heat for 7 minutes. Add to the blender, along with the annatto paste, and process to a paste. Set aside.

Mash the potatoes, using a fork. Mix in the melted pork lard and the blended paste, and season with salt.

Heat the banana leaves slightly in a pan or over a burner. Arrange the leaves in a cross. Add 2 tablespoons of the potato mixture and 2 pieces of meat. Close to create a rectangular package and tie to seal, by making a cross with the *cibaque* or string, as for a parcel.

Place the banana leaves trimmings in the bottom of a large pan, cover them with the water and bring to a boil. Place the *paches* in a single layer across the bottom of the pan, in the water, and let cook for 2 hours over medium heat, checking occasionally to make sure the water doesn't evaporate, and topping it up if necessary. Serve warm.

Spicy Potato Salad

Escribano
Peru

Preparation time: 15 minutes
Cooking time: 10 minutes
Serves: 4

A standard dish in the *picanterías* of Arequipa, the name *escribano* translates as "notary," referring to the lawyers, law clerks, and judges working in the southern city who would arrive late for lunch, when *los picantes*, the spicy main courses, had sold out. This simple salad was created with enough *rocoto* chile pepper so that patron still had his fill of spice, not to mention the consumption of *chicha* (corn beer) to cool down their palate.

2 lb (900 g) potatoes, peeled and cut into chunks
1 cup/5½ oz (160 g) peeled and diced tomatoes
½ cup/2 oz (60 g) cored, diced *rocoto* chile
1 tablespoon parsley, chopped
2 tablespoons olive oil, plus an extra dash to serve
4 tablespoons white wine vinegar
salt and ground pepper

Place the potatoes in a medium pan with enough salted water to cover, bring to a boil and cook for 10 minutes, or until tender. Drain, then place in a bowl and mash with a fork.

Add the diced tomatoes and chile, and the parsley, and mix well. Season with salt and pepper, then finish by adding the oil and vinegar. Serve at room temperature, with a dash of olive oil on top.

Huancayo-Style Potatoes

Papas a la huancaína
Peru

Preparation time: 10 minutes
Cooking time: 20 minutes
Serves: 4

This recipe from the city of Huancayo in Peru's central Andes is now a national dish. The recipe is believed to be traced to the construction of the Central Railway, which connected the coast, where *ají amarillo* chiles are grown, with Huancayo, where cheese and potatoes are common. The sauce has become so popular that it's sold in bottled form like mayonnaise and used as a dip. In southern Peru, you are more likely to find this dish with *Salsa ocopa* (Huacatay Sauce, page 407) rather than *huancaína*.

1 slice of white bread
¼ cup/2 fl oz (60 ml) evaporated milk
¼ cup/2 fl oz (60 ml) vegetable oil
½ red onion, sliced
3 *ají amarillo*, cored and sliced
1 cup/4 oz (120 g) crumbled *queso fresco*
8 potatoes (ideally *papas amarillas*), peeled and cut into 2-inch (5-cm) chunks

To serve
black olives
2 hard-boiled eggs, quartered

In a bowl, soak the bread in the evaporated milk, slightly breaking it up.

Meanwhile, heat the oil in a frying pan and sauté the onion and *ají amarillo* over low heat for 6 minutes.

Add the bread and milk to the frying pan and cook for 1 minute. Turn off the heat and let it cool slightly. While still warm, add to a blender with the cheese and blend until smooth.

Cook the potatoes in boiling, salted water for 12 minutes or until soft. Drain, then slice the potatoes, lay them on a plate, and pour the sauce on top. Serve with the black olives and hard-boiled eggs.

Potatoes Cooked in an Earthen Oven

Huatía
Bolivia, Chile, Peru

Preparation time: 45 minutes
Cooking time: 30 minutes
Serves: 12

During harvest season in the Andes of Southern Peru, Bolivia, and northern Chile, puffs of smoke can be seen wafting out of mounds of dirt in the middle of potato fields. The mound, or *huatía*, is a dome of dirt and stones with a fire heating it from within. Kindling, usually dried stalks and leaves from the field, gets added to the fire from an opening on one side until it is on the verge of collapse, then potatoes are added within, and sometimes other tubers, and broad beans too. The *huatía* is broken down into a steaming pile of earth, cooking the tubers in the very field from where they came. After they cook, they are symbolically harvested again, and laid out on a blanket, then peeled. They are eaten with *Uchucuta* (Andean Chile Sauce, page 408) and glasses of *Chicha de jora* (Corn Beer, page 388). The ritual serves as lunch for those working in the field, but also as a tribute to Pachamama, or Mother Earth. If you lack access to a potato field and native Andean tubers, the same process can be achieved with the tubers native to your area in a backyard garden.

16 lb (7 kg) earth from a potato field (clay, mud, and dirt)
4 lb (1.8 kg) dry twigs and branches from plants such as quinoa, *kiwicha*, potato, or mashua
2 lb (900 g) potatoes
1 lb (450 g) mashua
1 lb (450 g) oca
8 oz (225 g) fava (broad) beans (still in pods)
Uchucuta (Andean Chile Sauce, page 408), to serve

In a flat, open field, pile the hunks of clay, mud, and dirt into a cone or igloo-like shape, with an open space in the bottom.

Place all the dry twigs inside and light a fire. Let it burn for 30 minutes, heating the earthen oven until it is charred and near collapse. Place all the tubers and the beans inside, on the fire, then cover them with a clean tea towel. Quickly break the oven apart, collapsing it over the tubers and beans, and let the hot earth steam them for 30 minutes.

Carefully remove all of the dirt and clay and remove the tubers and beans from the fire. Clean them with a clean tea towel, and serve with *uchucuta*. Peel the potatoes as you eat them.

Spicy Potato, Pork, and Beet Stew

Puca picante 🔲
Peru

Preparation time: 20 minutes
Cooking time: 50 minutes
Serves: 4

A favorite dish in the Andean region of Ayacucho, Peru, the name *puca picante* is a combination of the Quechua word for red and Spanish word for spicy. Originally, it was made to nourish communal activities like harvests, or the building of houses and roads.

2 lb (900 g) pork belly, cut into 2-inch (5-cm) chunks
1 teaspoon vegetable oil
1 white onion, chopped
3 garlic cloves, minced
½ cup/4 fl oz (120 ml) *ají panca* paste
1 medium tomato, peeled and diced
1 teaspoon ground cumin
½ cup/2¼ oz (70 g) toasted peanuts, coarsely chopped
1 beet (beetroot), peeled, cooked, and chopped
½ cup/4 fl oz (120 ml) water
1 lb (450 g) small potatoes, washed
2 cups/16 fl oz (475 ml) beef stock
salt and ground pepper

In two batches, sear the pork belly in its own fat in a medium pan over high heat for 4 minutes on each side, or until golden brown. Remove the meat from the pan, and set aside.

In the same pan, heat 1 teaspoon of the vegetable oil over medium-high heat. Sauté the onion and garlic for 7 minutes, then add the *ají panca* paste with the tomato, stirring continuously. Add the cumin, and season with salt and pepper.

Blend the peanuts with the beet (beetroot) and water to a purée, then add to the onion pan with the browned meat, the potatoes, and stock. Stir well and cook for 20 minutes, or until the potatoes are soft. Serve hot, with white rice and a side salad.

Spicy Potato, Pork, and Beet Stew

Venezuelan Potato Soup

Pisca andina
Venezuela

Preparation time: 15 minutes
Cooking time: 25 minutes

Serves: 5–6

A typical breakfast in Mérida, a mountainous city in the Venezuelan Andes, *pisca andina* is a nourishing mix of chicken broth, potatoes, cheese, and a poached egg. Ladle the rich broth over cheese for a soft, gooey consistency.

    1 tablespoon butter
    ½ white onion, chopped
    1 scallion (spring onion), finely chopped
    2 garlic cloves, chopped
    4 cups/32 fl oz (1 liter) chicken stock
    4 potatoes, peeled and cut into cubes
    1 cup/8 fl oz (250 ml) milk
    10½ oz (300 g) *queso blanco ahumado*, cut into
    ½-inch (1-cm) cubes (or use smoked mozzarella)
    2 tablespoons cilantro (coriander), chopped
    5 eggs, poached

Heat the butter in a pan over high heat. Add the onion, scallion (spring onion), and garlic and sauté for 7 minutes or until soft. Add the stock and bring to a boil, then add the potatoes and let cook for 10 minutes or until soft.
    Add the milk and bring to a boil, then reduce to a simmer, add the cheese for a further 5 minutes.
    Place cheese in each serving bowl and ladle the soup over it. Add the cilantro (coriander), season with salt and pepper, and serve, with one egg per serving.

Chuño

In the high Andes of Peru and Bolivia, after a potato harvest in Quechua and Aymara communities, the best potatoes are set aside for consumption and sale or trade, with the remainder transformed into *chuño*. Also called *tunta*, *moraya*, and *papas secas*, these potatoes are laid out on hay-covered earth to freeze in the frigid night-time air of the altiplano, then to dehydrate during sunny days. After three days and nights the potatoes are laid out in fields and trampled on, an activity enjoyed by entire families, expelling any liquid and removing the skins. These potatoes may be sun-dried, which makes black *chuño*, or washed or soaked in water and then dried in the sun for approximately one week, to make white *chuño*.

This natural form of freeze-drying results in a potato that is light yet nutritious, and can be stored for a period of years, far longer than the month or two of fresh potatoes, making them integral to survival in periods of crop failure. Evidence of *chuño* dates back prior to the Incas' arrival in the thirteenth century, though it helped them to expand from a small band of warriors near Cusco to an empire of twelve million people that stretched from southern Colombia to northern Argentina in a relatively short period of time. By moving and storing large amounts of *chuño* in *qullqa*, or roadside storehouses, along with beans, quinoa, and dried alpaca meat called *charqui*, they were able to feed their armies as they marched across the Andes.

Chuño can be eaten on its own with a slice of fresh cheese or dipped into sauces, as well as used to thicken sauces, or rehydrated in stews like *carapulcra*.

Freeze-Dried Potatoes with Eggs

Chuño phuti
Argentina, Bolivia, Chile, Peru

Preparation time: 15 minutes, plus overnight soaking
Cooking time: 15 minutes

Serves: 4

Chuño phuti is a common dish prepared across the Andean altiplano. With its long shelf life, *chuño* is almost always available in rural communities, and the dish can be adapted to whatever vegetables are in season.

    8 oz (225 g) black *chuño*
    1 tablespoon vegetable oil
    ½ white onion, chopped
    2 tomatoes, peeled and diced
    3 eggs, beaten
    2 cups/6 oz (180 g) shredded *queso fresco*

Place the *chuño* in a bowl and add enough cold water to cover. Let soak overnight. Change the water at least once.
    The next day, peel any remaining skin off the *chuño* and rinse in cold water. Cook the *chuño* in boiling, salted water for 15 minutes until tender. Drain and cut into pieces or shred into chunks when cool enough to handle.
    In another pan, heat the oil and stir-fry the onion for 7 minutes, or until soft and brown. Add the tomatoes and continue cooking for a further 7 minutes, then add the cooked *chuño* and beaten eggs and mix together.
    Serve hot, sprinkled with the *queso fresco*.

Aymara Stew

Chairo
Bolivia, Chile, Peru

Preparation time: 15 minutes, plus overnight soaking
Cooking time: 45 minutes

Serves: 4

A hearty soup common among the Ayamara people found in numerous variations in the highlands of Bolivia, southern Peru, and northern Chile, *chairo* was traditionally made with ingredients that could last for long periods of time, such as freeze-dried potatoes and dried meat. It could be made in the fields, adding in fresh herbs and whatever other bits of meat or vegetables were around. After conquest, Old World ingredients like beef, lamb, and wheat were added into many preparations.

    5 black *chuño*
    1 lb (450 g) ossobuco
    1½ oz (40 g) *cecina* (salted pork)
    3 oz (80 g) goat tripe, cut into 2-inch (5-cm) cubes
    4 goat loins, cut into 2-inch (5-cm) chunks
    3 tablespoons vegetable oil
    ½ cup/2 oz (60 g) chopped white onion
    1 garlic clove, minced
    1 teaspoon *ají panca* paste
    ½ cup/2 oz (60 g) carrots, diced
    1 lb (450 g) boiled potatoes, cut into 2-inch (5-cm) cubes
    1 cup/5½ oz (160 g) *mote*, cooked (or use hominy)
    ½ cup/2 oz (60 g) shelled fava (broad) beans
    1 teaspoon ground cumin
    1 teaspoon fresh oregano, chopped

Roots and Tubers

Place the *chuño* in a bowl and add enough cold water to cover. Let soak overnight.

The next day, peel any remaining skin off the *chuño* and rinse in cold water.

Bring a large pan of salted water to a boil, add the ossobuco, cecina, tripe, and goat, and cook for 8 minutes. Take the meat out and reserve. Strain the water to remove any impurities, and keep the stock.

Heat the oil in a medium pan over medium heat, and sauté the onion, garlic, and *ají panca* paste for 7 minutes, stirring continuously. Pour in the reserved stock and bring to a boil, then add the *chuño*, carrots, potatoes, *mote*, and fava (broad) beans. Season with salt and pepper, and add the cumin and oregano. Reduce to a simmer for 20 minutes, then add the meats and simmer for a further 7 minutes.

Check the seasoning and serve hot.

Other Latin American Tubers

While the potato went on to conquer the world, most other Andean tubers haven't traveled quite as far from their ancestral homeland. Many of these native tubers have spectacular nutritional qualities, not to mention beautiful colors and delicious flavors. Plus, most have high yields and are companion crops to potatoes.

Mashua (*Tropaeolum tuberosum*), also called *añu* and *cubio*, is grown throughout the Andes of Bolivia, Colombia, Ecuador, and Peru at altitudes between 8,000 and 14,000 feet (2,400 and 4,300 meters), often alongside potato crops as they have an extraordinary ability to repel pests. Raw *mashua* has a strong peppery flavor, though it's often left in the sun for four or five days after harvest, letting the starches convert to sugar, making them sweeter. When they are boiled or roasted, the flavor becomes quite mild and their stems, branches, and shoots are also edible. Known to have anaphrodisiac effects, they were notoriously fed to Inca armies to keep them focused, and the stigma around *mashua* being a threat to their masculinity persists among men in the Andes today.

Rich in proteins and carbohydrates, *olluco* (*Ullucus tuberosus*), also called *papalisa* or *ullucus*, has been cultivated throughout the high Andes since around 5,500 BC. They tend to be orange or yellow with red, pink, or purple freckles. They stay crisp when cooked and are mostly eaten fresh, pickled, or freeze-dried and stored long periods of time. Additionally, the leaves are also edible and are often added to stews or salads.

Domesticated alongside the potato and *olluco*, oca (*Oxalis tuberosa*) is mostly cultivated at elevations between 10,000 and 12,000 feet (3,000 and 3,600 meters) and is found in a vast array of colors such as pink, yellow, orange, purple, and black. High in vitamin C, oca is sometimes sweetened by being dried in the sun, though it is mostly eaten raw or cooked. It's grown commonly in New Zealand, where it is called the New Zealand yam, and also found in Mexico under the name *papa ratonera* or *papa amarga*.

Grown between 7,000 and 10,000 feet (2,200 and 3,000 meters), *yacón* (*Smallanthus sonchifolius*) has a high water content and a pulp that varies from mild to extremely sweet. Conquest-era chroniclers noted indigenous communities ate the root raw and fresh, though today it's often added to juices. In Ecuador, it's sometimes called *jicama*, though it should not be confused with the root vegetable of the same name that is common in Mexico.

Domesticated in the lower Andes, *arracacha* (*Aracacia xanthorriza*) is mostly grown at altitudes between 6,000 and 8,000 feet (1,800 and 2,500 meters), from Venezuela to northern Chile and Argentina, though it is also common in highland areas of Central America. Its shape is similar to a squat carrot or parsnip and it can have a white, yellow, or purple interior. Much like a potato, it cannot be eaten raw. It can be baked in ashes, boiled and chopped, or used to make purées, ground into flour to make bread, or grated into a paste and cooked in cane syrup to make *rallado de arracacha*, as is done in Peru's Cajamarca department.

Maca (*Lepidium meyenii*), sometimes called Peruvian ginseng for its ability to increase fertility and sex drive, grows mostly at high altitudes, from 12,000 to 13,000 feet (3,800 to 4,000 meters). They resemble a radish in shape and the roots can be colored cream-yellow, black, or purple. When dried, they can be stored for years. The roots, which have flavors that can range from bitter to sweet, can be roasted, boiled, mashed, or ground into a flour that can used to make breads, cakes, or porridges.

Minced Arracacha

Picadillo de arracache
Costa Rica

Preparation time: 25 minutes
Cooking time: 30 minutes

Serves: 6

Picadillo de arracache, which can also be vegetarian, is a common dish found in *sodas*, the no-frills traditional eateries and lunch counters around Costa Rica. It is found under numerous names around the region, like *apio criollo* and *virraca*, and in Costa Rica is usually served with corn tortillas to make *gallos* (Costa Rican tacos), or can be part of a *casado* (lunch plate).

 2 tablespoons vegetable oil
 1 large onion, finely chopped
 4 garlic cloves, finely chopped
 1 red bell pepper, cored, seeded, and finely chopped
 3 tablespoons cilantro (coriander), chopped
 2 teaspoons ground annatto
 3 large tomatoes, peeled and cut into cubes
 2 lb (900 g) ground (minced) beef (or 1 lb/450 g ground beef and 1 lb/450 g ground pork or chorizo)
 1 cup/8 fl oz (250 ml) chicken stock
 3 lb (1.3 kg) *arracacha*, peeled and diced (or use cassava)
 salt and ground pepper

Heat the oil in a large pan and sauté the onion, garlic, bell pepper, cilantro (coriander), and annatto. Cook for 5 minutes over medium heat.

Add the tomatoes, meat, stock, and *arracacha* to the pan. Cook for 15 minutes or until the sauce is thick. Season with salt and pepper and cook for a further 10 minutes over medium heat, or until the *arracacha* is tender and most of the liquid has been absorbed. If using cassava, cook for at least 30 minutes or until soft.

Oca with Spicy Tamarillo Sauce

Ibias con ají de tomate de árbol
Colombia

Preparation time: 5 minutes
Cooking time: 25 minutes

Serves: 4

This simple recipe from the Colombian Andes takes on various forms from kitchen to kitchen. It can be adapted to use a mix of native tubers, like *ollucos* or potatoes.

6 *tomates de árbol* (tamarillos)
½ cup/4 fl oz (120 ml) water
2 scallions (spring onions), chopped
2 chiles (serrano, habanero, or a *jí amarillo*), chopped
2 sprigs cilantro (coriander), chopped
2 hard-boiled eggs, chopped
2 teaspoons salt
1 tablespoon olive oil
1 lb 2 oz (500 g) oca, washed

Preheat the oven to 400°F/200°C/Gas Mark 6.
To make the *ají*, cook the tamarillos for 5 minutes in boiling water, or until their skins start to come off. Drain and add to a blender with the measured water. Add the scallions (spring onions), chiles, cilantro (coriander), eggs, and salt and blend until smooth.
Spread the oca out on a baking sheet and drizzle them with the olive oil. Cook in the oven for about 20 minutes, or until tender. Serve with the *ají*.

Ollucos with Dried Meat

Olluquito con charqui, ulluku with ch'arki
Peru

Preparation time: 20 minutes
Cooking time: 1 hour

Serves: 6

This simple preparation that combines two indispensable Andean ingredients, *ch'arki* and *olluco*, is one of the oldest in Peruvian gastronomy, likely dating back more than a millennia. The *ch'arki*, a general term for dehydrated meat, was traditionally made with alpaca meat, or to a lesser extent llama. An alternative version, *olluquito con carne*, uses fresh meat. This is typically served with white rice.

1 tablespoon olive oil
½ cup/2 oz (60 g) chopped white onion
2 garlic cloves, minced
2 tablespoons *ají panca* paste
1 lb (450 g) *charqui*, soaked and shredded (or use beef jerky)
1 cup/8 fl oz (250 ml) beef stock
2 lb (900 g) *ollucos*, julienned
1 tablespoon parsley, chopped
salt and ground pepper

Heat the oil in a pan over medium heat and sauté the onion and garlic for 5 minutes. Add the *ají panca* paste and cook for a further 6 minutes over low heat. Add the *charqui*, stir well and then pour in the stock. Keep the heat low and cook for 30 minutes or until the *charqui* is cooked. Add the *ollucos*, season with salt and pepper, and add the chopped parsley. Continue simmering for 20 minutes, then serve hot, in a deep dish.

Boyacá Stew

Cocido boyacense 🍲
Colombia

Preparation time: 15 minutes
Cooking time: 45 minutes

Serves: 6

While eaten throughout Colombia with several variations, *cocido boyacense* originated in the mountainous Boyacá region northeast of Bogotá. It grew out of *la olla podrida*, a Spanish stew made from a variety of meats and vegetables, which was common during the colonial period. With many of the vegetables being unavailable in Colombia, native tubers like *ibia* (oca), *chugua* (ulluco), and *cubium* (mashua) were used in their place.

3 tablespoons vegetable oil
2 scallions (spring onions), chopped
4 tomatoes, peeled and chopped
1 teaspoon ground cumin
1 lb (450 g) pork chops
1 lb (450 g) chicken breasts, each cut in three
1 lb (450 g) short ribs, cut into 2-inch (5-cm) chunks
4 potatoes (ideally a mix of varieties)
4 ocas
4 ears of corn, halved widthways
6 cups/3 pints (1.5 liters) water
½ cup/2 oz (60 g) shelled fava (broad) beans
1 cup/5½ oz (155 g) fresh peas
salt and ground pepper

To serve
cooked white rice
avocado slices

Heat 2 tablespoons of the oil in a frying pan over medium heat and stir-fry the scallions (spring onions) and tomatoes for 5 minutes or until soft. Add the cumin and set aside.
Heat the remaining tablespoon of oil in a large pan, and sear all the meat for about 4 minutes per side, to brown. Add the scallion and tomato mixture, the potatoes (if large, cut in half), ocas, and corn. Pour in the water, stir well, and add the fava (broad) beans and peas. Lower the heat and simmer for 30 minutes, or until all the ingredients are cooked. Season with salt and pepper.
Serve with white rice and avocado slices.

Roots and Tubers

Boyacá Stew

Cassava

Cassava. Yuca. Manioc. These three words all mean exactly the same thing and can be used interchangeably, though we use cassava for consistency. Native to South America, cassava (*Manihot esculenta*) was domesticated around 10,000 years ago in Brazil and within 5,000 years it had spread throughout the region. It is widely cultivated for its edible starchy root, a major source of carbohydrates in tropical and sub-tropical regions of Latin America and the Caribbean.

Please note that cassava is not the same as yucca. Yucca is a shrub in the Asparagaceae family, which is a common garden plant with pointy leaves, similar to agave, and found in dry climates in the Americas. If you ever encounter a recipe in a book that calls for yucca, it's probably a misspelling; however, its seeds and flower petals are actually edible.

Cassava cannot be eaten raw as it contains cyanogenic glycosides, so it needs to be boiled, fermented, or dried to avoid cyanide poisoning.

Today cassava is a staple crop throughout the region and its culinary uses are seemingly endless. Most often, sweet varieties are simply boiled like a potato, though they can also be fried, mashed, or baked. It can be ground into a flour, called *farinha*, of which the coarseness can vary from a fine powder to larger pearls. That flour can be toasted to make *farofa*, used to make breads and cookies, or sprinkled onto other dishes. Cassava can also be fermented to make alcoholic drinks like *masato* or *cauim*, or its juice can be extracted in a long woven tube called a *tipiti* and fermented to make *tucupí*, which can be further reduced to make sauces like *tucupí preto* or *cassareep*.

A by-product of the flour is tapioca, a curd-like starch, which gets processed into flakes, sticks, and pearls. Tapioca takes its name from the Tupí word *tipi'óka* and is used to make breads, formed into crepes that get filled with sweet and savory ingredients, or to make gelatinized spheres used in desserts, especially in Asia in things like the balls, or *boba*, in bubble tea.

Cheesy Cassava Skewers

Sonso de yuca 〇
Bolivia

Preparation time: 45 minutes
Cooking time: 55 minutes
Makes: 10

In Santa Cruz de la Sierra and elsewhere in lowland Bolivia where cassava is cultivated, *sonso de yuca* is a common afternoon snack. It's made by mashing the cassava, mixing in milk and cheese (a mix of hard and soft cheeses works best), and then either baked, fried in a pan like a pancake, or shaped into a log then skewered and grilled over charcoal.

  3 lb (1.3 kg) cassava
  2 cups/1 lb (450 g) shredded mozzarella
  4 cups/1 lb (450 g) shredded *queso chaqueño*
  (or another hard cheese)
  2 tablespoons butter
  1 egg, slightly beaten
  1½ tablespoons warm milk
  salt

Peel the cassava and cut into 1½-inch (4-cm) cubes. Rinse under cold water, then add to a pan and cover with cold water. Add salt and bring to a boil, then reduce the heat and simmer for about 35 minutes until tender. Drain the cassava, purée with a mouli or potato masher, and add to a bowl.
  When the cassava is cool enough to handle by hand, add the shredded cheeses and knead the dough by hand. Gradually work in the butter, egg, and milk, kneading until you have a uniform, firm dough.
  Divide into 10 equal logs and spear them one per skewer. Place the skewers on a hot grill (barbecue) and cook, turning, until golden brown all over, about 15–20 minutes. Serve hot.

Cheesy Cassava Skewers

Dried Beef and Cassava Stew

Caribeu pantaneiro
Brazil

Preparation time: 15 minutes
Cooking time: 35 minutes　　　　Serves: 5–6

This dried beef and cassava stew is typical of the Brazilian states of Mato Grosso and Mato Grosso do Sul, a region home to a tropical wetland called the Pantanal, which extends into parts of Bolivia and Paraguay. Even before the Portuguese brought cattle to the region, the indigenous Terena people made it with dried game meat.

    2 tablespoons olive oil
    1 white onion, chopped
    1 lb (450 g) *carne de sol* (sun-dried shredded beef),
    cut into 1½-inch (4-cm) cubes
    1 red bell pepper, cored, seeded, and diced
    1 lb (450 g) cassava, cut into 1-inch (2.5-cm) chunks
    2 tomatoes, peeled, seeded, and diced
    1 cup/1½ oz (40 g) parsley leaves, chopped
    1 cup/1½ oz (40 g) cilantro (coriander), chopped
    salt and ground pepper
    cooked white rice, to serve

Heat the oil in a medium pan over medium heat, then add the onion and sauté for 7 minutes. Add the meat and sear for 6 minutes, flipping once. Add the bell pepper, cassava, and tomatoes, and continue cooking for a further 5 minutes.

Pour in enough water to cover the ingredients and cook over medium heat for 15 minutes or until the cassava is soft and the sauce is thick. Add the parsley and cilantro (coriander), with salt and pepper to taste. Serve hot, with rice on the side.

Toasted Cassava Flour

Farofa
Brazil

Preparation time: 5 minutes
Cooking time: 20 minutes　　　　Serves: 6

Farofa, or toasted cassava flour, is eaten throughout Brazil, often sprinkled on grilled meats and heavy stews, as well as eaten on its own. It is made by cooking the flour, called *farinha*, in oil or animal fat. Sometimes bits of meat, eggs, or greens are mixed in. Cornstarch can also be used in place of cassava flour.

    2 tablespoons olive oil
    1 onion, finely diced
    salt
    1½ cups/5 oz (140 g) cassava flour
    ¼ cup/⅓ oz (10 g) parsley or cilantro (coriander),
    to serve

Heat the oil in a pan over low heat. Add the onion and cook for 10 minutes or until softened. Season with salt, pour in the flour and stir continuously until the flour has dried and browned to sand-colored. Serve with parsley or cilantro (coriander) sprinkled over.

Jungle Tamales

Juanes de yuca
Bolivia, Colombia, Ecuador, Peru

Preparation time: 15 minutes,
plus 24 hours soaking
Cooking time: 1 hour 15 minutes　　　　Serves: 4

The *juane de yuca* combines the basics of the Amazonian diet—fish and cassava—which are wrapped in a *bijao* (banana) leaf and then boiled or grilled. A sort of jungle tamale, it's one of the most typical dishes of the Amazon and comes in a seemingly endless parade of names and variations that might add ingredients like pork, heart of palm, peanuts, corn, eggs, chicken, and innards. Traditionally, *juanes* were something that could be taken on hunting trips or on visits to other communities, though now you're more likely to see them sold in markets and by street vendors throughout the region.

    1 lb (450 g) salted paiche (or use salt cod)
    2 tablespoons lard
    1 cup/4 oz (120 g) chopped white onion
    1 tablespoon minced garlic
    2 tablespoons *ají amarillo* paste
    1 teaspoon *palillo* (ground turmeric)
    3 lb (1.3 kg) cassava, peeled and grated
    2 *ají dulce,* sliced
    4 tablespoons olive oil
    ½ cup/¾ oz (20 g) *sachaculantro* or cilantro
    (coriander)
    1 cup/8 fl oz (250 ml) fish stock
    8 *bijao* or banana leaves
    salt and ground pepper

Place the salted paiche (or salt cod) in a bowl and cover with cold water. Let soak for 24 hours, changing the water three times.

Melt the lard in a medium pan over medium heat, add the onion, and cook for 4 minutes until it becomes translucent. Add the garlic, *ají amarillo* paste, and *palillo* (ground turmeric), and continue cooking for a further 5 minutes. Season with salt and pepper, and cook until it caramelizes; set aside.

Place the cassava in a bowl, add the onion mixture and combine, then add the *ají dulce*, oil, *sachaculantro*, and the stock. Mix well with your hands, and season with salt and pepper. Incorporate the dried fish and check the seasoning. Divide into 4 equal pieces.

Form a cross with two *bijao* leaves and place one portion of the cassava mix in the middle of one. Close the leaves and tie using string, and repeat the process with the remaining leaves and 3 portions.

Bring enough water to cook the *juanes* to a boil in a pan. Add the *juanes* and cook over medium heat for 1 hour. Remove the *juanes*, open, and serve warm.

Cassava Fries

Mandioca frita, yuca frita, yuquitas frita
Brazil, Colombia, Peru, Venezuela

Preparation time: 10 minutes
Cooking time: 30–50 minutes   Serves: 4

When done right, it's hard to find a French fry that stands up to cassava fries. They are creamier than French fries and they only need one fry to get them nice and crispy. You can serve them with a dip like guacamole or *huancaína* sauce. Note: It's important to use fresh cassava, as frozen doesn't fry nearly as well.

3 lb (1.3 kg) cassava
vegetable oil, for deep-frying
salt

Peel the cassava and cut crosswise into 4-inch (10-cm) chunks. Bring a pan of salted water to a boil, add the cassava pieces and simmer for 20 minutes, then drain. When cool enough to handle, using your hands, break them into sticks, and remove the hearts.

Pour enough vegetable oil for deep-frying into a large, heavy pan, making sure it is no more than two-thirds full, and heat to 360°F/182°C.

Deep-fry the sticks in batches for 10 minutes or until brown and crispy on the outside. Remove with a skimmer, salt them while still hot, and serve warm.

Cassava Mush

Chibé
Brazil

Preparation time: 5 minutes,
plus 10 minutes resting   Serves: 3–4

This slightly acidic, soup-like porridge isn't cooked but is made by simply soaking cassava flour and seasoning the mixture. *Chibé* is a staple of remote Amazonian communities, where it can be prepared easily with some river water on long journeys or hunting trips.

2 cups/10 oz (280 g) cassava flour
2 cups/16 fl oz (475 ml) water
½ cup/2 oz (60 g) chopped white onion
1 teaspoon *jiquitaia* (ground *Baniwa* chile blend)
juice of 1 lime
1 teaspoon salt

Mix the cassava flour with the water. Let it rest for 10 minutes to let the flour hydrate, then add the remaining ingredients, season well and serve room at temperature.

Tapioca Crepes

Beiju de tapioca, chamado de tapioca, tapioquinha
Brazil

Preparation time: 10 minutes
Cooking time: 10 minutes   Makes: 2

Written evidence of *beiju de tapioca* dates back to Ambrósio Fernandes Brandão's 1618 book *Diálogos das Grandezas do Brasil*, though indigenous groups in northern Brazil were eating this grainy tapioca pancake long before. Typically, they're made with fresh grated coconut or *queijo de coalho*, though they can be filled with any sweet (*doce*) or savory (*salgado*) filling, then folded over just like a crepe. Today, street vendors called *tapioqueiras* are symbolic of northeastern cities like Fortaleza and Olinda. Serve with any kind of filling like cheese, or just spread with salted butter, or as an accompaniment to any dish.

1 cup/4 oz (120 g) *polvilho doce* (sweet manioc starch)
1 teaspoon salt
½ cup/4 fl oz (120 ml) water

Sift the *polvilho* into a medium bowl, add the salt and slowly add the water while kneading with your hands, until it forms a dough (you may not need all the water, and if it's too liquid, add more *polvilho*).

Heat a frying pan over medium heat and spread the mixture in the bottom of the pan, forming a tortilla. Cook for 2 minutes on each side, or until you see the *polvilho* start to stick together.

Fried Tapioca Cubes

Dadinhos de tapioca 🖾
Brazil

Preparation time: 10 minutes,
plus at least 3 hours resting
Cooking time: 30 minutes

Serves: 4

Translating as "little dice," these fried cubes of tapioca and cheese were created by Rodrigo Oliveira at the São Paulo restaurant Mocotó, but have quickly become a national bar snack. They are usually served with some sort of dip, like pepper jelly or sweet and sour sauce.

    vegetable oil, for greasing and deep-frying
    1½ cups/6 oz (180 g) tapioca flour
    1½ cups/5 oz (150 g) shredded *queijo coalho* (or use halloumi cheese)
    1 teaspoon salt
    pinch of ground pepper
    1¾ cups/14 fl oz (410 ml) whole milk

Lightly grease a lipped oven tray, 6 x 6 x 1½ inches (15 x 15 x 4 cm).
    Place the tapioca flour, shredded cheese, salt, and ground pepper in a large mixing bowl. Mix well, using a wooden spoon.
    Heat the milk in a small pan until hot, without letting it boil, and gradually add it to the tapioca and cheese mixture, stirring continuously until you have a lumpy texture. Pour the mixture into the prepared oven tray, pat down the mixture using the back of a spoon so that it is evenly spread, cover the tray with plastic wrap (clingfilm) and let rest in the refrigerator for at least 3 hours, or overnight.
    Once the mixture is cold and solid, turn it out onto a cutting board and cut into 1-inch (2.5-cm) cubes.
    Pour enough vegetable oil for deep-frying into a large, heavy pan, making sure it is no more than two-thirds full, and heat to 340°F/171°C.
    Fry the cubes in small batches for 7–10 minutes, or until crispy and brown. Remove from the oil and place on paper towels to absorb excess oil. Serve warm.

Cassava Porridge

Pirão, angu
Brazil

Preparation time: 5 minutes
Cooking time: 10 minutes

Serves: 4

This salty porridge can be served hot or cold. It is usually served alongside meat or fish, using the broth that they're cooked in, giving it a slight viscosity.

    1½ cups/7½ oz (210 g) cassava flour
    2 cups/16 fl oz (475 ml) beef stock
    salt and ground pepper

In a small pan, dissolve the cassava flour in a little cold water, to prevent lumps. Slowly add the hot stock and cook over low heat for 5 minutes, stirring continuously, until thick but soft. Season with salt and pepper, and serve.

Cassava Gnocchi

Nhoque de mandioca
Brazil

Preparation time: 15 minutes
Cooking time: 30 minutes

Serves: 4

Swapping out potatoes for cassava in gnocchi is something that Italian restaurants in Brazil and elsewhere in Latin America have been doing for several decades. Cassava, which is similarly gluten-free, adds subtle variations in flavor and texture to the preparation, though you can use the same sauces for either.

    2 lb (900 g) cassava
    1 egg
    1 tablespoon butter
    2 tablespoons all-purpose (plain) flour, plus extra for dusting
    dash of olive oil
    salt

Peel the cassava and cut it into chunks. Cook in boiling, salted water for 20 minutes or until soft, then drain, and mash it using a potato masher. Place in a medium bowl and knead with your hands as you add the egg, butter, and flour.
    Season with salt, place on a floured surface, and continue kneading until uniform, then shape into tubes ½ inch (1 cm) in diameter. Cut each tube into small, equal pieces, 1 inch (2.5 cm) long.
    Bring a large pan of water to a boil, with a dash of olive oil and a hint of salt added. Cook the gnocchi for 7 minutes, or until they rise to the surface. Remove from the water and serve on their own, with some butter or olive oil, or a sauce.

Fried Tapioca Cubes

Cassava and Cheese Croquettes

Enyucados
Costa Rica

Preparation time: 5 minutes
Cooking time: 35 minutes
Makes: 6–8

Typically sold in traditional restaurants and snack bars called *sodas*, Costa Rican *enyucados* are a baked or fried finger food and should not be confused with other cassava-based recipes with the same name, which are often more cake-like. Note that ground beef is also commonly used with or in place of the cheese in the filling.

> 1 lb (450 g) cassava
> 4 eggs
> ½ cup/2¼ oz (65 g) all-purpose (plain) flour, plus extra for coating
> 3 jalapeño peppers, cored, seeded, and chopped
> 1 cup/4 oz (115 g) shredded cheese (or use mozzarella)
> vegetable oil, for deep-frying
> salt

Peel the cassava and cut into 2-inch (5-cm) chunks. Cook in boiling, salted water for 15–20 minutes, then drain and mash to a purée. Add the eggs and flour, with salt to taste.

Mix the jalapeños with the shredded cheese; set aside.

Shape the dough into about 6–8 balls, 2 inches (5 cm) in diameter. Slightly press a ball with a spoon and place ½ teaspoon of the cheese and jalapeño filling in the dent. Re-shape the ball and coat with a little flour. Repeat the process with the remaining dough and filling.

Pour enough vegetable oil for deep-frying into a large, heavy pan, making sure it is no more than two-thirds full, and heat to 360°F/182°C.

Fry the cassava balls, in batches, for 3 minutes or until crispy and brown on the outside. Serve warm.

Cassava with Slaw and Pork Crackling

Vigorón
Costa Rica, Nicaragua

Preparation time: 15 minutes
Cooking time: 20 minutes
Serves: 4

Kiosks around Parque Colón in Granada, Nicaragua, famously sell this snack, which was invented by a street vendor named María Luisa Cisneros Lacayo, aka La Loca, in 1914. Selling it mostly at baseball games, she named it after seeing a poster for a medicinal tonic, *vigorón*, and it quickly caught on.

> 2 lb (900 g) cassava
> 1 white cabbage
> 2 carrots
> ¾ cup/6 fl oz (175 ml) white vinegar
> 3 tomatoes, sliced
> 2 banana leaves, each cut into 2 pieces
> 1 lb (450 g) *Chicharrón* (Pork Cracklings/crispy pork skin; page 276 for homemade or can be store-bought)
> salt and ground pepper

Peel the cassava and cut crosswise into 1-inch (2.5 cm) chunks. Place in a pan with enough salted water to cover. Place over medium heat and cook for about 20 minutes from the moment it starts boiling, or until soft. Drain and let cool.

For the *curtido* relish, thinly slice the cabbage and rinse it twice under cold water, then set aside. Peel the carrots, grate them, and mix them with the cabbage. Add the vinegar and season with salt and pepper. Finish by adding the tomatoes.

Place the cassava in the middle of a piece of banana leaf, then add the *curtido*, and crumble the *Chicharrón* on top.

Cassava Fritters

Carimañola, empanada de yuca
Colombia, Panama

Preparation time: 10 minutes
Cooking time: 45 minutes
Makes: 10

A *carimañola de yuca* is similar to the more common *papas rellenas*, though made from mashed and fried cassava. They can be stuffed with ground (minced) beef, shredded chicken, or cheese, and are usually served with hot sauce or *suero costeño*.

> 1 lb 8 ounces (675 g) cassava
> 2 tablespoons butter
> vegetable oil for deep-frying, plus 2 tablespoons
> 1 garlic clove, minced
> ½ cup/2 oz (60 g) chopped onion
> ¼ cup/1 oz (25 g) cored, seeded, and chopped red bell pepper
> 1 scallion (spring onion), chopped
> ½ teaspoon ground cumin
> 8 oz (225 g) ground (minced) beef
> 1 tablespoon tomato paste (purée)
> salt and ground pepper

Peel the cassava and cut into large chunks. Add to a large pan with some salt, and enough water to cover. Bring to a boil, reduce and simmer for about 20 minutes, or until tender. Drain the cassava and mash with the butter, then cover and set aside.

In a large frying pan, heat the 2 tablespoons of oil over medium-high heat. Add the garlic, onion, and bell pepper, and cook for about 3 minutes, until soft. Add the scallion (spring onion), cumin, and some salt and pepper, and cook for a further 1 minute, stirring continuously. Add the beef and cook for about 7 minutes. Add the tomato paste (purée) and cook for 2 minutes more. Remove from the heat, adjust the seasoning and let cool.

Divide the cassava mixture into 10 balls. Make a cavity in the center of each ball. Add about 1 tablespoon of the meat filling to the cavity, gently close the ball, and form it into an oval, or torpedo, shape.

Pour the vegetable oil for deep-frying into a large, heavy pan, making sure it is no more than two-thirds full, and heat to 350°F/177°C . Add the *carimañolas* in batches and cook for about 2–3 minutes until golden brown. Remove and place on paper towels to absorb excess oil. Serve warm with hot sauce.

Roots and Tubers

Cassava with Slaw and Pork Crackling

Cassava Coconut Porridge

Sahau, sahou
Belize, Honduras, Nicaragua

Preparation time: 20 minutes
Cooking time: 15 minutes

Serves: 4

Served warm or cold, this sweet, thick porridge is eaten for breakfast or dessert later in the day in Garifuna communities, who live along Central America's Caribbean coast. The amount of sweetener tends to be adjusted as to when it is eaten. Mashed banana or papaya, or cooked and mashed pumpkin, can be added just before serving. It's also possible to add some lard, wrap the *sahau* in banana leaves and boil like a tamale. A similar recipe called *gungude* replaces the cassava with sun-dried green plantains, which are ground and sold commercially as *gungude* powder, and also mixes the coconut milk with condensed milk.

 1 lb (450 g) cassava
 2–2½ cups/16–20 fl oz (475–550 ml) water
 1 coconut
 2 cinnamon sticks
 2 teaspoons ground nutmeg
 2 teaspoons vanilla extract
 honey or sugar, to taste
 1 teaspoon ground cinnamon

Peel and grate the cassava, and place in a bowl. Add the measured water, then strain through a cheesecloth, reserving the liquid. Discard the solids or find another use for them.
 Shell and grate the coconut, and place in a bowl. Add 2–2½ cups/16–20 fl oz (475–550 ml) water, then strain through a cheesecloth, reserving the liquid. Discard the solids or find another use for them.
 Set about ½ cup/4 fl oz (120 ml) of the coconut milk aside, then mix the remaining strained liquids together in a medium pan. Add the cinnamon, nutmeg, and vanilla and cook over low heat, stirring regularly, and adding the reserved coconut milk as needed. When thick, remove from the heat and let cool. Add honey or sugar if desired, then sprinkle with the ground cinnamon, and serve.

Tucupí

While cooking bitter cassava is one way to remove the cyanide that is found within it, fermenting its juice is another. To make *tucupí*, cassava is peeled, grated, and then the juice is squeezed out through a basket-like instrument called a *tipiti*. The juice is left to rest for several days so that the starch and liquid separate. At this point the juice is still poisonous, so it must be further boiled to make it safe to ingest. *Tucupí*, a bright yellow orange color and acidic in flavor, can then be used in sauces or soups. It's used in numerous regional dishes, such as *tacacá* and *pato no tucupí*. You'll see *tucupí* in markets throughout the Amazon, especially in northern Brazil, often sold in plastic soda bottles.

Tucupí can also be further reduced to make *tucupí preto*, a heady black sauce and marinade that is found throughout the northern Amazon under various regional names like *ají negro*, *tucupí negro*, *casaramá*, and *ualako*. Every community tends to have a recipe for *tucupí preto* that's a little bit different. For some it's almost a paste, which can be rubbed on meats or fish before being grilled. For others it's more liquidy, resembling soy sauce, and gets dropped into a soup like a shot of umami. Some add peppers, seeds, or insects for additional flavor, either during the reduction process or after.

Shrimp, Jambu, and Fermented Cassava Soup

Tacacá
Brazil

Preparation time: 15 minutes
Cooking time: 30 minutes

Serves: 4

Street vendors, called *tacacazeiras*, appear in the afternoons throughout cities in the Brazilian Amazon like Manaus and Belém do Pará. Some have been around for decades and have grown cult followings for their recipes of *tacacá*, a pungent broth made by boiling *tucupí* with salt and aromatic herbs like chicory or *manjericão*, a regional variety of basil. *Tacacá* can be overwhelming to those who have not grown up with it. A small sip out of a *cuia*, a small bowl made from a dried gourd that's wrapped in a woven basket so you don't burn your hands, and your senses are sent racing in different directions. There's the sourness of the *tucupí*, the saltiness of the shrimp, and the tongue-tingling sensation of the *jambu*, a green herb, otherwise known as paracress, or the toothache plant. Even then, some add dashes of chile-infused vinegar. Then there's the spoonful of *goma de mandioca*, a gel made from hydrated cassava starch, that gives the broth a strange, silky texture. Plus, it's served steaming hot in what is generally a rather humid environment.

 1 lb 9 oz (700 g) dried, salted shrimp (prawns) with shells
 6 cups/3 pints (1.5 liters) *tucupí*
 3 garlic cloves, minced
 6 endive (chicory) leaves, chopped
 1 teaspoon salt
 1 cup (70 g) *jambu* leaves, coarsely chopped
 ½ cup (2 oz/60 g) cassava starch, dissolved in ½ cup/4 fl oz (120 ml) cold water

Blanch the dried shrimps (prawns) in a pan of boiling water, remove with a skimmer, then rinse in cold water. Repeat this process two more times.
 Heat the *tucupí* in another pan with the garlic, endive (chicory), shrimp, and salt. Cover and cook over low heat for 30 minutes.
 Meanwhile, heat the *jambu* leaves in a dry frying pan until they soften and shred.
 In a *cuia* or small bowl, pour in some of the *tucupí* broth, the *jambu*, shrimp, and the cassava starch, and stir. Serve hot.

Shrimp, Jambu, and Fermented Cassava Soup

Corn

A Mixteca family walks through a forested path in the rugged hills of the state of Oaxaca to reach a small clearing. Here they tend to their *milpa*, a pre-Hispanic intercropping system where they grow corn, squash, and beans, as well as root vegetables. In this distinct microclimate, each plant helps the other survive in the sloped soil fed only with rainfall. The corn grown here is specific to this village and reflects the region's astonishing biodiversity. Despite many obstacles, they're ensuring that this corn survives for their children to one day plant.

The crops grown will feed the family for much of the year. Some will be eaten fresh, while the rest will be dried and nixtamalized (see page 120). Now softer, more fragrant, and nutritious, they'll grind treated corn kernels on a stone *metate* until there is no hint of grittiness, rolling the stone pin back and forth, sprinkling water on the kernels to keep the masa moist. They'll light a fire beneath the *comal*, a cast-iron griddle set within a mud brick frame. One of them will roll a handful of masa into a ball and flatten it until perfectly round, then place it on the hot griddle. When the tortilla smokes, they'll flip it over. Both sides will be speckled with brown marks. They'll place it in a cloth-lined basket, then repeat the process to make dozens of tortillas, as well as *gorditas* and *tlayudas*.

The cultural connection to corn (*Zea mays*) is integral to the Latin American experience. If a single ingredient could be pointed to as the backbone of cooking in the Americas, corn would be it. Since its wild ancestor, *teocintle* (*Zea perennis*), was domesticated by indigenous groups in southern Mexico between 7,500 and 12,000 years ago, corn has become a staple food for the entire world. It's the only grain that needs human intervention to reproduce.

In Mexico alone, there are 59 locally adapted, traditional varieties of corn, which have an estimated 2,000 uses. From Mexico, maize cultivation spread north and south to the far reaches of the continent. With each culture that the crop came into contact with, new uses developed. In rural areas, it is eaten three times a day. Corn is part of Mayan creation myths, and Inca armies carried toasted kernels with them as they marched across the Andes.

Corn is roasted over fires. Kernels are toasted, ground into flour, and baked into breads. In the Andes, kernels are fermented to make *chicha*, a low-alcohol beer. In Colombia and Venezuela, corn is beaten with wooden mortars called *pillones*, then ground into flour to make arepas and *hallacas*. In southern Brazil, it is boiled with milk and sugar to make a pudding called *canjica*. In Costa Rica, the Bribri allows the masa to mold to use as a starter for another type of *chicha*. Corn masa is used to make all sorts of recipes, not just tortillas. In El Salvador, it is formed into patties stuffed with pork, beans, or cheese to make *pupusas*. In most countries, the masa is stuffed inside of a corn husk or banana leaf to make tamales. By encouraging the varieties and rituals surrounding its cultivation, from planting to harvesting to consumption, it is an act of defiance against a world that is increasingly pushing them to the fringes. We are not just preserving them, we are preserving the identity of those who made them possible.

Stewed Corn

Humita en olla
Argentina

Preparation time: 15 minutes
Cooking time: 25 minutes　　　　　Serves: 5–6

Usually when you see a recipe called *humita*, it's a *humita en chala*, as they say in northern Argentina, where corn masa gets wrapped in corn husks and boiled. However, from the same region, there are also *humitas en olla*, where grated corn is stewed in a pot. In the Tucumán and Catamarca provinces, grated squash (*zapallo criollo*) is often mixed in with the corn.

    16 ears of corn
    3 tablespoons butter
    2 tablespoons vegetable oil
    1 white onion, finely chopped
    2 red bell peppers, peeled, cored, seeded,
    and chopped
    1 lb (450 g) tomatoes, peeled and chopped
    ½ cup/4 fl oz (120 ml) whole milk
    1 teaspoon brown sugar
    ½ cup/2 oz (60 g) cubed (1 inch/2.5 cm) *queso fresco*
    salt and ground pepper

Start by grating the corn on the large holes of a box grater into a bowl, along with any creamy liquid that is released, then set aside in a bowl.
　　In a medium pan, heat the butter with the oil over medium heat. Add the onion and bell peppers and cook for 7 minutes, or until the onions are transparent, then add the tomatoes. Cook for a further 5 minutes over medium heat, then add the grated corn, and milk. Add the sugar, and season with salt and pepper. Let simmer for 10 minutes to reduce the liquid, then add the cheese and serve hot.

Brazilian Polenta

Angú
Brazil

Preparation time: 5 minutes
Cooking time: 20 minutes　　　　　Serves: 4

The word *angú* is West African in origin and once referred to a yam porridge. In the sixteenth century, when the Portuguese introduced corn from the New World to the Congo Basin, the recipe was adapted to include it, and the recipe then traveled across the Atlantic through the slave trade. In Brazil, *angú* referred to porridges made from cassava flour or cornmeal, though over time cassava flour porridge became known as *pirão* (Cassava Porridge, page 100). Today, *angú* has two primary regional variations: *baiano* and *mineiro*. The Bahian version is moister and creamier, while the version from Minas Gerais is firmer.

    1 tablespoon vegetable oil
    1 cup/4 oz (120 g) chopped white onion
    2 garlic cloves, minced
    2 cups/16 fl oz (475 ml) vegetable stock
    1 cup/8 fl oz (250 ml) water
    1½ cups/8 oz (225 g) *fubá* (yellow cornmeal)
    2 tablespoons butter
    salt

In a medium pan, heat the oil over medium heat, add the onion and garlic, and sauté for about 4 minutes, or until soft. Pour in the stock and water, and bring to a boil. Add the cornmeal, while stirring vigorously so that it doesn't get lumpy.
　　Season with salt and cook for 10 minutes over low heat, or until thick and sticky. Turn off the heat and add the butter. Check the seasoning and serve hot.

Corn Pancakes

Chorreadas (Costa Rica), cachapas (Colombia, Venezuela) 📷
Costa Rica, Colombia, Venezuela

Preparation time: 10 minutes
Cooking time: 20 minutes　　　　　Serves: 6

Often sold from highway food stalls in Venezuela and parts of Colombia, the *cachapa* is the underappreciated cousin of the arepa. Thicker and larger, usually a mix of ground fresh corn and flour, it's more like a savory pancake, and usually stuffed with a soft white cheese called *queso de mano*. In Costa Rica, *chorreadas*, extremely similar to *cachapas* though without the cheese, are an indigenous recipe, traditionally using fresh corn and little else. As they were adapted into modern society, flour and other ingredients, sweet or savory, have been added. They are almost always served with *natilla*, Costa Rican sour cream. Note: Corn in Latin America tends to have more starch than in North America, so you can add a few tablespoons of cornstarch (cornflour) to thicken the batter if needed.

    2 cups/8 oz (230 g) fresh corn kernels
    ½ cup/2¼ oz (70 g) *masarepa* (precooked corn flour/
    maize flour)
    2 eggs
    4 tablespoons melted butter
    ½ cup/4 fl oz (120 ml) milk
    1 tablespoon dried oregano
    1 garlic clove, peeled
    8 oz (225 g) *queso de mano* (or use mozzarella),
    sliced

Put most of the corn kernels except for a few spoonfuls in a food processor or mixer, add the *masarepa*, eggs, half the melted butter, the milk, oregano, and garlic, and process until it forms a smooth, thick batter. Stir in the remaining corn kernels.
　　Heat the remaining butter in a frying pan, then fry the batter just like you would for pancakes. Cook until golden brown, about 4 minutes each side.
　　While still hot, sandwich the cheese between two *cachapas* or fold one in half and place the cheese inside. Serve hot.

Corn Pancakes

Chilean Corn Pie

Pastel de choclo ▢
Chile

Preparation time: 30 minutes   Serves: 8
Cooking time: 2 hours

Pastel de choclo is one of the most representative dishes of Chilean cuisine, if not Latin American cuisine as a whole. It's a peasant dish that has likely existed throughout the region since colonial times, though it started to become popularized in Chile in the 1830s when it was served during fiestas celebrating the beginning of the corn harvests. The filling of minced beef, onions, and spices is called *pino*, which is also used for empanadas. Slices of hard-boiled eggs, raisins, and olives are often added too. Traditionally, *pastel de choclo* is prepared and served in clay pots called *librillos*.

    1 tablespoon vegetable oil
    2 lb (900 g) beef shank (shin), chopped
    1 tablespoon *merkén* (smoked chile powder)
    ½ teaspoon ground cumin
    1 cup/8 fl oz (250 ml) beef stock
    3 white onions, chopped
    2 tablespoons all-purpose (plain) flour
    1 tablespoon brown sugar, for sprinkling
    salt and ground pepper

    For the corn batter
    8 ears of corn
    2 tablespoons lard
    ½ cup /4 fl oz (120 ml) whole milk
    1 teaspoon *merkén* (smoked chile powder)
    3 tablespoons corn (maize) flour

Heat the oil in a medium pan over high heat, and sear the beef for 5 minutes, stirring occasionally. Add the *merkén* and cumin, and season with salt and pepper. Cook for 3 minutes then add the stock. Bring to a boil, then lower the heat and simmer for 20 minutes. Add the onions and cook for 20 minutes, until soft. Add the flour, whisking to avoid any lumps. Check the seasoning and remove from the heat, then transfer the mixture to a bowl and let cool.

For the corn batter, grate the corn on the large holes of a box grater into a bowl, along with any creamy liquid that is released. Melt the lard in a medium pan over medium heat. Add the corn and cook for 10 minutes, then add the milk and season with salt, pepper and the *merkén*. Cook for a further 10 minutes, then pour into a blender with the corn (maize) flour and blend. Pour the mixture back into the pan and simmer for 5–10 minutes, or until it thickens. Check the seasoning.

Preheat the oven to 400°F/200°C/Gas Mark 6.

Spread the meat filling out in a baking dish, 8 x 8 x 1½ inches (20 x 20 x 4 cm) or serving-sized clay pots, and cover with the corn mixture. Sprinkle brown sugar over the top and bake in the oven for 40 minutes or until golden brown. Serve warm.

Old Indian Stew

Indio viejo, marol
Nicaragua

Preparation time: 20 minutes   ※ ⊘
Cooking time: 25 minutes   Serves: 5–6

One of Nicaragua's most emblematic dishes, *Indio viejo* was said have been made with all of the ingredients of the indigenous diet, though it has been adapted in the centuries since conquest. It's often served with white rice, fried plantains, and pickled cabbage slaw called *ensalada de repollo*.

    ½ cup/4 oz (120 g) lard
    1 white onion, chopped
    5 garlic cloves, minced
    2 yellow bell peppers, cored, seeded, and diced
    4 tomatoes, peeled and diced
    3 tablespoons coarsely chopped mint
    ½ cup/¾ oz (20 g) coarsely chopped cilantro
    (coriander)
    1 lb (450 g) *cecina de res* (salt-cured beef), shredded
    1½ cups/6½ oz (190 g) *masa harina*
    1 cup/8 fl oz (250 ml) water
    2 cups/16 fl oz (475 ml) beef stock
    1 tablespoon annatto paste, diluted in
    2 tablespoons water
    salt

Heat the lard in a medium pan over medium heat. Once melted, add the onion, garlic, and a pinch of salt and sauté for 5 minutes. Add the bell peppers and tomatoes and cook for a further 4 minutes. Add the mint, cilantro (coriander), and cecina, and simmer for a further 5 minutes.

Dilute the *masa harina* with the water and pour into the pan with the stock. Add the diluted annatto paste and cook for 10 minutes or until it thickens. Serve hot.

Chilean Corn Pie

Chiriqui-Style Corn and Cheese Fritters

Almojábanos con queso
Panama

Preparation time: 20 minutes
Cooking time: 25 minutes

Makes: 25–30

Beloved in Panama's Chiriquí region, where they are served daily alongside coffee in the morning, or with steak and onions or fried pork for lunch, *almojábanos* are fried, S-shaped (like Panama) pieces of corn and cheese masa.

    1 teaspoon salt
    1 teaspoon sugar
    4 cups/32 fl oz (950 ml) water
    1½ cups/7½ oz (210 g) masarepa
    1½ cups/7½ oz (210 g) corn (maize) flour
    2½ cups/9 oz (250 g) shredded *queso blanco* (or use
    another semi-soft white cheese)
    vegetable oil, for deep-frying

Start by diluting the salt and sugar in the water in a bowl. Slowly add the masarepa and corn (maize) flour and cheese, while kneading with your hands for 10 minutes, or until you get a smooth dough. Divide the dough equally into 25–30 pieces, and shape each into a ball. Stretch each into a log and gently fold the tips to make an "S" shape.

Pour enough oil for deep-frying into a large, heavy pan, making sure it is no more than two-thirds full, and heat to 350°F/180°C.

Deep-fry the *almojábanos* in small batches, for 3 minutes each side or until they become slightly brown and crisp, placing on a plate lined with paper towels, to absorb excess oil. Serve warm.

Grilled Street Corn

Elote
El Salvador, Guatemala, Mexico

Preparation time: 5 minutes
Cooking time: 15 minutes

Serves: 4

Grilled street corn is found throughout Mexico and parts of Central America. The recipe below is the most common variation, which makes a great side dish to any barbecue. Toppings can vary tremendously. Some add chopped herbs like cilantro (coriander) or basil. In El Salvador, where it's often called *elote loco*, some street vendors add sauces like ketchup and salsa Perrins, or Worcestershire sauce, which the country uses a tremendous amount of.

    4 ears of corn, husks removed but leave the stem
    ½ cup/4 oz (120 g) mayonnaise
    1 cup/5 oz (150 g) crumbled *cotija* cheese (or use
    shredded *queso fresco* or parmesan)
    2½ teaspoons chile powder
    lime wedges, to serve

Grill (barbecue) the corn until slightly charred all around, about 5 minutes per side. Let cool slightly, then slather with mayonnaise, followed by some *cotija* cheese and chile powder. Serve with lime wedges.

Street Corn Salad

Esquites, elote en vaso, chasca ▢
Mexico

Preparation time: 15 minutes
Cooking time: 15 minutes

Serves: 6

Like ice cream, served in a cone or in a cup, Mexican grilled street corn is served on the cob (*elotes*) or in a cup (*esquites*). The name is derived from the Nahuatl word *ízquitl*, which translates as "toasted corn."

    2 tablespoons butter
    ½ white onion, chopped
    4 fresh epazote leaves, chopped (or use 1 teaspoon
    dried epazote)
    4 cups/1 lb 7 oz (650 g) fresh corn kernels
    ⅓ cup/2½ fl oz (75 ml) water
    ½ cup/4 oz (120 g) mayonnaise
    salt

    To serve
    1 lime, cut into wedges, plus the juice of 2 limes
    ½ cup/2½ oz (75 g) crumbled *cotija* cheese (or use
    shredded *queso fresco* or parmesan)
    ground chile, to taste

In a pan, heat the butter over medium heat, add the onion and sauté for 5 minutes, or until soft. Add the epazote and stir well. Add the corn kernels and water, and cook until soft, no more than 10 minutes, stirring occasionally. Season with salt.

Take off the heat, and stir in the mayonnaise. Serve warm in cups, with a splash of lime juice squeezed over, the cheese scattered on top and the ground chile sprinkled over. Serve with a lime wedge.

Street Corn Salad

Little Corn Balls in Soup

Vorí vorí blanco ⬚
Paraguay

Preparation time: 15 minutes
Cooking time: 30 minutes

Serves: 5–6

One of Paraguay's most beloved dishes, *vorí vorí*—little corn flour and cheese balls served in a rich soup—is a riff on the Spanish dish *sopa de bolitas*. In Guaraní the name was pronounced "borita," then shortened to just "vori." Repeating a word in Guaraní signifies abundance, so it became "vorí vorí." The balls can vary slightly in size depending on the person making the soup, and when they are especially small, they call them "tu'i rupi'a" or "parakeet eggs." The color can vary as well, depending on the type of corn, and sometimes different colors will appear in the same soup. A version called *vorí vorí de gallina* adds confit chicken, while below is the recipe for *vorí vorí blanco*. It is typically made during the winter months.

    1 tablespoon lard
    1 white onion, chopped
    2 green bell peppers, cored, seeded, and chopped
    3 cups/25 fl oz (750 ml) water
    5 scallions (spring onions), chopped
    2 cups/10½ oz (280 g) corn (maize) flour
    1 tablespoon wheat flour
    2 cups/9 oz (250 g) crumbled *queso fresco*
    1 cup/8 fl oz (250 ml) whole milk
    1 tablespoon dried oregano
    salt

Heat the lard in a pan over medium heat, add the onion and bell peppers, and stir-fry for 10 minutes until soft, then add the water and let simmer.

In a bowl, mix the corn (maize) flour and wheat flour with 1 teaspoon of salt and half of the *queso fresco*. Slowly add 1 cup/8 fl oz (250 ml) of vegetable cooking water to the flours, and mix with a wooden spoon until it cools slightly until warm enough to handle. Knead into a dough; it will be somewhat dry. Divide the mixture into 15–20 pieces, shape into balls and transfer them to the vegetable pan for 15–20 minutes or until the balls start rising to the surface, then remove from the heat.

Finish by adding the remaining *queso fresco*, the milk, and oregano. Check the seasoning and serve hot, in a deep plate.

Cusco-Style Creamed Corn

Saralawa, lawa de maíz
Peru

Preparation time: 20 minutes
Cooking time: 30 minutes

Serves: 4–6

This creamy corn soup is one of the staple dishes in Peru's Cusco region. Some variations dry the corn in the sun for several days and then grind it into a flour that gets mixed in, though during the harvest season when corn is fresh, the below version is more common.

kernels from 5 ears of *choclo* (large-kernel corn)
2 tablespoons chopped *huacatay* (Peruvian black mint)
2 tablespoons chopped *olluco* leaves (or use spinach)
1 tablespoon ground *ají mirasol*
6 cups/48 fl oz (1.4 liters) water
3 tablespoons vegetable oil
1 white onion, finely diced
5 medium potatoes, peeled and diced
1 cup/4 oz (120 g) fava (broad) beans, peeled
2 eggs, beaten
2 cups/4 oz (120 g) cubed *queso fresco*, (½-inch/1-cm cubes)
salt
1 tablespoon chopped parsley, to serve

In a food processor or blender, blend the corn with the *huacatay*, *olluco* leaves, chile, and ½ cup/4 fl oz (120 ml) of the water. Strain and reserve.

In a pan, heat the oil over medium heat, add the onion and sauté for 7 minutes, or until browned and soft. Pour in the remaining water and add the potatoes and fava (broad) beans. Turn up the heat to high and cook for 12 minutes, or until the potatoes and beans are soft and cooked. Add the corn mixture, stir well, and let simmer over low-medium heat for 10 minutes, until thick. Season with salt.

Add the beaten eggs and whisk, then add the *queso fresco*.

Serve in a deep plate, with the parsley sprinkled on top.

Toasted Andean Corn Kernels

Cancha serrana
Bolivia, Ecuador, Peru

Preparation time: 5 minutes
Cooking time: 10 minutes

Serves: 6

These toasted corn kernels are served throughout Peru as a bar snack, in a small bowl when you sit down at a *cevichería*, or directly within a bowl of ceviche.

    1 tablespoon vegetable oil
    15 oz (425 g) *maíz chulpe* (dried corn kernels)
    salt

Heat the oil in a deep pan, about 5 inches (12.5 cm) diameter, over medium heat. Add the corn kernels and cover with a lid. Start moving the pan, being careful not to remove the lid. Once the corn kernels start popping, lower the heat and let the corn pop for 6 minutes, moving the pan constantly.

Place on a plate lined with paper towels to absorb excess oil. Season with salt to serve.

Little Corn Balls in Soup

Maíz Trillado

There's another variation of corn that does not go under the process of nixtamalization (see page 120), though still has the hulls removed. Large wooden mortars called *pillones* are used to pound dried corn kernels, though modern machinery also makes this possible on a large scale. The resulting cracked kernels, white or yellow, are sold as is or precooked and ground into flour, which is used for breads, arepas, tamales, and *hallacas*.

This flour goes by a variety of names throughout Latin America as well as *maíz trillado*: *maíz cascado*, *canjiquinha*, or *maíz pulverizado*. It's often confused with cracked hominy, which is nixtamalized, though they can be swapped in a pinch.

Brazilian Corn Mash

Canjiquinha, xerém
Brazil

Preparation time: 15 minutes, plus overnight soaking
Cooking time: 30 minutes

Serves: 3–4

Canjiquinha is a cracked, dried white corn that's used mostly in Minas Gerais. It's often served alongside pork ribs.

  1 tablespoon butter
  ½ white onion, chopped
  1 garlic clove, minced
  1 cup/1 oz (200 g) *canjiquinha* (cracked dried corn), rinsed and soaked in water overnight, then drained
  2 cups/16 fl oz (475 ml) vegetable stock
  1 tablespoon *cachaça*, optional
  1 cup /8 fl oz (250 ml) cream
  2 tablespoons chopped chives
  salt and ground pepper

Heat the butter in a pan over medium heat. Add the onion and garlic, and sauté for 5 minutes. Add the drained *canjiquinha* (cracked dried corn) and stock and bring to a boil, while whisking. Add the *cachaça*, if preferred, and the cream. Season with salt and pepper, lower the heat, and simmer for 20 minutes, or until it has a creamy consistency.
  Stir in the chopped chives before serving.

Corn Rice

Arroz de maíz
Costa Rica

Preparation time: 10 minutes
Cooking time: 40 minutes

Serves: 8

From Costa Rica's northern Pacific region of Guanacaste, *arroz de maíz* doesn't actually have any rice in it. The name refers to the resemblance of *maíz trillado*, or cracked hominy, to rice. Often cooked during communal events, this stew demands continuous stirring, making it quite the work-out when made traditionally in large cauldrons over a wood fire.

  2 lb (900 g) *maíz trillado* (cracked hominy)
  1 tablespoon butter
  1 white onion, chopped
  4 garlic cloves, minced
  1 cup/4½ oz (130 g) chopped celery
  1 red bell pepper, cored, seeded, and chopped
  1 teaspoon ground cumin
  1 teaspoon ground achiote (annatto)
  2 lb (900 g) chicken breasts
  1 cup/1½ oz (40 g) chopped cilantro (coriander); or use *culantro coyote*
  salt and ground pepper

Wash the corn in 4 changes of cold water, and keep the last water used. Heat the butter in a large pan over medium heat. Add the onion, garlic, celery, and bell pepper, and sauté for 8 minutes, stirring continuously. Add the drained corn and stir it for a couple of minutes. Add the cumin and achiote (annatto) and season with salt and pepper. Add the reserved corn water, making sure it is covering the ingredients.
  Bring to a boil and add the chicken breasts. Reduce to a simmer and cook for 20 minutes, stirring frequently, and adding more water if it starts to dry out, ensuring that there's always enough to cover all the ingredients.
  When the chicken is cooked, remove and shred it, then stir it back into the pan. Serve hot, with the cilantro (coriander) scattered on top.

Corn

Arepas

Hundreds of years ago, indigenous groups in present day Colombia and Venezuela made these corn patties that became a staple food. They are made in the streets of both countries, eaten at any time of the day, served with a variety of fillings. In Colombia, arepas tend to be flatter and occasionally made with yellow corn, while in Venezuela they tend to be more rounded and are often crowned with brown crust, called *concha*.

Most arepas are made from nixtamalized, precooked corn flour, called *masarepa*, though some regional variations use fresh, grated corn. Like the tortilla, the arepa often serves as a vehicle for serving other dishes, like *reina pepiada* (page 118), especially in Venezuela.

Basic Corn Arepas

Arepa de maíz
Colombia, Venezuela

Preparation time: 5 minutes
Cooking time: 30 minutes

Makes: 12

    2 cups/8 oz (240 g) *masarepa* (precooked corn
    flour/maize flour)
    1 cup/8 fl oz (250 ml) warm water
    1 teaspoon salt
    2 tablespoons melted butter or olive oil

Preheat the oven to 400°F/200°C/Gas Mark 6.
    Using your hands, mix the *masarepa*, warm water, salt, and 1 tablespoon of the melted butter or oil in a bowl. If the dough sticks to your hands, dampen your hands with water. Once the dough is ready, form 12 equal-sized balls. Flatten all the balls into arepas, roughly 4 inches (10 cm) in diameter.
    Heat the remaining tablespoon of butter or oil in a frying pan over medium heat, then sear the arepas for 2–3 minutes each side, or until golden brown or even slightly charred.
    Transfer to a baking sheet and bake them in the oven for 10–15 minutes until cooked through. Serve hot.

Fried, Egg-Stuffed Arepas

Arepas de huevo
Colombia

Preparation time: 5 minutes,
plus 10 minutes resting
Cooking time: 10 minutes

Makes: 4

These fried, egg-filled arepas come from Colombia's Caribbean region, where the art of frying has been perfected by the Afro-Colombian population there. There, street vendors, often with large piles of yellow masa, fry them so they're crisp on the outside, but the egg inside is still a bit runny and never overcooked.

    1 cup/4 oz (120 g) corn (maize) flour
    ½ teaspoon salt
    ½ teaspoon sugar
    1 cup/8 fl oz (250 ml) warm water
    vegetable oil, for deep-frying
    4 eggs

In a medium bowl, mix the corn (maize) flour, salt, and sugar. Slowly add the warm water, while kneading, to form a soft dough. Cover with a clean tea towel and let rest for 10 minutes.
    Divide the dough in 4 equal pieces with one extra smaller portion to keep aside. Shape the 4 pieces into balls, and flatten with your hand to a ¼ inch (5 mm) thickness.
    Pour enough vegetable oil for deep-frying into a large, heavy pan, making sure it is no more than two-thirds full, and heat to 350°F/177°C.
    Lower the arepas into the oil and cook for 2 minutes each side, then remove with a skimmer to a plate lined with paper towels, to absorb excess oil. Once cool enough to handle, cut a small incision on the side of each arepa, to create a space inside. Carefully place an egg inside (you can break it into a small bowl first and then put it inside the arepa, to make it easier). Close the arepa by gently pressing one piece of the small portion of dough left into the gap. Repeat with the other arepas.
    Deep-fry the arepas again for 4 minutes, so the egg on the inside will cook. Remove with a skimmer to a plate lined with paper towels, then serve warm.

Boyacá-Style Arepas

Arepa Boyacense
Colombia

Preparation time: 5 minutes
Cooking time: 30 minutes   Serves: 6

Amid the rolling green hills of the Boyacá department, as well as in nearby Bogotá, you will come across this smallish, dense, cheese-filled arepa that's a mix of corn and all-purpose (plain) flours. In rural areas it's cooked directly over charcoal, wrapped in a *bijao* (banana) leaf.

> 2 cups/8 oz (240 g) *masarepa* (precooked corn flour/maize flour)
> 5 tablespoons (55 g) all-purpose (plain) flour
> 1 cup/8 fl oz (250 ml) warm water
> ½ cup/4 fl oz (120 ml) milk
> ¼ teaspoon salt
> 2 tablespoons (30 g) sugar
> 3 tablespoons melted butter or olive oil
> 2 cups/8 oz (200 g) shredded *queso fresco* or *quesito*

Preheat the oven to 400°F/200°C/Gas Mark 6.

Using your hands, mix the flours, milk, salt, sugar, and 2 tablespoons of the melted butter or oil in a bowl. Gradually add enough water to make a soft, slightly sticky dough. If the dough sticks to your hands, dampen your hands with water. Once the dough is ready, form 12 equal-sized balls. Flatten all the balls into arepas, roughly 4 inches (10 cm) in diameter.

Heat the remaining tablespoon of butter or oil in a frying pan over medium heat, then sear the arepas for 1–2 minutes each side, or until golden brown or even slightly charred.

Divide the cheese into 6 portions. Take one arepa and place one portion of cheese in the middle, then cover with another arepa and seal by pressing around the edges with your fingers.

Transfer to a baking sheet, then bake them in the oven for 10–15 minutes, until cooked through. Serve hot.

Curvy Queen Arepas

Arepa reina pepiada
Venezuela

Preparation time: 10 minutes
Cooking time: 20 minutes   Serves: 4

When Miss World 1955, Venezuela's Susana Duijm, walked into a restaurant, the owner created a new arepa, stuffed with chicken and avocado, in her honor. The *arepa reina pepiada*, or the curvy queen arepa, has become a national favorite.

> 4 Basic Corn Arepas (page 117)
> 1 tablespoon vegetable oil
> 2 chicken breasts
> 1 white onion, chopped
> 2 garlic cloves, minced
> 1 avocado
> 3 tablespoons mayonnaise
> salt and ground pepper

Fry the arepas for 4 minutes each side, following the method on page 117. Set aside and keep warm.

In a frying pan, heat half the oil over medium heat, add the chicken breasts and cook for 12 minutes, turning them halfway, or until cooked through. Set aside to cool, then shred.

Meanwhile, in another frying pan, heat the remaining oil. Add the onion and garlic, and sauté for 5 minutes. Add the chicken to the pan and mix well. Transfer the mixture to a bowl.

Cut the avocado in half, remove the pit, scoop the flesh into the bowl with the chicken. Mix in the mayonnaise, adding salt and pepper to taste.

Cut the arepas in half, fill them with the chicken and avocado mix, and serve warm.

Maracaibo-Style Arepas

Arepa tumbarrancho
Venezuela

Preparation time: 15 minutes
Cooking time: 15 minutes   Serves: 4

The Venezuelan city of Maracaibo has created the breakfast sandwich version of an arepa. The *arepa tumbarrancho* is battered and stuffed with mortadella then fried, then stuffed again with cheese, which oozes out of it on the plate. This arepa is named after a firework of the same name because they are said to cause gas. Maracuchos, as people from Maracaibo are called, are known for their idiosyncratic behavior.

> 4 Basic Corn Arepas (page 117)
> 8 oz (225 g) mortadella (4 slices)
> ½ cup/2 oz (60 g) all-purpose (plain) flour
> 2 eggs
> 1 teaspoon salt
> 1 tablespoon mustard
> ½ cup/4 fl oz (120 ml) whole milk
> vegetable oil, for deep-frying
> 1 lb (450 g) *queso de mano* (or use mozzarella), cut into pieces
> 1 cup/2 oz (60 g) sliced white cabbage
> 2 tomatoes, peeled and sliced
> mayonnaise, ketchup, and mustard, to serve

Fry the arepas for 4 minutes each side, following the method on page 117. Cut them in the middle halfway through, and tuck a slice of mortadella inside. Close and set aside.

Put the flour, eggs, salt, mustard, and milk into a bowl. Whisk well and if needed to create a smooth consistency, slowly pour in a ½ cup/4 fl oz (120 ml) water.

Pour enough vegetable oil for deep-frying into a large, heavy pan, making sure it is no more than two-thirds full, and heat to 360°F/182°C.

Dip the arepas one by one in the batter and deep-fry them for 4 minutes, or until browned on all sides. Remove with a skimmer and place them on a plate lined with a paper towel to absorb the excess oil.

Open the arepas while still hot and place the cheese, cabbage, and tomatoes inside. Slather with the different sauces and serve warm.

Curvy Queen Arepas

Nixtamal

Tasting a tortilla that has been made from masa made from nixtamalized heirloom corn, passed warm from the *comal* to your hands, can be life-changing. Flavors come to life that you never realized corn could have. It's as if this seemingly basic ingredient, one of the most widespread on this planet, used in everything from breakfast cereals to biofuels, is not at all what you thought it was.

The process of nixtamalization originated in Mesoamerica, possibly in Guatemala or southern Mexico, several thousand years ago. The procedure steeps the corn in water mixed with cal (calcium hydroxide, sometimes called slaked lime) or ash (potassium hydroxide), which partially dissolves pericarp, the hull or hard skin of the corn, making it more digestible, easier to work with, and far tastier. The process makes it easier for niacin to be absorbed into the body, thus reducing the risk of pellagra, plus can provide additional calcium from the alkali used.

There's no exact recipe for this. The particular quantities of water and cal can vary depending on the type of corn and the desired results. More cal means a slightly bitter taste, which some appreciate, not to mention a longer lasting tortilla. Less cal can mean more natural flavors and colors. Similarly, the ratio of water, cooking temperature, and steeping times can all be tweaked to produce a particular result. When the pericarp, or hull, is just starting to come off, usually after a half day to a day of soaking, it becomes nixtamal.

Not every type of corn is appropriate to make nixtamal and that includes sweet corn. You want starchy corn, like field, flint, or dent. Most industrial tortilla-making outfits use white corn, which might be consistent in terms of its quality, though lacks flavor. Landrace corn, open pollinated varieties, the ones usually produced by small farmers using the milpa system, will result in the most flavorful food.

Nixtamal, called hominy in English, and also a staple of the cuisine of the southern United States, can be used directly in salads or stews, such as *pozole*, or made into masa to make tortillas.

Pozole

When the Aztecs would make *pozole*, it would be done on special occasions. Specifically, human sacrifices. The priest would offer the hearts to the gods, while the rest of the body would be stewed with corn and chiles and served to those in attendance. When the Spanish arrived, cannibalism became less socially acceptable than it was in pre-Columbian times, so pork became the preferred meat in the stew. *Pozole* remains a celebratory dish, eaten on New Year's Eve and other special occasions.

Pozole can be made red (*rojo*) or green (*verde*), which depends on the types of chiles used for the base of the stew. It can also be made white (*blanco*), when no chiles are added. It's often served with a variety of sides like shredded lettuce, sliced radishes, avocados, lime wedges, tostadas for dipping, or *chicharrón* to crumble on top.

You can make *pozole* from fresh nixtamal kernels, which are sometimes sold from *tortillerías*, though most likely you will be working with dried or canned varieties. When buying dried *maíz para pozole* (as it is labeled in Mexico) or hominy, it needs to be soaked in water for at least 6 hours and drained before being cooked. Canned varieties do not need soaking.

There are dozens of regional variations of *pozole* throughout much of central and northern Mexico, as well as the American southwest, not to mention individual preferences.

Red Hominy Stew

Pozole rojo 🍲
Mexico

Preparation time: 15 minutes, plus 25 minutes soaking
Cooking time: 3 hours 45 minutes

Serves: 6

While vegetarian versions exist, traditional preparations of *pozole rojo*, especially in the state of Jalisco, include pork bones in some form to give the stew its rich texture and flavor. We use pork ribs, though bones from the head, neck, shank, or even feet are commonly used.

    2 lb (900 g) pork shoulder, diced
    1 lb (450 g) pork ribs, cut into pieces
    1½ white onions, quartered
    12 garlic cloves, peeled
    8½ pints/135 fl oz (4 liters) water
    5 ancho chiles, seeded and veins removed
    5 guajillo chiles, seeded and veins removed
    ½ teaspoon Mexican oregano
    2 tablespoons vegetable oil
    6 cups/48 fl oz (1.4 liters) canned hominy, rinsed
    and drained (or 2 cups/16 fl oz (475 ml) dried hominy,
    soaked for at least 6 hours)
    salt and ground pepper

    To serve
    sliced radishes
    sliced white onion
    lettuce leaves
    lime wedges

Place the pork shoulder, pork ribs, 1 onion, 6 garlic cloves, and some salt in a large pan. Pour over the measured water, bring to a boil, then lower the heat. Cook for about 2 hours 30 minutes, or until the meat comes off the bone. Remove the surface layer of foam and grease that forms on the broth as it cooks. If necessary, add more hot water to keep the level of broth in the pot. Remove the cooked meat and set aside, reserving the stock.
   To prepare the sauce, soak all the chiles in enough water to cover for 25 minutes. Once soft, drain and place in a blender, with the remaining garlic, onion, and the oregano. Add a little of the stock to blend until smooth.
   Heat the oil in a small pan over medium-high heat, then add the sauce, and season with salt. Reduce the heat and simmer for about 25 minutes, then strain and mix in with the reserved cooking stock. Bring to a boil, then add the meat and lower the heat, letting it simmer for 10 minutes. Add the hominy and season with salt and pepper. Continue cooking until the hominy is completely cooked, about 40 minutes.
   Serve warm in a deep dish and garnished with radish, onion, lettuce, and lime wedges.

Corn

Red Hominy Stew

Green Hominy Stew

Pozole verde
Mexico

Preparation time: 15 minutes
Cooking time: 2 hours 15 minutes
Serves: 6

Green from a mix of serrano chiles and tomatillos, *pozole verde* is a favorite preparation in the state of Guerrero. Some cooks there like to add wild herbs such as *axoxoco*, better known as sorrel, into the blended mixture to add acidity.

8 tomatillos
2 serrano chiles
½ cup/¾ oz (20 g) chopped cilantro (coriander)
½ cup/¾ oz (20 g) chopped parsley
3 sprigs epazote
½ white onion, cut into 2 quarters
7 garlic cloves, peeled
1 tablespoon oil
¼ teaspoon Mexican oregano
2 cups/16 fl oz (475 ml) dried hominy, soaked for at least 6 hours (or 6 cups/48 fl oz (1.4 liters) canned hominy, rinsed and drained)
1 bay leaf
½ cup/¾ oz (20 g) fresh thyme sprigs
4 cups/32 fl oz (950 ml) water
4 cups/2 lb 3 oz (1 kg) pork leg, diced
salt and ground pepper

To serve
radishes
sliced white onion
lime wedges
Mexican oregano
lettuce leaves
corn tostadas

In a medium pan of water, boil the tomatillos and chiles for 20 minutes, or until the tomatillos change color. Drain and transfer to a blender with the cilantro (coriander), parsley, epazote, 1 onion quarter, and 1 garlic clove, along with ½ cup/4 fl oz (120 ml) of boiling water. Blend until smooth then strain and add to a pan with the oil. Place over medium heat, bring to a boil and cook for 15 minutes. Add the oregano and season to taste with salt and pepper, then set aside.

Put the hominy and remaining garlic cloves in a medium pan, add the remaining onion, the bay leaf, and thyme. Add the measured water and cook until the grain bursts, about 40 minutes. Remove the vegetables and herbs from the cooking stock, add the green sauce and pork to the stock, and simmer until the meat is soft, about 1 hour, topping up with more water if necessary. Season to taste.

Serve with radishes, onion slices, wedges of lime, oregano, lettuce leaves, and corn tostadas.

Mote

Several varieties of corn in the Andes also undergo the process of nixtamalization, just like with nixtamal. This subset goes by various names, most commonly *mote*, as well as *maíz pelado*, *maíz cascado*, or in English, Andean hominy. It's not used for making masa, but it is the principal ingredient in dozens of Andean dishes, such as *patasca* and *mote pillo*.

In Chile, *mote* specifically refers to husked wheat grain, which is made in a similar process to nixtamal and used in dishes like *mote con huesillos* and *catuto*.

Andean Hominy Stew

Patasca, phatasqa
Argentina, Bolivia, Chile, Peru

Preparation time: 15 minutes,
Cooking time: 3 hours
Serves: 6

Patasca is a hominy stew found throughout the high Andes, adapted to the meats and vegetables at hand. The biggest difference is the protein used, which varies from country to country. For example, in Chile they use *charqui* (dried alpaca meat) while in Bolivia they opt for beef tongue, and in Argentina veal shank is preferred.

6 cups/48 fl oz (1.4 liters) canned *mote* (Andean hominy), rinsed and drained (or 2 cups/16 fl oz (475 ml) dried *mote*, soaked for at least 6 hours)
1 veal shank
1 lb (450 g) beef tripe
3 tablespoons mint leaves
1 tablespoon vegetable oil
1 white onion, chopped
1 tomato, peeled and diced
2 tablespoons *ají panca* paste
1 tablespoon dried oregano
1 tablespoon cilantro (coriander) leaves
4 potatoes, peeled and cut into cubes
salt and ground pepper

To serve
¼ cup/⅓ oz (10 g) chopped mint
½ cup/¾ oz (20 g) chopped chives
¼ cup/1 oz (30 g) chopped *rocoto* chile

Rinse the *mote*, then add to a large pot and cover with salted water. Bring to a boil over medium heat and cook for about 2 hours, stirring occasionally. Add additional water if needed. Drain and let cool.

Place the *mote*, veal shank, beef tripe, and mint in a large pan. Cover with water and add a hint of salt. Place over high heat and bring to a boil, then cook for 20 minutes, or until the *mote* starts opening. Remove from the heat and take the meat out to a cutting board. Cut the meats into 1-inch (2.5-cm) cubes and set aside. Drain the *mote*, reserving the cooking stock.

In a separate pan, heat the oil over medium heat and sauté the onion, tomato, and *ají panca* paste for 8 minutes. Add both meats and the oregano and cilantro (coriander). Stir well and add the drained *mote*, with the potatoes. Pour in the reserved cooking stock, season with salt and pepper, and cook for a further 20 minutes.

Check the seasoning before serving, scattered with the mint, chives, and chopped *rocoto*.

Corn

Hominy with Eggs

Mote pillo
Ecuador

Preparation time: 5 minutes
Cooking time: 2 hours 50 minutes Serves: 2–4

Typical of the Azuay province in southeastern Ecuador, *mote pillao* is often served on its own for breakfast or alongside soups or meats for lunch.

> 3 cups/24 fl oz (700 ml) canned *mote* (Andean hominy), rinsed and drained (or 1 cup/8 fl oz (240 ml) dried *mote*, soaked for at least 6 hours)
> 2 tablespoons *mapahuira* (or use lard or bacon fat)
> 1 cup/4 oz (120 g) finely chopped white onion
> 2 garlic cloves, crushed
> ¼ teaspoon ground achiote (annatto)
> ¼ cup/2 fl oz (60 ml) milk
> 4 eggs, beaten
> 2 tablespoons finely chopped scallion (spring onion)
> 1 tablespoon finely chopped cilantro (coriander)
> salt

Rinse the *mote*, then add to a large pot and cover with salted water. Bring to a boil over medium heat and cook for about 2 hours 30 minutes, stirring occasionally, until the corn is soft and starts to pop. Add additional water if needed. Drain and let cool.

Heat the *mapahuira* in a medium pan over high heat, add the onion, garlic, achiote (annatto), and some salt, and sauté for about 5 minutes, or until the onion is soft. Add the *mote* and cook for a further 2 minutes, then add the milk and cook for 8 minutes, or until the milk is absorbed. Add the eggs and mix well for about 5 minutes.

Check the seasoning before serving, scattered with the scallion (spring onion) and cilantro (coriander).

Corn Masa

After the nixtamal is washed, it can be ground to make masa, essentially a dough, which can then be used to make an array of traditional foods. The best way to grind nixtamal for home use is with a *metate*, a lava rock grinding stone with a stone rolling pin, which has been used throughout Mesoamerica for thousands of years. It's a labor-intensive process perfected by Mexican grandmothers, though most of us are not nearly as tough. Other possibilities of grinding nixtamal include hand-cranked mills, food processors, and tabletop grinders and mixers, and they can make a reasonable masa, though none quite right.

Masa can also be made from *masa harina*, dough flour. Making tortillas in this way is still better than the often tasteless, store-bought tortillas, though the flavor, not to mention nutrients, lack when compared to masa made with nixtamal. Note that however you make your masa, it's best to use it within a day of making it.

As you can see, the process from the field to masa is a tremendous amount of work when done right. Keep that in mind whenever someone insists that tortillas and other *antojitos* (snacks) should be inexpensive. You get what you pay for.

Corn Masa

Masa de maíz
Mexico

Preparation time: 30 minutes, plus at least 8 hours soaking
Cooking time: 15 minutes Makes: 1 lb 4 oz (560 g)

This recipe is for fresh corn masa, which you can also buy from a *tortillería*. To make nixtamal, simply refrain from grinding the corn in the final step. Additionally, you can make an equivalent amount of masa by mixing 1½ cups/6 oz (180 g) *masa harina* with 1 cup/8 fl oz (250 ml) warm water, and then leaving it to rest for 20 minutes.

> 1 lb (450 g) dried corn kernels (field, flint, or dent)
> ¼ oz (5 g) cal (slaked lime)

Rinse the corn in cold water and remove any debris. Place in a large pan with the cal (slaked lime) and add cold water to cover; it should be 1–2 inches (2.5–5 cm) above the corn. Bring to a boil, then lower the heat to medium and let simmer. Once the pericarp of the corn starts to dissolve (it should easily peel off), after about 10 minutes or so, remove from the heat. Add additional water if any evaporated, ensuring it is still the same level above the corn. Cover and let soak overnight, or for at least 8 hours.

Drain the kernels and peel the pericarp, and you are left with nixtamal. To turn it into masa, mash the nixtamal with a stone grinder (alternatively you can use a food processor), adding water or *masa harina* if needed, until you achieve the desired consistency.

Oval-Shaped Masa Cakes

Huaraches
Mexico

Preparation time: 20 minutes
Cooking time: 25 minutes   Serves: 9–10

Flattened by hand into an oval shape, sort of resembling a sandal, hence the name, *huaraches* are similar to *sopes* or *tlacoyos*, just a bit bigger and topped with nearly anything, such as mashed pinto beans, chorizo, potatoes, or various salsas. They first appeared at a food stall run by a woman named Carmen Gómez Medina in Mexico City in the 1930s, when a man asked for a couple of ribs on a *gordita*. She enlarged the masa to fit the meat and the nickname took off.

    3 fresh poblano chiles
    1 jalapeño pepper
    9 tomatoes
    1 onion, peeled and halved
    2 garlic cloves, peeled
    2 lb (900 g) fresh Corn Masa (page 123)
    2 tablespoons lard
    1 cup/9 oz (250 g) Refried Black Beans (page 172)
    ½ cup/¾ oz (20 g) finely chopped cilantro (coriander)
    1 cup/3½ oz (100 g) shredded *queso añejo* (or use *queso fresco*)
    salt

In a dry pan, toast the chiles and tomatoes until fully cooked. Place in a blender with half the onion and the garlic. Season with salt, blend to a sauce, and set aside.

In a deep bowl, mix the masa with the lard. Divide into balls about the size of an orange. Press in the middle of each ball and add a spoonful of refried beans. Close the dough over the filling, place each ball between plastic separators, and flatten the dough with your hands. Repeat for each ball. Heat a *comal* or frying pan and cook the huaraches for about 1–2 minutes per side, until golden brown.

Finely chop the remaining onion. Serve the *huaraches* with the tomato and chile sauce, onion, cilantro (coriander), and shredded cheese.

Central American Corn Cakes

Riguas, güirila 🖻
El Salvador, Nicaragua

Preparation time: 5 minutes
Cooking time: 30 minutes   Serves: 4

Riguas can be made from fresh corn or masa, which is then cooked on or folded within a piece of corn husk or banana leaf, though never wrapped like a tamal. Cheese or refried beans are sometimes mixed with the corn.

    3 cups/13 oz (375 g) fresh corn kernels
    ½ tablespoon sugar
    1 teaspoon salt
    2 tablespoons butter
    8 banana leaves (10-inch/25-cm squares), cleaned and dried

Put the corn in a grinder and process to crush (this used to be done with a mortar and a pestle). Add the processed corn, sugar, salt, and butter to a blender and blend together until it makes a uniform batter.

Place 1 tablespoon of the corn mixture in the middle of each banana leaf, and fold the leaf in half.

Heat a frying pan over medium heat and place a *rigua* on one side of the pan. Cook for 10 minutes each side, or until the banana leaf starts to brown and the corn thickens. Repeat with all the *riguas*.

Serve warm.

Corn Masa Cakes

Bocoles
Mexico

Preparation time: 15 minutes
Cooking time: 15 minutes   Serves: 8

From Mexico's gulf region of Huasteca, *bocoles* are primarily an inexpensive street food of masa mixed with beef tallow or lard. The masa can be mixed with or cut open after cooking and stuffed like an arepa with ingredients like refried beans, *chicharrón*, shredded beef, or stewed meat.

    3 *morita* chiles, seeded and veins removed
    1½ cups/5 oz (150 g) shredded *queso fresco*
    2 tablespoons lard
    2 lb (900 g) fresh Corn Masa (page 123)
    2 cups/1 lb 2 oz (500 g) Refried Black Beans (page 172)
    1 lb (450 g) *Chicharrón* (Pork Cracklings/crispy pork skin; page 276 for homemade or can be store-bought)
    salt

Place the chiles and cheese in a blender and mix well for 4 minutes on medium speed. Pour into a bowl, stir in the lard and season with salt. Add the masa and knead well for 7 minutes until you have a uniform, soft dough, adding a little water if necessary. Shape into 8 equal-sized balls. Press them slightly into discs ½ inch (1 cm) thick.

Heat a frying pan over medium heat and sear the tortillas for 3–4 minutes per side, or until they are golden brown. Cut them open with a knife and fill them with refried beans and *Chicharrón*.

Central American Corn Cakes

Salvadoran Corn Patties

Pupusas
El Salvador

Preparation time: 15 minutes
Cooking time: 15 minutes

Serves: 12

It's believed that *pupusas* originated with Pibil, or Cuzcatlec, people who inhabited parts of western El Salvador, and evidence of their preparation has been uncovered at Joya de Cerén, a Mayan village near San Salvador that was buried in the ash of a volcanic eruption. Originally, they were half-moon shaped, much like an empanada. Until the 1940s, they were still a rather obscure dish concentrated in the central parts of the country, but migration quickly transformed them into a national dish.

In modern El Salvador, *pupusas* are ubiquitous. They are grilled on street-side *comales* in every part of the country and the simplest are plain or filled with beans, though oozing *quesillo* cheese, *loroco* buds, and *chicharrón* are common additions.

2 lb (900 g) fresh Corn Masa (page 123)
1½ cups/6 oz (180 g) chopped *quesillo* (or use mozzarella)
Curtido (Salvadoran Cabbage Relish, page 402), to serve

Shape the masa into 12 equal-sized balls. Press down with your thumb in the middle of the ball to create a cavity that is large enough to place a tablespoon of the cheese, then pinch the dough over the cheese. Flatten each ball lightly into a disc ¼ inch (5 mm) thick.

Heat a *comal* or frying pan over medium heat. Add the *pupusas* and cook for 6 minutes each side, or until golden brown and the cheese inside is melted.

Serve hot, with *curtido*.

Corn and Bean Tortillas

Tayuyos
Guatemala

Preparation time: 15 minutes
Cooking time: 10 minutes

Makes: 10

You'll see *tayuyos* being sold in almost any village market in Guatemala, usually with tomato sauce, often with small, corn-husk-wrapped tamales called *chuchitos*. Another variation, called *tayuyos to'om*, uses a *piedra de moler*, or grinding stone that is more typical in Mayan villages, to make the masa, then wraps it in corn husks or fresh corn leaves and steams it like a tamal.

2 lb (900 g) fresh Corn Masa (page 123)
1 cup/9 oz (250 g) Refried Black Beans (page 172)
1 tablespoon vegetable oil
salt

Mix the masa with the refried beans, seasoning with salt. Shape the dough into 10 equal-sized balls. Flatten each ball lightly into a disc ¼ inch (5 mm) thick.

Heat the oil in a frying pan over medium heat. Add the tortillas and fry for 4 minutes each side.

Serve warm.

Fried, Puffed Tortillas with Shredded Chicken

Salbutes
Belize, Mexico

Preparation time: 20 minutes
Cooking time: 45 minutes

Serves: 4

Common in Mexico's Yucatán peninsula and Belize, these fried and puffed, hand-made tortillas are usually topped with shredded chicken or turkey and served as a snack before or between meals. Other regional foods like *cochinita pibil* and *relleno negro* may also be used as toppings. *Panuchos*, usually sold by the same vendors, are quite similar, though they slice open the puffed tortilla and stuff fried black beans, as well as other toppings, inside.

3 chicken breasts
1 teaspoon dried oregano
2 cups/4 oz (105 g) chopped red onion
1 jalapeño pepper, cored, seeded, and sliced
¼ cup/2 fl oz (60 ml) white vinegar
2 lb (900 g) fresh Corn Masa (page 123)
1 teaspoon achiote paste (or annatto paste dissolved in 2 tablespoons water)
vegetable oil, for deep-frying
salt and ground pepper

For the topping, season the chicken breasts with salt, pepper, and half the oregano. Place in a pan, add enough water to cover, and bring to a boil. Simmer for 20–25 minutes, or until cooked. Remove the chicken from the cooking water (keep this), let cool, then shred using your hands.

Bring the cooking water to a boil, then add the onion, chile, vinegar, and the remaining oregano. Let cook for 3 minutes, then remove from the heat, cover, and let cool for 10 minutes. Drain, reserving the onion and chile.

Knead the masa with the achiote paste in a bowl. Shape the masa into 12 equal-sized balls. Flatten each ball between two pieces of plastic wrap (clingfilm), using a tortilla press or a flat utensil such as the flat side of a frying pan, pressing down evenly to form discs 4 inches (10 cm) in diameter and ⅓ inch (8 mm) thick.

Pour enough oil for deep-frying into a large, heavy pan, making sure it is no more than two-thirds full, and heat to 350°F/177°C.

Fry the *salbutes* in small batches, 2 or 3 at a time, and cook for about 1–2 minutes, or until brown, then flip them over and cook for a further 1 minute. Remove with a skimmer to a plate lined with paper towels, to absorb excess oil.

To serve, place the *salbutes* on a serving plate and press down slightly to flatten, then top them with a little shredded chicken, onion, and chile.

Fried, Topped Tortillas

Garnachas
Belize, Guatemala, Mexico

Preparation time: 20 minutes
Cooking time: 30 minutes

Makes: 4

Garnachas are a basic street snack that changes as you move across the region. In Oaxaca and Guatemala, they are made from masa with pinched sides that have been fried. In Belize, they are almost always topped with refried black beans. In Veracruz, they are larger, almost twice as big as other states. In Mexico City, the term *garnacha* is often used to refer to any *antojito* (snack) with a corn base that has been fried. In many cases they are topped with shredded meat, though they can also be vegetarian, like these.

> ½ cup (140 g) fresh Corn Masa (page 123)
> vegetable oil, for frying
> 1 white onion, chopped
> 1 garlic clove, minced
> 1 tomato, peeled and diced
> 1 *ancho* chile, seeded and veins removed
> 1 *guajillo* chile, seeded and veins removed
> 1 *chilacate* chile, seeded and veins removed
> pinch of dried oregano
> 1 cup/5 oz (150 g) shredded *cotija* cheese
> 1 cup/2 oz (50 g) shredded lettuce
> salt

Divide the masa into 4 equal-sized balls. Shape each ball into a small disc, about 3 inches (7.5 cm) wide and ⅓ inch (8 mm) thick. Heat a frying pan or a comal over medium heat, add the discs, and cook for about 1–2 minutes on each side, or until golden brown. Set aside.

Heat 1 tablespoon of vegetable oil in a pan over medium heat. Add half the onion and the garlic, and sauté for 7 minutes, then add the diced tomato, all the chiles, and the oregano and cook for 10 minutes. Transfer to a mixer and blend to a soft paste. Strain to remove any lumps, season with salt, and set aside.

In a frying pan, heat 3 tablespoons of vegetable oil and add the *garnachas*. Spoon some of the oil on top, then some of the sauce, and fry for about 5 minutes, or until the bottoms are crisp. Remove from the oil and place on a plate lined with paper towels, to absorb excess oil. Sprinkle with the cheese, the remaining chopped onion, and lettuce.

Tamales

From the Náhuatl word *tamalli*, which means wrapped, tamales are a family of recipes found in nearly every corner of Latin America. They are one of the oldest forms of cooking in the region and they act as portable meals, which have been used by hunters, travelers, and marching armies, as well as a ritual food for celebrations for several thousand years. They remain widely consumed.

Everything about tamales tends to be highly regional, though the one constant is that they are cooked within a wrap, such as a dried corn husk, banana leaf, *bijao* leaf, or avocado leaf. The wrap can be rolled, stuffed, or folded and then is usually tied crosswise and or lengthways and then the edges can be pinched together and tied at the top with a string.

The interior of a tamal is usually corn based, either fresh corn or a masa made from nixtamalized corn or cornflour, though rice and rice-based masa, plantains, cassava, and other fillings can also be found. Some have little seasoning, just a touch of salt or sugar, while others might add annatto, coconut milk, pork fat, peanuts, chiles, or mole. Pork, chicken, squash blossoms, potatoes, peas, carrots, or leafy greens are common ingredients.

While they can be boiled, grilled or baked, in most cases tamales are steamed. This is done much like you would steam vegetables, by placing them in a basket over a covered pan of simmering water.

Bean, Chipilín, and Loroco Tamales

Ticucos
El Salvador, Honduras

Preparation time: 20 minutes
Cooking time: 1 hour 15 minutes

Makes: 10

Found in the western regions of El Salvador and Honduras, especially in Lenca communities, *ticucos* can be made with fresh corn or corn (maize) flour, or sometimes a mix of the two, as we have done. They are especially popular to make during Christmas and Semana Santa (the Spanish celebration for Holy Week, leading up to Easter).

> 2 lb (900 g) fresh corn kernels
> 1 lb (450 g) corn (maize) flour
> 1 lb (450 g) butter or lard, softened
> 2 cups/10½ oz (300 g) beans, half-cooked (in El Salvador they use either white or red beans)
> 10 corn husks
> 1 tablespoon chopped *chipilín* (or use baby watercress)
> 3 oz (85 g) *loroco* (edible flowers), chopped
> salt

Cook the corn kernels in a pan of boiling water for 15 minutes or until soft. Drain and blend in a mixer to a soft batter. Tip into a bowl, add the corn (maize) flour and mix, kneading well for 7 minutes. Season with salt and slowly add the butter while kneading, for about 5 minutes. Add the beans and continue kneading until you have a soft dough.

Take one corn husk, place 1 tablespoon of dough in the middle, flatten it a little and place ½ teaspoon of *chipilín* and 1 or 2 *loroco* flowers on the dough. Place another tablespoon of dough on top and close the husk, folding in the sides, and then up and down. Close with a string.

Pour about 2 inches (5 cm) of water into a steamer, and bring to a boil. Add the steamer basket (make sure the boiling water doesn't touch the basket), place the tamales in the basket and cook for 1 hour. Open them and serve hot.

Salvadoran Hen Tamales

Tamales de gallina
El Salvador

Preparation time: 20 minutes
Cooking time: 2 hours ✳ Ø
Makes: 20

Served during holidays and special events, these tamales can be made with either chicken or game hen/poussin.

2 white onions, coarsely chopped
3 tomatoes, peeled and diced
5 garlic cloves, chopped
1 carrot, chopped
7 cups/60 fl oz (1.75 liters) water
1 game hen, cut into 4 pieces
1 lb (450 g) potatoes, washed
3 lb (1.5 kg) fresh Corn Masa (page 123)
1 lb (450 g) lard, plus extra if needed
10 banana leaves, cut in half
salt and ground pepper

For the salsa
½ cup/4 fl oz (120 ml) vegetable oil
4 bay leaves
10 tomatoes, peeled and diced
2 red onions, chopped
2 green bell peppers, cored, seeded, and diced
4 garlic cloves, minced

Put the onions, tomatoes, garlic, and carrot in a large pan. Pour over the measured water and bring to a boil. Once boiling, add the hen pieces and simmer for 30 minutes, or until tender. Remove the hen pieces, cut half into small (1-inch/2.5-cm) pieces and shred the other half. Strain the cooking liquid and reserve.

Meanwhile, boil the potatoes in a medium pan of salted water for 15 minutes, or until cooked but firm. Peel and dice. Set aside.

Place the masa in a large pan and slowly mix in 6 cups/50 fl oz (1.5 liters) of the reserved cooking stock while stirring continuously. Mix in the lard and cook over medium heat for 30 minutes, stirring continuously, or until the liquid is absorbed. Season with salt and pepper. Place a small teaspoon of the mix on a banana leaf. If the dough easily slips, then it is ready; if not, add more lard and continue stirring and cooking.

To make the salsa, heat the oil in a frying pan over medium heat, fry the bay leaves for 4 minutes, then take them out. Add the tomatoes, red onions, bell peppers, and garlic, and fry for 10 minutes over medium heat. Add the shredded hen meat and season with salt and pepper.

To prepare the tamales, take a banana leaf half and add 1 tablespoon of the masa mixture to the middle. Add ½ tablespoon of the salsa, a couple of pieces of hen meat and potato, and cover with another tablespoon of masa mixture. Close the tamal by folding it in three parts, first the bottom, then the top, and then all around. Press well so the dough doesn't slip on the sides. Repeat the process with all the dough and banana leaves.

Pour about 2 inches (5 cm) of water into a steamer, and bring to a boil. Add the steamer basket (make sure the boiling water doesn't touch the basket) and place the tamales in the basket. Cook for 40 minutes, or until the banana leaves are soft and cooked. Open them and serve hot.

Squash Blossom Tamales

Tamales de flor de calabaza 🔲
Mexico

Preparation time: 20 minutes
Cooking time: 1 hour ✳ Ø
Makes: 20

Known as *flores de calabaza*, squash blossoms are found throughout Mexico and are used in dozens of preparations. Even if they are a little bit withered, they will work for this recipe. *Huitlacoche* or shrimp can also be mixed in alongside the flowers.

1 cup/8 oz (225 g) lard
2 lb (900 g) fresh Corn Masa (page 123)
½ teaspoon salt
1 cup/4 oz (120 g) cubed squash (½-inch/
2.5-cm cubes)
½ cup/2 oz (60 g) pepitas (hulled squash or
pumpkin seeds), chopped
20 corn husks, soaked for 30 minutes in warm water
15 squash blossoms

Using a whisk, beat the lard in a bowl for 3–5 minutes. Add half the masa and beat until incorporated. Add the remaining masa and the salt, and beat until it has a soft texture, like a frosting or fudge (a tablespoonful should float in a glass of water). Check the seasoning; it should be slightly salty as it will leach during cooking. Using your hands or a spatula, fold the cubed squash and chopped pepitas into the dough.

Drain the corn husks. Place a squash blossom in the middle of each husk and add 2 tablespoons of the dough on top of the flower. Close the husk, doubling the pointed end over the bottom half.

Pour about 2 inches (5 cm) of water into a steamer, and bring to a boil. Add the steamer basket (make sure the boiling water doesn't touch the basket) and place the tamales in the basket, standing with the rounded ends up. Cook for 45 minutes to 1 hour, topping up with boiling water if necessary, until the tamales easily come off the husks when opened.

Squash Blossom Tamales

Loja-Style Tamales

Tamal Lojano
Ecuador

Preparation time: 20 minutes,
plus 24 hours soaking time
Cooking time: 1 hour 35 minutes

Makes: 10

Fast-food restaurants, cafés, hotel breakfast buffets, markets, and street corner vendors throughout the city of Loja in southern Ecuador sell this large, regional tamal. Generally, they are served with *ají de maní* (Spicy Peanut Sauce, page 410), which, in Loja, they often make with fig-leaf gourd seeds instead of with peanuts.

> 3 lb (1.4 kg) *maíz pelado* (husked yellow corn, kernels only), soaked for at least 24 hours
> 1 lb (450 g) pork shoulder
> 8 oz (225 g) lard
> 1 teaspoon butter
> 1 oz (30 g) baking powder
> 4 eggs, beaten
> 2 tablespoons vegetable oil
> 2 white onions, chopped
> 1 cup/4½ oz (130 g) peas
> 1 cup/4 oz (120 g) chopped carrots
> 1 lb (450 g) chicken breasts, cut into 2-inch (5-cm) chunks
> 1 cup/5 oz (140 g) raisins
> 10 achira leaves (or use banana leaves)
> 3 hard-boiled eggs, sliced
> 1 cup/1½ oz (40 g) chopped cilantro (coriander)
> salt

Drain the corn kernels and process in a grinder until smooth. You may need to run the corn through the grinder two or three times. Set aside.

Meanwhile, place the pork in a medium pan with enough water to cover it, and a pinch of salt. Cook for 25 minutes, then remove the meat, let cool slightly, and cut into 1-inch (2.5-cm) chunks. Retain the cooking water.

In a bowl, mix the ground corn, including the solids, with the lard and butter. Knead well for 5 minutes, or until uniform. Slowly add enough of the pork stock, starting with one cup, to give a uniform dough, kneading vigorously for 5 minutes. Add 1 teaspoon of salt and the baking powder, then the eggs. Knead well to a soft dough, then cover with a tea towel and set aside.

For the filling, heat the oil in a large frying pan, add the onions and sauté for 4 minutes, then add the peas and carrots and cook for a couple more minutes. Add the pork and chicken breast chunks. Stir well and add the raisins, then cook over low heat, stirring occasionally, for 15–20 minutes, or until the chicken is cooked.

Take an achira leaf and place 2 tablespoons of the dough in the middle. Flatten it a little and place 1 tablespoon of the filling, a slice of hard-boiled egg, and some cilantro (coriander) on top. Close the tamal by bringing the edges to the middle, and tie together with string.

Pour about 2 inches (5 cm) of water into a steamer, and bring to a boil. Add the steamer basket (make sure the boiling water doesn't touch the basket) and place the tamales in the steaming basket. Cook for 40 minutes. Open just before serving.

Guatemalan Tamales

Chuchitos, takamäles
Guatemala

Preparation time: 20 minutes
Cooking time: 1 hour

Makes: 10

Beloved by all walks of life in Guatemala, *chuchitos* are one of the country's most emblematic dishes. Called *takamäles* by the Kaqchikel people in the highlands of western Guatemala, they usually contain some combination of local ingredients like *chipilín* leaves, *loroco* or *izote* buds, and chiles.

> 14 oz (400 g) lard
> 2 lb (900 g) fresh Corn Masa (page 123)
> 1 cup/8 fl oz (250 ml) chicken stock
> 2 lb (900 g) chicken breasts
> 1 tablespoon vegetable oil
> 1 white onion, chopped
> 7 tomatoes, peeled and diced
> 3 red bell peppers, cored, seeded, and chopped
> 4 oz (120 g) *loroco* (edible vine)
> 15 corn husks, soaked for 30 minutes in warm water
> 2 oz (60 g) *queso duro* (or use any salty fresh cheese), shredded
> salt

Using a whisk, whip the lard in a bowl for 3–5 minutes, then add the masa and combine. Knead, while slowly pouring in the stock, until you get a uniform and soft dough. Set aside.

Cook the chicken in salted, simmering water for 20 minutes. Remove and shred.

Heat the oil in a frying pan over medium heat. Add the onion, tomatoes, and bell peppers, and sauté for 10 minutes until soft and cooked. Transfer to a blender with the *loroco*, and blend to a sauce on medium speed for 4 minutes.

Drain the corn husks, and place a 4-inch (10-cm) disc of dough in the middle of each of 10 of them. Add some shredded chicken and a tablespoon of the blended sauce to the dough disk. Close the dough to seal (you can add a little bit more dough if needed). Wrap the corn husks around the dough and then, using a string made with the remaining husks, tie the ends to seal.

Place 4 corn husks across the base of a large pan, and add the *chuchitos* around the edges, making a circle. Pour water into the middle and heat until it starts simmering, then cover. Cook for 30 minutes. Remove the chuchitos and open. Serve hot, with cheese sprinkled on top.

Corn

Guatemalan Tamales

Nicaraguan Meat-Filled Tamales

Nacatamales
Nicaragua

Preparation time: 20 minutes
Cooking time: 4–5 hours

Makes: 6

Nacatamales, Nahuatl for "meat-filled tamales," are wrapped in plantain leaves and boiled instead of steamed in corn husks. They are heavy, with a lard-infused corn masa and usually more than a dozen other ingredients, such as annatto-rubbed pork or chicken, rice, potatoes, chiles, tomatoes, onions, olives, mint, and dried fruits, among others. In Nicaragua, where they are ubiquitous on Sunday mornings, they are often eaten with bread or tortillas and coffee.

    1 tablespoon pork lard
    6 oz (175 g) pork jowl, cut into 1-inch (2.5-cm) chunks
    2 lb (900 g) pork ribs, deboned and cut into chunks
    1/2 white onion, chopped
    4 garlic cloves, minced
    1 tablespoon annatto paste
    1 tablespoon ground cumin
    1/2 cup/4 fl oz (125 ml) bitter orange juice
    1 cup/8 fl oz (250 ml) water
    12 banana leaves
    2 potatoes, peeled and sliced
    1 white onion, sliced
    6 pitted green olives
    1/2 cup/2 1/4 oz (70 g) prunes, chopped
    1/4 cup/1 oz (30 g) peanuts, shelled
    12 capers
    6–12 congo chiles (or use habanero)
    salt and ground pepper

    For the dough
    7 1/4 cups/2 lb (900 g) *masa harina*
    3 cups/25 fl oz (750 ml) warm water
    1/2 cup/4 fl oz (125 ml) bitter orange juice
    3 cups/1 lb 8 ounces (675 g) pork lard, melted

Heat 1 tablespoon of pork lard a large pan over medium heat and add the pork jowl and ribs. Sear well for about 8 minutes, then add the onion, garlic, annatto paste, cumin, and half of the bitter orange juice. Season with salt and pepper, add the water, cover and reduce the heat to low. Cook slowly for 1 hour or until the meat is tender. Check the seasoning and remove from the heat.

Prepare the dough by placing the *masa harina* in a bowl. Add the warm water and remaining bitter orange juice and knead to mix. Slowly add the melted lard and season with salt, kneading until the dough is smooth and uniform.

Heat the banana leaves lightly over a gas burner for 20 seconds per side while moving them around. Take 2 banana leaves and cross them over each other. Place 3 tablespoons of dough in the center where they meet, and slightly flatten with the back of a spoon. In the middle of the dough, add a piece of rib meat and 2 chunks of pork jowl. Cover with 1 tablespoon of sauce from the pan the pork was cooked in. Next, add 1 slice of potato, and some sliced onion. Continue by adding an olive, a prune, a few peanuts, 2 capers, and 1–2 chiles. Close the tamales by overlapping the leaves, ensuring the ingredients are well enclosed. Tie with a string to keep closed.

Pour about 2 inches (5 cm) of water into a steamer, and bring to a boil. Add the steamer basket (make sure the boiling water doesn't touch the basket), place the *nacatamales* in the basket. Cover and cook over medium heat for 3–4 hours, topping up the hot water every 20 minutes. Remove and let cool for 10 minutes before unwrapping to serve.

Tolima-Style Tamales

Tamales Tolimenses
Colombia

Preparation time: 20 minutes
Cooking time: 4 hours

Makes: 8

Every region of Colombia has a tamal that defines it, often just a subtle variation from one to the other. The tamales from Tolima region are set apart by their use of cooked rice to make a masa that can pocket a mix of meats and vegetables. These tamales are quite similar to the *fiambres* of the adjacent Valle del Cauca region, which also include rice, but all of the ingredients are wrapped within the banana or *bijao* leaf separately, rather than formed into a tamal.

    2 lb (900 g) pork ribs, cut into 2-inch (5-cm) chunks
    8 chicken thighs or legs
    1 lb (450 g) bacon, cut into pieces
    1 tablespoon butter
    5 scallions (spring onions), chopped
    3 garlic cloves, minced
    1/2 cup/3/4 oz (20 g) chopped cilantro (coriander)
    1 teaspoon annatto paste
    3 1/2 cups/1 lb (450 g) corn (maize) flour
    4 3/4 cups/2 lb (900 g) cooked rice
    8 banana leaves, cut into 12-inch (30-cm) squares
    4 potatoes, peeled and sliced 1/2 inch (1 cm) thick
    5 carrots, peeled and sliced 1/2 inch (1 cm) thick
    1 cup/4 1/2 oz (130 g) peas
    5 hard-boiled eggs, sliced
    salt and ground pepper

Put all the meat in a large pan and cover with water. Bring to a boil and simmer for 40 minutes. Remove the meat, then strain the cooking stock and reserve. Cut the ribs and bacon into 1-inch (2.5-cm) cubes and set aside.

In a frying pan, heat the butter over medium heat and sauté the scallions (spring onions) and garlic for 7 minutes. Add the cilantro (coriander) and annatto paste, season with salt and pepper, and set aside.

Place the corn (maize) flour and cooked rice in a bowl, and mix. Slowly add 1 cup/8 fl oz (250 ml) of the reserved cooking stock, while kneading, then add the cooked scallions and garlic and continue kneading.

Heat the banana leaves lightly over a gas burner for 20 seconds per side while moving them around. When all the banana leaves have been warmed, place 2 tablespoons of the dough on each, along with 2 pieces of bacon, 2 pieces of pork rib, and a piece of chicken. Spread the potatoes, carrots, peas, and eggs evenly on each tamal. Cover the mixture with 2 more tablespoons of dough, then bring all the edges of the banana leaf together and tie them with cabuya fiber or a string.

Add the remaining stock and the tamales to a large pan; the liquid must cover the tamales, so if there's not enough, top up with water. Bring to a boil, then lower the heat and cover. Simmer for 3 hours, or until cooked. Serve hot.

Corn

Steamed Corn Rolls

Bollos de mazorca, tamal de elote
Colombia

Preparation time: 5 minutes
Cooking time: 40 minutes　　　　Makes: 4

Using fresh corn, *bollos de mazorca*, a type of tamal from Colombia's Caribbean coast, appear during the harvest season. Steamed in fresh corn husks, they are similar to Andean *humitas* and Brazilian *pamonhas*. They are sold by informal street vendors and in small shops, usually for breakfast. In the city of Barranquilla, they are almost always sold alongside a slice of a regional cheese like *queso costeño*, though elsewhere along the coast you might find them with *suero* (similar to sour cream), fried beef, liver, *chicharrón*, or *huevos pericos* (Scrambled Eggs with Scallions and Tomatoes, page 205). Other variations of bollos, which are also found in neighboring Panama, include *bollos limpios* (made of hominy), *bollos de yuca* (made with cassava), and the *bollos de coco* (made with corn, shredded coconut, and anis).

　　10 ears of corn with husks
　　2 tablespoons sugar
　　½ teaspoon salt
　　2 tablespoons corn (maize) flour, optional
　　butter, and shredded *queso fresco*, to serve

Remove the husks from the corn carefully, in order to keep them whole, then place them in water until use. Cut the kernels off of the corn with a knife and mix them in a food processor with the sugar and salt. If the mix is too watery, add the corn (maize) flour. Strain, reserving only the solid part. Drain the corn husks and dry them.
　　Take one corn husk and place 4 tablespoons of the corn mixture in the middle. Roll the husk and tie a string on each side, securing the dough in the middle. Repeat the process until the dough is finished.
　　Pour about 2 inches (5 cm) of water into a steamer, and bring to a boil. Add the steamer basket (make sure the boiling water doesn't touch the basket), place the *bollos* in the basket and steam for 40 minutes. Remove and serve warm with butter or *queso fresco*.

Piura-Style Green Tamales

Tamales Verdes, tamalitos verdes
Peru

Preparation time: 25 minutes
Cooking time: 1 hour　　　　Makes: 8

Turned green by cilantro that is mixed in with the masa, these smallish tamales originated in Peru's Piura region on the north coast of the country. They are often served alongside other regional dishes like *Seco de cabrito* (Goat Stew, page 334).

　　5 cups/1 lb 10 oz (625 g) fresh corn kernels
　　3 tablespoons chopped cilantro (coriander)
　　1 *ají amarillo*, seeded and chopped
　　2 scallions (spring onions), green part only, chopped
　　3 tablespoons vegetable oil
　　16 green corn husks
　　2 chicken breasts, poached and chopped
　　salt and ground pepper
　　Salsa criolla (Creole Sauce, page 406), to serve

Using a mortar and pestle, mash the corn with the cilantro (coriander), chile, and scallions (spring onions) to a uniform paste. Add the oil and season with salt and pepper.
　　Overlap 2 of the corn husks side by side, and add 2 tablespoons of the corn mixture and 1 tablespoon of the chopped chicken to the middle, then cover with another 2 tablespoons of the corn mixture. Close the husk and seal the tamal with a string. Repeat the process with the rest of the husks and filling.
　　Place the tamales in a pan half filled with water. Bring to a boil, then lower the heat and simmer for 1 hour. Remove the tamales, pat dry, and open.
　　Serve with the *Salsa criolla* on the side.

Michoacán Triangular Tamales

Corundas
Mexico

Preparation time: 20 minutes
Cooking time: 1 hour 25 minutes,   Makes: 15
plus 20 minutes resting

These smallish, triangular tamales are found mostly in the northern reaches of the state of Michoacán, and their origins can be traced back to the Purépecha empire. The name is derived from the Purépecha word *k'urhaunda*, which means tamal, and *corundas* were served for Purépecha nobility during ceremonies. In Michoacán, they are prepared in someone's honor on their passing, as well as for Día de los Muertos. *Corundas* are wrapped with the leaves of the corn plant stem, not the husks, and they can be made free of fillings, or stuffed with beans or chiles. They are often served alongside pork, mole, or *salsa roja*.

1 lb 8 ounces (680 g) lard
2 lb (900 g) fresh Corn Masa (page 123)
1 tablespoon baking powder
1½ teaspoons salt
½ cup/4 fl oz (120 ml) water
15 milpa (fresh green corn) leaves, cleaned and dried
¾ cup/6 oz (180 g) *crema mexicana* (or use sour cream), to serve

For the sauce
1 tablespoon lard
1 onion, chopped
1 garlic clove, minced
3 poblano chiles, seeded and cut into thin strips
4 tomatoes, roasted, peeled, seeded, and blended to a purée
½ cup/4 fl oz (120 ml) chicken stock

Start by preparing the sauce. Heat the lard in a frying pan and sauté the onions for 5 minutes over medium heat, then add the garlic and chiles. Cook for 8 minutes, then add the tomato purée and chicken stock. Simmer for 10 minutes or until reduced by half. Set aside and keep warm.

For the dough, beat the lard with a whisk for 5 minutes or until smooth. Add the masa and knead well for 5 minutes. Dissolve the baking powder and salt in the water and slowly pour it into the dough. Continue kneading for a further 5 minutes or until you get a soft dough. Separate the dough into 15 equal pieces and shape each into a small ball. Take one milpa leaf from the thickest part and fold it to make a cone. Place one masa portion inside and press it slightly. Fold by rolling up the sides while keeping a triangle shape. In the last fold, tuck the edge into one of the folding sides to close it. Repeat with the remaining dough and leaves.

Pour about 2 inches (5 cm) of water into a steamer, and bring to a boil. Add the steamer basket (make sure the water doesn't touch the basket), place the tamales in the basket and cook for 1 hour, or until the milpa leaves easily come off the dough. Remove from the heat and rest for 20 minutes before serving.

Once warm, transfer to a plate. Serve with the warm sauce and *crema mexicana*.

Small Corn Tamales

Humitas, pamonhas, uchepos
Brazil, Mexico, Peru

Preparation time: 15 minutes
Cooking time: 1 hour 5 minutes   Makes: 6

Often sold from baskets set up on sidewalks, *humitas* are one of the staples of Andean life. Prepared *dulce* (sweet) or *salada* (salty), *humitas* can be cooked in boiling water, baked in an adobe oven, or steamed. To make *humitas dulces*, just swap the onion, chile paste, and pepper for a few tablespoons of sugar. Inca Garcilaso de la Vega noted in his book *Comentarios Reales de los Incas* (1609) that corn would be ground on a *batán* (grinding stone) to make *humitas* (he spelled them *humintas*), which were eaten during celebrations. However, the exact same recipe would be prepared for sacrifices, though it would then be called *sancu*.

They are quite similar to several other preparations in the region. In Brazil there are *pamonhas*, which may add shredded meats or come in sweeter versions with coconut milk. They are often eaten at Festas Juninas celebrations honoring the birth of John the Baptist. In the Mexican state of Michoacán, *uchepos* are usually served with salsa verde and *cotija* cheese.

4 tablespoons lard
½ cup/2 oz (60 g) chopped white onion
3 tablespoons *ají amarillo* paste
kernels from 4 ears of corn
½ cup/4 fl oz (120 ml) whole milk
6 corn husks
salt and ground pepper
Salsa criolla (Creole Sauce, page 406), to serve

Heat the lard in a frying pan over medium heat. Add the onion and the *ají amarillo* paste and sauté for 5 minutes. Take off the heat.

In a food processor, blend the corn kernels with the milk and place in a bowl with the onion mixture. Season with salt and pepper and mix well.

Take a corn husk and place 1 tablespoon of the corn mixture in the middle. Close the husk on the right side, then the left side, then close from the bottom and top parts. Tie the *humita* with a string, then repeat with the remaining husks and corn filling.

Place the *humitas* in a pan half filled with water. Bring to a boil, then lower the heat, cover, and simmer for 1 hour. Remove the humitas and pat dry. Open and serve warm with the *Salsa criolla* on the side.

Small Corn Tamales

Small, Sweet Corn Tamales

Tamalitos de elote
Guatemala, Honduras

Preparation time: 5 minutes
Cooking time: 55 minutes   Makes: 10

These small, slightly sweet tamales are usually prepared during the corn harvest season.

    kernels from 10 ears of corn
    ½ cup/2½ oz (70 g) corn (maize) flour
    2 cups/16 fl oz (475 ml) milk
    4 oz (120 g) lard
    1 teaspoon salt
    ¼ cup/1¾ oz (50 g) sugar
    12 corn husks, soaked for 30 minutes in warm water

Place the corn, corn (maize) flour and half the milk in a blender and mix on medium speed to a soft and uniform batter.
    In a pan, melt the lard over medium heat, then add the corn mixture and stir. Add the salt and sugar, and remaining milk, and continue cooking for 10 minutes, stirring frequently, or until all the ingredients are blended and there is not much liquid remaining.
    Dry the corn husks, and place 2 tablespoons of the corn mixture in the middle of 10 husks. Fold in half, then fold the sides to the middle. Tie with a string to seal.
    Place the remaining corn husks in the bottom of a pan, then place the tamales in a circle around the edge. Pour enough water into the pan to half cover the tamales. Bring to a boil then lower the heat and simmer for 40 minutes. Remove from the water and pat dry. Open and serve hot.

Tortillas

Making corn tortillas from masa is quite straightforward: take a bit of masa with your hands, roll it into a ball, flatten it, and then cook it.

As always, everyone has their own technique. It's possible to flatten masa with your hands, which is generally more common with thicker recipes like *sopes* and *pupusas*, though those who make tortillas regularly usually invest in a tabletop tortilla press (the heavier the better), which can flatten the masa into a desired thickness.

If you don't have a tortilla press, it's no problem. You can flatten tortillas by laying a sheet of plastic (like half of a plastic baggy/food bag) or parchment paper above and below the masa and use a rolling pin, or even the bottom of a pan, to flatten it. As for the size, they can range from small, about 3 inches (7.5 cm) or so for tacos, to large, 12-inch (30-cm) tortillas for *tlayudas*.

Once your tortillas are ready, you just need to cook them. The most traditional way is on a *comal*, a round thin pan that can be heated to a high temperature. Cast-iron pans and skillets (frying pans) will also work. Preheat the *comal*, add your tortilla and cook for about 30 seconds per side, or until they are dried. Brown spots and puffed up tortillas are just fine.

As an alternative, there has been a rise of *tortillerías* in Mexico, as well as in the United States, with stone mills that ensure consistently perfect tortillas, often made from landrace corn. Most will even sell you high-quality masa to make the tortillas yourself.

Also, wheat flour tortillas are common in the northern Mexican states of Sonora, Sinaloa, and Chihuahua.

Corn Tortillas

Tortillas de maíz
Mexico

Preparation time: 10 minutes
Cooking time: 8 minutes per tortilla   Makes: 20–40

    1 lb 4 oz (680 g) fresh Corn Masa (page 123)

Separate the masa into small balls and use a tortilla press to flatten them to the desired diameter and thickness.
    Heat a *comal* or large frying pan over medium heat, add a tortilla and cook for about 30 seconds each side, or until brown air pockets appear. Cover with a tea towel to keep warm while you cook the rest.

Flour Tortillas

Tortillas de harina
Mexico

Preparation time: 10 minutes
Cooking time: 15–20 minutes   Makes: 8–10

    2½ cups/12 oz (340 g) all-purpose (plain) flour
    1 teaspoon salt
    ½ teaspoon baking powder
    ⅓ cup/2½ oz (75 g) lard
    1 cup/8 fl oz (250 ml) warm water

Mix the dry ingredients in a bowl. Add the lard and knead with your hands. Slowly pour in the warm water (you might not need all of it), kneading until it forms a soft dough. Separate the dough into 8 equal-sized pieces, shape each piece into a ball, and press them using a tortilla press, flattening into the desired diameter.
    Heat a *comal* or large cast-iron skillet (frying pan) over medium heat, add a tortilla, and cook for about 30 seconds each side, or until brown spots and air pockets appear. Cover with a tea towel to keep warm while you cook the rest.

Egg-Stuffed Tortillas Dipped in Squash Seed and Tomato Sauce

Papadzules
Mexico

Preparation time: 30 minutes
Cooking time: 40 minutes

Serves: 10

This enchilada-like dish from Mexico's Yucatán peninsula is one of the hallmarks of Mayan cuisine. There is debate as to the etymology of the name. It is said to refer to "food of the lords," though it could also be derived from the Mayan word *papak*, which roughly means to smear and drench. What exactly the pre-Columbian preparation was is also a mystery. The thickness of the tortillas has been debated, as has the filling, for which chicken eggs were unavailable prior to the arrival of the Spanish. It has been suggested that the Mayans may have used turkey, duck, or iguana eggs for the filling, or crab meat, or *chaya* (tree spinach).

4 tomatoes
1 habanero chile
2 tablespoons corn oil
2 onions, chopped
2 cups/16 fl oz (475 ml) water
½ cup/1 oz (30 g) chopped epazote
12 oz (350 g) *pepitas* (hulled squash or seeds, ideally green)
4 tablespoons vegetable oil
24 x 5-inch (13-cm) Corn Tortillas (page 136)
12 hard-boiled eggs, grated
salt and ground pepper

Place the tomatoes on a dry, hot frying pan over medium heat. Roast, turning frequently, until the skins are black and blistered. Remove from the heat and let cool, then peel off the skin. Place the tomatoes in a blender with the habanero and blend until smooth. Strain into a bowl to remove the seeds.

Heat the corn oil in a frying pan, add the onions and cook for a few minutes over medium heat. Add the chile and tomato purée, season with salt and pepper, and remove from the heat.

Boil the water in a small pan, add some salt and the epazote, and cook for 10 minutes. Remove from the heat and set aside.

In a frying pan, toast the seeds over high heat for about 3 minutes. They should inflate, but not brown. Allow to cool. Place in a food processor or spice grinder and process until they form a thick, shiny paste, scraping down the sides as needed. Add the paste to a bowl and mix with the epazote and its cooking water. Using a spatula or whisk, mix to a smooth, thick sauce.

Heat the vegetable oil in a frying pan over medium heat. Fry the tortillas on both sides until golden brown, then dip the tortillas in the pumpkin seed sauce, ensuring that they are covered on all sides.

Add some grated egg to the center of each, roll them up, and place in a serving dish. Pour over the tomato salsa and sprinkle the remaining grated egg on top.

Fried Tortillas with Beans and Cheese

Catrachitas
Honduras

Preparation time: 10 minutes
Cooking time: 15 minutes

Serves: 6

Catrachitas, often served in a clay pot, could be called Honduran nachos. They are easy to prepare and often set out on a tray during parties and get-togethers. Another variation are *chilindrinas*, where the tortillas are cut into strips and fried, then topped with cheese and tomato sauce.

2 cups/15 oz (420 g) cooked red silk beans, cooking water reserved
½ red onion, roughly chopped
2 tablespoons lard
3 cups/75 fl oz (750 ml) vegetable oil
12 x 5-inch (13-cm) Corn Tortillas (page 136)
8 oz (225 g) *queso seco*, shredded (or use *queso fresco* or cotija)
salt

Blend the cooked beans in a food processor with the chopped onion. Heat the lard in a frying pan over medium heat, add the beans and onions, season with salt, and cook for 2–3 minutes until soft. Remove from the heat. You can add a little of the bean cooking water if necessary.

In a separate medium frying pan, heat the oil and fry the tortillas one at a time for about 30 seconds on each side, or until golden brown. Transfer to a plate lined with paper towels to absorb any excess oil.

Spread the bean mixture over the tortillas and sprinkle with the shredded cheese to serve.

Rolled Tacos

Tacos dorados, flautas, taquitos
Mexico

Preparation time: 30 minutes
Cooking time: 30 minutes
Serves: 6

The terms *tacos dorados*, *flautas*, and *taquitos* tend to be used interchangeably, though they do have subtle differences, which might change by the region. While all are made of rolled and fried stuffed tortillas, *flautas* tend to be made with larger tortillas than *tacos dorados*, resulting in a more flute-like shape. *Taquitos*, on the other hand, was a name given to this preparation in the southwestern United States. The chimichanga is also quite similar, though made with wheat tortillas.

4 cups/32 fl oz (950 ml) vegetable oil, plus
1 tablespoon for cooking
½ large onion, diced
2 chicken breasts, cooked and shredded
6 x 5-inch (13-cm) Corn Tortillas (page 136)
½ cup/2 oz (60 g) shredded cheese
salt

To serve
½ lettuce, chopped
½ cup/2 oz (60 g) shredded cheese
Pico de gallo (page 404)
⅓ cup/2½ fl oz (80 ml) cream
hot sauce

Heat the 1 tablespoon of oil in a pan over medium heat, then add the onion and sauté for 10 minutes until browned. Add the shredded chicken and cook for 5 minutes. Add salt to taste and set aside.

Warm the tortillas, add a scoop of the chicken mixture and some cheese to each, then roll up.

Heat the oil in a medium pan to 350°F/180°C. Lower the *flautas* into the oil with the seam side down and fry for about 5–7 minutes, or until crispy and golden brown, turning a few times. Place on a plate lined with paper towels to absorb any excess oil.

Serve with chopped lettuce, shredded cheese, *Pico de gallo*, cream, and hot sauce.

Yucatecan Fried Tortillas

Panuchos
Mexico

Preparation time: 15 minutes
Cooking time: 45 minutes
Serves: 6

These crispy fried tortillas are schmeared with refried black beans and topped with slaw and pickled red onions. They originated in Yucatecan markets sometime in the early 1900s, where vendors would make use of day-old beans by puréeing them and slathering them on fried tortillas with hard-boiled egg and some onions. As their popularity grew, more focused *panucherías* opened up around the region, and the toppings expanded to include things like *Pavo en escabeche oriental* (Yucatán-Style Turkey and Onion Stew, page 312) or shredded chicken.

1 red onion, thinly sliced
¼ teaspoon black peppercorns
¼ teaspoon cumin seeds
½ teaspoon dried oregano
2 garlic cloves, finely chopped
⅓ cup/2½ fl oz (75 ml) cider vinegar
6 x 5-inch (13-cm) Corn Tortillas (page 136)
3 cups/1 lb 2 oz (500 g) cooked black beans
⅔ cup/5 fl oz (150 ml) vegetable oil
1 lb (450 g) Mexican chorizo
salt and ground pepper

To serve
3 tomatoes, peeled and chopped
2 avocados, peeled, pitted, and mashed
1 lettuce, finely shredded
2 jalapeño peppers, cored, seeded, and chopped

First, pickle the onion slices. Place in a pan, cover with water and a pinch of salt, bring to a boil, cook for 1 minute, then drain. Grind the black peppercorns and cumin seeds together in a mortar, then add them to a small pan with the oregano, garlic, vinegar, drained onions, and ¼ teaspoon of salt. Pour in enough water to just cover, bring to a boil and cook for 3 minutes. Set aside until ready to serve.

Heat a large frying pan over medium-high heat. Add one tortilla at a time and flip frequently until it becomes stiff and leathery, puffing in the middle. Using a small knife, cut along the sides of each cooked tortilla, about a third of the way around. Carefully open the pocket, trying not to tear it. Place 1 tablespoon of beans inside each pocket and spread them around by pressing down gently on the top of each tortilla.

Pour the oil into a large frying pan over medium-high heat. One at a time, add the stuffed tortillas and cook on each side for about 2–3 minutes, or until crisp.

Meanwhile, cook the chorizo in another frying pan over medium heat for 8 minutes, turning occasionally. Remove and coarsely chop.

Place the *panuchos* on a plate and sprinkle with the chorizo and drained pickled onions. Serve with chopped tomatoes, mashed avocado, shredded lettuce, and chopped jalapeños.

Corn

Yucatecan Fried Tortillas

Honduran Tacos

Baleadas
Honduras

Preparation time: 10 minutes
Cooking time: 15 minutes

Makes: 10

In El Salvador there are *pupusas*. In Mexico there are tacos. In Honduras there are *baleadas*. The simple version consists of a flour tortilla (though sometimes corn) that has been warmed on a grill, then slathered in refried red beans and a bit of cheese, then folded over. *Baleadas* are an any-time-of-the-day snack. You can have one for breakfast and add eggs or chorizo. Usually they are served from *casetas*, streetside stalls often set near night spots and areas of high pedestrian traffic. In urban areas of Honduras like San Pedro Sula and Tegucigalpa, fast-food *baleada* restaurants offer dozens of toppings to fill "Super Baleadas," such as avocado slices, plantains, bell peppers, onions, shredded pork, or jalapeños.

> 10 Flour Tortillas (page 136)
> 1 lb (450 g) refried red silk beans
> 10 tablespoons *mantequilla blanca* (or use sour cream)
> 8 oz (225 g) *queso duro*, shredded (or use *cotija*)
>
> To serve, optional
> sliced avocado
> scrambled eggs
> chorizo

Heat the tortillas in a hot frying pan or grill (barbecue). Spread refried beans on top, followed by a tablespoon of *mantequilla blanca*, a few spoonfuls of the shredded cheese, and any other ingredients you would like to add. Fold in half and serve.

Oaxacan Corn Flatbread

Tlayuda, clayuda
Mexico

Preparation time: 20 minutes
Cooking time: 1 hour

Serves: 6

Some of the most flavorful ingredients of any place in Mexico, if not the world, hail from Oaxaca. *Tlayudas* serve as a vehicle for those ingredients. Aside from the masa that the large, thin tortillas are made out of, the *tlayuda* serves as a base for the region's chiles, cheeses, and meats. Like a taco, there is no firm idea of toppings or how it's served. They can be eaten open like a pizza or folded in half like a quesadilla.

> 1 tablespoon *asiento* (unrefined lard)
> 3 cups/1 lb 10 oz (750 g) Refried Black Beans (page 172)
> 1 garlic clove, finely chopped
> ½ white onion, coarsely chopped
> 2 *pasilla* chiles, seeded and coarsely chopped
> 1 teaspoon ground cumin
> 1 lb (450 g) *tasajo* (dried beef), cut into strips
> 1 tablespoon vinegar
> 6 x 12-inch (30-cm) Corn Tortillas (page 136)
> 1 cup/4 oz (120 g) crumbled *queso Oaxaca*
> salt and ground pepper
>
> To serve
> shredded cabbage
> 2 avocados, peeled, pitted, and sliced
> ½ cup/2 oz (60 g) crumbled *queso fresco*
> 4 radishes, sliced and quartered
> any red chile sauce

Heat the lard in a frying pan over medium heat. Add the refried black beans, garlic, chopped onion, chiles, and cumin, season with salt and pepper, and sauté for 7 minutes.

Mix the *tasajo* (dried beef) with the vinegar in a small pan. Season with salt and pepper and cook over medium heat for 10 minutes, until tender.

Heat a *comal* or frying pan over medium-high heat. Once hot, add the tortillas one at a time and warm for 2–3 minutes, then flip it over and spread the beans, *queso Oaxaca*, and *tasajo* on top. Cook for a further 5–10 minutes until the toppings are hot and the tortilla is crispy around the edges.

Top with shredded cabbage, a few avocado and radish slices, and some crumbled *queso fresco*. Serve as is or folded, with chile sauce on the side.

Nicaraguan Tostadas

Repocheta
Nicaragua

Preparation time: 15 minutes,
plus 1 hour resting
Cooking time: 40 minutes

Serves: 10

These fried tortillas topped with beans, cheese, and slaw are a typical Nicaraguan street food. Often, the tortillas are fried in advance and can be slathered with toppings in less than a minute. They can also be made with fresh masa, formed into thick patties and then fried.

2 cups/4 oz (120 g) sliced white cabbage
2 tomatoes, peeled and diced
1/4 white onion, chopped
2 tablespoons vinegar
1 tablespoon olive oil
vegetable oil, for deep-frying
10 x 5-inch (13-cm) Corn Tortillas (page 136)
2 cups/1 lb 2 oz (500 g) Refried Black Beans (page 172), warm
1 cup/3½ oz (100 g) shredded *queso fresco*
salt
crema mexicana (or use sour cream), to serve

Mix the cabbage, tomatoes, and onion in a bowl. Season with the vinegar, olive oil, and some salt. Let rest for 1 hour, draining just before serving.

Pour enough vegetable oil for deep-frying into a large, heavy pan, making sure it is no more than two-thirds full. Heat to 350°F/177°C. Fry the tortillas in batches for 4 minutes each side or until crispy. Place on a plate lined with paper towels to absorb any excess oil.

To serve, spread the tortillas with refried beans. Top with the cheese and the drained cabbage salad, then drizzle with *crema mexicana* to serve.

Guanajuato-Style Enchiladas

Enchiladas mineras
Mexico

Preparation time: 20 minutes
Cooking time: 45 minutes

Makes: 16

The name is derived from the Spanish word *enchilar*, which means "to add chile to," and in their most basic form, they are just tortillas dipped in sauce. A recipe for enchiladas was included in the first Mexican cookbook, *El Cocinero Mexicano*, published in 1831, and today they are a dish found across the globe. In most recipes, they are rolled and stuffed, and can use a wide variety of fillings and sauces, including, meat, chicken, cheese, mole, chiles, and *Salsa verde* (Spicy Tomatillo Salsa, page 406). This particular recipe comes from the state of Guanajuato, and dips the tortillas in the sauce before frying, giving them a unique texture and flavor.

3 *guajillo* chiles, seeded and halved lengthways
3 *ancho* chiles, seeded and halved lengthways
2 red bell peppers, cored, seeded, and diced
2 garlic cloves, roasted
3 tomatoes, roasted and peeled
2 cups/16 fl oz (475 ml) water
1 tablespoon dried oregano
vegetable oil, for frying
16 x 5-inch (13-cm) Corn Tortillas (page 136)
2 chicken breasts, poached and shredded
½ white onion, chopped
1 cup/4 oz (120 g) crumbled *queso fresco*
salt and ground pepper
cilantro (coriander), to serve

Toast the chiles and bell peppers in a frying pan for 4 minutes on each side, then add to a food processor with the roasted garlic, tomatoes, and measured water, and process to a sauce. Add the oregano and season with salt and pepper.

Heat 2 tablespoons of oil in a frying pan over high heat. Dip the tortillas in the red sauce, one at a time, then fry in the oil for about 45 seconds each side. They should be lightly fried, not crispy. Keep the cooked ones warm while you cook the rest, adding new oil every three tortillas.

To each cooked tortilla, add 1 tablespoon of shredded chicken, some onion and cheese, then roll them up and add some more of the sauce. Sprinkle with cilantro (coriander) and serve.

Braised Meat and Melted Cheese Tacos

Gringa ⬚
Mexico

Preparation time: 30 minutes, plus at least 8 hours resting
Cooking time: 50 minutes

Serves: 4

A Mexico City taqueria favorite, the *gringa* is a perfect combination of braised meat and melted cheese. Urban legend says that an American girl, a "gringa," asked for a white (flour) tortilla with melted cheese and the preparation caught on. Some taqueros will melt the cheese right on the grill while they cook the meat, though others make it more like a quesadilla.

    7 small *guajillo* chiles, seeded
    1 white onion, quartered
    2 garlic cloves, peeled
    1 teaspoon dried oregano
    1 teaspoon dried cumin
    1 tablespoon annatto paste
    1 clove
    ½ cup/4 fl oz (120 ml) sour orange juice
    ⅓ cup/2½ fl oz (75 ml) apple cider vinegar
    1 lb (450 g) beef loin or pork leg, cleaned and minced (finely chopped)
    2 tablespoons butter or vegetable oil
    8 Flour Tortillas (page 136)
    10 oz (275 g) *queso Oaxaca*, shredded
    salt and ground pepper

    To serve
    ½ white onion, sliced
    1 cup/1½ oz (40 g) chopped cilantro (coriander)
    1 cup/5 oz (150 g) chopped pineapple
    lime wedges

Bring a small pan of water to a boil. Take off the heat, add the chiles, and leave for 8 minutes, then drain, transfer to a bowl of iced water, drain, and set aside.

To make the marinade, place the onion, garlic, and chiles in a blender or food processor. Add the oregano, cumin, annatto paste, clove, orange juice, and vinegar. Season with salt and pepper then blend until smooth.

Place the meat in a large bowl and cover with the marinade. Cover and let rest for 8 hours or overnight in the refrigerator.

Heat 1 tablespoon of the butter or oil in a large cast-iron pan over high heat. Sear the meat with the marinade for 10 minutes, stirring, until evenly browned.

Spread 1 tablespoon of the meat on a tortilla, sprinkle with shredded *queso Oaxaca*, and then cover with another tortilla. Repeat with all the tortillas.

Heat the remaining butter or oil in a large frying pan. Fry the *gringas* one at a time, for 3 minutes each side, or until browned and the cheese is melted and gooey.

Cut each *gringa* into quarters and serve immediately with the onion slices, cilantro (coriander), pineapple, and lime wedges.

Gallos

In Costa Rica, a taco is called a *gallo* or *gallito*. The white or yellow corn tortillas, not any different to average Mexican 5-inch (13-cm) corn tortillas, are filled with typical Costa Rican ingredients like *Picadillo de arracache* (Minced Arracacha, page 93), *queso Turrialba*, or heart of palm.

Huitlacoche

In many parts of the world, *huitlacoche* (*Ustilago maydis*), a fungus that causes corn kernels to swell up into blue-black galls, is seen as a nuisance. However, in Mexico it is seen as a delicacy and has been used since the time of the Aztecs, if not longer. For it to be edible, *huitlacoche*, also spelled *cuitlacoche*, needs the galls to be harvested within a few weeks of the infection taking place, while they still retain moisture and delicate, earthy flavors. It can be consumed fresh, puréed for soups and sauces, or sautéed and used in tacos and quesadillas.

Corn Fungus Quesadillas

Quesadillas de huitlacoche
Mexico

Preparation time: 25 minutes
Cooking time: 20 minutes

Serves: 6

Huitlacoche can be substituted for mushrooms in many recipes. There may not be a better use for their subtle smoky, earthy flavors than paired with melted cheese, especially inside a quesadilla.

    2 tablespoons vegetable oil
    ½ cup/2 oz (60 g) finely chopped onion
    2 garlic cloves, finely chopped
    ¼ cup/¾ oz (20 g) finely chopped epazote
    7 oz (200 g) *huitlacoche*
    6 x 9-inch (23-cm) Corn Tortillas (page 136)
    1 cup/4 oz (120 g) shredded *queso Oaxaca*
    salt

Heat 1 tablespoon of the oil in a pan over medium heat. Add the onion, garlic, and epazote and sauté for 4 minutes. Add the *huitlacoche* and cook for a further 1 minute. Remove from the heat and season with salt to taste.

Spread each tortilla with the *huitlacoche* mixture and the shredded cheese. Fold to close. Heat the remaining tablespoon of oil in a medium frying pan and fry the quesadillas until golden brown on both sides.

Braised Meat and Melted Cheese Tacos

Garden Vegetables

Beneath the shadows of the Santa María and Santiaguito volcanoes in Guatemala's Western Highlands, families have gathered in a cemetery near Quetzaltenango for Día de los Santos, or All Saints' Day. With them, they have brought *fiambre*, a cold salad that may have as many as 50 different ingredients, and they unpack it around the graves of their loved ones, decorated with flowers and candles. *Fiambre* is said to have grown out of the tradition of bringing the favorite foods of the deceased to a cemetery. The feast among families resulted in all sorts of different foods being prepared, so *fiambre* was a way to combine them all together.

For much of the week before the making of *fiambre*, countless members of the family played a role in its making. Someone goes to the market to buy pacaya palm flowers, peas, carrots, green beans, and cauliflower. Others cook them, chop them, or pickle them. Someone slaughters a chicken. Someone prepares a vinegar-based dressing, called *caldillo*. The recipe gets passed down from generation to generation, always changing yet somehow always the same.

At the cemetery they fly kites and speak of memories. They pass plates around and visit with other friends and neighbors. They taste *fiambre* made by their neighbors, and share some of their own. The dead are there too, taking it all in. They'll do the same the next day, for *Día de los Muertos* too. *Fiambre* is the tie, the thing that connects them all together, through life and death.

Guatemalan Cold Salad

Fiambre
Guatemala

Preparation time: 25 minutes,
plus overnight chilling
Serves: 10

Every Guatemalan family has their own version of *fiambre*, which translates roughly to "served cold." Some leave out the meat or beets, while others might add in sardines. If there's something in the recipe that you dislike, leave it out. If there's something you want to add, go right ahead. Some like to prepare *fiambre desarmado*, where the ingredients are served separately.

> 5 carrots, peeled, cut into ½-inch (1-cm) cubes, and cooked
> 1 lb (450 g) green beans, cooked and drained
> 8 oz (225 g) peas, cooked and drained
> 1 red cabbage, shredded and blanched
> 1 white cabbage, shredded and blanched
> 1 cauliflower, cut into small florets and blanched
> 3 beets (beetroot), baked and sliced
> 2 *pacayas* (palm blossoms), chopped
> 8 oz (225 g) Brussels sprouts, cooked and drained
> 3 chiles, chopped
> 12 green olives, pitted
> ½ cup/1¾ oz (50 g) baby corn, pickled
> 1½ cups/8 oz (225 g) cooked white beans
> 1½ cups/8 oz (225 g) cooked red beans
> 1½ cups/7½ oz (210 g) cooked chickpeas
> 4 blood sausages, cut into small pieces
> 4 chorizo *colorado* (red chorizos)
> 1 lb (450 g) cecina (smoked and salt-cured beef), cut into ½-inch (1-cm) cubes
> 4 chicken breasts, cooked and shredded
>
> For the dressing
> 2 cups/16 fl oz (475 ml) chicken stock
> 1 hard-boiled egg
> 2 chiles
> juice of 8 bitter oranges
> 4 tablespoons mustard
> ½ cup/4 fl oz (120 ml) red vinegar
> 2 tablespoons olive oil
> ½ teaspoon sugar
> ½ teaspoon salt
>
> To serve
> 1 lettuce, leaves separated
> 8 oz (225 g) sliced ham
> 8 oz (225 g) cheddar cheese, sliced
> 8 oz (225 g) *queso fresco*, crumbled

For the dressing, put the stock, hard-boiled egg, chiles, bitter orange juice, mustard, vinegar, olive oil, sugar, and salt in a blender, and process. Strain.
 Combine all the cooked and prepared vegetables, and legumes (pulses) in an extra-large bowl or tray and coat with the dressing. Cover and refrigerate overnight.
 To serve, mix the meats into the dressed vegetables. On a large serving plate, place the lettuce on the bottom, then spread the salad on top and decorate with the ham and cheese slices. Finish by sprinkling the *queso fresco* on top. Serve chilled.

Toasted Okra

Quiabos tostados
Brazil

Preparation time: 20 minutes
Cooking time: 25 minutes
Serves: 4

Okra, brought to Brazil from West Africa during the slave trade, is eaten throughout the country. If you have fresh okra, just picked up from a farmers' market, this is a great way of preparing it. The secret is to simply not overcook the okra, so it stays crisp and doesn't become slimy.

> 1 lb (450 g) okra
> juice of 1 lime
> 3 tablespoons olive oil
> 1 onion, chopped
> 1 garlic clove, minced
> salt and ground pepper

Wash the okra, then mix with the lime juice in a bowl and set aside for 15 minutes. Rinse under cold water, then slice each okra lengthways.
 Heat the oil in a frying pan and sauté the onion and garlic for 7 minutes, until the onion is transparent. Add the okra and cook for about 8–10 minutes, or until lightly charred, turning occasionally. Season with salt and pepper. Serve.

Chilean Mixed Pickles

Pichanga fría
Chile

Preparation time: 10 minutes,
plus overnight chilling
Serves: 8

Pichangas were created by butcher shops wanting to use some of the leftover bits of pork they couldn't sell. They diced them up, mixed them with cheese and pickles and sold them directly to customers to eat with toothpicks or forks. They have become a common bar snack in the *picadas* of Santiago, to be picked at alongside a beer before the larger plates come. In some markets and butcher shops you'll find buckets filled with *pichanga* that gets scooped out and sold by weight.
 In southern Chile, a hot version of *pichanga* is served over French fries, similar to the *Chorrillana* (Chilean Disco Fries, page 88).

> 7 oz (200 g) assorted pitted olives
> 7 oz (200 g) assorted pickled vegetables: onions, cauliflower, carrots
> 7 oz (200 g) ham, cubed
> 7 oz (200 g) mortadella or beef bologna, cubed
> 7 oz (200 g) cheese, cubed
> optional: roasted tomatoes, fresh carrots, diced and boiled potatoes

Mix everything in a bowl. Cover and refrigerate overnight, then serve with fresh bread.

Garden Vegetables

Toasted Okra

Stuffed Pacaya Palm Flowers

Rellenos de pacaya, envueltos de pacaya
El Salvador, Guatemala

Preparation time: 10 minutes
Cooking time: 30 minutes
Serves: 4

Resembling long strings of baby corn, the clusters of flowers of the pacaya palm (*Chamaedorea tepejilote*) are a delicacy in much of Central America. They are sometimes used in salads, but the most common preparation is to stuff them and fry them in an egg batter. Sometimes they are covered in tomato sauce.

> 3 cups/25 fl oz (750 ml) water
> 4 pacaya palm flowers, ideally fresh
> 4 oz (120 g) *quesillo* cheese, shredded (or use mozzarella)
> 2 oz (60 g) *crema Salvadoreña* (or use sour cream)
> 2 eggs
> 2 tablespoons flour
> 2 tablespoons vegetable oil
> salt

Pour the water into a small pan, add salt, and bring to a boil. Drop the pacayas in the boiling water and cook for about 5 minutes, then remove and pat dry. If using canned or preserved pacayas, skip this step.

Once the pacayas are cool, cut them almost entirely in half, leaving them connected near the stem. Take a quarter of the cheese, squeeze it together and place in the middle of the strings of each pacaya, using a little bit of *crema* to make the cheese mixture stick to the pacaya better.

In a small bowl, beat the eggs, add the flour and a pinch of salt, and mix.

Heat the oil in a medium frying pan over medium heat. Dunk the *pacayas* in the egg mixture, then add to the pan and fry until golden brown on both sides. Transfer to a plate lined with paper towels, to absorb excess oil, then serve.

Braised Peas with Eggs

Colchón de arvejas
Argentina

Preparation time: 5 minutes
Cooking time: 25 minutes
Serves: 6

While it's often served as a side dish in Argentina, *colchón de arvejas* is meaty and filling enough for an entire meal.

> 2 cups/9 oz (260 g) peas
> 2 tablespoons olive oil
> 3 onions, chopped
> 1 garlic clove, minced
> 1 leek, chopped
> ³/₄ lb (340 g) smoked bacon lardons
> 6 eggs
> salt and ground pepper

Cook the peas in boiling, salted water until tender, then drain.

Add the oil to a frying pan over medium heat, sauté the onions, garlic, leek, and bacon until the onion is transparent. Add the peas, lower the heat, and season with salt and pepper. Press the peas with a wooden spoon, then break the eggs on top. Cover the pan and cook until the eggs are set. Serve as a side or with slices of toasted bread.

October Stew

Jopara kesu, Yopará
Argentina, Paraguay

Preparation time: 10 minutes, plus 8 hours soaking
Cooking time: 40 minutes
Serves: 4

Meaning "mixing" in Guaraní, also referring to the combination of Spanish and Guaraní that is spoken in Paraguay, *jopará* is a stew of different vegetables and legumes from the Old World and the New. It's famously cooked every October 1st in Paraguay and northern Argentina, for good luck, in hope of scaring away *Karaí Octubre*, a mythological creature with a straw hat and a bag full of misery. Some families cook *jopará* outside, in front of their homes, to show *Karaí* they have enough food and won't partake in his misery.

> 1½ cups/10 oz (280 g) dried hominy
> 1½ cups/9 oz (250 g) dried white beans
> 4 tablespoons vegetable oil
> 1 white onion, chopped
> 4 garlic cloves, minced
> 1 red bell pepper, cored, seeded, and diced
> 1¼ cups/10 fl oz (300 ml) milk
> salt
> *queso Paraguay*, shredded, to serve

Soak the hominy and beans for 8 hours in cold water. Drain and place in a medium pan with enough water to cover by ½ inch (1 cm). Cook for about 40 minutes over medium heat.

Meanwhile, in a frying pan, heat the oil over medium-high heat, add the onion, garlic, and bell pepper and sauté for 7 minutes, or until soft and the onion is browned. When the beans and hominy are about half way cooked (so after 20 minutes), add the sautéed vegetables to the pan, and season with salt. Cook until the beans and corn are completely cooked, adding the milk 10 minutes before they are ready.

Serve hot, with the cheese sprinkled on top.

Braised Peas with Eggs

Chilean Summer Stew

Porotos granados
Chile

Preparation time: 20 minutes,
plus overnight soaking
Cooking time: 1 hour

Serves: 8–10

Straight from the central Chilean countryside, this light stew uses all pre-Columbian ingredients and has probably existed in a similar form long before the arrival of the West. It's most common during the summer, after the squash and corn harvest.

  2 cups/12 oz (350 g) dried cranberry (borlotti) beans
  3 tablespoons vegetable oil
  1 medium white onion, finely chopped
  1 green bell pepper, cored, seeded, and finely chopped
  1 red bell pepper, cored, seeded, and finely chopped
  3 medium tomatoes, peeled, seeded, and finely diced
  2 tablespoons paprika
  2 cups/9 oz (250 g) fresh corn kernels
  1 cup/8 fl oz (250 ml) blended corn kernels
  1 cup/4½ oz (130 g) cubed squash (½-inch/1-cm cubes)
  3 cups/1¼ pints (700 ml) water
  dried oregano, to taste
  salt and ground pepper
  fresh basil, chopped, to serve

Soak the beans in plenty of water overnight.
  Drain and rinse the beans. Heat the vegetable oil in a pan. Add the onion and bell peppers and sauté for 8 minutes, or until the vegetables are soft and the onion is transparent. Add the tomatoes and paprika, cook for a further 3 minutes, then add the corn kernels, blended corn, squash, drained beans. Pour over the measured water. Bring to a boil, then simmer over low heat for 1 hour, adding more water if necessary, checking occasionally to see if the beans are soft and cooked.
  Season with salt, pepper, and oregano. Just before serving, add the chopped basil.

Guyanese Sautéed Spinach

Bhaji
Guyana

Preparation time: 10 minutes
Cooking time: 40 minutes

Serves: 4

Bhaji is a dish found in different parts of the southern Caribbean and Guyana and quite similar to saag bhaji in India. In Guyana, they mostly use *poi bhaji*, malabar spinach, a type of spinach with thick leaves, though any variety of spinach or leafy green will do. It is often eaten with shrimp, added to soups, or served with rice.

  2 lb (900 g) *poi bhaji* (or spinach), leaves only
  1 tablespoon vegetable oil
  1 white onion, chopped
  2 garlic cloves, minced
  1 *wiri wiri* chile, chopped
  1 tomato, peeled and chopped
  ½ teaspoon paprika
  3 green mangoes, peeled and finely diced
  ½ cup/4 fl oz (120 ml) coconut milk
  salt and ground pepper

Rinse the *bhaji* leaves, dry, then coarsely chop and set aside.
  In a pan, heat the oil over medium heat, then add the onion, garlic, and chile, and sauté for 5 minutes. Add the tomato and continue cooking for a further 4 minutes.
  Once the vegetables are soft, add the *bhaji* and cook for 10 minutes. Add the paprika, and season with salt and pepper, then add the mango and coconut milk, lower the heat and simmer for 20 minutes or until the *bhaji* becomes soft and dark.

Mixed Vegetables with Spicy Peanut Sauce

Gado-gado
Suriname

Preparation time: 30 minutes

Serves: 4

When Suriname was a Dutch colony, Indonesian and East Indian laborers arrived in droves, bringing with them recipes for dishes like gado-gado, which remains a staple dish. Translating as "mish-mash," the dish is a combination of raw and lightly cooked vegetables that are drizzled or dipped in peanut sauce.

  1 cup/2 oz (60 g) beansprouts
  2 large carrots, boiled and sliced
  7 oz (200 g) green beans, lightly boiled
  2 potatoes, boiled and cut into chunks
  4 hard-boiled eggs, halved
  ½ cup/2 oz (60 g) peanuts, chopped
  2 limes, cut into wedges, to serve

  For the sauce
  ⅓ cup/2½ oz (75 g) peanut butter
  1 tablespoon finely chopped fresh ginger
  1 garlic clove, finely chopped
  3 tablespoons water
  2 tablespoons soy sauce
  4 tablespoons lime juice
  ½ teaspoon brown sugar

For the sauce, place the peanut butter in a medium bowl with the ginger and garlic. Start whisking while slowly adding the water, and continue whisking while adding the soy sauce, lime juice, and sugar.
  Arrange the vegetables on a platter with the hard-boiled eggs. Sprinkle over the chopped peanuts, drizzle with the sauce and serve with extra sauce, and lime wedges, on the side.

Mixed Vegetables with Spicy Peanut Sauce

Surinamese Vegetable Salad with Coconut

Goedangan
Suriname

Preparation time: 15 minutes
Cooking time: 15 minutes
Serves: 8

An adaptation of the Indonesian *Gado-gado* (Mixed Vegetables with Spicy Peanut Sauce, page 150) by Javanese immigrants in Suriname, *goedangan* is a salad with fresh vegetables and sweet tropical flavors.

    1 white cabbage, cored and sliced
    8 oz (225 g) mung bean sprouts
    1 lb (450 g) green beans
    1 cucumber, sliced
    6 hard-boiled eggs, halved
    1 cup/3½ oz (100 g) fresh shredded coconut
    salt and ground pepper

    For the dressing
    ½ cup/4 fl oz (120 ml) coconut milk
    ½ cup/7½ oz (215 g) yogurt
    1–2 tablespoons brown sugar
    juice of 1 lime
    1 teaspoon chopped cilantro (coriander)
    1 hot chile, seeded and chopped

Blanch the cabbage in boiling water for 5 minutes, then plunge into iced water. Repeat with the mung bean sprouts for 3 minutes, and the green beans for 4 minutes. Drain and set aside.

In a bowl, whisk the coconut milk, yogurt, sugar, and lime juice together for the dressing. Add salt and pepper to taste, then stir in the cilantro (coriander) and chile.

On a large platter, arrange the blanched vegetables and decorate with the sliced cucumber and hard-boiled eggs. Top with the shredded coconut, then either drizzle over the dressing, or serve it on the side.

Radish, Mint, and Pork Rind Salad

Chojín
Guatemala

Preparation time: 10 minutes
Serves: 4

This Guatemalan salad is eaten on its own, with warm tortillas, or as a topping for tacos. When the pork rinds are left out, it is called *picado de rabano*.

    15 radishes, finely chopped
    ½ medium onion, finely diced
    3 tablespoons mint, chopped
    1 serrano chile, finely chopped
    ⅓ cup/2½ fl oz (75 ml) bitter orange juice
    6 oz (175 g) *Chicharrón* (Pork Cracklings/crispy skin;
    page 276 for homemade or can be store-bought)
    salt and ground pepper

In a bowl, mix the radish, onion, mint, and chile. Add the bitter orange juice, and salt and pepper to taste. Stir well. Crumble the *Chicharrón* on top to serve.

Cheese, Corn, and Lima Bean Salad

Solterito
Peru

Preparation time: 20 minutes
Serves: 2

This cold salad from Arequipa is common in the city's *picanterías*. There's a similar version from the Cusco region called *soltero*.

    ½ cup/2 oz (60 g) crumbled *queso fresco*
    1 cup/5 oz (140 g) cooked corn kernels
    ½ cup/2 oz (60 g) diced red onion
    ½ cup/3 oz (80 g) peeled and diced tomatoes
    1 cup/4 oz (120 g) fava (broad) beans, cooked
    and peeled
    2 small rocoto chiles, seeded, and chopped
    ½ cup/6 oz (175 g) pitted black olives, chopped
    1 cup/5 oz (140 g) cooked diced potatoes
    1 tablespoon parsley, chopped
    2 tablespoons olive oil
    4 tablespoons white vinegar
    1 teaspoon dried oregano
    salt and ground pepper

Place all the ingredients in a bowl, with salt and pepper to taste. Mix well with a spoon.

Amaranth Soup

Sopa de Bledo
Guatemala

Preparation time: 5 minutes
Cooking time: 55 minutes
Serves: 4

Called *bledo* in Guatemala, amaranth grows wild in Bajo Verapaz and neighboring regions. The plant's nutritious green leaves are most typically eaten in stews or soups, such as this one.

    1 tablespoon vegetable oil
    ½ cabbage, finely chopped
    1 onion, finely chopped
    1 teaspoon ground cumin
    4 cups/32 fl oz (950 ml) water
    2 tomatoes, chopped
    ½ chayote, chopped
    3 potatoes, chopped
    bunch of amaranth leaves
    salt
    3½ oz (100 g) parsley, chopped, to serve

In a medium pan, heat the oil then add the cabbage, onion, and cumin. Sauté for 8 minutes, stirring frequently, then remove from the heat.

In a medium pan, bring the water, with salt added, to a boil over medium heat, then add the tomatoes, chayote, and potatoes. Cook for 5 minutes, stirring occasionally, then add the sautéed cabbage and onion and cook for a further 8 minutes.

Add the amaranth leaves and cook, uncovered, for 25–30 minutes. Add salt to taste, and serve in soup bowls, garnished with the parsley.

Amaranth Soup

Heart of Palm

For many years the heart of palm industry was highly unsustainable, where the hearts were removed from wild, single stemmed palms, resulting in the death of the tree. Today, most palm hearts, often called *chonta* or *palmito*, come from multi-stemmed palm trees, like the peach palm or açaí palm, allowing hearts to be removed from one stem at a time while the others grow.

Processed forms of palm hearts are pickled, bottled, or canned, though in areas where palms are grown, they are available fresh and have a far superior flavor and texture. They have a delicate flavor and don't need much preparation. It is becoming increasingly common to slice them into noodles.

Palm Heart Salad

Ensalada de chonta, salada de palmito 📷
Brazil, Costa Rica, Ecuador, Peru

Preparation time: 20 minutes   ❋ ∅ 🜂 Ⓥ ꙍ ⚘
                                       Serves: 4

If you have access to fresh heart of palm, simple recipes like this that don't mask its flavor make for an excellent side dish.

    1 heart of palm
    juice of 2 limes
    1 tablespoon olive oil
    1 teaspoon salt
    1 teaspoon ground pepper
    ¼ cup/1 oz (30 g) Brazil nuts

Remove the hard part from the heart of palm. Cut the heart into strips about 3 inches (7.5 cm) long. Season with the lime juice, olive oil, salt, and pepper, and grate the Brazil nuts on top.

Cohune Cabbage

Belize

Preparation time: 5 minutes   ❋ ∅ 🜂 Ⓥ ⚘
Cooking time: 25 minutes   Serves: 4

In Belize, the large fronds of the cohune palm (*Attalea cohune*) are used for thatched roofs, and its seeds are used for oil, while the heart is eaten like a vegetable. There's no cabbage in the dish, just the diced and seasoned heart of palm, turned golden in color from turmeric, often called yellow ginger in Belize and introduced by the waves of East Indians who came to work in the country throughout the 1900s. It's typically served over white rice or with tortillas. A portion of meat may be added on the side to make it a meal.

    1 fresh heart of palm
    2 tablespoons coconut oil
    1 onion, chopped
    10 garlic cloves, chopped
    1 tablespoon ground turmeric
    1 teaspoon salt
    ¼ teaspoon black pepper
    3 culantro leaves, chopped (or use cilantro/coriander)
    2 dried oregano leaves

Remove the hard part from the heart of palm. Pour about 2 inches (5 cm) of water into a steamer, and bring to a boil. Add the steamer basket (make sure the water doesn't touch the basket) and place the heart of palm in the basket. Cover and steam for about 7 minutes, or until tender. Drain, cool, then dice.
    Heat the coconut oil in a medium pan over medium heat, then sauté the onion and garlic until tender, about 5 minutes. Add the diced heart of palm, turmeric, salt, pepper, culantro, and oregano. Cover and simmer for 10 minutes. Serve warm.

Palm Heart Salad

Nopales

Wander through Mexico City's seemingly never-ending *Mercado La Merced*, and at one point you'll come across an entire row of plastic crates filled with the flat paddles of prickly pear cacti, called *nopales*. In clearings hidden within all of those crates, women and men adorned in aprons sit with a flat board and a paddle, ferociously scraping the *nopales* with a small knife to clean them of their spines. They then cut them into slices or cubes. Eaten like a vegetable, with a flavor that resembles green beans or asparagus, *nopales* are usually grilled or boiled. They are great with a little bit of salt and lime.

Cactus Paddle Salad

Nopalitos
Mexico

Preparation time: 5 minutes
Cooking time: 15 minutes

Serves: 4

Serve as a salad, on a tortilla, or with eggs.

    10 *nopales*, cleaned and cut into ½-inch (1-cm) cubes
    2 tablespoons vegetable oil
    1 red onion, finely diced
    2 tablespoons cilantro (coriander), chopped
    2 tomatoes, diced
    juice of 2 limes
    4 tablespoons shredded *queso añejo* (or use pecorino)
    10 pickled jalapeño peppers, sliced
    salt

Cook the cubed *nopales* in a pan of salted, boiling water for 10 minutes over medium heat. Drain, rinse, and cover with a damp tea towel to cool down.

Heat the oil in a small pan over medium heat, add the *nopales* and cook for 5 minutes (this will make sure there's no mucilage left). Set on a clean tea towel to cool down.

In a bowl, mix the red onion, cilantro (coriander), tomatoes, lime juice, and *nopales*. Season with salt and serve with cheese and sliced jalapeños.

Squash

Cucurbita, a genus of the gourd family, are native to the Andes and Mesoamerica and are grown for their edible fruits, better known as squash. Along with companion plants corn and beans, squash has been an integral part of nutrition throughout the Americas for thousands of years. Once wild and bitter, it was domesticated, even before corn, and became sweeter.

Dozens of species and sub-species of squash were shaped by climate and geography. There's the *Cucurbita maxima*, which includes the giant *zapallos* of Argentina and Bolivia, as well as the smaller yet flavorful *zapallo loche* in Peru. There's the *Cucurbita pepo*, from Mexico, one of the oldest species, which includes orange Halloween pumpkins and the small, round *calabacitas*. There are also distant cousins, part of the larger *Cucurbitaceae* family, like chayote (*Sechium edule*), a tropical squash with a flavor that hints at zucchini or green beans.

The preparations of squash in the Americas are as diverse as the varieties. They can be boiled, baked, puréed, stewed, or roasted in the coals of a fire. In Peru, dough made from squash is fried like donuts. In Mexico, squash seeds, called *pepitas*, are ground into a paste to make sauce or used to thicken stews.

Fried Pumpkin with Shrimp

Pumpkin talkari, pumpkin choka
Belize, Guyana

Preparation time: 20 minutes
Cooking time: 1 hour

Serves: 2

Variations of this stewed and seasoned pumpkin recipe spread across the Caribbean when migrant workers from India came to the region after the abolition of slavery, taking on local flavors as it found new homes. For instance, in Belize, coconut milk and turmeric were added, while in Guyana, small, white-bellied shrimp and *wiri wiri* chiles found their way into the dish. The *calabaza* or West Indian pumpkin is most often used. It's usually served with roti, tortillas, or white rice.

    2 tablespoons vegetable oil
    1 white onion, chopped
    5 garlic cloves, minced
    2 *wiri wiri* chiles, chopped (or use habanero)
    1 tomato, peeled and chopped
    1 lb 8 oz (680 g) pumpkin, peeled, seeded, and chopped into chunks no bigger than ½ inch (1 cm)
    1 sprig thyme
    ½ teaspoon curry powder
    ¼ teaspoon garam masala
    ½ teaspoon brown sugar
    ½ cup/4 fl oz (120 ml) water
    4 oz (120 g) small shrimp (prawns)
    salt and ground pepper

Heat 1 tablespoon of the oil in a pan over medium-high heat, add the onion, garlic, and chiles, and sauté for 6 minutes. Add the tomato, lower the heat and cook for 8 minutes or until the tomato starts dissolving and the consistency begins to look like a thick sauce. Add the pumpkin and cook for 10 minutes over medium heat. Add salt to taste, then add some black pepper, the thyme, curry powder, garam masala, and sugar, then cook for a further 15 minutes. Add the water and continue to cook for 20 minutes until the pumpkin is soft like a purée and there is little water left in the pan.

Meanwhile, heat the remaining oil in a nonstick frying pan over medium-high heat and sear the shrimp (prawns). Cook for 4 minutes or until all the water has evaporated. They should look dry and crispy.

Add the shrimp to the pumpkin, and finish by mashing the pumpkin with a fork. Serve hot.

Garden Vegetables

Peruvian Squash Stew

Locro de zapallo
Peru

Preparation time: 15 minutes
Cooking time: 45 minutes

Serves: 4

Beloved by the Moche and a staple of north coastal cuisine in Peru, the *zapallo loche*, a landrace of *Cucurbita moschata*, is small with a bright orange flesh. Commercial agriculture was causing it to disappear, though gastronomy circles in Peru have helped bring it back.

    1 tablespoon vegetable oil
    1 cup/4 oz (120 g) chopped white onion
    1 tablespoon minced garlic
    2 tablespoons *ají amarillo* paste
    2 lb (900 g) *loche* squash (you can use butternut),
    peeled and cut into 1-inch (2.5-cm) chunks
    2 ears of corn, cut into 2-inch (5-cm) chunks
    2 cups/16 fl oz (475 ml) vegetable stock
    ½ cup/½ oz (15 g) *huacatay* (Peruvian black mint)
    leaves
    ½ cup/2 oz (60 g) fresh fava (broad) beans
    1 cup/5 oz (140 g) cubed *papa amarilla* (yellow
    potatoes)
    ½ cup/4 fl oz (120 ml) milk
    1 cup/4 oz (120 g) crumbled *queso fresco*
    salt and ground pepper

In a frying pan, heat the oil over medium heat, and sauté the onion and garlic for 5 minutes. Add the *ají amarillo* paste and cook for a further minute before adding the squash, corn, and stock. Season with salt, pepper, and the *huacatay* and cook for 15 minutes.

Add the fava (broad) beans and potatoes and cook for 15 minutes or until the potatoes are soft. To finish, pour in the milk and *queso fresco*. Stir well and simmer for 5 minutes. Check the seasoning before serving with white rice and fried eggs.

Pumpkin Purée with Dried Meat

Escondidinho de abóbora com carne seca
Brazil

Preparation time: 1 hour 30 minutes
Cooking time: 20 minutes

Serves: 8

You might snack on this tasty dish with a caipirinha in a Rio de Janeiro *botequim*, the laid-back bars with inexpensive food that are slowly fading into the city's memory. The pumpkin (or squash) and the *carne seca* can be baked together, as in this recipe, though it's quite common to serve them one on top of the other or side by side on a plate, sometimes with white rice.

    2 lb (900 g) pumpkin (or butternut squash), peeled,
    seeded, and diced
    7 garlic cloves, peeled
    1 tablespoon butter
    1 tablespoon water
    1 lb (450 g) dried meat (beef jerky), chopped
     2 tablespoons oil
    1 onion, finely chopped
    1 teaspoon ground cumin
    2 tomatoes, finely chopped
    1 bell pepper, cored, seeded, and finely chopped
    1 cup/8 oz (225 g) shredded *quejjo de coalho*
    (or use mozzarella)
    ½ cup/1½ oz (40 g) grated parmesan
    salt and ground pepper

Preheat the oven to 400°F/200°C/Gas Mark 6.

Put the pumpkin into a large pan, cover with water and place over high heat. Bring to a boil and cook until soft, then drain, and smash with a fork or pass through a potato masher.

Crush or grate 5 of the garlic cloves. Melt the butter in a frying pan over medium heat, then add the crushed garlic and brown. Add the water, then stir in the pumpkin. Season with salt and pepper, and stir. Set aside.

Place the dried meat in a medium pan, cover with water and bring to a boil. Drain, cover with fresh water and repeat twice (to remove excess salt). Shred the meat and set aside.

Heat the oil in a frying pan, sauté the onion until transparent, then grate in the remaining 2 garlic cloves, and cook until golden brown. Add the shredded meat and cook until the meat begins to brown and the moisture is gone. Season with pepper and the cumin, then add the tomatoes and bell pepper, and cook for 2 minutes. Add the cheese, stir for 2 minutes, then remove from the heat.

Spread half the pumpkin purée in a deep baking pan, then distribute the filling evenly on top. Cover with the remaining purée and sprinkle the parmesan on top. Bake in the oven for 20 minutes, then serve warm, with rice.

Creole Stew

Locro criollo 🍲
Argentina

Preparation time: 20 minutes,
plus overnight soaking
Cooking time: 2 hours 20 minutes

Serves: 4

Linked to 25 de Mayo celebrations, the anniversary of the Argentine revolution, *locro* is a form of hearty, vegetable-driven stews found throughout the Andes. Argentine versions tend to be meatier, often adding in offal.

    1 cup/6 oz (180 g) dried hominy
    8 oz (225 g) salted pork belly, cut into cubes
    100 g (3½ oz) flank steak, cut into cubes
    100 g (3½ oz) Boston butt (pork shoulder),
    cut into cubes
    50 g (2 oz) chorizo, cut into cubes
    1 white onion, chopped
    ½ red onion, thinly sliced
    ½ red bell pepper, cored, seeded, and chopped
    kernels of 8 ears of corn
    1 lb (450 g) butternut squash, cut into cubes
    salt and ground pepper

Put the hominy in a bowl, cover with cold water and let soak overnight.

In a medium pan, sear the pork belly over medium heat for 4 minutes, turning the pieces to color on every side. Add the other meats, the onions, and bell pepper and cook for a further 10 minutes. Add the drained hominy and enough water to cover the ingredients by 2 inches (5 cm). Add the rest of the vegetables, cover, bring to a boil, then reduce the heat to low and simmer for 2 hours, stirring every 20 minutes, adding more water if necessary.

Mash the vegetables with a wooden spoon and stir, until the *locro* has a thick consistency. Season with salt and pepper. Serve hot in a soup dish.

Squash Polenta

Quibebe, kivevé
Argentina, Brazil, Paraguay

Preparation time: 20 minutes
Cooking time: 30 minutes

Serves: 4

This savory squash purée, typical in Paraguay and neighboring countries, gets its name from the Guaraní word for a reddish color, because its base is a winter squash they call *andai* (*Cucurbita moschata*), with a deep red pulp (butternut squash and *calabaza* are cultivars and can be used in its place).

In northeastern Brazil, it is usually served alongside a meat course, and coconut milk and chile paste are often added into the recipe.

    1 lb (450 g) *andai* squash (or butternut or *calabaza*),
    peeled, seeded, and cut into small pieces
    1½ cups/12 fl oz (350 ml) water
    2 tablespoons sugar
    1 teaspoon salt
    ½ cup/4 fl oz (120 ml) milk
    3 tablespoons lard
    1 cup/5 oz (140 g) corn (maize) flour
    6 oz (175 g) *queso paraguayo* (or use ricotta),
    crumbled

Place the squash in a small pan with the measured water, sugar, and salt. Bring to a boil, cover, and cook over very low heat for 20 minutes, or until the squash becomes soft. Mash with the cooking water (or purée with a hand blender), adding more water if necessary, then bring to a boil again. Add the milk and lard and stir, then add the corn (maize) flour a little at a time, mixing until fully incorporated. Cook for 1–2 minutes or until slightly thickened.

Finally, add the cheese and stir, then remove from the heat and serve warm. If it's too thick, add additional water or milk to loosen.

Almost Locro

Guascha locro
Argentina

Preparation time: 15 minutes
Cooking time: 3 hours 45 minutes

Serves: 6

Families in the Salta province in northern Argentina, where corn, beans, and potatoes are more prevalent in the diet than the south, prepare this winter dish with regularity. The Quechua word *guascha* or *huascha* roughly translates as "something missing," meaning the ingredients are a bit lighter and less expensive than a true *locro*.

    1 lb (450 g) beef flank
    4 cups/32 fl oz (950 ml) water
    2 tablespoons olive oil
    2 onions, chopped
    ¼ cup/1½ oz (40 g) dried hot chiles
    3 lb (1.3 kg) butternut squash, peeled, seeded,
    and chopped
    6 ears of corn, kernels only
    1 teaspoon chile powder
    2 tablespoons sweet paprika
    1 tablespoon fresh thyme
    2 tablespoons ground cumin
    juice of 1 lime
    3 scallions (spring onions), chopped
    salt and ground pepper

Place a medium pan over medium heat, add the meat and cover with the water. Add some salt, bring to a boil, and cook over low heat for 3 hours, skimming off the foam occasionally. Remove the meat from the water, reserving the cooking stock, let cool, then cut into cubes.

Heat 1 tablespoon of the oil in a separate medium pan. Sauté half the chopped onion for about 7 minutes until transparent, then add the dried chiles. Add the reserved cooking stock, the cubed meat, and the squash. Cook, stirring, for about 15–20 minutes until the squash becomes a purée, forming a thick consistency. Add the corn and continue cooking for a further 5 minutes or until tender. Add salt and pepper to taste.

Heat the remaining oil in a frying pan, add the remaining chopped onion, the chile powder, paprika, thyme, and cumin, and sauté for 7 minutes. Add the lime juice and season with salt and pepper

Serve the *guascha locro* with the onion mixture on top, garnished with the scallions (spring onions).

Creole Stew

Nicaraguan Squash Stew

Guiso de pipián
Nicaragua

Preparation time: 10 minutes
Cooking time: 25 minutes

Serves: 4

In Nicaragua, this stew is made from *pipián* (*Cucurbita argyrosperma*), a winter squash that's sometimes called the cushaw pumpkin outside of the region. It's also found in El Salvador, where it is often used in *pupusas*.

    2 pipián (white squash), peeled, seeded, and cut
    into small squares
    1 cup/3 oz (80 g) breadcrumbs
    3 cups/25 fl oz (750 ml) milk
    1 cup/8 fl oz (250 ml) cream
    ½ cup/4 oz (115 g) butter
    2 garlic cloves, minced
    ½ white onion, chopped
    2 tomatoes, peeled and chopped
    ½ red bell pepper, cored, seeded, and diced
    1 teaspoon annatto paste
    salt and ground pepper

Cook the squash in a pan of boiling, salted water over medium heat for 8 minutes, or until soft.

Meanwhile, in a medium bowl, mix the breadcrumbs with the milk and cream, and set aside.

Heat the butter in a pan over high heat, add the garlic and onion, and sauté for 5 minutes, or until soft. Add the tomatoes and bell pepper and cook for a further 4 minutes over medium heat. Add the squash and breadcrumb mixture, stir well, then add the annatto paste. Season with salt and pepper and continue cooking for a further 8 minutes over low heat, or until thickened. Serve hot.

Stuffed Caigua

Caigua rellena, achojcha rellena
Bolivia, Peru

Preparation time: 20 minutes
Cooking time: 45 minutes

Serves: 4

Caigua (*Cyclanthera pedata*), sometimes called the slipper gourd, was depicted on the ceramics of the Moche civilization on the north coast of Peru, where it remains widely consumed. They have a flavor a bit like a cucumber and are often pickled, sautéed, or stuffed.

    4 caiguas
    1 tablespoon olive oil
    ½ cup/2 oz (60 g) chopped white onion
    1 garlic clove, chopped
    1 lb (450 g) ground (minced) meat
    ½ cup/2½ oz (70 g) raisins
    ½ cup/2½ oz (70 g) cooked peas
    ¼ cup/1 oz (30 g) cubed carrot
    ¼ cup/2 fl oz (60 ml) red wine
    1 cup/8 fl oz (250 ml) beef stock
    ¼ cup/1 oz (30 g) chopped black olives
    4 hard-boiled eggs, chopped
    salt and ground pepper

Preheat the oven to 350°F/180°C/Gas Mark 4.

Cut off the tops of the caiguas and remove the seeds and veins. Blanch in boiling water for 5 minutes, then plunge in iced water and remove. Set aside.

Heat the oil in a large pan over high heat, add the onion and garlic, and sauté for 4 minutes, or until transparent and soft. Add the meat and cook, stirring, over high heat for 3–5 minutes, then add the raisins, peas, and carrot. Season with salt and pepper, add the wine and stock, then lower the heat and cook slowly for 20 minutes. Add the black olives and eggs and cook for a further 1–2 minutes, then remove from the heat.

Spoon the filling into the caiguas and place on an oven tray. Bake in the oven for 10 minutes, then serve warm with white rice.

Stuffed Chayote

Chancletas
Costa Rica

Preparation time: 10 minutes
Cooking time: 15 minutes

Serves: 2

Chayote is one of the most consumed vegetables in Costa Rica, a country known for its abundance of fresh produce, which can be picked up from the spectacular network of weekly farmers' markets. The recipe for *chancletas*, named after sandals because of their shape, can be either sweet or savory.

    2 chayotes
    ½ cup/4 oz (115 g) soft cheese
    ¼ cup/1¾ oz (50 g) brown sugar
    1 tablespoon butter
    ½ cup/4 fl oz (120 ml) heavy (double) cream
    ½ cup/2 oz (60 g) shredded queso palmito (or use
    mozzarella)
    salt

Preheat the oven to 350°F/180°C/Gas Mark 4.

Cut both chayotes in half lengthways and remove all the seeds. Cook in boiling, salted water for 5 minutes, strain, then plunge into iced water. Carefully remove the flesh without ripping the skin. Place the empty chayote skins in an oven tray lined with parchment paper.

Put the chayote pulp in a medium bowl, and mix in the soft cheese, sugar, butter, and cream. Add 1–2 tablespoons of the mixture to each chayote half, and sprinkle over the shredded cheese. Bake in the oven for 7 minutes or until the top turns golden brown. Serve hot.

Stuffed Caigua

Pickled Chayote

Encurtido de chayote
Costa Rica

Preparation time: 5 minutes,
plus 1 hour pickling
Cooking time: 10 minutes

Serves: 4

Chayote holds its form and flavor quite well when pickled. Use this *encurtido* (pickle) as part of a *casado* (lunch plate), in a *gallo* (taco), or on its own.

 2 cups/16 fl oz (475 ml) distilled white vinegar
 1 onion, thinly sliced
 3 garlic cloves, peeled
 2 cloves
 1 star anise
 1 teaspoon coriander seeds
 ½ cup/1 oz (25 g) *chaya* (tree spinach) leaves, stems removed, chopped
 2 tablespoons sea salt
 2 teaspoons sugar
 2 chayotes, seeded and sliced

In a medium pan, combine the vinegar, onion, garlic, cloves, star anise, coriander seeds, *chaya*, salt, and sugar. Bring to a boil, just enough to dissolve the salt, then turn off the heat. Add the chayote and cool completely.

Transfer everything to a sterilized jar and refrigerate for at least 1 hour or up to 3 days.

Peppers and Chiles

The genus *Capiscum* has been cultivated for thousands of years in Latin America, and chile peppers have given birth to tens of thousands of different varieties that have been integral pieces of cuisine the world over. They can be defined by their heat, like Mexico's *morita* and habanero; by their fruity qualities, like Peru's *ají amarillo* and *ají limo*; or can be sweet, like Venezuela's *ají dulce*. They might be smoked, dried, and ground into spice blends like *jiquitaia* in the Upper Amazon or *merkén* in southern Chile, or eaten raw, blistered, roasted, pickled, toasted, and mashed. Stuffed, like *rocoto* in Peru and Bolivia or *poblano* in Mexico, they make some of the region's most characteristic dishes.

Chile peppers are generally sold fresh, as paste, dried, or ground. In this book we use all four variations as all have individual strengths. The heat of chiles is mostly concentrated in the interior ribs and the locules that the seeds are attached to. The seeds tend to be bitter, as well as spicy. Sometimes we want the flavors of a chile but not necessarily all of the heat, so we might remove those parts in some recipes.

Fresh chile peppers can add color, fruit and floral notes, and spice to a dish, however, when a pepper is dried, it opens up another world of complexity, a wider scope of rich flavors from smoky to sweet. Additionally, most dried chiles take on a new name. For instance, the red jalapeño becomes chipotle when dried, while *ají amarillo* becomes *ají mirasol*. Dried chiles need to be soaked in boiling water before use, for about 20 minutes, then mashed or blended, though they can also be fried in oil from dried, for about 30 seconds, or toasted in a pan or on a *comal* before being mashed, which is common

in moles. Keep in mind that dried and ground chiles are best within a few months of being dried, and don't last forever.

Chile and Meat Stew

Suban'ik
Guatemala

Preparation time: 20 minutes
Cooking time: 1 hour

Serves: 4

A ceremonial dish of the Kaqchikel Maya from San Martín Jilotepeque in Guatemala's Chimaltenango department, suban'ik is a chile and meat stew that is wrapped in *maxán* leaves (*Calathea lutea*), bound and tied with a natural fiber rope called *cibaque*, and steamed in a pot with a little bit of water. The chiles, of which a handful of varieties are used, are ground in a mortar with the tomatoes into a paste, similar to a mole. Usually a mixture of chunks of meat (pork, turkey, game hen, or beef) are used as well. *Maxán* leaves can be swapped for banana leaves, which are similar in size and strength. Suban'ik is usually served alongside tamales.

 2 cups/16 fl oz (475 ml) water
 1 lb 8 oz (680 g) turkey parts
 8 oz (225 g) beef bones
 1 lb (450 g) pork loin, cut into 3-inch (7.5-cm) cubes
 1 lb (450 g) tomatoes, peeled, cored, and diced
 1½ oz (40 g) tomatillos
 1 red bell pepper, cored, seeded, and chopped
 2 dried *pasa* chiles, stemmed and cored
 2 dried *sambo* chiles, stemmed and cored
 1 dried *guajillo* chile, stemmed and cored
 4 banana leaves
 1 *cibaque* (or cotton string)
 salt and ground pepper

In a medium pan, bring the water to a boil. Add the turkey parts and beef bones and bring to a boil again. Skim the surface of the water with a spoon, add the pork, and simmer for 40 minutes. The water should always cover half of the meat pieces, so add more water if and when necessary.

Meanwhile, place the tomatoes, tomatillos, bell pepper, and dried chiles in another pan. Pour water in to cover, bring to a boil, cover with a lid, and reduce the heat. Let simmer for 30 minutes until soft, then use a skimmer to transfer the vegetables and chiles to a mortar. Smash with a pestle to a smooth paste. (If necessary, do this process in two parts.) Season with salt and pepper and set aside.

Line the bottom of a large pan or clay pot with the banana leaves, making sure you have a thick surface where the water will not drain. Add the drained turkey and pork pieces and pour the sauce on top of the meat. Bring the edges of the banana leaves together to shape a basket and use the string to close it. Pour a small amount of water on the bottom of the pot and cook over medium heat for 20 minutes, until the meats are tender. Check the seasoning and serve while still warm, with white rice on the side.

Chile and Meat Stew

Roasted Peppers in Oil

Morrones asados
Argentina

Preparation time: 5 minutes
Cooking time: 30 minutes

Serves: 6–8

This is a good solution when you have more peppers in your garden than you know what to do with. Preserved in oil, they are great with a slice of grilled bread, or toast, or can be added to pizzas or pasta.

    2 green bell peppers
    2 red bell peppers
    2 yellow bell peppers
    3 cups/25 fl oz (750 ml) olive oil
    3 garlic cloves, peeled
    sea salt

Preheat the oven to 375°F/190°C/Gas Mark 5.
    Spread all the peppers out on a baking tray and add a generous drizzle of the oil. Roast in the oven for about 30 minutes, turning them occasionally, until the skin is brown and wrinkled (alternatively, the peppers can be held directly over a flame). Remove from the oven and let cool slightly.
    Peel the peppers. An easy way of doing this is to allow them to cool inside a plastic bag; the steam will detach the skin easily. Cut in quarters and remove the seeds. Season with salt and place inside a sterilized glass jar. Add the garlic, cover with oil, and seal.

Blistered Chiles

Chiles toreados
Mexico

Preparation time: 5 minutes
Cooking time: 5 minutes

Serves: 3–4

You will find bowls of *chiles toreados* served alongside grilled meats or tacos across Mexico.

    8 serrano chiles or jalapeño peppers
    1 tablespoon vegetable oil
    juice of 1 lime
    salt

With the back of a spoon, slowly press the chiles without breaking them. In a frying pan, heat the oil over medium heat and sear the chiles for 2 minutes each side, or until they start to blister. Remove from the heat and place in a small bowl. Season with lime juice and salt, and serve at room temperature.

Stuffed Poblano Chiles with Walnut Sauce

Chiles en nogada
Mexico

Preparation time: 15 minutes
Cooking time: 30 minutes

Serves: 6

One of the most emblematic dishes of the state of Puebla, *chiles en nogada* appear on restaurant menus and in homes when pomegranates appear in markets in central Mexico. The colors of the dish represent the Mexican flag: green parsley, white walnut sauce, and red pomegranate seeds. The origins of the dish's popularity date to 1821, when general Agustín de Iturbide came to Puebla, just after signing the Treaty of Córdoba, which established Mexico's independence from Spain. The Augustine nuns at Santa Mónica convent served him the dish, which had been made in the city's convents since the late eighteenth century, when pomegranates were brought to the region.

    ⅓ cup /2½ fl oz (75 ml) vegetable oil
    ½ cup/2 oz (60 g) chopped white onion
    2 garlic cloves, minced
    8 oz (225 g) pork loin, cut into small cubes
    1lb (450 g) tomatoes, peeled, seeded, and chopped
    3 cups/25 fl oz (750 ml) beef stock
    2 red apples, cored and cut into ½-inch (1-cm) cubes
    2 pears, cored and cut into ½-inch (1-cm) cubes
    3 peaches, pitted and cut into ½-inch (1-cm) cubes
    ½ cup/2½ oz (70 g) raisins, hydrated in warm water
    2 teaspoons sugar
    4 oz (100 g) lime confit, diced
    1⅓ cups/10½ fl oz (325 ml) dry sherry
    ½ teaspoon each of saffron, ground cloves, ground cumin, and ground cinnamon
    3 cups/25 fl oz (750 ml) vegetable oil
    6 poblano chiles, toasted
    2 pomegranates
    salt

    For the walnut sauce
    3 cups/10½ oz (300 g) walnuts
    1 cup/4 oz (120 g) shredded *queso fresco*
    1 cup/8 fl oz (250 ml) cream
    2 cups/16 fl oz (475 ml) whole milk

For the filling, heat the oil in a pan over medium heat. Add the onion and garlic, and sauté for 5 minutes. Once they start searing, add the pork and cook for a further 5 minutes. Add the tomatoes and cook for a couple more minutes. Pour in the stock and simmer for 15 minutes or until the liquids have evaporated.
    Mix the apples, pears, and peaches with the raisins, sugar, confit lime, and sherry. Season with salt and add the spices. Make sure the mixture has thickened before removing from the heat. Set aside.
    For the sauce, place all the ingredients in a blender. Process to a sauce, adding more milk if it is too thick.
    Pour the vegetable oil into a heavy pan, and heat to 360°F/182°C. When hot, fry each poblano chile for no more than 1 minute each side. Remove with a skimmer to a plate lined with paper towels, then place in a plastic bag for 5 minutes before they cool. Peel each chile, then make a small incision in the bottom and scrape out the seeds. Fill the chiles with the meat and fruit fillings, and place on a dish. Cover with the sauce and scatter over the pomegranate seeds. Serve at room temperature.

Stuffed Rocoto Chiles

Pimentão recheado, rocoto relleno
Brazil, Bolivia, Peru

Preparation time: 20 minutes
Cooking time: 30 minutes
Serves: 4

Peruvian writer Carlos Herrera wrote a fictional short story about the origins of *rocoto relleno*, a stuffed version of the fiery red Peruvian chile pepper. The tale goes that local cook Manuel Masías, who some claim actually invented the dish sometime in the late eighteenth century, had to go to hell to rescue the soul of his daughter Delphine, who died quite young. He served the dish to Lucifer and earned his daughter's release from hell. It's likely that forms of stuffed *rocotos* were being made in southern Peru prior to Masías' alleged dance with the devil, though they began appearing in Arequipa's *picanterías* stuffed with what is essentially Spanish *picadillo* around then. Today they are the city's most symbolic dish. Most preparations boil the chiles in water and vinegar long enough to remove much of the heat, so usually they aren't terribly spicy. In Cusco, as well as in much of the highlands of Bolivia, *rocoto relleno* is prepared quite differently. There, the chiles are battered and fried rather than baked, and they are sold in markets and street corners in the morning hours. To make Brazilian stuffed peppers, *pimentão recheado*, just replace the chiles with a bell pepper.

    8 cups/64 fl oz (1.9 liters) water
    1 cup/8 fl oz (250 ml) vinegar
    1 cup/7 oz (200g) sugar
    1 cup/8½ oz (240 g) salt
    4 *rocoto* chiles, cored and seeded
    1 tablespoon olive oil
    1 cup/4 oz (120 g) chopped white onion
    1 tablespoon minced garlic cloves
    2 *ají amarillo* chiles, seeded and diced
    1 tablespoon *ají panca* paste
    1 lb (450 g) beef sirloin, minced
    ½ cup/2 oz (60 g) cooked fava (broad) beans, peeled
    ½ cup/2½ oz (70 g) raisins, soaked
    ¼ cup/1 oz (30 g) chopped black olives
    2 tablespoons peanuts, chopped
    1 hard-boiled egg, chopped
    1 teaspoon ground cumin
    ½ cup/4 fl oz (120 ml) red wine
    1 cup/8 fl oz (250 ml) beef stock
    4 slices of *queso paria* (or use *queso fresco*)
    salt and ground pepper

Preheat the oven to 350°F/180°C/Gas Mark 4.
    Pour the water into a pan, add the vinegar, sugar, and salt, and bring to a boil. Place the chiles in a heatproof bowl and pour over 1½ cups/12 fl oz (350 ml) of the boiling water; let soak for 5 minutes, then drain and repeat the process 4 more times. Set the drained chiles aside.
    In a frying pan, heat the oil over high heat. Sauté the onion, garlic, and *ají amarillo* for 5 minutes. Mix in the *ají panca* paste, beef, fava (broad) beans, drained raisins, olives, and peanuts and cook for a further 4 minutes. Add the chopped egg and cumin, and season with salt and pepper, then pour in the wine and simmer for 2 minutes before adding the stock. Cook for a further 5 minutes, and check the seasoning.
    Place the *rocotos* on an oven tray and fill them with the meat stuffing. Place one slice of fresh cheese on top of each filled chile, then bake for 10 minutes or until the cheese is melted. Serve hot.

Moles

Coming from the Nahuatl word *molli*, meaning mixture, moles are an entire class of sauces found primarily in Mexican cuisine, particularly in the states of Oaxaca and Puebla. They can be red, yellow, green, or black, as well as spicy, smoky, fruity, or sweet. Their exact origins are murky, though they likely grew out of simple, pre-Hispanic purées of chiles. Over time, other ingredients such as nuts, seeds, herbs, and fruits were added, based on location and season, and with the introduction of new ingredients by the Spanish, they grew even more complex. Thick, chocolatey *mole poblano* and seven classic moles of Oaxaca (*negro, colorado, coloradito, amarillo, verde, chíchilo negro,* and *manchamanteles*) can have upwards of thirty different ingredients. Exact recipes change from family to family, so even within a single village there are rarely two moles that taste the same.

Green Mole

Mole verde
Mexico

Preparation time: 20 minutes
Cooking time: 1 hour
Serves: 6

Ground *pepitas*, or pumpkin seeds, tomatillos, and green chiles give this classic mole its color. It's usually served with chicken or pork, and with tortillas on the side.

    2 lb (900 g) pork ribs, cut into ¾-inch (2-cm) pieces
    1 bay leaf
    6 green tomatillos, peeled
    ⅔ cup/3¼ oz (90 g) *pepitas* (pumpkin seeds), toasted
    ½ cup/2½ oz (70 g) sesame seeds, toasted
    3 serrano chiles
    2 garlic cloves, peeled
    ½ white onion, chopped
    3 lettuce leaves
    2 *hoja santa* (Mexican pepperleaf), chopped
    4 tablespoons cilantro (coriander), chopped
    1 cup/8 fl oz (250 ml) chicken stock
    1 zucchini (courgette), cut into 1-inch (2.5-cm) cubes
    ½ cup/4 fl oz (120 ml) water
    salt

Place the pork and bay leaf in a medium pan and cover with water. Bring to a boil, then reduce the heat, cover, and simmer for 15 minutes, then remove the lid and cook for a further 15 minutes. The water should evaporate, and the pork will cook in its own fat.
    Meanwhile, place the tomatillos in another pan and cover with water. Bring to a boil, then reduce the heat and simmer for 7 minutes, or until soft. Drain and place in a large mortar or a blender. Add the toasted *pepitas* and sesame seeds, the chiles, garlic, onion, lettuce, *hoja santa*, cilantro (coriander), and stock. Pound or blend to a smooth paste. Season with salt.
    Pour the mixture into the pan with the meat and stir. Simmer over medium heat for 15 minutes, then add the zucchini (courgette) and water. Cook for a further 8 minutes, or until the sauce is thick and the vegetables are cooked. Serve hot.

Reddish Mole

Mole coloradito ⬡
Mexico

Preparation time: 10 minutes,
plus 20 minutes soaking
Cooking time: 1 hour 30 minutes

Serves: 8

The combination of chocolate, chiles, and spices give this classic Oaxacan mole, which generally has a dark red color, a sweet and spicy flavor. Serve with turkey or chicken.

    3 tomatoes
    12 dried *ancho* chiles, cored and seeded
    6 dried *chilcostle* chiles, cored and seeded
    1 tablespoon vegetable oil
    1 white onion, chopped
    5 garlic cloves
    2 cloves
    2 tablespoons sesame seeds
    1 teaspoon dried oregano
    1 teaspoon ground cinnamon
    3 cups/25 fl oz (750 ml) chicken stock
    2 tablespoons lard
    1½ oz (40 g) dark chocolate (*chocolate de mesa*)
    1 teaspoon sugar

Preheat the oven to 350°F/180°C/Gas Mark 4. Place the tomatoes on a lined baking sheet and roast for about 25 minutes, or until blistered. Set aside.

Heat a comal or frying pan and toast the chiles for about 2 minutes each side. Place the chiles in a bowl with the hot water, soak for 20 minutes. Drain and pat dry, then place in a blender.

Heat the oil in a large pan over medium heat, add the onion and garlic, and sauté for 7 minutes, or until transparent and soft.

Chop the tomatoes and add to the blender, along with the onion, garlic, cloves, sesame seeds, oregano, and cinnamon. Season with salt and blend until smooth, slowly adding a little of the chicken stock to loosen, if necessary.

Heat the lard in a medium pan or clay pot over medium heat and pour in the blended mix. Add the chicken stock, chocolate, and sugar. Reduce the heat to low and cook for 45 minutes, stirring occasionally. Check the seasoning and serve warm.

Puebla-Style Mole

Mole poblano
Mexico

Preparation time: 30 minutes
Cooking time: 3 hours

Serves: 16

While there are plausible theories the Aztecs made sauces that mixed chiles and chocolate, the modern form of *mole poblano*, like many other of Puebla's most famous recipes, was likely born in a convent. In the sixteenth century, possibly at the Convent of Santa Rosa in Puebla, a meal was being prepared for the visiting Archbishop. Because they had little to offer, or perhaps because of the tension of the preparation, as many as twenty ingredients (chiles, spices, bread, nuts, chocolate) were mixed together and reduced to a thick, rich, fragrant mole. They served it with turkey, allegedly the only meat they had that day. It quickly became one of Mexico's most revered dishes.

    1½ cups/12 oz (340 g) lard, plus 2 tablespoons
    9 oz (250 g) *mulato* chiles, cored seeded
    4 oz (120 g) *pasilla* chiles, cored and seeded
    4 oz (120 g) *ancho* chiles, cored and seeded
    18 cups/9 pints (4.25 liters) chicken stock
    1 cup/4½ oz (130 g) almonds
    2 tablespoons peanuts, peeled and roasted
    ½ cup/2 oz (60 g) each pecan nuts and pumpkin seeds
    2 tablespoons sesame seeds
    1 lb (450 g) tomatillos, coarsely chopped
    1 lb (450 g) tomatoes, coarsely chopped
    1 ripe plantain, sliced and fried
    ⅔ cup/3 oz (90 g) raisins
    1 teaspoon each black peppercorns and cumin seeds
    ½ teaspoon each anise seeds and dried thyme
    1 tablespoon dried oregano
    1 cinnamon stick
    12 garlic cloves, roasted
    1 white onion, roasted and quartered
    1 *bolillo* (bread roll), sliced and fried
    3 Corn Tortillas (page 136), sliced and fried
    4½ oz (130 g) dark chocolate (*chocolate de mesa*), crushed
    1 cup/7 oz (200 g) brown sugar

Heat 1 cup/9 oz (225 g) of the lard in a frying pan and fry the *mulato* chiles for 3 minutes. Remove with tongs and set aside. Repeat with the *pasilla* and *ancho* chiles. Turn off the heat and reserve the lard.

Place the chiles in a pan with 7 cups/3½ pints (1.6 liters) of the stock, bring to a boil and cook for 20 minutes, or until soft. Let cool. Divide the chiles into three batches and mix each batch with 2 cups/16 fl oz (475 ml) of the stock they were boiled in. Blend each batch for 2 minutes, or until smooth. Strain and set aside.

In a pan or clay pot, heat the reserved lard over medium heat. When it starts to smoke, reduce the heat to low and add the chile mixtures. Cook for 30 minutes, stirring continuously. The mixture should be thick, but you must see the bottom of the pot.

Meanwhile, heat the 2 tablespoons of lard in a frying pan. Fry the almonds for 3 minutes, or until lightly brown. Add the peanuts and pecans and fry for a further 3 minutes, then reduce the heat and add the pumpkin seeds, continuing to stir. When the pumpkin seeds puff up, add the sesame seeds and cook for a further 3 minutes. Turn off the heat and let cool. Place all the fried ingredients in a blender with 3 cups/25 fl oz (750 ml) of the remaining stock. Mix on medium speed to a smooth paste, about 3 minutes. Add the paste to the pan or pot with the chiles and continue cooking over low heat.

In another pan, heat the remaining ½ cup/3 oz (115 g) lard over medium heat. Add the tomatillos and tomatoes. Cook for 30 minutes, stirring continuously, until it has the consistency of a purée. Add the fried plantain and raisins and cook for a further 15 minutes over low heat. Take off the heat and let cool, then place in a blender with 4 cups/32 fl oz (950 ml) of the remaining stock and blend until smooth. Pour it into the pot, and stir.

Place the peppercorns, cumin, anise, thyme, oregano, cinnamon, garlic, and onion in a blender. Mix to a smooth paste with 2 cups/16 fl oz (475 ml) of the remaining stock. Pour into the pan or pot and stir well.

Continue cooking the mole for a further 30 minutes over low heat, stirring continuously. Season with salt.

Blend the *bolillo* and tortillas with the remaining 2 cups/16 fl oz (475 ml) of stock for 2 minutes then pour it into the mole. Continue cooking for 15 minutes, then add the chocolate and sugar and cook for a further 20 minutes, or until thick. If necessary, add more stock, or continue reducing. Check the seasoning for sugar and salt. Serve warm over chicken, turkey, or enchiladas.

Garden Vegetables

Reddish Mole

Tablecloth Stainer

Manchamanteles
Mexico

Preparation time: 15 minutes,
plus 20 minutes soaking
Cooking time: 1 hour 25 minutes

Serves: 4

More stew-like than other Oaxacan moles, *mancha-manteles* literally translates as "tablecloth stainer." The deep red color—made from a combination of chiles, tomatoes, and several fruits—can indeed dye a garment. The addition of the acidity from the fresh and dried fruits give this mole a heady mix of sweet, spicy, and sour flavors. It's usually made for the feast of Corpus Christi.

 6 tomatoes
 8 dried *ancho* chiles, cored and seeded
 ²⁄₃ cup/5 oz (150 g) lard
 ³⁄₄ cup/3¹⁄₂ oz (100 g) whole almonds
 6 garlic cloves, halved
 1 white onion, chopped
 2 teaspoons dried oregano
 1 lb 8 oz (680 g) pork loin, cut into cubes
 6 cloves
 ¹⁄₂ teaspoon ground nutmeg
 4 cups/32 fl oz (950 ml) chicken stock
 3 teaspoons apple cider vinegar
 1 tablespoon sugar
 1 cinnamon stick
 8 black peppercorns
 2 bananas, peeled and cut into chunks
 1 pear, peeled and diced
 ¹⁄₂ pineapple, peeled, cored and diced
 salt
 cooked white rice, to serve

Preheat the oven to 350°F/180°C/Gas Mark 4. Place the tomatoes on a lined baking sheet and roast for about 25 minutes, or until blistered. Set aside.

Meanwhile, heat a *comal* or frying pan and toast the chiles for about 2 minutes each side. Place the chiles in a bowl with enough hot water to cover, soak for 20 minutes, then drain. Set aside the chiles and ¹⁄₄ cup/2 fl oz (60 ml) of the chile-soaking water.

Once cool enough to handle, remove the skins and seeds from the roasted tomatoes.

Heat the lard in a pan over medium heat, add the almonds and sear for 5 minutes, stirring. Lower the heat and add the garlic, onion, oregano, and roasted tomatoes. Stir, and cook for 2 minutes, then add the pork and let brown on all sides, stirring occasionally, for 5 minutes.

In a blender, add all of the ingredients in the pan except the pork, as well as the chiles, cloves, nutmeg, and ¹⁄₂ cup/4 fl oz (120 ml) of the chicken stock. Blend for 2 minutes on medium speed, or until smooth. Strain and add back to the pork in the pan.

Add the remaining stock, the vinegar, sugar, cinnamon, and peppercorns to the pan, stir well, and bring to a boil over medium heat, then lower the heat and mix in the bananas, pear, and pineapple. Let cook for about 30–45 minutes, or until the liquid is reduced and a thick sauce is formed. Remove the cinnamon stick and peppercorns and season with salt. Serve warm, with white rice.

Black Mole

Mole negro Oaxaqueño
Mexico

Preparation time: 30 minutes ,
plus 30 minutes soaking
Cooking time: 1 hour 40 minutes

Serves: 8

Perhaps the most elaborate of all of the moles, Oaxaca's *mole negro* is served mostly on special occasions, such as Día de los Muertos. The dark color comes mostly from charred chiles (not just toasted) and chocolate, which help give it a rich tang. These recipes are passed down among family members like deeds to a house. It's often served with chicken, turkey, tamales, or enchiladas.

 20 black *chilhuacle* chiles
 8 *mulato* chiles
 2 tablespoons sesame seeds
 1 Corn Tortilla (page 136)
 1 dried avocado leaf
 3 tomatoes
 8 tablespoons lard
 1 cup/3¹⁄₂ oz (100 g) walnuts
 1 cup/4¹⁄₂ oz (130 g) almonds
 ¹⁄₂ cup/2 oz (60 g) cashews
 1 cinnamon stick
 6 cloves
 5 black peppercorns
 1 teaspoon ground nutmeg
 1¹⁄₂ cups/5 oz (140 g) raisins
 3 oz (80 g) dark chocolate (*chocolate de mesa*), crushed
 1 tablespoon dried oregano
 6 cups/50 fl oz (1.5 liters) chicken stock
 salt

Heat a *comal* or frying pan over high heat. Toast all the chiles on all sides for 4 minutes, or until blisters appear. Remove from the pan, core and seed, reserving the seeds of the *chilhuacle* chiles. Place all the chiles in a bowl, cover with hot water and season with salt. Let soak for 30 minutes, or until soft. Remove, pat dry, and set aside.

Meanwhile, in the same *comal* or frying pan, toast the *chilhuacle* seeds with the sesame seeds for 8 minutes, or until slightly burnt. Set aside. Repeat with the tortilla and avocado leaf. Set aside. Add the tomatoes to the same pan and roast for 15 minutes, or until the skin starts to peel. Transfer the tomatoes to a blender and blend for 2 minutes, or until smooth. Pass the mix through a strainer and set aside.

In a small pan, heat 4 tablespoons of the lard and cook the walnuts, almonds, cashews, cinnamon, cloves, peppercorns, nutmeg, and the burnt tortilla. Fry for 8 minutes, stirring, or until all the ingredients are crispy. Transfer to a blender and add the raisins, burnt sesame and *chilhuacle* seeds, and avocado leaf. Blend well for 2 minutes, and set aside.

In a frying pan, heat 2 tablespoons of the lard over medium heat and cook the soaked and dried chiles for 5 minutes. Pour in the blended nut mixture and simmer over low heat for 10 minutes, stirring frequently, until thick.

Heat the remaining 2 tablespoons of lard in a medium pan or clay pot, and add the nut, chile, and tomato mixtures, the crushed chocolate, oregano, and stock. Stir well and simmer for 40 minutes over low heat, or until the sauce thickens.

Garden Vegetables

Yellow Mole

Mole amarillo
Mexico

Preparation time: 20 minutes,
plus 20 minutes soaking
Cooking time: 2 hours 30 minutes   Serves: 6

Usually just called *amarillo*, this classic Oaxacan *mole*
is technically more of a light red or orange. Lacking
chocolate and fruits, it's not very sweet, but earthy
and vibrant. Different herbs like *hoja santa* and *pitiona*,
varying with the exact microclimate it is being made,
help define its flavor. It's often served over chicken,
with tamales, or as a stew with meats and vegetables.

    1 whole chicken (2 lb/900 g), cut into pieces
    4½ cups/36 fl oz (1 liter) chicken stock
    8 oz (225 g) potatoes, peeled and sliced
    8 oz (225 g) green beans
    6 baby zucchini (courgettes), halved
    1 chayote, peeled and diced
    6 *chilcostle* chiles, cored and seeded
    2 *ancho* chiles, cored and seeded
    5 *costeño* chiles, cored and seeded
    4 cups/32 fl oz (950 ml) hot water
    10 tomatoes
    5 tomatillos
    3 cloves
    6 black peppercorns
    1 teaspoon dried oregano
    1 white onion, chopped
    5 garlic cloves, peeled
    1 tablespoon lard
    4½ oz (125 g) fresh Corn Masa (page 123)

Put the chicken pieces and stock in a large pan and
place over high heat. Bring to a boil, reduce the heat,
cover, cook for 30 minutes, or until the meat is tender.
Remove the chicken from the stock and set aside.
Add the potatoes, green beans, zucchini (courgettes),
and chayote to the stock and cook for 30 minutes, or
until all the vegetables are soft. Remove and set aside.
    Heat a *comal* or frying pan and toast the *chilcostle*
for 7 minutes, or until blistered. Repeat with the *ancho*
and *costeño*. Place all the chiles in a bowl and cover with
the hot water. Soak for 20 minutes, then remove the
chiles, reserving the water. Place the chiles in a blender,
add 1 cup/8 fl oz (250 ml) of the reserved water, and blend
on medium speed to a smooth paste. Strain and set aside.
    Place the tomatoes and tomatillos in a pan, add water
to cover, and bring to a boil. Cook for 10 minutes, or until
soft. Peel the tomatoes. Place both in the blender.
    Heat a *comal* or frying pan over medium heat. Toast
the cloves, peppercorns, and oregano for 3 minutes.
Add them to the blender with the tomatoes, then add
the onion and garlic, and 1 cup/8 fl oz (250 ml) of the
reserved chicken stock. Blend for 2 minutes to form a
smooth paste. Pass through a strainer and reserve.
    In a medium pan, heat the lard over high heat and
pour in the chile paste. Stir well for 10 minutes, then
lower the heat to medium. Add the tomato paste and
continue cooking for a further 15 minutes, stirring often.
    Place the masa in a blender with 1 cup/8 fl oz (250 ml)
of stock. Blend for 1 minute, or until soft. Pour the tomato
mixture into the pan with the remaining stock. Let thicken
for 15 minutes over low heat. Season with salt. The *mole*
should be thick. If necessary, add more stock.
    Before serving, add the chicken and vegetables to
the mole to warm through, then serve warm.

Almond Mole

Mole almendrado
Mexico

Preparation time: 20 minutes,
plus 10 minutes soaking
Cooking time: 1 hour 30 minutes   Serves: 10

The village of San Pedro Atocpan in the Milpa Alta
borough of Mexico City has become known as a
production center for commercial moles, though it's
also the birthplace of the grainy, almond-based mole
almendrado. The exact set of 26 to 28 ingredients can
vary, though it always includes *mulato*, *pasilla*, and
ancho chiles.

    2 oz (60 g) *mulato* chiles, cored and seeded
    2 oz (60 g) *pasilla* chiles, cored and seeded
    2 oz (60 g) *ancho* chiles, cored and seeded
    9 oz (250 g) tomatoes
    9 oz (250 g) tomatillos
    3½ cups/29 fl oz (870 ml) chicken stock
    ½ white onion
    2 garlic cloves
    ½ cup/2 oz (60 g) sesame seeds, toasted
    2 cloves
    1 teaspoon black peppercorns
    1 teaspoon dried oregano
    1 teaspoon cumin seeds
    1 cinnamon stick
    3 tablespoons lard
    ½ cup/2 oz (60 g) almonds
    ½ cup/2 oz (60 g) peanuts
    ⅔ cup/2 oz (60 g) raisins
    1 ripe plantain, sliced
    1 *bolillo* (bread roll)
    1 tablespoon brown sugar
    salt

In a *comal* or dry frying pan, toast all the chiles with
the tomatoes and tomatillos over medium heat, turning
to toast evenly, and removing the chiles after 2 minutes.
Toast the tomatoes and tomatillos for a further
3 minutes.
    Place the chiles in a bowl, cover with hot, salted water,
and let soak for 10 minutes, then transfer to a blender.
    Roast the garlic cloves and onions in a dry frying pan
over high heat for 5 minutes, then transfer to the blender.
    Place the tomatoes and tomatillos in a medium pan
and cover up to halfway with chicken stock, reserving
1 cup/8 fl oz (250 ml) of the stock. Bring to a boil and
cook for 20 minutes, or until it has the consistency of a
purée. Let cool, then tip into the blender with the chiles,
roasted onion and garlic, sesame seeds, cloves, black
pepper, oregano, cumin, and cinnamon stick. Blend to
a smooth paste, for 3 minutes on medium speed.
    Heat half the lard in a clay pot or pan over medium
heat. Once it starts to smoke, reduce the heat to low and
add the blended mixture. Cook for 20 minutes, stirring.
Season with salt.
    Meanwhile, in a frying pan, heat the remaining lard
and fry the almonds, peanuts, raisins, and plantain for
7 minutes or until slightly brown. Place the ingredients
in the blender with the *bolillo* bread and of chicken
stock. Blend on medium speed until smooth, then add
it into the clay pot or pan. Season with salt and add
the sugar. Reduce the heat and simmer for 20 minutes,
or until the sauce thickens. Check the seasoning and
serve warm over chicken or enchiladas.

Beans and Lentils

On the streets of Salvador de Bahia, Brazilian women known as *Baianas do acarajé*, wearing layered white lace dresses, headscarves, and beaded jewelry, drop scoops of mashed black-eyed peas into a reddish palm oil known as *dendê* to make *acarajé*. Their dress is an homage to the Afro-Brazilian religion of Candomblé. Originating among slaves in the early 1800s, mixing West African, indigenous, and Roman Catholic beliefs, worship of Candomblé was kept secret by its followers until recent decades, now estimated at around two million. The *Baianas* slice open the *acarajé* and stuff them with shrimp and spicy pastes like *vatapá* and *caruru*, passing it from their hands to yours while still hot. Usually they'll also sell other saintly foods like *abará*, which uses the same black-eyed pea mixture but wraps it in a banana leaf and steams it rather than frying it, as well as shredded coconut sweets called *cocadas*.

Slaves brought the *acarajé* to Brazil from West Africa, where it has a variety of names, like *akará* and *kosai*. The name *acarajé* is derived from the Yoruba language, a combination of "akará" (ball of fire) and "jé" (to eat), and its consumption is tied to the origins of Candomblé, as an offering to Xangô's wives, Oxum and Iansã. The common version of *acarajé* sold by street vendors of Salvador are an offering to Iansã, the goddess of the winds and storms, though ritual versions come in other sizes, each designed as an offering to specific Orishas, or deities. Larger, round *acarajé* are for Xangô, while the smallest ones are for child spirits called Erês. The fritter is closely related to *acaçá*, another ritual food made from steamed and mashed white corn (for Oxala) or yellow corn (for Oxossi), which get placed on a *pegi*, or Candomblé altar. Prior to the abolition of slavery in Brazil in 1888, selling *acarajé* was done by *escravas de ganho*, earning slave women, who were allowed to keep some of the income to support their families and even buy their freedom. Today several thousand vendors, many who have tended their stalls for decades, preserve this legacy.

For many in Latin America, beans and lentils are a more important source of protein than meat. They come in a rainbow of colors and an array of sizes, are cheap, are easy to grow even in poor soil, and can be stored for long periods. They are prepared in tens of thousands of different ways in this part of the world—our short sample doesn't do them justice. Beans need to be cooked until soft, though there are endless discussions on exactly how you make that happen. Some swear by clay pots, as the alkaline in the clay makes the skins more tender. Choosing to soak or not to soak dried beans is one dilemma. While pressure cookers, multicookers, and simply boiling for ten minutes before simmering shortens the cooking time for dried beans, much of Latin America is old school. They like soaking beans. There's something beautifully simplistic about leaving them in water in the morning or the night before. It's a practice that connects us to thousands of years of everyday life in this part of world. For some smaller beans, like black-eyed peas and black beans, not to mention lentils, soaking doesn't have that much of an effect. For larger beans, however, soaking is a good idea. If you have forgotten to soak the beans, you can still cook them, just understand it will take a bit longer.

Black-Eyed Pea Fritters

Acarajé
Brazil

Preparation time: 35 minutes,
plus overnight soaking
Cooking time: 30 minutes

Makes: 12–15

In nearly any town in the Brazilian state of Bahia, you'll come across a woman dressed in white selling *acarajé*. Rules have been enacted by Brazil's institute of historical heritage to protect not just the recipe of *acarajé*, but the techniques and rituals surrounding it, such as the ways the beans are peeled, what the fritter can be stuffed with, and the typical dress of the *Baianas*.

2¼ cups/1 lb (450 g) dried black-eyed peas (beans)
3 onions, 2 roughly chopped, 1 thinly sliced
1 garlic clove, peeled
1 small *malagueta* chile, seeded
1¾ cups/14½ fl oz (425 ml) *dendê* oil (or use groundnut oil with 1 tablespoon ground annatto, though not ideal)
1 teaspoon chile powder
12 oz (340 g) raw, peeled small shrimp (prawns)
1½ cups/12 fl oz (350 ml) vegetable oil
salt and ground pepper

In a large bowl, cover the black-eyed peas (beans) with cold water and let soak overnight, or for up to 24 hours.

At the end of their soaking time, rub the peas between your hands to remove the outer skin. Discard the skins, and change the water as many times as needed to remove all the skins. This process will take a while. (While it's not technically following the cultural rules of making *acarajé*, you can skip this step by using peeled or canned peas.)

In a food processor, blend the peeled peas, the 2 chopped onions, garlic, and fresh chile. Season with salt and pepper, and mix the batter using a wooden spoon until light and fluffy.

For the *vatapá* (filling), heat 2 tablespoons of the *dendê* oil in a frying pan, and add the sliced onion with some salt and the chile powder. Cook over low heat until soft and golden. Add the shrimp (prawns) and cook for 4 minutes, until pink. Remove from the heat and set aside.

In a heavy pan, heat the remaining *dendê* oil with the vegetable oil to 375°F/190°C. In small batches, shape balls of batter using two spoons, drop carefully into the hot oil, and fry for about 3 minutes on each side or until bright and crispy. Remove to a plate lined with paper towels to absorb excess oil. Cut the fritters lengthways and fill with the shrimp and onion mixture. Serve.

Refried Black Beans with Bacon

Tutu à Mineira 🔲
Brazil

Preparation time: 15 minutes,
plus overnight soaking
Cooking time: 1 hour 20 minutes

Serves: 6

Prepared *à Mineira*, or in the style of the inland state of Minas Gerais, Brazil, this recipe for refried black beans gets added flavor from bits of meat, and is thickened with cassava flour. It can be served with white rice, simple sautéed collard greens, fried banana, or pork chops.

2¼ cups/1 lb (450 g) dried black beans
2 bay leaves
2 tablespoons vegetable oil
8 oz (225 g) *linguiça calabresa* (or smoked sausage or chorizo), thinly sliced
8 oz (225 g) thick-cut bacon, cut into chunks
3 garlic cloves, crushed
½ cup/2½ oz (70 g) cassava flour
4 hard-boiled eggs, sliced
salt and ground pepper
cooked white rice, to serve

Put the beans in a large bowl, cover with plenty of cold water and let soak overnight, or up to 24 hours.

Drain the beans and add to a medium pan with the bay leaves, enough water to cover generously, and some salt. Bring to a boil and cook for 10 minutes, then reduce to a simmer and cook covered for about 50 minutes until tender, adding more water if necessary. Strain, reserving both the beans and water (discard the bay leaves). In a food processor, blend the beans with enough of the cooking water to give a creamy consistency.

Meanwhile, heat the oil in a large pan. Sauté the sausage and bacon until golden brown. Set aside a few pieces of bacon or sausage for a garnish. Add the garlic, and some salt and pepper to the pan. Stir in the blended beans and bring the mixture to a boil. Lower the heat and slowly add the cassava flour until thick, stirring continuously. Remove from heat.

Garnish with hard-boiled egg slices and pieces of bacon or sausage. Serve warm, with white rice.

Refried Black Beans

Frijoles volteados, frijoles refritos
Guatemala

Preparation time: 10 minutes,
plus overnight soaking
Cooking time: 1 hour

Serves: 4-6

For many indigenous families in Guatemala, beans are the primary source of protein and *frijoles volteados* are one of the most common ways to prepare them. They are often eaten three times a day, slathered on tortillas or bread, or eaten with rice and a fried egg on the side.

1¼ cups/9 oz (250 g) dried black beans
1 bay leaf
8 cups/64 fl oz (1.9 liters) water
2 tablespoons olive oil
1 onion, finely diced
2 garlic cloves, minced
salt
½ cup/2 oz (60 g) crumbled *queso fresco*, to serve

Put the beans in a large bowl, add plenty of cold water to cover, and let soak overnight, or up to 24 hours.

Drain the beans and add to a medium pan with the bay leaf. Add the measured water and some salt, bring to a boil and cook for 10 minutes, then reduce to a simmer and cook covered for about 40 minutes, until almost tender. Strain, reserving the cooking water.

Add the beans and half the cooking water to a blender. Blend to a smooth, paste-like consistency, adding more of the water if needed.

Heat the oil in a medium frying pan, then sauté the onion and garlic. Add the bean paste and stir over medium heat for about 10 minutes. Sprinkle the *queso fresco* on top and serve.

Refried Black Beans with Bacon

Beans with Reins

Porotos con riendas
Chile

Preparation time: 20 minutes,
plus overnight soaking
Cooking time: 50 minutes

Serves: 6

The name of this common bean and noodle soup, served primarily in the winter, refers to how it is prepared in the Chilean countryside, with "reins," or pork skin (or in other words, leather). As it was adapted to city palates, the "reins" became noodles, though many still like to serve it with *chicharrón*.

> 2½ cups/13 oz (360 g) dried cranberry (borlotti) beans
> 1 pumpkin, peeled, seeded, and chopped
> 2 tablespoons vegetable oil
> 1 onion, finely diced
> 1 garlic clove, minced
> 1 celery stalk, finely diced
> ½ red bell pepper, seeded and finely diced
> 1 carrot, grated
> 1 tomato, grated
> 1 teaspoon *merkén* (smoked chile powder)
> 1 teaspoon ground cumin
> 2 *longaniza* sausages, sliced
> 7 oz (200 g) dried spaghetti
> 1 bunch chard, shredded
> 1 teaspoon oregano or parsley leaves
> salt and ground pepper

Put the beans in a large bowl, cover with plenty of cold water and let soak overnight, or up to 24 hours.

Drain the beans and add to a medium pan with enough water to cover generously, and some salt. Bring to a boil and cook for 10 minutes, then reduce to a simmer and cook covered for 25 minutes, then add the pumpkin and cook until the beans and pumpkin are tender.

Meanwhile, heat the oil in another medium pan over medium heat. Add the onion, garlic, celery, bell pepper, and carrot and cook, stirring, until tender, then add the tomato, *merkén* (smoked chile powder), and cumin. Cook for 1 minute, then add the *longaniza* and sauté for 3 minutes.

Add the mixture to the cooked beans and pumpkin, then add the spaghetti and cook for a further 6–8 minutes, until al dente. Add the chard just before serving. Serve hot, sprinkled with oregano or parsley.

Brazilian Beans, Sausage, and Greens

Feijao tropeiro
Brazil

Preparation time: 10 minutes,
plus overnight soaking
Cooking time: 1 hour

Serves: 6–8

Translating as "cattleman or cowboy beans," this dish from the state of Minas Gerais can be traced back to colonial times, when *tropeiros* would travel long distances on horseback through the rugged interior of Brazil. It's usually served with rice and *torresmos*, or pork crackling.

> 2¼ cups/1 lb (450 g) dried *carioca* (pinto) beans
> 2 bay leaves
> 6 cups/50 fl oz (1.5 liters) water
> 4 tablespoons olive oil
> 5 eggs, beaten
> 6 garlic cloves, minced
> 1 cup/2½ oz (70 g) chopped collard greens or kale
> 14 oz (400 g) *linguiça calabresa* (or smoked sausage or chorizo), sliced
> 8 oz (225 g) sliced bacon, diced
> 1 white onion, sliced
> 1 cup/5 oz (140 g) cassava flour
> ½ cup/1½ oz (40 g) chopped parsley
> ½ cup/1½ oz (40 g) chopped chives
> salt and ground pepper

Put the beans in a large bowl, cover with plenty of cold water and let soak overnight, or up to 24 hours.

Add the drained beans to a medium pan with the bay leaves, water, and some salt. Bring to a boil over medium-high heat and cook for 10 minutes, then reduce to a simmer and cook covered for about 35 minutes, until al dente (they should not be tender), adding more water if necessary. Drain and set aside.

Heat 2 tablespoons of the oil in a medium frying pan over medium heat. Add the eggs to the pan and cook, stirring, until scrambled. Set aside.

Heat the remaining oil in a large pan over medium heat. Add half the garlic and cook until golden, then add the chopped greens and cook until wilted. Season with salt and pepper, remove to a bowl, and set aside. In the same pan, brown the sausage. Remove and set aside.

Add the bacon to the pan and cook until golden brown, then add the onion and remaining garlic, followed by the drained beans, the sausage, eggs, and greens. Stir to combine, then add the cassava flour, a handful at a time, stirring until it is moist and fully incorporated. Remove from the heat and serve immediately, sprinkled with the parsley and chives.

Beef and Lentil Stew

Guiso de lentejas
Argentina

Preparation time: 20 minutes,
plus overnight soaking
Cooking time: 1 hour 45 minutes

Serves: 8

This hearty winter stew has no standard recipe. Most just toss in brown lentils with whatever is in their pantry.

> 4⅔ cups/2 lb (900 g) brown lentils
> 2 teaspoons baking soda (bicarbonate of soda)
> 2 tablespoons oil
> 2 bay leaves
> 10 oz (275 g) beef round roast (topside), chopped
> 7 oz (200 g) smoked bacon or pork belly, cut into chunks
> 1 chorizo *colorado*, cut into chunks
> 2 onions, finely diced
> 2 garlic cloves, minced
> 1 teaspoon sweet paprika
> 2 carrots, diced
> 1 each red bell pepper, green bell pepper, and yellow bell pepper, cored, seeded, and diced
> 2 tablespoons tomato paste (purée)
> 4½ cups/34 fl oz (1 liter) hot beef stock
> ½ cup/2 oz (60 g) chopped parsley
> salt and ground pepper

Beans and Lentils

Put the lentils in a bowl, add double their volume of water and the baking soda (bicarb), and let soak for 12 hours or overnight, then drain.

Heat 1 tablespoon of the oil in a pan over medium heat. Add the lentils and cook gently for 2 minutes. Add the water, bay leaves, and some salt. Boil for about 30 minutes, until the lentils become softer (not fully tender, as they will complete cooking later). Drain and set aside.

Heat the remaining tablespoon of oil in a medium pan and add the beef, bacon, and chorizo. Sauté for about 15 minutes until brown, then remove and set aside. In the same pan, add the onion, garlic, paprika, and some salt and pepper. Cook for 10 minutes until golden, then add the carrots and bell peppers, and cook for a further 5 minutes. Add back the beef, bacon, and chorizo, with the lentils and tomato paste (purée). Add the hot beef stock, cover, and cook for 40 minutes, or until the lentils are fully tender.

Serve in a deep dish or ceramic bowl, sprinkled with the parsley.

Brazilian Black Bean and Pork Stew

Feijoada
Brazil

Preparation time: 20 minutes, plus overnight soaking
Cooking time: 2 hours

Serves: 8

The name is derived from the Portuguese word for beans, *feijão*, and forms of *feijoada* are eaten throughout places once settled by the Portuguese, such as Macau, Mozambique, Angola, and Goa. In Brazil, this slow-simmered stew cooked in a clay pot is considered the national dish, eaten leisurely throughout a weekend afternoon. The most common forms of *feijoada* are found in the states of Minas Gerais and Rio de Janeiro, where it's usually prepared with black beans and a variety of different meats (the most traditional versions use pork scraps, like tails, feet, and trotters), though regional variations might change the types of beans or add in different vegetables. Wherever you are, it is usually served with a variety of sides like white rice, braised cabbage, *farofa* (toasted cassava flour), and orange slices.

2 cups/14 oz (400 g) dried black beans
½ cup/4 fl oz (120 ml) olive oil
8 oz (225 g) boneless smoked pork chops, cut into small chunks
8 oz (225 g) pork shoulder, cut into small chunks
8 oz (225 g) *linguiça* (or chorizo), sliced
7 oz (200 g) bacon, chopped
1 onion, chopped
1 garlic clove, minced
1 red bell pepper, cored, seeded, and chopped
1 green bell pepper, cored, seeded, and chopped
1 tomato, skinned and diced
½ cup/¾ oz (20 g) chopped parsley
½ cup/¾ oz (20 g) chopped chives
1 teaspoon paprika
1 teaspoon ground cumin
1 small red chile, seeded and chopped (or 1 teaspoon chile powder)
12 cups/100 fl oz (3 liters) water
1 orange
1 bay leaf
salt and ground pepper

Put the beans in a large bowl, cover with plenty of cold water and let soak overnight, or up to 24 hours.

Heat most of the oil in a large frying pan over medium heat. Sear the smoked pork chops and pork shoulder individually, removing to a plate as they are done. Lower the heat, add the sliced sausage, and cook for 6 minutes until lightly browned. Remove to a plate and set aside.

Wipe out the frying pan, place over low heat, and add the remaining oil and the bacon. Add the onion and garlic and let cook for 8 minutes. Add the peppers and tomato, parsley, chives, paprika, cumin, and chile. Cook for 10 minutes.

Meanwhile, drain the beans, place in a large pan, and cover with 12 cups of fresh water. Bring to a boil over high heat and, when it boils, add the whole, unpeeled orange and the bay leaf. Lower the heat and simmer for 20 minutes, skimming off the impurities and foam that will form. Add the meats, bacon, and sausage. Adjust the seasoning and cook for a further 30 minutes, then add the vegetables. Stir and cook over low heat for 40 minutes, or until the beans and pork are tender and the mix creamy.

Antioqueño-Style Beans

Frijoles antioqueños, Frijoles paisas
Colombia

Preparation time: 15 minutes, plus overnight soaking
Cooking time: 1 hour 55 minutes

Serves: 6

Frijoles antioqueños are a key part of the *bandeja paisa*, the oversized regional lunch platter, sometimes called Colombia's national dish, that also includes white rice, plantains, sausage, avocado, *chicharrón*, ground beef, a fried egg, and arepas. They can also be served in *cazuelitas*, small casserole dishes with the addition of corn, shredded beef, avocado, and ground pork rinds.

3½ cups/1 lb 2 oz (500 g) dried cranberry (borlotti) beans
6 cups/50 fl oz (1.5 liters) water
8 oz (225 g) ham hock or pork knuckle
3 tablespoons vegetable oil
1 tablespoon chopped onion
1 garlic clove, minced
2 cups/11 oz (320 g) diced tomatoes
¼ cup/¾ oz (20 g) chopped scallions (spring onions)
1 teaspoon cumin
¼ cup/⅓ oz (10 g) chopped cilantro (coriander)
2 carrots, grated
½ green plantain, sliced
salt

Put the beans in a large bowl, add plenty of cold water to cover, and let soak overnight, or up to 24 hours.

Drain the beans and add to a medium pan with the measured water, and some salt. Add the ham hock, bring to a boil over medium-high heat and cook for 10 minutes, then reduce to a simmer and cook covered for 35 minutes or until the beans are almost tender.

Heat the vegetable oil in a frying pan over medium heat. Add the onion and garlic, followed by the tomatoes and scallions (spring onions). Add the cumin and cilantro (coriander), and season with salt. Cook for 10 minutes.

When the beans are almost tender, add the cooked vegetables, grated carrot, plantain, and some salt. Cover and cook for a further 1 hour or until the beans are fully cooked. Serve with rice.

Black Bean Soup

Sopa negra
Costa Rica

Preparation time: 35 minutes,
plus overnight soaking
Cooking time: 1 hour 15 minutes

Serves: 6

There are variations of *sopa negra*, essentially black bean soup, found all across the Americas. The Tico version is always served with hard-boiled eggs, which are sometimes cooked in the soup, then removed and peeled before eating.

4½ cups/2 lb (900 g) dried black beans
10 cups/100 fl oz (3 liters) water
½ cup/¾ oz (20 g) cilantro (coriander)
1 onion, chopped
1 bell pepper, chopped
4 garlic cloves, peeled
2 tablespoons vegetable oil
1 celery stalk, chopped
½ cup/3¾ oz (110 g) tomato paste (purée)
3 green plantains, sliced
1 tablespoon ground cumin
3 hard-boiled eggs, halved or sliced
salt and ground pepper

Place the black beans in a large bowl and cover with plenty of cold water. Let soak overnight, or up to 24 hours.

Drain the beans and add to a medium pan with the measured water, and some salt. Bring to a boil and cook for 10 minutes, then reduce to a simmer and cook covered for about 50 minutes, until tender. Strain, reserving the cooking water.

Add half the beans and half the cooking water to a food processor or blender. Add half the cilantro (coriander), onion, bell pepper, and garlic. Blend until smooth.

Heat the oil in a pan over medium heat. Add the remaining cilantro, onion, bell pepper, and garlic, and the celery, and cook for 1 minute, then add the tomato paste (purée). Cook for 5 minutes, then add the blended bean mixture, followed by the remaining whole beans and cooking water, and the plantains. Add the cumin, season with salt and pepper, bring to a boil, and simmer for 8 minutes.

Serve in deep bowls with the hard-boiled eggs on top, with a side of rice.

Ecuadorian Easter Soup

Fanesca 🍲
Ecuador

Preparation time: 20 minutes,
plus overnight soaking
Cooking time: 1 hour 40 minutes

Serves: 10–12

Prepared only during Easter and Lent in Ecuador, the recipe for *fanesca* varies from region to region, family to family. It's a symbolic dish, with the twelve kinds of beans and grains, one for each of the twelve apostles, and the bacalao standing in for Jesus. Most often it's a midday meal on Good Friday, prepared and eaten among family and friends, and served with a spread of hard-boiled eggs, fried plantains, fresh chile peppers, pickled white onions, avocados, and empanadas.

½ cup/3¼ oz (90 g) yellow lentils
½ cup/3 oz (85 g) chickpeas
2 lb (900 g) salt (dried) cod (bacalao)
2 lb (900 g) sambo squash (also called *chilacayote* and *calabaza*), peeled, seeded, and chopped
1 lb (450 g) pumpkin, peeled, seeded, and chopped
1 cup/5 oz (130 g) cooked peas
1 cup/4¾ oz (150 g) cooked cranberry (borlotti) beans
8 cups/2 lb 1oz (920 g) cooked corn kernels
3 cups/13 oz (375 g) fava (broad) beans, cooked and peeled
1 cup/5 oz (150 g) cooked rice
¾ cup/3½ oz (100 g) butter
7 onions, finely chopped
8 garlic cloves, chopped
2 teaspoons ground achiote (annatto)
1½ cups/5 oz (150 g) ground peanuts
1 teaspoon chile powder
2 teaspoons ground cumin
1 cup/5 oz (150 g) cooked lupini beans
10 green cabbage leaves, cut into very thin strips
8 cups/40 fl oz (1.2 liters) milk
1 small bunch cilantro (coriander), chopped
1¼ cup/5 oz (150 g) *queso fresco*
salt

In separate bowls, soak the lentils and chickpeas in plenty of cold water overnight. Wash the salt cod and soak overnight in a large amount of cold water, to rid it of excess salt, changing the water every 6 hours. The next day, drain the legumes (pulses) and cook each separately in water for about 25 minutes, until tender. Drain and set aside.

Cook the squash and pumpkin for 15–25 minutes in a pan of boiling, salted water, or until tender. Drain and mash to a purée.

Put the cooked peas, lentils, chickpeas, cranberry (borlotti) beans, corn, fava (broad) beans, and rice in a large bowl. Mix well and set aside.

In a medium frying pan, heat the butter over medium heat and sauté the onions and garlic, then add the achiote (annatto), ground peanuts, spices, and lupini beans. Pour this mixture into a large pan, add the squash and pumpkin purée and the bean mixture, the cabbage, and milk. Mix well. Cook, covered, over low heat for 20 minutes.

Rinse the salt cod and place in a large pan. Cover with fresh water and cook gently until it breaks down into small pieces, then add it to the large pan of ingredients. Mix well, add the cilantro (coriander) and cook over low heat for 10 minutes. Either slice the *queso fresco* and use it to garnish the soup, or crumble the *queso fresco* and stir it into the soup to thicken. Serve warm.

Beans and Lentils

Ecuadorian Easter Soup

Legume Stew

Menestras
Ecuador

Preparation time: 10 minutes,
plus overnight soaking
Cooking time: 2 hours 10 minutes

Serves: 6–8

Typical of Guayaquil and the Ecuadorian coast, this hearty stew, which can be made of either lentils or beans, is never served on its own. It is always accompanied by white rice and a piece of fried meat, and sometimes fried plantains, *curtido* relish, and slices of avocado.

    2¼ cups/1 lb (450 g) brown lentils, rinsed
    3 tablespoons vegetable oil
    1 red onion, diced
    6 garlic cloves, minced
    3 tomatoes, diced
    1 bell pepper, cored, seeded, and diced
    1 teaspoon ground achiote (annatto)
    2 teaspoons ground cumin
    1 teaspoon chile powder
    8 cups/64 fl oz (1.9 liters) water
    4 tablespoons chopped cilantro (coriander)
    salt

Soak the lentils overnight in a bowl of water.
    Heat the oil in a large pan over medium heat, add the onion and garlic, and cook for 2–3 minutes.
    Add the tomatoes and bell pepper, then the achiote (annatto), cumin, and chile powder. Cook for 5 minutes, stirring occasionally. Add the water and bring to a boil, then add the drained lentils and simmer for 2 hours or until tender. Add salt to taste, then mix in the chopped cilantro (coriander) to serve.

Refried Beans in Anafre

Anafre de frijoles
Honduras

Preparation time: 20 minutes,
plus overnight soaking
Cooking time: 1 hour

Serves: 6

Anafre is a clay serving pot, with holes for air, found in Honduras where hot coals are placed beneath a clay bowl of beans to keep it warm. Usually, it's served as an appetizer with melted cheese and slices of jalapeños on top, as well as tortilla chips stuck right in the beans.

    1 cup/6 oz (180 g) *rojo de seda* (red silk) beans
    1 bay leaf
    1 tablespoon vegetable oil
    1 lb (450 g) chorizo, finely chopped
    ½ onion, finely diced
    1 garlic clove, minced
    ¼ teaspoon chile powder or cayenne pepper
    1 tablespoon chicken stock
    8 oz (225 g) shredded *queso fresco* or mozzarella
    salt and ground pepper

Put the beans in a large bowl, add plenty of cold water to cover, and let soak overnight, or up to 24 hours.
    Drain the beans and place in a medium pan with the bay leaf. Add plenty of cold water and some salt. Bring to a boil and cook for 10 minutes, then reduce to a simmer

and cook for about 35 minutes until almost tender. Drain, then mash.
    Heat the oil in a large pan over medium heat. Add the mashed beans and sauté, then add the chorizo and onion. Cook for about 3 minutes, then add garlic and chile, followed by the chicken stock. Continue stirring until it begins to bubble and then remove from the heat.
    Transfer the mixture to a clay bowl or serving dish. Mix, season with salt and pepper, and top with the cheese. You can place the bowl or dish on an *anafre* to keep it warm, otherwise just serve with warm tortillas or tortilla chips.

Piloy Bean Salad

Piloyada Antigüeña 🍲
Guatemala

Preparation time: 30 minutes,
plus overnight soaking
Cooking time: 1 hour 10 minutes

Serves: 6

One of Antigua, Guatemala's most traditional dishes is this bean salad, which is served cold, usually on Sundays. Its base is made up of large, reddish-brown piloy beans, a variety of scarlet runner bean found in this region.

    2¼ cups/1 lb (450 g) dried piloy beans
    1 bay leaf
    1 sprig thyme
    3 garlic cloves, minced
    ½ cup/4 fl oz (120 ml) vinegar
    2 tablespoons vegetable oil
    8 oz (225 g) pork shoulder
    4 cups/32 fl oz (950 ml) water
    6 chorizos
    6 *longaniza* sausages
    8 oz (225 g) tomatoes, diced
    1 onion, diced
    1 fresh chile, finely chopped
    1 bunch parsley, chopped
    2 tablespoons olive oil
    salt and ground pepper

    To serve
    4 tablespoons crumbled *queso seco* or *cotija* cheese
    3 hard-boiled eggs, sliced

Put the beans in a large bowl, cover with plenty of cold water and let soak overnight or up to 24 hours.
    Drain the beans and add to a pan with the bay leaf, thyme, garlic, half the vinegar, and some salt. Add enough water to cover, bring to a boil, and cook for 10 minutes. Reduce to a simmer and cook covered for 50 minutes or until almost tender. Drain and set aside.
    Meanwhile, heat 1 tablespoon of the vegetable oil in a pan over medium heat. Add the pork and sear all over. Add the water and some salt, cover, and cook for 45 minutes, or until the pork is fully done. Let cool and cut into 1–2-inch (2.5–5-cm) pieces.
    Heat the remaining oil in a pan over medium heat. Cook the chorizos and *longanizas* for 5 minutes, or until browned. Mix in the drained beans, pork, and remaining vinegar. Stir in the tomatoes, onion, chile, and parsley. Season to taste, and finish with the olive oil. Let cool.
    To serve, top with the crumbled cheese and slices of hard-boiled egg.

Beans and Lentils

Piloy Bean Salad

Bean Soup with Pork Ribs

Sopa de frijoles con costilla de cerdo
Honduras

Preparation time: 30 minutes,
plus overnight soaking
Cooking time: 2 hours

Serves: 4–6

This meaty bean soup is a Honduran staple. Typically, it uses *frijoles de seda*, small red beans that aren't overly starchy. You can serve it with a poached egg in the soup, as well as sides of rice, avocado, *queso fresco*, and tortillas.

    2½ cups/1 lb (450 g) dried *rojo de seda* (red silk) beans
    2 tablespoons olive oil
    ½ onion, very finely sliced
    3 garlic cloves, minced
    ½ bell pepper, seeded and cut into fine strips
    6 cups/50 fl oz (1.5 liters) water
    1 bunch cilantro (coriander)
    1 tablespoon pork lard
    1 lb (450 g) pork ribs or pork rinds
    1 teaspoon ground cumin
    1 lb (450 g) cassava, cut into 2-inch (5-cm) pieces
    3 *guineos* (green bananas), each sliced into 4
    salt and ground pepper

Put the beans in a large bowl, add plenty of cold water to cover, and let soak overnight, or up to 24 hours.

Heat the oil in a medium pan. Add the onion and cook for about 1 minute, then add the garlic and bell pepper and continue cooking. Add the drained beans and the measured water. Bring to a boil and cook for 10 minutes, then reduce to a simmer, add the cilantro (coriander), and cook for 1 hour, adding more water if needed. Add salt to taste.

Heat the lard in a medium frying pan over medium heat, then sear the pork ribs until medium done.

Add the pork ribs to the beans, add the cumin, and season with salt and pepper. Add the cassava and cook for 10 minutes, then add the bananas and continue cooking until the cassava begins cracking. Serve warm.

Bean and Cheese Toast

Molletes
Mexico

Preparation time: 10 minutes
Cooking time: 20 minutes

Serves: 4–6

A form of this open-faced breakfast sandwich can be traced back to Andalucia, where they are similar to Italian bruschetta. One of the simplest recipes in this entire book, *molletes* can be made in just minutes with the basics you have in your pantry: bread, beans, and cheese. A variety of toppings can be added such as chorizo, eggs, herbs, bacon, mushrooms, and salsas. In Puebla, there's a version called *molletes dulces* to celebrate the feast of Santa Clara: the rolls are filled with custard, sherry, or coconut and topped with sweetened *pepitas* (pumpkin seeds).

    10 oz (275 g) chorizo, diced
    4 *bolillos* or French rolls
    1 quantity Refried Black Beans (page 172)
    2½ cups/6 oz (180 g) shredded *queso ranchero*,
      grated (or use parmesan or Havarti)
    Pico de gallo (page 404), to serve

Preheat the oven to 350°F/180°C/Gas Mark 4.

Place a medium frying pan over medium heat. Add the chorizo and cook in its own fat for 4–5 minutes, until browned.

Cut the bread rolls in half. Spread with the refried beans, then add the cooked chorizo and cheese. Place on an oven tray and bake in the oven for about 15 minutes until the cheese has melted. Serve warm, with some *Pico de gallo*.

Mexican Cowboy Beans

Frijoles charros
Mexico

Preparation time: 20 minutes,
plus overnight soaking
Cooking time: 1 hour 45 minutes

Serves: 8–10

Named after *charros*, or Mexican horsemen, this soupy bowl of pinto beans is often served in the north of the country, sometimes alongside *carne asada*. Traditionally it was cooked for long hours over a campfire in a large pot, using many dried and preserved ingredients so it could keep for long periods of time. Another variation, called *frijoles borrachos* ("drunken beans") simmers the beans in beer.

    2¼ cups/1 lb (450 g) dried pinto beans
    4 tablespoons olive oil
    1 lb 4 oz (565 g) tomatoes, halved
    12 oz (350 g) bacon, diced
    1 white onion, diced
    2 chiles or 1 jalapeño pepper, minced
    3 garlic cloves, minced
    2 bay leaves
    2 sprigs epazote
    6 cups/50 fl oz (1.5 liters) chicken stock
    1 cup/1½ oz (40 g) chopped cilantro (coriander)
    salt

Put the beans in a large bowl, add plenty of cold water to cover, and let soak overnight, or up to 24 hours.

Preheat the oven to 400°F/200°C/Gas Mark 6.

Add 3 tablespoons of the oil, the tomatoes and some salt to a baking pan. Cover with aluminum foil, and roast in the oven for about 25 minutes until tender. Once cool enough to handle, remove the skins and seeds from the roasted tomatoes and dice the flesh.

In a medium pan or Dutch oven (casserole), add the remaining 1 tablespoon oil. Add the bacon and cook, stirring, until the fat is rendered and the bacon is brown. Add the onion and chiles and cook, stirring frequently. Add the garlic and diced roasted tomatoes.

Add the drained beans, bay leaves, epazote, and stock. Bring to a boil and cook for 10 minutes, reduce to a simmer and continue cooking for about 1 hour or until the beans are tender.

To serve, discard the bay leaves and top with the cilantro (coriander).

Spicy Fava Bean Stew

Pejtu de habas
Bolivia

Preparation time: 15 minutes,
plus overnight soaking
Cooking time: 1 hour 15 minutes

Serves: 4

Typical of the Valle de Cochabamba, though also prepared in many parts of the Bolivian highlands, *pejtu de habas* is a wholesome stew usually made from dried fava beans and dried meat. There's no definite preparation and some will opt for fresh fava beans and/ or meat if available. The potatoes can be served on the side or cooked with the other ingredients.

1 cup/8 oz (225 g) dried fava (broad) beans
1 lb (450 g) small potatoes, peeled
3 tablespoons vegetable oil
1 red onion, finely chopped
2 garlic cloves, minced
¼ teaspoon ground cumin
2 tablespoons *ají amarillo* paste
2 cups/16 fl oz (475 ml) beef stock
2 tablespoons chopped parsley
salt and ground pepper

Put the beans in a bowl with plenty of cold water to cover, and let soak overnight.

Drain the beans, and peel them. Fill a medium pan with water and bring to a boil. Add the beans and cook for 20 minutes, or until tender, then drain and set aside.

Meanwhile, put the potatoes in another pan of water, bring to a boil and cook for 15 minutes or until tender.

Heat the oil in a large pan over medium heat, add the onion and garlic, and sauté for 5 minutes, or until the onions are translucent. Add the cumin and *ají amarillo* paste and continue cooking for a further 10 minutes, stirring continuously. Add the stock, bring to a boil, then reduce to a simmer and cook for 30 minutes, or until it thickens. Add the potatoes and beans and cook for a further 10 minutes. Season with salt and pepper.

Serve hot with the chopped parsley on top.

Fava Bean Soup

Kapchi de habas
Peru

Preparation time: 30 minutes
Cooking time: 35 minutes

Serves: 4–6

The word *kapchi* in Quechua, translates as "cheese," which helps form the base of this nutritious, vegetarian meal that's prepared in the wintertime in the Peruvian Andes. During the rainy season in Cusco, wild mushrooms, such as Slippery Jacks (*Suillus luteus*), are gathered high in the mountains and are used instead of or in addition to the beans to make *kapchi de setas*, which otherwise uses the exact same ingredients.

1 lb 2 oz (500g) potatoes, peeled and cut into chunks
1 cup/4 oz (120 g) fresh fava (broad) beans
2 tablespoons vegetable oil
½ onion, chopped
4 garlic cloves, minced
1 tomato, chopped
1 teaspoon *ají panca* paste

1 cup/8 fl oz (250 ml) water
1 cup/8 fl oz (250 ml) milk
2 eggs, beaten
½ cup/2 oz (60 g) crumbled *queso fresco*
1 bunch *huacatay* (Peruvian black mint)
salt

Place the potatoes in a pan with water to cover, and some salt. Bring to a boil, then reduce the heat and cook for 20 minutes, until tender, then drain. In a separate pan, cook the fava (broad) beans until tender, then drain.

Heat 2 tablespoons of the oil in a medium pan, add the onion, garlic, tomato, and *ají panca*, and season with salt. Add the water, potatoes, and beans. Stir in the milk, eggs, cheese, and *huacatay*. Cook for a few minutes until the eggs are cooked, then serve, with quinoa on the side.

Tarwi

An edible lupin bean, tarwi (*Lupinus mutabilis*) was domesticated in the Andes around 1,500 years ago. It has a bitter taste, which can be easily removed by simmering for about an hour and a half in salted water, then being soaked overnight. They are eaten much like soybeans and made into flour or pressed for oil. Rich in protein and full of amino acids, tarwi has not only been an essential for a healthy diet in the Andes, but it's good for the soil too. Its honey-scented flowers attract beneficial insects and it helps pump nitrogen into the soil, which is why it is often planted near native tubers.

Tarwi Ceviche

Ceviche de tarwi, ceviche de chochos
Ecuador, Peru

Preparation time: 10 minutes,
plus two days overnight soaking
Cooking time: 3 hours

Serves: 4

This preparation of tarwi is rather common in the Ancash region of Peru, though it can be encountered in similar forms throughout the Peruvian and Ecuador Andes as well. The recipe is quite similar to a traditional fish-based ceviche and it's sold in highland market stalls and street carts.

10 oz (285 g) dry tarwi
½ red onion, finely chopped
juice of 5 limes
2 tablespoons chopped cilantro (coriander)
1 tablespoon rocoto chile paste
1 tomato, peeled and diced
1 tablespoon olive oil
salt and ground pepper

Place the dry tarwi in a large pot and cover generously with salted water. Bring to a boil, then reduce the heat and simmer for 90 minutes (the tarwi will soften, but will not become completely tender). Drain the water and rinse the tarwi. Let the tarwi soak in a bowl of salted water overnight. The next day, cover the tarwi with more salted water, bring to a boil, then reduce the heat and simmer for 90 minutes. Drain and rinse the tarwi again.

In a bowl, mix all the ingredients together, and season with salt and pepper. Serve immediately, in a cold dish or plate.

Fruit

At the edge of a finca in the green mountains east of Popayán, Colombia, a mestizo farmer watches an Andean motmot (*Momotus aequatorialis*) pick a lizard off of the trunk of a papaya tree as her horse drinks water from a stream. Brightly colored birds like the motmot, with its green feathers and neon blue tail and strip of its crown, are a common sight amidst the dozens of fruits she grows. There are granadillas, a type of passion fruit, as well as bananas, oranges, blackberries, lulo, guanabana, and nispero. She sells what she can, trades what she can, and preserves what she doesn't eat. Anything left over is for the birds, which help disperse the seeds.

Entire swaths of some Latin American countries have been turned into banana and pineapple plantations, producing fruits with homogeneous flavors and textures. At various points in the region's history, plantation owners have grown quite powerful, not just disrupting the environment, but entire economic and political landscapes. These fruits are designed for export, but they see little life in the places where they are grown. The alternatives are far superior.

There are starchy *chontaduras*, sweet *pitayas*, and sour *arazás*. Some grow on tree trunks, some grow on cactuses, some look like eyeballs. There are single trees overloaded with so many mangoes they could fill supermarkets. Some fruits are available year-round, while others appear only for weeks or days. Many are eaten raw or juiced, used to start a day or replace dessert. Others are treated more like vegetables, getting mashed, cooked, or fried.

Awara Broth

Bouillon d'awara 🍲
French Guiana

Preparation time: 20 minutes,
plus overnight soaking
Cooking time: 4 hours 30 minutes

Serves: 4

There is a saying that goes: "Si tu manges du bouillon d'awara, en Guyane tu reviendras." Or "If you eat awara broth, you will return to Guiana." The fruit of the awara palm (*Astrocaryum vulgare*), called *tucumã* in Brazil, is native to the upper Amazon and has seeds covered with an orange, oily pulp that is used in dozens of traditional recipes in northern Brazil, Suriname, and French Guiana. To extract the pulp from the skin and seed, it takes hours of smashing the fruit with a wooden pestle. At Easter, in French Guiana, the juice of the pulp is used as the base of this stew that gets very slowly cooked, often for several days. Any ingredients that are around can and will be tossed in the pot too, like salted and smoked meats, fish, cassava and other vegetables, banana leaves, and various spices. Everyone's recipe is a little different. The process is so laborious that many buy their stew from other families or informal vendors. Awara broth is usually served over white rice.

    4 oz (120 g) pig tails
    4 oz (120 g) pig snout
    4 oz (120 g) salt (dried) cod
    2 lb (900 g) awara pulp
    2½ cups/20 fl oz (600 ml) hot water
    4 oz (120 g) smoked ham
    4 oz (120 g) smoked bacon
    1 red bell pepper, cored, seeded, and cut into strips
    ½ cabbage, cored and sliced
    4 oz (120 g) maroon cucumber (*Cucumis anguria*), peeled and diced
    8 oz (225 g) spinach, rinsed and stemmed
    4 oz (120 g) eggplant (aubergine), diced
    8 oz (225 g) green beans, halved lengthways
    8 oz (225 g) smoked chicken thighs
    8 oz (225 g) raw shrimp (prawns), shell on
    salt and ground pepper

Put the pig tails, snout, and cod in separate bowls of water and soak overnight, changing the water a couple of times.
Place the awara pulp in a large pan and cover with the hot water. Stir well and simmer for 45 minutes over low heat, keeping the consistency smooth and thick. Strain the pig tails and snout, then add to the pan and simmer for 1 hour. If any black oil rises to the top, skim and discard. Add the ham, bacon, and bell pepper, bring to a boil and simmer for 1 hour over low heat.
Add the cabbage, cucumber, and spinach and cook for 30 minutes over low heat, stirring occasionally. Add the eggplant (aubergine) and green beans and cook for 15 minutes. Strain the cod and add to the pot. Cook for a further 30 minutes over medium heat, adding a cup of water if needed. Finish by adding the chicken and shrimp (prawns). Bring to a boil and simmer for 20 minutes.
Check the seasoning. Serve hot, in bowls, over white rice with an extra helping of just the broth on the side.

Açaí

The multi-stemmed açaí palm (*Euterpe oleracea*), pronounced "ah-sah-ee," grows along the shady edges of rivers and streams of the Amazon rainforest. Once harvested, cylindrical machines, *batedores de açaí*, remove the thin outer layer of the super-fruit from the pit and turn it into a pulp, which is traditionally eaten as a porridge or served with fish (Paiche with Açaí, page 240).

Few fruits have been surrounded by as much confusion as açaí. A hearty, nutritious food of the poor in the Brazilian states of Pará and Amazonas, it has seen its price soar as demand across the world has surged, mostly because of misleading claims of it being a wonder berry that can help one lose weight fast or cure diseases. While some *ribeirinhos*, the people who live along Amazon waterways where açaí has long been a staple of their diet, have had to buy less of the fruit, others, especially when working with fair trade suppliers, have improved their lifestyles dramatically. For years the supply of açaí couldn't keep up with demand, so there were experiments with growing açaí palms plantation style, but so far, they have not panned out. The trees require organic matter and the protection from insects that only biodiversity can provide.

Açaí Bowl

Açaí na tigela
Brazil

Preparation time: 10 minutes

Serves: 2

While traditional preparations of açaí in northeastern Brazil are warm (see *Pirarucu com açaí* on page 240), juice and beach bars began serving the mashed, frozen, and sweetened form of the pulp in other parts of the country in the 1970s, and its popularity has since gone global. Toppings tend to vary from region to region and may include slices of bananas, granola, shaved coconut, tapioca, nuts, and other fruits.

    7 oz (200 g) frozen açaí pulp (unsweetened)
    2 tablespoons guarana syrup or honey
    1 banana, sliced
    2 tablespoons tapioca pearls
    2 tablespoons toasted coconut

Blend the frozen açaí pulp with the guarana syrup or honey, then divide the mixture into two bowls. Top with slices of banana, tapioca pearls, and toasted coconut.

Awara Broth

Breadfruit

Native to the Pacific, breadfruit (*Artocarpus altilis*) was introduced to the Caribbean by British and French sailors in the late eighteenth century. The name was given because when ripe and cooked, breadfruit smells of freshly baked bread; it is often called *masapan* by Mayan communities. As each tree can produce as much as 450 lb (200 kg) of fruit per year, it is an inexpensive, staple food in many parts of tropical Latin America, especially along the Caribbean coast of Central America and northern Brazil. In the region, the soccer-ball-sized fruit is consumed boiled in soups, mashed with coconut milk, fermented, baked, roasted whole in a fire, and fried.

Sliced and Fried Breadfruit

Fruta de pan frita
Belize, Costa Rica, Guatemala, Honduras, Nicaragua, Panama

Preparation time: 10 minutes
Cooking time: 10 minutes

Serves: 4

Along the Caribbean coast and island communities of Central America, breadfruit is commonly sliced and fried and used as a replacement for bread.

 1 green breadfruit
 vegetable or coconut oil, for frying
 salt

Cut out the stem of the breadfruit then cut off the hard green exterior. Cut in half lengthways, then remove the hard inner core. Cut the halves into slices no thicker than ¼ inch (5 mm).
 In a medium frying pan, heat enough oil for shallow-frying. Place the breadfruit slices in the hot oil and cook until golden brown and crisp on both sides. Remove to a plate lined with paper towels to absorb excess oil. Sprinkle with salt and serve.

Mangoes

Native to South Asia, mangoes were introduced by the Portuguese to Salvador de Bahia, Brazil, in the sixteenth century. The stone fruit now grows in the tropical and subtropical regions across Latin America, everywhere from Mexico to northern Chile. They are commonly seen sliced on roadsides, often with a squeeze of lime and chile powder.

Jicama and Mango Salad

Belize

Preparation time: 20 minutes

Serves: 2–4

While peeled and sliced mangoes, doused in salt, lime, and ground chile, can be found in many places in Latin America, roadside fruit vendors in Belize sell them in plastic bags mixed with jicama.

 1 mango
 1 jicama (yam bean)
 1 teaspoon chile powder
 1 teaspoon salt
 juice of 1 lime

Peel the mango and jicama, then slice both into strips. Place in a bowl and mix with the chile, salt, and lime juice.

Green Mango Salad

Salada de mango verde, kalawang
Belize, French Guiana

Preparation time: 10 minutes,
plus 15 minutes chilling

Serves: 4

Unripe mangoes, with their high acidity, allow them to pair well with other fruits and some vegetables. In Brazil, they are often sliced, cut into chunks, or thinly cut on a mandolin into noodles for salads, which can also stand in as relishes or salsas. The preparation is similar in French Guiana's *kalawang*, though garlic, herbs like cilantro or parsley, and chile peppers, are added too.

 4 green mangoes, peeled and thinly sliced
 ½ red onion, thinly sliced
 2 tablespoons finely chopped cilantro (coriander)
 1 tablespoon lime juice
 salt and ground pepper

Mix all the ingredients in a bowl, with salt and pepper to taste, and refrigerate for 15 minutes before serving.

Green Mango Salad

Bananas

The Portuguese first brought bananas to the Americas in the sixteenth century, and they have quickly become a staple food crop that is available year round. In countries such as Ecuador, Guatemala, Costa Rica, Colombia, and Honduras, among others, banana exports are a major part of the economy, for better or worse. While export markets are dominated by just a few varieties of banana, markets in much of tropical Latin America feature dozens of different shapes and colors. They might be short and stubby or long and brawny, yellow, red, or orange. Besides being eaten raw, they are used in purées and tamales. Unripe green bananas, where the starches have not yet been converted into sugars, are often used in cooked dishes, especially in Caribbean coastal areas.

Green Banana and Coconut Milk Tamales

Darasa, bimena
Belize, Honduras

Preparation time: 20 minutes
Cooking time: 1 hour   Serves: 6

In their most basic form these tamales made in Garifuna communities on the coast of Belize and Honduras are made of just green bananas, peeled and grated with a wooden grater called an *egi*, mashed with coconut milk, which is most likely made from fresh coconuts. It's a labor-intensive process made from some of the most abundant ingredients in these communities that results in a rather delicious snack. *Darasa* is often served with fried fish or fish soup.

    6 banana leaves, cut into 10-inch (25-cm) squares
    7 green bananas, peeled and grated
    ½ *ají dulce* chile, finely chopped
    ½ medium onion, finely chopped
    ¾ cup/6 fl oz (175 ml) coconut milk
    2 tablespoons lime juice
    1 teaspoon salt
    ½ teaspoon ground pepper

Clean the banana leaves with a warm, damp tea towel, and set aside.
    Place the grated banana in a bowl and add the chile, onion, ½ cup/4 fl oz (120 ml) of the coconut milk, the lime juice, salt, and pepper. Mash everything with a mortar or wooden spoon until it forms a paste, adding in the remaining coconut milk if needed. Divide the mixture into 6 portions and place each in the middle of a banana leaf. Fold the leaves over four times by getting all the edges to the middle. Seal with a string made by cutting off a strip of the same banana leaves.
    Pour about 2 inches (5 cm) of water into a steamer, and bring to a boil. Add the steamer basket (make sure the water doesn't touch the basket), place the tamales in the basket and steam for 1 hour. Remove from the basket and let cool before serving.

Rapa Nui-Style Banana Bread Pudding

Po'e
Chile

Preparation time: 30 minutes
Cooking time: 1 hour   Serves: 6

Found in much of eastern Polynesia, including the Chilean territory of Rapa Nui, or Easter Island, *po'e*, naturally sweet, is usually served at barbecues and alongside savory dishes.

    9 oz (250 g) pumpkin or squash
    10 ripe bananas, mashed
    3 cups/14 oz (400 g) all-purpose (plain) flour
    1 cup/8 oz (225 g) butter, room temperature
    ½ cup/1½ oz (40 g) powdered milk
    1 cup/2½ oz (70 g) grated fresh coconut
    2 cups/14 oz (400 g) sugar
    coconut oil, for greasing

Preheat the oven to 350°F/180°C/Gas Mark 4.
    Coarsely grate the pumpkin or squash into a large bowl, add the mashed banana, and slowly mix in half of the flour, using your hands. Mix in the butter, powdered milk, grated coconut, sugar, and the remaining flour. Keep mixing well, using your hands, for about 5 minutes until you get a uniform dough.
    Grease an 8½ x 4½ x 2½-inch (22 x 11 x 6-cm) loaf pan (tin) with a little bit of coconut oil, and tip the dough into the pan. Bake for 1 hour until firm and a toothpick poked inside comes out clean, then remove from the oven and let cool before taking it out of the pan. If desired, drizzle with coconut cream or sprinkle over some grated coconut before serving.

Green Banana Porridge

Wabul bata de plátano verde
Honduras, Nicaragua

Preparation time: 10 minutes
Cooking time: 30 minutes   Serves: 4

In Miskito and Mayangna communities living along the Mosquito Coast of Honduras and Nicaragua, *wabul* can be eaten for any meal. At its most basic level, it is just cooked bananas or plantains, boiled or roasted, that are mashed with water or coconut milk using a wooden mortar and pestle called a *tuscaya*. Some versions use breadfruit, mango, or corn and the majority of preparations are sweet and thin, served like a drink, and sprinkled with ground cinnamon, cloves, or nutmeg. However, *wabul* can also be thicker, more like a porridge, and take on a savory flavor from the addition of stock made from fish and/or wild game. *Bijagua* (*Calathea lutea*) leaves can be swapped for banana leaves, which are similar in size and strength.

    16 oz (450 g) green bananas or plantains
    salt
    2 *bijagua* or banana leaves
    1½ cups/12 fl oz (355 ml) fish or game stock
    1½ cups/12 fl oz (355 ml) coconut milk

Remove the skin from the bananas and cut into 2-inch (5-cm) pieces.

Add 2 cups of salted water to a small pan and bring to a boil. Place the bananas in the pan and cover loosely with *bijagua* or banana leaves, which allow some of the steam to release from the pan. Reduce the heat to low and simmer for 20–30 minutes, or until soft. Remove the bananas from the water and drain.

In a mortar, mash the bananas with the stock and coconut milk, adding additional water to reach the desired consistency. Serve warm.

Ripe Banana and Coconut Milk Porridge

Michilá
Panama

Preparation time: 5 minutes, plus 5 minutes resting
Cooking time: 15 minutes

Serves: 4

In the Caribbean archipelago of Bocas del Toro near Panama's border with Costa Rica, many families have a recipe for *michilá*. The recipe uses two of the most abundant ingredients almost everywhere in the islands: bananas and coconut milk. There's no standard recipe for combining the two and ripe plantains or breadfruit can even be swapped in for the bananas, which can be boiled, mashed, or blended with the coconut milk. The consistency can range from frothy to creamy to thick and it can be sipped from a cup or eaten with a spoon. Whatever spices are in the pantry get sprinkled on top.

    8 oz (225 g) very ripe bananas or plantains, mashed
    3 cups/25 fl oz (750 ml) coconut milk
    1 cinnamon stick
    ¼ cup/1¾ oz (50 g) sugar, optional
    ground nutmeg or ginger, to serve

Place the mashed bananas, coconut milk, and cinnamon stick in a medium pan. Bring to a boil, then reduce heat to low and simmer for 10 minutes. Remove from the heat, then add the sugar, if using, and stir until it dissolves and the mixture is smooth. Let cool for 5 minutes and sprinkle with nutmeg or ginger before serving.

Hashed Banana Flowers

Picadillo de chira
Costa Rica

Preparation time: 30 minutes
Cooking time: 20 minutes

Serves: 2

If you have ever spent any time around a banana tree, you've probably noticed a low hanging, tear-drop-shaped, purple- or magenta-skinned flower. The inner petals, or bracts of this flower, sometimes called the heart or blossom, are edible. When eaten raw, they can be rather bitter, so more often than not they are cooked and used in savory recipes. Banana flowers are widely used in Southeast Asian and Indian cooking, though not widely in Latin America aside of the occasional recipe, such as this one from Costa Rica, which can be mixed with ground beef or served on a tortilla.

    1 teaspoon salt
    1 teaspoon baking soda (bicarbonate of soda)
    1 *chira* (banana flower)
    1 tablespoon olive oil
    1 small white onion, finely chopped
    2 garlic cloves, finely chopped
    1 tomato, peeled and diced
    1 teaspoon annatto paste
    1 tablespoon chopped cilantro (coriander)
    1 teaspoon ground cumin
    1 banana leaf, cut in half, to serve

Bring a medium pan of water to a boil, with the salt and baking soda (bicarbonate of soda) added.

Meanwhile, remove the outer purple layers from the banana flower, until you reach the pink to white, tender leaves. Cut off the tips, chop into chunks, and immediately place in the boiling water. Cook until soft, about 4 minutes, then drain, and rinse well. (This process will remove the bitterness, and you need to do it quickly, so the leaves don't oxidize and turn gray.)

Heat the oil in a frying pan over medium heat, add the onion and garlic, and sauté for about 7 minutes, until slightly brown, then add the tomato, annatto paste, cilantro (coriander), cumin, and banana flower. Cook for a further 5–7 minutes until the tomatoes start to brown, then remove from the heat.

Serve on a banana leaf.

Breaded and Fried Bananas

Banana à milanesa
Brazil

Preparation time: 5 minutes
Cooking time: 5 minutes

Serves: 6

This sweet and salty recipe is served as a side dish in many parts of Brazil, sometimes alongside *feijoada*. It works best when the bananas are still a bit firm, somewhere in between ripe and green.

    6 bananas
    2 eggs
    1 cup/4 oz (120 g) breadcrumbs
    ½ cup/2¼ oz (65 g) cassava flour
    ½ cup/2¼ oz (65 g) all-purpose (plain) flour
    2 tablespoons vegetable oil
    ½ teaspoon salt

Peel the bananas and cut into the preferred shape (halved, quartered, cut lengthways, or left whole).

Beat the eggs in a bowl. In separate, shallow dishes, place the breadcrumbs, and the cassava flour mixed with the all-purpose (plain) flour.

Roll the bananas in the flour, then coat with the beaten egg, and finally cover with the breadcrumbs.

Heat the oil in a medium pan, then add the bananas in two batches to not overcrowd the pan. Fry the bananas for about 2 minutes, or until golden brown, turning once or twice to ensure they fry evenly. Remove with a slotted spoon and place on a plate lined with paper towel to absorb any excess oil. Sprinkle with salt before serving.

Plantains

There is no botanical difference between bananas and plantains; however, these varieties of banana tend to be starchier and have thicker skins, so they are generally used more for cooking. Fried or baked, they often replace potatoes as a side dish in many parts of the region. When yellow and ripe they can still be eaten raw, they just aren't nearly as sweet as the typical banana.

Ripe Plantain Arepas

Arepas de Plátano Maduro
Colombia, Venezuela

Preparation time: 25 minutes
Cooking time: 50 minutes
Makes: 10–15

This common alternative to the arepa, supplementing plantain for most of the corn flour, is eaten as a snack at any time, or served as a side to seafood and meat plates.

3 ripe plantains with skin on, cut into 3–4 pieces
2 teaspoons sugar
¾ cup masarepa (precooked corn flour/maize flour)
4 tablespoons milk
8 tablespoons melted butter
3 oz (90 g) shredded *queso blanco* or *queso fresco*
½ teaspoon salt
1 tablespoon vegetable oil

Bring a pan of water to a boil, add the plantain pieces, and cook for 30 minutes. Drain and let cool, then peel the plantains.

In a bowl or food processor, mash the plantains. Add the masarepa, milk, melted butter, half the cheese, and salt. Stir until incorporated evenly. If the dough is too moist, add a little more masarepa. If the dough is too dry, add a little more milk.

Form the mixture into 10–15 small balls, then flatten all the balls into arepas, roughly 4 inches (10 cm) in diameter.

Heat the oil in a frying pan over medium heat, then sear the arepas in batches for 3–4 minutes per side, or until golden brown. Remove the arepas and place them on a plate lined with a paper towel to absorb any excess oil.

Serve hot with the remaining cheese scattered over the top.

Ripe Plantain Fritters

Aborrajados de plátano maduro
Colombia, Venezuela

Preparation time: 10 minutes
Cooking time: 30 minutes
Makes: 12

These stuffed, battered, fried plantains are a typical dish of Colombia's Valle de Cauca. Guava paste, there called *bocadillo*, is often added into the filling. In the Zulia state in western Venezuela, there's a similar recipe called *yoyos de plátano*, where the plantains are sliced lengthways, fried, rolled around cheese, then battered and fried again.

4¼ cups/34 fl oz (1 liter) vegetable oil
3 ripe plantains, peeled and each cut into 4 pieces
6 oz (175 g) *queso de mano* or mozzarella, cut into strips
2 eggs
3 tablespoons milk
6 tablespoons all-purpose (plain) flour
3 tablespoons sugar
pinch of salt
miel de caña (cane syrup), to serve, optional

Pour the oil into a large, heavy pan, making sure it is no more than two-thirds full, and heat to 350°F/177°C. Fry the plantains for about 4 minutes, or until soft and golden brown. Remove to a plate lined with paper towels to absorb excess oil. Before they completely cool, place each piece of plantain between two nonstick plastic sheets (such as silpats) and crush them with something flat, like a pan base, until they are ½ inch (1 cm) thick.

Place the cheese in the middle (the amount depends on the size of your plantain patty), fold each plantain in half and gently press the edges to seal together. Use your hands to give the patties an oval shape. Set aside.

In a medium bowl, whisk the eggs and milk together. Add the flour, sugar, and salt, and mix. Dip the patties one by one in the batter, then transfer, using a skimmer, to the hot oil. Deep-fry until brown on the outside, then remove to a plate lined with paper towels. Serve warm, drizzled with *miel de caña* (cane syrup), if preferred.

Plantain Stew

Moqueca de banana de terra
Brazil

Preparation time: 10 minutes
Cooking time: 20 minutes
Serves: 6

This is a common vegan variation of a Capixaba-style moqueca from the state of Espírito Santo, in southeastern Brazil just north of Rio. It's a lighter version of the famed clay pot stew that uses neither coconut milk or *dendê* oil, but tomatoes and annatto that impart a reddish hue.

3 tablespoons olive oil
2 onions, chopped
6 garlic cloves, minced
5 tomatoes, peeled and chopped
1 red bell pepper, cored, seeded, and chopped
1–2 *malagueta* chiles, seeded and chopped
1½ tablespoons ground annatto
5 ripe plantains, peeled and cut diagonally into ½-inch (10-mm) slices
1 cup/1½ oz (40 g) chopped cilantro (coriander)
salt, to taste

Heat the olive oil in a clay pot or large pan over medium heat. Add the onions, garlic, tomatoes, bell pepper, chiles, and annatto. Cook for 10 minutes over medium heat, stirring occasionally.

Add the plantains and three-quarters of the cilantro (coriander). Season with salt to taste and mix well. Reduce the heat, cover, and cook for a further 10 minutes, or until the plantains are tender.

Serve hot, with the remaining cilantro scattered over the top, and with white rice on the side.

Ripe Plantain Fritters

Green Plantain Balls in Soup

Caldo de bolas de verde
Ecuador

Preparation time: 30 minutes,
plus 30 minutes chilling
Cooking time: 1 hour 15 minutes

Serves: 8

Prevalent along the Ecuadorian coast, the identifying element of this soup are the large spheres made of grated green plantains, which are often stuffed with meat. The trick is to not overcook the balls, otherwise they'll fall apart in the soup. Corn and cassava are usually found in the broth, though potatoes might be added as well. Lime wedges and a spicy *ají* sauce is usually served on the side.

    2 tablespoons vegetable oil
    1 white onion, chopped
    2 garlic cloves, minced
    3 tomatoes, peeled and diced
    ½ green bell pepper, cored, seeded, and diced
    2 teaspoons ground cumin
    1 teaspoon annatto paste
    2 tablespoons chopped cilantro (coriander)
    ½ tablespoon dried oregano
    2 teaspoons chile powder
    1 lb (450 g) beef bones
    1 lb (450 g) beef brisket, cut into chunks
    2 green plantains, peeled and halved
    8 cups/64 fl oz (1.9 liters) water
    1 cassava, peeled and cut into ½-inch (1-cm) cubes
    2 carrots, peeled and cut into thick strips
    4 ears of corn, halved
    lime wedges, to serve

    For the *bolas verdes*
    2 tablespoons vegetable oil
    ½ red onion, thinly sliced
    ½ green bell pepper, cored, seeded, and diced
    1 tomato, peeled and diced
    2 garlic cloves, minced
    1 tablespoon ground cumin
    1½ teaspoons annatto paste
    1 bunch cilantro (coriander), chopped
    ½ cup/2 oz (60 g) cooked peas
    ½ cup/4½ oz (130 g) peanuts, coarsely chopped
    and blended with ¼ cup/2 fl oz (60 ml) water
    2 green plantains, peeled and grated
    2 eggs
    salt and ground pepper

Heat the oil in a medium pan over medium heat and add the white onion, garlic, tomatoes, and the bell pepper. Cook for 2 minutes, stirring, then add the cumin, annatto paste, cilantro (coriander), oregano, and chile powder. Cook for a further 2 minutes, then add the beef bones and brisket, and the halved plantains. Sear the meat on all sides for 4 minutes. Add the water and bring to a boil, then lower the heat and simmer for 30 minutes. Add the cassava, carrot, and corn. Simmer for a further 15 minutes or until the vegetables are tender, then remove from the heat and let cool. Remove and discard the bones. Take the meat out and chop it finely.

For the filling, heat the vegetable oil in a frying pan over medium heat. Sauté the red onion, bell pepper, tomato, garlic, cumin, and annatto paste. Cook for

3 minutes, season with salt and add the chopped meat, cilantro, and peas. Stir with a wooden spoon and add the peanuts and 2 tablespoons of the liquid from the stew.

To prepare the dough for the *bolas verdes*, take the cooked green plantains from the stew and mash into a purée, adding a little of the stew liquid for moisture if necessary. Add the grated plantains and eggs, then season with salt and pepper. Shape the dough into medium-size balls, make an incision on the top and fill with the meat filling. Place in the refrigerator for 30 minutes.

Strain the stew, reserving the vegetables, and bring to a boil. Add the *bolas verdes* and cook over low heat for 15 minutes. A few minutes before serving, add the strained vegetables back, to heat them again. Serve hot with lime wedges on the side.

Cat's Head

Cabeza de gato
Colombia

Preparation time: 30 minutes
Cooking time: 35 minutes

Serves: 6

Don't worry. This isn't actually a cat's head. This mashed plantain dish from Colombia's Caribbean coast is primarily eaten for breakfast, sometimes with eggs (fried or scrambled), avocado slices, and whatever chunks of meat are around. A dish called *cayeye*, or *mote de guineo*, in the Magdalena department is made the same way, though specifically refers to using small green plantains called *guineos*.

    5 green plantains, peeled and cut into chunks
    3 tablespoons butter
    1 medium white onion, finely chopped
    2 scallions (spring onions), finely chopped
    2 garlic cloves, finely chopped
    2 medium tomatoes, peeled and diced
    ½ teaspoon annatto paste
    1 tablespoon vegetable oil
    6 eggs
    salt
    queso costeño or *queso fresco*, to serve

Cook the plantains in plenty of boiling water for 10–15 minutes, until soft. Drain and mash.

In a frying pan, melt the butter over medium heat, add the onion, scallions (spring onions), and garlic and sauté for 5 minutes, or until golden brown. Add the tomatoes and annatto paste and cook until soft, then add the mashed plantains. Season with salt, stir well, set aside, and keep warm.

Heat the oil in a frying pan and fry the eggs over medium heat for about 5 minutes, making sure that the yolks stay liquid.

Separate the *cayeye* mixture into 6 portions, add an egg on top of each, and grate the cheese over it to serve.

Fruit

Plantain Crisps

Chifles, tostoncitos, platanitos
Colombia, Ecuador, Peru, Venezuela

Preparation time: 15 minutes
Cooking time: 15 minutes   Serves: 5–6

Chifles are typical in the banana lands in northern Peru and Ecuador, though there are similar styles of plantain chips found throughout Latin America, like *tostoncitos* in Venezuela or *platanitos* in Colombia. They can be sliced across or lengthways and eaten as a snack, added to stews, or used as a garnish in dishes like ceviche.

2 cups/16 fl oz (475 ml) vegetable oil
3 green plantains
salt

Pour the vegetable oil into a small, heavy pan, making sure it is no more than two-thirds full, and heat to 350°F/177°C.

Peel the plantains and cut them into thin slices, ideally less than 1/10 inch (2 mm) thick (using a mandoline is ideal). Gently lower the slices into the hot oil, in batches, and fry for about 7 minutes, until crispy and golden brown, then remove with a skimmer and let dry in a bowl lined with paper towels.

Sprinkle with salt while still hot, then serve warm or at room temperature.

Tumbes-Style Mashed Plantains with Seafood

Majarisco tumbesino
Peru

Preparation time: 40 minutes
Cooking time: 25 minutes   Serves: 4

Majarisco is one of the most representative plates of the hot and tropical Tumbes province in the far north of Peru near the border with Ecuador, where bananas and seafood make up a significant part of the diet. The name is a combination of the verb *majar*, or to mash, with the end of the word for seafood, *marisco*. It's often served with boiled cassava, *Chifles* (Plantain Crisps, see above), and *Chicha de jora* (Corn Beer, page 388).

1³/₄ cups/14 fl oz (425 ml) vegetable oil
5 green plantains, peeled and cut into 1-inch (2.5-cm) cubes
2 medium red onions, 1 chopped and 1 finely sliced
1 medium red bell pepper, cored, seeded, and chopped
1 *ají amarillo* chile, chopped
1 lb (450 g) seafood, such as shrimp (prawns), mussels, scallops
1/4 cup/2 fl oz (60 ml) fish stock
4 tablespoons *ají panca* paste
2 teaspoons finely chopped cilantro (coriander)
1/2 cup/4 fl oz (120 ml) lime juice
1/2 *ají limo* chile, seeded and finely chopped
salt and ground pepper

In a small, heavy pan, heat 1¹/₂ cups/12 fl oz (350 ml) of the oil to 350°F/177°C. Fry the plantains for 4 minutes, remove from the oil and mash while still hot. Set aside.

In a pan or deep frying pan, heat 2 tablespoons of the oil over medium heat. Add the chopped red onion, bell pepper, and *ají amarillo* and sauté for 5 minutes, then add the prepared seafood and cook for a further 4 minutes. Remove the seafood and set aside. Add the fish stock and *ají panca* paste, and season with salt and pepper. Add the seafood back in, as well as the mashed plantain. Cook for a further 10 minutes, stirring continuously. Check the seasoning and finish by adding the cilantro (coriander). Keep warm.

Place the sliced onion in a bowl and add the lime juice, *ají limo*, and remaining oil. Season with salt, place in a serving dish, top with the sliced onion mixture, and serve.

Mashed Plantain Balls

Bolón de verde, tacacho
Ecuador, Peru

Preparation time: 10 minutes
Cooking time: 30 minutes   Serves: 4

These balls of mashed plantains fried in lard are a typical accompaniment to cecina, or salted pork, in Amazonian regions of Ecuador and Peru. The texture tends to be firm, often a bit dry, so sauces made from Amazonian fruits and peppers, such as *ají de cocona* are recommended.

lard, for deep-frying
4 green plantains, peeled and each cut into 5 pieces
7 oz (200 g) pork belly, cut into 2-inch (5-cm) pieces
salt

Melt enough lard for deep-frying in a small, heavy pan, and heat to around 200°F/93°C. Add the plantains and fry until soft, about 8 minutes. Remove with a skimmer to a plate lined with paper towels, to absorb excess grease. While the plantains are still warm, mash, ideally using a wooden tool (it sticks less). Set aside.

Add the pork belly to a dry frying pan and cook for about 10 minutes or until cooked through and crispy. Place on a plate lined with paper towels to absorb excess grease, then finely chop into smaller pieces, mix with the mashed plantains, and season with salt.

In a small, heavy pan, re-use and heat enough lard for deep-frying to around 350°F/177°C. Shape the plantain mixture into medium-sized balls, then fry for 4 minutes, or until golden brown. Remove with a skimmer to a plate lined with paper towels. Serve warm.

Fried Plantains

Patacones, tostones, tajadas
Throughout Latin America

Preparation time: 20 minutes
Cooking time: 20 minutes

Serves: 6

These smashed, fried plantains are an accompaniment to fish and meat dishes throughout Latin America and the Caribbean. They are mostly eaten plain, with just a little salt, though they can be topped with shredded beef, slathered in refried beans, or eaten with cheese.

    vegetable oil, for deep-frying
    4 green plantains, peeled and each cut
    into 4–5 pieces
    salt

Pour enough oil for deep-frying into a large, heavy pan, making sure it is no more than two-thirds full, and heat to 325°F/163°C.

Add the plantains to the oil gently and fry until soft, about 7 minutes. Remove and let cool down a little, then, one at a time, smash the plantains, using a *pataconera/tostonera* or between plastic sheets (or silpats) using the base of a pan or bowl, or anything with a flat bottom.

Once all the plantains are smashed, fry them again for about 5 minutes, or until brown and crispy. Remove them with a skimmer and place them in a bowl lined with paper towels, to absorb excess oil. Add a pinch of salt and serve warm.

Plantains with Spicy Peanut Sauce

Bakabana 🔲
Suriname

Preparation time: 40 minutes
Cooking time 15 minutes

Serves: 5–6

Bakabana are battered and fried, overripe (as in black) plantains that were brought to Suriname by immigrants from Indonesia, where it's called *pisang goreng*. There are subtle differentiations between the two countries, such as the variety of banana, the recipe for the batter, and the addition of sauce. In Suriname, they are usually served with a sometimes spicy peanut sauce on the side, or dusted in sugar.

    vegetable oil, for deep-frying
    2 cups/9½ oz (260 g) all-purpose (plain) flour
    4 tablespoons brown sugar
    pinch of salt
    2½ cups/20 fl oz (600 ml) water
    4 ripe plantains, peeled and sliced lengthways,
    about ⅓ inch (¾–1 cm) thick

    For the sauce
    ⅓ cup/2½ oz (75 g) peanut butter
    1 tablespoon finely chopped fresh ginger
    1 garlic clove, finely chopped
    3 tablespoons water
    2 tablespoons soy sauce
    4 tablespoons lime juice
    ½ teaspoon brown sugar
    crushed chile flakes, optional

For the sauce, place the peanut butter in a medium bowl with the ginger and garlic. Start whisking while slowly adding the water, and continue whisking while adding the soy sauce, lime juice, sugar, and chile flakes to taste, if desired.

Pour enough oil for deep-frying into a large, heavy pan, making sure it is no more than two-thirds full, and heat to 350°F/177°C.

Mix the flour, sugar, and salt in a medium bowl. Slowly pour in the water and mix until thick and smooth. Dip the plantain lengths in the batter one at a time, and add to the hot oil. Fry for 3–4 minutes each side, until golden brown. Remove with a skimmer to a plate lined with paper towels, to absorb excess oil. Keep warm while you fry all the slices.

Serve the *bakabana* warm with the sauce on the side.

Hashed Guineos with Chaya

Picadillo de guineo con chicasquil
Costa Rica

Preparation time: 1 hour
Cooking time: 1 hour

Serves; 6–8

Small green plantains called *guineos* are paired with the leafy green *chicasquil*, called *chaya* elsewhere in the region, in this homey Costa Rican dish. Like other *picadillos* in the country, it can be served on a corn tortilla to make a *gallo*.

    4 lb (1.8 kg) *chicasquil* (tree spinach) leaves
    2 lb (900 g) *guineo* plantains (unpeeled)
    3 tablespoons olive oil
    4 garlic cloves, minced
    2 onions, chopped
    2 pieces of celery, chopped
    1 *ají dulce* chile, chopped
    1 tablespoon dried thyme
    1 teaspoon ground cumin
    ½ cup/¾ oz (20 g) cilantro (coriander) leaves
    salt

Remove the veins from the *chicasquil* leaves, then rinse the leaves in water, and place in a large pan. Cover with water and cook over medium heat for about 1 hour. Drain and chop.

Meanwhile, cut the tips and ends off the *guineos* and cut each into 3 pieces. Cook in a pan of boiling, salted water for 15 minutes until almost tender, then drain, peel and chop.

Heat the oil in a medium pan, then sauté the garlic and onion until brown. Add the celery and mix, followed by the *ají dulce*, thyme, and cumin. Add the chopped *chicasquil* leaves and chopped *guineo*, then mix. Garnish with the cilantro (coriander). Serve with tortillas.

Plantains with Spicy Peanut Sauce

Avocados

In Spanish the name is *aguacate* (or *palta* in Peru and Chile), which is derived from the Nahuatl word *ahuacatl*, meaning testicle, likely referring to the shape of the fruit (and hopefully not the color). The earliest evidence of avocado consumption dates back nearly 10,000 years to Coxcatlan in the present-day state of Puebla, though domestication didn't occur until a few thousand years later with three different landraces in the highlands of Mexico (*Persea americana var. drymifolia*), the highlands of Guatemala (*P. americana var. guatemalensis*), and the lowlands of Guatemala (*P. americana var. americana*). From there avocados spread throughout the region and today there are about thirty different varieties.

For most of us in the region, avocados are something that are always around. We'll mash them and put them on bread or sandwiches, slice them on salads, or just eat them with a spoon with a sprinkle of salt. We'll buy them ripe, soft but not mushy, so they can be eaten right away, and then unripe, so we'll have them around when they are ready to eat a few days later. You can speed up the ripening process a little bit by wrapping them in newspaper, or preserve a half avocado by wrapping it tightly in plastic wrap (clingfilm) and putting it in the refrigerator.

Guacamole

Guacamole
Mexico

Preparation time: 10 minutes

Serves: 4

As long as humans have been eating avocados, there has likely been guacamole. In its basic form it is just mashed with a *molcajete y tejolote* (Mexican mortar and pestle).

  3 ripe avocados
  ½ red onion, chopped
  1 red chile (such as serrano), chopped
  1 tablespoon chopped cilantro (coriander)
  2 ripe tomatoes, peeled, seeded, and diced
  juice of 2 limes
  1 tablespoon olive oil
  salt and ground pepper

Place the avocado flesh in a bowl and mash it with a fork. Add the onion, chile, cilantro (coriander), and tomatoes, and season with the lime juice, olive oil, salt, and pepper.

Avocado Celery Salad

Ensalada de apio y palta
Chile

Preparation time: 20 minutes

Serves: 4

A salad made from avocado and celery just seems so obvious and simple. In Chile, it's a common side dish in homes or *fuente de sodas*.

  8 celery stalks, sliced
  2 large avocados
  juice of 1 lime
  3 tablespoons olive oil
  10 walnuts, chopped
  ½ cup/¾ oz (20 g) chopped parsley or cilantro (coriander) leaves
  sea salt

Place the celery in a bowl of cold water.
  Peel the avocados, remove the pits (stones) and slice lengthways. Sprinkle over some of the lime juice.
  Drain the celery and mix with the avocado. Season with lime juice, salt, and the olive oil. Top with the chopped walnuts and cilantro (coriander) to serve.

Stuffed Avocados

Palta reina
Chile

Preparation time: 10 minutes
Cooking time: 20 minutes

Serves: 2

As an alternative to stuffing the avocado with chicken, you can use tuna or shrimp.

  2 tablespoons olive oil, plus extra for dressing
  1 chicken thigh (or ½ breast)
  2 tablespoons mayonnaise
  ¼ red bell pepper, seeded and finely chopped
  6 lettuce leaves, chopped
  juice of 1 lime
  1 avocado, peeled and pitted
  2 olives
  salt and ground pepper

Heat the oil in a pan over medium heat, add the chicken and cook for about 6 minutes per side, or until fully cooked through. Let cool then shred.
  Mix the shredded chicken with the mayonnaise. Add the bell pepper and season with ground pepper.
  Dress the lettuce with salt, oil, and lime juice. Place on 2 serving plates, as a base. Place an avocado half on top of each, stuff with the chicken and top with an olive to serve.

Guacamole

Dairy and Eggs

While it's possible that limited amounts of llama milk were consumed by pre-Columbian people, significant milk consumption, not to mention the art of cheesemaking, didn't occur until after Spanish and Portuguese settlers brought cattle to the New World. While early styles were similar to those of Europe, they had to be adapted to the wide range of climates and elevations that exist in Latin America, developing an array of different cheeses. In terms of cooking, fresh white cheeses with a mild flavor, usually called *queso fresco*, are extremely common, used to thicken sauces or crumbled onto other foods. In Brazil, the firm but very lightweight *queijo coalho* is ever-present in breads, or grilled beachside on skewers. In Mexico, semi-firm *quesillo*, *queso Oaxaca*, or *queso asadero* are used for fillings or toppings in various antojitos. In Colombia and Venezuela, white, salty cheeses with high melting points like *queso de freír* or *queso blanco*, are used for *tequeños* or arepas. In Argentina, a variation of Provolone cheese gets melted right on the grill.

Even before the chickens were introduced to Latin America, the eggs of various birds such as turkeys, ducks, rheas, and countless seabirds, not to mention turtles and iguanas, were an important food source. Today, eggs come in countless forms around the region. There are the blue-shelled eggs of Araucana chicken in southern Chile and oversized rhea eggs in Argentina and Chile. Some are fried and slathered in spicy salsas in Mexico or scrambled with tomatoes and onions in Colombia. In Peru, Brazil, and Venezuela, boiled quail eggs are a common street food or used as hot dog or hamburger toppings.

Grilled Provolone Cheese

Provoleta 🔲
Argentina, Uruguay

Preparation time: 5 minutes
Cooking time: 10 minutes
Serves: 4

Usually served as one of the first courses of an *asado*, *provoleta*, in its most basic form, is provolone cheese seasoned with oregano and seared directly on the grates of a grill (barbecue) until browned and a little bit gooey. If not done right it will melt right through the grill and become just a puddle of melted cheese, so to prevent this, it's best to place it in an airy space for a day or at least a few hours before cooking, which will allow a core to form and help it maintain shape. You can also use a cast-iron pan, as here, which can double as a serving dish. It's mostly eaten family style, though specially designed *provoleteras*, cast-iron pans designed for a slice of provolone or with spaces for individual, bite-size servings, can be found online. Serve with bread.

      1 slice provolone cheese about 6½ oz (180 g), and
      1 inch (2.5 cm) thick
      2 tablespoons flour
      1 teaspoon crushed chile flakes
      1 teaspoon dried oregano
      2 tablespoons olive oil

Heat a cast-iron frying pan on a heated grill (barbecue); it should have strong heat but not direct fire. Cover the provolone slice with flour, then place in the hot pan. Allow a golden crust core to form, about 2–5 minutes, then flip and do the same on the other side.
      Mix the chile flakes and oregano with the olive oil, then add to the top of the *provoleta*. Serve on a warm plate or directly in the pan, with pieces of bread.

Brazilian Grilled Cheese Skewers

Queijo coalho em espetos
Brazil

Preparation time: 10 minutes
Cooking time: 10 minutes
Serves: 6–8

Vendors roam the beaches of Brazil carrying metal cans filled with hot charcoal, which they use to roast long skewers of the mild, white *queijo coalho*. Usually they are served as is, or sprinkled with a little oregano, or drizzled with a garlic sauce called *molho de alho*.

      1 lb (450 g) *queijo coalho*, cut into 6–8 equal sticks,
      about 5 inches (12 cm) long and 1 inch (2.5 cm) wide
      (or use halloumi)
      bamboo skewers, soaked in water

Poke the cheese with the skewers and place them directly on the grates of a heated grill (barbecue). Let cook for about 2–3 minutes or until browned, then repeat for each side. Serve immediately.

Humacha Cheese

Queso Humacha
Bolivia

Preparation time: 15 minutes
Cooking time: 30 minutes
Serves: 4

Traditional of La Paz, Bolivia, and typically eaten during Semana Santa, this chunky cheese sauce is used to cover boiled corn and potatoes.

      4 potatoes, washed
      4 ears of corn, husks removed
      ½ cup/4 fl oz (120 ml) vegetable oil
      1 garlic clove, minced
      1 onion, chopped
      3 *ají amarillo* chiles, chopped, or 1½ teaspoons *ají amarillo* powder
      1½ cups/9 oz (250 g) chopped tomato
      1½ cups/6½ oz (190 g) fava (broad) beans, peeled
      1 branch of *huacatay* (Peruvian black mint), coarsely chopped
      1 teaspoon ground cumin
      2 cups/16 fl oz (475 ml) water
      3 cups/25 fl oz (750 ml) milk
      1 lb 2 oz (500 g) *queso fresco*, cut into thin strips or small cubes
      salt and ground pepper

Place the potatoes in a medium pan and cover with cold water. Add salt and cook over medium heat for 15 minutes, or until tender. Drain, let cool, then peel. Cook the corn in boiling salted water until tender, then drain.
      Meanwhile, in a small pan, heat the oil over medium heat, add the garlic and onion and sauté for 7 minutes, or until golden and soft. Add the *ají amarillo* and tomato, and cook for a further 4 minutes. Add the fava (broad) beans, *huacatay*, cumin, water, and some salt and pepper. Let cook for 15 minutes or until the beans are tender, then add the milk and cheese and cook for a further 5 minutes.
      Serve the potatoes and corn with the warm cheese sauce.

Dairy and Eggs

Grilled Provolone Cheese

Nicaraguan Cheese Tortillas

Quesillo Nicaragüense 🔲
Nicaragua

Preparation time: 5 minutes,
plus 1 hour pickling
Cooking time: 15 minutes

Serves: 6

Two neighboring towns, La Paz Centro and Nagarote, both claim to have invented the quesillo, an easy-to-make snack using staples that nearly every Nicaraguan has in their pantry. In the early 1900s a woman from Nagarote created the tortilla with a thick layer of melted cheese that's sold wrapped in a banana leaf, though she did so in La Paz Centro. Vendors in both towns hawked them at their respective train stations and eventually a quesillo restaurant opened in each town, where both add pickled onions and drizzle the quesillo in *crema*.

Banana Vinegar (page 402)
1 tablespoon sugar
1½ teaspoons salt
1 cup/8 fl oz (250 ml) water
1 white onion, finely chopped
6 thick Corn Tortillas (page 136)
1 lb (450 g) *cuajada* cheese (or use *queso Oaxaca*)
8 oz (225 g) *crema mexicana* (or use sour cream)

Whisk the banana vinegar, sugar, salt, and water in a bowl until the sugar and salt are dissolved. Place the onion in a bowl or jar and pour the mixture over it. Let it sit for at least 1 hour before using.

Heat a *comal* or cast-iron frying pan over high heat. Warm a tortilla on one side, then flip and add a layer of cheese. When melted and gooey, remove with a spatula. Fold the tortilla, add a spoonful of the pickled onions, and drizzle with *crema*. Repeat with the other tortillas.

Cheese Soup

Sopa de queso
Nicaragua

Preparation time: 15 minutes
Cooking time: 35 minutes

Serves: 6

A common appearance during Semana Santa festivities in Nicaragua, *sopa de queso* is thick and creamy from a mixture of cheese and corn masa. *Rosquillas*, round fritters, also made of corn flour and cheese, add a crunchy texture to the soup.

2½ cups/12 oz (350 g) corn (maize) flour
6½ cups/52 fl oz (1.5 liters) water
1 teaspoon olive oil
1½ tablespoons annatto paste
3 cups/12 oz (350 g) shredded *queso fresco*
1 large onion, sliced
2 green bell peppers, cored, seeded, and sliced
2 red tomatoes, sliced
4 garlic cloves, minced
1 bunch mint
4 cups/32 fl oz (950 ml) whole milk
juice of 1 bitter orange
4 oz (120 g) cream, optional
1 cup/8 fl oz (250 ml) vegetable oil

In a mixing bowl, combine the corn (maize) flour and 2 cups/16 fl oz (475 ml) of the water, and knead into a dough. Mix the olive oil and annatto paste together, then add to the dough with the cheese and 1 teaspoon salt. Separate out about 1 cup of dough and add ½ cup/4 fl oz (120 ml) water to it. Mix and set aside.

Add the remaining water to a large pan over medium heat, and add the onion, peppers, tomatoes, garlic, and mint. Simmer for 10 minutes or until the vegetables are cooked. (If desired, you can remove the vegetables at this stage.)

Bring the milk to a boil in a small pan, then remove from the heat.

Add the reserved cup of dough to the soup, then add the milk, and stir. Remove from the heat and add orange juice to taste. If you like, add the cream, stirring vigorously.

For the fritters, heat the vegetable oil in a medium frying pan over medium heat. Shape the dough into palm-sized discs (like donuts). Fry until brown and crispy, then place on a plate lined with paper towels to absorb excess oil. Serve the soup with the fritters on the side or directly in the soup.

Colombian Cheese and Yam Soup

Mote de queso
Colombia

Preparation time: 20 minutes
Cooking time: 55 minutes

Serves: 4–6

A local yam called the *ñame criollo*, and salty, fresh white cheese called *queso costeño* are the signature ingredients of *mote de queso*, a common dish in the Caribbean coast areas in the Sucre and Córdoba administrative departments.

1 yam, peeled and chopped
7 cups/3½ pints (1.75 liters) water
2 tablespoons oil
½ cup/2 oz (60 g) diced white onion
4 scallions (spring onions), chopped
1 cup/5½ oz (160g) diced tomato
2 garlic cloves, minced
2 teaspoons ground cumin
1 cup/4 oz (120 g) crumbled *queso costeño*
or *queso fresco*
salt

To serve
juice of 1 lime
cilantro (coriander)
suero costeño (or use crème fraîche
or sour cream), optional

Place the yam in a medium pan, add the water and cook over medium heat for about 45 minutes, or until soft and tender.

Meanwhile, heat the oil in a frying pan over medium heat. Add the onion, scallions (spring onions), tomato, garlic, and cumin. Cook for 10 minutes, stirring frequently, until the onions are tender. Set aside.

Lower the heat of the yam pan and add the onion mixture, and the cheese. Cook for about a further 10 minutes. The consistency of the soup should be creamy with small, tender chunks of yam. Add more water if it is too thick. Add salt to taste, mix well, and serve in deep bowls with lime juice, cilantro (coriander) and some *suero costeño*, if desired.

Nicaraguan Cheese Tortillas

Fried Cheese Sticks

Tequeños
Venezuela

Preparation time: 20 minutes,
plus 30 minutes resting
Cooking time: 5 minutes

Makes: 20

Created in the town of Los Teques southwest of Caracas, *tequeños* are a favorite party food or school lunch snack in Venezuela. In Peru, *tequeños* often use wanton wrappers for the dough.

> 3 cups/14 oz (400 g) all-purpose (plain) flour, plus extra for dusting
> 1 teaspoon salt
> 1 cup/8 oz (225 g) butter, cubed
> 1 egg
> ½ cup/4 fl oz (120 ml) warm water
> 9 oz (250 g) *queso blanco* or *queso de freír* (or use paneer)
> vegetable oil, for deep-frying

> For the *gusacaca* sauce
> 1 cup/4½ oz (130 g) diced avocado
> 2 jalapeño peppers (or other chiles), seeded and chopped
> ¼ cup/1 oz (30 g) chopped onion
> ¼ cup/½ oz (10 g) cilantro (coriander)
> 1 garlic clove, peeled
> 3 tablespoons olive oil
> juice of 1 lime

Add the flour and the salt to a bowl and stir. Add the butter and cut until it is incorporated and coarse crumbs are formed. Add the egg and warm water and mix well, then turn out of the bowl and knead to a smooth, uniform dough. The dough should not stick to the surface, so add more flour if needed. Cover and let rest for 30 minutes.

Meanwhile, make the *gusacaca*. Add the avocado, jalapeño, onion, cilantro (coriander), and garlic to a blender. Add the oil, with lime juice and salt to taste. Blend until smooth, then set aside.

Spread the dough on a work surface and divide it into two equal portions, sprinkling with a little flour. Using a rolling pin, roll both out to rectangles ⅛ inch (5 mm) thick, then cut strips of dough lengthways. Cut the cheese into sticks and wrap each in a dough strip.

Pour enough vegetable oil for deep-frying into a large, heavy pan, making sure it is no more than two-thirds full, and heat to 350°F/177°C. Once the oil is hot, add the *tequeños* in batches, and deep-fry until golden brown, then remove to a plate lined with paper towels, to absorb excess oil. Serve hot with the *gusacaca*.

Fresh Cheese

Queso fresco
Various

Preparation time: 1 hour 45 minutes,
plus 30 minutes chilling
Cooking time: 5 minutes)

Makes: 8 oz
(225 g)

In much of Latin America, there's some form of fresh, unaged cheese with a mild flavor made from cow, or sometimes goat milk. It's a little bit salty, low in fat and sodium, and extremely versatile. It can be crumbled over grilled vegetables, into soups, over corn, on a tortilla, or as a filling for *chiles rellenos*. It can be eaten fresh or used as a replacement for cheeses like feta or ricotta. It doesn't melt easily when heated, though it can be used to thicken sauces or dips over low heat. It's a natural complement to chiles, helping balance out the heat. From one cheesemaker to the next, *queso fresco* has subtle variations in flavor and texture. It might be a little bit tangier, firmer, or it might have herbs added or be wrapped in banana leaves. It might even have a different name, such as *queso de pueblo*. It's not that different from simple farmer's cheese you'll find in other parts of the world. Store-bought versions are easy to come by, though many home cooks make their own. It's easy enough to make by heating whole milk, adding something acidic like lime juice or vinegar, leaving it to curdle, and then draining and straining it in cheesecloth. *Queso fresco* doesn't have a long life span, usually no more than a week, though you can stretch that out another week or so by storing it in an airtight container in the refrigerator.

> 8 cups/64 fl oz (1.9 liters) whole milk
> ⅔ cup/5 fl oz (150 ml) white vinegar
> 1 tablespoon apple cider vinegar
> 1½ teaspoons salt
> 3 cheesecloths
> 1 kitchen string

In a medium pan, bring the milk to 170°F/76°C, while stirring slowly. Turn off the heat and add both vinegars and the salt. Stir well and let sit for 40 minutes at room temperature.

Meanwhile, line a colander with 2 of the cheesecloths, one on top of the other, and place a bowl underneath. When the milk is curdled, stir gently to break up the pieces of curds. Slowly pour into the colander and let sit for 15 minutes. Gather the edges of the cheesecloths and use a string to close. Press it gently to remove the excess liquids. Allow the cheese to drip for 40 minutes (you can suspend it by the string directly over the bowl, if you like).

Gently open the cheesecloth and shape the cheese as desired in the third cheesecloth. Close the cloth gently and place it in the colander. Place the cheese in the refrigerator for 30 minutes. Remove the cheesecloth and place in a container. Keep refrigerated until use.

Dairy and Eggs

Chaya Scramble

Chaya con huevos
Belize

Preparation time: 10 minutes
Cooking time: 10 minutes   Serves: 4

Fast growing chaya (*Cnidoscolus aconitifolius*), a leafy green that originated in Yucatán Peninsula, can be found along roadsides in many parts of Belize, where it is used primarily in the masa of small tamales called *tamalitos*, or scrambled with eggs. Moringa leaves, callaloo, spinach, green beans, or okra can also be used in place of chaya. Serve with tortillas, Johnny cakes, or fry jacks.

    4 eggs
    2 tablespoons milk
    1 tablespoon vegetable or coconut oil
    3 cups/6 oz (180 g) chopped chaya
    ½ onion, chopped
    1 tomato, peeled and diced
    salt and ground pepper

In a medium bowl, beat the eggs and milk together well, and season with salt and pepper.
    Heat the oil in a frying pan over medium heat, then add the chaya, onion, and tomato, and sauté for 3–4 minutes, stirring continuously. Add the beaten eggs and cook for a further 3 minutes, then serve.

Rooster's Head

Cabeça do galo
Brazil

Preparation time: 5 minutes
Cooking time: 20 minutes   Serves: 4

This thick and wholesome stew is a favorite for alleviating hangovers, or just restore one's soul, in Brazil's northeastern states of Pernambuco and Paraíba.

    1 tablespoon vegetable oil
    1 medium onion, chopped
    4 garlic cloves, minced
    1 tomato, peeled, seeded and chopped
    1 green bell pepper, cored, seeded and chopped
    1 tablespoon ground annatto (or use sweet paprika)
    ¼ cup/½ oz (10 g) chopped cilantro (coriander), plus
    a few extra sprigs to serve
    3 eggs, lightly beaten
    4 cups/32 fl oz (950 ml) boiling water
    ½ cup/2½ oz (70 g) cassava flour (*farinha de
    mandioca*)
    1 lime, quartered, to serve
    salt and ground pepper

Heat the oil in a pan over medium heat, add the onion, and cook until beginning to brown, then add the garlic, tomato, and bell pepper. Cook, stirring continuously, for 5 minutes. Add salt and pepper to taste, then add the annatto, cilantro (coriander), and beaten eggs.
    Remove the pan from the heat, then immediately pour the boiling water over the mixture. Stirring continuously, add the cassava flour and stir until thoroughly mixed. Replace on the heat and bring to a boil, about 5 minutes. Serve immediately in deep bowls, with cilantro leaves and quarters of lime.

Scrambled Eggs with Scallions and Tomatoes

Huevos pericos
Colombia, Venezuela

Preparation time: 10 minutes
Cooking time: 20 minutes   Serves: 2

This is the standard preparation of scrambled eggs in Colombia and Venezuela. It's often served with an arepa, a slice of salty cheese, and hot chocolate.

    ¼ cup/2 oz (60 g) butter
    5 scallions (spring onions), chopped
    2 medium tomatoes, cut into small chunks
    4 eggs, beaten
    Basic Corn Arepas (page 117) or bread, to serve

Put the butter in a frying pan and melt over medium high heat, then add the scallions (spring onions) and tomatoes. Stir until the scallions are golden, about 7 minutes. Add the beaten eggs, then lower the heat to medium. Let the eggs cook slowly for 5–10 minutes, stirring occasionally, until the desired consistency. Serve warm with arepas or bread.

Divorced Eggs

Huevos divorciados
Mexico

Preparation time: 30 minutes
Cooking time: 20 minutes   Serves: 6

Similar to huevos rancheros, *huevos divorciados* are eggs served with two different sauces: one red, one green. Sometimes the eggs are separated by a row of refried beans or *chilaquiles*.

    2 tablespoons vegetable oil
    12 eggs

    For the red sauce
    3 medium tomatoes, cut into ½-inch (1-cm) chunks
    ½ white onion, chopped
    4 green serrano chiles, chopped
    6 tablespoons finely chopped cilantro (coriander)

    For the green sauce
    18 green tomatillos, halved
    ½ white onion, finely chopped
    2 garlic cloves, finely chopped
    4 serrano chiles, thinly sliced
    1 teaspoon sugar
    4 tablespoons finely chopped parsley

In a mortar, gently mash the tomatoes for the red sauce with the onion and chiles, and season with salt. Add the cilantro (coriander) and set aside in the refrigerator.
    For the green sauce, mash the tomatillos in the mortar. Add the onion, garlic, and chiles, stir together and season with the sugar, and salt if needed. Add the parsley and set aside at room temperature.
    Heat the oil in a medium frying pan and fry the eggs in batches over medium heat, keeping the yolks creamy.
    To serve, place 2 eggs on each plate and pour the red sauce over one and the green over the other.

Charcoal-Cooked Rhea Egg

Huevos de choique al rescoldo ▢
Argentina, Chile, Paraguay

Preparation time: 10 minutes
Cooking time: 25 minutes   Serves: 1

The Greater Rhea (*Rhea americana*)—also called the *suri*, *choique*, and *'ñandú*—standing about four feet tall, is the largest flightless bird in South America. A distant cousin to the ostrich and emu, the rhea and smaller puna rhea are threatened in their native ranges, which extend from southern Peru to Patagonia. As their meat is low in cholesterol and they lay, big beautiful eggs, a cottage industry of farm-raised rheas has popped up in Argentina and Paraguay. We do realize that many of you don't have access to the eggs of flightless birds in South America, though ostrich eggs, which are often available in gourmet meat suppliers in many parts of the world, are a good alternative. Their eggs are about twice as big, though, so you'll need to double the seasoning and adjust the cooking time. This recipe is made with the heat of charcoal and ash, so make sure the coals and ashes stay hot while cooking.

    1 rhea egg
    ⅛ oz (5 g) garlic, chopped
    2 tablespoons chopped parsley
    salt and ground pepper

Make a small incision on top of the egg (½ inch/1 cm in diameter). With a straw or a long spoon, mix the egg yolk and white inside. Take a little bit out of the egg so it won't spill while cooking. Add the chopped garlic and parsley to the inside of the egg. Season with salt and pepper.

    Place the egg in the middle of a pile of hot charcoal and ash, ensuring that the bottom half is surrounded. Let cook for about 5 minutes, then stir the egg inside with a long spoon or a stick. Repeat the process of leaving to cook then stirring 4 more times, or until the egg is cooked (it should have the consistency of a poached egg). To serve make a larger incision in the egg shell and spoon it out or tip it into a bowl.

Eggs with Huacho Sausage

Huevos con salchicha Huachana
Peru

Preparation time: 10 minutes
Cooking time: 15 minutes   Serves: 5–6

Huacho is a small community a few hours north of Lima that is famous for its pinwheels of sometimes spicy pork sausages that get their deep red color from annatto seeds. They have been exported to North America and Europe on a small scale, though you can swap them out with chorizo or another sausage if you can't find it. Usually they are eaten for breakfast with eggs, often on a French roll.

    8 eggs
    4 Huacho sausages
    salt and ground pepper

Whisk the eggs in a medium bowl and add salt and pepper to taste. The sausages tend to be salty, so go easy.

    Place the sausages in a medium frying pan, and sear over medium heat until they burst. Remove the casing and crumble the sausage in the pan. Take out half of the fat in the pan from the sausages, and mix with the beaten eggs, then add the mixture back in.

    Leave over medium heat for about 30 seconds without touching them then, using a silicone spatula, slowly move and scrape the bottom of the pan to mix the cooked and liquid parts of the eggs, until they reach the consistency you want. Remove from the heat, mix, and serve hot.

Motul-Style Eggs

Huevos Motuleños
Mexico

Preparation time: 15 minutes   Serves: 4
Cooking time: 45 minutes

A common breakfast offering on Mexico's Yucatán Peninsula, *huevos Motuleños* originated in the town of Motul, east of Mérida.

    4 medium tomatoes, peeled and coarsely chopped
    1 small white onion, coarsely chopped
    1 garlic clove, chopped
    7½ tablespoons vegetable oil
    1 green plantain, peeled and sliced diagonally into 8 pieces
    4 Flour Tortillas (page 136)
    4 eggs
    4 slices of ham
    ½ cup/2 oz (60 g) crumbled *queso fresco* (or use *cotija* cheese)
    1 cup/4½ oz (130 g) cooked peas
    1 habanero chile, sliced
    salt

Put the tomatoes, onion, and garlic in a blender and blend together.

    Add 2 tablespoons of the oil to a small pan over medium heat, then pour in the blended mixture. Turn the heat to low and cook for about 10 minutes, stirring occasionally. Season with salt, remove from the heat, and keep warm.

    Heat 1 tablespoon of oil in a frying pan, add the plantain and cook for about 8 minutes, turning every 2 minutes or so, until golden brown on both sides. Set aside.

    Clean the frying pan, add a ½ tablespoon of oil, and place over medium-high heat. Once hot, add the tortillas and fry for 2 minutes each side, or until crispy on each side. Wrap in a tea towel to keep warm, and set aside.

    Add another 1 tablespoon of oil per egg to the frying pan, and fry one at a time, making sure to not let the yolk firm up.

    To serve, place a tortilla on each plate and set a fried egg on top with a slice of ham, a few spoonfuls of the cheese, and a dollop of the warm tomato sauce. Sprinkle a few spoonfuls of peas on the plate and 1–2 slices of habanero, then serve.

Dairy and Eggs

Charcoal-Cooked Rhea Egg

Colombian Egg and Milk Soup

Changua ▢
Colombia

Preparation time: 15 minutes
Cooking time: 10 minutes

Serves: 2

This nourishing soup is commonly served for breakfast in the Colombian administrative departments of Boyacá and Cundinamarca, which includes the capital Bogotá. It's usually served with an arepa or *calado*, a dry bread that softens in the soup. It also does wonders for a *resaca*, otherwise known as a hangover.

    1 cup/8 fl oz (250 ml) water
    1 cup/8 fl oz (250 ml) milk
    4 eggs
    2 tablespoons chopped cilantro (coriander)
    2 small scallions (spring onions), chopped
    salt and ground pepper
    2 Basic Corn Arepas (page 117), to serve

Pour the water and milk into a small pan and place over medium heat. When it begins to boil, carefully crack the eggs into the pan without breaking the yolks. Boil for about 3 minutes, then continue cooking over low heat, add the cilantro (coriander) and scallions (spring onions). Slowly stir until the white is set, and season with salt and pepper.

Divide the broth between 2 bowls, making sure there are two eggs in each. If desired, you can add more scallions and cilantro to the bottom of each bowl before adding the broth and egg. Serve immediately, with Basic Corn Arepas (page 117).

Caesar's Mushrooms in Egg

Choros enhuevados
Honduras

Preparation time: 10 minutes
Cooking time: 5 minutes

Serves: 4

No one is quite sure how the dreamy red *Amanita Caesarea* mushroom, native to southern Europe and northern Africa, came to the misty forests near La Esperanza and Intibucá, Honduras, but they are now commonplace during the rainy season in May and June. The Lenca community there has adapted them as their own and they're included in a handful of recipes. They grill them with a touch of lime and eat them with tortillas, stew them, or batter and fry them, but for breakfast they are served in eggs.

    2 tablespoons lard
    1½ cups/3½ oz (100 g) chopped Caeser's
    mushrooms (or use chanterelles)
    ½ onion, finely chopped
    2 tablespoons chopped epazote
    3 eggs, beaten
    salt and ground pepper

In a medium frying pan, heat the lard then add the mushrooms, onion, and epazote. Sauté for 1 minute, then add the beaten eggs with salt and pepper to taste, and cook until your desired consistency.

Colombian Egg and Milk Soup

Fish and Seafood

On a tiny spit of sand on the north coast of Honduras, between the Caribbean Sea and a lagoon lined with a tangled web of mangroves, a Garifuna man sets off in his canoe, paddling just before the dawn as the sky full of stars begins to fade into the blue. What the water provides is a means of survival for his isolated village of just a few dozen families, descendants of mixed groups of escaped West African slaves who intermarried with native Arawak people on St. Vincent before being exiled to the island of Roatán in 1798.

His dugout canoe, hollowed out from a tree trunk, wobbles amidst the waves as he moves further from shore. He scoops out the water that has gathered beneath his bare feet with a plastic soda bottle that has been cut in half, as he paddles out to the *bajos*, the patches of reef that are his preferred fishing grounds. With hook and line baited with marsh clams (*Polymesoda placans*) found in the lagoon, he pulls in a few snapper and amberjack, and when the sun moves higher in the sky, he brings them back to his family on shore.

His wife grates and strains coconuts for the milk and grinds bright red achiote seeds that grow in the trees beside their house. She tosses them with the fish into a pot to make a stew called *hudutu*. She serves it with boiled green and ripe plantains that her husband has mashed with a wooden mortar and pestle into a paste, as well as cassava bread. Other days she might fry the fish whole with *patacones* (plantain fritters) grill it, or, when there is more than the family needs, they'll salt it or smoke it over nance wood to use another day. Sometimes they'll dive for lobster or conch, which they'll dice and marinate in lime and onion to make ceviche. The recipes they create have been shaped by the species they catch and the flora they grow or forage. From the Atlantic to the Pacific to Lake Titicaca to the rivers of the Amazon Basin, this is how small fishing communities have lived for centuries.

The use of fish and seafood has changed extensively over the past century. Ice and refrigeration has allowed seafood to be preserved for longer periods of time, enabling it to reach inland areas and fulfill the demand of towns and cities. The efficiency of fishing methods, such as specialized nets and larger boats that go further from shore, has increased hauls, sometimes with disastrous consequences. Even as large trawlers clear the oceans of fish and disrupt ancestral supply chains, small communities like this one still survive on what the sea can bring them each day.

Garifuna Fish and Coconut Milk Stew with Plantains

Hudutu
Belize, Guatemala, Honduras, Nicaragua

Preparation time: 20 minutes
Cooking time: 40 minutes
Serves: 4

This fish stew with mashed plantains is common among the Garifuna who live in small communities in remote corners of the Caribbean coast of the northern half of Central America. Typically, women make this stew, while the men mash the plantains in a method similar to African fufu. When served with rice instead of plantains, it's called "fish seré."

    2 lb (900 g) skin-on kingfish fillets
    2 tablespoons vegetable oil
    2 green plantains, peeled and chopped
    2 ripe plantains, peeled and chopped
    1 white onion, sliced
    2 garlic cloves, minced
    1 carrot, peeled and diced
    1½ cups/12 fl oz (350 ml) coconut milk
    1½ cups/12 fl oz (350 ml) water
    1 teaspoon ground cumin
    ½ teaspoon ground annatto
    4 sprigs culantro, chopped (or use cilantro/coriander)
    2 basil leaves, chopped
    2 cups/4 oz (120 g) chopped okra
    salt and ground pepper

Cut each fish fillet into about 4 pieces.
Heat 1 tablespoon of the oil in a frying pan and sear the fish pieces, skin side down, for 3 minutes. Set aside.
Add the green plantains to a small pan of boiling, salted water and boil for 10 minutes over medium-high heat, then add the ripe plantains and boil for a further 5 minutes, or until tender. Drain and let cool. The traditional method for mashing the plantains is to put them into a *hana*, or wooden mortar, and then pound with a *uduwa*, a long stick. Alternatively, blend in a food processor, adding enough water to give a smooth paste.
Heat the remaining oil in a pan. Add the onion, garlic, and carrot, and sauté for 8 minutes over medium heat. Add the coconut milk and water, then the cumin, annatto, culantro, and basil. Season with salt and pepper. Stir until it starts steaming. When it's about to simmer, add the fish and okra. Cook over medium heat, stirring occasionally, for 10 minutes or until the fish is tender. Serve hot with the plantains on the side, or dropped into the soup.

Grated Plantain and Fish Chowder

Bundiga
Belize

Preparation time: 15 minutes
Cooking time: 30 minutes
Serves: 4

A Garifuna recipe with ingredients similar to *hudutu*, *bundiga* is a fish porridge thickened with grated plantains and coconut milk. Serve with *Arroz con coco* (Coconut Rice, page 63) or cassava bread.

2 lb (900 g) red snapper or kingfish fillets, cut into large chunks
5 cups/40 fl oz (1.2 liters) coconut milk
2 garlic cloves, chopped
1 medium onion, chopped
3 basil leaves
4 green plantains, peeled and grated
½ cup/1 oz (30 g) okra
salt and ground pepper

Season the fish with salt and pepper and set aside.
In a medium pan, bring the coconut milk to a boil, stirring continuously, and just before it boils, add the garlic, onion, and basil. Continue to stir to prevent sticking, and cook for a further 10 minutes. Add the grated plantains one spoonful at a time (these can also be formed into dumplings), then simmer for about 7 minutes, stirring continuously. Add the okra and fish and cook for 10 minutes, or until tender. Adjust the seasoning, and serve hot.

Run Down

Rondón 🅾
Colombia, Costa Rica, Nicaragua, Panama

Preparation time: 25 minutes
Cooking time: 40 minutes
Serves: 4
(if using pressure cooker; 1 hour if not)

This seafood and coconut stew is found primarily in Antillean communities living along the Caribbean coast of Central America and the Colombian Caribbean, brought from Jamaica by immigrants working on the railroads and Panama Canal. It's called run down, pronounced *rondón* in Jamaican patois, because it uses whatever fish and seafood is leftover. Clams, mussels, conch, sea snails, and any other seafood around can be added to the recipe. Serve with rice, *Tostones* (Fried Plantains, page 194), and/or lime wedges.

    1 lb (450 g) pig tail, cut into 1-inch (2.5-cm) chunks
    3 lb (1.4 kg) seabass (or other firm white fish)
    1½ cups/12 fl oz (350 ml) coconut milk
    1 onion, diced
    4 garlic cloves, minced
    1 cassava, peeled and cut into cubes
    1 yellow yam, peeled and cut into cubes
    1 lb (450 g) pumpkin, peeled and cut into cubes
    2 carrots, peeled and sliced
    2 sweet potatoes, peeled and cut into cubes
    2 green plantains, peeled and sliced
    1 tablespoon minced fresh ginger
    1 small chile, seeded and minced
    1 tablespoon curry powder
    1 tablespoon dried oregano
    salt and ground pepper

Cook the pig tail in water with a pinch of salt added, either in a pressure cooker for 15 minutes, or for 35 minutes from boiling in a pan on the stove. Drain.
Meanwhile, clean and fillet the fish, removing the skin. Season with salt and pepper, and set aside.
Put the coconut milk in a large pan over medium heat, add the onion and garlic, and cook for 3 minutes. Add the cassava, yam, pumpkin, carrots, sweet potatoes, and plantains, and simmer for 15 minutes. Add the fish fillets and pig tail, then the ginger, chile, curry powder, and oregano. Cook for a further 5 minutes, or until the fish is tender.

Fish and Seafood

Run Down

Ecuadorian Fish and Onion Soup

Encebollado ecuatoriano
Ecuador

Preparation time: 10 minutes
Cooking time: 30 minutes
Serves: 5–6

A national dish of Ecuador, *encebollado* is especially common on the southeastern coast, in the provinces of Guayas and Manabí. It can be eaten at any time of the day, though it is often prepared in the early morning to revive your soul.

1 red onion, sliced
juice of 1 lime
2 tablespoons white vinegar
1 lb (450 g) cassava, peeled and cut into chunks
1 tablespoon olive oil
1 white onion, chopped
2 tomatoes, peeled and diced
2 lb (900 g) fresh albacore tuna, cut into steaks or large chunks
1 teaspoon chile powder
2 teaspoons ground cumin
4 tablespoons chopped cilantro (coriander)
salt and ground pepper

Start by mixing the red onion with the lime juice and vinegar in a small bowl. Season with salt and pepper, and set aside for at least 20 minutes.

Meanwhile, in a medium pan, boil the cassava in plenty of water for 25 minutes, until tender, then drain and return to the pan.

While the cassava is cooking, heat the oil in a large pan over high heat, add the onion and tomatoes, and cook for 5 minutes. Add the fish with enough water to cover, with a pinch each of salt and pepper, the chile powder, cumin, and half the cilantro (coriander). Cook for 15 minutes until the fish is cooked through, then remove the pieces of fish from the stock and strain the liquid into a bowl. Pour the strained cooking liquid into the pan with the drained cassava and coarsely mash the cassava. Add the fish, check the seasoning, and simmer for a further 5 minutes.

Serve hot with the pickled onions and remaining chopped cilantro.

Guna Coconut Fish Stew

Tule masi
Panama

Preparation time: 15 minutes
Cooking time: 20 minutes
Serves: 4

The name of this dish translates to "people's food" in Guna, the language of the indigenous people who live primarily in an autonomous zone that consists of several hundred small islands off the Caribbean coast of Panama. There is no set recipe for this soup, which has a base of grated coconut, plantains, and boiled tubers like cassava, taro, or yams, and usually includes boiled, smoked, or fried fish, or sometimes game. Serve with *Arroz con coco* (Coconut Rice, page 63) or *Patacones* (Fried Plantain, page 194).

1 coconut
7 cups/5 fl oz (1.6 liters) water
1 green plantain, peeled and sliced
1 cassava, peeled and sliced
3 lb (1.4 kg) red snapper fillets, cut into large chunks
juice of 2 limes
salt

Heat a charcoal grill (barbecue).

Grate the coconut pulp (flesh) and place in a filter, such as a coffee filter, set over a bowl or pitcher (jug). Pour the water over the grated coconut, and when it has all passed through, pour the strained coconut water into a pan and place on the grill to heat.

Add the plantain and cassava, bring to a boil, cook for 10 minutes, then add the snapper pieces. Continue cooking for a further 10 minutes or until the cassava is soft and the snapper cooked. Add the lime juice to taste, season with salt, and serve hot.

Blue Fish Stew

Peixe azul marinho
Brazil

Preparation time: 15 minutes
Cooking time: 20 minutes
Serves: 4

When the tannins from green bananas meet with the iron of the pan, a chemical reaction occurs, turning the broth of this recipe as blue as the sea. The stew, a cultural tradition of the Caiçara culture in southeastern Brazil, works best with the São Tomé or dwarf bananas, and also includes fish and *angu* or *Pirão* (Cassava Porridge, page 100). It's usually served with cassava flour.

1 lb 8 oz (680 g) grouper or snapper fillets
juice of 4 limes
1 tablespoon vegetable oil
½ white onion, chopped
4 garlic cloves, minced
½ red bell pepper, seeded and chopped
½ green bell pepper, seeded and chopped
1 *malagueta* chile, seeded and chopped
4 cups/32 fl oz (950 ml) fish stock
4 green bananas (ideally Sao-Tomé style), unpeeled, each sliced into 5 pieces
4 tomatoes, peeled and diced
2 tablespoons chopped cilantro (coriander)
4 tablespoons chopped parsley
3 tablespoons cassava flour
salt and ground pepper

Season the fish fillets with lime juice, salt, and pepper and set aside.

Heat the vegetable oil in a cast-iron pan over medium heat, add the onion, garlic, bell peppers, and chile, and sauté for 10 minutes, or until slightly caramelized.

Add the fish to the pan, pour in the fish stock, and add the banana slices. Turn the heat to high and bring to a boil. As soon as the stock has become blue-ish, remove the bananas, peel them, and add the pulp back to the pan. Add the tomatoes, cilantro (coriander), and parsley.

Transfer 3 cups/25 fl oz (750 ml) of the stock to a small pan and bring to a boil, then slowly add the cassava flour, whisking to prevent any lumps. Once the mixture has thickened, add it to the soup. Stir well and serve hot.

Yucatecan Fish

Tikin xic
Mexico

Preparation time: 15 minutes,
plus 5 hours marinating
Cooking time: 20 minutes

Serves: 4

Similar to *Cochinita pibil* (Yucatán-Style Barbecued Pork, page 286), another pre-Hispanic dish from the Yucatán Peninsula, *tikin xic* uses a marinade of bitter oranges and annatto, with the fish wrapped in a banana leaf and baked in an earthen oven.

    1 whole grouper, about 5 lb (2.2 kg), guts removed
    3 tablespoons annatto paste
    1 cup/8 fl oz (250 ml) bitter orange juice
    1 large banana leaf
    2 green bell peppers, cored, seeded, and sliced
    2 red bell peppers, cored, seeded, and sliced
    3 tomatoes, sliced
    2 red onions, sliced
    1 teaspoon dried oregano
    ½ bottle lager (4½ fl oz/125 ml)
    ¼ cup/2 fl oz (60 ml) olive oil
    salt and ground pepper

Clean the fish by rinsing it under ice-cold water. Dry well inside and out using paper towels, and place on a tray. Season with salt, inside and out.

Dilute the annatto paste in the bitter orange juice and, using a brush, cover the whole fish with the mixture. Marinate for at least 5 hours in the refrigerator.

Heat a charcoal grill (barbecue).

Lay the banana leaf on the grill and let it soften for about 3 minutes, then flip. Place the fish in the middle of the banana leaf and add the bell peppers, tomato, onion, and oregano on top. Pour over the lager and oil, season with salt and pepper, and close the banana leaf.

Place on the grill for 20 minutes, or until the flesh can easily be shredded from the bones. Serve on a platter, to share.

Salt Cod Fritters

Bolinhos de bacalao
Brazil

Preparation time: 20 minutes,
plus 24 hours soaking
Cooking time: 45 minutes

Makes: 20

Originally from Portugal, *bolinhos de bacalao* have been firmly integrated into Brazilian tradition. You'll see them served alongside beer at pubs called *botecos* or eaten at home on Fridays and during Lent.

    1 lb (450 g) salt (dried) cod (bacalao)
    1 lb 8 oz (680 g) potatoes, peeled and cut into 2-inch (5-cm) pieces
    1 tablespoon olive oil
    ½ white onion, chopped
    2 garlic cloves, minced
    2 eggs, separated
    3 tablespoons chopped parsley
    vegetable oil, for deep-frying
    salt and ground pepper

Soak the salt cod in cold water for 24 hours, changing the water frequently (about every 6 hours).

Rinse the cod well, place in a pan with fresh water, and boil over medium heat for 10 minutes. Remove the cod and shred the meat, reserving the water. Add the potatoes to the cod cooking water, bring to a boil and cook for 20 minutes, or until completely tender.

Meanwhile, heat the olive oil in a frying pan over medium heat and sauté the onion and garlic for 15 minutes, or until soft. Remove from the heat and set aside.

When the potatoes are cooked, drain, and mash well. Mix in the shredded fish, egg yolks, parsley, and fried onion and garlic. Season with salt and pepper. Whisk the egg whites into stiff peaks, then fold them into the potato mix.

Pour enough vegetable oil for deep-frying into a large, heavy pan, making sure it is no more than two-thirds full, and heat to 350°F/177°C.

Shape the potato and cod mixture into balls, about 2 inches (5 cm) in diameter. In batches, deep-fry in the hot oil for 4–5 minutes or until golden brown. Remove with a skimmer to a plate lined with paper towels to absorb excess oil. Serve warm.

Venezuelan Seafood Soup

Fosforera
Venezuela

Preparation time: 20 minutes
Cooking time: 2 hours 15 minutes

Serves: 4

Every town along Venezuela's eastern coast has its own recipe for this seafood soup, named because of the high amounts of phosphorous in the ingredients.

    10 cups/5 pints (2.4 liters) water
    2 fish heads
    ½ white onion, chopped
    5 garlic cloves, minced
    ½ red bell pepper
    2 *ají dulce* chiles, seeded and chopped
    1 leek (white part only), chopped
    4 tomatoes, peeled and chopped
    1 lb (450 g) shrimp (prawns), heads removed and reserved for stock
    1 lb (450 g) calamari, cleaned and sliced into rings
    1 lb (450 g) clams, cleaned
    1 lb (450 g) scallops, cleaned
    2 crabs
    3 tablespoons chopped cilantro (coriander)
    salt

In a stockpot, bring the water to a boil over high heat. Add the fish heads, onion, garlic, bell pepper, chiles, leek, tomatoes, and shrimp (prawn) heads. Simmer for 2 hours, stirring occasionally and making sure there's always enough water to cover. Strain into a large pan, pressing on the solids to extract all the liquid.

Bring to a boil over high heat, add the shrimp, calamari, clams, scallops, and crabs, and simmer for 15 minutes. Season with salt and add the cilantro (coriander). Serve hot in deep dishes.

Bahian Seafood Stew

Moqueca baiana
Brazil

Preparation time: 10 minutes,
plus 15 minutes chilling
Cooking time: 45 minutes

Serves: 4

Moqueca is believed to have originated in the state of Espírito Santo, where seafood—fish, shrimp, skate, crabs, or a mix—is cooked in a broth of tomatoes and annatto. That version, combining Portuguese and indigenous ingredients, is lighter than the rich version from Bahía, below, which has arguably become better known, and adds coconut milk, peppers, and *dendê* oil, giving it a distinctive orange-red color. The typical pot for cooking *moqueca* is a *panela de barro*, a clay casserole made by applying mangrove sap to clay to make it waterproof. Indigenous groups have been making them long before conquest. *Moqueca baiana* is typically served with several sides, such as white rice, cilantro, farofa, chiles, and *Pirão* (Cassava Porridge, page 100) made by thickening the broth from the *moqueca* with cassava flour.

  8 oz (225 g) shrimp (prawns)
  1 lb (450 g) fish fillets (any firm white fish, such as seabass, swordfish, or grouper)
  juice of 1 lime
  2 tablespoons olive oil
  2 tablespoons *dendê* oil
  1 onion, chopped
  3 garlic cloves, minced
  3 tomatoes, peeled and diced
  1 red bell pepper, cored, seeded, and sliced
  1 tablespoon each paprika and dried cumin
  1 cup/8 fl oz (250 ml) fish stock
  1½ cups/12 fl oz (350 ml) coconut milk
  2 tablespoons chopped cilantro (coriander)

On a plate, rub the shrimp (prawns) and fish fillets with the lime juice and olive oil. Season with salt and pepper, cover, and chill in the refrigerator for 15 minutes.

Heat 1 tablespoon of the *dendê* oil in a frying pan over medium heat. Add the fish fillets and cook for 3 minutes each side, or until golden. Remove from the pan, heat the remaining *dendê* oil and add the onion, garlic, tomatoes, and bell pepper. Cook for 8 minutes over medium heat, then season with the paprika and cumin. Pour in the fish stock and coconut milk, stir well and bring to a boil. Lower the heat and simmer, whisking occasionally, for 20 minutes, or until the broth thickens. Add the fish fillets and shrimp to the broth and cook for a further 10 minutes. Sprinkle with the cilantro (coriander) and serve hot.

Return to Life

Vuelve a la vida
Mexico, Venezuela

Preparation time: 30 minutes
Cooking time: 30 minutes

Serves: 4

This seafood cocktail, which, along with similar versions called *siete potencias* (seven powers) and *rompe colchón* (mattress breaker), are sold from jars on Venezuelan beaches and are believed to be aphrodisiacs. Similar versions are sold in Mexico as well.

  8 oz (225 g) shrimp (prawns), peeled and deveined
  8 oz (225 g) squid, cleaned
  ½ octopus, cleaned
  12 mussels
  1 cup/8 fl oz (250 ml) lime juice
  2 tablespoons white vinegar
  1 cup/8 fl oz (250 ml) water
  3 tablespoons tomato purée
  1 tablespoon Worcestershire sauce
  1 red onion, chopped
  1 hot chile, finely chopped
  5 *ají dulce* chiles, finely chopped
  ½ cup/¾ oz (20 g) chopped cilantro (coriander)
  salt and ground pepper

Add the shrimp (prawns) and squid to a pan of salted boiling water. Remove the squid after 2–3 minutes and the shrimp after 3–4 minutes. As soon as they are ready, transfer them to an iced water bath to stop cooking and cool them. Cut the squid into rings.

Add the octopus to boiling salted water, then reduce the heat and simmer for 15–20 minutes, until tender. Let cool and cut into chunks.

Rinse the mussels in cold water. Pour about 1 inch (2.5 cm) of water in a medium pot over high heat. Add the mussels to the pot, cover and let cook for 5–7 minutes. Remove from the heat and when cool enough to handle remove the mussels from their shells. Set aside.

Mix the lime juice with the vinegar, water, tomato purée, and Worcestershire sauce. Season well with salt and pepper, then add the onion, chiles, *ají dulce*, and cilantro (coriander).

Place all the seafood in a bowl, mix with the sauce, and let sit for 10 minutes. Mix well before serving in cold cups or dishes.

Salt-Baked Grunt

Chita al sal
Peru

Preparation time: 20 minutes
Cooking time: 30 minutes

Serves: 6

Chita is an ocean bottom-dwelling grunt that's found off South America's Pacific Coast, from the Galapagos Islands to northern Chile. The salt case helps trap the moisture of the fish within, preserving its delicate flavor. It was created by Humberto Sato at Costanera 700, the Lima restaurant he founded in 1975, which helped lay the groundwork for modern Nikkei cuisine in which Japanese culinary techniques are applied to local Peruvian ingredients.

  1 *chita*, cleaned (or use any grunt)
  4 lb (1.8 kg) fine sea salt
  aluminum foil

Preheat the oven to 350°F/180°C/Gas Mark 4.

In an oven tray, lay out enough aluminum foil to cover the tray and the fish. Place a third of the salt in the bottom of the tray and spray water from a spray bottle, to humidify it, making it more solid. Place the fish on top of the salt and cover it with the remaining salt, spraying water to create a solid mix. Cover the fish and salt with the foil and bake for 30 minutes.

Remove from the oven and take off the foil. Break the salt with a knife, and carefully brush the salt from the fish before serving.

Sinaloa-Style Grilled Fish

Pescado zarandeado estilo Sinaloa
Mexico

Preparation time: 20 minutes,
plus 15 minutes soaking
and marinating
Cooking time: 15 minutes

Serves: 4

This grilled fish dish is found along much of Mexico's Pacific Coast in one form or another. It's often butter-flied and grilled in a *zaranda*, a wire cage used to cook fish over open fires, which gives the recipe its name. Alternatively, it can also be wrapped in a banana leaf with the sauce or cooked in a pan. Serve with Corn Tortillas (page 136) and/or white rice.

    2 dried *ancho* chiles, seeded
    2 dried *guajillo* chiles, seeded
    3 cups/25 fl oz (750 ml) water
    1½ tablespoons soy sauce
    2 teaspoons Worcestershire sauce
    2 teaspoons tomato paste (purée)
    juice of 1 lime
    1 teaspoon dried oregano
    ½ teaspoon ground cumin
    4 garlic cloves, peeled
    1 snapper, grouper, or snook, about 3 lb (1.4 kg)
    ¼ teaspoon salt
    oil, for brushing

Put the chiles and water in a pan and bring to a boil, then remove from the heat and let soak for 10 minutes. Drain, reserving 2 tablespoons of the soaking liquid. Add the liquid and the chiles to a food processor or blender, with the soy sauce, Worcestershire sauce, tomato paste (purée), lime juice, oregano, cumin and garlic. Blend until smooth.

Cut the fish in half along the backbone, then cut diagonally along the flesh side of the fish, about ¼ inch (5 mm) deep. Season the fish with the salt and spread the blended chile mixture on both sides. Let sit for 5 minutes.

Heat a grill (barbecue); if charcoal, let the flames die down. Place a barbecue basket on the grill to get hot, then brush with oil. Add the fish to the basket and close, then cook for about 12–15 minutes, turning every 3 minutes or so. Remove the fish from the basket, place on a platter, and serve hot.

Steamed Pejesapo

Pejesapo al vapor
Peru

Preparation time: 15 minutes,
plus 30 minutes soaking
Cooking time: 15 minutes

Serves: 4

Pejesapo (*Sicyases sanguineus*), or frogfish, is a fatty, traditionally seen as ugly looking, gelatinous feeder fish that lives off the Pacific coast of South America from central Peru to central Chile. A member of the Gobiesocidae family, like monkfish, men called *pejesaperos* catch them by using long poles with nets or hooks to pick them from rock walls and tidal pools. It's a delicate fish and if overcooked, which doesn't take a lot, it falls apart. Most typically, pejesapo is cooked in a stew with tomatoes, onions, and other ingredients called *caldillo de pejesapo* or *chupín de pejesapo*. In Lima, pejesapo is served in *chifas* and Nikkei restaurants.

    2 medium pejesapo fish
    4 cups/32 fl oz (950 ml) boiling water
    ⅓ cup/⅓ oz (10 g) dried shiitake mushrooms
    ½ cup/4 fl oz (120 ml) soy sauce
    2 teaspoons minced fresh ginger
    1 teaspoon sugar
    1 tablespoon sesame oil
    ½ cup/1¼ oz (35 g) chopped scallions (spring onions)

Slice the fish underneath lengthways, from mouth to tail, removing the guts and the gills. Rinse in cold water.

Pour the boiling water over the shiitake mushrooms in a heatproof bowl. Cover with plastic wrap (clingfilm) and soak for 30 minutes. Strain and reserve the liquid. Cut the mushrooms into slices or, if small, leave whole.

Place the fish belly side down in a bowl with the mushrooms around it. Mix the warm mushroom broth with the soy sauce, ginger, sugar, and sesame oil, and pour it over the fish. Cover with aluminum foil and let steam in the bowl for about 15 minutes. Remove from the bowl, place the fish on a platter and spoon some of the sauce over it. Sprinkle with the scallions (spring onions) and serve immediately.

Uruguayan Fish Soup

Chupín de pescado
Argentina, Paraguay, Uruguay

Preparation time: 10 minutes,
plus 30 minutes marinating
Cooking time: 25 minutes

Serves: 4

This tomato and fish soup was first made in Uruguay by Italian immigrants who came to the country during World War I. It's adapted from the classic Genoese soup *ciuppin*, which was made by fishermen on their boats with low value fish they couldn't sell.

    juice of 2 lemons
    1 teaspoon salt
    2 lb (900 g) white fish fillets (such as seabass), cut
    into 2-inch (5-cm) pieces
    2 tablespoons olive oil
    2 white onions, chopped
    2 garlic cloves, minced
    3 tomatoes, peeled and diced
    1 red bell pepper, cored, seeded, and diced
    5 potatoes, peeled and cut into ½-inch (1-cm) cubes
    ½ cup/4 fl oz (120 ml) white wine
    1½ cups/12 fl oz (350 ml) fish stock

Mix the lemon juice and salt in a medium bowl and add the fish. Let marinate for 20–30 minutes.

In a pan, heat the oil over medium heat, add the onions and garlic, and sauté for 5 minutes. Add the tomatoes and bell pepper, and continue cooking for a further 4 minutes. Add the potatoes, stir, then pour in the wine and stock. Let boil for 5 minutes, then lower the heat, add the fish fillets, and cover the pan. Let the fish cook for 8 minutes or until cooked through but still soft. Serve the fish with the sauce spooned on top.

Curry Fried Snapper

Pargo frito al curry 📷
Panama

Preparation time: 15 minutes,
plus 1 hour marinating
Cooking time: 10 minutes

Serves: 4

Afro-Antillean communities in Colón, Bocas del Toro, and the El Chorrillo neighborhood in Panama City prepare fried red snapper with a touch of curry and *ají chombo*. Serve with *Tostones* (Fried Plantains, page 194) or *Arroz con coco* (Coconut Rice, page 63).

    juice of 1 lime
    1 snapper (pargo), about 3 lb (1.4 kg)
    1 red onion, finely sliced
    2 garlic cloves, minced
    2 *ají chombo* chiles, chopped
    2 tablespoons curry powder
    ½ cup/4 oz (115 g) all-purpose (plain) flour
    vegetable oil, for frying

Squeeze lime juice over the flesh of the fish and cut 4 or 5 slices into the flesh, about 1 inch (2.5 cm) apart. Place in a bowl and add the onion, garlic, chiles, and 1 table-spoon of the curry powder. Season with salt and pepper, and leave in the refrigerator to marinate for 1 hour.

Mix the remaining curry powder and flour. Remove the fish from the bowl and roll in the seasoned flour.

Heat enough oil for shallow-frying in a frying pan over medium heat. Fry the fish for 3 minutes each side, or until golden and crispy. Remove to a plate lined with paper towels to absorb excess oil.

Fish in Tomato Sauce

Pimentade
French Guiana

Preparation time: 15 minutes,
plus 2 hours marinating
Cooking time: 20 minutes

Serves: 8

There are variations of *pimentade*, fish stewed in tomato sauce seasoned with lime and served over white rice, found across the Guyanas. In French Guiana, catfish is often used, though tilapia or flounder are substitutions. Some add coconut milk or annatto to the sauce. Serve with white rice and *Tostones* (Fried Plantains, page 194).

    3 garlic cloves, 2 crushed and 1 chopped
    juice of 2 limes
    1 teaspoon salt
    2.2 lb (1 kg) catfish, cut into 4-inch (10-cm) pieces
    1 tablespoon olive oil
    2 tomatoes, peeled, seeded, and cut into chunks
    3 white onions, sliced into rings
    1 tablespoon chopped bay leaves
    1 tablespoon chopped thyme leaves
    1 teaspoon cloves
    2 tablespoons chopped basil
    1 cup/8 fl oz (250 ml) hot water
    1 red bell pepper, cored, seeded, and chopped

Add the 2 crushed garlic cloves to a bowl, and mix in the lime juice and salt. Add the fish pieces to the marinade to coat. Marinate in the refrigerator for 2 hours.

In a medium pan, heat the oil and sauté the tomatoes and onions for 5 minutes. Add the bay leaves, thyme, cloves, basil, and chopped garlic, along with the hot water. Bring to a boil slowly over low heat, then add the fish (reserve the marinade) and bell pepper. Cover and cook over high heat for 10 minutes. Beat the remaining marinade in the bowl to thicken, then add it into the pan.

Cusk Eel Chowder

Caldillo de congrio
Chile

Preparation time: 20 minutes,
plus 30 minutes soaking
Cooking time: 1 hour 25 minutes

Serves: 5–6

"In the storm-tossed Chilean sea lives the rosy conger, giant eel of snowy flesh," wrote Chilean Nobel laureate Pablo Neruda in his poem *Oda al Caldillo de Congrio*, on his return to Chile from exile in Italy. Much of the poem describes a recipe for the chowder (skinning the eel; sautéing the garlic, onion, and tomato; steaming prawns; stirring in the cream), then closes with a grand proclamation "...that in this dish, you may know heaven." The traditional recipe for *caldillo de congrio* uses the *congrio dorado* (*Genypterus blacodes*), or *congrio colorado* (*Genypterus chilensis*), red and pink cusk-eel species common in the Chilean Pacific, which can be substituted with other cusk eel, such as ling or whiting.

    1 cusk eel, head, tail, and guts removed
    1 carrot, roughly chopped
    2 white onions, 1 chopped, 1 sliced
    1 celery stalk, chopped
    2 cups/16 fl oz (475 ml) white wine
    ½ cup/4 fl oz (120 ml) olive oil
    9 garlic cloves, minced
    2 red bell peppers, cored, seeded and sliced
    6 tomatoes, peeled and diced
    1 teaspoon each dried oregano and ground cumin
    1 tablespoon chopped cilantro (coriander)
    5 potatoes, peeled and cut into ½-inch (1-cm) slices
    2 tablespoons chopped parsley
    1 cup/8 fl oz (250 ml) cream
    1 egg yolk

To prepare the eel, remove the head, tail, and guts, discarding the guts. Submerge the fish and head under cold water for 30 minutes. Drain, cut the fish into 3-inch (7.5-cm) chunks, pat dry, and place in the refrigerator.

Add the head and tail to a large pan over high heat and cover with cold water. Add the carrot, chopped onion, and celery. Once the stock begins to boil, add the wine and simmer for 30 minutes. Strain the stock into a bowl.

Preheat the oven to 350°F/180°C/Gas Mark 4.

Heat 1 tablespoon of the olive oil in a pan over medium heat, add the sliced onion, garlic, and bell peppers, and sauté for 15 minutes, stirring frequently. Add the tomatoes, oregano, cumin, and cilantro (coriander), and season with salt and pepper.

Add the remaining oil to a *paila de greda* (clay dish) or 13 x 9 x 2-inch (33 x 23 x 5-cm) oven dish, and place in the oven for 7 minutes. Once hot, cover the dish with the sliced potatoes, then add the sautéed vegetables. Cover with stock then bake in the oven for 10 minutes. Remove from the oven and add the fish chunks, seasoned with salt and pepper, then sprinkle with the parsley. If needed, add more stock and cook in the oven for a further 20 minutes, or until the fish starts to peel off. Remove from the oven. Stir in the cream and egg yolk. Serve hot in deep dishes.

Fish and Seafood

Curry Fried Snapper

Peruvian Seafood Soup

Parihuela
Peru

Preparation time: 15 minutes
Cooking time: 45 minutes

Serves: 6

Peru's answer to a Galician *caldeirada* or a Provençal bouillabaisse, this fragrant, sometimes spicy, soulful soup is eaten by fishermen after a day at sea. It can be, and generally is, made with whatever fish or shellfish is available. Beer or *Chicha de jora* (Corn Beer, page 388) may be used for acidity in place of the wine. When using only crab, it's called *concentrado de cangrejo*.

    3 stone crabs
    1 fish head (about 28 oz/800 g)
    ½ white onion
    8 oz (225 g) mussels in shells, cleaned
    2 tablespoons chopped parsley
    2 tablespoons olive oil
    1 red onion, chopped
    2 garlic cloves, minced
    1 teaspoon minced fresh ginger
    2 tablespoons *ají amarillo* paste
    1 tablespoon *ají panca* paste
    2 tomatoes, peeled and diced
    ½ teaspoon ground cumin
    1 cup/8 fl oz (250 ml) white wine
    8 oz (225 g) shrimp (prawns)
    1 lb (450 g) seabass fillets
    3½ oz (100 g) seaweed (such as yuyo)

    To serve
    1 *rocoto* chile; seeded and sliced
    1 scallion (spring onion), chopped
    Cancha serrana (Toasted Andean Corn Kernels, page 114)
    lime wedges

Submerge the crabs in a bowl of iced water for 3–5 minutes to stun them, then keep them on ice until use.

Place the fish head in a pan with the onion, mussels, crabs, and parsley, and cover with cold water. Bring to a boil over high heat, then lower and simmer for 30 minutes. Strain the stock, reserving the crabs and mussels.

In a large pan, heat the oil, add the red onion, garlic, ginger, both chile pastes, tomatoes, and cumin and sauté for 7 minutes over medium heat, stirring frequently. Pour in the wine and the reserved stock and bring to a boil. Once boiling, add the mussels, crab, shrimp (prawns), and fish fillets. Cover the pan and cook for 8 minutes, or until all the seafood is cooked. Check the seasoning and add the seaweed.

Serve hot with the chile slices and scallions (spring onions) sprinkled on top. Serve with the toasted corn and lime wedges on the side.

Peruvian Sweated Fish

Sudado de pescado
Ecuador, Peru

Preparation time: 15 minutes
Cooking time: 20 minutes

Serves: 4

Like a Spanish *estofado*, *sudados* are stews that are slow cooked in covered pots, which braise the protein in its own juices, essentially causing it to sweat. Along the north coast of Peru they are especially common and based on a recipe that dates to the Moche, adding native chile peppers and *Chicha de jora* (Corn Beer, page 388), to the broth. In Barranquilla, Colombia, a traditional stew made with chicken—*pollo sudado*—follows a similar technique.

    2 tablespoons olive oil
    ½ red onion, chopped
    4 garlic cloves, chopped
    2 tablespoons *ají amarillo* paste
    1½ cups/12 fl oz (350 ml) *Chicha de jora* (Corn Beer, page 388)
    ½ white onion, chopped
    3 tomatoes peeled, seeded, and diced
    1 scallion (spring onion), chopped
    1 lb 5 oz (600 g) grouper or seabass fillets
    1 cup/8 fl oz (250 ml) fish stock
    juice of 1 lime
    salt and ground pepper
    4 sprigs cilantro (coriander), to serve

Heat the oil in a medium pan over medium heat and sauté the red onion and garlic for 7 minutes. Add the *ají amarillo* paste and stir well. Pour in the *Chicha de jora* (Corn Beer) and let simmer for 5 minutes. Add the white onion, tomatoes, and scallion (spring onion) and spread the mixture to cover the bottom of the pan. Place the fish fillets on top and pour in the stock. Cover the pan and cook for 7 minutes over low heat.

To finish, pour in the lime juice, mix well and check the seasoning. Serve hot, garnished with the cilantro (coriander), with white rice on the side.

Skate Omelet

Tortilla de raya
Peru

Preparation time: 15 minutes, plus overnight soaking
Cooking time: 25 minutes

Serves: 4

In artisan fishing communities of the Lambayeque province in northern Peru, such as Pimentel, Puerto Eten, San José, and Santa Rosa, such *tortilla de raya* is found on the menu of every *cevichería*. The manta ray, or skate, was once worshipped by the Moche, but here is served as an omelet that, when done right, comes out brown and crisp along the edges, while moist in the center. Some restaurants will add diced up bits of shrimp, fish, and squid to join the skate. Though this is a traditional omelet in every sense of the term, it is rarely eaten for breakfast, but for lunch.

1 lb (450 g) dried skate meat (or use fresh skate)
12 eggs
½ cup/2 oz (60 g) chopped white onion
2 red bell peppers, cored, seeded, and cut into
½-inch (1-cm) dice
2 *ají amarillo* chiles, sliced
½ cup/1¼ oz (35 g) chopped scallions (spring onions)
2 tablespoons chopped cilantro (coriander)
½ teaspoon ground cumin
1 tablespoon olive oil
salt and ground pepper
Salsa criolla (Creole Sauce, page 406), to serve

Place the skate in a bowl of cold water and let soak overnight in the refrigerator. As an alternative, you can soak it in acidulated water (1 cup/8 fl oz/250 ml vinegar to 8 pints/3.8 liters water) for at least 30 minutes. Drain and shred. Note: if using fresh skate, bring a medium pot of salted water to a boil, then add the skate, and reduce to a simmer. Let cook for 10 minutes. Remove the water, pat dry, and shred the meat.

Whisk the eggs in a medium bowl, then add the shredded skate, onion, bell peppers chiles, scallions (spring onions), and cilantro (coriander). Mix well, add cumin to taste, and season with salt and pepper.

Heat the oil in a frying pan. Once hot, pour in the egg mixture and lower the heat. Let cook for 7 minutes, or until it forms a crust on the bottom. Flip and let it cook for a further 4 minutes over medium heat. Serve warm with *Salsa criolla*.

Mollusks

You might encounter the occasional raw oyster or uncooked clam in ceviche, though most mollusks aren't served raw in the region. Sea snails, mussels, clams, scallops, octopus, and all sorts of other mollusks from Latin American waters are often grilled or baked or find their way into soups, stews, and sauces.

Sea Snails in Soy Sauce

Caracoles al sillao
Peru

Preparation time: 15 minutes
Cooking time: 1 hour 5 minutes   Serves: 4

Sea snails are best served nearly raw or slowly stewed, like *caracoles al sillao*, a favorite recipe from the port city of Callao, a result of the Japanese influence on Peruvian food.

   24 sea snails (with shell)
½ cup/3½ oz (100 g) sugar
1 tablespoon minced fresh ginger
1 turnip, peeled and sliced
1 cup/8 fl oz (250 ml) soy sauce
½ cup/4 fl oz (120 ml) pisco
2 tablespoons finely diced, seeded *rocoto* chile
2 tablespoons chopped scallions (spring onions)

Rinse the sea snails well and place in a medium pan with enough cold water to cover. Bring to a boil and cook for 3 minutes, then drain and rinse in iced water.

Add the sea snails back to the pan and cover with enough water to half cover the snails, about 1 inch (2.5 cm). Add the sugar, ginger, turnip, soy sauce, and pisco, and bring to a boil, then lower the heat and

simmer over low heat for 1 hour. Once cooked, remove the snails from the pan one at a time. Remove the snail meat from the shells using a toothpick or snail fork, then add back to the pan and mix with the sauce.

Serve them warm, back in the shells or in a bowl, garnished with the chile and scallions (spring onions).

Olive Octopus

Pulpo al olivo
Peru

Preparation time: 10 minutes
Cooking time: 30 minutes   Serves: 4

In 1987, a client who happened to own a well-known car filter factory told Japanese-Peruvian chef Rosita Yimura at her restaurant in Callao that he had tried an octopus dish with a sauce the color of lead. It caught her attention and she began experimenting with a sauce, made from mayonnaise and olives, resulting in this recipe that is now found at every *cevichería* in Peru. Dark purple or black olives that grow in coastal Peru called *aceitunas de botija*, named after the clay vessels they were once stored in, are typically used for the sauce.

   1 carrot, chopped
1 white onion, chopped
1 celery stalk, chopped
2 tablespoons salt
1 octopus (about 3 lb/1.4 kg), head removed
2 cups/1 lb (450 g) mayonnaise
1 cup/3½ oz (100 g) pitted *botija* olives
juice of 1 lime
¼ cup/2 fl oz (60 ml) olive oil
2 teaspoons dried oregano

Place the carrot, onion, and celery in a large pan with enough cold water to cover, add the salt. Bring to a boil, dunk the octopus in and out of the water five times, then place it in the pan and cook for 25 minutes. Remove from the pan and let cool, then refrigerate.

Meanwhile, prepare the sauce by slowly blending the mayonnaise in a food processor or blender, adding the olives one at a time, not letting the mayonnaise liquefy. Season with the lime juice and emulsify with the olive oil.

Cut the octopus tentacles into thin slices and place on a platter. Cover with the sauce, sprinkle with the oregano, and serve cold.

Parmesan Scallops

Conchas a la parmesana ▣
Peru

Preparation time: 15 minutes
Cooking time: 10 minutes
Serves: 4

Scallops are both plentiful and inexpensive on the Peruvian coast, and this is one of the simplest recipes in all of Peruvian gastronomy. It is also one of the biggest crowdpleasers at a backyard barbecue.

    12 live bay scallops in shells
    1 tablespoon melted butter
    1 garlic clove, minced
    1½ cups/4 oz (120 g) grated parmesan
    juice of 2 limes

Clean the scallops and open them, leaving just one shell with the scallop. Place on an oven tray. Mix the butter with the garlic and season with a pinch of salt and pepper, then spread using a brush on top of the scallops. Sprinkle the grated parmesan evenly on top and broil (grill) for 5–10 minutes, or until the cheese is melted and golden brown. Squirt a few drops of lime juice on each scallop, and serve.

Salvadoran Shellfish Soup

Mariscada
El Salvador

Preparation time: 30 minutes
Cooking time: 1 hour 15 minutes
Serves: 6

This shellfish soup can be found along the Salvadoran coast, often served in small bowls with cooked crabs, shrimp, and other shellfish hanging out of it.

    3 lb (1.4 kg) whole fish (typically *mojarra*)
    1 lb (450 g) clams
    1 lb (450 g) black clams (cockles)
    4 crabs
    3 cups/24 fl oz (710 ml) water
    2 cups/16 fl oz (475 ml) fish stock
    1 white onion, chopped
    5 garlic cloves, minced
    3 tomatoes, peeled and diced
    8 oz (225 g) squid, cleaned and cut into rings
    6 langoustines, heads removed
    1 lb (450 g) shell-on shrimp (prawns), heads removed
    6 scallions (spring onions), chopped
    3 tablespoons chopped cilantro (coriander)

Start by cleaning the fish. Remove the heads and tails, reserving the heads. Remove the guts and cut the fish into 3-inch (7.5-cm) chunks. Set aside in the refrigerator.

Soak the clams and cockles in separate bowls of fresh water for about 30 minutes to purge of sand. Drain and set aside.

Submerge the crabs in a bowl of iced water for 3–5 minutes to stun them, then keep them on ice until use.

Put the water, stock, and fish heads in a pan over high heat. Add the onion, garlic, tomatoes, and some salt and pepper, and bring to a boil. Lower the heat and simmer for 30 minutes. Remove the fish heads and tip what's left of the stock into a food processor or blender, and process. Return to the pan and place over medium

heat. Once hot, add the crabs, squid, and langoustines. If necessary, add more water to cover all the seafood.

Increase the heat and bring to a boil, then lower the heat and simmer for 20 minutes. Add all the clams, the shrimp (prawns), and fish chunks, and continue simmering the soup for a further 15 minutes.

Finish by adding the scallions (spring onions) and cilantro (coriander) and check the seasoning. Serve hot in soup dishes.

Sailor-Style Clams

Almejas a la marinera
Chile

Preparation time: 30 minutes
Cooking time: 30 minutes
Serves: 4

"Sailor style" recipes from Galicia arrived in South America by way of Spanish settlers after conquest and were adapted to local bivalves, such as mussels, clams, and razor clams.

    1 teaspoon olive oil
    ½ white onion, diced
    2 garlic cloves, minced
    ¾ cup plus 1 tablespoon/7 fl oz (200 ml) white wine
    2 teaspoons chopped parsley, plus extra to garnish
    12 razor clams
    1 teaspoon salt

Soak the clams in a bowl of fresh water for about 30 minutes to purge of sand. Drain and set aside.

In a sauté pan, heat the oil over low heat. Add the onion and garlic and let brown for 10 minutes over low heat. Add the wine and parsley and let cook for a further 2 minutes. Place the razor clams in the pan, and cover them with the sauce. Cook until they begin to open.

Serve in a deep dish with the razor clams beside each other, and with a spoon of the sauce inside and sprinkled with parsley.

Scallops in Pil Pil Sauce

Ostiones al pil pil
Chile

Preparation time: 10 minutes
Cooking time: 5 minutes
Serves: 4

Garlicky pil pil sauce, brought to South America by Basque settlers, has taken on new life in Chile, where it's often used with chicken, shrimp, and other seafood. Here, the local *cacho de cabra* is used, which you can alternatively swap out for the spice blend *merkén*, made of the same chile pepper.

    ¼ cup/2 fl oz (60 ml) olive oil
    5 garlic cloves, minced
    1 *cacho de cabra* chile, seeded and chopped
    1½ teaspoons chopped parsley
    1 cup/8 fl oz (250 ml) white wine
    24 scallops, shells removed

Heat the olive oil in a pan over high heat. Add the garlic and stir vigorously, then add the chile, parsley, and wine. Continue stirring vigorously for a further 2 minutes, or until the sauce thickens. Add the scallops, season with salt, and cook for 2 minutes. Serve hot.

Fish and Seafood

Parmesan Scallops

Chilean Seafood Soup

Paila marina
Chile

Preparation time: 15 minutes,
plus 30 minutes soaking
Cooking time: 25 minutes

Serves: 5–6

The hot version of the *mariscal frío*, using most of the same ingredients, is this light stew. It's almost always served in an earthenware bowl called a *paila*, made from a brown clay called *greta*, most famously in the town of Pomaire outside of Santiago. It can be heated in an oven, on charcoal, or directly over a flame. It's usually served with bread, such as *pan marraqueta* (Crusty Chilean Rolls, page 26).

  2 lb (900 g) clams in shells
  12 razor clams
  2 tablespoons olive oil
  ½ white onion, finely chopped
  4 garlic cloves, minced
  4 tomatoes, peeled and diced
  1 teaspoon dried oregano
  1 lb (450 g) mussels in shells, cleaned
  1 cup/8 fl oz (250 ml) white wine
  3 cups/25 fl oz (750 ml) fish or shellfish stock
  4 cusk eels, cleaned, cut into 4-inch (10-cm) chunks
  1 tablespoon chopped cilantro (coriander)
  1 teaspoon chopped parsley
  ¼ teaspoon *merkén* (smoked chile powder)
  salt and ground pepper

Soak the clams and razor clams in a bowl of fresh water for 30 minutes to purge of sand. Drain and set aside.
   Heat the oil in a large pan over medium heat, add the onion, garlic, and tomatoes, and sauté for 10 minutes. Add the oregano, season with salt and pepper, then add the clams and mussels. Cook for 2 minutes before adding the wine, stock, and eel chunks. Cook for 10 minutes, then sprinkle in the cilantro (coriander) and parsley. Add the razor clams and cook for a further 3 minutes. Check the seasoning and add the *merkén* (smoked chile powder). Serve hot in a *paila* or soup bowl.

Conch Soup

Sopa de caracol
Belize, Honduras, Nicaragua

Preparation time: 20 minutes
Cooking time: 35 minutes

Serves: 6

"Watenegui consup, yupi pa ti, yupi pa mi," or: "What a good soup, here's some for you, here's some for me," goes the surprise 1991 international hit *Sopa de Caracol*, which was performed in Spanish and Garifuna by Honduran musical group Banda Blanca. This coconut-scented dish is found throughout the north coast of Honduras and the Bay Islands, as well as elsewhere in the Caribbean. The queen, or pink, conch (*Lobatus gigas*), a mollusk often seen on reefs and beds of seagrass throughout the Caribbean, is a delicacy in this part of Central America. Conch can be breaded and fried for fritters or diced for ceviche, though soups and chowders are the most common preparation. It's especially important to clean the conch well without over tenderizing it or overcooking it. Also, if possible,

use fresh coconut milk, as is mostly done in this part of the world. Serve with warm Corn Tortillas (page 136) and your preferred hot chile sauce.

  1 tablespoon vegetable oil
  1 white onion, chopped
  3 garlic cloves, chopped
  1 green bell pepper, cored, seeded, and chopped
  4 cups/32 fl oz (950 ml) fish stock
  1 lb (450 g) cassava, peeled and cut into 1-inch (2.5-cm) chunks
  2 green plantains, cut into ½-inch (1-cm) slices
  2 carrots, peeled and sliced
  2 lb (900 g) conch meat, tenderized with a mallet, and cut into ½-inch (1-cm) chunks
  2 cups/16 fl oz (475 ml) coconut milk
  1 cup/8 fl oz (250 ml) water
  ½ bunch cilantro (coriander), leaves only
  salt and ground pepper

Heat the oil in a large pan over medium-high heat. Add the onion, garlic, and bell pepper, and cook for 5–7 minutes or until the onion is soft. Add the stock, cassava, plantain, and carrots, and bring to a boil. Reduce the heat to low and simmer for 20 minutes, or until the vegetables are cooked through but still firm. Stir in the conch meat, followed by the coconut milk, water, and cilantro (coriander). Season with salt and pepper and simmer for 5 minutes, checking the conch every 2 minutes and making sure it isn't overcooked.
   Serve hot in large bowls.

Callao-Style Mussels

Choritos a la chalaca
Peru

Preparation time: 15 minutes
Cooking time: 5 minutes

Serves: 4

These mussels served on the shell are served *a la chalaca*, or in the style of the Peruvian port city of Callao, which means loaded with chopped onions, tomatoes, corn, and chile peppers. Sometimes so overloaded you won't taste the mussels. They are usually served at the start of a meal at a *cevichería* with a beer or pisco sour while waiting for the ceviche and heavier plates to arrive.

  12 mussels in shells, cleaned
  2 bay leaves
  2 tomatoes, finely diced
  ½ red onion, finely chopped
  1 garlic clove, minced
  1 cup/5 oz (140 g) cooked corn kernels
  ½ *ají limo*, seeded and finely chopped
  1 cup/8 fl oz (250 ml) lime juice
  2 tablespoons chopped cilantro (coriander)
  salt

Place the mussels and bay leaves in a medium pan and add water to come halfway up the mussels. Cover, place over high heat, and cook for 5 minutes, or until all of the mussels are open. Drain, and open all the mussels, keeping just the shell halves with the meat. Place on a platter and keep in the refrigerator.
   In a bowl, mix the tomatoes, onion, garlic, corn, *ají limo*, and lime juice together. Add the cilantro (coriander) and season with salt. Mix well, then spread the mix evenly over the mussels. Serve cold.

Fish and Seafood

Conch Soup

Curanto in a Pan

Curanto en Olla, Pulmay
Argentina, Chile

Preparation time: 10 minutes,
plus 30 minutes soaking
Cooking time: 2 hours

Serves: 8

One of the oldest forms of cooking on the South American continent, *curanto* involves building a fire in a hole that's several feet deep, then cooking an array of meats, fish, shellfish, vegetables, and potato dumplings called *milcaos* (Chilote Potato Dumplings, page 84) and *chapaleles* (also page 84) over the hot stones inside, layered between *nalca* leaves, then covered in wet burlap sacks and buried. It's still quite common in the Chiloé Archipelago, though forms of it have migrated with the Chilote people to other parts of Chile and Argentina. This more modern adaption, called either *curanto en olla* or *pulmay*, uses many of the same ingredients, though it's cooked in a large pot.

    2 lb (900 g) clams in shells
    3 cups/25 fl oz (750 ml) white wine
    7 garlic cloves, crushed
    2 lb (900 g) mussels in shells, cleaned
    1 whole chicken, cut into 8 pieces
    1 lb (450 g) *longaniza* sausages or chorizo, cut into
    1-inch (2.5-cm) chunks
    6 smoked pork chops or ribs
    6 potatoes, sliced
    2 white cabbages, leaves separated
    1 cup/1½ oz (40 g) parsley leaves
    salt and ground pepper

Soak the clams in a bowl of fresh water for about 30 minutes to purge of sand. Drain and set aside.
    Place half of the wine with the garlic in a 30-qt (30-liter) stock pot, bring to a boil then add the mussels and clams on one half of the bottom. On the other half, place the chicken skin side down, and season with salt and pepper. Next, add the sausage chunks and pork in a layer. Add the sliced potatoes to create a third layer, and season with salt and pepper. Finish by pouring in the remaining wine. The liquids should cover three-quarters of the ingredients; if necessary, top up with hot water. Add as many cabbage leaves as necessary to cover all the ingredients. Cover the pan and cook for 2 hours over low heat.
    Serve all of the ingredients on a platter, scattered with the parsley to garnish, alongside *milcaos* and *chapaleles*. Serve the broth in cups.

Shrimp

Shrimp (prawn) consumption is widespread in much of Latin America and comes in endless preparations. West African shrimp stews brought to the region throughout slavery were adapted with local vegetables and chiles. Dried and salted, their strong flavor can add a funky kick to stews like *tacacá*, or they can be grilled and slathered in cheese, and served on a taco.

Shrimp with Coconut Sauce

Encocado de camarones
Ecuador

Preparation time: 10 minutes
Cooking time: 15 minutes

Serves: 4

In 1533, a slave ship headed to Peru was wrecked along Ecuador's northern coast and the escaped Africans fled into the jungle, setting up maroon settlements that merged with the indigenous groups already living there. As the community grew and expanded throughout the Esmeraldas province, they created a distinct Afro-Ecuadorian culture with its own music, art, and cuisine. The *encocado*, often pronounced *encoca'o*, is part of this heritage. It can be made with shrimp, fish, crabs, or other seafoods, as well as a combination of several. It's often made with chicken or game meat too. Serve with a side of cooked white rice and/or *Tostones* (Fried Plantains, page 194).

    2 fresh coconuts
    2 tablespoons olive oil
    1 white onion, chopped
    3 garlic cloves, minced
    ½ red bell pepper, cored, seeded, and diced
    ½ green bell pepper, cored, seeded, and diced
    2 lb (900 g) shrimp (prawns), peeled and deveined
    1 teaspoon ground cumin
    2 tablespoons chopped culantro (or use cilantro/coriander)
    2 tablespoons chopped oregano
    2 tablespoons *chirarán* (purple basil), chopped
    salt and ground pepper

Crack open the coconuts, drain all the liquid from inside, and place in a blender. Cut the coconut flesh into chunks and add to the blender along with ½ cup/4 fl oz (120 ml) water. Blend until smooth, then strain the liquid through a strainer (sieve) into a bowl, and set aside.
    Heat the oil in a medium pan over high heat, add the onion, garlic, and bell peppers, and sauté for 7 minutes, stirring frequently. Once the vegetables are cooked, add the reserved coconut milk. Simmer for 3 minutes, then lower the heat and add the shrimp (prawns), cumin, culantro, oregano, and chirarán. Cook for 3 minutes, stirring. Season with salt and pepper.
    Serve hot.

Fish and Seafood

Shrimp with Coconut Sauce

Shrimp Bobo

Bobó do camarão
Brazil

Preparation time: 15 minutes
Cooking time: 30 minutes   Serves: 4

A staple in the state of Bahia in northern Brazil, this stew of shrimp, cassava purée, and coconut milk is a variation of the West African dish *ipetê*. The word *bobó* comes from the Ewe people from Ghana and Togo, though there it refers to a dish made with beans, while in Brazil it refers to cassava. White rice is served on the side. Occasionally, restaurants serve it in a coconut husk or pumpkin.

    2 tablespoons butter
    1 white onion, chopped
    2 garlic cloves, minced
    2 lb (900 g) cassava, peeled and grated
    2 cups/16 fl oz (475 ml) coconut milk
    3 cups/25 fl oz (750 ml) water
    4 tomatoes, peeled and chopped
    1 *malagueta* chile, seeded and chopped
    2 tablespoons tomato paste (purée)
    1 lb 8 oz (680 g) shrimp (prawns), peeled, deveined and cut into 1-inch (2.5-cm) pieces
    1 tablespoon chopped cilantro (coriander)
    1 tablespoon *dendê* oil

Heat 1 tablespoon of the butter in a frying pan over medium heat, and sauté the onion and garlic for 5 minutes. Add the grated cassava, coconut milk, and water. Cook for 10 minutes, or until the cassava is soft. Mash the cassava with a fork and keep warm.

In a pan, heat the remaining tablespoon of butter over medium heat and sauté the tomatoes, chile, and tomato paste (purée) for 10 minutes. Add the shrimp (prawns) and stir, then add the mashed cassava mixture and cilantro (coriander) and season with salt. Just before removing from the heat, stir in the *dendê* oil. Serve hot.

Bahian Shrimp and Okra Gumbo

Caruru de camarão
Brazil

Preparation time: 15 minutes
Cooking time: 25 minutes   Serves: 4

In the Afro-Brazilian religion of Candomblé, *caruru* is known as *amalá*, a favorite of Xangô, the deity of fire and lightning. As the story goes, every time Xangô wanted to eat *amalá*, the deity Exu would steal it. Upset, he would cause the ground to shake and rain lightning down upon the earth. Xangô's twin sons, the Ibejis, challenged Exu, who didn't realize they were twins, to a dance off. Whenever one got tired, the other replaced him without Exu knowing, until he collapsed. From that point on he never took Xangô's *amalá* again, and every September 27th in Bahia, *caruru* is served as an offering to the Ibejis twins, which are synonymous with the twin saints of Cosmas and Damian in Catholicism. During the festivities, it is often served alongside other dishes like *Acarajé* (Black-Eyed Pea Fritters, page 172), *Vatapá* (Bahian Shrimp Stew, this page), and popcorn, however, in everyday use it's commonly served with *acarajé*.

    1 lb (450 g) okra, cut into 1-inch (2.5-cm) pieces
    1 tablespoon white vinegar
    ¼ cup/1¼ oz (35 g) cassava flour
    1 cup/8 fl oz (250 ml) warm fish stock
    2 tablespoons olive oil
    1 white onion, chopped
    2 garlic cloves, minced
    ¼ cup/1 oz (25 g) chopped cashews
    ¼ cup/1 oz (25 g) chopped peanuts
    1 lb (450 g) shrimp (prawns), peeled and deveined
    ½ teaspoon *dendê* oil
    salt and ground pepper

Add the okra and vinegar to a pan and cover with cold water. Bring to a boil and cook for 4 minutes, then drain the okra and set aside.

Meanwhile, mix the cassava flour with the warm stock in a pan, and cook for 4 minutes, stirring continuously.

In a frying pan, heat the olive oil over medium heat, add the onion, garlic, cashews, and peanuts, and sauté for 10 minutes. Add the shrimp (prawns) and cook for 2 minutes, then mix with the stock. Season with salt and pepper and cook for a further 3 minutes. Add the okra to the stew, along with the *dendê* oil. Serve warm, with rice on the side.

Bahian Shrimp Stew

Vatapá
Brazil

Preparation time: 15 minutes
Cooking time: 25 minutes   Serves: 4

This typical Bahian dish mashes bread or cassava flour, shrimp, coconut milk, ground nuts, and *dendê* oil into a creamy paste or sauce that's often eaten with *caruru* (this page) or as a filling for *Acarajé* (Black-Eyed Pea Fritters, page 172). When it is prepared in other parts of northern Brazil, such as the states of Amazonas or Pará, it's often served with white rice and peanuts, and other ingredients are sometimes left out.

    1 tablespoon vegetable oil
    1 white onion, finely chopped
    3 scallions (spring onions), thinly sliced
    2 garlic cloves, minced
    2 *malagueta* chiles, seeded and chopped
    ½ cup/1¼ oz (35 g) dried shrimp (prawns)
    3 cups/25 fl oz (750 ml) fish stock
    ¼ cup/1 oz (25 g) chopped cashews (unsalted)
    ¼ cup/1 oz (25 g) ground peanuts (unsalted)
    1 cup/5 oz (140 g) cassava flour
    8 oz (225 g) shrimp (prawns), peeled and deveined
    2 cups/16 fl oz (475 ml) coconut milk
    ¼ cup/2 fl oz (60 ml) *dendê* oil
    salt and ground pepper

Heat the vegetable oil in a frying pan over medium heat. Stir in the onion, scallions (spring onions), garlic, chiles, and dried shrimp (prawns), and cook for 5 minutes. Once all the liquid has been absorbed, place in a blender and purée well on medium speed for 4 minutes.

Add the blended mixture to a pan over medium heat. Pour in the stock and whisk in the cashews and peanuts, followed by the cassava flour. Season with salt and pepper, then bring to a boil. Reduce to medium-low and simmer for 5–8 minutes. Stir in the shrimp (prawns) and coconut milk. Simmer for a further 5–6 minutes. Remove from the heat, stir in the *dendê* oil, and serve hot.

Bahian Shrimp and Okra Gumbo

Garlic Shrimp

Camarones al ajillo
Belize, El Salvador, Honduras, Nicaragua

Preparation time: 10 minutes
Cooking time: 10 minutes   Serves: 4

If you go into any beachside seafood restaurant on either coast of Central America there is a good chance you will find some form of this dish, which was adapted from the Spanish *gambas al ajillo*. Here, it is served with white or fried rice and/or *Tostones* (Fried Plantains, page 194).

    1 tablespoon butter
    4 garlic cloves, chopped
    1 tablespoon lime juice
    2 lb (900 g) shrimp (prawns), peeled and deveined
    ½ teaspoon salt
    ½ teaspoon ground pepper
    ¼ cup/2 fl oz (60 ml) white wine
    1 tablespoon chopped cilantro (coriander)

Melt the butter in a pan over high heat, then add the garlic and sauté for 3 minutes. Add the lime juice and stir well, letting the sauce thicken. Add the shrimp (prawns), salt, and pepper, then pour in the wine. Cook for a further 3 minutes over high heat, sprinkle with cilantro (coriander) and serve hot.

Spicy Shrimp and Crab Stew

Chilpachole de jaiba y camarón
Mexico

Preparation time: 15 minutes,
plus 20 minutes soaking
Cooking time: 30 minutes   Serves: 4

From the Sotavento region in the state of Veracruz, this rich and smoky stew can be made with shrimp and/or blue crabs from the Gulf of Mexico. It can be thickened with corn flour and is sometimes served with *chochoyotes*, or small balls made from corn masa, that are cooked within the broth.

    2 *ancho* chiles, seeded
    2 *guajillo* chiles, seeded
    3 tomatoes, chopped
    2 garlic cloves, peeled
    ½ white onion, chopped
    1 cup/8 fl oz (250 ml) shrimp (prawn) stock
    4 cups/32 fl oz (950 ml) fish stock
    ¼ cup/2 fl oz (60 ml) vegetable oil
    1 lb (450 g) crabmeat
    1 lb (450 g) shrimp (prawns), peeled and deveined
    ¼ cup/2 fl oz (60 ml) lime juice
    2 tablespoons chopped epazote

Place all the chiles in a dry frying pan or comal over medium heat and toast for 2 minutes per side. Place the chiles in a bowl with hot water, soak for 20 minutes, then transfer the chiles to a blender.
    Add the tomatoes, garlic, onion, shrimp (prawn) stock, and fish stock to the blender with the chiles, and blend well on medium speed until smooth.

Heat the oil in a medium pan over medium heat, add the blended mixture and cook for 3 minutes. Add the crabmeat and shrimp (prawns) and cook for 5 minutes. Add the lime juice and epazote, then cook for a further 10 minutes. Check the seasoning, and serve hot.

Shrimp Chowder

Chupe de camarones
Peru

Preparation time: 20 minutes
Cooking time: 25 minutes   Serves: 6

Thick, chunky chowders with a potato base called *chupes* are beloved in Peru, and can be made from anything from squash to tripe. None, however, is held in as high esteem as the *chupe de camarones* from Arequipa, a city with a different *chupe* for every day of the week, plus others for festivals and holidays. While this recipe uses shrimp, the classic recipe uses red crayfish, which live in coastal rivers of Peru and were considered sacred by the Moche people.

    ½ cup/4 fl oz (120 ml) vegetable oil
    1 white onion, chopped
    4 garlic cloves, minced
    1 tomato, peeled and chopped
    6 cups/50 fl oz (1.5 liters) fish stock
    1 lb (450 g) potatoes, peeled and cut into 1½-inch (4-cm) cubes
    2 ears of corn, cut into 3-inch (7.5-cm) chunks
    1 cup/4 oz (120 g) fava (broad) beans
    1 cup/4 oz (120 g) cubed squash (½-inch/ 1-cm cubes)
    2 tablespoons chopped epazote
    2 lb (900 g) shelled raw shrimp (prawns)
    1 cup/8 fl oz (250 ml) evaporated milk
    2 cups/9 oz (250 g) shredded *queso fresco*
    salt and ground pepper
    6 poached or fried eggs, to serve, optional

Heat the oil in a pan over high heat. Add the onion, garlic, and tomato, and sauté for 5 minutes, then tip in the stock and potatoes. Bring to a boil and cook for 5 minutes, then add the corn and cook for a further 5 minutes. Add the fava beans, squash, and epazote. Mix well, season with salt and pepper, lower the heat and cook for a further 5 minutes. Add the shrimp (prawns), bring to a boil then and add the milk and cheese. Stir and remove from the heat. Serve hot, in bowls, with a poached or fried egg added to each bowl, if preferred.

Seepweed in Mole with Shrimp

Romeritos en mole con camarones
Mexico

Preparation time: 15 minutes
Cooking time: 35 minutes

Serves: 4

Romerito (*Suaeda spp.*), a type of seepweed that looks a bit like rosemary and has a slightly sour, citrusy taste, grows wild near marshy areas, and also is grown as part of the "Milpa" system, appearing in Mexico in the late autumn and early winter.

In central Mexico, *romeritos* are the main ingredient of this Christmas recipe, often just called *romeritos*. The dried shrimp gets rehydrated in the dish, though other variations prepare the shrimp as fried patties on the side. They were eaten in pre-Columbian times, with *ahuahutle*, the eggs of aquatic insects known as *axayacatl*, which live in the same environment as the *romeritos*. While wild plants and insects were marginalized during the Vice Royalty in the eighteenth century in Puebla, it's said that a creative convent with an empty pantry tossed the *romeritos* in a pot with potatoes, *nopales*, and *mole poblano*, and this dish—which they called *revoltijo*—was the result.

    2 lb (900 g) *romeritos*
    1 lb (450 g) *nopales*, cut into strips
    ½ white onion, chopped
    pinch of baking soda (bicarbonate of soda)
    1 lb (450 g) potatoes, peeled and cut into chunks
    1 tablespoon olive oil
    ½ cup/4 fl oz (120 ml) *mole poblano* paste (see page 166)
    2 cups/16 fl oz (475 ml) chicken stock
    2 cups/5 oz (145 g) dried shrimp (prawns)
    salt

Wash the *romeritos* and boil for 5 minutes in salted water. Drain and set aside.

In another pan, bring the *nopales*, onions, baking soda (bicarbonate of soda), 1 teaspoon of salt, and enough water to cover to a boil over high heat. Lower the heat and cook for 10 minutes or until soft. Drain and reserve.

Cook the potatoes in a medium pan of boiling, salted water for 15 minutes or until soft (but not broken). Drain and reserve.

In a medium pan, heat the oil, add the *mole* paste, and sauté for 3 minutes, then pour in the stock. Add the *nopales* and potatoes, season with salt, and cook for 2 minutes, then add the *romeritos* with the shrimp (prawns). Stir well, check the seasoning, and serve hot.

Crab

There are mangrove crabs (*Ucides cordatus*) dug out of the muddy mangrove forests of Belize and Brazil that find their ways into stews. The sweet meat of king crabs fished from the deep, frigid waters off Patagonia that get baked in a casserole. Popeye crabs on coastal Peru are stuffed or stewed. Along the coasts of the Americas, crabs of all shapes and sizes have been collected for as long as humans have lived in the region.

King Crab Pie

Pastel de centolla
Chile

Preparation time: 20 minutes
Cooking time: 30 minutes

Serves: 8

Centolla (*Lithodes santolla*), or southern king crab, is found in the deep, cold waters of Patagonia. It's often served on its own with butter, though in southern Chile it's commonly prepared as a chowder or casserole.

    2 tablespoons olive oil
    1 white onion, finely chopped
    2 garlic cloves, minced
    1 red bell pepper, cored, seeded, and chopped
    2 carrots, peeled and grated
    1 leek, finely sliced
    1 potato, peeled and cut into ½-inch (1-cm) cubes
    ½ cup/4 fl oz (120 ml) dry white wine
    3 eggs
    1¼ cups/10 fl oz (300 ml) heavy (double) cream
    2 lb (900 g) king crab meat, shredded
    ½ cup/2 oz (60 g) shredded mozzarella
    1 tablespoon chopped parsley
    salt and ground pepper

Preheat the oven to 350°F/180°C/Gas Mark 4.

Heat the oil in a medium pan over medium heat, add the onion, garlic, and bell pepper, and sauté for 5 minutes. Add the carrots, leek, and potato. Pour in the wine, cook for 2 minutes, then remove from the heat.

In a bowl, whisk the eggs with the cream. Add the shredded crabmeat and the cooked vegetables, and season with salt and pepper.

Transfer the mix to a *paila* or 8 x 12-inch (20 x 30-cm) oven dish, sprinkle the shredded cheese evenly over the top, and bake for 15–20 minutes, until the cheese is melted and bubbling. Sprinkle parsley on top and serve hot.

Bursted Crabs

Cangrejos reventados
Peru

Preparation time: 15 minutes
Cooking time: 15 minutes

Serves: 4

If you spend any time along the waterfront of Huanchaco, an ancient beach near the northern Peruvian city of Trujillo, where woven reed fishing rafts called *caballitos de totora* are still used by the fishermen there, as they have for several thousand years, *cangrejos reventados* will enter into your vocabulary. It's one of the signature dishes at all of the *cevicherías* that line the *malecón* esplanade, and there are many. The type of crab used is typically the *cangrejo popeye* (*Menippe frontalis*), a type of stone crab. Some variations of the dish use egg, some don't. There is no right or wrong. *Cangrejos reventados* are often served partially covered by or bursting out of the broken crab shell, with boiled cassava on the side.

    2 tablespoons vegetable oil
    2 red onions, chopped
    2 tablespoons minced garlic
    2 tablespoons *ají mirasol* paste
    2 tomatoes, peeled and diced
    2 lb (900 g) stone crabmeat, shredded
    1 cup/8 fl oz (250 ml) fish stock
    ½ cup/4 fl oz (120 ml) *Chicha de jora* (Corn Beer,
    page 388)
    8 eggs, beaten
    3 oz (80 g) fresh seaweed (such as yuyo)
    salt and ground pepper

Heat the oil in a pan over medium heat, add the onions and garlic, and sauté for 5 minutes. Add the *ají mirasol* paste and cook, stirring, for 3 minutes. Add the tomatoes and crabmeat, stir, then add the fish stock with the *Chicha de jora* (Corn Beer), and cook for 5 minutes. Add the beaten eggs, mix well, then add the seaweed and cook for a further 2 minutes. Season with salt and pepper and serve hot, with boiled cassava on the side.

Stuffed Crab Shells

Casquinha de siri
Brazil

Preparation time: 15 minutes
Cooking time: 25 minutes

Serves: 4

These Brazilian crab cakes with a crispy crust are often served as a starter or beachside in their shell, with lime wedges, especially in the state of Bahía.

    1 lb (450 g) crabmeat
    juice of 2 limes
    ½ cup/2 oz (55 g) breadcrumbs
    ½ cup/4 fl oz (120 ml) milk
    2 tablespoons butter
    ¼ white onion, very finely chopped
    1 garlic clove, minced
    2 egg yolks
    2 tablespoons chopped parsley
    8 scallop shells or small crab shells, cleaned
    1½ cups/4 oz (120 g) grated parmesan
    salt and ground pepper

Preheat the oven to 350°F/180°C/Gas Mark 4.
    In a bowl, mix the crabmeat with the lime juice and season with salt and pepper. Set aside.
    Put the breadcrumbs and milk in a bowl and set aside to soak.
    Heat the butter in a frying pan over medium heat, add the onion and garlic, and sauté for 5 minutes. Lower the heat and add the breadcrumbs and the crabmeat. Cook for 8 minutes, stirring occasionally. Remove from the heat, then stir in the egg yolks and parsley. Check the seasoning and divide the mixture between the shells. Sprinkle with the cheese and place on an oven tray. Bake for 8 minutes, or until the cheese is golden brown. Serve hot.

Sea Urchins

Large, red sea urchins (*Loxechinus albus*) are found on the coasts of southern South America, from Ecuador to Argentina and the Falkland Islands. They are fried in tortillas (the Spanish-style omelet version), served with a touch of lime for ceviche, cooked in stews, or eaten raw. In Baja California, Mexico, there's also the red sea urchin (*Mesocentrotus franciscanus*), often eaten on tacos and tostadas.

Sea Urchins in Salsa Verde

Erizos en salsa verde
Chile

Preparation time: 15 minutes

Serves: 4

Despite their large size, Chilean sea urchins don't lack flavor, so they are best served very simply, if not raw. Adding just a touch of lime and some onion and cilantro is a common preparation in market stalls and typical restaurants along the country's 2,600-mile (4,000-km) coastline.

    8 sea urchins (45 tongues)
    1 white onion, chopped
    4 tablespoons chopped cilantro (coriander)
    juice of 4 limes
    2 tablespoons chopped parsley
    salt

Clean the sea urchins to get the tongues and set them on a plate.
    In a bowl, mix the onion, cilantro (coriander), and lime juice together, and season with salt. Place the sea urchin tongues on a cold platter, cover them with the green sauce and sprinkle with parsley. Serve at room temperature.

Fish and Seafood

Sea Urchins in Salsa Verde

Ceviche

Crude forms of ceviche made of raw fish marinated in the juice of the banana passion fruit (*Passiflora mollissima*), also called *tumbo* or *taxo*, were seen by Spanish conquistadors on the north coast of Peru in the 1500s, though using acidity to coagulate proteins in seafood is a culinary technique that likely existed in the region long before. Along the Pacific coast of Latin America, from Mexico to Chile, pre-Columbian people used souring agents like fruits and fermented beverages, not to mention salt and chile peppers, to flavor seafood. Thousands of recipes have developed over the ensuing centuries.

While ceviche is Peru's national dish and a form of it has become emblematic of that country, there's no direct evidence it originated there. However, Lima is where the dish underwent its two great transformations. The first occurred when the Spanish settled in Latin America and established the Vice Royalty in Lima. They introduced bitter oranges, limes, and onions to the region and those were soon incorporated into ceviche. Was it the Moorish slaves from Granada who worked in their kitchens trying to replicate adding vinegar for *escabeche*, a common dish in Spain? It's hard to say. The second transformation occurred in the twentieth century as Japanese migrants flocked to Peru to work in coastal plantations. Some became cooks, and in the second half of the century began experimenting with the form of ceviche. They cut the fish into uniform chunks and shortened the time it came into contact with the acidity from a few hours to just a few seconds before serving, helping to balance the acidity. This continues to be the standard form throughout Peru and increasingly elsewhere in the region. There are many theories regarding the origins of the word ceviche, which is spelled more often in Peru as "cebiche" and less frequently as "seviche". The term *sibech* in Arabic, which means "sour food" and was the basis for the name of *escabeche*, may have played a part. Or it may have been the bastardization of the word *siwichi*, the Quechua term for fresh fish.

If you ask any of the *cevicheros* what the best fish is to use for ceviche, they'll tell you the freshest fish. When a fish is removed from water and especially when it is frozen, its cellular structure and flavors change. Many insist on eating ceviche in the morning when the fish is fresher, and even today most *cevicherías* close after lunch. That said, some fish work better than others when making ceviche. Firm-fleshed fish tend to hold up best when marinated. Generally, white-fleshed fish like *corvina* (seabass) or *lenguado* (sole) are preferred, though oily fish like bonito or mackerel or even freshwater salmon or trout with pink flesh can also make a good ceviche. Shellfish are commonly used as well. Shrimp are often mixed in with fish, as can be squid, which is often seen fried, adding a slight crunch to the dish. Black clams (cockles) called *conchas negras* in Peru and Ecuador or *pianguas* in Colombia, make a terrific ceviche, though their strong flavor can be off-putting to some. Lobsters, oysters, razor clams, octopus, sea urchins, geoduck, and *percebes* (goose barnacles) can all be used for ceviche.

Paying attention to acidity when making ceviche is important, as it can easily throw off the balance of the dish. Smallish Peruvian limes, with a thin rind and light green to yellowish color, tend to be highly acidic. To avoid bitterness, it's important to squeeze only half the lime. Instead of lime, other souring agents can be used, such as grapefruit, oranges, lemons, passion fruit, tomato, *tamarillo*, and even *chicha*, a fermented maize beer.

Not all ceviche is spicy. In fact, most of it isn't. In Baja, ceviche *tostadas* are served with hot sauce on the side, or at the most, a few slices of optional jalapeño that can be picked off. In Chile, most ceviches have no spice at all. In Peru, and sometimes Ecuador, Andean chiles with strong aromas like *rocoto* or *ají limo* are chopped into thin slices or bits and sprinkled on top of the ceviche at serving. Many classic ceviches have some *ají amarillo* puréed and mixed in with the *leche de tigre*, while in the Amazon, tiny and fruity *ají charapita* are sometimes mixed with cocona fruit to add a slight, fruity kick. Still, even in Peru, most ceviches are not overly spicy unless requested.

What else goes into a bowl of ceviche is what really sets it apart. Most regions use whatever they have around them. The classic *Limeño* ceviche will add boiled cassava, glazed sweet potatoes, *choclo* (boiled corn), *cancha* (toasted corn kernels), onions, some cilantro, and seaweed. On the north coast near Piura, they'll add canary beans into the mix. In Ecuador, there might be tomatoes, popcorn, and *chifles* (plantain chips). In Mexico and Central America, tortilla chips are served on the side. More recently, some restaurants have added exotic ingredients, like edible flowers and *cushuro*, a cyanobacteria from the Andes.

In many ceviches, especially in Peru, sprinkled in the *leche de tigre* is a bit of monosodium glutamate. It's optional, though an alternative is adding some dried kombu to the *leche de tigre* stock, turning it into almost a dashi, as many Nikkei chefs do.

Street Cart Ceviche

Ceviche carretillero 🍲
Peru

Preparation time: 20 minutes

꙰ 🚫 ❄
Serves: 4

Street cart ceviche is the most straightforward, common form that you will find in Lima's *cevicherías*, not to mention in beach shacks and market stalls. It can also be served with mixed seafoods, which vary depending on region and time of year. Shrimp, octopus, squid, and scallops are common. Some like to fry one of the ingredients, usually the squid, which adds a crunchy texture to the dish.

2 cups/16 fl oz (475 ml) lime juice
1 celery stalk, chopped
½ red onion, sliced
1 garlic clove, minced
1 teaspoon minced fresh ginger
8 oz (225 g) fish trimmings
½ *ají limo*, seeded and chopped
2 tablespoons chopped cilantro (coriander)
1 lb 8 oz (680 g) fresh white fish fillets (such as seabass or sole), cut into ¾-inch (2-cm) chunks

To serve
Cancha serrana (Toasted Andean Corn Kernels, page 114)
boiled corn kernels
boiled sweet potato (½-inch/1-cm) slices

Put the lime juice, celery, half of the onion, garlic, ginger, and fish trimmings in a blender, with a couple of ice cubes. Blend for 3 minutes on high speed. Strain into a bowl. Add the *ají limo*, remaining onion, and cilantro (coriander), then season with salt. In another bowl, pour the mixture over the fish and mix together. Serve immediately with the *Cancha serrana*, corn kernels, and sweet potato on the side.

Street Cart Ceviche

Tiger's Milk

Leche de tigre
Peru

Preparation time: 20 minutes

Serves: 4

The basic Peruvian *leche de tigre*, or tiger's milk, is a milky base of lime juice, onions, salt, leftover fish and/or fish stock, and chile peppers, that is blended and used to apply the acidity to the fish or shellfish, a process that some claim qualifies as "cooking" it, depending on your interpretation of the word. Many believe that *leche de tigre* can cure a hangover and will order it in a small glass to start the meal. It's possible to add chunks of fish and/or shellfish, as well as seaweed, to the glass if desired.

    2 cups/16 fl oz (475 ml) lime juice
    1 celery stalk, chopped
    ½ red onion, sliced
    1 garlic clove, minced
    1 teaspoon minced fresh ginger
    1 lb (450 g) fish trimmings
    ½ *ají limo*, seeded and chopped
    2 tablespoons chopped cilantro (coriander)
    salt

Add the lime juice, celery, onion, garlic, ginger, fish trimmings, and a couple of ice cubes to a blender. Process for 3 minutes on high, then strain. In a bowl, mix the liquid with the chopped *ají limo* and cilantro (coriander), and some salt. Serve in a cup or a glass.

Cold Seafood Ceviche

Mariscal frío
Chile

Preparation time: 15 minutes,
plus 20 minutes marinating

Serves: 5–6

This bowl of mixed seafood is said to have been created on the fishing piers on Chile's central coast. Clams, mussels, fish, sea squirts, lobster, and shrimp tails that weren't sold were tossed in a bowl with some lime, salt, onions, and herbs and eaten by the fishermen who caught them, who also believed it could cure a hangover.

    1 lb 8 oz (680 g) shelled razor clams (about 36 in total)
    1 lb (450 g) shelled *piure*, optional
    1 lb (450 g) shelled clams (about 24)
    1 lb (450 g) shelled mussels
    ½ cup/4 fl oz (120 ml) lemon juice
    1 white onion, chopped
    2 tablespoons chopped cilantro (coriander)
    slices of toast, to serve

Clean all the seafood well to get rid of any sand.
    Soften the razor clams by pounding them a few times with the back of a knife.
    Cut all the seafood in two and place in a cold dish. Pour the lemon juice over to cover, and season with salt. Place in the refrigerator for 20 minutes to macerate.
    Mix the onion with the cilantro (coriander) and, once the seafood is ready, mix everything together. Serve cold with slices of toast.

Shrimp in Chile Water

Aguachile
Mexico

Preparation time: 10 minutes,
plus 15 minutes marinating

Serves: 3–4

In the indigenous version of *aguachile*, which translates as "chile water," from Sinaloa in northwestern Mexico, sun-dried game meats were marinated in water with *chiltepín*, a small but pungent chile that grows wild in the hills. However, in recent decades, *aguachile*, now found in nearly every *marisquería* in Mexico, refers to the modern version below, which is usually made with shrimp.

    1 lb (450 g) shrimp (prawns), peeled and deveined
    juice of 9 limes
    5 *chiltepín* or serrano chiles
    2 tablespoons olive oil
    3 tablespoons chopped cilantro (coriander)
    1 small cucumber, peeled and thinly sliced
    ½ red onion, sliced
    1 avocado, peeled, pitted, and sliced

Cut the shrimp (prawns) lengthways (butterfly cut) and place in a medium bowl. Add enough of the lime juice to cover, then place in the refrigerator.
    Meanwhile, add the serrano chiles, oil, remaining lime juice, and half the cilantro (coriander) to a blender. Blend on high speed until smooth, then season with salt and transfer to a bowl.
    Add the shrimp to the blended mixture, and stir gently. Check for seasoning and add some salt and ground pepper. Finish by adding the cucumber and onion slices and marinating for 15 minutes. Garnish the dish with the remaining cilantro and the sliced avocado. Serve cold with *tostadas* or saltine crackers.

Rapa Nui-Style Tuna Ceviche

Ceviche de atún estilo Isla de Pascua
Chile

Preparation time: 15 minutes

Serves: 1

On the Chilean territory of Rapa Nui, known as Easter Island, there is a form of ceviche that is prepared more like elsewhere in Polynesia, where it might be called *'ota 'ika* or *poisson cru*, than it is on the mainland. In Hanga Roa restaurants, raw fish, usually tuna but sometimes *kana kana* (barracuda), is diced into small chunks and marinated in lime juice and coconut milk until opaque. It's garnished with carrots, cucumber, and sweet potato or taro.

    8 oz (225 g) tuna fillet, cut into ½-inch (1-cm) dice
    1 tablespoon chopped red bell pepper
    ¼ red onion, chopped
    1 tomato, peeled, seeded, and diced
    1 tablespoon peeled, chopped cucumber
    juice of 1 lime
    1 teaspoon soy sauce
    1 tablespoon coconut milk

Mix all the ingredients in a bowl with a pinch of salt just before serving. Serve cold.

Shrimp in Chile Water

Yellow Chile Tiradito

Tiradito al ají amarillo
Peru

Preparation time: 15 minutes
Serves: 4

While there may have been rustic forms of preparing thinly sliced fish in a sauce made of citrus and chile peppers centuries ago, the modern form of this recipe that would come to be known as *tiradito* was developed in recent decades with the rise of Nikkei cuisine in Lima. The cut of the fish, similar to Usuzukuri-style sashimi, and the short marination time, are a direct result of Japanese influence. However, *tiradito* is not only served at Nikkei restaurants, but *cevicherías* around the country. Nobu Matsuhisa, the famed Japanese chef who once lived and worked in Lima, gave *tiradito* international recognition when he began serving it on the menu of Nobu. Other sauces, based on soy sauce or other chiles like *rocoto*, can be used instead of, or alongside, the *ají amarillo*-based sauce.

 8 oz (225 g) fresh white fish fillets (such as seabass or sole)
 ⅔ cup/5 fl oz (150 ml) lime juice
 2 tablespoons *ají amarillo* paste
 2 garlic cloves, minced
 ½ teaspoon minced fresh ginger
 2 tablespoons chopped cilantro (coriander)
 1 *ají limo*, seeded and chopped
 salt

Cut the fish fillets into thin slices, like sashimi. Place the slices on a platter and rest in the refrigerator.
 In a blender, mix the lime juice with the *ají amarillo* paste, garlic, and ginger, and season with salt.
 Add the blended mixture to a bowl, and mix in the cilantro (coriander) and chopped *ají limo*.
 Remove the fish from the refrigerator, sprinkle with salt, then slather the chile mixture on top. Serve cold.

Fish Ceviche Tostadas

Tostadas de ceviche de pescado
Mexico

Preparation time: 20 minutes,
plus 20 minutes macerating
Makes: 6

Stalls in Ensenada on Mexico's Baja peninsula, where fishing vessels haul in an astounding array of seafood each day, sell dozens of variations of these *tostadas*, adding ingredients like *pulpo* (octopus), *camarón* (shrimp), *erizo* (sea urchin), *pata de mula* (black clam), *caracol* (sea snail), or *pepino de mar* (sea cucumber).

 1 lb (450 g) cod, cut into ½-inch (1-cm) dice
 juice of 10 limes
 2 tomatillos, peeled and diced
 ½ cup/2¼ oz (70 g) sliced red onion
 2 serrano chiles, seeded and finely chopped
 ½ cup/¾ oz (20 g) chopped cilantro (coriander)
 2 tablespoons olive oil
 6 *tostadas* (fried tortillas)
 1 ripe avocado, halved, peeled, pitted, and sliced

Mix the diced fish with the lime juice. Season with salt and add the tomatillos, onion, serrano chiles, and cilantro (coriander). Place in the refrigerator for 20 minutes to macerate.
 To serve, add the oil and check the seasoning. Place the *tostadas* on a plate and spread the ceviche over evenly. Place 2 or 3 slices of avocado on each *tostada*.

Ecuadorian Shrimp Ceviche

Ceviche de camarón ecuatoriano
Ecuador

Preparation time: 15 minutes
Cooking time: 5 minutes
Serves: 5–6

Near Guayaquil and elsewhere along the Ecuadorian coast, rectangular shrimp farms have become so numerous that they can be seen from space. The country has become the largest producer in the Western Hemisphere, which can be a mixed blessing. Still, shrimp-centric ceviches are popular throughout the country and it usually comes with sides like plantain chips, *Patacones* (Fried Plantains, page 194), and popcorn.

 2 lb (900 g) shrimp (prawns), peeled and deveined
 3 red onions, sliced
 1½ cups/12 fl oz (350 ml) lime juice
 ½ cup/4 fl oz (120 ml) bitter orange juice
 6 tomatoes, peeled and blended
 3 tablespoons olive oil
 2 tablespoons cilantro (coriander), chopped
 salt

Cook the shrimp (prawns) for 4 minutes in boiling water, with one-third of the onions and a pinch of salt. Drain, reserving ½ cup/4 fl oz (120 ml) of the cooking water.
 Soak the remaining red onions in iced water for 10 minutes. Drain well and place in a bowl with ½ cup/ 4 fl oz (120 ml) of the lime juice, and some salt.
 Mix the remaining lime juice with the orange juice, blended tomatoes, and reserved cooking water. Whisk in the olive oil for a thicker sauce, and season with salt.
 Add the shrimp, cilantro (coriander), and the seasoned onions to the bowl, and serve cold.

Black Clams

Black clams (*Anadara tuberculosa*), or cockles, live in the mangrove forests along the Pacific Coast of Latin America, from northern Peru to Mexico, and go by a handful of names, such as *concha negra*, *pata de mula*, *concha prieta*, and *piangua*. Many populations are threatened because of overharvesting and a loss of habitat, resulting in seasonal bans in much of the region. There is a strong cultural heritage associated with collectors of this clam, such as the *piangueras*, along the Pacific Coast of Colombia, all of them female, who wade into the mangrove when the tide comes down, often with their children and usually smoking tobacco to avoid the *jején*, a small insect with a nasty bite. They are often served in ceviche, *encocado* (with coconut milk), or raw with lime or orange wedges. Note: don't get these confused with blood clams, sometimes also called *conchas negras*, found in the Gulf of Mexico, which get their color from a high level of hemoglobin in them, or chocolate clams (*Megapitaria squalida*), common in Baja.

Ecuadorian Shrimp Ceviche

Black Clam Ceviche

Ceviche de piangua, ceviche de conchas negras
Colombia, Ecuador, Peru

Preparation time: 20 minutes

Serves: 4

Black clam ceviche is one of the most emblematic dishes along the Pacific coast of Colombia, Ecuador, and northern Peru. The flavor of these clams can be quite strong for some, as evident in how they turn the *leche de tigre* black, so some mix black clams with shrimp or other seafood to dilute them. In Colombia and Ecuador, it's common to swap out the tomatoes with ketchup, while in Peru tomatoes are rarely used. Garnishes for this ceviche might include plantain chips, *Cancha serrana* (Toasted Andean Corn Kernels, page 114), popcorn, or saltine crackers.

    24 black clams
    ½ red onion, finely chopped
    1 *ají limo*, finely chopped
    2 tomatoes, seeded and diced
    ½ cup/4 fl oz (120 ml) lime juice
    2 tablespoons chopped cilantro (coriander)
    salt and ground pepper

Start by opening the black clams, reserving and straining the juices that come out from them. In a bowl, mix the clam flesh with the onion, *ají limo*, and tomatoes. Add the lime juice and cilantro (coriander), season with salt and pepper, then add the clam juice slowly, to taste. Serve cold.

Freshwater Fish

In an oxbow lake in the Ecuadorian Amazon, several Cofán men pull an adult paiche (*Arapaima gigas*) they caught with a net to shore to be butchered. The fish, called *pirarucu* in Brazil, can grow up to three meters in length and has helped sustain indigenous communities across the northern Amazon for centuries. Over-exploitation during the past century from commercial fishing operations has pushed indigenous communities such as the Cofán to raise them in ponds, taking pressure off of wild populations.

In markets around the region it can be seen salted like bacalao and rolled up, later to be rehydrated in stews or fried to eat with *açaí*. Fresh, it can be chopped up and steamed inside of a *bijao* leaf with rice or cassava for *juanes*, or just cooked on a grill. Even its bony tongue is used for grating guarana, which is then mixed with water to kill intestinal worms.

From tiny *pepescas* of El Salvador, which are fried in oil and served with cassava and *curtido*, to the enormous *tambaqui* in the Amazon and Orinoco basins, whose large ribs and succulent meat resemble pork, Latin America is a center of megadiversity of freshwater fish. Inland fisheries such as high-altitude lakes, wetlands, and tropical river systems have been an integral source of protein for local populations for thousands of years, helping shape the region's gastronomy.

Paiche with Açaí

Pirarucu com açaí 📷
Brazil

Preparation time: 20 minutes,
plus 20 hours soaking
Cooking time: 20 minutes

Serves: 6

In Belem do Pará, the epicenter of the *açaí* trade, the pulp of trendy palm fruit *açaí* isn't served sweetened or cold. The thin pulp purée is left mostly alone, adding just a touch of salt. The flavor is earthy, almost bean-like. In stands at the Ver-o-peso market it's served alongside fried fish, usually salted *pirarucu* (paiche).

    2 lb (900 g) salted paiche fillets
    juice of 2 limes
    2 teaspoons all-purpose (plain) flour
    ½ cup/4 fl oz (120 ml) vegetable oil
    ½ teaspoon sea salt
    2 lb (900 g) unsweetened *açaí* pulp (room temperature)
    farinha d'água (fermented cassava flour), optional

Place the paiche fillets in iced water for 20 hours, changing the water every 5 hours (3 times). Alternatively, if you are using fresh paiche, you can skip this step.
    Dry the fillets and spread lime juice all over the fish, then roll in the flour.
    Heat the oil in a frying pan to 325°F/162°C. Fry the fillets for 3 minutes each side, or until golden brown and crispy. Remove to a plate lined with paper towels to absorb any excess oil.
    In a bowl, stir the salt into the *açaí* pulp. Serve the warm fish with the *açaí* and, if using, the *farinha d'água* (fermented cassava flour) on the side.

Fried Fish with Cassava

Pescaditas, pepescas con cassava
El Salvador

Preparation time: 10 minutes
Cooking time: 50 minutes

Serves: 5–6

Called *pescaditas* or *pepescas* (*Brachyrhaphis olomina*), these tiny freshwater fish found throughout Central America are always served in a bunch, often over fried or boiled cassava and some *Curtido* (Salvadoran Cabbage Relish, page 402).

    1 lb 8 oz (680 g) cassava, peeled and cut into 4-inch (10-cm) chunks
    vegetable oil, for deep-frying
    1 lb (450 g) *pepescas* (or use baby sardines)
    Curtido (Salvadoran Cabbage Relish, page 402), to serve

Boil the cassava in salted water for 30 minutes, or until soft. Drain and cut into thick strips. Pour enough oil into a heavy pan, making sure it is no more than two-thirds full. Heat to 350°F/177°C. Fry the cassava in the hot oil for 5 minutes, turning occasionally, or until golden and crispy. Remove with a skimmer to a plate lined with paper towels to absorb excess oil. Season with salt and set aside. In the same pan, deep-fry the fish in batches, for 3 minutes, or until crispy. Place on a plate lined with paper towels to absorb any excess oil. Serve the fried cassava on a plate with the *pepescas* on top and *curtido* on the side.

Paiche with Açaí

Grilled Boga

Boga para caranchear
Argentina

Preparation time: 20 minutes
Cooking time: 25 minutes

Serves: 4

In the Río Paraná, running more than 3,000 miles (4,800 km) across northern Argentina, Brazil, and Paraguay, the boga (*Leporinus obtusidens*), called *piapara* in Portuguese, is prized for its firm texture and mild flavor. The name of the preparation refers to a local bird of prey called the *El Carancho*, the southern crested caracara (*Caracara plancus*), which is often seen on riverbanks and streams perched on a whole fish while pecking a boga apart. The whole fish is served, often on a wooden board, in the middle of the table, and can be picked apart by diners. The term, which is sometimes used with other fish or small animals, is commonly used in north-eastern Argentine provinces like Santa Fe, Entre Ríos, Corrientes, and Misiones.

    1 boga, about 5 lb (2.3 kg)
    1 tablespoon vegetable oil
    2 garlic cloves, minced
    2 scallions (spring onions), chopped
    1 tablespoon diced red bell pepper
    1 tablespoon olive oil
    1 cup/1½ oz (40 g) chopped parsley
    juice of 2 limes, optional
    salt and ground pepper

Prepare a grill (barbecue).
    Cut the head and tail off the fish and clean the insides by removing the guts. Make an incision on the belly of the fish and open it through the bones on both sides to debone it, being careful to not cut the entire fish so it will stay just "open" (butterfly cut). Leave the scales on the fish. Refrigerate.
    In a frying pan, heat the vegetable oil over medium heat, add the garlic, scallions (spring onions), and bell pepper, and sauté for 5 minutes. Season with salt and pepper, remove from the heat, and set aside.
    Season the fish with the olive oil, and some salt and pepper. Place scale side down on the grill over low heat. Let cook for 20 minutes, without turning it, then place on a serving dish, add the vegetable mixture on top, and sprinkle with parsley, and lime juice if desired.

Fish Steamed in a Banana Leaf

Patarashca
Colombia, Peru

Preparation time: 10 minutes
Cooking time: 20 minutes

Serves: 2–4

From the Quechua word *pataray*, meaning to fold or wrap, *patarashca* is a dish found in Peru's northern Amazon and parts of Colombia. While frogs, salamanders, and game meat were once typical fillings, today's *patarashcas* are usually made with fish from Amazonian waterways with herbs and seasoning, which are wrapped in a *bijao* or banana leaf. They can be grilled, baked, or cooked directly over hot coals. Serve with *Patacones* (Fried Plantains, page 194).

Sacha culantro is a wild form of culantro that grows in Amazon regions. It can be substituted with regular culantro or just cilantro.

    1 *gamitana* or paiche fillets, about 4 lb (1.8 kg)
    2 large banana or *bijao* leaves
    3 sacha culantro leaves
    ½ white onion, sliced
    3 tomatoes, diced
    3 garlic cloves, minced
    1 *ají charapita*, chopped
    1 teaspoon ground cumin
    1 tablespoon vegetable oil
    salt and ground pepper

Prepare a grill (barbecue).
    Descale the fish and remove the guts. Rinse under iced water for 15 minutes and dry well. Place the fish on the banana or *bijao* leaf and season with salt and pepper.
    In a bowl, mix the sacha culantro, onion, tomatoes, garlic, *ají charapita*, cumin, and oil, and season with salt and pepper. Spread the mixture on and around the fish and close the banana leaf. Wrap a second banana leaf around the fish so that it is sealed and no liquid leaks out, then tie with a long strip of the leaf or kitchen twine. Place the wrapped fish on the grill and cook it for 20 minutes, until done. Serve family style.

Grilled Tambaqui Ribs

Costela de tambaqui na brasa
Brazil

Preparation time: 5 minutes
Cooking time: 30 minutes

Serves: 4

The freshwater tambaqui (*Colossoma macropomum*), sometimes called *pacu* or *gamitana*, is found throughout the Amazon and Orinoco basins and can also be sustainably farm raised. They survive on fruits and seeds, which they disperse under the water much like birds do in the air, and can grow to more than 70 pounds (32 kilos). They have a fatty, white flesh and long ribs that, when grilled, can resemble pork in flavor and texture. If desired, you can glaze them with BBQ sauce just like you would pork ribs.

    2 tambaqui ribs
    juice of 3 limes
    2 tablespoons white vinegar
    salt and ground pepper

Prepare a grill (barbecue) on low to medium heat.
    Rub the ribs with the lime juice and vinegar and rinse well with iced water. Dry well and season with salt and pepper. Secure the ribs with wooden skewers and place on the grill. Cook the ribs for 30 minutes, rotating every 5 minutes or so to cook them evenly. Remove from the grill and serve.

Grilled Tambaqui Ribs

Painted Fish Stew

Mojica de pintado
Brazil

Preparation time: 15 minutes
Cooking time: 30 minutes

Serves: 4

Found in major river systems throughout much of South America, Pseudoplatystoma is a genus of large, striped or spotted, shovel-nosed catfish that go by local names like *surubí*, *doncella*, and *bagre*. In the southwestern Brazilian state of Mato Grosso, they're called pintado and are the key ingredient of several traditional recipes, such as *pintado a urucum*, where it's fried and covered in a sauce of coconut milk, annatto, and cheese. Of indigenous origin, *mojica* means "what comes from the river with cassava," and the chunky stew is flavored with regional chiles like the fruity, piquant *cheiro*.

    2 tablespoons vegetable oil
    2 garlic cloves, minced
    ½ white onion, chopped
    1 red bell pepper, cored, seeded, and diced
    2 tomatoes, peeled and diced
    1 teaspoon annatto paste
    2 *cheiro* chiles, chopped
    1 lb (450 g) pintado or catfish fillets, cut into 2-inch (5-cm) pieces
    1 cup/8 fl oz (250 ml) coconut milk
    ½ cup/4 fl oz (120 ml) water
    ½ cup/2¼ oz (70 g) cassava flour
    juice of 1 lime
    salt and ground pepper

In a pan, heat the oil over medium heat and stir-fry the garlic, onion, and bell pepper for 8 minutes. Add the tomatoes, annatto paste, and chiles, and continue cooking for a further 5 minutes. Add the fish and increase the heat to high. Pour in the coconut milk and water, then slowly stir in the cassava flour, lower the heat and simmer for 10 minutes, stirring frequently. Season with salt and pepper, add the lime juice, and serve hot.

Lake Yojoa-Style Fried Fish

Pescado frito estilo de Yojoa
Honduras

Preparation time: 10 minutes
Cooking time: 10 minutes

Serves: 1–2

About halfway between Honduras' two largest cities, San Pedro Sula and Tegucigalpa, right off highway CA 5, a string of fish shacks look out over Lago de Yojoa, the country's largest lake, surrounded by steep, pine-covered mountains. These small, open-air eateries specialize in fish from the lake, mostly largemouth bass or tilapia, that's fried alongside *Tajadas* (Fried Plantains, page 194), also called *tostones*, and pickled onions. Elsewhere in the country, the term "estilo de Yojoa" refers to this preparation of fish fried whole.

    1 *lobina negra* (largemouth bass)
    vegetable oil, for shallow-frying
    salt

    To serve
    1 lime, cut into wedges
    Patacones (Fried Plantains, page 194)

Clean the fish by opening it from the belly and removing the guts. Rinse under iced water to clean it, then pat dry with a paper towel.

Heat about 2 inches (5 cm) of oil in a frying pan that's large enough for the whole fish. Once hot, slowly place the fish in the oil. Fry for 10 minutes, turning occasionally, until brown and crispy on the outside. Remove the fish from the oil and place it on a plate lined with paper towels to absorb excess oil. Season with salt.

Serve warm with lime wedges and *Patacones*.

Paraguayan Fish Soup

Pira caldo
Paraguay

Preparation time: 20 minutes
Cooking time: 20 minutes

Serves: 4

Pira caldo is one of the many recipes that arose after the Paraguayan War, when the scarcity of food resulted in recipes packed with calories, adding fat and cheese. *Pira*, the Guarani word for fish, is usually *surubí*, though armored catfish and other small river fish are also used.

    2 tablespoons beef tallow
    1 leek, white part only, finely chopped
    2 celery stalks, finely chopped
    2 white onions, chopped
    2 carrots, peeled and chopped
    1 green bell pepper, cored, seeded, and diced
    2 red bell peppers, cored, seeded, and diced
    1 bay leaf
    1 lb 8 oz (680 g) *surubí* fillets (or use catfish)
    1 cup/8 fl oz (250 ml) white wine
    1 cup/8 fl oz (250 ml) water
    1½ cups/12 fl oz (350 ml) milk
    2 tablespoons tomato paste (purée)
    3 tomatoes, peeled and chopped
    5 oz (150 g) Paraguayan cheese, shredded
    2 tablespoons chopped cilantro (coriander)
    salt and ground pepper

Heat the beef tallow in a large pan over high heat. Add the leek, celery, onions, carrots, bell peppers, and bay leaf. Cook for 3 minutes, stirring occasionally. Lower the heat and cook for 5 minutes. Add the fish, cover, and cook for 5 minutes, stirring occasionally. Remove the fish from the pan and add the wine. Stir well, then add the water, milk, tomato paste (purée), and chopped tomatoes, and stir for 2 minutes. Return the fish to the pan.

To finish, add the shredded cheese and cilantro (coriander) and turn off the heat. Season with salt and pepper and serve hot, after the cheese is completely melted.

Lake Yojoa-Style Fried Fish

Beef

In a clearing amidst a small vineyard in the Uco Valley outside of Mendoza, a group of winemakers, and their friends, and their families gather in the afternoon with an *asado* to celebrate the start of the grape harvest. The sky is bright blue and the snowy peaks of the cordillera shimmer like diamonds off in the distance.

As the first guests arrive, wine is poured and they nibble on a *picada* of cured meats, cheeses, olives, and figs. Chorizos and *achuras*, or offal meat, like *mollejas* (sweetbreads) and *chinchulines* (chitterlings), are the first cuts to be pulled off of a hot metal grate hovering above a pile of slow-burning wood and charcoal by the *asador*. The chorizos are sliced up and eaten on crusty rolls, while the offal gets slathered in *salsa criolla*, a sauce made of chopped tomato, onion, and parsley in vinegar. There are discs of *provoleta* right on the grate, *asado de tira* (short ribs) perched on a metal stand angled over one side of the parrilla, and a concave pot with legs set over the coals cooking carrots, corn, and potatoes. The largest cuts, which were put on the grill first, like *vacío* (flank steak) and *bife de chorizo* (sirloin), will come off last.

The first cattle in the New World arrived in Veracruz, Mexico in 1525 and by 1536 they were in Argentina. The hunger for beef has transformed the region's landscape, creating lifeless plots of grass at the expense of rich, tropical forests, while it also gave an identity to immense grasslands, from Los Llanos in Colombia and Venezuela to the pampas of Argentina and southern Brazil, turning them into hubs of cattle culture, where many of the first recipes with beef in this new land were formed.

The art of the *asado* didn't begin until the eighteenth century in the prairies of the southern cone. There, gauchos, horsemen, often nomadic, who worked the plains rounding up cattle, survived on a diet that was almost entirely beef cooked over *quebracho* wood, and drinking *maté*. The *asado* has evolved to include different forms of grilling and cuts have been adapted to different regions and to backyard barbecues, yet the very essence of the ritual, the act of cooking and eating together, remains the same.

Argentine Short Ribs

Asado de Tira ⌾
Argentina, Uruguay

Preparation time: 10 minutes
Cooking time: 1 hour 30 minutes   Serves: 5–6

An almost obligatory cut for an Argentine *asado*, the *asado de tira* is sold as a long, thin strip of chuck ribs cut flanken style, so it's not quite a traditional cut of short ribs. In 1882, The River Plate Fresh Meat Company, a meat processing facility in Campana, north Buenos Aires, started cutting the ribs with a saw to split the bone, as their mostly English buyers preferred cuts with less bone. The *asado de tira* was essentially a discarded cut that was given to employees. For a more tender meat, seek out the cuts with the smaller, rounder, bones, which signify they're from a younger cow. On the pampas, this cut is often cooked almost vertically, with the rib side facing the heat. Serve warm with a simple salad or fries.

    5 lb 8 ounces (2.5 kg) *asado de tira*
    tallow, for greasing
    coarse salt

Start by preparing the grill (barbecue), lighting small pieces of wood and newspapers and letting burn until the charcoal has stopped smoking. Smear some of the tallow or a hunk of fat from the beef over the grate to prevent the meat from sticking.

Season the meat with salt and set it on the grill, bone side down, and cook until it starts to brown, about 50 minutes. Flip the meat and cook it for about a further 20 minutes. Depending on the thickness of the meat, the total cooking time might vary from 1–1½ hours. The inside of the meat should be warm, juicy, and slightly brown, but not red.

Remove the meat from the grill and cut into pieces of 2 or 3 ribs per person.

Beef Stew in a Squash

Carbonada
Argentina, Chile, Uruguay

Preparation time: 10 minutes
Cooking time: 1 hour   Serves: 4

The *carbonada* is a beef stew made with common vegetables, and sometimes a fruit or two, found through the Southern Cone of South America. While the squash can be chopped up and cooked in the pot with the meat, some variations, like this one, use it as a serving dish.

    2 medium squash
    1½ cups/12 fl oz (350 ml) milk
    2 tablespoons vegetable oil
    1 white onion, chopped
    ½ red bell pepper, seeded and chopped
    2 lb (900 g) beef sirloin, cut into 1½-inch (4-cm) cubes
    1½ cups/12 fl oz (350 ml) beef stock
    2 sweet potatoes, peeled and cut into chunks
    3 ears of corn, cut into chunks
    3 peaches, pitted and diced
    2 cups/9 oz (250 g) diced *queso fresco*
    salt

Preheat the oven to 350°F/180°C/Gas Mark 4.

Cut the top off each squash and reserve. Remove the pulp and seeds, then pour half of the milk inside each. Cover the squash with foil and cook in the oven for 15 minutes, then lower the heat to 325°F/165°C/Gas Mark 3 and continue cooking for a further 20 minutes, or until it becomes tender, and the skin starts peeling. Remove the squash that falls off the skin and reserve.

Meanwhile, heat the oil in a frying pan over medium heat, add the onion and bell pepper, and sauté for 5 minutes. Add the beef and sear well for 10 minutes. Add the stock, sweet potatoes, and corn, then season with salt, lower the heat and simmer for 20 minutes. Add the peaches and the squash that fell from the skin. Cook over low heat for 10 minutes then place everything back inside the squash.

Add the *queso fresco* to the top of the filling for each, and cover each squash with the top removed at the beginning. Place on a lined baking sheet and bake in the oven for 10 minutes, then remove and place the squash on a plate.

Serve hot in soup dishes from the squash.

Flank Steak with Creole Sauce

Sobrebarriga a la criolla
Colombia

Preparation time: 20 minutes
Cooking time: 3 hours   Serves: 4

Translating as "over belly," the *sobrebarriga*, or flank (skirt) steak, is one of the most common cuts of beef in Colombia. With its different textures and degrees of fat, it can be a difficult cut to cook, but after being simmered for hours, tissue breaks down and it becomes quite tender.

    1 veal *sobrebarriga*, about 2 lb (900 g)
    8 cups/64 fl oz (1.9 liters) water
    1 white onion, halved
    3 garlic cloves, crushed
    salt and ground pepper

    For the sauce
    2 tablespoons vegetable oil
    3 white onions, chopped
    2 garlic cloves, minced
    1 red bell pepper, cored, seeded, and cut into small chunks
    4 tomatoes, peeled and diced
    ½ teaspoon annatto paste
    ½ teaspoon ground cumin

    To serve
    2 avocados, peeled, halved, and pitted
    cooked white rice

Place the meat in a large pan with the water, onion, and garlic. Season with salt and pepper, then bring to a boil and simmer over low heat for 3 hours or until the meat is tender. Remove the meat from the pan and set aside.

Meanwhile, heat the oil in a pan, add the chopped onions, minced garlic, and bell pepper, and sauté for 5 minutes, then add the tomatoes and annatto paste, cumin, and salt and pepper to taste. Cook for a further 10 minutes over low heat, stirring frequently.

Cut the meat into four equal pieces and place one piece in each dish. Serve with the sauce spread on top, avocado halves, and rice on the side.

Argentine Short Ribs

Brazilian-Style Rump Cap

Picanha, tapa de cuadril
Argentina, Brazil, Paraguay

Preparation time: 10 minutes
Cooking time: 1 hour

Serves: 4

If you have ever been to a Brazilian *churrascaria*, you are probably familiar with picanha, the large hunks of beef with a C-shaped cap of fat being sliced off a large metal skewer. North American butchers usually break down the picanha into other cuts like rump, round, and loin, and aren't always familiar with it. You might need to ask for the "rump cap" or "cap of top sirloin," and request for the fat cap to be left on. In Argentina and Paraguay, where it's less common, the cut is called *tapa de cuadril*. While the cut likely originated on the pampas of southern Brazil, it had little commercial value in Brazil and was being exported as a by-product elsewhere in the region. The only demand was from Eastern European immigrants working at a Volkswagen plant in São Paulo to make a stew called tafelspitz in the 1960s, but a decade later a restaurant called Dinho's started selling *bife de tira*, a cut of the picanha, on their menu, and popularized it. The cut is near where cattle in southern Brazil are branded with an iron, which is called a "picanha."

2–2 1/2 lb (900–1.1 kg) picanha, room temperature
salt
1 *rodizio* sword or large skewer

Use a knife to score the fat side of the picanha in a cross-hatch pattern, then let rest as you prepare a charcoal grill (barbecue) until the coals have a layer of white ash.

Place the picanha on a cutting board and cut horizontally into 4 pieces. Bend the pieces of meat into semi-circles and pierce them through the fat cap on both sides with the sword or skewer. Season with salt and let sit for 5 minutes.

Place the sword or skewer about 6 inches (15 cm) over the fire, with the fat side up. Cook for 10 minutes, then turn the meat and cook for a further 15 minutes. Raise the meat to about 16 inches (40 cm) from the fire with the fat side up, and continue cooking, turning occasionally, until the internal temperature is 125°F/52°C.

Thinly slice the meat and serve, with or without the fat cap.

Rolled Flank Steak

Matambre relleno
Argentina, Uruguay

Preparation time: 20 minutes
Cooking time: 20 minutes, plus 20 minutes resting

Serves: 6

Matambre is a combination of the Spanish words *matar*, to kill, and *hambre*, hunger. So it means hunger killer. It's made from a cut of beef taken between the skin and the ribs, sort of flank steak. It gets layered with fillings, which vary from recipe to recipe, though usually include eggs and carrots, then rolled and held together with twine or pins. There are several options for cooking, such as grilling (barbecuing) or boiling it in water or milk and then roasting it. When it is grilled it is sliced and served warm, but when boiled it is chilled first and then sliced and served cold, sometimes on bread.

1 *matambre* or flank (skirt) steak, about 2 lb (900 g)
2 garlic cloves, minced
3 tablespoons chopped parsley
3 hard-boiled eggs, halved
1 red bell pepper, cored, seeded, and sliced
3 carrots (ideally long and thin), peeled
salt and ground pepper
Chimichurri (page 400), to serve

Spread the steak on a flat surface. Butterfly the steak by cutting it with a sharp knife along three sides, keeping the knife level with the surface. Unfold the steak and open it up flat, pounding it with a mallet if necessary.

Season the meat with salt and pepper. In a bowl, mix the garlic and parsley, then rub the mix all over the steak. Place the egg halves to form a line across the steak, near one of the edges, then do the same with the bell pepper slices and carrots. The fillings will only cover one part of the steak. Roll it up, wrap butcher's twine around the rolled steak four times at even intervals, to secure it well.

Prepare a grill (barbecue). When hot (400°F/200°C), cook the steak for 20 minutes, rolling it several times.

Let rest and cool for 20 minutes before slicing about 1/2–1 inch (1–2.5 cm) thick and serving with *chimichurri*.

Bolivian Schnitzel Topped with a Fried Egg

Silpancho
Bolivia

Preparation time: 30 minutes
Cooking time: 10 minutes

Serves: 2

Created in the highland city of Cochabamba in 1946 by local cook Celia la Fuente Peredo, *silpancho* is a classic Bolivian meal with a thin cut of beef that has been pounded, breaded, and fried like schnitzel. In restaurants in that city, some of which only sell *silpancho*, lights turned on outside indicate there's some available. If they are turned on and covered, it's being prepared.

2 thin top sirloin steaks
1/2 cup/1 1/2 oz (40 g) fine breadcrumbs
1 tablespoon vegetable oil
2 tomatoes, diced
1 *rocoto* chile, seeded and chopped
1 white onion, diced
1 tablespoon chopped cilantro (coriander)
2 tablespoons vinegar
salt and ground pepper

To serve
cooked white rice
2 fried eggs
1 potato, sliced and fried

Cover the steaks with the breadcrumbs and pound them with a meat tenderizer, adding more breadcrumbs if necessary. Season with salt and pepper.

Heat the oil in a frying pan over medium heat. Once hot, sear the steaks for 3 minutes each side, or until golden brown. Remove from the pan and set aside.

In a bowl, mix the tomatoes, chile, onion, and cilantro (coriander). Season with salt, pepper and the vinegar.

To serve, top a layer of rice with a steak, followed by a fried egg, and the salsa with fried potato slices on the side.

Bolivian Schnitzel Topped with a Fried Egg

Bone Marrow

Caracú, tuétano
Argentina, Chile, Paraguay, Uruguay

Preparation time: 5 minutes
Cooking time: 10 minutes   Serves: 4

Caracú, a word of Guaraní origin meaning marrow bone, is an accepted term throughout the southern cattle lands of South America. It's the heart of stews, like the *puchero*, though it makes a nice starter roasted lightly with a little salt during an *asado* while waiting for the meats to cook.

    4 marrow bones, either split lengthways or across
    (ask your butcher)
    salt
    toasts, to serve

Preheat the oven to 400°F/200°C/Gas Mark 6.
    Place the bones in an oven tray, sprinkle with salt, and bake for about 8 minutes, or until the marrow is soft. (Alternatively, you can place them directly on a preheated grill/barbecue for about 20 minutes.)
    Serve an entire bone per person, with a few toasts.

Breaded and Fried Beef

Milanesa de res
Argentina, Uruguay

Preparation time: 10 minutes
Cooking time: 10 minutes   Serves: 2

The Latin American version of the Italian dish *cotoletta alla Milanese*, or veal Milanese, arrived in Argentina and Uruguay with Italian immigrants sometime in the late nineteenth century, though today you can find it nearly everywhere in Latin America. It can be made with thinly sliced beef, though chicken, pork, or veal are often used. There are dozens of variations. When served with an egg on top, it's called a *caballo*, or "on horseback." When served with tomato sauce and cheese, and sometimes ham, it's called *a la Napolitana*, or Neapolitan style. In Mexico, they are often eaten on *tortas* and *cemitas*. Serve with French fries or mashed potatoes.

    1 lb (450 g) beef top round (topside), sliced into
    2 thin steaks
    2 eggs
    2 garlic cloves, minced
    2 tablespoons chopped parsley
    1 lb (450 g) breadcrumbs
    vegetable oil, for shallow-frying
    salt

Trim the steaks of any fat or sinew and soften them with a meat tenderizer. In a bowl, beat the eggs and mix them with the garlic and parsley. Season with salt and tip into a shallow dish. Spread the breadcrumbs on a plate.
    Soak one steak in the egg mixture, slowly remove it, letting any excess egg drip off, and place in the bread-crumbs, covering the whole steak with the breadcrumbs on both sides. Repeat with the remaining steak.
    Add enough oil to cover the coated steaks to a frying pan and heat to 350°F/177°C. Fry the steaks, in batches, for 3 minutes each side, or until golden brown. Place on a plate lined with paper towels, to absorb excess oil.
    Serve warm.

Clay Pot Beef Stew

Barreado
Brazil

Preparation time: 20 minutes
Cooking time: 8 hours   Serves: 4

In Brazil's Paraná state this slow-cooked beef stew fuels Carnival parties for days. The stew, made with inexpensive, tough, fatty cuts of meat, gets cooked inside a clay pot that's sealed with a cassava flour dough, turning it into a slow cooker and trapping moisture inside. Some will keep the pot fired for as long as two days. It's common to serve the meat in a bowl, on top of a little bit of *pirão* (Cassava Porridge, page 100), made using the liquid from the stew, along with white rice and slices of banana.

    2 lb (900 g) beef chuck steak or bottom round
    (silverside), cut into 1-inch (2.5-cm) chunks
    1 teaspoon dried cumin
    1 tablespoon vinegar
    2 tablespoons corn oil
    3 white onions, chopped
    3 tomatoes, peeled and chopped
    2 garlic cloves, minced
    1 lb (450 g) bacon
    2 cups/16 fl oz (475 ml) water
    1 bay leaf
    salt and ground pepper

    For the paste
    4 cups/1 lb 2 oz (560 g) cassava flour
    2 cups/16 fl oz (475 ml) water

    To serve
    Pirão (Cassava Porridge, page 100)
    cooked white rice
    thickly sliced bananas

Prepare a paste by mixing the cassava flour and water. Set aside.
    Season the meat with the cumin, vinegar, and some salt and pepper. Set aside. Add the oil to a clay pot (8 inch/20 cm diameter), and cover the bottom with the vegetables, followed by a layer of bacon and a layer of meat. Repeat the process until the ingredients are finished.
    Pour the water into the pot with the bay leaf. Bring to a boil, then lower the heat. Add the lid and use half the cassava dough to seal the pot, pressing it around the edges of the lid where it meets the pot. Cook over low heat for 4 hours, then break open the seal, remove the lid, stir well, and check the seasoning. Add more water if necessary (it should cover the ingredients). Reseal the lid with more cassava dough, and cook for at least a further 4 hours, still over low heat. Remove from the heat and open the pot. The meat should be mostly shredded. Check the seasoning one more time.
    Serve the *barreado* on top of some *pirão*, with rice and bananas on the side.

Clay Pot Beef Stew

Brazilian Fried Cowboy Steak

Frito do vaqueiro, marajoara frito
Brazil

Preparation time: 10 minutes
Cooking time: 2–3 hours　　　　Serves: 8

Cowboys in the wilds of Marajó Island in northern Brazil eat this meat—which is steamed in its own fat—for breakfast with coffee in the field. They are known to store it in cans beneath a horse's saddle to keep warm.

    2 lb (900 g) flank (skirt) steak (ideally water buffalo)
    2 lb (900 g) eye of round (silverside) steak
    salt and ground pepper
    Farofa (Toasted Cassava Flour, page 98), to serve

Cut all the meat into 2-inch (5-cm) chunks and season with salt and pepper. Place in a cast-iron pot and cover with a lid. Cook over a low fire or low heat for 2–3 hours, or until the meat is tender and brown, but not dried out, stirring every 30 minutes to prevent the meat from sticking. Serve hot with *farofa* on the side.

Brazilian Beef Croquettes

Kibe, quibbe
Brazil

Preparation time: 20 minutes,
plus 2 hours soaking
Cooking time: 30 minutes　　　Makes: about 20

In Brazil, these deep-fried and stuffed fritters made of ground and spiced beef and bulgur wheat, which in Brazil is labeled *trigo para quibe*, or "wheat for kibbeh." You'll mostly see them served as snacks from *lanchonetes*, sometimes with a creamy cheese called *requeijão*. They were introduced in the late nineteenth and early twentieth century by immigrants who came to Brazil from Lebanon and Syria, where it is known as kibbeh and eaten throughout the Levant. There it is generally made from bulgur wheat and ground lamb, though beef, goat, or camel meat is used as well.

    8 ounces (225 g) bulgur wheat, soaked in water
    for 2 hours
    1 lb 8 ounces (680 g) ground (minced) beef
    1½ white onions, chopped
    4 mint leaves, chopped
    2 teaspoons salt
    1½ teaspoons ground black pepper
    2 tablespoons olive oil
    2 garlic cloves, minced
    2 tablespoon chopped parsley
    vegetable oil, for deep-frying
    lime slices, to serve

Start by preparing the dough. Drain the bulgur wheat and use a cheesecloth to squeeze out any excess water. In a bowl, mix it with 1 lb (450 g) of the beef, 1 of the chopped onions, the mint, 1 teaspoon of the salt, and 1 teaspoon of the black pepper. Pass the mix through a food processor to mix well. Set aside.

For the filling, heat the olive oil in a pan over medium heat, add the remaining onion and the garlic, and sauté for 5 minutes, or until soft and transparent. Add the beef and cook, stirring, for 15 minutes, or until cooked and dry. Season with the remaining salt and pepper, and stir in the parsley. Mix well, then remove from the heat.

Divide the dough into 20 equal pieces and shape each into a 1-inch (2.5-cm) ball. Press each ball in the middle with one finger to make a cavity, place a tablespoon of the filling inside and close the dough over the filling to seal. Form into a torpedo shape, and set aside.

Pour enough vegetable oil for deep-frying into a large, heavy pan, making sure it is no more than two-thirds full, and heat to 350°F/177°C. Once the oil is hot, fry the croquettes in small batches for 3 minutes each side, or until golden brown. Place on a plate lined with paper towels to absorb excess oil.

Serve warm with slices of lime.

Short Rib and Cassava Stew

Vaca atolada
Brazil

Preparation time: 20 minutes
Cooking time: 1 hour 30 minutes　　Serves: 4

Translating as a "cow stuck in the mud," *vaca atolado* is a thick chunk of beef, such as a short rib, that's cooked and served in a thick sauce. It hails from the state of Minas Gerais in the seventeenth century, when adventurers from São Paulo would set off in search of gold. During the rainy season, when the cattle would be stranded, they are said to have taken breaks and prepared a stew with beef that had been preserved in fat, with cassava and herbs. Serve with white rice.

    2 lb 8 ounces (1.1 kg) beef ribs
    5 cups/40 fl oz (1.2 liters) water
    5 sprigs parsley
    2 scallions (spring onions)
    2 bay leaves
    3 tablespoons olive oil
    1 large onion, diced
    1 green bell pepper, cored, seeded, and diced
    3 garlic cloves, minced
    2 cups/11 oz (320 g) diced tomatoes
    1 tablespoon ground annatto
    1 lb 12 ounces (800 g) cassava, peeled and cut
    into cubes
    2 tablespoons chopped parsley
    salt and ground pepper

Place the beef ribs and water in a large pan. Make a bouquet garni by tying together the sprigs of parsley, scallions (spring onions), and bay leaves, and add to the ribs. Heat, and once it starts to boil, reduce to a simmer and cook for 20 minutes. Drain and set aside, reserving the cooking stock.

Heat the oil in a large pan, add the onion, bell pepper, and garlic, and cook for about 5 minutes until softened, then add the meat and cook for a further 5 minutes until browned. Add 3 cups/24 fl oz (675 ml) of the cooking stock, the tomatoes, and annatto and mix gently. Bring to a boil, then reduce to a simmer and let cook uncovered for 40 minutes.

Add the cassava and cook for 20 minutes, or until you can mash the cassava. Extract a few pieces of cassava and mash until smooth, then add them back to the pot. If you find the sauce too light, repeat with a few more pieces of cassava (leaving some intact cassava pieces). Mix in the parsley and check the seasoning.

Serve warm.

Costa Rican Lunch Plate

Casado
Costa Rica

Preparation time: 10 minutes
Cooking time: 35 minutes   Serves: 4

Translating as "married," no one really knows if this typical Costa Rican meal was named because all of the ingredients live together on the plate or because it's something you would eat at home for lunch with your spouse. The exact build of a *casado* will vary by region, time of year, and whims of the cook, but generally you will find rice, beans, salad, plantains, tortillas, and a protein, which might be beef, pork, chicken, or fish.

2 lb (900 g) sirloin steak, in 4 pieces
2 garlic cloves, minced
2 tablespoons vegetable oil
1/2 cup/4 fl oz (120 ml) beef stock
2 ripe plantains, peeled and cut into thick slices
1 iceberg lettuce
2 tomatoes, sliced
1 carrot, peeled and grated
2 teaspoons white vinegar
2 tablespoons olive oil
salt and ground pepper

To serve
4 fried eggs
2 cups/9 oz (250 g) cooked white rice
2 cups/12 oz (350 g) cooked black beans
1 cup/4½ oz (130 g) cubed *queso fresco*
Corn Tortillas (page 136, for homemade)

Season the steaks with salt, pepper, and garlic. In a frying pan, heat 1 tablespoon of the vegetable oil over high heat, then sear the steaks for 3 minutes each side.

Remove the steaks to a plate, pour the stock into the pan and reduce until thick. Keep warm.

In another frying pan, heat the remaining 1 tablespoon of vegetable oil and fry the plantain slices for 4 minutes each side, or until golden brown. Remove to a plate lined with paper towels, to absorb excess oil.

With your hands, tear the lettuce into pieces and place in a salad bowl with the tomatoes and grated carrot. Prepare a vinaigrette by whisking the vinegar into the olive oil. Season with salt and pepper, pour it over the salad, and mix well.

Prepare 4 plates to serve with a piece of steak and some sauce, as well as some fried plantain slices, salad, a fried egg, rice, beans, *queso fresco*, and tortillas.

Stuffed Pot Roast

Muchacho relleno
Colombia

Preparation time: 40 minutes,
plus 3 hours marinating   Serves: 8
Cooking time: 2 hours

In some Caribbean-facing countries, *muchacho* (meaning "boy") describes the eye of round, or pot roast. (Note: it's called *lagarto* in Brazil and *peceto* in Argentina.) Fillings vary, so the *muchacho* can be rolled and filled like a *matambre relleno* (Rolled Flank Steak, page 250), have only hard-boiled eggs inside, or infused with seasonings.

6 lb (2.7 kg) pot roast (silverside)
½ cup/4 fl oz (120 ml) Worcestershire sauce
1 tablespoon red vinegar
4 garlic cloves, minced
2 teaspoons dried oregano
10 green beans, trimmed
1 carrot, cut into slices the size of the green beans
4 oz (120 g) ground (minced) pork
15 oz (450 g) *Hogao* (Colombian Sofrito, page 400)
1 egg
2 tablespoons breadcrumbs
2 tablespoons vegetable oil

Using a long knife, cut 4 holes through the roast from one end to the other, stopping before you reach the other side. Do the same horizontally, making another 6 holes.

Prepare a marinade with the Worcestershire sauce, vinegar, garlic, oregano, and some salt and pepper. Rub the marinade on the outside of the beef and inside the holes. Set aside for at least 3 hours.

Cook the green beans for 5 minutes in boiling, salted water. Drain and plunge into iced water. Cook the carrot slices in the same way.

Mix the ground (minced) pork with *hogao*, egg, and breadcrumbs. Season with salt and pepper. Stuff the green beans and carrot slices into the shorter holes in the beef. Spread the pork mixture into the longer holes. Roll the beef, wrap butcher's twine several times around it, and tie it. Preheat the oven to 350°F/180°C/Gas Mark 4.

Heat the oil in a large frying pan over medium heat. Sear the beef for 5 minutes each side, or until brown, then place in an oven dish (13 x 9 x 2 inches/33 x 23 x 5 cm) with all of the marinade juices and 2 cups/16 fl oz (475 ml) water. Cover with aluminum foil and bake for 1½ hours, or until the meat is tender. Remove from the oven, place the meat on a plate, and let cool. Blend the juices left in the oven dish to make a sauce. Serve the *muchacho* cut into ½-inch (1-cm) slices, with the sauce poured over.

Beef, Corn, and Tomato Stew

Tomaticán
Chile

Preparation time: 20 minutes
Cooking time: 30 minutes   Serves: 4

Served during the summer months, when fresh corn and tomatoes are available, *tomaticán* is the very essence of seasonal comfort food in the countryside of central Chile.

2 tablespoons vegetable oil
1 white onion, thinly sliced
1 garlic clove, minced
1 lb (450 g) bottom sirloin (rump), cut into 4 slices
½ teaspoon each paprika and dried oregano
4 tomatoes, peeled and diced
1 cup/4½ oz (125 g) fresh corn kernels
2 tablespoons chopped parsley
cooked white rice, to serve

Heat the oil in a pan over medium heat. Sauté the onion and garlic for 5 minutes, then add the meat and sear well. Add the paprika, oregano, and tomatoes. Season with salt and pepper, stir, bring to a boil, then lower the heat, cover, and cook for 15 minutes. Add the corn and ½ cup/4 fl oz (120 ml) water and bring to a boil again. Lower the heat and cook for a further 10 minutes. Stir through the parsley. Serve hot, with rice on the side.

Hot Stone Soup

Calapurca, k'ala phurka
Argentina, Bolivia, Chile, Peru

Preparation time: 30 minutes,
plus overnight soaking
Cooking time: 3 hours

Serves: 4

The signature characteristic of this otherwise rather straightforward soup is that small volcanic stones that have been heated over charcoal are dropped into the soup before serving. Generally used to warm the soup before serving rather than cook it, the soup bubbles as the stone is dropped in, anywhere from a few seconds to a few minutes depending on the temperature of the stone. Warning: every stone retains heat differently and if it is too hot the soup can splash, so be sure to cautiously test out a bowl before serving. *Calapurca* is found primarily in an Aymara speaking territory that extends throughout much of the altiplano, and the ingredients may change considerably from one place to the next. Usually some form of corn, chile pepper, potatoes, and meat, either fresh or dehydrated, are used.

1 whole chicken, cut into pieces
4 lb (1.8 kg) beef bones
2 lb (900 g) thick beef flank (skirt), cut into 1-inch (2.5-cm) chunks
1 onion, chopped
2 lb (900 g) *mote* (Andean hominy), soaked overnight
3 tablespoons vegetable oil
3 garlic cloves, minced
2 scallions (spring onions)
2 tablespoons chopped cilantro (coriander)
1 teaspoon dried oregano
2 lb (900 g) potatoes, peeled and boiled
salt and ground pepper

Place the chicken, beef bones, beef pieces, and onion in a large pan. Season with salt and pepper, mix well, and add enough water to cover all the ingredients. Cover and cook over medium heat for 1–2 hours, stirring every 30 minutes and checking the meat has not stuck to the bottom. Add the drained *mote*, and continue cooking for a further 30 minutes, adding another cup or so of water if necessary. When the beef starts to fall apart, remove all of the bones from the cooking stock. Continue cooking over medium heat as you complete the next step.

Heat the oil in a pan over medium heat, add the garlic and scallions (spring onions) and sauté for 5 minutes. Add the cilantro (coriander) and dried oregano and cook for a further 5 minutes. Add to the pan with the meats, and stir well, adding more water if it's too dry. Using your hands, break the potatoes and add them to the soup.

Pour the soup into bowls and, just before serving, take a small stone, no larger than a golf ball, directly out of a fire where it has been heating and drop it into the soup. Make sure the hot broth isn't splashing out before putting it front of anyone. Alternatively, you can bring a pot to a boil then serve.

Colombian Braised Beef

Posta negra 🍲
Colombia

Preparation time: 20 minutes,
plus 24 hours marinating
Cooking time: 2 hours 30 minutes

Serves: 4

The many rich layers of flavors in the marinade and sauce of *posta negra* corresponds with the amalgam of cultures—indigenous, African, and Spanish—found in Cartagena and around the Caribbean coastal region of Colombia where the recipe is from. Almost like a Mexican *mole*, it can be sweet, spicy, salty, and bitter all at the same time. There's not one standard recipe for the marinade. Typically, *salsa negra*, a commercial liquid seasoning that resembles a less salty soy sauce, is used, though Worcestershire sauce makes a good substitute. While cola has become an accepted ingredient, Colombia's neon-red soda Kola Román might be there instead, as might bitter orange juice, tamarind pulp, or vinegar. The cut of beef is usually the *punta de anca*, which is the same as picanha in Brazil or called the cap of top sirloin elsewhere. Chuck or pot roasts can be used as a substitute. Serve with *tostones* (Fried Plantains, page 194), *yuca frita* (Cassava Fries, page 99), or *arroz con coco* (Coconut Rice, page 63).

2–2 lb 8 ounces (900g–1.1 kg) cap of top sirloin, fat cap removed
3 tablespoons vegetable oil
4 cups/32 fl oz (950 ml) water
salt and ground pepper

For the marinade
1/2 cup/3 1/2 oz (100 g) panela sugar (or use light muscovado)
1 white onion, cut into big cubes
1 carrot, cut into chunks
3 garlic cloves, chopped
3 bay leaves
2 sprigs thyme
8 cloves
1 cinnamon stick
2 tablespoons *salsa negra* (or Worcestershire sauce)
4 cups/32 fl oz (950 ml) cola

For the marinade, mix the sugar, onion, carrot, garlic, bay leaves, thyme, cloves, cinnamon, *salsa negra*, and cola in a dish. Season the meat with salt and pepper and spread the marinade over the meat. Leave to marinate in the refrigerator for 24 hours.

The following day, heat the oil in a frying pan over medium heat. Sear the meat for 4 minutes each side, or until browned. Place the seared meat in a pan and pour the marinade and the water over it. Bring to a boil, then lower the heat, cover, and simmer for 2 hours, stirring often, or until the meat is tender. (Alternatively, you can do this in a pressure cooker, reducing the cooking time to 1 hour.)

Remove the meat from the pan and let rest for 10 minutes, then cut into slices. Add the slices back into the cooking liquid and cook over medium heat for 15 minutes.

Serve the meat with any additional sauce poured over it.

Colombian Braised Beef

Ecuadorian Beef and Potato Stew

Timbushca
Ecuador

Preparation time: 20 minutes
Cooking time: 3 hours 30 minutes

Serves: 6

Found mostly in the Ecuadorian highlands in the Imbabura and Chimborazo provinces, this traditional stew is thickened with cream and peanuts. Some variations are meatier, while others exploit the beef bones primarily to flavor the broth.

8 cups/64 fl oz (1.9 liters) water
1 lb (450 g) brisket with bone
8 oz (225 g) beef chuck
4 scallions (spring onions), 2 whole, 2 chopped
3 tablespoons chopped parsley
2 tomatoes peeled, seeded, and chopped
2 garlic cloves, minced
1 teaspoon ground cumin
1 tablespoon annatto oil
1 white onion, chopped
2 tablespoons chopped cilantro (coriander)
¼ cup/1 oz (30 g) peanuts, toasted and chopped
½ cup/4 fl oz (120 ml) cream
2 lb (900 g) potatoes, peeled and chopped
½ white cabbage, chopped
1 hard-boiled egg, chopped
salt and ground pepper

Bring the water to a boil in a large pan. Once boiling, add all the meat, the whole scallions (spring onions), parsley, tomatoes, garlic, and cumin. Season with salt, cover and simmer for 3 hours, or until the meats are tender.

Meanwhile, heat the annatto oil in a pan over medium heat. Add the chopped scallions, onion, and cilantro (coriander) and sauté for 5 minutes. Mix the peanuts with the cream, add to the pan, and cooking for a further 5 minutes. Remove from the heat and set aside.

Once cooked, remove the meat from the stock. Add the potatoes, cabbage, and peanut mixture to the stock and cook for 20 minutes. Cut the meat into 1-inch (2.5-cm) chunks and place them back in the stock. Check the seasoning and continue to cook until the soup is thick.

Serve hot, with the chopped egg scattered on top.

Meat, Tuber, and Vegetable Stew

Sancocho, sancocho de res
Colombia, Ecuador, Honduras, Panama, Venezuela

Preparation time: 20 minutes
Cooking time: 1 hour 30 minutes

Serves: 6

Sancocho is a hearty meat and vegetable stew that was introduced by the Spanish and adapted to New World ingredients like cassava and arracacha. It's the national dish of several countries in the region. The following variation is most similar to *sancocho paisa*, a regional dish found in Colombia's central and western Andes. Using essentially leftovers from the week, the slow-simmered stew is served for Saturday lunches. Chopped cilantro, onions, and lime wedges are usually served as garnishes.

2 lb (900 g) beef back ribs
1 lb (450 g) pork ribs
5 scallions (spring onions), trimmed
2 tablespoons chopped parsley
4 tablespoons chopped cilantro (coriander)
10 cups/5 pints (2.4 liters) water
2 ears of corn, cut into three chunks each
2 green plantains, peeled and cut into chunks
8 oz (225 g) carrots, peeled and cut into chunks
8 oz (225 g) arracacha, peeled and cut into chunks
2 lb (900 g) potatoes, peeled and cut into chunks
1 lb (450 g) cassava, peeled and cut into chunks
salt and ground pepper
cooked white rice, to serve

Place the meats in a large pan with the whole scallions (spring onions), parsley, cilantro (coriander), and measured water. Season with salt and pepper, bring to a boil over high heat, then lower the heat and simmer, covered, for 40 minutes.

Add the corn and plantains to the pan and cook for 15 minutes. Add the carrots, arracacha, potatoes, and cassava and simmer for a further 20 minutes. Remove the spring onions and stir. When all the ingredients are tender, remove from the heat.

Serve hot in a soup dish, with rice on the side.

Beef Rib Broth

Caldo de costilla
Colombia

Preparation time: 20 minutes
Cooking time: 1 hour 45 minutes

Serves: 4

In parts of Bogotá and other highland Colombian cities, you'll see small restaurants and stalls near high concentrations of bars and clubs selling bowls of this soulful broth made of beef ribs. The hot soup is said to give a second wind to keep the party going, or, when eaten in the morning, to cure a hangover.

½ teaspoon annatto paste
15 cups/7½ pints (3.5 liters) water
3 lb (1.4 kg) beef back ribs (cut and separate all the ribs)
1 teaspoon ground cumin
5 garlic cloves, peeled
1 white onion, chopped
6 scallions (spring onions), chopped
½ cup/¾ oz (20 g) chopped cilantro (coriander)
1 lb (450 g) potatoes, peeled and sliced
2 carrots, peeled and sliced
salt and ground pepper

Dilute the annatto paste in the water. Separate 1 cup/8 fl oz (250 ml) out from the rest and set aside.

Season the ribs with salt, pepper, and the cumin, then sear them in a large pan over medium heat, with no oil, for 7 minutes. Pour in the annatto water (except the separated smaller quantity) and increase the heat. Bring to a boil, then lower the heat and simmer for 1 hour.

Put the garlic, onion, and scallions (spring onions) in a blender with the reserved annatto water, and a quarter of the cilantro (coriander). Process for 1 minute on high speed. Pour the blended mixture into the pan, stir well, and simmer for 20 minutes. Add the potatoes and carrots and cook for 20 minutes, or until tender.

Sprinkle over the remaining cilantro and serve hot in soup bowls.

Stewpot

Puchero
Argentina, Paraguay, Uruguay

Preparation time: 15 minutes
Cooking time: 1 hour

Serves: 4

Originally from Spain, *puchero* was adapted to the Río de la Plata area, where beef is cheap and plentiful. On both sides of the ocean it's a peasant dish, cooked slowly, allowing the ingredients to release their full flavors.

    1 tablespoon vegetable oil
    1 garlic clove, minced
    1 lb (450 g) ossobuco
    6 cups/50 fl oz (1.5 liters) water
    2 white onions, chopped
    1 carrot, cut into 1-inch (2.5-cm) cubes
    3 ears of white corn
    1/2 cup/3¼ oz (90 g) uncooked rice
    salt

Heat the oil in a frying pan over medium heat, add the garlic and meat, and sear the meat for 2 minutes each side. Remove from the heat and set aside.

Bring the measured water to a boil in a medium pan, add the onions, carrot, and corn, and simmer for 40 minutes, then add the meat and rice and cook for a further 15 minutes, until the meat and vegetables are tender, and the rice is cooked.

Serve hot.

Spicy Beef and Vegetable Stew

Churipo
Mexico

Preparation time: 20 minutes
Cooking time: 1 hour 45 minutes

Serves: 8

This Purépecha recipe from the Mexican state of Michoacán dates to pre-Hispanic times, when it was made with game meats, though beef or pork have become standard. It's usually served with triangular tamales called *corundas* (Michoacán Triangular Tamales, page 134).

    3 *guajillo* chiles
    3 *pasilla* chiles
    2 tablespoons vegetable oil
    2 lb (900 g) beef bottom round (silverside), cut into
    1½-inch (4-cm) cubes
    2 lb (900 g) *carne seca de res* (dried beef)
    1 lb (450 g) beef bones, cut into 2-inch (5-cm) chunks
    8 cups/4 pints (1.9 liters) water
    3 ears of corn, halved
    1 lb (450 g) zucchini (courgettes), diced
    1 lb (450 g) carrots, peeled and diced
    1 lb (450 g) white cabbage, shredded
    salt

Soak all the chiles in warm water.

Meanwhile, heat the oil in a medium pan over high heat and sear the cubed meat for 3 minutes each side, or until brown. Add the dried beef and beef bones, then pour in the measured water and simmer for 40 minutes.

Drain the chiles and grind on a *metate*, or blend them. Add the mixture to the stock. Add the corn and cook for 15 minutes.

Meanwhile, cook the vegetables separately in boiling, salted water: 4 minutes for the zucchini (courgettes), 10 minutes for the carrots, and 5 minutes for the cabbage. Add the vegetables to the soup, cook for 30 minutes, or until the meat is tender.

Serve hot.

Olancho-Style Meat Stew

Tapado Olanchano
Honduras

Preparation time: 20 minutes,
plus overnight soaking
Cooking time: 2 hours 30 minutes

Serves: 8

In the wild, Honduran cowboy country of Olancho, various cuts of meat and vegetables are simmered in a coconut milk broth. It's a variation of the seafood based *tapado costeño*, found among Garifuna communities along the Caribbean coast of Honduras and Guatemala. Serve with white rice and tortillas.

    3 lb (1.4 kg) dried salted beef
    2 lb (900 g) pork ribs
    4 garlic cloves, 2 crushed, 2 minced
    1 tablespoon lard
    1/2 white onion, chopped
    1 sweet chile, seeded and chopped
    1/2 cup/⅜ oz (20 g) cilantro (coriander) leaves
    3 culantro leaves
    1 teaspoon annatto paste
    1 cup/8 fl oz (250 ml) chicken stock
    2 tablespoons Worcestershire sauce
    2 tablespoons tomato paste (purée)
    2 cups/16 fl oz (475 ml) coconut milk
    4 ripe plantains
    2 lb (900 g) cassava, peeled and cut into 1-inch
    (2.5-cm) chunks
    2 green plantains, peeled and sliced

Soak the dried beef in cold water overnight, then drain and rinse. Add to a medium pan and cover with fresh, cold water. Cook for 30 minutes over medium heat, or until soft, then cut into 1-inch (2.5-cm) chunks.

Meanwhile, add the pork ribs and the crushed garlic to a medium pan and cover with salted water. Bring to a boil, then reduce the heat to simmer and cook for 45 minutes. Remove from the heat and set aside, reserving the cooking water.

Heat the lard in a pan, add the minced garlic, onion, chile, cilantro (coriander), and culantro, and sauté for 8 minutes over medium heat. Add the annatto paste, stock, Worcestershire sauce, and tomato paste (purée). Continue cooking for 10 minutes, stirring frequently. Pour in the coconut milk and bring to a boil, then stir well and remove from the heat.

Peel the ripe plantains, retaining as much of the peel as possible. Cut the plantains into 1-inch (2.5-cm) chunks. Place half the plantain peel in the bottom of a large pan, about 8 inches (20 cm) diameter, and layer up the cassava, beef, pork ribs, sautéed vegetables, and plantain slices and chunks. Add the pork rib cooking water and top with a layer of plantain peels. Cover the pan and cook over low heat for 1 hour, or until the cassava and plantains are soft.

Serve hot.

Paraguayan Beef Soup

Soyo
Paraguay

Preparation time: 15 minutes,
plus 1 hour soaking
Cooking time: 30 minutes

Serves: 2

Short for the Guaraní word *so'o josopy*, or crushed meat, the beef is traditionally smashed in a mortar into a paste before being cooked. It's a humble recipe that's often made in family homes and served by market vendors.

  8 oz (225 g) ground (minced) beef, smashed in a mortar
  1 tablespoon vegetable oil
  ½ white onion, chopped
  1 carrot, peeled and chopped
  2 garlic cloves, minced
  2 tomatoes, peeled and chopped
  1 bay leaf
  2 sprigs oregano
  bread, to serve

Place the smashed beef in a bowl and cover with cold water. Let soak for 1 hour.
  In a pan, heat the oil, add the onion, carrot, and garlic, and sauté for 10 minutes. Add the tomatoes and cook for a further 5 minutes over medium heat. Add the beef with the soaking water, bay leaf, and oregano. Cook, stirring occasionally, for 15 minutes, or until the meat is cooked through. Season with salt and pepper. Serve hot.

Chopped Beef Braised in Spicy Tomato Sauce

Bistec picado
Panama

Preparation time: 20 minutes,
plus 30 minutes marinating
Cooking time: 10 minutes

Serves: 4

Chinese immigration to Panama was integral in helping build the railroads and later the Panama Canal, but its influence on Panamanian cuisine was pronounced as well. *Bistec picado*, a direct result of that influence, is seasoned in soy sauce and almost like a Panamanian stir-fry.

  1 lb (450 g) steak (flank, skirt, or hanger), sliced
  1 teaspoon dried oregano
  1 tablespoon soy sauce
  1 tablespoon Worcestershire sauce
  1 tablespoon olive oil
  1 white onion, sliced
  1 red bell pepper, cored, seeded, and sliced
  1 green bell pepper, cored, seeded, and sliced
  ½ cup/4 fl oz (120 ml) red wine
  salt and ground pepper

Place the meat in a bowl and season with a pinch each of salt and pepper. Add the oregano, soy sauce, and Worcestershire sauce. Mix well with your hands and let marinate for 30 minutes in the refrigerator.
  Heat the oil in a medium pan over high heat. When hot, add the meat and cook for 3 minutes. Add the onion and bell peppers, mix well, then pour in the wine. Cover, lower the heat and cook for 5 minutes. Serve hot.

Beef, Plantains, and Cassava Cooked in Banana Leaves

Vaho, baho
Nicaragua

Preparation time: 30 minutes,
plus overnight marinating
Cooking time: 4 hours

Serves: 8

One of the cornerstones of Nicaraguan cuisine, *vaho*, which originated in the colonial era, is the result of the mix of cultures—indigenous, Spanish, African—that make up the country. It's typically served at Sunday family gatherings.

  4 lb (1.8 kg) beef brisket, cut into large strips
  5 white onions, halved and sliced
  5 garlic cloves, crushed
  1 cup/8 fl oz (250 ml) bitter orange juice
  2 banana leaves
  4 lb (1.8 kg) cassava, peeled and cut into 1-inch (2.5-cm) chunks
  6 ripe plantains, cut into 1-inch (2.5-cm) chunks
  3 green plantains, into 1-inch (2.5-cm) chunks
  3 tomatoes, peeled and cut into strips
  1 red bell pepper, cored, seeded, and cut into strips
  1 green bell pepper, cored, seeded, and cut into strips
  2 cups/16 fl oz (475 ml) water
  salt and ground pepper

  For the cabbage salad
  ½ white cabbage, shredded
  4 tomatoes, peeled, seeded, and diced
  2 tablespoons vinegar
  juice of 2 limes
  salt

Place the beef strips in a bowl and season with salt and pepper. Add the onions, garlic, and orange juice. Cover and marinate in the refrigerator overnight.
  Line the bottom of a pan with the banana leaves, large enough to fold over and enclose the ingredients, and thick enough so the water won't drain out. Add a circle of cassava chunks around the edges of the pan, followed by the plantains, and finally the meat in the middle. Cover with the tomatoes, bell peppers, and the onions from the marinade. Enclose by folding over the banana leaves and pour the water around the sides. Bring to a boil and cook for 2 hours over medium heat, covered, then lower the heat and cook for a further 2 hours.
  Meanwhile, mix the cabbage with the diced tomatoes and season with the vinegar, lime juice, and salt.
  Once the *vaho* is cooked, remove the lid, unfold the banana leaves, and serve one piece of each ingredient per person, with the cabbage salad on top.

Beef

Shredded Beef in Spicy Tomato Sauce

Hilachas
Guatemala

Preparation time: 20 minutes
Cooking time: 1 hour 30 minutes

Serves: 8

Quite similar to *ropa vieja* found in parts of the Caribbean, *hilachas* is a tomato-based, shredded beef stew that's typical of the city of Salamá in the Guatemalan department of Baja Verapaz. Some serve it with crusty bread, which is used to soak up the sauce and thicken it, rather than adding flour.

> 2 lb (900 g) beef flank (skirt), cut into 2-inch (5-cm) chunks
> 1 white onion, sliced
> 2 cups/16 fl oz (475 ml) chicken stock
> 4 tomatoes, chopped
> 2 *guajillo* chiles, seeded
> 6 tomatillos, chopped
> 3 garlic cloves, minced
> 1 tablespoon annatto paste
> 1 tablespoon vegetable oil
> 1/2 teaspoon ground cumin
> 1 potato, peeled, cooked and cut into 1-inch (2.5-cm) cubes
> salt
> cooked white rice, to serve

Place the beef in a medium pan with the onion, and season with salt. Cover with the chicken stock (if necessary, add more water) and cook for 45 minutes to 1 hour, or until tender. Remove the meat from the cooking stock, reserving the stock, and let cool before shredding.

Add the tomatoes, chiles, tomatillos, and garlic to the cooking stock, and cook for 20 minutes over medium heat. Add the contents of the pan to a blender, with the annatto paste, and blend well for 1 minute on high speed.

In a pan, heat the oil over medium heat, then pour in the blended mixture. Add the cumin and let reduce for 10 minutes. (If the sauce is too thin, you can add 2 tablespoons flour and whisk well to prevent the lumps.) Add the shredded meat and potato, and stir. Check the seasoning.

Serve hot, with rice on the side.

Stir-Fried Beef and Potatoes

Lomo saltado
Peru

Preparation time: 15 minutes
Cooking time: 10 minutes

Serves: 2

Beginning in the mid-nineteenth century, Chinese laborers from Guangdong province came to work on coastal plantations after the abolition of slavery, and in the 1920s the first *chifas*, the Chinese restaurants now ubiquitous across Peru, started to appear on Calle La Concepción in what is now Lima's Barrio Chino. It was here that *lomo saltado*, a simple beef stir-fry, was served alongside other Cantonese dishes. Over the ensuing decades as the dish migrated outside the *chifa* and into Peruvian kitchens, which quietly absorbed the use of soy sauce and cooking with woks, native ingredients like potatoes and *ají amarillo* were incorporated into the recipe.

> 1 lb (450 g) beef sirloin, cut into strips
> 1/2 cup/4 fl oz (120 ml) vegetable oil
> 1 red onion, thickly sliced
> 2 *ají amarillo*, seeds removed and sliced
> 4 tomatoes, cut into quarters
> 1/4 cup/2 fl oz (60 ml) soy sauce
> 4 tablespoons white vinegar
> 1/2 cup/4 fl oz (120 ml) beef stock
> 1/2 cup/3/4 oz (20 g) chopped chives
> 1 tablespoon chopped cilantro (coriander)
> salt and ground pepper
> cooked white rice and French fries, to serve

Season the beef with salt and pepper.

Heat the oil in a wok over high heat. When hot, stir-fry the beef for 5 minutes, or until well seared. Add the onion, chiles, and tomatoes, and continue stirring briskly for no more than a minute. Pour in the soy sauce and vinegar with the beef stock and let bubble for 1 minute. Check the seasoning, then stir in the chives and cilantro (coriander).

Serve hot with rice and French fries on the side.

Rolled Steaks

Niños envueltos
Argentina, Chile, Uruguay

Preparation time: 20 minutes
Cooking time: 55 minutes

Serves: 4

Translating as "wrapped children," *niños envueltos* are like a Cono Sur, or Southern Cone, version of pigs in a blanket, though not nearly as lazy. Some variations wrap and cook the meat with rice inside cabbage leaves.

> 2 lb (900 g) beef bottom round (silverside), cut into thin steaks
> 2 garlic cloves, minced
> 1 tablespoon chopped parsley
> 8 oz (225 g) cooked ham, cut into 1/3-inch (8-mm) slices
> 1 carrot, peeled and cut into thin sticks
> 3 tablespoons vegetable oil
> 1 cup/8 fl oz (250 ml) red wine
> 1 cup/8 fl oz (250 ml) beef stock
> grated nutmeg, to taste
> salt and ground pepper
> cooked white rice, to serve

Remove any extra fat from the steaks, season with salt and pepper, and rub with the garlic and parsley. Place a piece of ham and a piece of carrot in one of the edges of each and roll up the steaks. Spear them with toothpicks to secure.

Heat the oil in a frying pan over medium heat and sear the rolled steaks for 5 minutes on each side. Pour in the wine and let reduce for 5 minutes over high heat. Add the beef stock, then reduce the heat to low and cook for 40 minutes, rolling the *envueltos* every 10 minutes for even cooking. If the sauce reduces too much, add more stock. Season with salt, pepper, and nutmeg.

Serve warm, with rice on the side.

Dark Beef Roast

Asado negro
Venezuela

Preparation time: 20 minutes
Cooking time: 3 hours 30 minutes   Serves: 7

Served during holidays in Caracas, *asado negro* is a fatty roast that is slow cooked in caramel and served beneath a thick, dark sauce. Serve with *Tostones* (Fried Plantains, page 194) or white rice.

    2 lb 8 ounces (1.1 kg) beef bottom round (silverside)
    4 garlic cloves, crushed
    ¹/₂ cup/4 fl oz (120 ml) vegetable oil
    1 cup/7 oz (200 g) grated *papelón* (panela sugar; or use light muscovado)
    1 white onion, coarsely chopped
    3 *ají dulce* chiles
    6 tomatoes, peeled, halved, and seeded
    1 cup/8 fl oz (250 ml) red wine
    1 cup/11 oz (320 g) *malta* (malt beer)
    salt and ground pepper

Season the beef all over with salt and pepper. Rub a quarter of the garlic over the meat and set aside.

Heat the oil in a medium pan over medium heat, then add the sugar and let it caramelize for 4 minutes. Place the beef in the pan and sear well for 5 minutes on each side, stirring the sugar to prevent it from burning. Add the onion, remaining garlic, chile, and tomatoes. Continue stirring, season with salt and pepper and pour the wine, *malta* (malt beer), and enough water to cover the meat. Cover the pan and cook over low heat for 3 hours.

Remove the meat from the liquid in the pan, and let cool down, then cut into slices and place back into the pan. Continue cooking over low heat for 10–15 minutes, until the sauce thickens.

Serve the slices hot, with the sauce on the top.

Beef Salad

Salpicón de res 🔲
El Salvador, Guatemala, Honduras, Mexico, Nicaragua

Preparation time: 20 minutes,
plus 30 minutes chilling   Serves: 8
Cooking time: 1 hour

Found in parts of Mexico and Central America, *salpicón de res* is a finely chopped or shredded beef salad and used as a topping for *tostadas* or to stuff peppers.

    4 lb (1.8 kg) beef flank (skirt), cut into 2-inch (5-cm) chunks
    2 garlic cloves, crushed
    1 white onion, chopped
    ¹/₂ cup/¹/₂ oz (15 g) chopped mint
    5 radishes, chopped
    ¹/₂ cup/4 fl oz (120 ml) lime juice
    salt and ground pepper
    chopped cilantro (coriander), to serve

Place the meat in a medium pan and add enough water to cover, a pinch of salt, and the garlic. Bring to a boil and cook for 20 minutes, then lower the heat and skim the foam off the top. Add half the onion and simmer for 30 minutes. Once the meat is completely cooked, remove from the water and let cool. Finely chop the cold meat and place in a bowl.

Add the mint, radishes, and the remaining onion. Season with the lime juice, salt, and pepper. Mix well and refrigerate for at least 30 minutes before serving.

Serve cold, garnished with cilantro (coriander).

Uruguayan Beef and Noodle Soup

Ensopado
Uruguay

Preparation time: 10 minutes
Cooking time: 40 minutes,   Serves: 4
plus 15 minutes resting

Typical in rural areas in the interior of Uruguay, the *ensopado* is a humble mix of meats and noodle soup served on summer days that's reminiscent of the *puchero* (Stew Pot, page 259), but with more liquid.

    2 tablespoons vegetable oil
    1 white onion, chopped
    2 garlic cloves, minced
    ¹/₂ red bell pepper, seeded and chopped
    1 carrot, peeled and chopped
    1 lb 8 ounces (680 g) beef flank (skirt), cut into 1-inch (2.5-cm) chunks
    3¹/₂ oz (100 g) bacon, cubed
    3 tablespoons tomato paste (purée)
    1 leek, sliced
    ¹/₂ sweet potato, cut into 1-inch (2.5-cm) chunks
    2 ears of corn, cut into 2-inch (5-cm) chunks
    1 lb (450 g) short pasta

Heat the oil in a pan over medium heat. Once hot, add the onion, garlic, and bell pepper, and sauté for 5 minutes, then add the carrot and stir. Add the meat with the bacon to the pan and sear well on every side. Add the tomato paste (purée) and season with salt.

Pour enough water to cover all the ingredients and stir, then add the leek, sweet potato, and corn. Cook for 20 minutes over medium heat until the vegetables are soft, then add the pasta and cook for a further 12 minutes.

Check the seasoning, remove from the heat, and let rest for 15 minutes.

Serve warm in soup dishes.

Beef Salad

Dried Beef

There is a long history of drying meat for preservation in the Andes. Partial carcasses or cuts of meat from llamas, alpacas, guanacos, and game were preserved through exposure to sun, wind, smoke, or salt to make *charqui*, a word later adapted to "jerky" elsewhere in the world. This meat could last for days, weeks, and months beyond the slaughter of an animal. When cattle were introduced into the region and up until the adoption of refrigeration in the nineteenth century, dried and salted beef was the first real industry in countries like Argentina and Uruguay. While exact preparations vary from region to region, the practice is widely used as a means to preserve meat, and the products are integral to countless recipes.

Sun-Dried Beef

Carne-de-sol 🔲
Brazil

Preparation time: 10 minutes, plus 2 days of curing and drying

Serves: 10

With no access to refrigeration in the hot, semi-arid, windy landscape in northeastern Brazil, *carne-de-sol* was a practical solution for what to do with freshly slaughtered beef or goat meat before it spoiled. The name is somewhat misleading as the meat is usually hung in a covered place. The process gives the meat a salty exterior, though the interior remains quite tender in most cases, and slabs of it are often grilled like fresh meat. It can be shredded or chopped and is used in a wide variety of dishes in the *sertão*, the Brazilian backcountry.

    2 lb (900 g) sirloin or rump steak
    1 cup/7 oz (200 g) coarse salt
    3 tablespoons panela sugar (or use light muscovado)

Remove any excess fat or sinew from the meat, then cut into three equal-sized pieces. Use a mortar to crush the coarse salt and mix it with the sugar. Place the meat on a dish and cover with the salt and sugar mix on all sides. Cover the dish with a clean tea towel and place in the refrigerator overnight, or for a minimum of 8 hours.

Remove the meat and use a clean tea towel to wipe away any excess salt and sugar. Once clean, take 3 medium hooks and hang each piece by one end in a clean and open space, for 1 day. Remove the meat from the hooks, cover with a clean tea towel, and refrigerate until use.

Semi-Dried Salted Beef

Tasajo
Mexico

Preparation time: 10 minutes, plus 4–6 hours resting
Cooking time: 5 minutes

Serves: 4

In the Pasillo de Humo inside Oaxaca's 20 de Noviembre market, clouds of smoke waft from a narrow passageway lined with wood-fired grills. A flurry of hawkers waving menus encourage passersby to pick out their cuts and go take a seat at one of the tables

at one end. There are plump, red chorizos and adobo-marinated cecina, or salted pork, but the stand-out choice are the sheets of beef draped over the grills, called *tasajo*, which have been pounded thin and cured in salt for hours before being grilled. In the market they serve it as is, with tortillas on the side, but in homes around Oaxaca, it's often stewed with onions, tomatoes, and chiles. It's also used to top *tlayudas* (thin toasted tortillas) and *memelas* (thin masa cakes).

    2 lb 8 ounces (1.1 kg) flank (skirt) steak
    6 tablespoons salt

Slice the steak as thinly as possible, about ¼ inch (5 mm) thick. Place on a cutting board and, using a meat tenderizer, pound the slices to as thin as possible, without breaking the meat. You should be able to see through parts of it. Set the meat on a plate and sprinkle with the salt on both sides. Let sit in a cool place for 4–6 hours.

Prepare a grill (barbecue) to high heat and, when hot, place the *tasajo* on it. Sear quickly, just a minute or two each side.

Shredded Sun-Dried Beef with Cassava Flour

Paçoca de carne seca
Brazil

Preparation time: 15 minutes, plus 1 hour soaking
Cooking time: 1 hour 40 minutes

Serves: 4

In the seventeenth century, this adaption of *carne-de-sol* was used by *tropeiros*, the muleteers taking caravans of goods into the interior of the country. Crushed in a *pilão*, or mortar, then sautéed with onions, garlic, and cassava flour, it was a quick meal made with little effort and ingredients that travel well. It's sometimes served alongside white rice, braised cabbage, plantain purée, or boiled cassava.

    1 lb (450 g) *Carne-de-sol* (Sun-Dried Beef, see opposite)
    ½ teaspoon clarified butter
    1 white onion, chopped
    2 garlic cloves, minced
    ⅓ teaspoon *Farofa* (Toasted Cassava Flour, page 98)
    salt

Cut the *carne-de-sol* into cubes and soak for 1 hour in a bowl of iced water. Drain.

Add ¼ teaspoon of the clarified butter to a pan over medium high heat, then add the meat. Cook for 3 minutes, stirring continuously. Add 1 cup of water and reduce the heat to low and cook for 1 hour, or until tender, adding more water if needed. Drain the meat and let cool.

Shred, or use a mortar to crush the meat well, for 5–10 minutes.

Heat a frying pan over medium heat and add the remaining clarified butter, followed by the onion. Sauté for 10 minutes, then add the garlic and cook for a further 5 minutes, stirring frequently.

Add the shredded or pounded meat, lower the heat, and cook for 15 minutes. Finish by adding the *farofa* and cooking for 2 minutes.

Season with salt and serve.

Sun-Dried Beef

Sunny Beef

Carne asoleada
Honduras

Preparation time: 10 minutes,
plus 9 hours marinating and drying
Cooking time: 10 minutes

Serves: 5–6

This variation of Honduran *carne asada*, where the beef is hung to cure for hours after sitting in a marinade, adds a concentration of flavor and a layer of texture to the exterior of the meat that you wouldn't get from just grilling it. Note: In Panama, there's a preparation of dried meat also called *carne asoleada*, though it's more of a form of smoking meat over a fire that's found in rural areas throughout Latin America.

2 lb 8 ounces (1.1 kg) flank (skirt) steak
3 garlic cloves, peeled
¼ cup/2 fl oz (60 ml) olive oil
½ cup/4 fl oz (120 ml) bitter orange juice
1 teaspoon annatto paste

Cut the steak into slices ½ inch (1 cm) thick.
Blend the garlic with the oil, orange juice, and annatto paste in a blender for 2 minutes on high speed. Add salt and rub the mixture on the steaks and let marinate for 1 hour. Then, using hooks, leave the steaks hanging in the open air for at least 8 hours. Once the meat is dry, remove it from the hooks.
When ready to cook, prepare a grill (barbecue) and when hot, add the meat and cook for about 3–5 minutes each side.

Beef Tongue

Intimidating to some, *lengua*, or beef tongue, is a relatively easy meat to cook, and is prepared in dozens of ways across the region. Slow cooked, the fatty meat can become quite tender. In Latin America you will find it in stews, pickled, on tacos, or sliced thin like a deli meat and used in sandwiches.

Tongue in Vinaigrette

Lengua a la vinagreta
Argentina, Paraguay, Uruguay

Preparation time: 20 minutes,
plus overnight marinating
Cooking time: 1 hour

Serves: 4

Cooked, sliced thin, and pickled, *lengua a la vinagreta* is commonly served as a quick meal, alongside salads and potatoes, in small restaurants and *bodegones* throughout the Río de la Plata area.

8 cups/4 pints (1.9 liters) water
1 lb (450 g) beef tongue
1 garlic clove, minced
1 white onion, minced
1 tablespoon finely chopped parsley
1 teaspoon finely chopped red bell pepper
4 tablespoons olive oil
¼ cup/2 fl oz (60 ml) white wine vinegar
2 eggs, hard-boiled and chopped

Add the water to a medium pan, with salt, and bring to a boil. Add the tongue and simmer for 1 hour, or until tender. Remove from the water and let cool to warm, then use a small knife to peel off the skin. Thinly slice the tongue and set aside.
For the marinade, mix the garlic, onion, parsley, bell pepper, oil, vinegar, and eggs together in a bowl, and season with salt and pepper.
Place the sliced tongue on a plate, spread the marinade on top of the slices and refrigerate overnight.
Serve cold or at room temperature, with some of the marinade on top.

Stewed Tongue

Lengua guisada 🍲
Panama

Preparation time: 20 minutes
Cooking time: 3 hours 30 minutes

Serves: 4

In homes and casual restaurants called *fondas* around Panama, beef tongue is most often stewed until tender in a rich sauce.

1 beef tongue, cleaned and trimmed
5 cups/2½ pints (1.2 liters) water
2 leeks, white parts only, finely chopped
1 white onion, chopped
3 garlic cloves, minced
1 bay leaf
1 green bell pepper, cored, seeded, and diced
3 carrots, peeled and diced
2 tomatoes, peeled and diced
2 cups/16 fl oz (475 ml) white wine
2 cups/16 fl oz (475 ml) beef stock
2 tablespoons olive oil
1 teaspoon dried thyme
8 oz (225 g) peas, blanched
1 tablespoon chopped parsley
salt and ground pepper
cooked white rice, to serve

Fill a medium pan with water, and salt, and bring to a boil. Add the tongue and simmer for 1 hour, or until tender. Remove from the water and let cool to warm, then use a small knife to peel off the skin.
Add the tongue back to the pan with the measured water, leeks, onion, garlic, bay leaf, bell pepper, carrots, and tomatoes. Place over low heat and cook for 1½–2 hours. Take out the tongue and cut it into 1-inch (2.5-cm) slices.
Pour the cooking liquid from the pressure cooker into a blender, add the wine and beef stock, and blend until smooth.
Heat the oil in a pan over medium heat and sear the tongue slices for 2 minutes each side. Pour the blended mixture into the pan, add the thyme, and season with salt and pepper. Lower the heat and simmer for 30 minutes, then add the peas. Check the seasoning. Mix in the chopped parsley.
Serve hot, with rice on the side.

Stewed Tongue

Offal

Achura, or offal, needs more care and love than the average cut of steak that can be just seasoned and tossed on a grill, yet for many they are the best parts of the animal, offering up an immense display of different flavors and textures.

Sweetbreads

Mollejas ⬚
Argentina, Paraguay, Uruguay

Preparation time: 10 minutes
Cooking time: 25 minutes

Serves: 10

Of all the *achura*, or offal, of an asado, perhaps none excite a meat aficionado as much as *mollejas*, or sweetbreads. Made of the soft, white thymus glands of a calf, which comes in two parts, the more desired heart and the throat, they are relatively simple to prepare. When done right, they have a slightly crispy exterior and a delicate flavor.

10 sweetbreads
6 cups/50 fl oz (1.5 liters) cold water
1 cup/8 fl oz (250 ml) white vinegar
2 tablespoons salt
2 limes, 1 juiced and 1 cut into wedges
salt

Start by heating a charcoal grill (barbecue). On an Argentine-style *parrilla*, you would lift the grate to mid-height and have a consistent, medium heat.

Rinse the sweetbreads well and place them in a pan with the water, vinegar, and salt. Bring to a boil over high heat, then reduce to a simmer and cook for about 10 minutes. Drain, and place the sweetbreads in a bowl of iced water. Once cold, remove the sweetbreads from the water and pat dry gently.

Season the sweetbreads with salt and place on the grill for about 5 minutes, then flip, season again, and cook for a further 5 minutes. Before removing from the grill, sprinkle the sweetbreads with the lime juice.

Serve hot, with the lime wedges.

Beef Heart Skewers

Anticuchos de corazón
Bolivia, Peru

Preparation time: 20 minutes,
plus at least 3 hours marinating
Cooking time: 10 minutes

Serves: 8

When night falls in Lima, charcoal grills are set up on sidewalks and in parking lots. Skewered three to a *palito* (bamboo skewer), beef hearts, cut into chunks and seasoned with garlic, *ají panca*, pepper, vinegar, cumin, and salt, are grilled, just a few minutes per side, as they are brushed with more marinade. A small boiled potato and a chunk of large-kernel corn are served with an order, along with spicy sauces based in native chile peppers, like *rocoto* or *ají amarillo* with *huacatay* (Peruvian black mint). Some vendors have grown cult followings and sell out of meat not long after the first

orders are filled. These *carretillas*, or street carts, started to appear on Lima's streets as early as the 1830s, though the origins of the recipe date back far earlier. While conquistadores found Quechua people in the highlands cooked skewers of meat over open fires, the modern version of *anticuchos* can be traced to the time of slavery in Peru, when slaves in hacienda kitchens would make use of offal meats that would otherwise be thrown out. It is usually served with corn on the side.

1 beef heart
1 cup/9 oz (250 g) *ají panca* paste
2 tablespoons roasted garlic paste (purée)
$1/4$ cup/2 fl oz (60 ml) red vinegar
1 tablespoon dried oregano
1 teaspoon ground cumin
$1/2$ cup/4 fl oz (120 ml) vegetable oil
salt and ground pepper

Start by cleaning the beef heart, cutting off any fat and sinew. Cut into $1^1/2$-inch (4-cm) cubes and skewer onto wooden skewers, 3 to a skewer. Place in a dish or tray.

In a blender, mix the *ají panca* with the garlic paste (purée), vinegar, oregano, and cumin for 2 minutes on medium speed, while pouring in the oil. Season with salt and pepper, and pour the mixture onto the skewers, making sure to cover the meat completely. Marinate for at least 3 hours, even better overnight, in the refrigerator. Remove the skewers from the refrigerator 1 hour before cooking.

Prepare a grill (barbecue) over high heat. Cook the skewers over direct heat for 3–4 minutes each side, brushing them continually with the marinade as they cook.

Serve hot, with hot sauce on the side.

Grilled Beef Intestines

Chinchulines
Argentina, Paraguay, Uruguay

Preparation time: 10 minutes,
plus 2 hours soaking
Cooking time: 25 minutes

Serves: 5–6

It's said that small beef intestines, called *chinchulines*, were first used on a grill in Patagonia during the winter, when the isolated location forced them to be used. Slow to cook, they are usually one of the first cuts of meat to be used during an *asado*.

1 lb (450 g) small beef intestines
8 cups/64 fl oz (1.9 liters) water
2 tablespoons white vinegar
$1/2$ cup/4 fl oz (120 ml) lemon juice
coarse salt

Wash the intestines and soak them for 2 hours in a bowl with the water and vinegar. Drain, rinse and pat dry, then cut into 5-inch (12-cm) lengths.

Prepare a charcoal grill (barbecue) to medium heat. Season the intestines with coarse salt and place on the grill, not directly over the flame. Cook for 15 minutes, or until crispy, then flip and cook for a further 10 minutes.

Remove to a plate, drizzle the lemon juice over them, and serve warm.

Sweetbreads

Brazilian Beef Offal Stew

Panelada
Brazil

Preparation time: 20 minutes
Cooking time: 2 hours 30 minutes   Serves: 6

For *panelada*, found throughout Brazil, intestines, and occasionally tripe and other offal meats, are slowly simmered in a rich sauce that masks the sometimes funky smell associated with cooking beef innards.

1 lb (450 g) beef intestines
1 lb (450 g) beef tripe
2 bay leaves
2 tablespoons olive oil
1 white onion, chopped
4 garlic cloves, minced
1 red bell pepper, cored, seeded, and chopped
2 tomatoes, peeled and chopped
1 tablespoon crushed chile flakes
1 tablespoon annatto paste
1 tablespoon chopped parsley
salt and ground pepper

Cut the intestines and tripe into 1-inch (2.5-cm) squares, then place them in a medium pan and cover with cold water. Bring to a boil over high heat, then add the bay leaves and simmer for 2 hours, stirring occasionally, or until the meat is tender. Remove from the heat and let cool until the fat floats to the surface. Skim off the fat, and reserve the liquid and meat.

Heat the oil in another pan, add the onion, and sauté for 10 minutes over medium heat. Add the garlic and bell pepper and cook for a further 10 minutes, then add the tomatoes and, once it starts boiling, add the drained meat with 1 cup/8 fl oz (250 ml) of the cooking stock. Add the chile flakes and annatto paste, and season with salt and pepper. Bring to a boil, then stir in the parsley.

Serve hot.

Ecuadorian Tripe Stew

Guatita, papas con librillo
Ecuador

Preparation time: 20 minutes
Cooking time: 2 hours 30 minutes   Serves: 6

Served on the weekends throughout Ecuador, *guatita* is a tripe stew made with peanuts and other spices, and thickened or served over potatoes.

2 lb (900 g) beef tripe
3 scallions (spring onions)
2 garlic cloves, minced
1 tablespoon chopped parsley
10 cups/80 fl oz (2.4 liters) water
2 tablespoons vegetable oil
1 teaspoon annatto paste
1/2 white onion, chopped
1 *ají amarillo*, cored, seeded, and chopped
4 oz (120 g) unsalted peanuts, toasted
6 cups/50 fl oz (1.5 liters) milk
1 tablespoon chopped cilantro (coriander)
4 lb (1.8 kg) potatoes, peeled
2 hard-boiled eggs, chopped
salt and ground pepper

Rinse the tripe under cold water, then soak for 15 minutes. Place in a pan with the scallions (spring onions), garlic, and parsley. Cover with the measured water and bring to a boil. Reduce the heat to low and cook for 2 hours, or until the tripe is soft. Drain and coarsely chop.

In a pan, heat the oil with the annatto paste over medium heat. Add the onion and *ají amarillo*, and sauté for 10 minutes.

Meanwhile, process the peanuts in a blender for 2 minutes or until it becomes a paste (you can add a little of the milk to help it mix better). When the onion and *ají amarillo* are soft, add the peanut paste, milk, and tripe to the pan. Sprinkle in the cilantro (coriander) and season with salt and pepper. Simmer for 25 minutes over low heat, stirring occasionally.

While the stew is simmering, boil the potatoes in salted water. Drain and cut into chunks, then keep warm.

Remove the stew from the heat and stir in the chopped eggs. Place the warm potato pieces on a plate and pour the tripe stew over.

Serve warm.

Tripe Stew

Brazil: *dobradinha*; Costa Rica, Nicaragua, Venezuela: *sopa de mondongo*; El Salvador: *sopa de pata*; Mexico: *menudo*; Panama: *mondongo a la culona*; Peru: *cau cau*

Preparation time: 30 minutes
Cooking time: 2 hours   Serves: 6

Versions of tripe stewed with vegetables are found throughout Latin America. They are flavorful recipes, which are rarely the same, even within a particular region. They're said to cure hangovers. The following is a basic tripe stew. You can keep it as is or add additional seasonings and ingredients based on the desired region. For instance, for Mexican *menudo*, add hominy and chiles. For Peruvian *cau cau*, you'll want potatoes, *ají amarillo* paste, and turmeric. For Brazilian *dobradinha*, be sure to add white beans. For a Salvadoran *sopa de pata*, don't forget chayote and cow feet. For some Central American versions, you can toss in chickpeas and chorizo.

1 lb (450 g) honeycomb beef tripe
2 bay leaves
1 tablespoon olive oil
1/2 white onion, chopped
2 garlic cloves, minced
1 teaspoon dried cumin
2 lb (900 g) potatoes, peeled, boiled, cut into chunks
2 tablespoons chopped cilantro (coriander)
salt and ground pepper
cooked white rice, to serve

Rinse the tripe under cold water, then soak for 15 minutes. Place in a pressure cooker with the bay leaves, and add cold water to cover (around 8 cups/64 fl oz/1.9 liters). Season with salt and pepper and cook over medium heat for 1 1/2 hours from when full pressure is reached, or until the tripe is soft. Release the pressure and open the lid. Drain the tripe, reserving 6 cups/50 fl oz/1.5 liters of the cooking stock. Cut the tripe into 1/2-inch (1-cm) squares.

Heat the oil in a pan over medium heat. Add the onion and garlic, then sauté for 10 minutes, or until well colored and soft. Add the tripe and reserved stock. Add the cumin, season with salt and pepper, and cook for 10 minutes. Add the potato pieces and cook for a further 15 minutes. Stir through the cilantro (coriander).

Serve warm, with rice on the side.

Colombian Oxtail Stew

Guiso de cola
Colombia

Preparation time: 20 minutes,
plus overnight marinating
Cooking time: 4 hours

Serves: 6

While it's sometimes more bone than meat, the fatty meat that does surround the tail of cattle can become beautifully tender and add complex flavors to a stew when braised slowly. *Guiso de cola*, not nearly as spicy as other oxtail recipes in the region, is the kind of stew that sticks to your ribs. A typical weekend meal in the Colombian Andes, it is usually served with rice or boiled cassava or potatoes.

    4 lb (1.8 kg) oxtail, sliced
    1 white onion, chopped
    3 scallions (spring onions), white part only, chopped
    4 garlic cloves, minced
    3 cups/25 fl oz (750 ml) beef stock
    1 cup/6 oz (170 g) chopped tomatoes
    2 carrots, peeled and roughly chopped
    4 potatoes, peeled and cut into chunks
    1/2 teaspoon ground cumin
    1/4 teaspoon annatto paste
    1/4 cup/1/3 oz (10 g) chopped cilantro (coriander)
    salt and ground pepper

In a large bowl, season the oxtail with salt and pepper, then add the onion, scallions (spring onions), and garlic. Refrigerate overnight, mixing occasionally.

Transfer the mixture to a large pan and add the beef stock; if the meat is not covered, top up with cold water to cover. Bring to a boil over high heat, then reduce the heat, cover, and simmer for 2 hours. Add the tomatoes and continue cooking for 1 1/2 hours, stirring occasionally. Add the carrots, potatoes, cumin, and annatto paste, stir well, and simmer, covered, for a further 30 minutes, or until the ingredients are soft. Finish by mixing in the cilantro (coriander). Check the seasoning.

Serve hot.

Tacna-Style Spicy Offal Stew

Picante a la tacneña
Peru

Preparation time: 20 minutes,
plus 20 minutes soaking
Cooking time: 2 hours 30 minutes

Serves: 4

This spicy offal stew hails from the department of Tacna in the far south of Peru near the border with Chile. Prior to the introduction of cattle and other European ingredients, a form of this thick, fragrant stew was made with the innards of camelids, like guanacos and llamas.

    1 cow's foot
    1 lb (450 g) beef tripe
    7 oz (200 g) shredded *charqui* (dried llama meat or beef jerky)
    2 tablespoons olive oil
    1/2 white onion, chopped
    3 garlic cloves, minced
    1/2 cup/4 1/4 oz (125 g) *aji panca* paste
    1 teaspoon ground cumin
    1 teaspoon dried oregano
    2 lb (900 g) potatoes, peeled, boiled, and cut into chunks

Place the cow's foot and tripe in a pan of salted water. Place over high heat, bring to a boil, then lower the heat and simmer for 2 hours, or until the tripe is tender and the meat of the foot detaches easily from the bone. Drain, reserving 3 cups/25 fl oz (750 ml) of the cooking stock. Remove the meat from the foot, and cut the tripe into long slices.

In a frying pan over medium heat, toast the *charqui* for 2 minutes each side, then place in a bowl of iced water and let soak for 20 minutes. Drain.

Meanwhile, heat the oil in a pan over medium heat, add the onion and garlic, and sauté for 10 minutes. Add the *aji panca*, cumin, and oregano, and season with salt and pepper. Stir, then add the reserved cooking stock, the *charqui*, the meat from the foot, tripe, and potatoes and cook for a further 15 minutes. Check the seasoning.

Serve hot.

Guyanese Pepperpot

Guyanese pepperpot ☐
French Guiana, Guyana, Suriname

Preparation time: 20 minutes
plus overnight marinating
Cooking time: 2 hours 30 minutes

Serves: 8

The secret ingredient in this rich Guyanese stew is the molasses-like cassareep, a black liquid made by reducing the juice extracted from bitter cassava that has been flavored with spices. It acts as a browning agent and adds a beautiful burnt sugar flavor to the meat in the stew. Originally, the thick sauce was used by indigenous communities to not just flavor meat but preserve it for multiple days during long river journeys or hunting excursions. Early forms of pepperpot consisted of game meats, fish, or vegetables being simmered with cassareep in clay pots over open fires, and the recipe was adapted throughout the southern Caribbean, as well as New England in the US. It has been known to be kept in pots for indefinite lengths of time, even years, just adding more cassareep whenever more meat is added. Today, it's mostly eaten on Christmas Day or on holidays in Guyana and is usually served with rice or roti.

1 lb (450 g) oxtail, sliced
1 lb (450 g) bottom round (silverside), cut into 1-inch (2.5-cm) chunks
1 garlic clove, minced
1 white onion, diced
1 teaspoon fresh thyme leaves
1 teaspoon salt
1 teaspoon ground pepper
1 teaspoon brown sugar
2 scallions (spring onions), chopped
2 wiri wiri chiles, whole (or use scotch bonnet)
½ cup/4 fl oz (120 ml) cassareep
1 cinnamon stick
2 tablespoons chopped parsley

Mix the oxtail and pork in a large bowl with the garlic, onion, thyme, salt, and ground pepper, and set aside in the refrigerator to marinate, ideally overnight.

Place a heavy pan over medium heat. When hot, add the sugar and continue stirring until it caramelizes and begins to turn a deep brown, about 4 minutes. Add the beef chunks and brown for about 5–6 minutes, stirring occasionally. Remove from the pan and set aside. Repeat the process with the oxtail until brown. Set aside.

Add the marinade mixture, scallions (spring onions), and chile. Cook for about 5 minutes, then pour in half the cassareep, mix and continue cooking for about 2 minutes. Return the oxtail to the pan and add enough water to cover, along with the cinnamon stick. Bring to a boil, then reduce the heat and simmer for 40 minutes. Return the beef chunks to the pan, along with the other half of the cassareep. If necessary, add more water (it shouldn't be above the meat). Continue cooking for 1 hour 30 minutes, or until the meats are tender and the sauce is thick. Check the seasoning.

Serve hot, garnished with chopped parsley.

Cow's Foot Soup

Caldo de mocotó, cowheel soup, sopa de pata de vaca
Belize, Brazil, Guyana, Panama

Preparation time: 20 minutes
Cooking time: 4 hours 30 minutes

Serves: 6

There's debate as to whether slaves working in Charqueadas in Rio Grande do Sul were the first to heavily season cow's feet for *caldo de mocotó*, or if it was an adaptation of a Portuguese recipe from early settlers. However, in the rural, often impoverished, corners of Brazil, this fatty stew was born out of necessity, utilizing a cut that was sold for nearly nothing or just given away. In places like the *sertão* (backcountry), *caldo de mocotó* was the food of survival, and its comforting flavors have been ingrained in Brazil's national memory. Similar preparations of cow's foot soups, though with different seasonings, can be found in Caribbean-facing countries, such as Belize, Guyana, and Panama.

2 lb (900 g) cow's feet, cleaned and cut into rounds (by the butcher)
juice of 1 lime
1 white onion, chopped
2 garlic cloves, minced
½ cup/¾ oz (20 g) chopped cilantro (coriander), plus extra to serve
3 tablespoons chopped parsley
2 tablespoons chopped mint
1 *malagueta* chile
2 teaspoons ground annatto
2 teaspoons ground cumin
1 tablespoon tomato paste (purée)
6 cups/50 fl oz (1.5 liters) water
salt and ground pepper
chopped scallions (spring onions), to serve

Place the cow's feet pieces in a large pan and add cold water to cover. Season with salt and add the lime juice. Bring to a boil over high heat, then discard the liquid and clean the pan. Rinse the feet pieces and return them to the pan. Cover again with water, bring to a boil over high heat, then reduce to a strong simmer and cook for 3–4 hours, until the feet pieces are tender. Strain, reserving the cooking stock, and let cool.

Meanwhile, add the onion, garlic, cilantro (coriander), parsley, mint, chile, annatto, cumin, and tomato paste (purée) to a blender. Add ½ cup/4 fl oz (120 ml) of the reserved cooking stock and process until smooth.

Separate the meat from the bones and cut it into large chunks.

In a large pan, mix the remaining cooking stock with the water, meat, and the blended mixture, and bring to a boil over medium heat. Reduce to a simmer and cook for a further 30 minutes, adding more water depending on the desired thickness. Season with salt and pepper.

Serve in soup bowls, with chopped cilantro and scallions (spring onions).

Guyanese Pepperpot

Pork

The highway winds west from San Salvador, passing through whitewashed colonial towns and rolling green hills of coffee plantations. A heavy rain has just stopped and steam rises from the pavement in the town of Juayua, where a woman with a white apron stands beside a table on the sidewalk beneath a flowered umbrella, as she has done for decades. A dozen pots and canisters are laid out in front of her, covered with paper towels. She crosses two pieces of banana leaf and forms them into a bowl with a plastic bag at the bottom. She scoops *chicharrón*, salty chunks of pork fried with the fat and skin left on, and places it in the center of the green leaves alongside strips of fried cassava. From another bowl, she scoops out *curtido*, a lightly fermented slaw, and drops it over the meat before handing it to the first of a growing line of clients who arrive as the clouds above dissipate.

The *conquistadores* introduced pigs in the 1500s and they were quickly absorbed across the region. Different breeds that were brought intermingled and adapted to different landscapes, creating distinct new breeds. It's hard to imagine the region without them now, as their versatile meat is used in innumerable ways. Its skin is fried in enormous cauldrons, its innards are stewed, its feet are pickled, and lard is used for frying. It's roasted whole on spits or in a *caja china*. It's turned into sausages and cooked with flowers or layered on sandwiches with slices of sweet potato. Mayan communities marinate it in citrus and spices and bury it in steaming hot pits. If this is what can be done here with pork in 500 years, just imagine what will happen in 500 more.

Pork Cracklings

Chicharrón, torresmo
Various

Preparation time: 10 minutes,
plus 1 hour salting
Cooking time: 1 hour

Serves: 8

The definition of *chicharrón*, or *torresmo* in Portuguese, expands and contracts as you move around Latin America. It's made almost everywhere there are pigs, and at its basic understanding it signifies fried pork. In some countries that signifies only fried pork skin, while in others—Brazil, Colombia, and Peru—it might also mean fried chunks of pork, usually with the skin and fat attached. In some places, like Bolivia, it's pork ribs, cooked in their own fat.

> 4 lb (1.8 kg) pork belly, skin attached
> 1 cup/9 oz (250 g) sea salt
> 1 tablespoon lard
> 2 garlic cloves, crushed
> 2 bay leaves
> 2 limes, cut into wedges, to serve

Rub the pork belly with the salt and let sit for 1 hour.
Rinse well under cold water, pat dry, and cut into roughly 2 x 1/2-inch (5 x 1.5-cm) chunks.
In a heavy pan, melt the lard over medium heat. Once hot, add the garlic and bay leaves. Stir well for 2 minutes, then add the pork belly. Reduce the heat to low and cook for 45 minutes, turning the meat every 15 minutes.
Increase the heat and sear every side of the pork pieces over high heat for a further 15 minutes. Remove the pork and cut it into smaller chunks.
Serve hot with lime wedges.

Nicaraguan Pork Tenderloin

Lomo de cerdo pinchado
Nicaragua

Preparation time: 20 minutes,
plus 20 minutes resting
Cooking time: 2 hours

Serves: 6

The word *pinchado* means pricked or punctured, and in this case, it's a method to help the meat absorb the marinade. In Nicaragua, pork recipes, such as this one, are usually eaten during the Christmas season.

> 2 white onions, chopped
> 2 red bell peppers, cored, seeded, and cut into strips
> 2 chayotes, cored and chopped
> 1 celery stalk, chopped
> 1 carrot, peeled and chopped
> 2 tablespoons vinegar
> 1 teaspoon annatto paste
> 3 lb (1.4 kg) pork tenderloin
> 1/2 cup/4 oz (115 g) butter
> 5 potatoes, peeled and diced
> 2 tomatoes, peeled and chopped
> 1 cup/8 fl oz (250 ml) water
> sugar, to taste
> salt and ground pepper
> cooked white rice, to serve

In a bowl, mix the onions, bell pepper, chayotes, celery, and carrot. Add the vinegar and annatto paste, and season with salt and pepper. Cut large incisions into the pork and cover it with vegetable mix, getting as much into the incisions of the pork as possible. Let rest for 20 minutes.
Melt the butter in a large pan over medium heat, then add the pork and sear for 5 minutes each side, or until golden brown. Add the rest of the chopped vegetables, the potatoes, tomatoes, and water. Lower the heat, cover, and cook for 1 hour and 45 minutes, or until the meat is soft. Check the seasoning: if it's too acidic, add a pinch of sugar and salt.
Remove the pork from the pan and cut into slices. Serve warm, with rice on the side.

Brazilian Sausage with Cassava

Linguiça com mandioca, chouriço com mandioca
Brazil

Preparation time: 10 minutes
Cooking time: 35 minutes

Serves: 4

The pairing of cassava with fatty cured pork sausages like *linguiça*, seasoned with garlic and paprika, or the mildly seasoned *chouriço*, which is sometimes made with blood like morcilla, is Brazil's idea of sausage and potatoes. It's eaten for breakfast or as a snack at a *botequim*.

> 1 lb 8 ounces (680 g) cassava, peeled
> 1 tablespoon butter
> 1 lb (450 g) *linguiça* or *chouriço*, sliced
> 1/2 red onion, chopped
> 1/2 white onion, chopped
> 2 garlic cloves, crushed
> 2 tablespoons chopped parsley
> 6 chives, chopped
> salt and ground pepper

Place the cassava in a medium pan and cover with water. Bring to a boil, then reduce the heat and simmer for about 20 minutes, or until tender. Drain and cut into chunks.
In a large pan, melt the butter over medium heat, then fry the sausage for about 5 minutes. Add the onions and garlic and sauté for 6 minutes. Add the cassava, parsley, and chives, and cook for a further 4 minutes. Season with salt and pepper.
Serve warm.

Brazilian Sausage with Cassava

Spicy Pork Stew

Fricasé
Bolivia

Preparation time: 20 minutes,
plus overnight soaking
Cooking time: 3 hours 15 minutes

Serves: 6

This spicy, meaty stew, strikingly similar to a Mexican *pozole*, is usually served in the mornings in the Bolivian Andes. Dating back to the colonial period, it's an adaptation of a French fricassee, using local ingredients like chile, *chuño*, and *mote*.

    8 oz (225 g) dried *mote* (Andean hominy)
    12 oz (340 g) *chuño* (freeze-dried potatoes), peeled
    3 lb (1.4 kg) pork loin (with skin)
    4 cups/32 fl oz (1 liter) water
    1 teaspoon fresh oregano leaves
    3½ tablespoons *ají amarillo* paste
    1 teaspoon dried cumin
    4 garlic cloves, minced
    2 tablespoons breadcrumbs (optional)
    salt and ground pepper

Put the *mote* in a bowl, add cold water to cover, and soak overnight. Do the same with the *chuño* in another bowl. Cook for the *mote* for 40 minutes in its soaking water in a pan over medium heat (if needed, adding more water to completely cover the kernels), or until the kernels open. Drain and set aside.

Meanwhile, rinse the *chuño* for as long as it takes for the water to run clear, then add to a pan of boiling, salted water and cook for 20 minutes, or until soft. Drain and set aside.

Cut the pork loin into 2½-inch (6-cm) pieces. Rinse with iced water and place in a pan. Cover with the measured water , season with salt, add the oregano, and bring to a simmer, then reduce the heat to low. Cook for 1½–2 hours or until tender.

Prepare the spices for the meat by placing the *ají amarillo* paste, cumin, garlic, lime juice, and pepper to taste in a blender. Process well.

When the meat is cooked, pour in the spice mixture. Continue cooking over medium heat for 20 minutes. If the sauce is too thin, add the breadcrumbs. Stir well and cook for 15 minutes.

Serve the *mote* and *chuños* on a plate with pieces of pork and the warm sauce spooned over.

Ground Cassava Leaves with Pork

Maniçoba
Brazil

Preparation time: 20 minutes
Cooking time: 5 days

Serves: 10

While the leaves of the cassava plant, called *maniva*, can be quite tasty, they also contain cyanide, which is why they need to be finely ground and boiled for about a week to be able to eat. As *maniçoba*, a cassava leaf and pork stew made in the Brazilian states of Pará and Bahia, takes days to prepare, it's usually done in large batches (this is a small one!) and served at family gatherings or festivals.

    6 lb (2.7 kg) cassava leaves
    1 lb (450 g) bacon, cut into 1-inch (2.5-cm) chunks
    1 lb (450 g) *Carne-de-sol* (Sun-Dried Beef, page 264, for homemade)
    1 lb (450 g) *linguiça calabresa*, sliced
    1 lb (450 g) *chouriço*, sliced
    1 lb (450 g) *paio* (Brazilian cured sausage), sliced
    1 lb (450 g) lard
    1 lb (450 g) ham, cut into 2-inch (5-cm) chunks
    1 lb (450 g) pork loin, cut into 2-inch (5-cm) chunks
    1 lb (450 g) pork tail, cut into 1-inch (2.5-cm) chunks
    1 lb (450 g) pig ears
    8 garlic cloves, minced
    ground pepper
    cooked white rice, to serve
    Farofa (Toasted Cassava Flour, page 98), to serve

Remove the veins and stems from the cassava leaves, then rinse them. Grind them as fine as possible in whatever way you are able: blending in batches, grinding in a hand mill or a meat grinder, or pounding in a wooden mortar. Place the pulp in a large pan and cover with water. Bring to a boil, then reduce the heat to a light simmer and continue cooking for at least a full day. Note: When cooking at night you can turn off the burner, though during daylight hours you want to continue simmering until the evening and picking back up again in the morning. When necessary, add more water to keep the leaves completely covered.

After 1 day, add the bacon to the cassava pulp. Bring to a boil, then lower the heat and continue simmering for a further 2 days, adding more water when needed.

On the fourth day, add the other meat pieces to the stew. Simmer for 1 more day, adding water when needed.

On the morning of the fifth day, add the garlic and ground pepper. Boil for 6 hours or until the meat is tender. Check the seasoning. Serve warm with rice and *farofa*.

Paulista Lunch Plate

Virado à paulista
Brazil

Preparation time: 20 minutes,
plus 6 hours soaking
Cooking time: 1 hour 15 minutes

Serves: 8

In São Paulo, the *virado à paulista* is what you eat for your work lunch, often on Mondays, and is meant to fill you up for the day. It's usually an inexpensive *prato feito*, or special, at restaurants in the Centro, combining lots of simple foods that have been around since the colonial era.

    2½ cups/22 oz (625 g) dried black beans
    9 cups/3½ pints (2 liters) water
    7 oz (200 g) bacon, chopped
    1 white onion, chopped
    2 *linguiça*, cut into 1-inch (2.5-cm) chunks
    5 garlic cloves, minced
    1 cup/5 oz (140 g) cassava flour
    8 pork chops
    2 tablespoons chopped parsley
    2 tablespoons olive oil
    2 tablespoons butter
    salt and ground pepper

    To serve
    sautéed kale
    8 fried eggs
    cooked white rice
    ripe plantain, peeled, sliced, and fried

Place the black beans in a bowl, add water to cover and soak for 6 hours, or overnight. Drain the beans and add to a medium pan with the measured water, and some salt. Bring to a boil and cook for 10 minutes, then reduce to a simmer and cook, covered, for about 50 minutes, until tender. Drain, reserving half the cooking water, and divide the beans into 2 equal parts.

Add one part of the beans to a blender and process on medium speed for 1 minute with enough of the reserved cooking water to make a soft paste.

Heat a pan over medium heat and add the bacon. Stir well for 8 minutes, or until well seared. Add the onion, linguiça, and half the garlic. Continue cooking for 5 minutes. Add the puréed beans and the whole beans, then the cassava flour. Stir well, and season with salt and pepper. Cook over low heat, stirring occasionally.

Meanwhile, season the pork chops with the remaining garlic, salt, pepper, and the parsley. In a frying pan, heat the olive oil and sear the chops for 5 minutes each side, or until golden brown.

To serve, place one pork chop on each plate, with some kale, beans with sausage, a fried egg, rice, and fried plantain slices.

Pig's Head and Entrail Stew

Revolcado
Guatemala

Preparation time: 20 minutes
Cooking time: 3 hours 30 minutes   Serves: 6

This earthy, red stew that dates to the colonial period in Guatemala is made from the leftover parts of a pig, namely the head, though often other pieces of offal, such as entrails, heart, and liver too.

        1 pig's head
        8 oz (225 g) pig entrails
        3 black peppercorns
        8 oz (225 g) tomatillos, quartered
        2 lb (900 g) tomatoes, quartered
        1 white onion, chopped
        3 *pasilla* chiles, seeded
        1 *guaque* chile
        4 garlic cloves, crushed
        1 tablespoon ground annatto
        salt
        12 Corn Tortillas (page 136, for homemade), to serve

Rinse the pig's head and entrails in cold water. Once clean, place them in a large pot, cover with water, add salt and the peppercorns, and cook over medium heat for 2 hours 30 minutes, topping up the water when needed so they stay covered.

Remove the head and entrails from the pot, detach the meat from the bones of the head and cut it and the entrails into approximately 1½-inch (4-cm) pieces and set aside.

In a dry frying pan, cook the tomatillos and tomatoes for 10 minutes over medium heat. Repeat the process separately with the onion, chiles, and garlic. Add all the toasted ingredients to a blender with the annatto and process on medium speed until it is a smooth paste, adding a little water if needed. Pour the paste into a pan over medium heat and stir, then add the meat and the entrails and cook for 15 minutes. Check the seasoning.

Serve hot with tortillas on the side.

Ecuadorian Fried Pork

Fritada
Ecuador

Preparation time: 15 minutes
Cooking time: 1 hour 35 minutes   Serves: 6

The *fritada*, chunks of pork that have been boiled and then fried in their own fat, is served in small traditional restaurants called *huequitos* and roadside stalls around Ecuador, though especially the sierra. Side plates are particular to every cook, though might include *llapingachos* (Ecuadorian Potato Pancakes, page 86), potatoes, *mote*, fava beans, or hunks of cheese.

        5 garlic cloves, minced
        1 white onion, coarsely chopped
        2 teaspoons salt
        ¼ teaspoon ground pepper
        ¼ teaspoon ground cumin
        2 cups/16 fl oz (475 ml) water
        2 lb (900 g) pork belly, cut into 2-inch (5-cm) squares

Place all the ingredients except the pork in a large heavy pan over high heat. When the water starts to boil, add the meat to the pan. Lower the heat and simmer for 1 hour, stirring occasionally, or until the water is completely absorbed. Continue cooking the pork in its own fat until golden brown on all sides, about 35 minutes.

Serve hot.

Izote Flowers with Chorizo

Flor de izote con chorizo
El Salvador

Preparation time: 10 minutes
Cooking time: 25 minutes   Serves: 4

Throughout Central America, flowers, such as bright red *pito* or pink *madre cacao* flowers, are often integral to some recipes, not merely consumed as garnishes. In El Salvador, the white petals of izote flowers, which grow on the spineless yucca cactus (*Yucca elephantipes*), often used as an ornamental plant, are used quite a bit. They might be stewed, fried with eggs, pickled, or used to fill *pupusas*. Please note that it's important to only use the petals, as the pistils and stamen can be quite bitter.

        8 cups (2 liters) izote flower petals
        2 tablespoons olive oil
        1 white onion, chopped
        3 garlic cloves, minced
        10 cherry tomatoes, halved
        ½ jalapeño pepper, cored and chopped
        1 lb (450 g) chorizo, cut into 1-inch (2.5-cm) pieces
        cooked white rice, to serve

Bring a pan of water to a boil, add the petals and cook for 5 minutes. Drain and set aside.

In a large pan, heat the oil over high heat, add the onion and garlic and sauté for 5 minutes. Add the tomatoes and jalapeño, then lower the heat to medium and cook for 5 minutes. Add the chorizo, lower the heat again and cook for 3 minutes. Add the boiled petals and cook for a further 3 minutes over low heat. Mix well.

Serve warm, with rice on the side.

Las Tablas-Style Chorizo

Chorizo tableño
Panama

Preparation time: 40 minutes,
plus overnight marinating
Cooking time: 4 hours 10 minutes

Makes: 10

The colonial city of Las Tablas, amid the ranches and rainforest of the Azuero peninsula, is perhaps Panama's folkloric capital. Families in the surrounding villages are known for their spicy, smoked pork sausages that are red from the annatto inside. They are usually fried in their own fat and eaten with corn tortillas and *queso blanco*, or chopped up and eaten with rice.

    1 lb (450 g) pork shoulder, finely chopped
    15 oz (425 g) pork belly, finely chopped
    3 garlic cloves, minced
    1 red onion, finely chopped
    1/2 red bell pepper, cored, seeded, and finely chopped
    1/2 tablespoon chopped culantro leaves (or use cilantro/coriander)
    1 tablespoon annatto oil
    1 *ají chombo*, cored, seeded, and chopped
    sausage casing, about 5 feet (1.5 m) in length
    salt and ground pepper

In a large bowl and using your hands, mix the meats with the garlic, onion, bell pepper, culantro, annatto oil, and chile. Season with salt and pepper, cover with plastic wrap (clingfilm), and marinate in the refrigerator overnight.
    The next day, prepare a grill (barbecue) or open fire.
    Soak the sausage casing in warm water for 30 minutes, then drain and place the open end over a sausage stuffing tube and push three quarters of the casing over it. Turn the stuffer on a slow setting and slowly guide the meat into the casing until it is fully stuffed, being sure not to stuff too tightly. Twist the sausage into 10 equal portions, tying the ends with kitchen string. Hang all the chorizos above the grill or fire and let smoke for a minimum of 4 hours.
    When the chorizos are ready, they will be soft on the inside, and tender. The annatto oil will cover the chorizos and they become bright red. Store in the refrigerator until use.
    To serve, cut the chorizos into slices and fry with no oil in a frying pan for 3 minutes over medium heat, or until browned on each side.

Rolled Pork Shoulder

Arrollado huaso
Chile

Preparation time: 20 minutes,
plus 5 hours marinating
Cooking time: 2 hours

Serves: 4

During Chile's colonial period, a *huaso* was considered a skilled horseman, a cowboy essentially, often seen wearing a poncho. By the twentieth century they had established themselves as an integral part of Chilean folklore, and this dish, which can be traced back to Spain, was named in homage to them. Different cuts of pork may be used and the outer layer, for example, might be either pork skin or *malaya*, part of the skirt.

    2 lb (900 g) pork loin
    7 oz (200 g) bacon
    1/2 cup/4 fl oz (120 ml) red wine vinegar
    1 teaspoon ground cumin
    1 tablespoon dried oregano
    1 tablespoon *merkén* (smoked chile powder)
    1 garlic clove, minced
    2 lb (900 g) pork skin (in a 10-inch/25-cm square)
    16 cups/32 fl oz (4 liters) beef stock
    cooked white rice, to serve

Cut the pork loin and bacon into strips 1 inch (2.5 cm) thick. In a bowl, mix the vinegar, cumin, oregano, *merkén*, and garlic. Season with salt and pepper. Add the meats and mix well. Marinate for at least 5 hours in the refrigerator.
    Lay the pork skin on a clean surface. Place the strips of bacon and pork loin on the bottom part of the skin and start rolling and pressing to shape into a cylinder. Tie at intervals to secure, using butcher's twine. Wrap the rolled pork in a clean tea towel, and close the ends so it is sealed inside, using additional twine if needed.
    Place the wrapped pork in a pan, pour over the beef stock, and place over high heat. Bring to a boil, then lower and simmer, covered, for 2 hours, turning the meat after 1 hour. Set aside in the stock until cool enough to handle.
    Remove the pork, open the tea towel, and cut the twine. Cut the pork into slices 1 inch (2.5 cm) thick.
    Serve warm, with rice.

Pork Spine and Bulgur Wheat Soup

Cuchuco de trigo con espinazo de cerdo
Colombia

Preparation time: 20 minutes
Cooking time: 1 hour 15 minutes

Serves: 8

Made in the highland departments of Cundinamarca and Boyacá in central Colombia, *cuchuco* is a hearty soup that dates to the Muisca people. The word *cuchuco* is a Chibcha word referring to broken grains, such as cracked corn or bulgur wheat, that occur during the milling process. Upon arrival of the Spanish, the soup transitioned into a fusion of Old and New World ingredients, where potatoes and fava beans were cooked with pork and wheat.

    2 lb (900 g) pork back bones, cut into 3-inch (7.5-cm) chunks
    3 scallions (spring onions), green part only, chopped
    8 oz (225 g) bulgur wheat
    3 garlic cloves, minced
    10 cups/5 pints (2.4 liters) water
    8 oz (225 g) potatoes, peeled and cut into chunks
    1 lb (450 g) *papas criollas*, washed (or use any small, yellow potato)
    8 oz (225 g) peas
    4 oz (120 g) fava (broad) beans
    5 cabbage leaves, sliced
    4 tablespoons wheat flour

Place the bones in a large pan with the scallions (spring onions), bulgur, and garlic. Cover with the water, bring to a boil over high heat and cook for 40 minutes. Remove the bones and add all the potatoes, the peas, and fava (broad) beans. Season with salt and pepper. Cook for 15 minutes over medium heat. Add the cabbage leaves, slowly stir in the flour, and return the bones to the pan. Lower the heat, cover, and cook for a further 20 minutes. Check the seasoning. Serve hot.

Pork Spine and Bulgur Wheat Soup

St. John's Stew

Estofado de San Juan
Chile

Preparation time: 20 minutes
Cooking time: 2 hours 15 minutes   Serves: 8

This stew from central and southern Chile is eaten primarily the night before St. John's Day, which coincides with the winter solstice in the Southern Hemisphere, the Mapuche New Year, called *Wiñoy Tripantu*. Initially, quail and other small game birds were included in the stew, which was served in clay dishes.

    2 tablespoons olive oil
    7 white onions, 3 chopped, 4 sliced
    ½ cup/3 oz (80 g) dried *guindas* (sour cherries)
    2 lb (900 g) smoked pork ribs, cut into individual ribs
    6 garlic cloves, chopped
    2 lb (900 g) smoked pork chops
    2 lb (900 g) smoked pork sausages, cut into 1-inch
    (2.5-cm) pieces
    3½ cups/29 fl oz (870 ml) white wine
    1¾ cups/14 fl oz (425 ml) white vinegar
    3 bay leaves
    1 teaspoon *merkén* (smoked chile powder)
    1 teaspoon ground cumin
    8 chicken thighs
    salt and ground pepper

Heat the oil in a frying pan over medium heat. Sauté the chopped onions for 10 minutes, or until soft. Set aside.
    In a heavy pan, layer the sliced onions, then the *guindas*, then the ribs, and top with the sautéed onions. Next add a layer of garlic, then the pork chops, and finally the sausage pieces. Pour in the wine and vinegar, add the bay leaves, *merkén*, and cumin, and season with salt and pepper. Bring to a boil, without stirring, place a lid on the pan, then lower and simmer for 1 hour 30 minutes. Add the chicken thighs and cook for a further 30 minutes, still covered. Check the seasoning.
    Serve hot.

Pork Ribs Dusted with Corn Flour

Chicharô hu'itî
Paraguay

Preparation time: 10 minutes
Cooking time: 30 minutes   Serves: 4

This heavy, morning meal is meant to provide enough energy to get someone through a full day of work in the fields. To make it, just three ingredients are often used. Pork, usually ribs, are doused in lime juice then baked, grilled, or fried, then coated in toasted corn flour. Fresh herbs like oregano can also be added.

    1 lb 8 ounces (680 g) pork ribs, separated and cut
    into 2-inch (5-cm) chunks
    ½ cup/4 fl oz (120 ml) lime juice
    8 oz (225 g) corn (maize) flour
    salt
    4 pieces of boiled cassava, to serve
    lime wedges, to serve

Season the pork ribs with salt and pour the lime juice over them. Heat a frying pan over medium heat and add the rib pieces and fry in their own fat for 20 minutes, or until golden brown, flipping occasionally.
    Meanwhile, toast the corn (maize) flour in a dry frying pan over medium heat for about 6 minutes, stirring occasionally. Reserve in a large bowl.
    Once cooked, add the ribs to the bowl and coat them well in the toasted corn flour.
    Serve hot with the boiled cassava, and lime wedges to squeeze over.

Meat and Hominy Stew

Mute
Colombia

Preparation time: 30 minutes,
plus overnight soaking   Serves: 6
Cooking time: 4 hours

Mute is sometimes used as a general term for any hominy soup in Colombia, though in the northern central Boyacá and Santander departments, it's more specific. It's a heavy stew utilizing different cuts of meat, corn, beans, vegetables, and pasta.

    ½ cup/3 oz (85 g) dried black beans
    ½ cup/3 oz (85 g) dried chickpeas
    1 lb (450 g) beef tripe, cut into 1-inch (2.5-cm) squares
    ½ cup/4 fl oz (120 ml) lime juice
    1 lb (450 g) pork ribs, cut into individual ribs
    1 lb (450 g) beef tenderloin, cut into 1-inch
    (2.5-cm) chunks
    1 lb (450 g) pork loin, cut into 1-inch (2.5-cm) chunks
    1 tomato, peeled and chopped
    2 scallions (spring onions), chopped
    ¼ cup/1 oz (30 g) chopped white onion
    1 garlic clove, minced
    ½ teaspoon ground cumin
    ¼ teaspoon ground annatto
    1 cup/3½ oz (100 g) peeled, chopped squash
    1 carrot, peeled and sliced
    4 potatoes, peeled and cut into ½-inch (1-cm) cubes
    1 cup/6 oz (170 g) hominy
    ½ cup/2½ oz (75 g) elbow macaroni
    salt
    1 tablespoon chopped cilantro (coriander), to serve

Place the beans and chickpeas in separate bowls. Cover with water and soak overnight. Drain.
    Rinse the tripe in iced water with the lime juice added, then place in a pan and cover with salted water. Bring to a boil, then lower the heat and simmer for 2 hours, or until soft. Drain and set aside.
    In a larger pan, add all of the meats together, including the cooked tripe, as well as the beans, chickpeas, tomato, scallions (spring onion), chopped onion, garlic, cumin, and annatto paste. Add enough water to cover and bring to a boil over high heat. Lower the heat and simmer for 1 hour 30 minutes, then add the squash, carrot, potatoes, and hominy and cook for a further 20 minutes. Finish by adding the pasta and cook for 8 minutes, or until all the ingredients are soft. Check the seasoning.
    Serve hot, with the chopped cilantro (coriander) scattered over.

Pork Ribs Dusted with Corn Flour

Crispy Pork, Rice, and Beans

Chifrijo
Costa Rica

Preparation time: 30 minutes,
plus 40 minutes marinating
Cooking time: 20 minutes
Serves: 4

In 1979, Miguel Cordero, the owner of Cordero's Bar in Tibás on the outskirts of San José, claims to have been the first to serve *chifrijo*, which is now found in nearly every cantina in Costa Rica. The name is a combination of the letters of its signature ingredients: *chi* for *chicharrón* and *frijo* for *frijoles*. The beans are usually *frijoles tiernos*, or red beans, though others are commonly used. The *chicharrón* can either be pieces of fried pork or the fried skin. It's eaten like nachos with tortilla chips and served with *chilera*, a homemade mixture of pickled vegetables. Over the last couple of decades, the preparations have mutated, and many versions include a base of rice and extra toppings like avocados.

1/2 tablespoon salt
1 teaspoon chile powder
1 teaspoon dried thyme
1 tablespoon dried oregano
4 tablespoons vegetable oil
8 oz (225 g) pork ribs, cut into 1-inch (2.5-cm) chunks
8 oz (225 g) pork leg, cut into 1-inch (2.5-cm) chunks

To serve
3 cups/13 oz (375 g) cooked white rice
3 cups/1 lb 10 oz (730 g) Refried Black Beans (page 172)
1 1/2 cups/13 oz (375 g) Pico de Gallo (page 404)
Corn Tortillas (page 136, for homemade)
1 avocado, halved, peeled, pitted, and sliced
lime slices
1 jalapeño pepper, sliced

In a bowl, mix the salt, chile powder, thyme, and oregano. Use this mix to season all the pork pieces and let marinate for 40 minutes.

Heat the oil in a frying pan over high heat. Add the pork and lower the heat to medium. Sear well for 20 minutes, until they become golden brown and crispy, flipping once. Remove to a plate lined with paper towels to absorb excess oil.

To serve, layer the rice first in small bowls, then the beans, pork, and *pico de gallo*. Serve with tortillas, and slices of avocado, lime, and jalapeño on the side.

Arabic Tacos

Tacos árabes
Mexico

Preparation time: 20 minutes,
plus at least 2 hours marinating
Cooking time: 15 minutes
Serves: 4

A restaurant serving Middle Eastern food called La Oriental, which opened in 1933 in front of Puebla's Cathedral, though has since moved, is believed the first to serve *tacos árabes*. While they intended to cook lamb, thinly sliced and spit-roasted shawarma-style on a *trompo* spit, it was expensive, so they switched to pork, which was readily available. The marinade for the pork remained the same as it was with lamb, though the yogurt-based sauces were replaced by chipotle sauce. Rather than a tortilla they use a flatbread called *pan árabe*, which is somewhere between pita and lavash. The recipe eventually moved to Mexico City, where it was adapted into *tacos al pastor*.

1 lb (450 g) pork loin, cut into thin strips
5 tablespoons vegetable oil
4 *pan árabe* flatbreads

For the marinade
1 white onion, sliced
1 cup/1 1/2 oz (40 g) chopped parsley
1 tablespoon dried oregano
3 bay leaves
2 tablespoons fresh thyme
2 garlic cloves, minced
1 teaspoon ground cumin
juice of 3 limes
2 teaspoons white vinegar
1/2 cup/4 fl oz (120 ml) water

For the sauce
5 tablespoons chipotle sauce
1 tablespoon dried oregano
2 garlic cloves, chopped
1 tablespoon tomato paste (purée)
4 tablespoons white vinegar
1 teaspoon salt

Place all the marinade ingredients in an oven dish, add the pork and mix, making sure all the meat is covered. Marinate in the refrigerator for at least 2 hours, or overnight.

Meanwhile, prepare the sauce by placing all the ingredients in a blender and blend well on high speed until you have a soft paste.

Heat the oil in a frying pan over high heat. Drain the meat from the marinade, add to the hot oil and cook for 10–15 minutes, stirring frequently.

To serve, place the meat in the middle of the *pan árabe* flatbreads and spread the sauce on top.

Pork

Crispy Pork, Rice, and Beans

Yucatán-Style Barbecued Pork

Cochinita pibil 🍲
Mexico

Preparation time: 20 minutes,
plus overnight marinating
Cooking time: 4 hours

✳ ⌀
Serves: 6–8

Cochinita refers to a whole baby pig, while *pibil* means "buried" in Mayan. While the traditional recipe calls for burying a whole pig and roasting it slowly in a hot, stone-lined pit, cooking just the shoulder on a grill or in the oven is more common in many small restaurants and home kitchens.

    6 tablespoons annatto seeds
    2 tablespoons dried oregano
    2 tablespoons black peppercorns
    1½ tablespoons ground ginger
    1½ teaspoons cumin
    1 teaspoon cloves
    2 tablespoons ground cinnamon
    1 teaspoon salt, plus extra to season, if needed
    12 large garlic cloves, roughly chopped
    1½ cups/12 fl oz (350 ml) bitter orange juice
    1 bone-in pork shoulder, 5–6 lb (2.2–2.7 kg), cut into
    3-inch (7.5-cm) wide sections
    6 banana leaves, rib removed and cut in half

    To serve
    pickled red onions
    habanero chile sauce
    Corn Tortillas (page 136, for homemade)

Put the annatto seeds, oregano, peppercorns, ginger, cumin, cloves, and cinnamon into a mortar (or spice grinder), and grind to a powder (work in batches if necessary).

In a blender, combine the ground spice mixture with the salt, garlic, and bitter orange juice. Blend until it forms a slightly gritty paste. Put the pork into a large bowl, pour over the marinade, mix, and refrigerate overnight.

Light a charcoal grill (barbecue) and let burn until the coals are hot and covered in ash (or preheat an oven to 325°F/165°C/Gas Mark 3).

Roast the banana leaves on the grill for 1–2 minutes to make them more pliable, then use them to line the bottom and sides of the roasting pan, overlapping them and letting them hang over the edges of the pan. Set the pork in the middle and slather the marinade over it. Fold the banana leaf edges over the meat. Use more banana leaves to cover the meat completely. Make sure the package is well sealed, so the liquid does not run out.

Set the pan on the grill (or in the oven) and close the lid. Cook until the meat is tender, about 3 hours 30 minutes–4 hours. To maintain an even temperature, add more charcoal regularly.

Season with salt, if necessary. Cut the largest pieces of meat into more manageable chunks for serving. You can even remove the bones.

Serve warm, with pickled red onions, habanero chile sauce, and corn tortillas.

Spicy Marinated Pork

Tatemado de Colima
Mexico

Preparation time: 25 minutes,
plus 3 hours marinating
Cooking time: 2 hours 45 minutes

✳ ⌀
Serves: 6

In Colima, *tatemado*, a spicy pork stew, gets its distinct flavor from coconut vinegar, which is made from fermented *tuba*, or coconut sap. If unavailable, Southeast Asian coconut vinegar or other mild vinegars, such as apple cider vinegar, can be substituted in a pinch.

    1 lb 8 ounces (680 g) pork shoulder, cut into chunks
    1 lb 8 ounces (680 g) pork ribs, cut into individual ribs
    ½ cup/4 fl oz (120 ml) coconut vinegar or apple
    cider vinegar
    6 *guajillo* chiles
    ½ teaspoon coriander seeds
    3 *ancho* chiles
    1 tablespoon lard
    3 garlic cloves, peeled
    ½ teaspoon ground cumin
    3 cloves
    ½ teaspoon ground pepper
    ½ tablespoon minced fresh ginger
    2 cups/16 fl oz (475 ml) water
    3 scallions (spring onions), white part only, halved
    ¼ teaspoon ground nutmeg
    salt

    To serve
    Corn Tortillas (page 136, for homemade)
    4 radishes, quartered

Mix the pork shoulder, ribs, vinegar, and some salt in a bowl and let marinate for at least 3 hours.

Preheat the oven to 350°F/180°C/Gas Mark 4.

Remove the cores of the *guajillo* chiles but retain the seeds. Toast the seeds with the coriander seeds in a dry frying pan over high heat for 8 minutes, moving the pan constantly to prevent the seeds burning. Tip into a mortar and crush. Set aside.

Bring a small pan of water to a boil over high heat, add the *ancho* and *guajillo* chiles, and blanch for 5 minutes. Drain and place in iced water. Remove and pat dry.

Heat the lard in a pan over medium heat and fry the chiles for 4 minutes each side, then place in a blender with the garlic, cumin, cloves, ground pepper, ginger, and crushed chile and coriander seed mixture. Add the water and blend to a paste, then strain.

Place the pork in an oven dish. Season with salt and cover with the blended chile paste. Cover the dish with aluminum foil and bake in the oven for about 2 hours, or until the meat is tender. Remove the foil and broil (grill) for 15 more minutes.

Place the scallions (spring onions) on top of the meat, sprinkle the nutmeg over them and broil (grill) for a further 5 minutes.

Serve warm, with corn tortillas and radishes on the side.

Yucatán-Style Barbecued Pork

Arequipa-Style Pork Stew

Adobo Arequipeño 🍲
Peru

Preparation time: 15 minutes,
plus overnight marinating
Cooking time: 1 hour 40 minutes

Serves: 6

Found throughout Latin America, though most commonly in Peru and Mexico, *adobos* are thick, pepper-based pastes that were used as a marinade for meats. When the Spanish arrived in the New World they introduced vinegar into the preparation, often replacing the *chicha*, or maize beer, that accompanied the chiles. In regions of Peru like Cusco and Arequipa, informal eateries called *picanterías*, serve their *adobos* rather soupy and they have a deep red color brought on by the dark *ají panca*.

- 2 lb (900 g) pork shoulder
- 1 tablespoon roasted garlic paste (purée)
- 3 tablespoons *ají panca* paste
- ¼ cup/2 fl oz (60 ml) red wine vinegar
- 4 cups/32 fl oz (950 ml) *Chicha de jora* (Corn Beer, page 388, for homemade)
- 8 tablespoons white onion paste (blended boiled onion)
- 4 allspice berries
- 1 tablespoon dried oregano
- 1½ cups/8 oz (225 g) thickly sliced red onion
- 1 *rocoto* chile
- salt and ground pepper
- fresh oregano leaves, to serve

Cut the pork into 4 equal parts and season with salt and pepper. Mix them in a bowl with the garlic and *ají panca* pastes, vinegar, *chicha de jora* (corn beer), and the onion paste. Ensure that the pieces are completely covered, and marinate in the refrigerator overnight, for at least 12 hours.

Place the pork and its marinade in a pan and add the allspice and oregano. Cover and bring to a boil over high heat, then lower the heat to low and simmer for 1 hour 30 minutes. Add the sliced onions, stir and cook for 5 minutes. Add the chile, increase the heat to a boil, and cook for 5 minutes. Remove the chile, stir well, and check the seasoning.

Serve hot, with fresh oregano leaves sprinkled over.

Pork and Dehydrated Potato Stew

Carapulcra
Peru

Preparation time: 20 minutes,
plus overnight soaking
Cooking time: 4 hours 30 minutes

Serves: 4

In its oldest form, *carapulcra* was a stew made of dehydrated chunks of potatoes, called *papas secas*, and dehydrated meat, called *charqui,* as well as peanuts, chiles, and other seasonings. These were foods that could be preserved for long periods of time and eaten well beyond the harvest season. After conquest, Old World ingredients were introduced into the recipe, such as pork and onions. It is often served with *Sopa seca* (Dry Soup, page 307) or white rice.

- 1 lb (450 g) *papas secas*
- 2 tablespoons lard
- 2 lb (900 g) pork ribs, cut into individual ribs
- ½ white onion, chopped
- 1 tablespoon garlic paste (purée)
- 1 tablespoon *ají mirasol* paste
- 2 tablespoons *ají panca* paste
- 2 cloves
- 1 small cinnamon stick
- ½ cup/4 fl oz (120 ml) red wine
- 2 cups/16 fl oz (475 ml) beef stock
- 4 tablespoons peanuts, chopped
- 1 teaspoon ground cumin
- 1 teaspoon ground oregano
- salt and ground pepper
- *Salsa criolla* (Creole Sauce, page 406), to serve

Place the *papas secas* in a bowl and cover with cold water. Let soak overnight.

In a clay pot or pan, heat 1 tablespoon of the lard over medium heat. Add the pork ribs and sear well for 5 minutes on each side, or until golden brown. Remove the meat from the pot and set aside.

Heat the remaining lard in the same pot, and sauté the onion for 8 minutes. Add the garlic paste (purée) and chile pastes and continue stirring. Add the cloves and cinnamon and continue cooking over medium heat for 10 minutes, or until it caramelizes.

Drain the *papas secas* and add to the pot, along with the pork ribs. Add the wine, stock, chopped peanuts, cumin, and oregano. Season with salt and pepper, lower the heat and cook, covered, for 4 hours. Check the seasoning and stir well.

Serve warm in soup bowls, garnished with the *Salsa criolla.*

Arequipa-Style Pork Stew

Pig's Feet

In the tradition of using every part of the animal in the region, *patitas*, or pig's feet or trotters, are used in dozens, if not hundreds of recipes. Their gelatinous meat can be pickled or used to flavor stocks or thicken sauces. Depending on the butcher, they might need to be cleaned before use, by pulling out or burning off the hairs.

Afro-Antillean Pig's Feet

Saus de patitas de puerco
Panama

Preparation time: 20 minutes,
plus 3 hours marinating
Cooking time: 25 minutes

Serves: 8

Saus, also spelled *sao* or *sous*, is an Afro-Antillean form of cooking pig's feet. The combination of the acidity, the spice of the *ají chombo*, and the fatty meat of the feet, is a surprisingly pleasant combination. It's usually served as an appetizer, often at festivals and gatherings.

    4 lb (1.8 kg) pig's feet, cleaned and halved
    (ask your butcher)
    2 cups/16 fl oz (475 ml) lime juice
    ³/₄ cup/6 fl oz (175 ml) white vinegar
    3 *ají chombo*, cored and chopped
    2 lb (900 g) cucumber, peeled and thinly sliced
    3 garlic cloves, minced
    2 white onions, sliced
    1 tablespoon chopped cilantro (coriander)
    salt

Place the pig's feet in a large pan and add enough cold water to cover. Bring to a boil and cook for 10 minutes, then drain. Remove any excess fat or blood. Add new water to cover, this time with salt. Bring to a boil and cook for 15 minutes. Remove the feet.
    Pour the lime juice and vinegar into a large bowl, then add the chiles, cucumber, garlic, and onions. Season with salt and add the pig's feet with the cilantro (coriander). Mix well and leave to marinate for at least 3 hours at room temperature.
    Serve warm in a bowl.

Pig's Feet with Peanut Sauce

Patita con maní 🍲
Peru

Preparation time: 15 minutes
Cooking time: 4 hours 5 minutes

Serves: 4

Spicy, fatty, and a little bit sweet, *patita con maní* is one of the great undiscovered dishes of Peruvian gastronomy. As occurred with *anticuchos* (page 268), *sangrecita* (page 308), and other dishes made from otherwise discarded animal parts, slaves during the Vice Royalty found a way to make pig's and cow's feet more delicious from the prime cuts that they were unable to eat. Snout, jowls, ears or other parts can be added into the stew too.

    1 lb (450 g) cow's feet
    2 pig's feet, cleaned
    2 tablespoons lard
    ¹/₂ white onion, chopped
    1 tablespoon roasted garlic paste (purée)
    2 tablespoons *ají panca* paste
    2 cups/16 fl oz (475 ml) beef stock
    1 teaspoon ground cumin
    1 teaspoon dried oregano
    ¹/₂ cup/2 oz (50 g) chopped peanuts
    2 lb (900 g) potatoes, peeled and cut into 1-inch
    (2.5-cm) cubes
    ¹/₄ cup/¹/₄ oz (8 g) chopped mint
    salt and ground pepper
    cooked white rice and salad, to serve

Cook the cow's feet in a large pan of salted water over medium heat for 3 hours. Take out the foot and remove the meat from the bone. Cut into ¹/₂-inch (1-cm) cubes and set aside.
    Place the pig's feet in a large pan and add enough cold water to cover. Bring to a boil and cook for 10 minutes, then drain. Remove any excess fat or blood. Add new water to cover, this time with salt. Bring to a boil and cook for 15 minutes. Drain, reserving 4 cups/ 32 fl oz (950 ml) of the cooking water. Cut the pig's feet into ¹/₂-inch (1-cm) cubes and set aside.
    In a clay pot or pan, heat the lard over medium heat, add the onion with the garlic and *ají panca* pastes and sauté for 8 minutes. Add the meat, beef stock, and reserved cooking water, then the cumin and oregano, and season with salt and pepper. Mix well and add the peanuts. Cook for 15 minutes over medium heat, then add the potatoes and cook for a further 15 minutes. Check the seasoning and stir in the mint.
    Serve hot in shallow bowls, with rice and salad on the side.

Pig's Feet with Peanut Sauce

Poultry

A little bit after 11am the first clientele starts to appear at a small *fonda* beneath the shade of a mamoncillo tree at the edge of a sidewalk on Avenida Perú in Panama City. The metal box is painted red and has roll-up windows and a few counter seats. Selling only *pollo frito* and *patacones*, it is one of just a few such *fondas* on the busy avenue that haven't been displaced by high rises.

Inside is a basic kitchen set up with a pot full of hot oil. The *fondero* drops a piece of chicken in and it bubbles inside the vat until crisp. He removes it with a metal skimmer and places it on a paper plate with some *patacones*, and slides it across the counter to a woman from a nearby office building who is waiting. She douses it with a bottle of hot sauce and takes a bite. This interaction between vendor and client will replay again and again, hundreds of times until the late afternoon.

While chickens likely didn't arrive to Latin America until after AD 1500, from both the east and the west almost simultaneously, you can wander through any urban area and the chances are you are not very far from someone cooking chicken. You'll see whole chickens spinning on rotisseries, shredded breast meat being put on tacos and tortas, and parts of hens (adult female chickens) stewing leisurely in a pot. Even their gizzards are skewered and grilled and their blood is seasoned and fried.

Small native turkeys and Muscovy ducks were domesticated in the region long before contact with the Old World, which can be seen in the depth of the recipes that utilize them. Latin America's native poultry are often stewed with herbs and vegetables or braised in lively sauces made of chiles and spices.

Disco Chicken

Pollo al disco
Argentina

Preparation time: 30 minutes
Cooking time: 1 hour 55 minutes,
plus 10 minutes resting

Serves: 12

Usually made in large quantities during an *asado*, *pollo al disco* is made in a *disco de arado*, a round pan that's about 24 inches (60 cm) wide and at least 6 inches (15 cm) in depth. It's like a larger, deeper, and sturdier paella pan (a good substitute) that was originally made from no longer used steel discs attached to the harrows of a plough, which could be set right on a wood fire. Vegetables, such as corn and potatoes, can be cooked alongside the chicken if desired.

    2 cups/16 fl oz (475 ml) vegetable oil
    3 whole chickens, each cut into 8 pieces
    3 lb (1.4 kg) white onions, chopped
    5 garlic cloves, minced
    1 red bell pepper, cored, seeded, and julienned
    2 lb (900 g) carrots, peeled and julienned
    10 scallions (spring onions), white part only, chopped
    9½ cups/4 pints (2.2 liters) red wine
    1 tablespoon crushed chile flakes
    1 tablespoon dried oregano
    3 bay leaves
    3 cups/25 fl oz (750 ml) chicken stock (if needed)
    3 tablespoons chopped parsley
    salt and ground pepper

Prepare a charcoal fire and, when ready, heat the *disco de arado*. Slowly pour half the oil into the pan in a spiral, covering the entire surface. Heat for 5 minutes, then add the chicken pieces. Cook for 30 minutes until seared, stirring with a large wooden spoon every 10 minutes to prevent sticking. Remove from the pan and set aside.

Pour the remaining oil into the pan and heat for 5 minutes before adding the onions, garlic, and bell pepper. Stir well and cook for 15 minutes until the onions are transparent, then add the carrots and scallions (spring onions), and continue cooking for 20 minutes, stirring frequently. Add the chicken back to the pan with the wine and mix well. Add the chile flakes, oregano, and bay leaves, and season with salt and pepper. Let cook for 40 minutes, stirring frequently and occasionally checking; if it is too dry, gradually add the chicken stock.

Remove the chicken, add the parsley to the sauce, and check the seasoning. Remove the pan from the heat and let it rest for 10 minutes to cool down.

Serve the chicken pieces warm with some of the sauce on the top.

Belizean Stewed Chicken

Ariran guisou, stewed chicken
Belize, Honduras

Preparation time: 30 minutes,
plus overnight marinating
Cooking time: 1 hour

Serves: 6

This heavily seasoned chicken stew is comfort food for Garifuna families in Belize and Honduras. There's no set recipe, just chicken stewed with whatever is in the pantry and growing in the garden. It's usually served with rice and beans or *Arroz con coco* (Coconut Rice, page 63).

    3 lb (1.4 kg) chicken legs and thighs, skin removed
    2 tablespoons coconut oil
    1 cup/8 fl oz (250 ml) chicken stock
    salt

    For the marinade
    ¼ cup/2 fl oz (60 ml) lime juice
    3 tablespoons Worcestershire sauce
    2 teaspoons sugar
    2 teaspoons ground pepper
    1 tablespoon annatto paste
    1 bay leaf
    2 teaspoons ground turmeric
    1 teaspoon ground cumin
    4 garlic cloves, minced
    2 white onions, sliced

In a large bowl, mix the marinade ingredients together. Season with salt and add the chicken pieces. Mix well with your hands, making sure all of the meat is covered. Cover the bowl and marinate in the refrigerator overnight.

Heat the coconut oil in a pan over medium heat. Add the chicken pieces a few at a time (reserving the marinade) and sear for 5 minutes each side, or until golden brown. Place on a plate once they are seared.

In the same pan, add the reserved marinade and cook for 5 minutes over medium heat, stirring. Add the chicken back to the pan with the stock. Bring to a boil, then reduce the heat, cover, and cook for a further 30 minutes.

Serve hot.

Brazilian Chicken Croquettes

Coxinha
Brazil

Preparation time: 1 hour
Cooking time: 1 hour 15 minutes   Makes: 25–30

Unlike the chicken nugget, which uses shredded chicken meat and is reshaped into parts that don't resemble actual pieces of chicken, the Brazilian *coxinha* is shaped like a drumstick. As the tale goes, in the late nineteenth century, one of the sons of Princess Isabel in the town of Limeira would only eat chicken thighs. One day, lacking chicken thighs but having plenty of other chicken parts, the house cook shredded the meat and shaped it into a thigh. The young prince approved, and the legend of the *coxinha* spread. Today, there are countless regional variations, adding fillings such as cheese, corn, peas, and even jackfruit.

    4 large potatoes or cassava, washed
    2 chicken breasts, boneless
    2 celery sticks, chopped
    ¹/₂ cup/³/₄ oz (20 g) chopped parsley
    4 cups/1 lb 2 oz (520 g) all-purpose (plain) flour
    1 tablespoon olive oil
    1 onion, finely chopped
    2 garlic cloves, finely chopped
    4 tomatoes, peeled and chopped
    2 eggs
    2 cups/3¹/₂ oz (100 g) breadcrumbs
    6 cups/50 fl oz (1.5 liters) vegetable oil (or other neutral oil)
    salt and ground pepper

Place the potatoes and chicken in a large pan with enough water to cover. Add the celery, parsley, and some salt. Cook over medium heat for 20 minutes, or until the potatoes are soft, and the chicken is fully cooked. Remove the potatoes and chicken from the pan and let cool before peeling and mashing the potatoes. Shred the chicken on a plate and season with salt and pepper. Reserve the cooking liquid.

In a bowl, mix the mashed potatoes with the flour. Season with salt and pepper and knead to a dough, using enough of the cooking liquid (about 3 cups/ 25 fl oz/750 ml) to bring it together, until smooth. Then divide into 25–30 balls and set aside.

For the filling, heat the olive oil in a frying pan over medium heat. Add the onion and garlic, and cook until translucent. Add the tomatoes and cook until dry. Incorporate the shredded chicken and adjust the seasoning.

Using your hands, flatten each dough ball into a disc. Put about 1 tablespoon of chicken filling in the center of each disc. Pinch the top of the dough to seal, then shape into a teardrop.

In a bowl, beat the eggs. Place the breadcrumbs in a separate bowl. Pass the balls through the egg and then place in the breadcrumb bowl to coat completely.

Pour the vegetable oil into a large, heavy pan, making sure it is no more than two-thirds full, and heat to 350°F/177°C. Fry the *coxinhas*, in batches, for about 8 minutes, until golden brown. Remove to a plate lined with paper towels to absorb excess oil.

Serve hot.

Chicken Pie

Empadão de frango, pastel de polvorosa
Brazil, Venezuela

Preparation time: 30 minutes,   Serves: 8
plus 20 minutes chilling
Cooking time: 50 minutes

From bakeries to home kitchens, double-crust chicken empanadas are found in some form in most of Latin America. They can be round like a pie or rectangular to the shape of a baking dish. They can be personal size or sliced by the piece. There's a mini, hand-held version in Brazil, the *empadinha*, which is a favorite at birthday parties.

    2 tablespoons olive oil
    2 onions, finely chopped
    2 garlic cloves, minced
    2 tomatoes, chopped
    2 lb (900 g) chicken breast, cooked and shredded
    ¹/₂ cup/2 oz (60 g) chopped green olives
    1 cup/5 oz (140 g) corn kernels
    1 cup/4¹/₂ oz (130 g) peas
    1 cup/7¹/₂ oz (210 g) chopped heart of palm
    1 cup/8 oz (225 g) tomato sauce (passata)
    1 tablespoon hot sauce
    2 cups/16 fl oz (475 ml) chicken stock
    5 cups/1 lb 7 oz (650 g) all-purpose (plain) flour, plus 1 tablespoon
    ¹/₃ cup/2¹/₂ fl oz (75 ml) milk
    ¹/₂ cup/³/₄ oz (20 g) chopped parsley
    4 egg yolks, separated
    12 oz (350 g) butter, cut into smaller pieces
    ¹/₂ cup/4 fl oz (120 ml) cold water
    salt and ground pepper
    cooked white rice and salad, to serve

In a large pan, heat the oil over medium heat. Add the onions and garlic and sauté for about 2 minutes, until translucent. Add the chopped tomatoes and cook until softened, then add the shredded chicken, olives, corn, peas, and heart of palm. Stir in the tomato sauce (passata) and hot sauce until combined, then add the stock. Dissolve the 1 tablespoon of flour in the milk and stir into the mixture. Lower the heat to medium-low and cook, stirring often, for about 10 minutes. The filling should be creamy and slightly thickened. Stir in the parsley and season with salt and pepper. Remove from the heat and allow to cool completely.

In a bowl, combine the flour with 1 teaspoon of salt. Add 3 egg yolks and stir. Add the butter, and use your fingers to work the butter into the flour until the mixture crumbles into small pieces. Add enough of the cold water, a few tablespoons at a time and working the dough with your fingers, for it to come together. Wrap the dough in plastic wrap (clingfilm) and chill for 20 minutes.

Preheat the oven to 350°F/180°C/Gas Mark 4.

Cut off one-third of the pastry dough and reserve. Roll out the remaining dough using a rolling pin to a round that is large enough to line the base and sides of a 9-inch (23-cm) springform pan. Press the dough into the bottom of the pan, using a fork.

Add the cold filling and distribute it evenly across the base. Roll out the remaining dough and place it on top of the filling, sealing the edges together. Using a fork, prick the top of the dough so steam can escape. Brush with the remaining lightly beaten egg yolk. Bake for 25–35 minutes or until golden brown.

Serve hot, with rice or salad.

Chicken with Okra

Frango com quiabo
Brazil

Preparation time: 20 minutes,
plus 40 minutes marinating
Cooking time: 1 hour

Serves: 6

Chicken, introduced to Brazil by the Portuguese, and okra, brought by slaves, were easy ingredients to find in Minas Gerais in the nineteenth century, when the transportation of food and supplies from other regions was limited. Simple stews like this, usually accompanied by cassava flour, were typical of the period and remain so.

2 lb (900 g) chicken thighs, skin removed
5 garlic cloves, minced
1 teaspoon annatto paste
2 tablespoons lime juice
3 tablespoons olive oil
1 lb (450 g) okra, cut into 1/2-inch (1-cm) pieces
1 white onion, sliced
1 tomato, peeled, seeded, and chopped
1 tablespoon chopped parsley
salt and ground pepper
cooked white rice, to serve

Place the chicken thighs in a bowl, add the garlic, and season with salt and pepper. In a small bowl, mix the annatto paste with the lime juice and pour it over the chicken. Cover with plastic wrap (clingfilm) and place in the refrigerator to marinate for 40 minutes.

Meanwhile, heat 1 tablespoon of the oil in a frying pan over medium heat, then add the okra and cook, stirring, for 20 minutes, until no longer slimy. Let cool and drain, retaining only the okra.

Heat the remaining 2 tablespoons of oil in a pan over high heat, add the onion and sauté for 15 minutes, until brown and caramelized. Add the tomato and chicken and sear the chicken for 5 minutes each side, or until golden brown. Pour enough hot water to half cover half the chicken, season with salt, cover, and simmer over medium heat for 20 minutes. Add the okra and mix well. Check the seasoning.

Finish by sprinkling over the parsley, and serve warm, with rice on the side.

Bahian Chicken Stew

Xinxim de galinha 🍲
Brazil

Preparation time: 20 minutes,
plus 30 minutes marinating
Cooking time: 45 minutes

Serves: 6

Xinxim de galinha is like a who's who of Bahian ingredients: *dendê* oil, shrimp, peanuts, coconut milk. Dedicated to the goddess Oxum in Candomblé rituals, it's one of the most iconic Afro-Brazilian dishes and is usually eaten alongside other regional dishes like *caruru de camarão* (Bahian Shrimp and Okra Gumbo, page 228) or *vatapá* (Bahian Shrimp Stew, page 228).

1 whole chicken (4–5 lb/1.8–2.3 kg), cut into pieces
2 tablespoons lime juice
4 garlic cloves, minced
1 teaspoon ground pepper
1/2 cup/4 fl oz (120 ml) *dendê* oil
2 white onions, chopped
2 tablespoons chopped cilantro (coriander)
1/2 cup/1 3/4 oz (50 g) toasted and chopped peanuts
1/2 cup/2 oz (60 g) chopped cashews
2 tablespoons minced ginger
4 oz (120 g) dried shrimp (prawns)
1 cup/8 fl oz (250 ml) coconut milk
salt

On a plate, season the chicken pieces with the lime juice, garlic, ground pepper, and some salt. Let rest at room temperature to marinate for 30 minutes.

In a large pan, heat the oil over medium heat. Add the chicken pieces and sear for 10 minutes each side, stirring occasionally.

Meanwhile, place the onions, cilantro (coriander), peanuts, cashews, and ginger in a blender. Mix well on medium speed until it forms a smooth paste. Add to the chicken with the dried shrimp (prawns) and cook over medium heat for 20 minutes, or until the chicken is cooked. Add the coconut milk and bring to a boil. Check the seasoning.

Serve warm.

Bahian Chicken Stew

Guatemalan Pumpkin Seed and Tomato Stew

Pepián de pollo
Guatemala

Preparation time: 40 minutes
Cooking time: 1 hour 10 minutes
Serves: 4

The most beloved of all the Guatemalan *recados*, or stews, *pepián* is a thick and meaty stew with a potent mix of spices that have been roasted prior to cooking. It's made in homes but also commonly served at markets and by street vendors, who serve it with rice and tortillas.

    1 whole chicken, about 3 lb (1.4 kg), cut into 8 pieces
    3 peeled onions, 2 quartered, 1 whole
    2 dried *guaque* chiles, seeded
    2 dried *pasilla* chiles, seeded
    1½ cups/7½ oz (210 g) *pepitas* (hulled squash or pumpkin seeds)
    ¾ cup/3¾ oz (110 g) sesame seeds
    6 black peppercorns
    6 cloves
    1 tablespoon dried oregano
    ½ cinnamon stick
    1 teaspoon coriander seeds
    3 garlic cloves, peeled
    9 tomatoes
    ¼ cup/2 fl oz (60 ml) water
    1 chayote, thickly sliced
    3 potatoes, peeled and cut into chunks
    2 tablespoons cilantro (coriander), coarsely chopped
    salt
    cooked white rice, to serve

Place the chicken in a large pan and add enough water to cover. Season with salt, add the quartered onions, bring to a boil, then simmer for 25 minutes.

Meanwhile, roast the dried chiles in a dry frying pan over medium heat for 10 minutes, flipping once, then place in a bowl. Repeat the process with the *pepitas* and sesame seeds, peppercorns, cloves, oregano, cinnamon, coriander seeds, and garlic in the same pan, then add them to the bowl.

Roast the whole onion in the same pan for 7 minutes or until golden. Mix with the chiles and seeds, and repeat the process with the tomatoes.

Tip all the roasted ingredients into a blender with the water. Mix for 2 minutes on medium speed to form a paste. Add the paste to the chicken pan when it has simmered for 25 minutes, and simmer for a further 20 minutes, or until the sauce reduces. Add the chayote and potatoes and cook for 10 minutes or until tender. The sauce must be thin and light.

Serve hot, with the cilantro (coriander) scattered over and rice on the side.

Colombian Chicken and Potato Stew

Ajiaco
Colombia

Preparation time: 20 minutes
Cooking time: 1 hour 45 minutes
Serves: 8

There are hearty stews of meats and potatoes called *ajiaco* in Colombia, Cuba, and Peru. All are adaptations of local dishes upon the arrival of the Spanish, though each is unique. In Colombia, it's a highland stew that combines chicken with three types of Colombian potatoes: *criolla*, *pastusa*, *sabanera* (these can be substituted with Russet, red, and Yukon Gold potatoes). If there's a flavor you can't quite pick out, it's probably the Andean herb *guascas* (*Galinsoga parviflora*), sometimes called potato weed or gallant soldier in North America, which has a flavor reminiscent of bay leaves.

    3 chicken breasts, skin removed
    2 cups/16 fl oz (475 ml) water
    3 ears of corn, each cut in half
    3 scallions (spring onions), white part only, chopped
    2 garlic cloves, minced
    3 cups/25 fl oz (750 ml) chicken stock
    3 *sabanera* potatoes, peeled and thickly sliced
    8 *criolla* potatoes, whole
    3 *pastusa* potatoes, peeled and thickly sliced
    5 tablespoons *guascas* (potato weed)
    3 tablespoons chopped cilantro (coriander)
    salt and ground pepper

    To serve
    capers
    avocado slices
    crema mexicana (or use sour cream)

Place the chicken and measured water in a large pan. Add the corn, scallions (spring onions), garlic, and stock. Season with salt and pepper, bring to a boil, then lower the heat, cover and simmer for 40 minutes, or until the chicken is cooked.

Remove the chicken, shred into small pieces and set aside. Continue cooking the vegetables for a further 30 minutes, then add the potatoes and *guascas* and cook for a further 30 minutes (if necessary, gradually add more water).

Check the seasoning and add the chicken back to the pan. Add the cilantro (coriander) and heat well.

Serve hot with capers, avocado, and *crema mexicana*.

Colombian Chicken and Potato Stew

Annatto Hen

Gallina achiotada 🔲
Costa Rica

Preparation time: 20 minutes
Cooking time: 1 hour   Serves: 4

One of the most traditional recipes from Guanacaste in the northwestern corner of Costa Rica, *gallina achiotada* is often made for holiday dinners and social gatherings. It is usually served with corn tortillas and hard-boiled eggs.

    1 whole chicken, about 5 lb (2.3 kg)
    2 culantro leaves
    4 garlic cloves, 2 crushed, 2 minced
    2 tablespoons lard
    8 potatoes, peeled and cut into ½-inch (1-cm) slices
    4 oz (120 g) bacon, chopped
    1 white onion, chopped
    1 habanero chile, cored, seeded, and chopped
    2 tomatoes, peeled and diced
    1 cup/8 fl oz (250 ml) chicken stock
    1 teaspoon dried oregano
    2 sprigs parsley
    1 sprig thyme
    1 cup/8 oz (225 g) butter
    2 tablespoons annatto paste
    salt and ground pepper
    Corn Tortillas (page 136, for homemade)

Place the chicken in a large pan and add enough water to come three-quarters of the way up the chicken. Add some salt, with the culantro leaves and crushed garlic. Bring to a boil over high heat, then lower the heat and cook for 15 minutes. Flip the chicken, then cook for a further 15 minutes.

Meanwhile, heat the lard in a separate pan over high heat. Add the potatoes, lower the heat, and cook, stirring, for 10 minutes. Add the bacon, onion, chile, tomatoes, and minced garlic, and sauté for 10 minutes. Add the stock and oregano, and season with salt and pepper, then cook for a further 15 minutes, or until the stock evaporates. Remove from the heat and set aside.

Remove the chicken from its pan and fill the neck end cavity with the potato mixture. Add the parsley and thyme sprigs and close the skin over the cavity with the help of toothpicks or twine to keep it in place.

Heat the butter in a large pan over medium heat. Add the annatto paste, stir well, place the chicken on its side in the pan and sear for 15 minutes, spooning the annatto butter over it. Flip the chicken onto its other side and repeat the process, until the chicken is cooked and tender.

Serve warm with corn tortillas and lime wedges.

Rooster Stew

Gallo en chicha
El Salvador, Guatemala

Preparation time: 20 minutes,
plus 8 hours marinating
Cooking time: 2 hours   Serves: 4

Eaten primarily for special occasions in El Salvador and parts of Guatemala, this dish braises rooster or chicken in corn beer, fruits, and panela sugar. The resulting sauce is sweet, sour, and a little bit funky in the best way possible. It's like a Salvadoran coq au vin. Made from corn and pineapple rinds, Salvadoran *chicha* is like a cross between Andean *chicha de jora* (Corn Beer, page 388) and *tepache* (Fermented Pineapple Drink, page 390). You can substitute with one or the other, or just beer or cider.

    2 tablespoons lime juice
    2 cups/16 fl oz (475 ml) Salvadoran *chicha*
    ⅓ cup/3½ fl oz (100 ml) apple cider vinegar
    3 garlic cloves, minced
    ½ teaspoon mustard seeds
    1 teaspoon ground pink pepper
    1 whole rooster or chicken, about 5 lb (2.3 kg), cut into 8 pieces
    3 tablespoons lard
    8 oz (225 g) pork ribs
    3 cloves
    1 *chile dulce* chile, cored and chopped
    1 cup/8 fl oz (250 ml) white wine
    2 cups/10½ oz (300 g) chopped plums
    2 cups/10 oz (280 g) raisins, chopped
    3 potatoes, peeled and cubed
    1 cinnamon stick
    8 bay leaves
    4 tomatoes, peeled, seeded, and diced
    2 carrots, peeled and grated
    salt and ground pepper

In a bowl, mix the lime juice, *chicha*, apple cider vinegar, garlic, mustard seeds, and pink pepper. Season with salt, rub the mixture over the chicken pieces, cover, and marinate for 8 hours (or overnight) in the refrigerator.

Heat 2 tablespoons of the lard in a large pan over high heat. Remove the excess marinade from the chicken (reserve all the marinade) and add the pieces to the pan. Reduce the heat to medium and cook the chicken for about 5 minutes each side, or until browned. Remove from the pan and set aside.

In the same pan, heat the remaining tablespoon of lard and repeat the searing process with the pork ribs. Add the chicken back to the pan with the ribs, and add the cloves, chile, and the reserved marinade. Cover, bring to a boil (if necessary, add a cup of hot water), then reduce the heat and simmer for 1 hour.

Add the wine, plums, raisins, potatoes, cinnamon, bay leaves, tomatoes, and carrots. Stir well and let cook for a further 40 minutes over low heat. Check the seasoning.

Serve warm in deep plates.

Annatto Hen

Salvadoran Chicken and Onions

Pollo encebollado
El Salvador

Preparation time: 15 minutes,
plus 30 minutes marinating
Cooking time: 55 minutes

Serves: 6

You would be pressed to find a Salvadoran who, upon tasting this recipe for chicken smothered in onions, doesn't get transported into their mother's or grandmother's kitchen with a pot of *pollo encebollado* simmering on the stove and releasing its sweet aromas into the air. For *bistec encebollado*, just replace the chicken with beef.

> 3 dried *guajillo* chiles
> 2 tablespoons mustard
> 1¹/₂ tablespoons Worcestershire sauce
> 3 garlic cloves, minced
> 1 whole chicken, about 3 lb (1.4 kg), cut into 8 pieces
> 1 cup/8¹/₂ oz (235 g) butter
> 5 white onions, sliced
> ¹/₂ cup/4 fl oz (120 ml) white wine
> 1 bay leaf
> handful of breadcrumbs (if needed)
> salt and ground pepper
> cooked white rice, to serve

Pour boiling water over the chiles in a bowl and let soak for 10 minutes, then drain, remove the stems and seeds, and cut into small pieces.

Meanwhile, in a separate bowl, mix the mustard, Worcestershire sauce, and garlic, and season with salt and pepper. Rub the mixture onto the chicken pieces and let marinate for 30 minutes.

Heat 2 tablespoons of the butter in a pan over medium heat, add the chicken and sear well for 7 minutes each side, or until browned. Remove the chicken and set aside.

Add the remaining butter to the same pan and heat over high heat. Add the onions and sauté for 5 minutes, then add the chiles, and cook for a further 5 minutes, or until the onions become transparent and soft. Remove from the heat.

Place the seared chicken pieces in a medium pan with the onion mixture, wine, and bay leaf, and add enough water to cover. Season with salt and bring to a boil over high heat, then lower the heat to medium and cook for 20 minutes or until the chicken is cooked through. If the sauce is too thin, add some breadcrumbs and cook for a further 10 minutes.

Serve warm, with rice.

Chicken Colombo

Colombo de poulet
French Guiana

Preparation time: 20 minutes,
plus overnight marinating
Cooking time: 30 minutes

Serves: 4

Colombo de poulet is a Creole curry that originated in the French Caribbean in the nineteenth century, when it was made by indentured laborers from India who worked on sugar plantations. The tropical chicken stew with coconut milk is seasoned with a *poudre de colombo*, or colombo powder, a curry blend with no exact recipe, but generally made with spices that might include coriander seeds, fenugreek, turmeric, mustard seeds, black peppercorns, cumin, and cloves. Toasted, long-grain rice is also added, acting as a thickener. Commercial forms of colombo powder are available in Caribbean markets.

> 1 whole chicken, (4–5 lb/1.8–2.3 kg), cut into 4 pieces
> 2 tablespoons vegetable oil
> 1 tablespoon butter
> ¹/₂ shallot, chopped
> 2 garlic cloves, chopped
> ¹/₂ scotch bonnet chile, chopped
> 1 tablespoon cayenne pepper
> 2 tablespoons lime juice
> 1 zucchini (courgette), cut into ¹/₂-inch (1-cm) cubes
> 1 eggplant (aubergine), cut into ¹/₂-inch (1-cm) cubes
> 1 tablespoon chopped parsley
> 1 teaspoon dried thyme
> 1 chive, chopped
> 2 cups/16 fl oz (475 ml) chicken stock
> 1 cup/8 fl oz (250 ml) coconut milk
> salt and ground pepper
>
> For the marinade
> 3 tablespoons colombo powder (see above)
> ¹/₂ shallot, finely chopped
> 2 garlic cloves, finely chopped
> 1 teaspoon coriander seeds, ground
> 1 tablespoon white vinegar
> 1 cup/8 fl oz (250 ml) water
> cooked white rice, to serve

In a large dish, season the chicken pieces with salt and pepper. In a bowl, mix the marinade ingredients together, pour over the chicken to coat, and let marinate in the refrigerator overnight.

Heat the oil and butter in a pan over medium heat. Add the shallot, garlic, scotch bonnet, and cayenne pepper. Cook, stirring, for 10 minutes, or until the shallot is translucent. Remove the chicken from the marinade (reserving the marinade), carefully add to the pan and sear on both sides. Add the lime juice, zucchini (courgette), and eggplant (aubergine). Mix well then add the parsley, thyme, and chives. Pour in the marinade and the chicken stock and lower the heat. Cover and simmer for 15 minutes until the chicken is cooked, then stir in the coconut milk and check the seasoning.

Serve hot, with rice.

Chicken Colombo

Guatemalan Green Chicken Stew

Pollo en jocón
Guatemala

Preparation time: 20 minutes
Cooking time: 1 hour

Serves: 8

This fragrant stew made by simmering chicken in a sauce of tomatillos and cilantro is prevalent among Mayan communities in Guatemala. It's thickened with squash seeds, and sometimes corn tortillas or masa are used in the same way.

 ½ cup/2½ oz (70 g) pumpkin seeds, toasted
 ¼ cup/1¼ oz (35 g) *pepitas* (hulled squash or pumpkin seeds)
 5 lb (2.3 kg) chicken breasts, deboned and skin removed
 2 tomatoes, peeled and chopped
 2½ oz (75 g) cilantro (coriander), coarsely chopped
 1 lb 8 ounces (680 g) tomatillos
 3 tablespoons olive oil
 3 jalapeño peppers, cored, seeded, and sliced
 4 garlic cloves, minced
 2 green bell peppers, cored, seeded, and chopped
 1 white onion, chopped
 salt and ground pepper

 To serve
 avocado slices
 cooked white rice
 Corn Tortillas (page 136, for homemade)

Coarsely chop the pumpkin and *pepita* seeds, then crush them in a mortar into a powder.

Place the chicken and tomatoes in a large pan. Add enough water to cover, and season with salt. Bring to a boil over high heat, then lower the heat and simmer for 30 minutes. Remove the chicken, reserving the cooking stock, and let cool. Shred and set aside.

Put the cilantro (coriander) with the tomatillos and 1 cup/8 fl oz (250 ml) of the cooking stock into a blender, and blend on medium speed for less than a minute. Set aside.

In a large pan, heat the oil over medium heat. Add the jalapeño, garlic, bell peppers, and onion and sauté for 10 minutes, or until soft. Add 3 cups/25 fl oz (750 ml) of the cooking stock, and the blended cilantro and tomatillo mixture. Add the ground seeds and simmer for 10 minutes, or until thick. Continue by adding the shredded chicken to the sauce and cook for a further 10 minutes. Season with salt and pepper.

Serve with avocado slices, rice, and corn tortillas.

Brown Stew Chicken

Brown stew chicken
Guyana

Preparation time: 20 minutes, plus overnight marinating
Cooking time: 45 minutes

Serves: 4

Chicken browned and sweetened in a gravy made from brown sugar and seasonings is a typical preparation in much of the English-speaking Caribbean; however, the addition of reduced cassava extract known as cassareep makes this version distinctly Guyanese. Serve with roti or white rice.

 ½ teaspoon fresh ginger, minced
 4 garlic cloves, minced
 ½ teaspoon ground pepper
 1 teaspoon fresh thyme leaves
 ½ teaspoon paprika
 2 green onions (salad onions), chopped
 4 lb (1.8 kg) chicken thighs and legs, skin removed and cut into 1½-inch (4-cm) chunks (ask your butcher)
 3 tablespoons olive oil
 1½ tablespoons brown sugar
 ½ white onion, chopped
 2 *wiri wiri* chile, whole
 4 scallions (spring onions), minced
 1 tablespoon dried thyme
 2 cinnamon sticks
 10 cloves
 ½ tablespoon five-spice powder
 2 tablespoons Worcestershire sauce
 2 tablespoons soy sauce
 3 tablespoons cassareep
 2 cups/16 fl oz (475 ml) boiling water
 salt
 cooked white rice, to serve

In a bowl, mix the ginger, 1 teaspoon of the garlic, the pepper, fresh thyme, paprika, and green (salad) onions. Season with salt and add the chicken. Mix well with your hands and leave to marinate overnight in the refrigerator.

Heat the oil in a large pan over medium heat, add the sugar and stir continuously until it begins to foam. When it starts to caramelize, add the onion, remaining garlic, chile, and scallions (spring onions). Stir for 5 minutes, then add the marinated chicken, dried thyme, cinnamon, cloves, five-spice powder, Worcestershire, soy, and cassareep.

Lower the heat, cover, and cook for 20 minutes. Add the boiling water, uncover, and continue cooking for a further 15 minutes, or until the chicken is tender. Check the seasoning.

Serve hot in deep plates, with rice.

Poultry

Brown Stew Chicken

Guatemalan Highland Chicken Stew

Pulique
Guatemala

Preparation time: 20 minutes,
plus 1 hour soaking
Cooking time: 1 hour 15 minutes

Serves: 4

Native to Jalapa and Guazacapán in the Santa Rosa department in the highlands of Guatemala, *pulique* is mostly made with chicken, though beef, turkey, or any meat available can be substituted. Some variations found in coastal areas even use seafood. It's pre-Columbian in origin, though it was adapted to Spanish ingredients during the colonial period.

    1½ cups/10 oz (270 g) uncooked rice
    1 whole chicken, around 3 lb (1.4 kg), jointed
    8 cups/64 fl oz (1.9 liters) water
    1 lb (450 g) tomatoes, peeled and diced
    4 oz (120 g) tomatillos
    ½ white onion chopped
    1 *guaque* chile, slightly roasted
    2 garlic cloves, peeled
    1 sprig epazote
    2 tablespoons chopped cilantro (coriander)
    1 *güisquil* (chayote), cut into cubes
    2½ oz (75 g) green beans
    2 medium potatoes, peeled and cubed
    1 teaspoon annatto paste
    2 teaspoons corn (maize) flour
    4 peppercorns
    salt and ground pepper
    Corn Tortillas (page 136, for homemade)

Soak the rice in cold water for 1 hour.
    Meanwhile, place the chicken pieces and water in a large pan and season with salt. Bring to a boil over high heat, then simmer for 45 minutes.
    Drain the rice and place in a blender with the tomatoes, tomatillos, onion, chile, and garlic. Mix on medium speed for 1 minute, or until it becomes a smooth paste. Add the paste to the pan with the chicken and bring to a boil, then lower the heat. Add the epazote, cilantro (coriander), and chayote, stir well, and cook for 5 minutes. Add the green beans, potatoes, and annatto paste, and cook for a further 10 minutes.
    In a bowl, whisk the corn (maize) flour with ½ cup/ 4 fl oz (120 ml) of the cooking liquid, then add it back to the pan. Add the peppercorns, cover, and cook for a further 10 minutes.
    Check the seasoning. Remove the epazote, and, if necessary, the peppercorns.
    Serve warm in deep plates, with corn tortillas on the side.

Peruvian Spicy and Creamy Chicken Stew

Ají de gallina
Peru

Preparation time: 20 minutes
Cooking time: 1 hour

Serves: 6–8

Ají de gallina has its roots in medieval Spain with a dish called *manjar blanco*, where chicken was covered in a sweet, creamy sauce made of milk, sugar, almonds, rose water, and rice. It arrived in Lima in the sixteenth century, and over time it became more savory and was adapted to New World ingredients like *ají* chile peppers and pecans. Additionally, the recipe now known in Peru as *manjar blanco*, similar to *dulce de leche*, grew out of the original Spanish dish. Traditionally, non-egg-laying hens were used instead of chicken, though today chicken is almost universally used.

    1 whole chicken, about 4 lb (1.8 kg)
    8 garlic cloves, minced
    1 celery stalk, chopped
    1 bay leaf
    1 carrot, peeled and cut into chunks
    6 slices of white bread
    1 cup/8 fl oz (250 ml) milk
    2 tablespoons vegetable oil
    2 red onions, chopped
    6 tablespoons *ají amarillo* paste
    2 tablespoons (25 g) pecans, chopped
    1 lb (450 g) potatoes, cooked thickly sliced
    2 tablespoons grated parmesan
    3 hard-boiled eggs, halved
    10 purple olives
    cooked white rice, to serve, optional

Place the chicken in a medium pan with half the garlic, the celery, bay leaf, and carrot. Add enough water to cover the chicken, and season with salt. Bring to a boil and cook for 35 minutes, or until tender.
    Meanwhile, place the bread in a bowl with the milk and set aside to soak.
    Strain the chicken, reserving the cooking stock. Let the chicken cool before shredding.
    In a frying pan, heat the oil over medium heat, add the remaining garlic, the onions, and *ají amarillo* paste, and sauté for 10 minutes. Add the soaked bread and stir. If the sauce is too thick, gradually add some of the cooking stock, stirring. Add the shredded chicken and pecans to the pan and check the seasoning.
    Place the potatoes on a plate and cover them with the hot *ají de gallina* and the parmesan sprinkled over. Garnish with the hard-boiled eggs and olives.
    Serve warm, with rice on the side, if preferred.

Stuffed and Rolled Chicken

Pamplona
Uruguay

Preparation time: 30 minutes
Cooking time: 40 minutes

Serves: 4

The first Uruguayan *pamplona* is believed to have been created in 1963 by a butcher in the Florida Department, who is said to have rolled thinly sliced pork up with different ingredients as a way to market it. It caught on and is now eaten during *asados* or made in home kitchens across the country, usually with chicken. Some like to add an outer layer of bacon because, you know, bacon.

1 tablespoon butter
1/2 cup/3 1/2 oz (100 g) chopped heart of palm
1 red bell pepper, cored, seeded, and sliced
4 chicken breasts, deboned
1 teaspoon dried oregano
1 teaspoon paprika
2 garlic cloves, minced
4 thin slices of ham
8 oz (225 g) pancetta, diced
1/2 cup/2 oz (60 g) shredded mozzarella
1 tablespoon chopped parsley
salt and ground pepper

Prepare a charcoal grill (barbecue) to medium heat.
In a frying pan, heat half the butter over medium heat. Add the heart of palm with the red bell pepper, season with salt and sauté for 8 minutes. Set aside.
Cut each chicken breast in half horizontally, without cutting all the way through to the other side, then open them out. If necessary, to make them as thin as possible, lay plastic wrap (clingfilm) over them and lightly pound them with a meat tenderizer. Season with salt and pepper, sprinkle over the oregano and paprika, and rub in the garlic. On one end of each piece of chicken, place a slice of ham, some pancetta, and some of the heart of palm and bell pepper mixture. Sprinkle mozzarella and parsley over each.
Start rolling from the end of the chicken with the fillings, pressing gently as you roll. When you arrive at the end, tie them with butcher's twine to secure.
Grease the grill with the remaining butter and add the chicken. Cook for about 15 minutes each side, or until golden brown. When ready, place on a cutting board and slice.
Serve warm.

Yucatán-Style Lime Soup

Sopa de lima
Mexico

Preparation time: 10 minutes
Cooking time: 50 minutes

Serves: 4

The limes in *sopa de lima*, which is primarily a chicken and tomato stew, are known as *limas agrias*, or bitter limes, found throughout the Yucatán. They are dark green and less acidic than a standard lime, though you can substitute with key limes or a combination of lime and grapefruit juices. It is usually served with either tortillas or tortilla chips.

4 chicken breasts
4 oz (120 g) tomatoes
1/2 white onion, chopped
4 garlic cloves, peeled
3 black peppercorns
2 teaspoons dried oregano
1 cinnamon stick
3 cloves
2 star anise
juice of 2 *limas agrias* (bitter limes)
1 habanero chile
6 cups/48 fl oz (1.4 liters) chicken stock

Place the chicken breasts in a medium pan and season with salt. Cover the chicken with 1 inch (2 cm) of water and bring to a boil. Reduce to low and simmer for 10 minutes, or until tender. Remove the chicken from the stock and let cool, then shred. Set aside the stock.
In a dry frying pan, roast the tomatoes, onion, and garlic for 15 minutes over high heat, making sure they brown on all sides. Remove from the heat and set aside.
In another pan, toast the peppercorns, oregano, cinnamon, cloves, and star anise for 4 minutes, moving the pan constantly.
Place all the ingredients except the chicken in a large pan, along with the reserved stock. Bring to a boil, then lower the heat to medium and cook, covered, for 20 minutes, stirring every 5 minutes. Turn off the heat and strain the soup. Return to the pan and add the shredded chicken. Season with salt.

Dry Soup

Sopa seca
Peru

Preparation time: 20 minutes
Cooking time: 50 minutes

Serves: 4

This oxymoron of a recipe is prepared in Chincha and elsewhere along the south coast of Peru. It's so named because the broth is generally cooked in a clay pot until dry, though consistencies may vary. It's usually served alongside *carapulcra* (Pork and Dehydrated Potato Stew, page 288).

1 cup/8 fl oz (250 ml) vegetable oil
2 tablespoons annatto paste
2 white onions, chopped
5 garlic cloves, minced
4 chicken thighs, bone-in and skin-on
1 teaspoon ground cumin
4 tomatoes, peeled and diced
2 carrots, peeled and chopped
1 cup/1 1/2 oz (40 g) basil leaves
4 cups/32 fl oz (950 ml) chicken stock
4 tablespoons chopped parsley
2 lb (900 g) spaghetti

Heat the oil in a deep pan over medium-high heat. Add the annatto paste and cook for 2 minutes, then add the onions and garlic and sauté for 10 minutes.
Season the chicken with the cumin and some salt and pepper, then add to the pan and cook for 5–7 minutes each side. Remove and set aside. Add the tomatoes and carrots and cook for 6 minutes.
Put the basil and stock in a blender, blend until smooth, then pour into the pan. Bring to a simmer, then add the parsley and spaghetti. Return the chicken to the pan. Cook for 15 minutes, stirring frequently, until the chicken and spaghetti are cooked. Serve in a deep dish.

Theologian Soup

Sopa teóloga
Peru

Preparation time: 20 minutes   Serves: 8
Cooking time: 1 hour 30 minutes

In the mid-1500s, widowed Mochica women working in a Dominican convent are said to have first made this bread soup for the clergy around the time of the founding of the village of Moche, south of Trujillo along the north coast of Peru. It's usually prepared with either chicken or turkey, though it can also be prepared without meat.

    6 slices of white bread
    3 cups/25 fl oz (750 ml) fresh milk
    1 whole chicken, about 4–5 lb (1.8–2.3 kg), jointed
    1 leek, coarsely chopped
    2 celery stalks, chopped
    1 carrot, peeled and cut into chunks
    1 teaspoon dried oregano
    2 tablespoons olive oil
    1 white onion, chopped
    2 garlic cloves, minced
    2 *ají amarillo*, cored, seeded, and crushed
    1 tomato, peeled, seeded, and chopped
    3 potatoes, peeled and cut into small cubes
    8 oz (225 g) queso fresco, cut into 1/2-inch (1-cm) cubes
    1/2 cup/3/4 oz (20 g) chopped parsley
    salt and ground pepper

Put the bread in a bowl with 2 cups/16 fl oz (475 ml) of the milk, and set aside to soak.

    Meanwhile, place the chicken in a large pan with the leek, celery, carrot, and oregano. Add enough water to cover, and season with salt and pepper. Bring to a boil over high heat, then reduce the heat, cover, and simmer for 45 minutes until cooked. Remove the chicken from the pan, and strain and reserve the cooking stock.

    In a blender, put the soaked bread and 1 cup/8 fl oz (250 ml) of the cooking stock, and blend for 1 minute on high speed, or until it forms a paste. Set aside.

    Heat the oil in a large pan over high heat, add the onion, garlic, *ají amarillo*, and tomato. Cook for 8 minutes, stirring continuously. Lower the heat and add the soaked bread paste. Stir for 6 minutes, or until the sauce thickens. Pour in 4 more cups/32 fl oz (950 ml) of the cooking stock, bring to a boil, then simmer for 15 minutes. Add the potatoes and queso fresco, and cook for 10 minutes, or until the potatoes are soft. Add the remaining milk to the pan, along with the chicken. Check the seasoning.

    Sprinkle in the parsley and serve hot, in deep plates.

Hen Chowder

Chupe de gallina
Venezuela

Preparation time: 20 minutes
Cooking time: 1 hour 10 minutes   Serves: 6

The thick, potato-based chowders called *chupes* are most identifiable from Bolivia, Chile, and Peru, though the Andean regions of Venezuela also have their own. *Chupe de gallina*, traditionally made with hen, though chicken has become more prevalent in recent years, is a creamy chicken and potato stew that helps warm the soul on chilly mountain nights.

    1 whole chicken, about 4–5 lb/1.8–2.3 kg
    4 cups/32 fl oz (950 ml) chicken stock
    1 white onion, chopped
    2 garlic cloves, minced
    2 lb (900 g) potatoes, peeled and cut into cubes
    6 ears of corn, cut into 1-inch (2.5-cm) chunks
    1 red bell pepper, cored, seeded, and diced
    1 lb (450 g) queso fresco, cut into 1/2-inch (1-cm) cubes
    4 cups/32 fl oz (950 ml) milk
    1 cup/8 fl oz (250 ml) cream
    2 tablespoons chopped cilantro (coriander) leaves
    salt and ground pepper

Place the chicken in a large pan. Add the stock, onion, and garlic, and bring to a boil over high heat. Reduce the heat and simmer, covered, for 40 minutes. Remove the chicken and strain the stock into another pan. Debone the chicken and cut it into 2-inch (5-cm) pieces.

    Bring the stock to a boil then lower the heat to medium, add the potatoes, corn, and bell pepper, and cook for 15 minutes. Add the chicken pieces with the queso fresco, milk, and cream. Season with salt and pepper. Bring to a boil and cook for a further 15 minutes.

    Sprinkle in the cilantro (coriander) and serve hot, in deep plates.

Fried Chicken Blood

Sangrecita de pollo 🖻
Peru

Preparation time: 10 minutes
Cooking time: 20 minutes   Serves: 4

Rich in iron, this recipe for seasoned and fried chicken blood is an inexpensive and delicious way to help fight anemia, which is a significant health issue among children throughout much of Latin America. It's important not to overcook the blood; it should be more velvety than dried. *Sangrecita* is usually served over boiled cassava or potatoes, with bread, or can be one of the layers of a *causa* (see page 88).

    1/2 cup/4 fl oz (120 ml) water
    2 cups/16 fl oz (475 ml) chicken blood
    3 tablespoons vegetable oil
    1 white onion, chopped
    2 garlic cloves, minced
    2 *ají amarillo*, cored, seeded, and chopped
    1 scallion (spring onion), chopped
    1 teaspoon dried oregano
    1 teaspoon chopped mint
    1 tablespoon cilantro (coriander) leaves
    salt and ground pepper
    1 lb (450 g) cassava or potatoes, boiled and cut into thick chunks, to serve
    red onion and red bell pepper salad, to serve

Bring the measured water to a boil in a pan and add the chicken blood. Cook until it solidifies, about 1–2 minutes. Strain the blood and set it aside. Let cool then coarsely chop.

    In a frying pan, heat the oil over medium heat, add the onion, garlic, chiles, and scallion (spring onion), and sauté for about 10 minutes. Add the blood, oregano, mint, and cilantro (coriander). Continue stirring for a further 5 minutes, then remove from the heat. Check the seasoning.

    Serve warm, with the boiled cassava or potatoes and a salad of red onions and red bell pepper.

Fried Chicken Blood

Turkey Stew

Pepián de pavita
Peru

Preparation time: 30 minutes
Cooking time: 1 hour 25 minutes

Serves: 6

In Peru, the *pepián* is a type of thick stew that dates to the colonial period, when some of the earliest efforts of fusion between the New World and the Old were occurring. In some parts of the country, they are made of corn, usually served alongside a meat, such as rabbit or *cuy* (guinea pig); however, in the La Libertad region in the north, rice is the base ingredient with turkey its usual accompaniment.

> 2 lb (900 g) turkey breasts
> 1 leek, coarsely chopped
> 4 red onions, 1 coarsely chopped, 3 thinly sliced
> 1 carrot, peeled and cut into chunks
> 3 black peppercorns
> 3 cups/1 lb 1 oz (540 g) rice
> 2 tablespoons vegetable oil
> 7 garlic cloves, minced
> ³/₄ cup/6 oz (170 g) *ají panca* paste
> ³/₄ cup/6 oz (170 g) *ají amarillo* paste
> ¹/₂ cup/4 fl oz (120 ml) *Chicha de jora* (Corn Beer, page 388, for homemade)
> salt and ground pepper

Place the turkey breasts in a medium pan with the leek, chopped onion, carrot, and peppercorns. Add enough water to cover all the ingredients, bring to a boil, then lower the heat and simmer, covered, for 40 minutes. Remove from the heat, take out the turkey, and strain and reserve the cooking stock. Shred the turkey into large pieces.

Rinse the rice and spread out on a layer of paper towels. Using a rolling pin, slightly smash the rice, breaking but not completely crushing it.

Heat the oil in a large pan over medium heat, then add the sliced onions and the garlic, and sauté for 8 minutes. Add the *ají panca* and *amarillo* pastes and the *chicha de jora* (corn beer), then lower the heat and cook for 15 minutes. Pour in 12 cups/6 pints (2.8 liters) of the reserved cooking stock (top up with hot water if there is not enough) and increase the heat. Once the liquid starts boiling, add the rice, lower the heat to medium, and cook for a further 20 minutes. Check the seasoning.

To serve, place some of the shredded turkey in each dish and cover with the soup.

Black Turkey Stew

Pavo en relleno negro 🍲
Belize, Mexico

Preparation time: 30 minutes, plus overnight soaking
Cooking time: 1 hour 40 minutes

Serves: 6

The black color of this Yucatecan turkey stew with *buut*, or meatballs, inside, comes from *recado negro*, the dark-colored seasoning paste made of chiles and spices. In some Mayan communities in the region, it is prepared in a pot set in a *píib*, or earthen oven, with meatballs covering hard-boiled egg yolks stuffed inside the turkey.

> 30 *cha'wa* chiles (*chile de árbol*)
> 7 black peppercorns
> 7 *chile de chapa* chiles
> 4 cloves
> 1 tablespoon cumin seeds
> 1 tablespoon vegetable oil
> 3 garlic cloves, chopped
> 1 white onion, chopped
> 4 turkey breasts
> 8 oz (225 g) pork loin, minced
> 2 tomatoes, chopped
> 1 *xcatic* chile, cored and chopped
> 10 epazote leaves
> 9 oz (250 g) fresh Corn Masa (page 123)
> 2 cups/16 fl oz (475 ml) chicken stock
> 6 hard-boiled eggs
> salt and ground pepper

Toast the *cha'wa* chiles (*chile de árbol*) in a dry frying pan over high heat for 10 minutes, tossing them, or until completely charred. Place in a bowl, add cold water to cover, and some salt, and soak overnight.

The next day, in a dry frying pan over medium heat, add 4 of the black peppercorns and 4 of the *chapa* chiles with the cloves and cumin seeds. Toast for 5 minutes, moving the pan, until slightly toasted, then tip into a blender. Heat the oil in the same pan, then sauté the garlic and ¹/₂ onion until golden brown, around 6 minutes. Add them to the blender, along with the drained *cha'wa* chiles, and blend everything together on medium speed to a smooth paste. Set aside.

Place the turkey breasts in a medium pan with enough cold water to cover. Add the remaining peppercorns and *chapa* chiles, bring to a boil and cook over medium heat for 30 minutes. Remove the turkey and rub it with the blended paste.

In a frying pan, sear the turkey for 4 minutes each side. Let cool, then shred and place back in the pan. Reduce the heat and simmer for 10 minutes.

In a bowl, mix the minced pork with the tomatoes, the remaining onion, and *xcatic* chile. Season with salt and pepper and continue mixing with your hands. Shape into small golf-ball-sized balls. Add the epazote and meatballs to the pan and cook over medium heat for 20 minutes.

Dilute the corn masa with the chicken stock and add it to the pan, then cook for a further 10 minutes, or until the soup thickens. Check the seasoning.

Serve warm in deep dishes, dividing the turkey and meatballs between them. Place a hard-boiled egg in each dish.

Black Turkey Stew

Yucatán-Style Turkey and Onion Stew

Pavo en escabeche oriental
Mexico

Preparation time: 30 minutes
Cooking time: 1 hour 15 minutes
Serves: 6

This turkey stew is named because it is from the Yucatecan city of Valladolid, which is east, or *oriente*, of the peninsula's capital of Mérida, not because it has some sort of Asian influence. It utilizes what is known as *recado blanco*, a white seasoning paste most often used in Valladolid, which can used as a marinade or a rub.

2 lb (900 g) turkey breasts
1 white onion, quartered
5 garlic cloves, crushed
1 tablespoon dried oregano
8 cups/64 fl oz (1.9 liters) water
2 tablespoons white vinegar
6 *xcatic* or *güero* chiles
8 roasted garlic cloves
1/2 red onion, thinly sliced
1/4 cup/2 fl oz (60 ml) bitter orange juice
2 tablespoons vegetable oil
salt

For the *recado blanco*
3 tablespoons ground white pepper
1 tablespoon black peppercorns
2 teaspoons coriander seeds, toasted
4 tablespoons ground cumin
5 cloves
1 teaspoon ground cinnamon
2 teaspoons sea salt
1/4 cup/2 fl oz (60 ml) bitter orange juice

Place the turkey, onion, garlic, oregano, and water in a large pan. Season with salt and bring to a boil, then reduce the heat and simmer for 30 minutes, or until the meat is tender. Remove the turkey, and strain and reserve the cooking stock. When cool, cut the turkey into slices 1/2 inch (1 cm) thick.

To make the *recado blanco*, put all the ingredients in a mortar, grind well, and set aside.

Pour 3 cups/25 fl oz (750 ml) of the turkey cooking stock into a pan, and add 1 tablespoon of the *recado*. Add the vinegar, chiles, and roasted garlic. Bring to a boil over high heat, then lower the heat and simmer for 15 minutes. Add the red onion and cook for a further 15 minutes, then remove from the heat.

Take out the onions and chiles and put them in a bowl; set aside. Dilute the remaining *recado* in the mortar with the bitter orange juice, and rub it over the turkey slices.

Heat the oil in a frying pan and sear the turkey for 2 minutes each side over high heat.

Serve warm in a deep dish, with some of the cooking stock, and the onions and chiles on top.

Guatemalan Turkey Stew

Kak'ik
Guatemala

Preparation time: 30 minutes
Cooking time: 1 hour 10 minutes
Serves: 8

Most prevalent in Cobán, the capital of the department of Alta Verapaz in central Guatemala and home to a high concentration of Q'eqchi' Maya people, the country's largest ethnic group, the recipe for *kak'ik* has changed little in centuries. This spicy turkey soup has a distinctive set of flavors from the combination of tomatillos, annatto, herbs, and smoky chiles, like the *cobanero*. Local, seasonal ingredients like *tomate de árbol* and *samat*, a wild cilantro, are sometimes added too. It's generally served with rice, tortillas, or tamales.

1 whole turkey, about 10 lb (4.5 kg), deboned and separated into 8 pieces (ask your butcher)
6 sprigs cilantro (coriander)
10 sprigs mint
2 white onions, peeled; 1 quartered, 1 left whole
3 tablespoons sesame seeds
2 tablespoons *pepita* seeds (hulled squash or pumpkin seeds)
4 black peppercorns
4 pink peppercorns
1 red bell pepper, cored and seeded
2 *guaque* chiles
1 *pasilla* chile
6 garlic cloves, peeled
8 tomatoes, peeled and halved
4 oz (120 g) tomatillos
1 teaspoon annatto paste
1 teaspoon *cobanero* chile powder

Place the turkey in a large pot with the cilantro (coriander), mint, and quartered onion. Add enough water to cover all the ingredients, bring to a boil over high heat, then reduce to a simmer, cover, and cook for 45 minutes.

Meanwhile, in a dry frying pan, toast the sesame seeds, *pepita* seeds, and peppercorns over medium heat for 8 minutes, moving them constantly. Remove and set aside.

Lay the bell pepper, chiles, garlic, whole onion, tomatoes, and tomatillos on a baking sheet and place under a hot broiler (grill) for 3–4 minutes, or until they start to char, then flip and broil for a further 3 minutes.

Place the toasted and broiled ingredients in a blender with the annatto paste and chile powder, and blend for 2 minutes on high speed, adding a little of the turkey cooking stock if necessary. Add the blended mixture to the turkey pan, cook for 10 minutes, then check the seasoning.

Serve warm in deep dishes. Place one large piece of turkey in each dish.

Chiclayo-Style Green Rice with Duck

Arroz con pato a la Chiclayana
Peru

Preparation time: 20 minutes
Cooking time: 1 hour 5 minutes

Serves: 4

Arroz con pato, or duck with rice, is not a recipe limited to Peru, but the way it's made in Lambayeque in the north of the country is unlike anywhere else, with its green rice and use of beer (or *chicha*) in the broth.

1 tablespoon vegetable oil
1 duck, cut into 4 pieces
2 garlic cloves, minced
1 lb 8 ounces (680 g) peas
3 tablespoons *ají amarillo* paste
1½ cups/12 fl oz (350 ml) dark beer
1½ cups/2 oz (60 g) coarsely chopped cilantro (coriander) leaves
4 cups/32 fl oz (950 ml) chicken stock
1 lb (450 g) grated squash (*loche*)
1 cup/4 oz (120 g) diced pumpkin
2 lb (900 g) uncooked rice
salt and ground pepper

Heat the oil in a medium pan over high heat and sear the duck for 4 minutes each side, or until golden brown. Remove and set aside. In the same pan, sauté the garlic with the peas for 5 minutes, then add the *ají amarillo* paste and sauté for a further 5 minutes.

Place the beer and cilantro (coriander) in a blender and blend for 1 minute, then pour into the pan with the garlic, peas, and *ají amarillo paste*. Add the chicken stock, grated squash, and diced pumpkin. Season with salt and pepper, bring to a boil, then add the duck and cook for 20 minutes, or until soft and cooked. Remove the duck and keep warm. Add the rice to the pan (if necessary, add more water). Cook for 25 minutes over low heat until tender. Stir, and add the duck pieces. Check the seasoning.

Serve warm.

Duck Ceviche

Ceviche de pato
Peru

Preparation time: 20 minutes, plus 45 minutes marinating
Cooking time: 1 hour

Serves: 6

Ceviche de pato, made in coastal provinces north of Lima, as well as the Ancash region, stretches the very definition of the term ceviche. Aside of being made with duck, it's served warm. Some argue it's not a true ceviche, though the process of transformation of the protein through the acidity in bitter oranges and salt still occurs. The protein is just further cooked over heat.

1 cup/8 fl oz (250 ml) bitter orange juice
1 teaspoon cumin
4 garlic cloves, minced
2 *ají amarillo* chile, cored, seeded, and chopped
3 *ají mirasol* chile, cored, seeded, and chopped
2 *ají limo* chile, cored, seeded, and chopped
3 duck breasts
3 duck legs
3 tablespoons vegetable oil
1 white onion, coarsely chopped
2 red onions, thinly sliced
salt and ground pepper

To serve
1 lb (450 g) cassava, boiled and sliced
1 *rocoto* chile, cored and sliced

In a bowl, mix the bitter orange juice with the cumin, half the garlic, half the *ají amarillo* and *ají mirasol*, and the *ají limo*, and season with salt and pepper. Place all the duck pieces on a plate, rub them with the marinade and let marinate for 45 minutes.

Heat 1 tablespoon of the oil in a pan over medium heat, and sear the duck pieces for 5 minutes each side, or until golden brown. Remove and set aside.

In the same pan, heat the remaining oil and add the remaining garlic, the white onion, and the remaining *ají amarillo* and *ají mirasol*. Sauté for 10 minutes, then add the duck with the marinade, bring to a boil, then lower the heat and simmer for 15 minutes. Add the red onions, and cook for a further 15 minutes. Check the seasoning.

To serve, place slices of cassava on a plate with the duck. Pour over some of the sauce and garnish with *rocoto* slices.

Duck in Tucupí Sauce

Pato no tucupí ▣
Brazil

Preparation time: 45 minutes,
plus overnight marinating
Cooking time: 3 hours 30 minutes

Serves: 4

Like the soup *tacacá* (Shrimp, Jambu, and Fermented
Cassava Soup, page 104), also made in the state of
Pará in northern Brazil, this heady stew is made from
a mixture of the fermented yuca broth called *tucupí*
and the numbness-inducing herb *jambu*, or paracress,
yet it's far less overpowering, mellowed out with the
shredded duck, vegetables, and other seasonings. It is
usually served with white rice, chiles, and cassava flour.

    1 duck, about 3 lb (1.4 kg)
    2 tablespoons vegetable oil
    1 white onion, coarsely chopped
    1 carrot, peeled and sliced
    1 leek, sliced
    1 celery stalk, chopped
    1 sprig thyme
    1¹/₂ cups/12 fl oz (350 ml) white wine
    3 cups/25 fl oz (750 ml) *tucupí*
    1 bunch *jambu* leaves
    salt and ground pepper

    For the marinade
    1 white onion, coarsely chopped
    1 carrot, peeled and sliced
    1 leek, sliced
    1 bay leaf
    1 sprig thyme
    1¹/₂ cups/12 fl oz (350 ml) white wine

In a bowl, mix the marinade ingredients together and
season with salt and pepper. Rub the duck with the
marinade and let it marinate overnight in the refrigerator,
removing it to room temperature an hour before cooking.
 Preheat the oven to 320°F/160°C/Gas Mark 2.
Place the duck in an oven dish with the marinade, cover
with foil, and cook in the oven for 1 hour and 40 minutes,
or until the meat is soft and can easily detach from the
bones. Remove from the oven and, when cool enough
to handle, remove all the meat from the bones (keep
the bones).
 Increase the oven to 400°F/200°C/Gas Mark 6.
Place all the duck bones in the oven dish and bake for
40 minutes, turning them after 20 minutes to cook evenly.
 Heat the oil in a pan over high heat, add the onion,
carrot, leek, celery, thyme, and wine, and sauté for
15 minutes, stirring continuously. Add the roasted duck
bones, mix well, and add enough water to cover. Simmer,
covered, for 45 minutes, then strain, reserving the stock.
 In a pan, mix the *tucupí* and 2 cups/16 fl oz (475 ml)
of the reserved stock. Bring to a boil over high heat, then
add the *jambu* leaves and the duck meat. Check the
seasoning.
 Serve hot, in deep plates.

Duck in Chile Sauce

Pato en chirmol
Belize, Mexico

Preparation time: 25 minutes
Cooking time: 1 hour 15 minutes

Serves: 6

A combination of the Nahuatl words *chilli* and *molli*
(mix), *chirmol*, also spelled *chimol* or *chirmole*, is made
primarily in Tabasco, Chiapas, and the Yucatán, and
can vary considerably. At its heart, it's a chile sauce,
less complicated than a *mole* though no less profound.
There's usually some form of poultry, likely to be duck or
turkey, though chicken or even beef may also be used.

    2¹/₂ tablespoons vegetable oil
    1¹/₂ white onions, chopped
    4 garlic cloves, minced
    3 tomatoes, diced
    3 black peppercorns
    1 teaspoon dried oregano
    ¹/₂ cinnamon stick
    ¹/₃ cup/1³/₄ oz (45 g) pumpkin seeds
    4 *ancho* chiles, seeded and cut into strips
    1¹/₂ cups/12 fl oz (350 ml) duck stock
    3 x 4-inch (10-cm) Corn Tortillas (page 136, for
    homemade), stale or toasted
    1 whole duck, broken down into breasts and legs
    salt
    cooked white rice, to serve

In a frying pan, heat 1 tablespoon of the oil over high
heat and add the onions and garlic. Sauté for 8 minutes,
or until brown and soft. Add the tomatoes and cook for
5 minutes. Set aside.
 In another frying pan, toast the peppercorns,
oregano, cinnamon, and pumpkin seeds. Tip onto a plate
and set aside.
 Heat ¹/₂ tablespoon of the oil in the same frying pan
and toast the chiles over medium-high heat for 5 minutes,
then lower the heat and continue toasting for a further 10
minutes. Set aside.
 Add the onion mixture, the dry toasted ingredients,
the chiles, and ¹/₂ cup/4 fl oz (120 ml) of the stock to a
blender, and blend to a sauce, gradually crumbling the
tortillas into the blender as you mix, and adding more of
the stock if needed.
 Heat the remaining tablespoon of oil in a pan over
high heat, and sear the duck for 4 minutes each side,
or until golden. Pour the sauce onto the duck, add
the remaining stock, lower the heat, and simmer for
25 minutes, or until the meat is tender and the sauce
has reduced to your desired thickness.
 Serve hot, with rice.

Duck in Tucupí Sauce

Native Meats and Insects

In the Sacred Valley of the Incas outside of Cusco, a dozen or so men from the village of Urquillos dig a large hole and light a wood fire inside to make *pachamanca*, a ritual feast, a tribute to the ground it came from. Above the fire, set on a metal grate, are dozens of roundish, grapefruit-size river stones. When the stones are hot, they are used to line the pit. Native meats like alpaca and guinea pig, as well as pork, are marinated in a paste of *huacatay* and *ají amarillo*, then wrapped in banana leaves and tossed inside, along with cassava, sweet potatoes, various native tubers, and fava beans. Piles of freshly picked herbs like *paico*, oregano, and cilantro are layered throughout the mound of meats and vegetables and then all is covered with wet burlap tarps. Dirt and more hot stones are used to cover the *pachamanca*. Visibly, all that can be seen for the next few hours as the food cooks is a smoking pile of brown dirt.

After a few hours, the dirt is removed. Everyone joins in to dig up the stones and pile them off to the side. The burlap and herbs are tossed out, while any dirt is brushed off the meats and tubers and they are placed on a manta, a colorful blanket. *Uchucuta*, a chile sauce ground in a stone mortar while the food is cooking, is placed beside them. Together, everyone eats.

Rabbit

Rabbits, both native and introduced, are found throughout Latin America. While there is evidence that the Aztecs were breeding a considerable number of rabbits within the urban confines of the city of Teotihuacan, the consumption of rabbits has generally been more intermittent in the region.

Pickled Rabbit

Conejo escabechado 🍲
Chile

Preparation time: 15 hours,
plus 15 hours marinating
Cooking time: 45 minutes

※ ⊘
Serves: 4

The European rabbit (*Oryctolagus cuniculus* L.) was introduced to central Chile in the nineteenth century for breeding purposes, but they soon escaped, multiplied like, well, rabbits, and in the last century have become a considerable nuisance, wreaking havoc on native ecosystems and farmland through much of the central and southern parts of the country. Luckily, they're also delicious. This adaptation of a Spanish recipe, served cold or hot, is one of the most common preparations in the country.

    1 whole rabbit, cut into 8 pieces
    2 cups/16 fl oz (475 ml) red vinegar, plus 1 tablespoon
    4 cups/32 fl oz (950 ml) water
    3 garlic cloves, minced
    2 tablespoons fresh oregano
    ½ cup/4 fl oz (120 ml) olive oil
    2 red onions, thickly sliced
    1 carrot, peeled and sliced
    ½ red bell pepper, cored, seeded, and cut into strips
    ½ tablespoon ground cumin
    1 bay leaf
    1 cup/8 fl oz (250 ml) white wine
    salt and ground pepper

Place the rabbit pieces in a bowl with the 2 cups/16 fl oz (475 ml) vinegar and the water, and marinate in the refrigerator for 12 hours.

In a bowl, mix a third of the garlic with the oregano, the 1 tablespoon of vinegar, and some salt and pepper. Drain the meat, add to the bowl, coat in the marinade and set aside for 3 hours.

In a medium pan, heat the oil over medium heat and sear the meat for 3 minutes each side, or until golden brown. Remove and set aside. In the same pan, add the onions, remaining garlic, carrot, and bell pepper, and sauté for 8 minutes, then add the meat back to the pan. Add the cumin and bay leaf, and season with salt. Add the wine, lower the heat, cover, and simmer for 30 minutes, or until the meat is completely tender.

Serve either hot or cold.

Spicy Braised Rabbit

Picante de conejo
Bolivia, Chile, Peru

Preparation time: 20 minutes,
plus 10 hours brining
Cooking time: 1 hour 30 minutes

※ ⊘
Serves: 6

This highland recipe braises rabbit in a spicy broth that is usually adapted to the season and geography. There are always *ají* chile peppers, but you may also add peanuts, tomatoes, *chuño*, garlic, onions, and herbs. It's usually served over potatoes or with rice or quinoa.

    6 rabbit pieces (legs and saddle, approx. total weight 3–4 lb/1.4–1.8 kg)
    5 tablespoons vegetable oil
    4 garlic cloves, minced
    1 white onion, chopped
    1 carrot, peeled and grated
    ½ rocoto, finely chopped
    2 tablespoons *ají panca* paste
    2 tablespoons chopped cilantro (coriander) leaves
    3 cups/25 fl oz (750 ml) hot water
    1 tablespoon ground turmeric
    ½ teaspoon ground cumin
    2 lb (900 g) potatoes, boiled
    salt and ground pepper
    cooked white rice, to serve

    For the brine
    4 cups/32 fl oz (950 ml) cold water
    ¼ cup/3 oz (85 g) salt

In a large bowl, mix the water with the salt for the brine, and add the rabbit pieces. Leave in the brine for 10 hours, in the refrigerator. Remove the rabbit, rinse, and pat dry.

In a large pan, heat the oil over high heat and sear all the rabbit pieces for 5 minutes each side, or until golden brown. Remove and set aside. Add the garlic, onion, carrot, rocoto, and *ají panca* paste to the same pan and sauté for 8 minutes over medium heat. Add the cilantro (coriander) and cook for a further 5 minutes.

Return the rabbit pieces to the pan with the hot water. Add the turmeric and cumin, and season with pepper. Stir well, cover, and simmer for 1 hour, stirring every 15 minutes, until the rabbit saddle is cooked and tender. After 1 hour, remove the saddle pieces and set aside. Continue to cook the legs for a further 15–30 minutes, or until tender. Return the saddle pieces to the pan to reheat.

Peel the boiled potatoes and mash them with a fork. Add them to the pan, mix well to combine.

Serve warm, with rice.

Guinea Pig

Domesticated in the Andes more than 5,000 years ago, *cuyes*, or guinea pigs, are a low impact meat that remain an important source of protein in the region. High in protein and low in fat and cholesterol, *cuy* has a flavor similar to rabbit. In Andean households, they are often kept in kitchen enclosures, sometimes resembling small houses, and are fed vegetable scraps and alfalfa. It's not a meat that's eaten every day, but often on birthdays and special occasions. They can be grilled, roasted, fried, turned into pâté, cooked underground in a *pachamanca*, covered in peanut sauce, or paired with spicy potatoes.

Pickled Rabbit

Fried Guinea Pig

Cuy frito, cuy chactado 🍳
Colombia, Ecuador, Peru

Preparation time: 15 minutes,
plus 1 hour resting and
2 hours marinating
Cooking time: 10 minutes

Serves: 1

When fried, sometimes under the weight of a heavy stone, the skin of the guinea pig crisps up like *chicharrón*. It's usually served whole and flattened. As much as you can try to remove the meat with a knife and fork, the best way of eating *cuy* is to grab it by the hands and feet and just gnaw on it. Serve alongside boiled potatoes and potatoes, *salsa criolla* (Creole Sauce, page 406), *uchucuta* (Andean Chile Sauce, page 408), and a glass of *chicha de jora* (Corn Beer, page 388).

    1 whole guinea pig, guts removed
    1 cup/8 fl oz (250 ml) *Chicha de jora* (Corn Beer,
    page 388, for homemade)
    1/2 cup/4 fl oz (120 ml) lime juice
    2 garlic cloves, minced
    2 tablespoons *ají panca* paste
    1 teaspoon dried oregano
    4 cups/32 fl oz (950 ml) vegetable oil
    1 cup/5 oz (140 g) corn (maize) flour

Rinse the guinea pig under cold water for 5 minutes to remove any blood. Pat dry with paper towels and let rest for 1 hour at room temperature.

Meanwhile, in a bowl, mix the *chicha de jora* (corn beer) with the lime juice, garlic, *ají panca* paste, and oregano. Season the guinea pig with salt and pepper and rub it with the marinade. Rest for 2 hours.

Heat the oil in a large, heavy pan, making sure it is no more than two-thirds full, and heat to 375°F/190°C. Coat the guinea pig in corn (maize) flour, then carefully lower it into the oil, and deep-fry for 5–8 minutes, or until crispy and brown. Remove with a skimmer and place to a plate lined with paper towels to absorb excess oil.

Serve warm.

Spicy Braised Guinea Pig

Picante de cuy, cuy colorado
Peru

Preparation time: 15 minutes,
plus 1 hour resting
Cooking time: 15 minutes

Serves: 1

Cut in half and slathered in a thick, rich, red sauce made from chiles and peanuts, this version of guinea pig feels far less exotic than when it's served naked on the plate in its entirety. Call it the gateway *cuy*. It's most common in the central Andes of Peru, in provinces like Ancash, Junín, and Ayacucho.

    1 whole guinea pig, guts removed
    2 garlic cloves, minced
    4 tablespoons *ají panca* paste
    2 tablespoons vegetable oil
    2 potatoes, boiled thickly sliced
    1/4 cup/1 oz (25 g) ground peanuts (unsalted)
    1 teaspoon dried oregano
    cooked white rice, to serve

Rinse the guinea pig under cold water for 5 minutes to remove any blood. Pat dry with paper towels and let rest for 1 hour at room temperature.

Cut the guinea pig into 4 pieces and season it with salt and pepper. Rub the garlic and 1 tablespoon of the *ají panca* paste into the meat.

Heat the oil in a pan over medium heat and sear the meat for 4 minutes per side, or until crispy and brown. Remove and set aside.

In the same pan, add the sliced potatoes and the remaining *ají panca*, the peanuts, and the oregano, and season with salt and pepper. Cook for 3 minutes, add the guinea pig and mix well. Check the seasoning.

Serve hot, with white rice.

Insects

In many parts of Latin America, insects are an abundant and efficient source of protein and flavor. Eggs, nymphs, larvae, pupae, and adult insects are the basis of hundreds of recipes from Mexico to the Amazon. Salted and fried, they can add texture to a dish or be eaten on their own. They can be nutty, smoky, or taste like lemongrass, adding flavors to salads and sauces, or be used as a natural colorant.

Fried Grasshoppers

Chapulines
Mexico

Preparation time: 10 minutes,
plus 5 hours soaking
Cooking time: 5 minutes

Serves: 4

Collected mostly during the rainy season in parts of Central America and Mexico, especially in Oaxaca, the grasshoppers of the genus Sphenarium, known as *chapulines*, long supplemented pre-Columbian diets that included only small amounts of meat with protein. Submerged in boiling water and dried in the sun, they are sold in markets by the scoop from large baskets. They lack much flavor of their own, though they nicely absorb the flavors of garlic, lime, salt, and chiles when toasted on a *comal* or pan. Eat them as a snack or sprinkle them on top of tacos or *tlayudas*.

    4 cups/32 fl oz (950 ml) water
    1/4 cup/19 oz (550 g) cal (slaked lime)
    3 cups/15 oz (450 g) fresh *chapulines*, wings and
    legs removed
    2 tablespoons oil
    1 serrano chile, seeded and coarsely chopped
    salt
    1 lime, cut into wedges, to serve

Mix the measured water with the cal (slaked lime) and, gently, add the *chapulines*. Soak for 4 hours, then drain carefully and soak again in clean water for a further 1 hour. Dry well and set aside. Note: if using dehydrated *chapulines*, skip this step.

Put the oil and chile in a frying pan and place over high heat. Once hot, add the insects and fry for 4 minutes, constantly moving and searing. Remove to a plate lined with paper towels and season with salt.

Serve warm, with lime wedges to squeeze over.

Fried Guinea Pig

Maguey Worm Tacos with Tomatillos

Tacos de chinicuiles
Mexico

Preparation time: 20 minutes
Cooking time: 30 minutes

Serves: 6

Chinicuiles, also called *gusanos de maguey*, are the larvae of the Comadia redtenbacheri moth that live in the roots of agave plants. Collected during the rainy season, mostly in the central Mexican states of Tlaxcala and Hidalgo, they're one of the kinds of "worms" (actually a caterpillar) you might find in a bottle of cheap mezcal. They are always cooked, never eaten raw and usually alongside tomatillos in a taco, though can also be used in *moles* or ground up with salt and chiles to make a seasoning.

    20 tomatillos
    1 serrano chile
    1/2 white onion, chopped
    1 tablespoon chopped cilantro (coriander)
    2 garlic cloves, minced
    1 tablespoon olive oil
    2 cups/10 oz (300 g) maguey worms
    salt
    6 Corn Tortillas (page 136, for homemade),
    to serve

Roast the tomatillos in a dry frying pan for 3 minutes, turning frequently. Repeat the process with the chile and onion. Mash the tomatillos, chile, onion, cilantro (coriander), and half the garlic in a mortar and set aside.

In a pan, heat the oil and sauté the remaining garlic for 3 minutes. Add the maguey worms and cook, stirring, for 4 minutes, or until they are well toasted. Season with salt and remove from the heat.

To serve, heat the tortillas in a nonstick pan for 2 minutes on each side. Spread the tomatillo sauce evenly over the tortillas and top with the maguey worms.

Steamed Maguey Leaves with Ant Larvae

Mixiotes de escamoles
Mexico

Preparation time: 10 minutes
Cooking time: 20 minutes

Serves: 4

Mixiotes, steaming sauced and seasoned meats—such as rabbit, chicken, or beef—that have been wrapped in maguey leaves, come from the semi-arid, southern Mexican Highlands. One such filling can be *escamoles*, the larvae and pupae of Liometopum apiculatum ants, available only for a period of two to three months per year, between February and April. Sometimes called Mexican caviar for their limited supply and high price, they have a delicate, nutty flavor and cottage-cheese-like texture.

    2 tablespoons butter
    1/2 white onion, thinly sliced
    1 1/2 cups/13.5 oz (350 g) *escamoles* (ant larvae)
    1 poblano chile, roasted, seeded, and chopped
    1 tablespoon chopped epazote
    4 maguey leaves, cut into 7-inch (18-cm) squares

Heat the butter in a pan over medium heat. Add the onion and sauté for 5 minutes, then add the ant larvae and chile. Season with salt and add the epazote. Continue cooking over low heat for 10 minutes, stirring.

Divide the larvae mixture evenly between the middle of each maguey leaf. Fold over each leaf to close, and tie to secure with butcher's twine. Pour 2 inches (5 cm) of water into a steamer, and bring to a boil. Add the steamer basket (make sure the water doesn't touch the basket) and the maguey leave packages in the basket. Steam for 5 minutes, or until the leaves are soft. Serve warm.

Large-Bottomed Ants

Hormigas culonas
Colombia

Preparation time: 10 minutes
Cooking time: 5 minutes

Serves: 4

These large-bottomed leaf cutter ants (*Atta laevigata*), called *hormigas culonas*, are a delicacy in the Santander department of Colombia, a custom originating with the Guane culture. Only the females, with egg-filled abdomens, are consumed. They can be harvested for a period of several weeks each year in April and May, when they leave their nest and a rural family drop whatever they are doing to catch them. They are typically roasted alive then salted with their wings and legs removed. They have an earthy, nutty flavor that's a bit like popcorn.

    2 cups/7 oz (200 g) *hormigas culonas*, wings and
    legs removed
    2 tablespoons vegetable oil

Heat the oil in a large clay pot or pan over high heat and add the ants. Constantly move the pot for 5 minutes, or until the ants are well toasted. Remove from the pot and place on a plate lined with paper towels, to absorb any excess oil. Season with salt and serve warm.

Grilled Palm Weevil Larvae

Mojojoy, Suri
Bolivia, Brazil, Colombia, Ecuador, Peru, Venezuela

Preparation time: 15 minutes,
plus 1 hour marinating
Cooking time: 10 minutes

Serves: 8

In markets throughout the Amazon, the fat larvae of the South American palm weevil (*Rhynchophorus palmarum*), often harvested from inside the trunks of the aguaje palm, can be seen for sale wriggling in plastic buckets. They are primarily eaten skewered and grilled, though they can also be stewed in their own fat and a bit of water. They have a chewy skin and buttery interior, though their crunchy, black beak is bitter and best avoided.

    2 lb (900 g) palm weevil larvae
    5 garlic cloves, minced
    1/2 cup/4 fl oz (120 ml) vegetable oil

Rinse the larvae under cold water for 1 minute, then pat dry and place in a bowl. Add the garlic, oil, and some salt, mix well and marinate for 1 hour.

Preheat a charcoal grill (barbecue). Place the marinated larvae on skewers and set them on the grill. Cook for 5 minutes each side, or until crispy. Serve hot.

Native Meats and Insects

Dried, Shredded Venison

Venison

From tiny *pudú* of Chile to marsh deer of Brazil's Paraná, deer inhabit nearly every type of biome in Latin America, though many native species are endangered. The abundant white-tailed deer, in particular, was an especially important food source for the Maya and other pre-Columbian civilizations, and remains prevalent in many indigenous and rural communities.

Dried, Shredded Venison

Pisillo de venado (page 323)
Colombia, Venezuela

Preparation time: 15 minutes,
plus at least 5 hours soaking
Cooking time: 55 minutes
Serves: 8

In Los Llanos, the tropical grasslands that extend from eastern Colombia into western Venezuela, *pisillo* is made from deer or *chigüire*, better known as "capybara." After a hunt, the meat is sun-dried and salted, fried in lard and seasoned, then smashed with a stone or pestle. It can be used as filling for empanadas or arepas or eaten alongside white rice, beans, cassava, or plantains.

2 lb (900 g) salted and dried venison meat
1½ white onions, 1 thickly sliced, ½ chopped
2 tablespoons lard
5 garlic cloves, minced
1 hot chile, minced
½ green bell pepper, seeded and chopped
5 tomatoes, chopped
cooked white rice, to serve

Place the dried meat in a bowl and add cold water to cover. Let soak for at least 5 hours.

Drain the meat, place in a medium pan, and cover with new water. Add the sliced onion and bring to a boil. Cover and simmer for 30 minutes, or until the meat is soft.

Meanwhile, heat the lard in a large pan over medium heat. Add the chopped onion and garlic, and sauté for 7 minutes. Add the chile, bell pepper, and tomatoes. Continue cooking, while stirring continuously, for 10 minutes over low heat.

Drain the meat and leave until cool enough to handle, then shred it and add it to the pan with the vegetables. Increase the heat and cook for 5 minutes. Season with salt.

Serve warm, with rice on the side.

Yucatecan Spicy Venison Stew

Chocolomo de venado
Mexico

Preparation time: 30 minutes
Cooking time: 2 hours
Serves: 20

The roots of this recipe can be traced to Mayan offerings of a recently killed deer to the gods, which was a celebratory event where all parts of the animal were used. After cattle were introduced to the Yucatán, the festive atmosphere of bullfighting transitioned more readily to the dish, and it's now more commonly made with beef and organ meats. In fact, the name is a combination of the Mayan word *choko*, meaning hot, and the Spanish word *lomo*, or loin. Rabbit, duck, and other game meats also lend themselves well to *chocolomo*.

20 cups/15 pints (7 liters) water
2 tablespoons black peppercorns
2 garlic heads, cloves separated and crushed
2 *xcatic* chiles, seeded
2 sweet chiles, seeded
1 tablespoon mint leaves
1 sprig fresh oregano
1 cup/1½ oz (40 g) cilantro (coriander) leaves
4 lb (1.8 kg) venison loin, cut into 1-inch (2.5-cm) chunks
1 lb (450 g) venison heart, cut into 1-inch (2.5-cm) chunks
1 venison brain, cut into 1-inch (2.5-cm) chunks
1 lb (450 g) venison liver
2 tablespoons olive oil
2 white onions, chopped
8 tomatoes, coarsely chopped
4 habanero chiles, coarsely chopped
1 tablespoon dried oregano
1 cup/8 fl oz (250 ml) bitter orange juice

Pour the measured water into a large stockpot, add the peppercorns, garlic, all the chiles, the mint, and oregano. Set aside 1 tablespoon of the cilantro (coriander) and then and the remainder to the pot. Bring to a boil over high heat, then add the venison loin and heart. When it boils again, lower the heat, cover, and simmer for 40 minutes. Add then the brain and liver and simmer for 1 hour from when it comes back to a boil.

Meanwhile, heat the oil in a large pan over medium heat. Sauté the onions with the tomatoes and habanero chiles. Add the oregano, reserved tablespoon of cilantro, and some salt and pepper. Cook, stirring, for 8 minutes. Add the bitter orange juice and continue cooking for a further 5 minutes. Reduce the heat and keep warm.

Once the meats are tender, remove from the pot. For the liver, before serving, clean it by removing the inner white part, then cut it into pieces.

To serve, place all the meat pieces in deep plates and pour some of the stock over them. Spoon some of the chile sauce on top of each. Serve hot.

Native Meats and Insects

Yucatecan Spicy Venison Stew

Shredded Venison

Dzik de venado
Mexico

Preparation time: 15 minutes
Cooking time: 1 hour 15 minutes,
plus 30 minutes resting

Serves: 10

Cooked in a *pib*, or pit barbecue, then shredded and marinated in bitter orange, radishes, and herbs, *dzik de venado* is a form of *salpicón*, a salad-like mixture that's often used to top tacos and tostadas.

    2 garlic cloves
    1 oz (30 g) dried oregano
    1 tablespoon ground black pepper
    3 cloves
    2 tablespoons ground cumin
    1 cinnamon stick
    2 tablespoons coriander seeds
    1¼ cups/10 fl oz (300 ml) bitter orange juice
    2 banana leaves
    4 lb (1.8 kg) venison leg
    2 cups/3 oz (80 g) chopped cilantro (coriander)
    leaves
    1 white onion, chopped
    10 radishes, chopped
    tostadas or tortillas, to serve

Heat a dry frying pan or *comal* over medium heat, then add the garlic and roast for 10 minutes until lightly charred, turning occasionally.

Place the oregano, pepper, cloves, cumin, cinnamon, and coriander seeds in a frying pan over medium heat. Toast for 3 minutes, constantly moving the pan to prevent burning. Place the ingredients in a mortar with the roasted garlic and grind to a smooth paste. Dilute the mixture with 2 tablespoons of the bitter orange juice, and set aside.

Preheat the oven to 365°F/180°C/Gas Mark 4.

Quickly pass the banana leaves over a flame to soften. Rub the venison leg with the diluted mixture and season with salt and pepper. Wrap the banana leaves over the leg, place in an oven dish, and bake for 1 hour.

Remove from the oven and leave until cool enough to handle, then shred the meat and place in a bowl. Add the cilantro (coriander), onion, and radishes. Season with salt and pepper, and pour over the remaining bitter orange juice to cover. Let cool for 30 minutes. Serve at room temperature, with tostadas or tortillas.

Camelids

Llamas and alpacas were domesticated several thousand years ago in South America. The larger llamas were prized as pack animals, though their meat was eaten as well, often dehydrated to make *charqui*. Smaller than llamas, alpacas were raised primarily for their wool and meat, which is lean, a little bit sweet, and has a mild flavor similar to beef. Alpaca makes for a good substitute for beef in dishes like *Lomo saltado* (Stir-Fried Beef and Potatoes, page 261), just grilled over high heat like a steak (no more than medium or it gets very tough), or ground for burgers. The meat of their wild ancestors, guanacos and vicuñas, is less prevalent. While guanacos are hunted for their meat on occasion, vicuñas are protected and more sought after for their valuable fur.

Alpaca in Spicy Sauce

Adobo de Alpaca 🔲
Peru

Preparation time: 10 minutes,
plus overnight marinating
Cooking time: 50 minutes

Serves: 4

The mild alpaca meat absorbs the spicy, vinegar-based marinades called *adobos* of southern Peru quite well. It is usually served with boiled potatoes or quinoa.

    7 tablespoons vegetable oil
    ½ onion, peeled and chopped
    4 garlic cloves, finely chopped
    4 tablespoons *ají panca* paste
    ½ cup/4 fl oz (120 ml) white vinegar
    3 teaspoons salt
    ½ teaspoon ground pepper
    2 lb (900 g) alpaca loin, cut into chunks

Heat 6 tablespoons of the oil in a medium pan. Add the onion, garlic, and *ají panca* paste, then sauté for 5 minutes. Stir in the vinegar, salt, and pepper. Transfer to a food processor and blend. Pour the mixture into a bowl, add the alpaca and coat well. Refrigerate overnight.

Heat the remaining tablespoon of oil in a pan over medium heat. Remove the alpaca from the marinade and add to the pan. Cook for 2 minutes per side, or until browned. Remove from heat. Place the alpaca and marinade in a pan over low heat, cover, and simmer for 45 minutes, adding a little water if it starts to dry out.

Serve in a dish, covered with the sauce.

Llama Jerky

Charqui de llama
Bolivia, Chile, Peru

Preparation time: 7 days

Serves: 8–10

Derived from the Quechua word *charqui*, or *ch'arki*, jerky is the dehydrated meat of the South American altiplano. Here, it has been a staple ingredient for thousands of years. To reduce water content and prevent microbial growth, it's important to hang the meat in a well-ventilated place with lots of sun and cool nights, which is why the cold, dry conditions at altitude work so well. Traditionally made from camelids, such as llama, alpaca, or guanaco, jerky can be made with venison, beef, or lamb, It is eaten as is, rehydrated in stews, or shredded in other recipes.

    4 lb (1.8 kg) llama meat
    2 lb (900 g) salt

Remove any fat from the meat and place it in the freezer for 1–2 hours. Remove from the freezer and pound with a tenderizer, then cut against the grain into strips no more than ¼-inch (5 mm) thick. Add a layer of salt in a large tray, place the strips of meat on it, then cover with the remaining salt. Let sit for 1–2 days, or until the meat turns dark in color and completely dehydrates. Hang the meat strips in a sunny, dry, well-ventilated space that is protected from insects. Let hang for 5–7 days, turning the strips every day so they dry evenly. At night, cover with a tea towel or fiber bag to keep them from getting damp. When dry and brittle, take down and enjoy.

Native Meats and Insects

Alpaca in Spicy Sauce

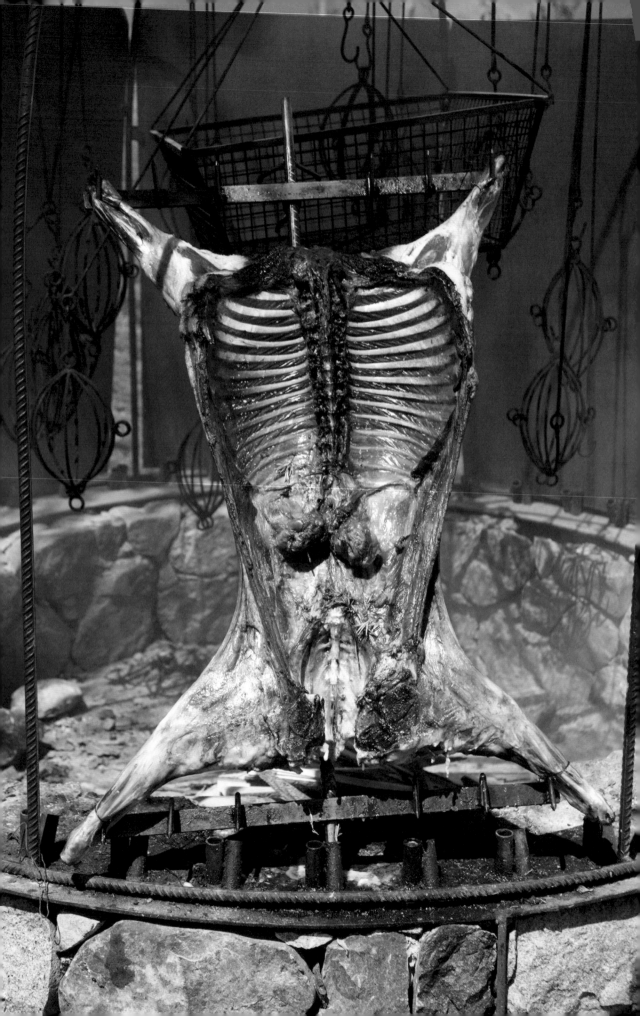

Lamb and Goat

The wind howls and a fire crackles before the dawn beside a lake in Patagonia. A rancher takes a sip of a cup of *maté* then piles on more lenga wood (*Nothofagus pumilio*) to fuel the flame. When it's hot, he walks to retrieve the lamb from a nearby shed, where it has been hanging for several days since its slaughter. He has already stripped off its wool and innards, and much of its blood that has dripped out has been mixed with *merkén*, salt, and lemon juice and left to coagulate before being cut into jelly-like cubes to eat with bread.

He cuts the lamb vertically, down the torso, and cuts some of the ribs to allow them to cook better. Using hooks, he attaches the carcass on an iron cross, pierces the thorax with a thin spike, and ties the legs back with wires. The lamb, with its back outwards, is set up a couple of feet from the fire. For the next four or five hours, he'll turn the lamb on occasion to make sure it cooks evenly. He'll drink beer as he adds more wood to the fire and douses the smoked meat in chimichurri for flavor, sometimes a bit of his beer too. After it seems like a whole day has gone by, it will be time to eat.

Lamb arrived en masse to the vast, sparsely inhabited grasslands of Chilean and Argentine Patagonia in the late nineteenth century. It attracted colonists from Europe and Chiloé, which forever changed the region's culture and cuisine.

Goats arrived in the Americas on Christopher Columbus' second voyage in 1493, spreading from the Caribbean to the rest of the region. In pockets of Latin America, often in marginal landscapes, goat is a staple meat, the base of many spectacular recipes.

Stake Roasted Lamb

Cordero al palo, asado al palo, asado a la estaca
Argentina, Chile, Uruguay

Preparation time: 20 minutes
Cooking time: 5 hours

Serves: 8–12

Lamb stretched out on an iron cross, roasting slowly beside a fire for hours, is perhaps the signature recipe in the grasslands of Patagonia. At times, multiple lambs are slaughtered and placed around the fire at a time. Note: It's possible to just use the ribs on the stake, which will shorten the cooking time considerably.

    1 whole skinned lamb, innards removed
    (6–10 months of age; 20–33 lb/9–15 kg)
    salt

You will need: an iron cross (made with stainless steel) and some steel wire

Start by preparing your fire. Use the hardest and driest firewood available, place it as a small, stone-ringed circle on the ground, and light it.

With a knife, mark the ribs of the lamb with 5 vertical cuts. Place the lamb on top of the cross (bone side touching the stake), attaching it vertically first and then horizontally with steel wire and/or hooks, depending on your stake. Sprinkle or spray a little bit of water on the lamb and sprinkle it with salt.

Place the stake in the ground, about 2 feet (60 cm) from the fire. Keep the meat about 30 inches (75 cm) above the ground, inclining the stake at 70 degrees; the bones must be facing the heat. Place your hand briefly between the lamb and the fire to check the heat is reaching the carcass. Keep a uniform high heat during the entire cooking time, adding more firewood as you need it. After 2–3 hours, turn the lamb and give it a further 1–2 hours of cooking. The lamb is ready when the bones come out easily.

Carefully remove the steel wire and remove the lamb stake away from the fire. Cut and serve while hot.

Grilled Rack of Lamb

Costillar de cordero
Uruguay

Preparation time: 5 minutes,
plus at least 3 hours marinating
Cooking time: 20 minutes,
plus 15 minutes resting

Serves: 4

Lamb is a fatty meat that is a typical addition to a backyard *asado* in Uruguay. It might be the ribs, shoulders, or legs and generally it's only lightly seasoned, often with little more than a sprinkling of salt.

    1 rack of lamb, French trimmed
    1 teaspoon salt
    3 garlic cloves, minced
    leaves from 2 sprigs rosemary
    grated zest of ½ lemon
    2 tablespoons olive oil
    salt and ground pepper

Trim the fat from the tip of the bones if that hasn't been done already, and remove the membrane between the ribs.

Season the lamb with salt, then make a marinade with the garlic, rosemary, lemon zest, and olive oil and use it to cover the lamb. Marinate for at least 3 hours.

Heat a charcoal grill (barbecue) until white ash can be seen on the coals. Wrap the tips of the lamb bones in aluminum foil.

Form a crown of embers around the center of the grill, leaving a thin amount of charcoal in the middle. When hot, place the rack rib side down in the center of the grill. Roast for about 10 minutes, then season with salt and pepper and flip the rack and cook for a further 8–10 minutes, or until a meat thermometer reads between 140 and 145°F/60 and 63°C. Remove from the heat and let rest for about 15 minutes.

Cut into individual ribs and serve while warm.

Lamb's Head Soup

Caldo de cabeza de cordero
Bolivia

Preparation time: 20 minutes
Cooking time: 1 hour 15 minutes

Serves: 4

Songs have been sung on the altiplano about Bolivia's *caldo de cabeza de cordero*, a hearty soup made from lamb's head that's usually eaten in the mornings. On the altiplano, rice and potatoes are often added to give the soup body, while elsewhere in the Andes some add *mote*, chiles, or wild herbs. A similar recipe, *thimpu de cordero*, swaps the lamb's head for its legs.

    1 head of lamb, cleaned
    4 cups/32 fl oz (950 ml) water
    1 carrot, sliced
    1 small white onion, chopped
    1 celery stalk, chopped
    1 sprig parsley
    1 sprig cilantro (coriander)
    ¼ cup/1¾ oz (45 g) rice
    8 *chuños* (dehydrated potatoes), soaked and peeled
    2 potatoes, peeled and halved
    salt

    To serve
    lime wedges
    Llajua (Bolivian Pepper Sauce, page 408)

Put the lamb head in a pot with the water. Add some salt and bring to a boil over medium heat, then add the carrot, onion, celery, parsley, and cilantro (coriander). Reduce to a simmer and cook for 45 minutes, then add the rice and *chuños* and continue cooking for 10 minutes. Add the potatoes and cook for a further 15 minutes, or until cooked through. Remove from the heat.

Remove the head and cut in half. Place the lamb's head pieces in a large, deep bowl and pour the broth and vegetables over it.

Serve family-style with lime wedges to squeeze over and a bowl of *llajua* on the side.

Lamb's Head Soup

Lamb Barbacoa

Barbacoa de borrego 🔲
Mexico

Preparation time: 15 minutes,
plus overnight soaking
Cooking time: 4 hours 30 minutes

Serves: 4

"Barbacoa" generally refers to a process of steaming meat inside of a brick-lined pit. The pit, which is a little more than 3 feet deep, is heated by lighting a wood fire, then once it is reduced to coals, is covered with roasted agave or avocado leaves, and topped with a pot of broth that is topped with a grill and the meat, which is wrapped in the same leaves. The meat is draped with a wet cloth and covered with dirt, plus more hot stones and charcoal, then left to cook for the next 8 hours or so. In Guanajuato, barbacoa will probably be made with goat, while in northern states like Sonora and Chihuahua you're more likely to find beef head. In central Mexico, lamb is the preferred meat, and *pancita*, made from the lamb's stomach that has been stuffed with viscera, is usually cooked in the pit too. Consommé, made from the broth and drippings, will usually be served as well. The following recipe doesn't require a pit, just a large pot or slow cooker.

    3 avocado or agave leaves
    1 large potato, peeled and quartered
    2 medium carrots, peeled and sliced
    1 medium white onion, diced
    4 garlic cloves, crushed
    2 tablespoons *guajillo* chile powder
    1 tablespoon *ancho* chile powder
    1 tablespoon cider vinegar
    1 tablespoon ground cumin
    1/4 teaspoon ground cinnamon
    1/2 teaspoon dried Mexican oregano
    1/3 cup/2 oz (55 g) dried chickpeas, soaked overnight
    1 bone-in lamb shoulder, about 4 lb (1.8 kg)
    6 cups/50 fl oz (1.5 liters) water
    salt

    To serve
    Corn Tortillas (page 136, for homemade)
    diced white onion and shredded cilantro (coriander)
    lime wedges

Slightly warm the avocado or agave leaves by placing them in the middle of a dry frying pan over medium heat for 4 minutes on each side. Remove and set aside.

At the bottom of a steamer pot, place all the ingredients except the lamb, water, half of the onion, and the leaves. Place the steamer grill on top of the ingredients. Salt the lamb and place it on top of the grill, then top that with the leaves. Pour in the water (don't let it cover the lamb). Cover the pot with aluminum foil and a lid. Place over medium heat and bring to a boil, then reduce the heat and simmer for 4 hours.

Discard the leaves and remove the bone from the lamb. Coarsely shred the meat and place on a platter.

For the sauce, skim the fat from the cooking liquid, pour into a pan, and add the remaining half onion. Cook over medium heat for about 20 minutes, adding salt if needed.

Mix the shredded lamb with the sauce and serve hot on warm corn tortillas, with a white onion and cilantro (coriander) salad on the side, and lime wedges to squeeze over.

Peruvian Cilantro Lamb Stew

Seco de cordero
Peru

Preparation time: 30 minutes
Cooking time: 3 hours 30 minutes

Serves: 5–6

Secos, found along the central and northern coast of Peru, are slow-cooked stews defined by their thick, rich sauces made with a heavy amount of herbs, plus *ají* chiles and a base of *chicha de jora* (Corn Beer, page 388).

    1/2 cup/4 fl oz (120 ml) vegetable oil
    4 lb (1.8 kg) lamb shoulder meat, cut into 2-inch (5-cm) chunks
    2 white onions, finely chopped
    1 tablespoon minced garlic
    4 tablespoons *ají amarillo* paste
    1 tablespoon *ají panca* paste
    1/2 tablespoon ground cumin
    1/2 cup/3/4 oz (20 g) chopped cilantro (coriander)
    1 cup/8 fl oz (250 ml) *Chicha de jora* (Corn Beer, page 388, for homemade) or dark beer
    2 cups/16 fl oz (475 ml) beef stock
    1 cup/4 1/2 oz (130 g) peas
    1 carrot, cut into 1/2-inch (1-cm) slices
    2 lb (900 g) potatoes, boiled
    salt and ground pepper

    To serve
    cooked white rice
    canary (pinto) beans

Heat half the oil in a medium pan over medium heat. Sear the meat for 2 minutes on each side, or until golden brown. Remove from the pan and set aside.

In the same pan, and adding more oil if needed, sauté the onions and garlic for 10 minutes, or until soft and transparent, then add the chile pastes, cumin, and cilantro (coriander). Season with salt and pepper and continue cooking for a further 15 minutes.

The oils and fat will separate from the solids. At this point, add the meat back to the pan with the beer. Add the stock to cover the meat, and close the lid. Simmer over low heat for several hours, checking every 30 minutes or so. The lamb should be soft enough you can shred it with a spoon.

About 15 minutes before removing the lamb from the heat, add the peas, carrot, and cooked potatoes. Check the seasoning.

Serve while hot, with rice and canary (pinto) beans.

Lamb Barbacoa

Goat Stew

Seco de chivo, seco de cabrito
Ecuador, Peru

Preparation time: 10 minutes,
plus overnight soaking and
1 hour marinating
Cooking time: 2 hours 10 minutes
Serves: 8

This stew made of kid goat has subtle differentiations between Ecuador and Peru. In Peru, *chicha de jora* or dark beer serves as the base of the sauce, and it's served with white rice and canary beans. Sometimes a *tamalito verde* (page 133) is on the plate too. In Ecuador, the *chicha de jora* is often replaced with a fruit juice, such as *naranjilla* or tamarind, and it's usually served with fried plantains and yellow rice.

    1 lb (450 g) dried canary (pinto) beans
    5 tablespoons vegetable oil
    1 white onion, chopped
    4 garlic cloves, minced
    1 teaspoon dried oregano
    1 teaspoon ground cumin
    1 cup/8 fl oz (250 ml) *Chicha de jora* (Corn Beer,
    page 388, for homemade) or dark beer
    1½ tablespoons *ají amarillo* paste
    4 lb (1.8 kg) kid goat, cut into 2-inch (5-cm) chunks
    ½ teaspoon ground turmeric
    1 cup/1½ oz (40 g) chopped cilantro (coriander)
    1 lb (450 g) cassava, cooked and cut into thick strips
    salt and ground pepper

Place the beans in a bowl, add cold water to cover, and let soak overnight. The following day, drain the beans and set aside.

In a medium pan, heat 2 tablespoons of the oil, add half the onion and half the garlic and sauté for 5 minutes. Add the oregano and cumin, season with salt and pepper, stir well, then add the drained beans. Add water to cover, then cover the pan and bring to a boil. Lower the heat and simmer for 1 hour 30 minutes, stirring every 20 minutes, until tender.

In a bowl, mix the beer with the remaining garlic and half of the *ají amarillo* paste. Season with salt and pepper, then add the goat meat and rub the marinade into the meat. Set aside somewhere cool for 1 hour.

Heat the remaining oil in a medium pan over medium heat. Stir in the remaining onion, *ají amarillo* paste, and turmeric. Sauté for 5 minutes, then add the marinated goat and cilantro (coriander). Stir well and add enough water to cover the meat. Cover the pan, bring to a boil, then lower the heat and simmer for a further 30 minutes. Remove from the heat and check the seasoning.

Serve hot.

Stewed Goat

Cabrito a la cacerola
Chile

Preparation time: 25 minutes
Cooking time: 40 minutes
Serves: 4

While goats are unheard of in much of Chile, they are plentiful in the arid Norte Chico. There it's cooked *al disco*, in a large, round pan, or cooked on an iron cross like a lamb in Patagonia (see page 330), as well as in this simple stew.

    4 pieces of suckling goat, 4 oz (120 g) each
    6 tablespoons vegetable oil
    ½ cup/4 oz (115 g) butter
    2 garlic cloves, minced
    2 scallions (spring onions), chopped
    1 tablespoon chopped parsley
    2 lb (900 g) potatoes, washed and cut into 1-inch
    (2.5-cm) cubes
    2 sprigs thyme
    salt and ground pepper

Season the pieces of goat with salt and pepper. In a pan, heat 4 tablespoons of the oil over high heat. Add the goat pieces and cook for 20–30 minutes over low heat, or until the meat is tender. Remove from the pan and set aside. Remove any excess oil and heat half the butter over medium heat. Stir in the garlic and scallions (spring onions) with the parsley and sauté for 8 minutes, then add the goat pieces back to the pan and remove from the heat.

Meanwhile, in another pan, heat the remaining butter and oil over medium heat. Add the potatoes and thyme, then lower the heat and cook, stirring frequently, for 30 minutes or until the potatoes are soft.

To serve, place the potatoes on a platter with goat pieces and a little bit of the liquid on the top.

Goat in Coconut Milk

Chivo al coco
Venezuela

Preparation time: 30 minutes
Cooking time: 1 hour 50 minutes
Serves: 4

In the Western coastal areas of Venezuela, goat meat is widely consumed. Shredded or cut into chunks and cooked with coconut milk, *chivo al coco* is a hearty lunch plate served alongside white rice or mashed green plantains.

    1 tablespoon vegetable oil
    ½ white onion, chopped
    3 garlic cloves, chopped
    ½ red bell pepper, cored, seeded, and chopped
    1 green bell pepper, cored, seeded, and chopped
    4 tomatoes, peeled, seeded, and diced
    1 teaspoon annatto paste
    3 cups/25 fl oz (750 ml) coconut milk
    2 lb (900 g) goat meat, cut into 1-inch (2.5-cm)
    chunks
    2 scallions (spring onions), green part only,
    finely chopped
    1 lime, cut into wedges
    salt and ground pepper

Heat the oil in a medium pan, add the onion, garlic, bell peppers, tomatoes, and annatto paste, and sauté for 7 minutes or until the vegetables are soft. Add the coconut milk and bring to a boil. Add the meat and bring to a boil again over high heat, then lower the heat to medium and cook for 10 minutes. Season with salt and pepper, then lower the heat once more and let simmer for 1 hour–1 hour 30 minutes, or until the meat is tender, whisking every 15 minutes or so to avoid lumps and burns. If necessary, gradually add hot water if it starts to stick. Check the seasoning.

Serve warm, with the scallions (spring onions) scattered over, and with lime wedges to squeeze over.

Goat in Coconut Milk

Curry Goat

Curry Goat
Guyana, Suriname

Preparation time: 20 minutes
Cooking time: 1 hour 5 minutes   Serves: 6

Goat is common in Caribbean countries, where it's served in stews or roasted, though in Guyana and Suriname it's almost always curried. There, goat means balancing ratios of masala and curry powder. Elsewhere in the Caribbean the masala is left out, so the flavor is unique.

    3 lb (1.4 kg) goat pieces, cut into 1-inch (2.5-cm) chunks
    ¼ cup/2 fl oz (60 ml) lime juice
    2 tablespoons white vinegar
    1½ tablespoons curry powder
    1 tablespoon each ground cumin and garam masala
    2 tablespoons olive oil
    ½ white onion, chopped
    6 garlic cloves, minced
    2 *wiri wiri* chiles, chopped
    3 scallions (spring onions), chopped

Season the pieces of goat with salt and pepper, then rub with the lime juice and vinegar, and set aside.
    In a bowl, mix the curry powder, cumin, and garam masala together, and gradually whisk in enough water to form a paste. Set aside.
    Heat the oil in a medium pan over high heat, then add the onion, garlic, and chiles. Lower the heat and add the curry paste. Stir well, cook for 2 minutes, then place the drained pieces of goat meat in the pan and mix well. Cover and cook for 20 minutes, or until the pieces of meat have released their own juices. Pour enough water to half cover the meat and cook, uncovered, for a further 40 minutes, or until the meat is tender. Check the seasoning.
    Serve while hot, scattered with the scallions (spring onions) and with rice or roti on the side.

Goat Innard Stew

Chirimpico
Peru

Preparation time: 30 minutes
Cooking time: 1 hour 40 minutes   Serves: 6

In the Lambayeque region in northern Peru, the tripe, liver, belly, entrails, heart, blood and nearly anything else gets chopped up, heavily seasoned, and stewed with loche squash and *chicha de jora* beer or lime juice. It's served with boiled cassava, slices of sweet potatoes, or sometimes *sangrecita* (page 308) made of goat blood.

    8 oz (450 g) goat tripe
    4 oz (225 g) goat heart
    4 oz (225 g) goat liver
    2 bay leaves
    3 tablespoons vegetable oil
    1 red onion, chopped
    3 garlic cloves, minced
    2 tablespoons *ají panca* paste
    2 tablespoons white vinegar
    1½ cups/6¾ oz (190 g) fresh corn kernels
    3 oz (80 g) goat blood
    3 cups/4 oz (120 g) cilantro (coriander) leaves
    salt and ground pepper

Rinse the tripe, heart, and liver well. Cut the heart and liver into 1-inch (2.5-cm) pieces and set aside.
    Place the tripe in a pan. Cover with salted water, add the bay leaves, and bring to a boil. Simmer for 1 hour, then remove from the pan and cut into 1-inch (2.5-cm) chunks. Reserve 2 cups/16 fl oz (475 ml) of the cooking stock.
    In a clay pot or pan, heat the oil over high heat. Sear the pieces of heart for 4 minutes and season with salt and pepper. Lower the heat to medium and add the onion, garlic, *ají panca* paste, and vinegar. Cook for 10 minutes, stirring often. Continue by adding the tripe and liver, then pour in the reserved cooking stock and the corn. Bring to a boil and cook for 7 minutes. Add the blood and cilantro (coriander) and cook for a further 15 minutes. Check the seasoning.
    Serve hot, in a deep dish.

Mexican Goat Stew

Birria de chivo 🍲
Mexico

Preparation time: 20 minutes,
plus overnight marinating
Cooking time: 4 hours 5 minutes   Serves: 8

In central Mexican states such as Jalisco and Zacatecas, goat is generally the meat of choice for *birria*, a type of *adobo*, or marinade, made from chiles, spices, and other seasonings. Beef and mutton are common alternatives to goat. While traditionally *birria* was roasted slowly in underground pits, today it's more likely coming out of an oven. In Jalisco, where the recipe originated, *birria* is served in clay dishes with chopped onion, salsa, and limes. It's usually served on special occasions, though in Guadalajara, as well as in Tijuana, it's a favorite of late-night taco stands, served with a broth called *consomé*.

    2 *ancho* chiles, seeded
    4 *guajillo* chiles, seeded
    8 *cascabel* chiles, seeded
    2 tablespoons black peppercorns
    8 garlic cloves, peeled
    ½ white onion, chopped
    1 teaspoon dried oregano
    1 tablespoon ground cumin
    4 cloves
    ½ cup/4 fl oz (120 ml) white vinegar
    4–4½ lb (1.8–2 kg) goat leg
    8 oz (225 g) tomatoes, roasted, peeled, and seeded
    salt
    Corn Tortillas (page 136, for homemade), to serve

Heat a frying pan over medium heat and roast the chiles and peppercorns for 5 minutes, or until the chiles blister. Tip into a blender and add the garlic, onion, oregano, cumin, cloves, and vinegar. Blend on medium speed, until smooth. If necessary, add water, but it must stay thick.
    Season the goat with salt and pepper, then place it in an oven tray, 11 x 7 x 2 inches (28 x 18 x 5 cm), and spread the paste over it. Cover with aluminum foil and let it marinate overnight in the refrigerator.
    Remove the meat from the refrigerator 1 hour before cooking. Preheat the oven to 350°F/180°C/Gas Mark 4.
    Place the covered oven tray in the oven, and cook for 4 hours, or until the meat is tender and falls from the bone. Remove from the oven. Scoop out 1 cup/8 fl oz (250 ml) of the cooking juices, add to a blender with the roasted tomatoes, and blend until smooth.
    Serve while hot, with the sauce on top and tortillas on the side.

Mexican Goat Stew

Sweets

The sun beats down on the backs of more than a dozen cane cutters of African and South Indian descent in a field of sugarcane near the coast of Guyana. They arrived in the early morning when there was little light, getting as much done as they can before 9am, when the sun begins to peak over the green leaves. The soil is too soft for heavy machines, so the cutters bend down and swing a cane machete with a wide blade near the root of the thick stalk. Venomous snakes lurk beneath the mud and fallen stalks, or the occasional caiman might appear from an adjacent canal. Each of the cutters lifts several tons of cane every day, carrying bundles of the long sticks tied with dried cane leaves, weighing as much as one hundred pounds, above their heads at a time. The cane is loaded onto a small barge that will be pulled by tractor to a nearby mill where it will be partially refined, turning it into large grains that maintain a golden-brown hue from the natural molasses within.

In the 1500s, the Guianas were one of the first places in the New World to grow sugarcane, along with Brazil and various Caribbean islands. With two rainy seasons intersected by dry seasons, there are two harvests per year here, helping fulfill what seemed to be a limitless demand from the Old World in the ensuing centuries, changing landscapes and responsible for bringing in millions of slaves and indentured workers.

Prior to the introduction of refined sugar, the craving for sweet things was satisfied with fruits, honey, and natural syrups. In the sixteenth century, Spanish and Portuguese convents and monasteries brought their dessert-making traditions with them to the Americas, adapting old recipes and creating new ones from the combinations of ingredients they found before them. They created caramel confections like dulce de leche and *cajeta*, egg-rich custards, and fried pastries. Sugar soon found its way into everything. It was added to chocolate, fruits, and shaved ice. Even vegetables like squash, corn, and beans can be sweetened.

Santa Fe-Style Alfajor

Alfajor Santafesino
Argentina

Preparation time: 30 minutes,
plus 30 minutes resting
Cooking time: 15 minutes

Makes: 10

The *alfajor* came to the New World in the sixteenth century from Andalusia, where it was finger shaped and filled with ground almonds, walnuts, and honey. Generally speaking in South America, the sweet takes on the form of a sandwich of two round wheat- or corn-based cookies with a dulce de leche or fruit-based filling, and in some places gets covered in sugar, meringue, shredded coconut, or chocolate. In Argentina's Santa Fe province, the cookies are flakier and usually add an extra layer of cookie and dulce de leche, and are then bathed in a white glaze.

> 3¹⁄₂ cups/16¹⁄₄ oz (460 g) all-purpose (plain) flour, plus extra for dusting
> 5 egg yolks
> 1 teaspoon salt
> 1 tablespoon anise liquor
> 6 tablespoons warm water
> ¹⁄₂ cup/4 oz (115 g) butter, diced
> 2 cups/1 lb (460 g) Dulce de Leche (page 374, for homemade)
>
> For the frosting (icing)
> 1 egg white
> 1¹⁄₃ cups/6³⁄₄ oz (190 g) confectioner's (icing) sugar
> 1 tablespoon lime juice
> 1 cup/6¹⁄₂ oz (200 g) superfine (caster) sugar
> 3 tablespoons water

Tip the flour in a mound onto a clean surface and form a well in the middle. Add the egg yolks, salt, anise liquor, and warm water to the well. Incorporate the wet ingredients into the dry, then knead briefly to bring it together. Add the butter and continue kneading for 10 minutes until it forms a smooth and elastic dough. Cover with plastic wrap (clingfilm) and rest for 30 minutes at room temperature.

Preheat the oven to 400°F/200°C/Gas Mark 6.

Sprinkle a little flour onto a clean surface and roll out the dough to ¹⁄₈ inch (3 mm) thick. Using a plain 3-inch (7.5-cm) cookie cutter, stamp out 20 discs from the dough and place them on an oven tray lined with parchment paper. Prick each disc with a fork and bake in the oven for 10–12 minutes, or until golden brown. Remove from the oven and leave to cool for a few minutes on the tray, before transferring to a wire rack to cool completely.

Spread the dulce de leche on to each cookie and sandwich two cookies together.

In a bowl, start whisking the egg white with the confectioner's (icing) sugar and lime juice until thick. Meanwhile, in a small pan over medium heat, heat the sugar and water until the sugar dissolves, then boil for 5 minutes. Slowly pour the sugar syrup into the egg white mixture, whisking continuously, until the glaze is a medium consistency. Drizzle the glaze over the *alfajores* until they are completely coated and then let dry on a wire rack.

Serve once the glazed *alfajores* have cooled to room temperature.

Chilean Sandwich Cookies

Alfajores de Matilla
Chile

Preparation time: 30 minutes
Cooking time: 45 minutes

Makes: 12

In the towns of Matilla and Pica on the north coast of Chile, the *alfajores* are large, thick, and lumpy with the three layers of dough hiding globs of *manjar* or other fillings and rolled in shredded coconut. They are a far cry from the uniform discs of commercial forms of *alfajores*. They are usually rolled up in paper and sold by the half dozen.

> 3¹⁄₄ cups/15 oz (425 g) all-purpose (plain) flour, plus extra for dusting
> 1 teaspoon salt
> 6 eggs
> ¹⁄₃ cup aguardiente
> 1 tablespoon butter
> 2 cups/14 oz (400 g) superfine (caster) sugar
> 1 teaspoon ground cinnamon
> ¹⁄₄ teaspoon ground cloves
> 2 cups/16 fl oz (475 ml) boiling water

Preheat the oven to 400°F/200°C/Gas Mark 6.

In a bowl, place 3 cups/14 oz (400 g) of the flour with the salt, eggs, aguardiente, and butter. Using your hands, mix together and knead well into a smooth and uniform dough.

Place the dough on a floured surface and roll out to a rectangle ¹⁄₄ inch (5 mm) thick. Fold in half and repeat the process twice more. Roll out one last time to the same thickness and use a plain 3-inch (7.5-cm) cookie cutter to cut out discs of dough; you should have about 36 in total.

Line two baking sheets with parchment paper and place the dough discs on the sheets, slightly apart to allow room to spread. Bake for about 10 minutes, or until golden brown. Remove from the oven and let cool.

Meanwhile, prepare the filling. Put the sugar, remaining flour, cinnamon, and cloves in a pan. Place over medium heat and cook, stirring, for 15–20 minutes or until the sugar starts to caramelize. Slowly pour in the boiling water, stirring, and cook for a further 15 minutes, or until thick. Remove from the heat and set aside to cool until warm.

Spread the warm filling on the cookies, stacking 3 layers of cookie for each *alfajor*, letting the filling overflow on the sides and using the crumbs of the dough to cover it.

Serve once the filled *alfajores* have cooled to room temperature.

Sweets

Santa Fe-Style Alfajor

Small Mistol Balls

Bolanchao
Argentina

Preparation time: 20 minutes
Cooking time: 10 minutes

Makes: 15–20

In the semi-arid Gran Chaco of northwestern Argentina, the red fruit of the mistol tree (*Ziziphus mistol*), sometimes used to make a fruit wine, gets ground in a mortar into a paste and formed into balls, which are coated in carob flour and baked until golden brown. It's an indigenous recipe, slowly disappearing, which can keep for long periods of time, essentially preserving the fruit.

2 lb (900 g) mistol
1 lb (450 g) toasted carob flour

Preheat the oven to 375°F/190°C/Gas Mark 5.

In a large mortar, mash all of the mistol, removing the seeds as you mash. Form into a rough, granulated mix, then shape the fruit pulp into golf-ball-sized balls and sprinkle carob flour on them to give them a firmer consistency. Place the balls on an oven tray and bake for 5–10 minutes, or until golden brown. Remove from the oven and let cool before serving.

Beaten Egg Yolks Soaked in Syrup

Huevos quimbos
Argentina, Chile

Preparation time: 20 minutes,
plus 1 hour chilling
Cooking time: 10 minutes

Makes: 15

Called *huevos moles* in Spain, where the preparation was typical in the provinces of Granada and Jaén, *huevos quimbos*, sort of soft egg cookies soaked in syrup, were introduced through convents across Latin America sometime in the eighteenth century. The recipe was developed as one of the ways to use egg yolks left over from making recipes that called for the whites, and which ranged from puddings to a binding agent in the mortar used in the construction of churches.

1 egg
6 egg yolks
1/2 teaspoon vanilla extract
1 tablespoon all-purpose (plain) flour
2 cups/14 oz (400 g) superfine (caster) sugar
2 cups/16 fl oz (475 ml) water

Preheat the oven to 350°F/180°C/Gas Mark 4.

In a bowl, whisk the whole egg with the egg yolks until the mixture doubles in size and turns pale in color. Add the vanilla extract. Slowly incorporate the flour with a spatula until the mixture is uniform. Transfer to a piping bag.

Pipe the dough into small half-sphere molds or small cupcake paper liners of 1 1/2 inch (4 cm) diameter. Bake in the oven for 7–10 minutes, or until golden brown. Remove from the oven and place on a wire rack to cool.

In a pan over medium heat, dissolve the sugar in the water to make a simple syrup. Pour the syrup over the egg cakes, let cool, then place in the refrigerator for an hour before serving.

Fruit Paste and Cheese

Fresco y batata, postre vigilante, Martín Fierro, 🔲
Romeu e Julieta, bocadillo con queso
Argentina, Brazil, Colombia, Uruguay

Preparation time: 5 minutes

Serves: 4

Argentinian author José Hernández was beloved for his stories about the life of South American gauchos, most famously Martín Fierro. He always ordered a dessert, usually made of equal layers of *dulce de membrillo*, or quince paste, and semi-firm white cheese. It happened to be the Uruguayan version of the Argentine dessert *vigilante*, which uses sweet potato paste, so it was named the Martín Fierro in his honor.

The simple combination of a sweet paste and semi-firm, white cheese is common in many parts of Latin America. The recipe is as simple as layering one on top of the other and there are many choices for cheeses and pastes. In Brazil and Colombia, where guava paste is used for the fruit, it's called *Romeu e Julieta*, after the Shakespeare play, and *bocadillo con queso*, respectively.

2 cups/9 oz (250 g) *queso colonia*, *queso fresco* (or any semi-firm white cheese)
9 oz (250 g) Guava Paste (page 370) or any other fruit paste, such as quince, or sweet potato etc.

Cut the cheese into squares or into your preferred shape. Cut the fruit paste into the same shape. Place the fruit paste on top of the cheese and serve with toothpicks.

Mashed Nance in Condensed Milk

Mashed craboo in condensed milk
Belize

Preparation time: 15 minutes

Serves: 4

The bright yellow fruit of the nance tree (*Byrsonima crassifolia*) is found in tropical climates from Mexico to Brazil and throughout the Caribbean. In Belize, where it is known as *craboo*, the stone fruit ripens from July through September. When ripe it can be quite sweet, so it's mostly eaten fresh in desserts, but also as ice cream, stewed with sugar and preserved in a jar, fermented to make a fruit wine, and occasionally in savory recipes, such as stuffing meats or added to stews. Mashing them in milk is the most typical preparation in Belizean home kitchens.

10 1/2 oz (300 g) nance
6 oz (170 g) condensed milk

Mash the nance with a wooden mortar until thoroughly muddled yet still chunky. Remove the seeds, then mix with the condensed milk. If preferred, serve chilled.

Fruit Paste and Cheese

Dulce de Leche Thousand-Layer Cake

Milhojas de dulce de leche, milhojas con arequipe 🄰
Argentina, Chile, Colombia, Uruguay

Preparation time: 1 hour 10 minutes,
plus 2 hours 30 minutes resting
Cooking time: 10 minutes

Serves: 6

Dozens of cultures around the planet make some form of multi-layered cake or pastry based on a French millefeuille. Within Latin America there are differing versions, though most use some form of thin, flaky pastry layered with dulce de leche, also called *manjar* or *arequipe*.

   1¹/₃ cups/6¹/₄ oz (175 g) all-purpose (plain) flour, plus extra for dusting
   ¹/₂ teaspoon salt
   ³/₄ cup/6 oz (170 g) cold butter, cut into small cubes
   6 tablespoons iced water
   1 tablespoon lime juice
   3 cups/1 lb 8 oz (690 g) Dulce de Leche (page 374, for homemade)
   1 cup/5 oz (140 g) confectioner's (icing) sugar
   Sprig mint, to decorate, optional

In a large bowl, mix the flour with the salt. Using a whisk, mix the butter into the flour to combine as much as possible. Add the water and lime juice and mix into a rough dough, using a wooden spoon.
   Sprinkle some flour on a clean surface and knead the dough with your hands, for no more than 5 minutes to prevent warming it. Shape into a square, cover in plastic wrap (clingfilm), and place in the refrigerator for 30 minutes.
   Flour the surface and roll the dough into a large rectangle, ¹/₄ inch (5 mm) thick. Bring one side to the middle of the dough and repeat with the other side, folding the dough into three layers. Cover again with plastic wrap and let rest in the refrigerator for 30 minutes.
   Place the dough with a folded end facing you and roll again into a rectangle. Fold over into three again, cover and let rest in the refrigerator for 30 minutes. Repeat the process, always turning a folded end in front of you, two more times, then cover and rest it the refrigerator for 1 hour.
   Preheat the oven to 375°F/190°C/Gas Mark 5. Line two baking sheets with parchment paper.
   Roll out the dough one more time and cut into 10–12 rectangles 5 x 10 inches (12.5 x 25.5 cm). Place the rectangles on the lined baking sheets and bake for 10 minutes, or until puffed and golden brown. Remove from the oven and let cool.
   Once cooled, spread dulce de leche on one of the rectangles and cover it with another pastry rectangle. Repeat the layers until the dough and dulce de leche are used up. Sift the confectioner's (icing) sugar on top through a fine sifter (sieve) and decorate with a sprig of mint, if preferred.
   Serve at room temperature.

Garifuna Pumpkin Cake

Fein tau weiyema
Belize, Honduras

Preparation time: 15 minutes
Cooking time: 15 minutes

Serves: 8

Garifuna families living along the coast of Belize and Honduras prepare this pumpkin cake, which has a dense, bread-pudding like texture.

   butter, for greasing
   ¹/₄ cup/2 fl oz (60 ml) vegetable oil
   1¹/₂ cups/10¹/₂ oz (300 g) superfine (caster) sugar
   ¹/₄ cup/2 fl oz (60 ml) milk
   1 tablespoon vanilla extract
   1¹/₂ teaspoons ground cinnamon
   ¹/₂ teaspoon salt
   2 lb (900 g) pumpkin purée
   2 cups/9 oz (260 g) all-purpose flour

Preheat the oven to 350°F/180°C/Gas Mark 4. Butter a round cake pan, 9 inches (23 cm) in diameter.
   In a bowl, and using a wooden spoon, stir together the oil, sugar, milk, vanilla, cinnamon, salt, and pumpkin purée. Stir in the flour and pour into the prepared pan, using a spatula to remove all the batter and smooth the top. Bake for 1 hour, or until a toothpick inserted in the center comes out clean. Let cool, then cut into slices.

Belizean Powder Buns

Powda buns
Belize

Preparation time: 20 minutes
Cooking time: 15 minutes

Makes: 15

Made from the basic staples in a Belizean pantry, these sweet, filling biscuits are eaten at any time of the day.

   2 cups/9 oz (260 g) all-purpose (plain) flour
   ¹/₂ cup/4 oz (115 g) softened unsalted butter, plus extra for greasing
   ¹/₂ cup/3¹/₂ oz (100 g) brown sugar, plus extra for sprinkling
   ¹/₂ cup/2¹/₂ oz (70 g) raisins
   1 teaspoon each ground cinnamon and ground nutmeg
   2 teaspoons baking powder
   1¹/₂ cups/3¹/₂ oz (100 g) finely shredded fresh coconut
   2 eggs
   1 teaspoon vanilla extract
   ¹/₂ cup/4 fl oz (120 ml) coconut milk

Preheat the oven to 350°F/180°C/Gas Mark 4.
   Sift the flour into a bowl and add the butter. Rub it in with your fingertips until combined and crumbly. Add the sugar, raisins, cinnamon, nutmeg, baking powder, and coconut. Knead well to combine evenly.
   In another bowl, beat the eggs, vanilla extract and coconut milk until combined. Add to the dry ingredients and knead well. The dough should be uniform and sticky.
   Line two baking sheets with buttered parchment paper. Using a greased spoon, drop large spoonfuls of dough evenly on the baking sheets, about 14 in total. Sprinkle brown sugar over them all and bake for 15 minutes or until golden brown. Remove from the oven and place the buns on a wire rack to cool.

Dulce de Leche Thousand-Layer Cake

Broken Underwear

Calzones rotos 🔲
Chile

Preparation time: 20 minutes
Cooking time: 10 minutes
Makes: 20

These fried pastries typical in Chile are sprinkled with powdered sugar, and can be thin and crispy or a bit thicker and more donut-like. Rumor has it that a woman on Santiago's Plaza de Armas selling these pastries was once confronted with a gust of wind that lifted up her skirt, revealing her torn underwear, and the name stuck.

  3 cups/14 oz (400 g) all-purpose (plain) flour, plus extra for dusting
  ½ cup/3½ oz (100 g) superfine (caster) sugar
  1 teaspoon baking powder
  3 tablespoons softened butter
  2 egg yolks
  1 egg
  1 teaspoon grated lime zest
  vegetable oil, for deep-frying
  confectioner's (icing) sugar, for dusting

Sift the flour into a bowl and mix in the sugar and baking powder. Add the butter, egg yolks, whole egg, and lime zest and mix well with a wooden spoon. Slowly add enough water, 1 tablespoon at a time, to make a firm, but soft dough.

Lightly flour a clean surface and roll out the dough to ⅛ inch (3 mm) thick. Cut the dough into rectangles 4 x 2 inches (10 x 5 cm). Make an incision lengthways in the middle of each rectangle, about 1½ inches (4 cm) long, then tuck one of the shorter ends through the incision and out the other side, stretching it gently back on itself. Place on a tray.

Pour enough oil for deep-frying into a heavy pan, making sure it is no more than two-thirds full, and heat to 350°F/177°C. Fry the *calzones* 3 or 4 at a time, for 1 minute each side, removing them with a skimmer to a plate lined with paper towels, to absorb excess oil.

When they have cooled to just warm, sprinkle with confectioner's (icing) sugar and serve.

Happy Custard Apple

Cherimoya alegre
Chile

Preparation time: 10 minutes
Cooking time: 20 minutes
Serves: 4

Called "the most delicious fruit known to men" by Mark Twain, the *cherimoya* (*Annona cherimola*), sometimes called the custard apple, is native to the Andes but now grown in tropical regions around the world. The green fruit's sweet, creamy white flesh makes it a favorite for use in desserts, such as this simple recipe from Chile that in its simplest form can be made with as few as two ingredients: orange juice and *cherimoya*.

  2 cups/16 fl oz (475 ml) orange juice
  1 cup/7 oz (200 g) granulated white sugar
  3 fl oz (90 ml) Cointreau
  2 *cherimoya* (custard apples)
  2 oranges, peeled

Add the orange juice and sugar to a pan, bring to a boil over medium heat, stirring until the sugar has dissolved. Simmer, uncovered, for 15 minutes then add the Cointreau and let cool.

Cut the *cherimoya* (custard apples) in half, pick out the seeds and scoop the pulp into a mixing bowl. Cut the oranges into small pieces, remove the seeds, and add into the bowl, along with the orange juice mixture. Mix well, and serve in cold dishes.

Chilean Blackberry Cake

Kuchen de mora
Chile

Preparation time: 20 minutes, plus 1 hour resting
Cooking time: 55 minutes
Serves: 8

An estimated 300,000 German colonists arrived in Chile between 1845 and 1914, completely changing the cultural makeup of the south of the country. It's for this reason that the word *kuchen*, of German origin, has become the term in Chile for a genre of cakes made of eggs, flour, and sugar. Usually, the cakes have a lattice or streusel crust, and seasonal fruits such as blackberries, murta berries, or apples are incorporated into the cakes in some form.

  1¼ cups/6 oz (170 g) all-purpose (plain) flour
  ½ teaspoon salt
  ¾ cup/3½ oz (100 g) confectioner's (icing) sugar
  ½ cup/4 oz (115 g) butter, cubed, plus extra for greasing
  3 egg yolks, beaten
  1 teaspoon vanilla extract
  2 eggs
  ½ cup/3½ oz (100 g) superfine (caster) sugar
  ⅓ cup/1½ oz (40 g) cornstarch (cornflour)
  3 tablespoons whole milk
  1⅓ cups/10½ fl oz (325 ml) cream
  1 lb (450 g) blackberries

Sift the flour into a bowl, add the salt and confectioner's (icing) sugar and mix. Add the butter and rub it in with your fingers to make a crumbly dough. Add the egg yolks and vanilla extract and continue kneading to a smooth, uniform dough. Place the dough between two pieces of parchment paper and roll out to a circle 10 inches (25 cm) in diameter. Transfer the dough to the refrigerator to rest for 1 hour.

Preheat the oven to 400°F/200°C/Gas Mark 6.

Lay the chilled dough in a greased pie mold, 9 inches (23 cm) in diameter and 1 inch (2.5 cm) deep, pressing along the edges. Prick the bottom of the dough with a fork and bake for 10 minutes, then remove from the oven.

Meanwhile, prepare the filling. In a large bowl, whisk the whole eggs with the sugar until paler in color and the sugar has dissolved. In another bowl, dilute the cornstarch (cornflour) with the milk and pour it into the mixture. Whisk well, while adding the cream, until all the ingredients are incorporated.

Reduce the heat to 350°F/180°C/Gas Mark 4. Spread the blackberries on the pastry crust and slowly pour in the cream mixture. Bake for 45 minutes until set and the custard is golden brown, then remove from the oven and let cool.

Serve at room temperature.

Broken Underwear

Peaches with Wheat Berries

Mote con huesillos 🍲
Chile

Preparation time: 5 minutes, plus overnight soaking and chilling
Cooking time: 1 hour 15 minutes

Serves: 6

For most Chileans, this cold snack made of *mote* (wheat berries) that are covered with *huesillos* (dried peaches) soaked in syrup is no doubt etched into your memory. There's a saying that goes "más chileno que el mote con huesillos," or "more Chilean than *mote con huesillos*." In the summertime, it's sold by street vendors and food stalls, bottled and sold in markets, or mixed in home kitchens.

9 oz (250 g) dried peaches
2½ oz (75 g) panela sugar (or use light muscovado)
peel of 1 orange
1 cinnamon stick
⅔ cup/4½ oz (130 g) granulated white sugar
9 oz (250 g) wheat berries

Rinse the peaches under cold water and place in a bowl. Cover with water and let soak overnight.

The following day, place the peaches and their soaking water in a pan with the *chancaca*, orange peel, and cinnamon stick. Bring to a boil over medium heat and simmer for 45 minutes, stirring frequently. Add the sugar and continue cooking, stirring constantly, for a further 30 minutes. Remove from the heat and remove the peaches, reserving the cooking syrup; set aside in the refrigerator.

Meanwhile, put the wheat berries in another pan, add water to cover, and bring to a boil over medium heat. Cover and cook for 30 minutes or until soft, then drain and let cool. Set aside in the refrigerator.

Add a large tablespoon of wheat berries to each of 6 large glasses, divide the peaches between them, and add some cooking syrup.

Serve cold.

Layered Cheese with Guava Paste

Queso en capas con bocadillo
Colombia

Preparation time: 15 minutes

Serves: 4

In Mompox, a lost colonial town on an island in Colombia's Magdalena river, *queso en capas*, a mozzarella-like cheese with an elastic consistency, is stretched into long, thin strips that get rolled up into squares and sold by roving street vendors. It pairs well with fruit pastes or candied fruits, and in Mompox they are sometimes rolled up with *bocadillo*, or guava paste. While *queso en capas* can be difficult to find, Mexican *queso Oaxaca* or *quesillo*, which has a similar flavor and texture, can be substituted.

10 oz (275 g) *queso en capas* or *queso Oaxaca*
4 oz (120 g) Guava Paste (page 370), cut into 4 pieces

Stretch the cheese into 4 separate, equal strips, as thin as possible without breaking it. Place a square of guava paste on the end of one strip of cheese. Fold the cheese over the square (by rolling it towards the other end) several times and then cut it. Turn the square and fold the strip of cheese over the exposed side of the guava paste several times. Repeat the process of cutting, turning, and folding until the strip is gone. Repeat the process with the remaining strips of cheese.

Corn, Pineapple, and Lulo

Champús
Colombia, Ecuador

Preparation time: 30 minutes, plus overnight soaking
Cooking time: 3 hours 15 minutes

Serves: 6

Popular in Colombia's Cauca Valley and over the border in Ecuador, *champús* is a cold, refreshing, chunky fruit concoction, frequently sold by street vendors, that's made of corn, panela sugar, pineapple, and the very tart and acidic fruit lulo, also called naranjilla, as well as additional herbs and spices. Another form of *champús* is made in Peru using other fruits, such as quince, guanabana, and apples.

2 cups/12 oz (340 g) dried corn kernels
1 cinnamon stick
8 oz (225 g) panela sugar (or use light muscovado)
5 cloves
2 teaspoons orange zest
1 cup/8 fl oz (250 ml) water
10 lulos, peeled and mashed
1 pineapple, peeled, cored, and cut into small cubes

Place the dried corn in a bowl and cover with water. Let soak overnight.

Rinse the soaked corn under cold water, place in a medium pan with the cinnamon and cover with water. Bring to a boil, then lower the heat and simmer uncovered for 3 hours, or until soft, stirring occasionally to prevent it from sticking to the bottom and adding more water if necessary.

Scoop a cup of the cooked corn into a blender, blend for 1 minute on medium speed, then pour it back into the pan.

In a bowl, mix the sugar, cloves, orange zest, and water, then add to the pan with the mashed lulo and cubed pineapple. Cook for 5 minutes over low heat to dissolve the panela. Remove from the heat and let cool, adding more sugar or water, if necessary.

Serve cold with ice.

Peaches with Wheat Berries

Corn Cookies

Totopostes
Costa Rica, El Salvador, Guatemala, Honduras, Nicaragua

Preparation time: 20 minutes
Cooking time: 50 minutes,   Makes: 12
plus 15 minutes resting

This pre-Columbian biscuit, still found throughout much of Central America, is made from a base of corn mixed with water and some form of fat, then wrapped in husks and roasted in ashes. In Costa Rica, *totopostes* are sweeter, ring shaped, and made with shredded coconut and cheese. They are known as a filling food famously consumed by soldiers during the 1921 war with Panama.

> 1 cup/8 oz (225 g) butter
> 1½ cups/12 fl oz (350 ml) whole milk
> ½ cup/3½ oz (100 g) white sugar
> 2 cups/8 oz (225 g) shredded cheese (any firm white cheese)
> ½ cup/2 oz (50 g) shredded coconut
> 1 teaspoon salt
> 1 lb (450 g) fresh Corn Masa (page 123, for homemade)

Preheat the oven to 350°F/180°C/Gas Mark 4.
Put the butter, milk, and sugar in a small pan and heat for 5 minutes, or until the sugar is dissolved; do not let it boil. Remove from the heat and let cool.
In a bowl, mix the cheese, coconut, salt and masa.
Make a small well in the middle of the dry ingredients and slowly pour in the butter and milk mixture, kneading to mix. Once the dough is soft and uniform, shape into 12 sticks, 6 inches (15 cm) long, and join the ends of each to form a ring. Place on a baking sheet lined with parchment paper and bake for 40 minutes, until golden brown. Remove from the oven and let cool for 15 minutes.
Heat a broiler (grill) to 375°F/190°C. Broil (grill) the *totopostes* for 5 minutes, until dark brown spots begin to form.
Serve warm.

Salvadoran Rice Flour Cookies

Salpores de arroz
El Salvador

Preparation time: 15 minutes
Cooking time: 20 minutes   Makes: 15

A cross between a biscuit and a cookie, *salpores* are a staple at Salvadoran *panaderías*. They can also be made with corn flour or cornstarch and come in a variety of shapes. Sometimes they are sprinkled with colored sugar.

> 3 cups/14 oz (400 g) rice flour
> 1 cup/6½ oz (200 g) superfine (caster) sugar, plus extra for sprinkling
> 1 teaspoon ground cinnamon
> 1 teaspoon salt
> 1 teaspoon baking powder
> ½ cup/4 oz (115 g) lard, at room temperature
> 2 eggs, beaten

Preheat the oven to 350°F/180°C/Gas Mark 4.
In a medium bowl, mix all the dry ingredients together. Add the lard and knead with your hands to combine. Slowly add the eggs, while kneading, until you have a soft, uniform dough. Divide into 15 equal pieces, roll into balls, and flatten into rounds or ovals ½ inch (1 cm) thick. Gently press the tops with a fork and sprinkle sugar on top.
Place on a baking sheet lined with parchment paper and bake for 20 minutes, or until golden.
Serve warm.

King Kong

King Kong
Peru

Preparation time: 30 minutes
Cooking time: 25 minutes   Serves: 4

In 1933, when the movie *King Kong* was being shown in the northern Peruvian region of Lambayeque, people started calling a regional sweet after the film. Previously called the *alfajor de Lambayeque*, a baker by the name of Victoria Mejia had created it a decade before because the typical *alfajor* just wasn't big enough. Instead of two layers of small cookies he placed four large cookies filled with *manjar blanco* and fruit preserves (usually strawberry or pineapple). Sometimes, *dulce de maní*—a paste made of ground peanuts cooked with *chancaca* (panela sugar), and sweet potatoes—is included too. Multiple bakeries specialize in the dessert, which can be either round or rectangular, and weigh up to several pounds.

> 12 cups/3 lb 8 oz (1.6 kg) all-purpose (plain) flour
> 3½ oz (100 g) chilled butter, cubed
> 6 egg yolks
> ½ cup/4 fl oz (120 ml) water
> pinch of salt
> *Manjar blanco* (page 374) or Dulce de Leche (page 374, for homemade)
> choice of two fillings: strawberry or pineapple preserves, quince or fig paste, or *dulce de maní*

Preheat the oven to 375°F/190°C/Gas Mark 5.
Sift the flour into a large bowl, add the butter and rub it in with your fingers to make a crumbly dough. Add the egg yolks, water, and a pinch of salt and knead into a soft and uniform dough. Roll out into a thin layer and cut into 4 equal-sized rectangles. Place the pieces of dough on a baking sheet lined with parchment paper and bake for about 25 minutes, or until golden brown. Remove from the oven and let cool.
Prepare the layers of cookies by smearing *manjar blanco* on one and the other fillings on the other two, then stack and use the clean cookie for the top.

Amaranth Bars

Alegrías
Mexico

Preparation time: 15 minutes
Cooking time: 30 minutes,
plus 5 minutes resting

Serves: 6–8

This sweet bar, which dates back at least to the Aztecs, who called it *tzoali*, was used in ritual offerings. Today it can be found in bakeries throughout Mexico.

> 1¹/₄ cups/9 oz (250 g) amaranth seeds
> ¹/₄ cup/1 oz (30 g) walnut pieces
> ¹/₄ cup/1 oz (30 g) peanuts
> ¹/₂ cup/2¹/₂ oz (70 g) *pepitas* (hulled squash or pumpkin seeds)
> 1 lb 3 oz (540 g) panela sugar (or use light muscovado)
> ¹/₂ cup/4 fl oz (120 ml) water
> ¹/₂ cup/5 oz (140 g) honey or agave syrup

Place a dry frying pan over medium heat. Toast the amaranth seeds until brown, then tip into a bowl. Toast the walnuts, peanuts, and *pepitas*, separately, in the same way, adding them all to the bowl.

Add the sugar, water, and honey or agave to a pan. Cook for about 15 minutes over low heat, stirring continuously, until a caramel forms, then let cool for 5 minutes, before adding to the dry mixture and stirring to mix.

Line a tray with aluminum foil. Spread the mixture out using a spatula, and let cool. Cut using a wet knife and serve.

Vermicelli Cake

Sawine
French Guiana, Guyana

Preparation time: 10 minutes
Cooking time: 30 minutes,
plus 2 hours chilling

Serves: 12

Similar to South Indian *paysum* or Pakistani *seviyan*, this vermicelli cake is prepared by Muslims in the Guyanas and Trinidad to celebrate Eid al Fitr, marking the end of Ramadan, though it can also be served at any special occasion or party.

> butter, for greasing
> 1 tablespoon vegetable oil
> 7 oz (200 g) vermicelli or another long, thin pasta
> 2 cups/16 fl oz (475 ml) water
> 2 cinnamon sticks
> 1 teaspoon salt
> ¹/₂ teaspoon ground nutmeg
> ¹/₂ teaspoon ground cardamom
> ¹/₂ teaspoon ground ginger
> 6 cups/50 fl oz (1.5 liters) condensed milk
> ¹/₄ cup/1³/₄ oz (50 g) superfine (caster) sugar
> 1¹/₂ teaspoons vanilla extract
> ¹/₄ cup/1¹/₄ oz (35 g) raisins
> ¹/₂ cup/2 oz (60 g) dried cherries, chopped

Grease a 9 x 13-inch (23 x 33-cm) serving dish with butter and set aside.

Heat the oil in a sauté pan over medium heat. Break the vermicelli into smaller pieces, add to the pan and cook, stirring frequently, until golden brown.

Meanwhile, in a medium pan over high heat, combine the water, cinnamon, salt, and spices, and bring to a boil. Reduce the heat to low, add the toasted vermicelli and cook for 15 minutes, or until the pasta is cooked through and the water has reduced by about two-thirds. Stir in the condensed milk, sugar, vanilla, raisins, and cherries and remove from the heat; it should have a pudding-like consistency. Transfer to the prepared dish, and refrigerate for at least 2 hours, until chilled.

Slice and serve cold.

Cassava Cake

Cassava pone
Guyana

Preparation time: 20 minutes
Cooking time: 1 hour

Serves: 10

At its most basic, this gummy, golden brown cake is made of primarily just shredded cassava and coconut, plus some sugar and spices. However, some cooks will add pumpkin and carrots, and raisins are sometimes included.

> 2 oz (60 g) shredded cassava
> 1¹/₂ oz (40 g) shredded fresh coconut
> ¹/₂ cup/3¹/₂ oz (100 g) superfine (caster) sugar
> 1 teaspoon vanilla extract
> 1 tablespoon ground cinnamon
> 1 teaspoon freshly ground black pepper
> 1 tablespoon ground nutmeg
> 3 tablespoons butter, softened, plus extra for greasing
> 1¹/₂ cups/12 fl oz (350 ml) evaporated milk (unsweetened)
> 1¹/₂ cups /12 fl oz (350 ml) condensed milk

Preheat the oven to 350°F/180°C/Gas Mark 4. Grease the bottom and sides of an 8-inch (20-cm) square baking pan, 1¹/₂ inches (4 cm) deep.

Place the cassava and coconut in a bowl and mix well with your hands. Add the remaining ingredients and mix until everything is well incorporated.

Tip the mixture into the prepared baking pan and bake for 1 hour, or until golden brown and a knife inserted in the center comes out smooth but still slightly sticky. Remove from the oven and let cool.

Once cold, cut into squares and serve.

Plantains in Mole

Plátanos en mole 🔲
Guatemala

Preparation time: 10 minutes
Cooking time: 30 minutes
Serves: 8

In Guatemala, mole is sweet. It's not for savory dishes, like in Mexico, but most usually served over fried plantains. There is a touch of spice from *pasilla* chiles, though fewer spices compared with Mexican moles and higher proportions of cinnamon, sesame, and chocolate.

    1 *pasilla* chile
    4 oz (120 g) sesame seeds
    1 cinnamon stick
    1 tablespoon *pepitas*
    2 tomatoes, peeled
    2 cups/16 fl oz (475 ml) water
    6 ripe plantains, peeled
    2 tablespoons vegetable oil
    8 oz (240 g) milk chocolate

Heat a *comal* or frying pan and toast the chile, sesame seeds, cinnamon stick, and *pepitas* for about 6 minutes, stirring occasionally. Set aside 1 tablespoon of roasted sesame to use later for the garnish. Place the rest of the ingredients in a blender.

Heat the same *comal* or frying pan over high heat, roast the tomatoes until they are well browned on every side. Place the roasted tomatoes in the blender with the other ingredients and the water. Mix well on medium speed until smooth.

Cut the plantains into diagonal slices. Heat the oil in a frying pan over medium heat and add the plantain slices and cook for 4 minutes on each side, or until golden. Remove them from the pan and place them on a plate with paper towel to absorb any excess oil.

Pour the blended mix in a pan and bring to a boil. Reduce the heat to low and add the chocolate. Cook until it melts, about 3–5 minutes, then stir and add the fried plantains and cook for a further 5 minutes.

Serve the plantains warm, covered in sauce, and the reserved sesame seeds sprinkled on top.

Chickpeas in Syrup

Garbanzos en miel
Guatemala

Preparation time: 15 minutes,
plus overnight soaking
Cooking time: 1 hour 15 minutes
Serves: 6

Introduced to Central America during the colonial era, chickpeas are served in a sweet syrup made from panela sugar in this recipe that's typical during Semana Santa.

    1 lb (450 g) dried chickpeas
    1/2 teaspoon salt
    2 cups/14 oz (400 g) panela sugar (or use light muscovado)
    1 cinnamon stick

Put the chickpeas in a bowl, add water to cover, add the salt, and let soak overnight.

Drain the chickpeas, rinse well, place in a pan and add water to cover. Bring to a boil and cook uncovered for 45 minutes over medium heat, or until soft. Drain and let cool.

Peel the chickpeas, add back to the pan, cover with water and bring to a boil. Add the sugar and cinnamon and continue cooking for 25 minutes, or until the consistency of the syrup is as thick as honey. Place the mixture in a deep dish and let it cool.

Serve cold.

Drunk Soup

Sopa borracha
Panama

Preparation time: 30 minutes,
plus 1 hour soaking
Cooking time: 1 hour 5 minutes,
plus 2 hours resting
Serves: 8

Sopa borracha is not a soup and it's not likely to get you drunk. However, these squares of alcohol-soaked sponge cake bathed in sweet syrup and dried fruits are typical of holiday parties and other festive events, where you very well may be drunk by the time it is set on the table.

    2 cups/10 oz (280 g) dried plums (prunes)
    2 cups/10 oz (280 g) raisins
    2 cups/16 fl oz (475 ml) rum
    2 cups/16 fl oz (475 ml) muscatel
    2 cups/16 fl oz (475 ml) brandy
    butter, for greasing
    9 eggs, separated
    1 1/2 cups/10 1/2 oz (300 g) superfine (caster) sugar
    3 cups/14 oz (400 g) all-purpose (plain) flour
    2 teaspoons baking powder
    1 teaspoon salt
    grated zest of 1 lime
    1/2 tablespoon vanilla extract
    2 cups/16 fl oz (475 ml) water
    2 cinnamon sticks
    1 1/2 cups/10 1/2 oz (300 g) brown sugar
    2 lime slices
    10 cloves

Place the dried plums (prunes) and raisins in a bowl and pour in the rum, muscatel, and brandy. Let soak for at least 1 hour.

Preheat the oven to 375°F/190°C/Gas Mark 5. Grease the bottom and sides of an 8-inch (20-cm) square baking pan, 1 1/2 inches (4 cm) deep.

Place the egg whites in a bowl and whisk until stiff. In a separate bowl, whisk the egg yolks with the superfine (caster) sugar until pale and airy, then slowly pour them into the bowl with the whites, while whisking. Mix the flour with the baking powder, salt, lime zest, and vanilla. Gradually fold into the egg mixture. These steps should be done quickly, to keep as much air in the mix as possible.

Pour the mixture into the greased pan and bake for 45 minutes, or until golden brown a knife inserted in the center comes out clean. Let cool.

Meanwhile, place the water, cinnamon, brown sugar, lime slices, and cloves in a pan, bring to a boil, reduce the heat and simmer for 20 minutes, or until thick. Drain and let it cool. When the syrup is cold enough, pour it into the bowl with the soaking fruits and mix well.

Remove the cooled cake from the pan and cut into 1-inch (2.5-cm) squares. Place the squares on a deep plate and strain over the syrup, making sure to cover all of the squares. Refrigerate for 2 hours, then serve the cake pieces with the soaked fruits.

Plantains in Mole

Paraguayan Sweet Polenta

Mbaipy he'ẽ, polenta dulce 🍲
Paraguay

Preparation time: 15 minutes
Cooking time: 20 minutes

Serves: 10

This corn-based cake has the texture of bread pudding, and is sweetened with cane syrup and served warm, often with hot chocolate.

½ cup/3½ oz (100 g) superfine (caster) sugar
5 tablespoons water
3½ cups/29 fl oz (870 ml) whole milk
1 lb (450 g) corn (maize) flour
1 cup/10 oz (280 g) molasses
grated zest of 1 orange

In a small pan, mix the sugar and water. Cook over medium heat for 10 minutes, while slowly swirling the pan (do not stir) until it turns a dark brown color. Remove from the heat.

Heat the milk in a pan over medium heat until it starts steaming, then slowly add the corn (maize) flour, while stirring, until it starts boiling. Add the molasses and orange zest, reduce the heat and cook for 5 minutes, stirring continuously.

Place the corn flour mixture in a bowl and slowly pour the caramel on top of it.

Serve warm.

Lucuma Ice Cream

Helado de lúcuma
Peru

Preparation time: 10 minutes,
plus 6 hours chilling and churning
Cooking time: 25 minutes

Serves: 4

Lucuma is found along the lower slopes of the western side of the Andes, and is one of the signature fruits of Peru (and northern Chile). The flavor, particularly in sweets, is unlike any fruit you have ever encountered. It is sometimes called eggfruit for its dry, orange-yellow flesh, which is similar in texture and color to a hard-boiled egg yolk but tastes more like a cross between pumpkin and brown sugar. The baseball-sized fruit has long been a staple of the indigenous cuisine; it is depicted on the ceramics of Peru's ancient coastal civilizations. It has a thin green skin that peels off when ripe and a brown seed. Lucuma ice cream regularly outsells strawberry and chocolate; even the fast-food chains have it on their menus. The best versions can be found on the side of the Pan-American Highway near the town of Chilca, south of Lima, the perfect pit stop en route to the beaches further south, where dozens of small ice cream stands sell ice cream made from lucuma, as well as figs and other local fruits.

2 cups/16 fl oz (475 ml) heavy (double) cream
6 egg yolks
⅔ cup/4½ oz (130 g) superfine (caster) sugar
½ cup/4 fl oz (120 ml) light corn syrup
1 cup (200 g) lucuma pulp
1 teaspoon vanilla extract

Heat 1⅓ cups/10½ fl oz (325 ml) of the cream in the top of a double boiler over simmering water over medium heat.

Meanwhile, whisk the egg yolks, sugar, and corn syrup in a metal mixing bowl. Pour ¼ cup/2 fl oz (60 ml) of the hot cream into the egg mixture, whisking continuously, then whisk the mixture back into the remaining cream in the double boiler. Cook, stirring with a wooden spoon, until the mixture begins to thicken and has a very slight boil, about 15 minutes. Strain into a clean bowl and place the bowl in an ice bath.

Add the lucuma pulp, vanilla, and remaining cream and whisk until blended. Refrigerate until cold, about 4–5 hours. Churn the mixture in an ice-cream maker according to manufacturer's directions.

Bojo Cake

Bojo
Suriname

Preparation time: 20 minutes,
plus overnight soaking
Cooking time: 1 hour 40 minutes

Serves: 10

In the time of slavery in Suriname (1651–1863), Afro-Surinamese women were often forced to raise their children alone. To support their families, they would sell different kinds of cakes, like this spongy, flourless cake made of shredded coconut and cassava, that they carried around on plates balanced on their head. Today, it's most served at parties, enlivened with rum, cinnamon, and other spices, and can be served warm or cold.

½ cup/3 oz (85 g) golden raisins (sultanas)
⅓ cup/2½ fl oz (75 ml) rum
12 oz (350 g) cassava, peeled, rinsed, and
cut into chunks
2 cups/7 oz (200 g) shredded coconut
⅓ cup/2¼ oz (65 g) superfine (caster) sugar
1 teaspoon ground cinnamon
1 teaspoon salt
2 eggs
¼ cup/2 fl oz (60 ml) coconut milk
1 tablespoon vanilla extract
2 teaspoons almond extract
4 tablespoons butter, melted, plus extra for greasing

Soak the golden raisins (sultanas) in the rum overnight.

Place the cassava in a pan and add water to cover. Bring to a boil then reduce the heat to medium and simmer uncovered for 40 minutes, or until tender. Drain, remove the core, and let cool. Once cold, grate it finely, using a cheese grater.

Preheat the oven to 325°F/165°C/Gas Mark 3. Grease the bottom and sides of an 8-inch (20-cm) baking pan, 2 inches (5 cm) deep.

In a large bowl, mix the cassava with the coconut. Stir in the sugar, cinnamon, and salt.

In a separate bowl, whisk the eggs, coconut milk, and vanilla and almond extracts, then pour the mixture into the cassava mix and stir. Finish by adding the melted butter and the raisins with the rum. Incorporate well and pour into the prepared baking pan.

Bake for 1 hour, or until golden brown. Remove from the oven and then from the pan while it's still warm.

Serve at room temperature.

Sweets

Paraguayan Sweet Polenta

Baked Quince

Membrillos al horno 🍲
Uruguay

Preparation time: 20 minutes
Cooking time: 35 minutes
Serves: 8

Quince, introduced to Uruguay during the colonial period, is grown mostly in the country's Montevideo and Canelones departments. This fruit is often mixed into cakes or made into jams, but the best preparation of quince might just be just baked and filled with a little bit of cream.

8 ripe quinces
juice of 2 limes
$^1/_2$ cup/4 oz (115 g) butter, plus extra for greasing
3 tablespoons heavy (double) cream
1 cup/5 oz (140 g) confectioner's (icing) sugar

Peel the quinces, then halve them and remove the cores. Place in a bowl, cover them with water and the lime juice (to prevent them oxidizing), and set aside for 10 minutes.

Preheat the oven to 350°F/180°C/Gas Mark 4. Line a baking sheet with aluminum foil, lightly greased with butter. In a bowl, whisk the butter, cream, and most of the sugar together, to a smooth and uniform batter. Drain the quinces, pat dry, and place on the baking sheet. Fill the quinces with even quantities of the cream mixture. Sprinkle the remaining sugar over the tops through a fine sifter (sieve), and bake for 35 minutes, until tender.

Remove from the oven and serve hot.

Bahian Coconut Candy

Cocada Baiana
Brazil

Preparation time: 15 minutes
Cooking time: 15 minutes
Makes: 50

Cocadas, found in many parts of Latin America, are baked coconut confections that come in hundreds of forms. They might be shaped like balls or cookies, garnished with nuts, or dyed with food coloring. In Bahia, they are formed into patties or balls and sold by street vendors, often alongside *acarajé* (Spicy Black-Eyed Pea Fritters, page 172) or by roving beach vendors. They are usually just made with only two ingredients rolled together: shredded coconut and sugar. They are usually white, but golden brown when the coconut is toasted, or a darker hue when made with brown sugar and burnt coconut.

butter, for greasing
1 cup/8 fl oz (250 ml) water
2 cups/14 oz (400 g) brown sugar
5 cups/13 oz (375 g) shredded coconut
$^1/_2$ cup/4 fl oz (120 ml) condensed milk

Line a tray with parchment paper, lightly greased.

Add the water and sugar to a pan. Mix well, bring to a boil without stirring, and let the sugar cook until it reaches 220°F/104°C. Add the shredded coconut and condensed milk, mix well, and remove from the heat.

Using two spoons, scoop full tablespoonfuls of the mixture onto the lined tray until you have 50 *cocadas*. Let cool until fully set. Use a spatula to remove the *cocadas* from the tray to serve.

Venezuelan Sticky Buns

Golfeado
Venezuela

Preparation time: 20 minutes,
plus 1 hour rising
Cooking time: 35 minutes
Makes: 6

The Venezuelan take on the cinnamon roll is filled with shredded cheese and glazed with a panela sugar-based syrup called *melado*. Nearly every bakery in Venezuela makes them and they are sometimes topped with an extra slice of *queso de mano*, a soft white cheese used in making arepas and *cachapas*.

$^3/_4$ oz (20 g) fresh yeast
$^1/_2$ cup (100 g) superfine (caster) sugar
1 tablespoon salt
$^1/_2$ cup/4 oz (115 g) butter
1 cup/8 fl oz (250 ml) warm milk
3 cups/14 oz (400 g) all-purpose (plain) flour, plus extra for dusting
2 eggs
2 cups/14 oz (400 g) panela sugar (or use light muscovado)
9 oz (250 g) *queso de mano*, shredded (or use mozzarella)
1 teaspoon anise seeds
$^1/_2$ cup/4 fl oz (120 ml) water

In a mixing bowl, place the yeast with the sugar and salt. Melt half of the butter and pour it and the warm milk into the bowl. Stir well with a wooden spoon and slowly add the flour until it forms a lumpy dough. Add the eggs and knead with your hands until incorporated.

Place the dough on a floured surface and continue kneading to a soft and uniform dough. Stretch out the dough and roll it into a rectangle, $^1/_4$ inch (5 mm) thick.

Spread the remaining butter over the dough and sprinkle it with three-quarters of the sugar, the cheese, and the anise seeds. Roll the dough into a tight log and cut into slices $1^1/_2$ inches (4 cm) thick. Place on a baking sheet lined with parchment paper, cover with a clean tea towel and let rise for 1 hour at room temperature.

Preheat the oven to 350°F/180°C/Gas Mark 4.

Bake the buns for 20 minutes, or until risen and golden brown.

Meanwhile, heat the remaining sugar with the water in a small pan. Bring to a boil then set aside and keep warm. Remove the buns from the oven and brush the syrup over them. Place back in the oven for a further 5–10 minutes.

Serve warm.

Baked Quince

Tarts

Recipes for sweet, baked pastries arrived in the region with European settlers, who adapted them to local fruits and other fillings. In most cases, they tend to be small, individual portioned pastries rather than full size pies, with fillings generally encrusted in pastry, though there are always exceptions.

Belizean Coconut Crusts

Coconut crusts
Belize

Preparation time: 30 minutes
Cooking time: 25 minutes
Makes: 20

Coconut forms the base of many Belizean sweets, such as the coconut crust and coconut tart, whose names are sometimes interchangeable. While the ingredients are more or less the same for either, in general the coconut crust is like a coconut empanada that's filled with shredded and caramelized coconut, while the tart is a round, open crust with the filling exposed.

2 fresh coconuts
2 cups/14 oz (400 g) white sugar
1 teaspoon vanilla extract
1 teaspoon minced fresh ginger
1/2 teaspoon ground nutmeg
4 cups/1 lb 3 oz (530 g) all-purpose (plain) flour
1 teaspoon salt
1/2 cup/4 oz (115 g) butter, cubed, plus extra for greasing

Preheat the oven to 400°F/200°C/Gas Mark 6.
Open both coconuts and reserve the milk. Grate all the flesh and place in a pan with the sugar, vanilla, ginger, and nutmeg. Place over medium heat, stirring constantly to prevent burning, for 15 minutes, or until the sugar starts to caramelize. Remove from the heat and set aside to cool.
Put the flour, salt and butter into a bowl. Rub the butter into the flour with your fingers to a sandy dough. Slowly add enough of the reserved coconut milk to bring the dough together, and knead until smooth and uniform. Shape the dough into about 20 golf-ball-sized balls and set aside.
Line a baking sheet with parchment paper. Grease a clean surface and flatten one of the dough balls with your hands. Place a spoonful of coconut filling in the middle and close the dough by folding it in half. Press the edges together with a fork to seal, then place on the lined baking sheet. Repeat with the remaining dough and filling.
Bake for 10 minutes, or until the crusts are golden brown and crispy. Remove from the oven, let cool a little.
Serve warm.

Pine Tarts

Pine tarts
Guyana

Preparation time: 30 minutes,
plus 1 hour chilling
Cooking time: 1 hour 5 minutes
Makes: 12

These triangular tarts filled with pineapple, not pine, are a staple in Guyanese bakeries. The recipe, as well as other baked goods like the cheese roll, were created during the British rule of Guyana.

1 medium, ripe pineapple, peeled, cored, and cut into chunks
4 tablespoons (50 g) white sugar
1/2 cup/3 1/2 oz (100 g) brown sugar
1/2 teaspoon ground nutmeg
1/2 teaspoon ground cinnamon
1 teaspoon vanilla extract

For the dough
3 1/2 cups/1 lb (450 g) all-purpose (plain) flour
2 teaspoons sugar
pinch of salt
1/3 cup/2 1/2 oz (75 g) butter
1/3 cup/2 1/2 fl oz (75 ml) vegetable oil
3/4 cup/6 fl oz (175 ml) cold water
1 egg white, beaten
2 eggs, beaten

Place the pineapple in a food processor and blend on medium speed until you have a smooth purée. Take out the purée and place in a small pan, and use the rest for another preparation. Add the white and brown sugar, nutmeg, cinnamon and vanilla extract, and bring to a boil. Simmer for 40 minutes over low heat, stirring frequently, or until it reaches a jam-like consistency. Remove from the heat and set aside to cool.
To make the dough, sift the flour into a mixing bowl with the sugar and salt. Add the butter and the oil. Using a pastry cutter or a spatula, mix the butter into the flour until lumpy. Slowly add the cold water and knead. Shape the dough into a log and place it on a sheet of plastic wrap (clingfilm). Roll with your hands until it is about 12 inches (30 cm) long. Enclose in the plastic wrap and refrigerate for at least an hour.
Preheat the oven to 350°F/180°C/Gas Mark 4.
Line a baking sheet with parchment paper. Cut the log into round slices (about 15 in total), 1 inch (2.5 cm) thick. Flatten each disc with your palm and roll into a round, 7 inches (18 cm) diameter. Brush the edges with egg white, place a tablespoon of pineapple filling in the middle of each round, about 1 inch (2.5 cm) from the edge, and fold 3 sides into the center to form a triangle, then place on the lined baking sheet.
Brush all the tarts with the beaten eggs and pierce the middle with a knife for steam to escape. Bake for 25 minutes or until golden brown. Remove from the oven and let cool for 30 minutes.
Serve warm.

Belizean Coconut Crusts

Quince Tart

Pasta frola de dulce de membrillo
Argentina, Paraguay, Uruguay

Preparation time: 10 minutes,
plus 15 minutes resting
Cooking time: 35 minutes

Serves: 8

The pasta frola is an adaptation of the *crostata alla marmellata*, which was brought to South America by Italian immigrants. It's a full-size pie with a shortcrust pastry and a thin-striped lattice exposing some of the quince paste inside. Normally, it is eaten during afternoon merienda with tea or *maté*.

> 4 cups/1 lb 3 oz (530 g) all-purpose (plain) flour, plus extra for dusting
> 1½ teaspoons baking soda (bicarbonate of soda)
> ½ teaspoon salt
> ½ cup/3½ oz (100 g) white sugar
> ½ cup/4 oz (115 g) butter, cubed, plus extra for greasing
> 1 teaspoon vanilla extract
> 1 egg
> 1 egg yolk
> 1 lb (450 g) membrillo (quince paste)
> ½ cup/4 fl oz (120 ml) Port wine or water
>
> To finish
> 1 egg, beaten

Sift the flour into a mixing bowl with the baking soda (bicarbonate of soda), salt, and sugar. Add the butter and rub it in with your fingers until you have a sandy dough. Add the vanilla, whole egg, and yolk and bring the mixture together. Place on a floured surface and continue kneading until soft and uniform. Cover with plastic wrap (clingfilm) and refrigerate for 15 minutes.

Preheat the oven to 350°F/180°C/Gas Mark 4. Grease a baking pan, 8 inches (20 cm) in diameter, with butter.

Put the quince paste in a pan with the Port wine or water, and heat for 3–5 minutes over medium heat, until melted enough that it can be spread. Set aside and keep warm.

Divide the dough into two parts, one using two-thirds of the dough and the other the remaining for the lattice. Roll out the larger part to a round ¼ inch (6 mm) thick. Place it in the baking pan, pressing the dough up against the sides. Prick the bottom with a fork and pour the quince over the dough.

Roll out the remaining piece of dough into a circle, and cut into strips, ½ inch (1 cm) thick. Place on top of the tart in a criss-cross pattern and pinch the ends into the base. Brush the dough strips with the egg wash and bake for 30 minutes, or until golden brown.

Fritters

The art of frying in Latin America also extends to sweets. Doughs can be made of wheat, corn, plantains, bananas, cassava, or squash. They can be covered in sugar or drizzled in honey or syrup, or filled with chocolate or dulce de leche.

Sweet Cornmeal Rings

Mandoca
Venezuela

Preparation time: 15 minutes,
plus 25 minutes resting
Cooking time: 35 minutes

Makes: 20

From the Zulia state, these sweet, deep-fried cornmeal and ripe plantain rings are eaten hot with butter and cheese, primarily for breakfast.

> 1 ripe plantain
> 1 cup/7 oz (200 g) panela sugar (or use light muscovado)
> 1 cup/8 fl oz (250 ml) water
> ½ teaspoon salt
> 1 teaspoon anise seeds
> 1½ cups/6 oz (180 g) shredded *queso fresco*
> 4 cups/1 lb 4 oz (560 g) corn (maize) flour
> vegetable oil, for greasing and deep-frying
> butter, to serve

Peel the plantain and cook in boiling water for 10 minutes, until tender. Drain, cool, and mash with a fork.

In a bowl, mix the sugar and water, whisking until the sugar dissolves completely. Add the salt, anise seeds, mashed plantain, and *queso fresco*, then slowly add the corn (maize) flour, mixing with a wooden spoon to a firm batter. If necessary, add more water or corn flour to achieve the correct consistency. Rest the batter in the refrigerator for 15 minutes.

Lightly grease a baking sheet.

Divide the dough into 20 equal-sized pieces, and shape each into a 3 x ½-inch (8 x 1-cm) stick. Bring the tips together, forming a tear-drop shape. Place on the greased tray and let sit for 10 minutes.

Pour enough oil to half-cover the *mandocas* into a large, heavy pan, making sure it is no more than two-thirds full, and heat to 365°F/185°C. Fry in batches for 3 minutes each side, or until golden brown and crispy. Remove with a skimmer to a plate lined with paper towels to absorb excess oil.

Serve warm, with butter on the side.

Costa Rican Sweet Fritters

Prestiños
Costa Rica

Preparation time: 20 minutes,
plus 30 minutes resting
Cooking time: 20 minutes

Makes: 15

Brought to Costa Rica by the Spanish, you'll see this adapted form of an Andalucian recipe for sale in plastic bags hanging from fruit stands along highways in northern Costa Rica. There, they are usually drizzled with *tapa de dulce*, a syrup made from unrefined cane sugar, though warm honey or maple syrup can be used too.

    3 cups/14 oz (400 g) all-purpose (plain) flour
    1 teaspoon salt
    1 egg, beaten
    vegetable oil, for deep-frying

    For the syrup
    1 cup/7 oz (200 g) white sugar
    1 cup/7 oz (200 g) brown sugar
    1/2 teaspoon salt
    1 cup/8 fl oz (250 ml) water

Mix the flour and salt together in a bowl. Add the beaten egg and combine, then add enough water, a little at a time, while kneading, to make a smooth, not sticky dough. Divide the dough into 15 equal parts, cover with a tea towel, and refrigerate for 30 minutes.

Roll each piece of dough into a thin disc.

Pour enough oil for deep-frying into a large, heavy pan, making sure it is no more than two-thirds full, and heat to 350°F/177°C.

Place both sugars, the salt, and water in a pan and stir. Bring to a boil over medium heat, then remove from the heat and set aside. Let cool a bit as you complete the next step.

Fry the *prestiños* in batches for about 3 minutes each side, or until golden brown and crispy. Remove with a skimmer to a plate lined with paper towels, to absorb excess oil. Drizzle with the syrup and serve hot.

Mashed and Stuffed Plantain Fritters

Rellenitos de plátano
Guatemala

Preparation time: 20 minutes,
plus overnight soaking
Cooking time: 1 hour 25 minutes

Makes: 15

A comforting sweet made throughout the year, these oval-shaped fritters are made of mashed ripe plantains and filled with a sweet purée of refried black beans, chocolate, and cinnamon. They are often sprinkled with sugar or drizzled with cream or honey.

    4 oz (120 g) dried black beans
    10 green plantains, peeled and cut into chunks
    vegetable oil, for frying
    1/2 cup/4 oz (120 g) superfine (caster) sugar
    1 teaspoon ground cinnamon
    brown sugar, for sprinkling
    salt

Put the beans in a large bowl, cover with plenty of cold water and let soak overnight, or up to 24 hours.

Drain the beans and add to a medium pan with enough water to cover generously, and some salt. Bring to a boil and cook for 10 minutes, then reduce to a simmer and cook covered for about 50 minutes, or until tender, adding more water if necessary. Drain and set aside.

Meanwhile, place the plantains in a pan, add water to cover, and bring to a boil. Cook for 15–20 minutes, or until soft. Drain (reserving the water) and add to a blender then blend well for 2 minutes, adding a little of the cooking water if necessary. Set aside to cool.

Blend the black beans, without water, in a blender to form a thick purée. Heat 1 tablespoon of the oil in a frying pan and add the black bean purée. Add the sugar and cinnamon and cook for 10 minutes over low heat. Take off the heat and set aside.

When the plantain has cooled, shape into about 15 golf-ball-sized balls. Flatten each with the palm of your hand and place 1/2 tablespoon of the black bean purée in the middle of each. Bring the edges together to enclose the filling, and gently shape into ovals.

Pour enough vegetable oil to cover the surface of the clean frying pan, and place over medium heat and fry the *rellenitos* for 2 minutes each side, or until golden brown and crispy. Remove from the pan and place on a plate lined with paper towels. Let cool a little, and serve warm with brown sugar sprinkled on top.

Cassava and Cheese Fritters

Buñuelos de yuca y queso
Colombia, Nicaragua, Panama, Venezuela

Preparation time: 20 minutes
Cooking time: 15 minutes
Makes: 20

Either round or disc-shaped, sweet fritters known as *buñuelos* are consumed in many parts of Latin America. Introduced to the region by the Spanish, who generally make them from a wheat-based yeast dough, here native ingredients like cassava or squash might be used in its place. Cassava, often with cheese, fried and drizzled in syrup, is a preparation found in several countries.

    1 cup/7 oz (200 g) brown sugar
    1 cinnamon stick
    juice of ½ lime
    1 cup/8 fl oz (250 ml) water
    4 cups/32 fl oz (950 ml) vegetable oil
    ½ cup/2 oz (60 g) shredded *cuajada* cheese (milk curd)
    2 cups/10½ oz (300 g) grated cassava
    2 eggs, beaten
    ¼ teaspoon salt
    1 teaspoon baking powder

Put the sugar, cinnamon, lime juice, and water in a pan. Bring to a boil then simmer for 10 minutes, or until the consistency of a syrup. Keep warm over low heat.

Heat the vegetable oil to 375°F/190°C in a heavy pan, making sure it is no more than two-thirds full.

Meanwhile, in a bowl, mix the cheese, cassava, beaten eggs, salt, and baking powder. Knead well with your hands until smooth and uniform. Use a spoon to drop portions of the dough into the hot oil and fry for 5 minutes, or until golden brown. Remove with a skimmer to a plate lined with paper towels to absorb excess oil.

Serve warm with the warm syrup drizzled on top.

Colombian Fried Bananas

Bananos calados
Colombia

Preparation time: 5 minutes
Cooking time: 10 minutes
Serves: 2–4

Bananas cooked in butter, bathed in a sugary sauce made from panela sugar, and topped with vanilla ice cream, is the ultimate Colombian comfort dessert.

    2 oranges
    2 tablespoons butter
    4 bananas, peeled and halved widthways
    4 tablespoons panela sugar (or use light muscovado)
    1 cinnamon stick

Finely grate enough orange zest to give 1 tablespoon. Halve both oranges and squeeze the juice, reserving ½ cup/4 fl oz (120 ml).

In a frying pan, heat the butter over medium heat until slightly brown. Add the bananas, sugar, orange zest and juice, and cinnamon. Cook for 4 minutes, spooning the hot butter over, until they are golden brown. Remove the bananas and cinnamon, and reduce the sauce to a syrup. Pour it over the bananas to serve.

Peruvian Squash Donuts

Picarones
Peru

Preparation time: 15 minutes,
plus 2 hours 15 minutes resting
Cooking time: 1 hour 20 minutes
Makes: 25–30

This form of the *buñuelo* was created by African slaves in Lima during the Vice Royalty of Peru, who adapted the dough to include squash and, sometimes, sweet potato. They are a common street snack around Peru and are drizzled in *miel de chancaca*, a syrup made from unrefined cane sugar.

    1 lb 8 oz (680 g) sweet potatoes
    1 lb 8 oz (680 g) squash
    1 tablespoon anise seeds
    ⅓ oz (10 g) fresh yeast
    1 tablespoon white sugar
    1 cup/8 fl oz (250 ml) warm water
    1 lb (450 g) all-purpose (plain) flour
    vegetable oil, for deep-frying

    For the *miel de chancaca*
    14 oz (400 g) panela sugar (or use light muscovado)
    1 cinnamon stick
    1 orange, halved
    1 ripe plantain, peeled
    1 fig leaf
    6 cloves

Peel the sweet potatoes and squash and cut into 2-inch (5-cm) chunks. Place in a medium pan with the anise seeds and add cold water to cover. Cook for 15–20 minutes, or until tender. Drain, then mash the squash and sweet potato to a purée.

In a separate bowl, mix the yeast and sugar with the warm water. Rest for 15 minutes.

In a large bowl, mix the purée with the yeast mixture. Slowly add the flour while kneading vigorously with your hands for 15 minutes, or until soft and uniform. Cover the dough with a clean tea towel and let rest for 2 hours.

Meanwhile, for the *miel de chancaca*, place the sugar, cinnamon, orange halves, plantain, fig leaf, and cloves in a pan. Add water to cover and cook uncovered over medium heat for 35 minutes, or until thick. Strain and keep warm.

Pour enough oil for deep-frying into a large, heavy pan, making sure it is no more than two-thirds full, and heat to 375°F/190°C.

Take small amounts of dough and form a hole in the middle of each to make a ring. Fry the rings in batches for 5 minutes, spooning oil on top. Remove with a skimmer to a plate lined with paper towels to absorb excess oil.

Serve hot with the *miel de chancaca* poured over the top.

Colombian Fried Bananas

Ices

Especially in tropical areas of Latin America, shaved ice gets treated well beyond just a few squirts of colored syrups. Toppings can change wildly from region to region, but expect any vendor to have an arsenal of fresh fruits, homemade syrups, drizzles of condensed milk, and a collection of nuts, cookies, and candy.

Popayán-Style Iced Blackberries

Salpicón de Payanés
Colombia

Preparation time: 15 minutes

Serves: 4

Also called *salpicón de Baudilia* after the creator, believed to be the descendant of slaves, the centuries-old original recipe of this refreshing drink from the western Colombian city of Popayán is said to have used shaved ice from the snow cap of the Puracé volcano southeast of town, which was sold in the city prior to refrigeration. South American liberator Simón Bolívar is said to have written letters about the emotion he had when tasting the icy combination of blackberries, lulo, and soursop. The recipe has changed little over the years, though some like to add condensed milk or orange peels.

    5 lulos (naranjilla)
    2 cups/1 lb (440 g) crushed ice
    3 cups blackberries, mashed and frozen
    2 cups/14 oz (400 g) white sugar
    1 cup/8 fl oz (250 ml) orange juice
    1½ cups/12 oz (340 g) guanabana (soursop) pulp
    1 orange, cut into wedges, to serve

Cut the lulos in half and extract the pulp with a spoon, reserve in the refrigerator.

In a large bowl, mix the crushed ice with the frozen blackberries and lulo pulp. Add the sugar and orange juice and stir with a long spoon. The mixture will be thick, though you can add water if preferred.

To serve, place large chunks of guanabana in the bottom of each glass and pour the mixture over it. Serve with an orange wedge to squeeze on top.

Colombian Shaved Ice

Cholado
Colombia

Preparation time: 30 minutes
Cooking time: 20 minutes

Serves: 6

In the sweltering heat of the Valle de Cauca, shaved ice is treated more like a sundae than a snow cone. It gets drizzled in colorful syrups flavored with passionfruit and blackberry and condensed milk, topped with chunks of fresh fruits like bananas and lulo, and wafer cookies.

2¼ cups/1 lb (450 g) white sugar
2 cups/16 fl oz (475 ml) water
3 drops food coloring (red, green, or yellow)
1 pineapple, peeled and cored
2 red apples, peeled and cored
3 bananas
2 lulos (naranjilla), peeled
pulp of 1 passionfruit
8 oz (225 g) blueberries
6 cups of ice
juice of 3 limes
6 tablespoons condensed milk

Place the sugar and water in a pan and heat gently to dissolve the sugar. Add the food coloring and boil to reduce to a syrup consistency, about 15–20 minutes. Remove from the heat and set aside.

Cut the pineapple, apples, bananas, and lulos into small pieces. Crush the ice and mix with the lime juice.

In each serving glass, place 2 tablespoons of the crushed ice and some colored syrup, then equally divide half the chopped fruit, passionfruit pulp and blueberries between them. Repeat to fill the glasses, finishing by adding 1 tablespoon each of syrup and condensed milk. Mix with a long spoon to serve.

Churchill

Churchill
Costa Rica

Preparation time: 5 minutes

Serves: 1

Drive along the waterfront in and around Puntarenas, Costa Rica, and you'll notice gatherings of carts and kiosks advertising a Churchill. A type of *granizado*, or shaved ice treat, it's believed that the creator of this refreshing snack was a shopkeeper who looked remarkably similar to Britain's then Prime Minister, Winston Churchill. He would walk along Puntarenas' Paseo de los Turistas always asking for the same ingredients: ice, a bright red fruity sweetener called kola syrup, and condensed milk. Over the years many variations were created, using powdered milk or adding toppings like chopped fruit, marshmallows, or candy.

    1 cup/8 oz (220 g) shaved (crushed) ice
    2 tablespoons kola syrup
    ½ cup/4 fl oz (120 ml) condensed milk
    1 tablespoon milk powder
    1 scoop vanilla ice cream

In a glass, place one scoop of shaved ice and cover with the kola syrup. Continue with another layer of shaved ice and cover it with the condensed milk and milk powder. Finish with the vanilla ice cream and serve immediately.

Popayán-Style Iced Blackberries

Puddings

Rice puddings, as well as cooked and sweetened purées of fruits, beans, and corn are typical homemade desserts around the region.

Sweet Plantain Pudding

Chucula 🍽
Ecuador

Preparation time: 5 minutes,
plus 45 minutes cooling
Cooking time: 30 minutes

Serves: 5–6

Among Amazonian communities in northeastern Ecuador, *chucula* is a staple food. At its most basic it is simply ripe bananas mixed with water, a few spices, and a sweetener such as panela sugar or honey. It's simple to prepare, just boiled in a pot, and can then be eaten warm or cold. The recipe has been adapted to other parts of the country and milk usually replaces the water, with the consistency becoming more like a smoothie.

    4 ripe plantains, peeled and sliced
    2 cups/16 fl oz (475 ml) whole milk
    2 cloves
    4 cinnamon sticks
    1 teaspoon vanilla extract
    2 tablespoons sugar
    bittersweet (dark) chocolate, to decorate

Put the plantains in a small pan with water to cover, and bring to a boil. Cook for 10–15 minutes, or until soft and tender, then drain and mash into a purée.

Meanwhile, in a separate pan, heat the milk with the cloves, cinnamon, and vanilla. Once boiling, remove the cinnamon and cloves and add the plantain purée and sugar. Stir well and continue cooking over medium heat for 15 minutes.

Remove from the heat and let cool for at least a few minutes. Decorate with bittersweet (dark) chocolate shavings before serving.

Purple Corn Pudding

Mazamorra morada, colada morada
Bolivia, Ecuador, Peru

Preparation time: 10 minutes
Cooking time: 1 hour 50 minutes

Serves: 12

The preparation of *mazamorra morada* is similar to making *Chicha morada* (Purple Corn Juice, page 390). It's common to make the *chicha* first and use any left over the next day for the pudding by boiling it with pineapple and dried fruits and then using sweet potato starch to thicken it. Usually, *mazamorra morada* is served alongside *Arroz con leche* (Rice Pudding, page 369), when it's called *sol y sombra*, or sun and shadow.

    4 lb (1.8 kg) dried purple corn kernels
    12¹/₂ cups/6¹/₄ pints (3 liters) water
    1 cinnamon stick
    8 cloves
    4 oz (120 g) dried peaches
    4 oz (120 g) dried apricots
    4 oz (120 g) dried cherries
    4 oz (120 g) dried plums (prunes)
    1¹/₂ cups/10¹/₂ oz (300 g) white sugar
    ³/₄ cup (110 g) sweet potato flour
    juice of 2 limes
    ground cinnamon, to sprinkle

Place the corn in a large pan with the water, cinnamon and cloves, and bring to a boil. Simmer covered for at least 1 hour, or until the water has a deep purple color. Strain and discard the solids, retaining the cooking water. Set aside 2 cups/16 fl oz (475 ml) of it, and place what's left in a pan.

Add the dried fruits to the pan with the purple corn liquid. Cook uncovered for 20 minutes, or until the fruits are purple. Add the sugar and continue cooking for a further 20 minutes.

Meanwhile, whisk the sweet potato flour into the reserved 2 cups/16 fl oz (475 ml) of cooking water, until it dissolves. Pour the mixture into the pan with the fruits, stir well, and bring to a boil. Once boiling, whisk in the lime juice and continue cooking uncovered over medium heat for 10 minutes, or until the mixture thickens. Remove from the heat.

Serve warm in cups, sprinkled with cinnamon.

Sweet Plantain Pudding

Sweet Oaxacan Corn Flan

Nicuatole
Mexico

Preparation time: 10 minutes,
plus 3 hours cooling and setting
Cooking time: 15 minutes

Serves: 12

This sweetened, gelatinous *atole* can be seen in Oaxacan markets, cut into squares and laid out on banana leaves, sometimes flavored with seasonal fruits like mangoes and pineapples. The most traditional form of *nicuatole* is made by cooking a mixture of cinnamon, ground corn or corn masa, and milk and then letting it cool in clay pots with red dye from cochineal insects. The original pre-Columbian form of the recipe most likely used maguey sap instead of sugar.

1 lb 5 oz (600 g) fresh Corn Masa (page 123, for homemade)
5 cups/40 fl oz (1.2 liters) water
2 cups/16 fl oz (475 ml) whole milk
1¼ cups/9 oz (250 g) white sugar
1 cinnamon stick

Place the corn masa and the water in a large bowl and mix with your hands until it becomes a smooth paste.

When ready, place the corn paste in a clay pot or pan with the milk, sugar, and cinnamon. Mix well and bring to a boil over medium heat and cook for about 15 minutes, stirring frequently, until it has a batter-like consistency. Remove from the heat and pour into 1 large mold or 6–12 smaller ones. Let cool for about 3 hours, or until completely coagulated.

Serve cold.

Banana and Coconut Milk Pudding

Chocao
Panama

Preparation time: 10 minutes
Cooking time: 15 minutes

Serves: 4

Bananas, the blacker the better, cooked with coconut milk, ginger, and a little honey or sugar is the basis of this recipe common in Panama's sparsely populated Darien province. Raisins or cinnamon are sometimes added, too.

2 cups/16 fl oz (475 ml) coconut milk
8 ripe bananas, peeled and sliced
1 teaspoon minced fresh ginger
1 teaspoon salt
½ cup/3½ oz (100 g) brown sugar
ground cinnamon, for sprinkling

Bring the coconut milk to a boil in a medium pan over medium heat. Once boiling, add the bananas and cook for 4 minutes, while mashing them. Add the ginger, salt, and sugar. Check and adjust the seasoning and continue cooking for about 10 minutes, until the milk has slightly evaporated and the mixture is thick.

Serve warm in cups, sprinkled with cinnamon.

Hominy Pudding

Canjica, mugunzá
Brazil

Preparation time: 15 minutes,
plus overnight soaking
Cooking time: 1 hour 40 minutes

Serves: 8–12

Canjica is rice pudding re-imagined with hominy. In the northeastern regions of Brazil, where it is called *mugunzá*, coconut or coconut milk are mixed in as well. The recipe is typically associated with *Festas Juninas*, the Brazilian winter celebrations held in June.

1 lb (450 g) dried corn kernels
7 cups/3½ pints (1.75 liters) water
7 cups/3½ pints (1.75 liters) whole milk
2 cups/14 oz (400 g) white sugar
3 cinnamon sticks
5 cloves
3 oz (80 g) shredded coconut
ground cinnamon, for sprinkling

Rinse the corn, place in a bowl with cold water to cover, and let soak overnight.

Drain the corn and place in a pan with the measured water and bring to a boil. Reduce the heat and simmer covered for about 1 hour, until soft and tender.

Drain the kernels and place in a pan with the milk, sugar, cinnamon, and cloves. Cook over low heat for 20 minutes, stirring constantly, then add the coconut and continue cooking for a further 15 minutes, until thick but moldable.

Spoon the *canjica* into a large bowl or serving glasses and cool in the refrigerator.

Serve cold, sprinkled with cinnamon.

Sweet Black Bean Pudding

Frejol colado
Peru

Preparation time: 20 minutes,
plus overnight soaking
Cooking time: 2 hours

Serves: 12

South of Lima in the Cañete and Chincha valleys, this sweetened and seasoned black bean pudding topped with toasted sesame seeds is an obligatory dish during Semana Santa, though it has become quite common any time of the year. The preparation dates to the Vice Royalty, when Afro-Peruvian communities sold it in dried out gourds that could be sealed with wheat paste during transport.

2 lb (900 g) dried black beans
7½ cups/3 lb 4 oz (1.5 kg) white sugar
1 teaspoon anise seeds
1 teaspoon ground cloves
1 teaspoon sesame seeds, toasted and ground, plus extra seeds to decorate
1 cup/8 fl oz (250 ml) whole milk

Rinse the beans and place in a bowl. Cover with cold water and let soak overnight.

Drain the beans and place on a surface. Put a clean tea towel over them and use a rolling pin to slightly mash them, to remove the skins. Clean the beans (discarding the skins) and place in a medium pan. Add water to cover and cook over medium heat for 1 hour, stirring frequently, or until completely tender.

Drain the beans and pass them through a fine mesh strainer (sieve) to make a purée, then place the purée in a pan with the sugar. Cook for 1 hour, stirring frequently with a wooden spoon to prevent burning, until the mixture is sticky and can easily detach from the sides of the pan. Add the anise seeds, cloves, and ground sesame seeds and mix well. Add the milk and mix well again. Bring to a boil and remove from the heat. Tip into a serving dish and sprinkle with sesame seeds.

Serve warm.

Rice Pudding

Arroz con leche
Various

Preparation time: 15 minutes
Cooking time: 25 minutes

Serves: 8–12

Rice pudding isn't a Latin American invention, though the creamy dessert is found in most parts of the region.

1 cup/7 oz (190 g) short-grain rice
5 cups/40 fl oz (1.2 liters) water
1 cinnamon stick
2 cups/16 fl oz (490 ml) evaporated milk (unsweetened)
2 cups/16 fl oz (490 ml) condensed milk
1 teaspoon vanilla extract
ground cinnamon, for sprinkling

Put the rice, water, and cinnamon in a medium pan and cook covered over medium heat for 15 minutes, until cooked but not soft. Add the evaporated milk and condensed milk, reduce the heat and cook, stirring constantly to prevent sticking, for a further 10 minutes uncovered, or until the rice is creamy. Add the vanilla and mix well. Remove the cinnamon stick.

Serve in cups or glasses, sprinkled with cinnamon.

Fruit Preserves

Aside of extending the shelf life of the vast varieties of fruits in the region, pastes, jams, marmalades, and other forms of fruit preserves have a wide variety of uses. They get spread on bread, used to fill pastries, sliced with cheese, or eaten on their own with a spoon.

Murta with Quince

Murta con membrillo
Chile

Preparation time: 15 minutes
Cooking time: 25 minutes,
plus 5 hours resting

Serves: 10

Chilean guava (*Ugni molinae*), called *murta*, *murtilla*, or *uñi* in Chile, is in the same family as guava, though it is considerably smaller, more like a dark red berry, with a flavor that resembles wild strawberries. Found in much of southern Chile it is often used to make a liquor and marmalades, or preserved and eaten with quince.

    5 cups/40 fl oz (1.2 liters) water
    3¹/₃ cups/1 lb 8 oz (680 g) white sugar
    1 cinnamon stick
    5 quinces
    35 oz (1 kg) *murta* berries

Sterilize a preserving jar large enough to store the preserved fruits.
    Put the water, sugar, and cinnamon into a pan. Stir well and bring to a boil over medium heat, then remove the cinnamon and set aside.
    Peel the quinces, core them, and cut them into thin slices. Remove the stems from the *murta* berries.
    Place the fruits in the jar and pour the syrup over them. Close the lid well to seal.
    Wrap the jar in a clean tea towel and place it in a pan. Add water to come three-quarters of the way up the jar and bring to a boil. Boil for 20 minutes, then remove from the heat. Remove the jar from the pan and let cool. Leave for at least 5 hours before eating.
    Consume within 1 year and keep in the refrigerator after opening.

Figs in Panela Syrup

Dulce de brevas, brevas caladas
Colombia

Preparation time: 15 minutes,
plus overnight soaking
Cooking time: 1 hour 40 minutes

Serves: 12

In 1560, the first figs were planted in Mexico and they slowly made their way down the continent. While not widely consumed, they are planted at low to mid-level altitudes in many corners of the region. In Colombia, they are most often consumed by splitting them lengthways and soaking them in water and lime juice overnight, then cooking them in a mixture of cinnamon and water. They are usually served with a slice of fresh cheese.

    24 figs
    juice of 1 lime
    1 lb (450 g) panela sugar (or use light muscovado)
    2 cinnamon sticks
    6¹/₂ cups/54 fl oz (1.6 liters) water

Make a cross incision in the top of each fig, without cutting right through. Place in a bowl, add cold water to cover, add the lime juice, and let soak overnight.
    Put the sugar and cinnamon in a pan with the water. Mix well and bring to a boil uncovered. Once the sugar has dissolved, add the drained figs. Lower the heat and cook over low heat for 1¹/₂ hours, stirring frequently, or until it has a syrup-like consistency. Remove from the heat and let cool before serving.

Guava Paste

Goiabada, bocadillo de guayaba, conserva de guayaba
Brazil, Colombia, Venezuela

Preparation time: 10 minutes
Cooking time: 1 hour 10 minutes,
plus 1 hour chilling

Serves: 10

Guava paste is a Latin American adaptation of the Spanish *dulce de membrillo*, or quince paste, that is often eaten with cheese. It's sometimes called *bocadillo de Veleño*, because the primary global center of production is in the Colombian town of Vélez in the Santander Department. In some places, it's wrapped in *bijao* leaves to help preserve its flavor.

    2 lb (900 g) guava, peeled and quartered
    4 cups/1 lb 12 oz (800 g) white sugar
    juice of 1 lime

Place the guava in a pan, add water to cover and cook covered for 30 minutes over medium heat, or until completely soft. Drain and place in a blender. Blend well into a paste then pass the paste through a fine mesh strainer (sieve). Place in a pan with the sugar and mix well. Cook over low heat, stirring, for 40 minutes, or until the mixture has a bright red color and you can see the bottom of the pot. Add the lime juice and mix well.
    Pour the guava paste into an 8-inch (20-cm) square pan, 2 inches (5 cm) deep, using a rubber spatula. Let cool then refrigerate for about 1 hour, to set.

Cayote Squash Preserve

Dulce de cayote
Argentina, Bolivia

Preparation time: 10 minutes
Cooking time: 2 hours 30 minutes

Makes: 3 or 4
1-pint jars

The stringy innards of the cayote squash (*Cucurbita ficifolia*), sometimes called the fig-leaf gourd, is used in for this sweet preserve that's typical in the far north of Argentina and southern Bolivia. It's often eaten with walnuts and slices of cheese.

    1 cayote squash
    sugar
    juice of 1 lime
    3 cloves
    1 teaspoon ground cinnamon

Place the whole squash over medium heat on a grill (barbecue) or in a clay oven. Cook for 30 minutes, turning occasionally to char the skin on all sides. Once the squash is soft on the inside, remove the burnt skin and the seeds.

Weigh the squash and measure out the same amount in sugar. Place both ingredients in a pan with the lime juice, cloves, and cinnamon, and mix well. Place the pan over low heat and cook uncovered until it has a jam-like consistency and honey color, about 1½–2 hours. Transfer the cooked jam to sterilized jars.

Consume within 1 year and keep in the refrigerator after opening.

Candied Acorn Squash

Miel de ayote
Costa Rica, El Salvador, Honduras, Nicaragua

Preparation time: 20 minutes
Cooking time: 1 hour 5 minutes

Serves: 8

While the name of this dish translates as "squash honey," it's more candied and caramelized than liquefied. Cooked with cinnamon and *tapa de dulce* (panela sugar) it's very rich and usually eaten on its own. Serve warm or cold.

    1 lb/450 g panela sugar (or use light muscovado)
    5 cups/40 fl oz (1.2 liters) water
    1 cinnamon stick
    4 cloves
    4 fig leaves
    peel of 2 oranges
    4 lb (1.8 kg) ripe acorn squash

Put the sugar, water, cinnamon, cloves, fig leaves, and orange peels in a pan, and place over medium heat to dissolve the sugar.

Meanwhile, peel the squash, remove the seeds and core, and cut into ¾-inch (2-cm) cubes.

Once the sugar has completely dissolved, add the squash cubes and cook uncovered for 1 hour, or until the liquid has turned into a syrup, with a darker color. Remove the fig leaves and cinnamon stick and serve warm.

Spaghetti Squash Honey

Conserva/miel de chiverre
Costa Rica

Preparation time: 20 minutes, plus 3 days
Cooking time: 2 hours 30 minutes

Makes: 8–12 oz
(230–240 g)

Cooked in butter and sugar, the flesh of the huge *chiverre* squash is cooked with *tapa de dulce*, the local panela sugar, making a sweet, dark brown paste that's used in a variety of ways in Costa Rican cuisine. It can be spread on bread, used as the filling in baked empanadas, to make candy, or as a glaze for meats.

    ¼ *chiverre* squash
    7 oz (200 g) panela sugar (or use light muscovado)
    1 cup/8 fl oz (250 ml) water
    1 cinnamon stick
    2 cloves

Preheat an oven to 350°F/180°C/Gas Mark 4.

Place the squash on a baking sheet and bake for 30 minutes, then remove from heat.

When cool enough to handle, cut the squash in half and remove the pulp, discarding the skin, seeds, and any loose strands. Chop the pulp into small pieces and mash with a meat mallet, then wrap it in a cheesecloth and squeeze all the water from it.

Place the sugar and water in a medium pan over medium heat until the sugar dissolves. Add the cinnamon and cloves, then add the squash and cook over low heat for about 2 hours, or until the squash has a honey color. Remove from the heat and place the squash in a serving dish to cool down.

Serve at room temperature.

Squash in Syrup

Zapallos en almíbar 🍲
Argentina, Uruguay

Preparation time: 20 minutes,
plus 2 hours, then overnight, resting
Cooking time: 30 minutes,
plus 1 hour cooling

🌿 🔪 🍳 ⓥ ❖

Serves: 8

Cubed and preserved in syrup, firm squash can have a crunchy exterior and soft interior. It almost tastes like candy and it's usually served as dessert on its own.

    2 lb 8 oz (1.1 kg) squash
    7½ cups/60 fl oz (1.75 liters) water, plus 1 cup/8 fl oz (250 ml) for the lime
    1½ oz (40 g) burnt lime (calcium oxide)
    5 cups/2 lb (900 g) white sugar
    1 teaspoon vanilla extract

Peel the squash, remove the seeds and core, and cut into 1-inch (2.5-cm) cubes. Place in a pan and add 3¾ cups/30 fl oz (900 ml) of the water (i.e. half the measured amount).
    Dilute the burnt lime in the cup of water and mix it into the pan with the squash. Let rest for 2 hours.
    Drain the squash and rinse well. Pat dry and place in a large bowl. Cover all over with the sugar and refrigerate overnight.
    Tip the squash with the sugar into a pan, and add the vanilla and remaining water, and cook uncovered over medium heat for 30 minutes, or until soft. Tip the squash and syrup into a serving dish and let cool for 1 hour.
    Serve at room temperature.

Bitter Orange and Molasses Preserves

Koserevá de apepú
Paraguay

Preparation time: 20 minutes
Cooking time: 3 hours 40 minutes

🌿 🔪 🍳 ⓥ ❖

Makes: 1 lb 13 oz (840 g)

Koserevá is made from *apepú*, or bitter orange, cooked in black molasses. It's primarily eaten on its own or with a slice of Paraguay cheese.

    12 *apepú* or bitter (Seville) oranges
    3 cups/1 lb 13 oz (840 g) molasses
    3 cloves
    6 cups/50 fl oz (1.5 liters) water

Peel the oranges, retaining the peel. Quarter the oranges and remove the white membrane; set aside. Place the peels in a pan and add water to cover. Bring to a boil, then strain. Repeat the process 4 times.
    In the same pan, mix the molasses and cloves with the water, peels, and orange pulp. Cook for 2–3 hours uncovered over low heat, or until shiny and thick, stirring occasionally. Remove from the heat and store in a jar.
    Serve at room temperature.

Papaya Preserves

Cabellitos de papaya biche, dulce de lechosa
Colombia, Venezuela

Preparation time: 5 minutes,
plus 1 hour soaking
Cooking time: 25 minutes

🌿 🔪 🍳 ⓥ

Serves: 4–6

Sweetened, preserved unripe papaya is a preparation found in different parts of the regions under a variety of names. In Venezuela, where it is called *dulce de lechosa* and used during Christmas time, chunks of it are preserved in syrup or mashed into a pudding. In Colombia, it's slightly less sweet and cut into thin strips.

    1 green (unripe) papaya
    5 cups/40 fl oz (1.2 liters) water
    1 teaspoon baking soda (bicarbonate of soda)
    7 oz (200 g) panela sugar or cane sugar
    5 cloves
    1 teaspoon ground cinnamon

Peel the papaya, cut in half, and remove the seeds. Cut into strips, about ¼ inch (5 mm) thick.
    Pour the water into a pan, then add the baking soda (bicarbonate of soda) and papaya. Let soak for about 1 hour, or until tender. Drain and discard all but 1 cup/ 8 fl oz (250 ml) of the cooking water.
    Add the reserved cooking water to a small pan, and add the sugar, cloves, and cinnamon. Bring to a boil over medium heat and, once the panela has dissolved, add the papaya. Cook over low–medium heat until dry. Let cool before serving.

Sweets

Squash in Syrup

Caramel Spreads

Caramel spreads, which come in a wide variety of forms, are used as a filling in countless pastries across the region, most notably *alfajores*. They are also drizzled on ice cream or *flan*, smeared on bread, used to fill churros, or just eaten with a spoon.

Dulce de Leche

Dulce de leche, doce de leite, arequipe, cajeta
Argentina, Brazil, Colombia, Mexico, Paraguay, Uruguay, Venezuela

Preparation time: 10 minutes
Cooking time: 2 hours 20 minutes

Makes: 1 lb 4 oz (565 g)

Dulce de leche is created by simmering milk (ideally raw milk) and sugar in a heavy pan over low heat, allowing it to caramelize and creating a Maillard reaction that gives it its distinctive flavor. It's a delicate process that requires constant attention and stirring so it doesn't burn. The cooking time can be reduced considerably by using a can of sweetened condensed in place of milk and sugar. There are subtle regional distinctions in the preparations and ingredients. Sometimes vanilla and other spices are added. For Mexican *cajeta*, goat milk is used. For *arequipe* in Colombia and parts of Venezuela, it tends to be lighter in color.

3½ cups/29 fl oz (870 ml) whole milk
1¾ cups/12 oz (350 g) white sugar
½ teaspoon baking soda (bicarbonate of soda)
½ teaspoon vanilla extract

Pour the milk into a heavy pan and add the sugar. Place over medium heat and stir well with a wooden spoon until the sugar dissolves. Add the baking soda (bicarbonate of soda) and vanilla and continue cooking over medium heat, stirring constantly with a wooden spoon, for about 2 hours, making sure it doesn't boil. Once thick, and the color turns brown, remove from the heat and continue stirring for 10 minutes. Pour into a dish and let cool.
Serve at room temperature.

Manjar Blanco

Manjar blanco, manjar
Chile, Ecuador, Panama, Peru

Cooking time: 1 hour 30 minutes, plus cooling

Makes: 1 lb 8 oz (680 g)

Called blancmange in Europe, this caramel spread typical in Peru and Panama, as well as parts of Ecuador and Chile, is sometimes used interchangeably with dulce de leche (see left), though there are subtle differences. It ends to be lighter in color, thicker, and sometimes lime and cinnamon are added. It's used as a filling for *alfajores*, *tejas*, and other pastries.

2 cups/16 fl oz (475 ml) whole milk
2 cups/16 fl oz (475 ml) evaporated milk (unsweetened)
1 teaspoon vanilla extract
1 teaspoon ground cinnamon

Put the milk, evaporated milk, vanilla, and cinnamon in a heavy pan. Bring to a boil over medium heat, stirring constantly with a wooden spoon. When it begins to boil, reduce the heat and continue stirring and scraping the bottom and sides of the pan so it does not burn, for about 1½ hours, until it thickens and you can see the bottom of the pan when moving the spoon. As soon as it reaches this point, remove from the heat (it's important not to overcook it). Let cool before serving.

Candy

While mass-produced candies and chocolates are everywhere in Latin American streets, the art of making homemade candies is alive and well. They often use natural sweeteners and are flavored with fruits. The effort is quite minimal in most cases and they make for an easy dessert.

Brazilian Fudge Balls

Brigadeiros
Brazil

Cooking time: 15 minutes,
plus 15 minutes cooling

Makes: 30

Served at every child's birthday party in Brazil (after the cake), the *brigadeiro* dates to a mid-1940s presidential campaign. Rather than selling election buttons, the supporters of the candidate Eduardo Gomes, whose military rank was brigadier, or *brigadeiro* in Portuguese, decided to sell candy at his rallies. Being just after World War II, milk and sugar were in short supply, so they used condensed milk, which they mixed with butter and chocolate. While Gomes lost the election, the recipe for *brigadeiros* quickly spread across the country. Countless variations were invented over the following decades, adding in passionfruit or coconut, or even filling them with cachaça.

> 3½ cups/29 fl oz (870 ml) condensed milk
> 4 teaspoons unsweetened cocoa powder
> 1 teaspoon (5 g) butter
> chocolate sprinkles, rainbow sprinkles, cocoa powder, shredded coconut, or ground hazelnuts, to coat

Mix the condensed milk, cocoa powder, and butter in a pan over medium heat, stirring continuously for about 15 minutes, or until the mixture becomes stiff yet still malleable. Tip the mixture into a bowl and let cool to room temperature, about 15 minutes.

Using an ice-cream scoop or tablespoon, scoop the mixture into small, walnut-sized balls. Roll each ball in chocolate sprinkles, rainbow sprinkles, cocoa powder, shredded coconut, or ground hazelnuts to coat.

Place in small paper liners and serve.

Brazilian Peanut Candy

Paçoca de amendoim
Brazil

Preparation time: 15 minutes
Cooking time: 5 minutes

Serves: 4

Peanuts, cassava flour, and sugar is all you need to make this simple round or square candy that's made in Minas Gerais, São Paulo, and Southeastern Brazil. Forms of *paçoca* were made prior to the arrival of the Portuguese, using peanuts and cassava flour. In traditional recipes, the peanuts are roasted and then ground in a *pilão*, or mortar, though blenders and food processors have become common. In northeastern Brazil, another form of the recipe, called *paçoca Sertaneja* or *paçoca de carne seca* (Shredded Sun-Dried Beef with Cassava Flour, page 264), grinds sun-dried beef in a mortar then cooks it with cassava flour.

> 9 oz (250 g) roasted and peeled peanuts (unsalted)
> 9 oz (250 g) cassava flour
> 5 tablespoons sugar

Preheat the oven to 350°F/180°C/Gas Mark 4. Place the peanuts in an oven pan and heat in the oven for 5 minutes to release the oils. Remove to a blender and blend for 1 minute into a thick paste. Add the cassava flour and sugar to the blender and continue mixing on medium speed until incorporated.

Spread the mixture on a flat surface, about 1 inch (2.5 cm) deep and cut into small squares to serve.

Drinks

At a gas station in a rural village southeast of Asunción, Paraguay, large tanks of water, both hot and cold, are set up beside the ones for gas. The driver gets out and refills his insulated flask. The tanks are sponsored by a brand of *yerba maté*, encouraging drivers to continue sipping on the bitter, herbal tea as they drive. Inside the car, his friend in the passenger seat fills up the *guampa*, a hollowed-out bull horn, with the *maté*, which has been mixed with herbs, and pours the cold water over it. He inserts the *bombilla*, a metal straw with a filter on one end, and passes the *tereré*, the cold form of *yerba maté*, to the passengers in the back. When finished, the co-pilot adds more water and passes the *guampa* to the driver. It gets refilled and passed around until they reach their destination.

Paraguay, Uruguay, Argentina, and Chile are countries with some of the highest amounts of tea consumption on earth, primarily because of the amounts of *yerba maté*, which was first cultivated by the Guaraní and Tupí people. In the 1650s, Jesuits domesticated the plant and started plantations in the region, leading to much wider use. It's one of a number of teas and infusions made from native herbs and plants in the region, which are used to stimulate, refresh, and cure minor ailments.

From fermented fruit and corn drinks to frothy chocolate pick-me-ups, liquid libations are some of the most overlooked pieces of Latin American gastronomy. They are used for respite from tropical heat and to awaken the bones in the cold of frigid mountain air. Latin American spirits—such as tequila, mezcal, pisco, cachaça, and rum—are now found worldwide, however, the region's cocktail culture dates back more than a century.

Dried Peach Drink

Refresco de mocochinchi
Bolivia

Preparation time: 10 minutes,
plus overnight soaking
Cooking time: 2 hours

Serves: 4

During summers in Bolivia, you'll find this drink made of dried peaches sold from glass jars by vendors perched out on street corners and plazas. Orange juice, raisins, lime zest, and other ingredients may be added.

3 cups/1 lb 5 oz (570 g) *mocochinchi* (dried peaches)
6 cups/50 fl oz (1.5 liters) water
1 cinnamon stick
1½ cups/10½ oz (300 g) sugar

Place the dried peaches in a bowl and add cold water to cover. Let soak overnight.
Drain and place the peaches in a medium pan. Add the measured water and bring to a boil, then reduce the heat, add the cinnamon stick, and simmer uncovered for 2 hours.
Approximately 15 minutes before the end of the simmering time, add the sugar to a dry frying pan over medium heat. Melt, stirring with a spatula until it turns thick and brownish. Pour the caramel into the peach pan and slowly stir until completely dissolved. Remove the pan from the heat, remove the cinnamon, and let cool.
Serve cold over ice.

Cane Sugar Water with Lime

Aguapanela con limón, papelón con limón
Colombia, Venezuela

Preparation time: 5 minutes,
plus chilling
Cooking time: 10 minutes

Serves: 8

This infusion from panela, or rapadura, that's often sold in blocks or cones, is like a Latin American version of iced tea without the tea. The following recipe is most similar to the Colombian version, and there it's often used as a base for the country's fruit *chichas*. There are subtle differentiations in the way it is prepared throughout the region. *Aguapanela* may also be served hot, and some like to add a slice of fresh cheese, milk, or black coffee to it. It's believed to be good for curing colds and other respiratory problems.

4 cups/32 fl oz (950 ml) water
8 oz (225 g) panela sugar (or use light muscovado)
juice of 2 limes
lime slices, to serve

In a medium pan, bring the water with the panela to a boil over medium heat, stirring until the panela is completely dissolved. Remove from the heat, pour into a pitcher (jug), and place in the refrigerator. When cold, add the lime juice, stir, and serve with slices of lime.

Coconut Limeade

Limonada de coco
Colombia

Preparation time: 5 minutes

Serves: 2

Spend any time in the sweltering heat along the Caribbean coast of Colombia and inevitably a glass of *limonada de coco* will come into your hands and, at least for that moment, you'll never want to drink anything else ever again.

1 cup/8 fl oz (250 ml) coconut milk
2½ cups/1 lb 3 oz (550 g) crushed ice
juice of 3 limes
3 tablespoons brown or panela sugar
1 lime, sliced, to serve

Blend all the ingredients (minus the lime slices) in a blender for 1 minute on high speed.
Serve cold with lime slices.

Sweet Corn and Milk Drink

Chicheme
Costa Rica, Panama

Preparation time, 10 minutes,
plus overnight soaking
Cooking time: 1 hour

Serves: 6

Made from *maíz trillado*, similar to cracked hominy, *chicheme* is a sweet drink, almost a cold porridge, found in parts of Panama and Costa Rica. In Guanacaste, *chicheme* refers specifically to a beverage made with *maíz pujagua*, or purple corn, that is fermented for several days before being drunk.

12 oz (340 g) *maíz trillado* (or use cracked hominy)
7 cups/56 fl oz (1.7 liters) water
3 tablespoons cornstarch (cornflour), dissolved in 1½ tablespoons water
1 cup/8 fl oz (250 ml) evaporated milk (unsweetened)
¾ cup/5 oz (150 g) panela sugar (or use light muscovado)
1 cup/7 oz (200 g) white sugar
6 cloves
1 tablespoon grated nutmeg
2 cinnamon sticks

Soak the hominy overnight in 7 cups of water.
Place the hominy and the water in a medium pan and bring to a boil over high heat, then reduce to medium and cook for 40 minutes. Remove from the heat and let soak until warm, about 10 minutes, then blend for 2 minutes on medium speed in a blender and add back to the pan.
Add the cornstarch (cornflour) mixture to the hominy liquid and stir with a whisk. Add the evaporated milk, panela, white sugar, cloves, nutmeg, and cinnamon. Heat, stirring occasionally, over medium heat for 10 minutes, or until the mixture thickens. Remove from the heat and let cool.
Serve cold.

Cane Sugar Water with Lime

Toad Water

Agua de sapo
Costa Rica

Preparation time: 10 minutes,
plus cooling
Cooking time: 5 minutes

Serves: 10

No toads are harmed in the making of this refreshing drink from the Limón province on Costa Rica's Caribbean coast.

> ³/₄ cup/5 oz (150 g) panela sugar (or use light muscovado)
> ¹/₂ cup/2 oz (50 g) chopped fresh ginger
> 4 cups/32 fl oz (950 ml) water
> 1 cup/8 fl oz (250 ml) lime juice

In a small pan, whisk the panela and chopped ginger with half the water. Bring to a boil over medium heat, then cook until the panela is completely dissolved, about 5 minutes. Remove from the heat and add the remaining water. Let cool down, then add the lime juice.
Serve cold over ice.

Spiced Cinnamon Firewater

Canelazo
Colombia, Ecuador

Preparation time: 5 minutes
Cooking time: 5 minutes

Serves: 6

Canelazo is sold by street vendors in the Andean highlands, especially during Christmastime, and is often consumed as an after-dinner drink. Sometimes it is mixed with fruit juices too, like passionfruit, blackberry, and *naranjilla* (lulo).

> 8 cinnamon sticks
> 1 cup/7 oz (200 g) panela sugar (or use light muscovado)
> 6 cups/50 fl oz (1.5 liters) water
> ¹/₄ cup/2 fl oz (60 ml) aguardiente

Mix the cinnamon, sugar, and water in a medium pan. Stir with a whisk and bring to a boil, then simmer for 5 minutes, stirring continuously, until the sugar has dissolved. Remove from the heat and add the aguardiente.
Serve hot.

Salad Punch

Refresco de ensalada
El Salvador

Preparation time: 30 minutes,
plus 1 hour chilling

Serves: 8

El Salvador's cure for hot summer days. It uses typical fruits of the region like cashew fruits (or their juice or pulp) and mamey, though if unavailable they can be left out.

> 1 medium pineapple, peeled and cored
> 3 mangoes, peeled and stone removed
> 2 green apples, peeled and cored
> 2 mamey fruit, peeled and seeded
> 5 oranges
> 2 cashew fruits
> pinch of salt
> 2 tablespoons sugar
> 8 cups/64 fl oz (1.9 liters) water
> 1 cup/2¹/₂ oz (75 g) chopped lettuce, optional

Dice the pineapple, mangoes, apples, and mamey into small cubes, less than ¹/₂ inch (1 cm), then place in a medium bowl. Squeeze the juice of the oranges and cashew fruits over the diced fruit, and add the salt and sugar. Stir and macerate in the refrigerator for about 1 hour.
To serve, add the water, and the lettuce, if desired, and serve cold.

Sangrita

Sangrita
Mexico

Preparation time: 10 minutes,
plus chilling

Serves: 4

Dating to the 1920s, the original *sangrita* recipe from Guadalajara is said to have been made with the strained, leftover juice from a local version of *pico de gallo*, a chile-spiked fruit salad eaten for breakfast. Its bright red color comes from the red chile powder and pomegranate juice, though many recipes, especially in the United States, use tomato juice instead, which doesn't quite have the same balance. Poured into tall shot glasses called *caballitos*, it is meant to be sipped alternately alongside a shot of good tequila blanco, not chased.

> ¹/₂ cup/4 fl oz (120 ml) fresh orange juice
> ¹/₄ cup/2 fl oz (60 ml) pomegranate juice
> 1 tablespoon lime juice
> pinch of *pequín* (or any other red) chile powder
> pinch of sugar, optional
> tequila blanco, to serve

Mix all the ingredients in a small bowl. Adjust the lime and chile powder to taste. You can also add a pinch of sugar. Let chill in the refrigerator.
Serve in tall shot glasses, with a shot of tequila blanco alongside.

Salad Punch

Morro Seed Horchata

Horchata de morro
El Salvador, Honduras, Nicaragua

Preparation time: 15 minutes
Cooking time: 25 minutes   Serves: 6

A general name given to a wide variety of plant milk-based beverages that can be traced to the Mediterranean, *horchata* was introduced to Latin America via Spain, particularly Valencia, where it is made with rice. It is widely consumed in Mexico and other parts of the region. The addition of ground, flat seeds of the morro or *jícaro* fruit, which grows in dry climates of Central America (and can be found in Hispanic markets and online), are the primary differentiation of this form of *horchata*.

    1 lb (450 g) morro seeds
    1 cup/6 oz (180 g) white rice
    ½ cup/2½ oz (70 g) sesame seeds
    1¼ cups/4½ oz (125 g) chopped peanuts
    ½ cup/2½ oz (70 g) pumpkin seeds
    ½ cup/2 oz (50 g) cacao powder
    cold water or milk

Toast the morro seeds in a dry frying pan over medium heat for 5 minutes, stirring continuously. Repeat the process with the rice, sesame seeds, peanuts, and pumpkin seeds, all separately. Once cool, tip the toasted rice, seeds, and nuts into a blender and process on high speed, scraping down the sides once or twice, until it becomes a powder. Add the cacao powder and mix everything together.
    For every ½ cup/4 fl oz (120 ml) of water or milk, add 1 tablespoon of the *horchata* powder. Strain the liquid and serve cold.

Tamarind Drink

Refresco de tamarindo
El Salvador, Guatemala, Nicaragua

Preparation time: 5 minutes,
plus chilling   Serves: 4
Cooking time: 1 hour

Native to Africa, tamarind was likely brought to the New World during the slave trade, and the trees spread quickly through tropical areas of the continent. On hot days in Central America, the sweet and sour pulp from the pods, sometimes sold in compressed cakes, is used to make this thirst-quenching drink.

    1 lb 4 oz (560 g) dried tamarind pods
    ½ cup/3½ oz (100 g) white sugar
    5 cups/40 fl oz (1.2 liters) boiling water
    pinch of salt

Remove the outer shells of the tamarind pods and any of the fibrous strings attached to them.
    Place the tamarind and sugar in a heatproof bowl and pour the boiling water over to cover. Let sit for 1 hour. Stir well, then remove the seeds, retaining only the pulp.
    Add the pulp and liquid to a blender and mix until smooth. If you prefer, you can strain out any remaining pulp and discard. Add salt, check the seasoning, pour into a pitcher (jug) or bottle and place in the refrigerator.
    Serve cold.

Icing Glass

Sea moss, isinglass, Irish moss
Panama

Preparation time: 15 minutes,
plus overnight soaking   Serves: 4
Cooking time: 45 minutes

This sweet, thick, high-protein tonic is found in various forms in several parts of the Caribbean, usually under the name Irish moss or sea moss. Its base is marine algae of genus Gracilaria or Eucheuma, which are dried in the sun after being harvested, and it was first made in Panama in the 1840s by migrants from Jamaica, Guadeloupe, and Barbados who came to work on the inter-ocean railroad. Roadside stalls and fondas in and around the Caribbean port town of Colón, as well as families in Bocas del Toro, sell the drink, occasionally in recycled liquor bottles out of coolers. The taste of the sea moss is quite strong, so a considerable amount of aromatic spices like cloves and nutmeg are usually mixed in to make it more palatable. The name isinglass, or icing glass, is derived from a Dutch word meaning fish gelatin, which is often added as a thickener. It's considered an aphrodisiac and good for the digestive system.

    2 oz dried Irish moss seaweed
    2 tablespoons lime juice
    2½ cups/20 fl oz (600 ml) water
    1 cinnamon stick
    1 clove
    2 teaspoons gum Arabic
    ½ teaspoon ground nutmeg
    ¾ cup plus 1 tablespoon/7 fl oz (200 ml) evaporated
    milk (unsweetened), plus extra if needed
    ¾ cup/6 fl oz (175 ml) condensed milk
    1 tablespoon sugar
    salt, to taste

Place the seaweed in a large bowl and add enough iced water to cover, and add the lime juice. Cover the bowl with plastic wrap (clingfilm) and place in the refrigerator. Let soak overnight.
    The next day, add the measured water to a pan with the cinnamon and clove. Bring to a boil, then add the seaweed and cook uncovered for 40 minutes over medium heat. Strain the seaweed, keeping only the water. Add the strained water back to the pan, along with the gum Arabic, nutmeg, and the evaporated and condensed milk. Stir well and bring to a boil. Add the sugar and a pinch of salt, then take off the heat. Check the seasoning, adding more sugar and/or salt if needed, and let it cool. When cold, if the mix is too thick, add more milk.
    Serve ice cold.

Atoles

For as long as there has been corn masa, there has probably been *atole*, also spelled *atol*. The name is derived from the Nahuatl word *ātōlli* and Spanish conquistadors found the forms of the warm beverage they encountered quite insipid. The oldest recipes would have called for simmering cooked and ground corn masa (page 123) in water at their most basic, though early forms were likely flavored with honey, vanilla, cinnamon, chocolate, chile, and/or various fruits as well.

Over time, unrefined cane sugar called *piloncillo* (panela sugar) became a standard sweetener, and in recent decades commercial corn flours and *masa harina* have mostly replaced the masa; a severe loss of quality. *Atole* remains widely consumed in much of Mesoamerica, often in the mornings, bought at street corners, markets, or made at home. They can be plain, sweet (chocolate, vanilla, pumpkin), nutty (almond, pecan, peanut), or fruity (pineapple, strawberry, mango). They can be made from fresh corn or toasted and ground corn called *pinole*. The corn can even be replaced with rice, oatmeal, or wheat.

Fresh Corn Atole

Atol de elote
El Salvador, Guatemala, Honduras, Mexico

Preparation time: 20 minutes
Cooking time: 20 minutes
Serves: 6

Made from fresh corn, this sweet *atole* can be found primarily during harvest times in Central American markets and street corners. There the corn kernels are often ground on a *metate* to give it a creamy texture. *Chileatole* from Mexico, also made from fresh corn, can be made with this recipe by taking out the milk and cinnamon in the recipe below and adding epazote and toasted and blended chiles.

    6 ears of yellow corn, husks removed
    2¹/₂ cups/18 fl oz (550 ml) water
    1 cup/7 oz (200 g) sugar
    2 cups/16 fl oz (475 ml) milk
    1 cinnamon stick
    pinch of salt

Rinse the corn and cut off the kernels. In a mixer, blend the kernels with the water for 2 minutes on high speed.
    Tip the mixture into a medium pan with the sugar, milk, and cinnamon, and cook over medium heat, stirring continuously. When it begins to boil, add the salt and continue cooking for a further 10 minutes.
    Serve warm.

Pineapple Atole

Atol de piña
El Salvador

Preparation time: 20 minutes
Cooking time: 25 minutes
Serves: 10

While Mexican versions of pineapple *atole* tend to be closer to a standard *atole* made with corn masa with some pineapple chunks tossed in, the Salvadoran version is made primarily of pineapple, using only a small amount of cornstarch as a thickener.

    3 medium pineapples
    2 cups/16 fl oz (475 ml) water
    2 cinnamon sticks
    6 allspice berries
    2 cups/14 oz (400g) panela sugar (or use light muscovado)
    4 tablespoons cornstarch (cornflour), dissolved in 2 cups/16 fl oz (475 ml) water

Peel the pineapples and remove the cores. Cut the flesh into small cubes, or use a blender and mix it on high speed to a chunky purée.
    Place the pineapple and water in a pan over medium heat, add the cinnamon, allspice, and panela. Simmer for 15 minutes, stirring with a wooden spoon every 5 minutes or so. Slowly add the cornstarch (cornflour) mixture to the pan and continue stirring for 5 minutes, or until it thickens.
    Serve hot.

Chocolate Atole

Champurrado
Mexico

Preparation time: 10 minutes
Cooking time: 30 minutes
Serves: 12

Dating to the Aztecs, early forms of *champurrado* were likely quite bitter, using cacao beans rather than processed chocolate that is common today. It's a favorite drink during Día de los Muertos festivities, as well as during Christmastime, though it's quite common to have *champurrado* for breakfast on any given day alongside a tamal or churro.

    6 cups/50 fl oz (1.5 liters) water
    ¹/₂ cup/7 oz (100 g) panela sugar (or use light muscovado)
    1 cinnamon stick
    7 oz (200g) Mexican chocolate, broken into pieces
    7 oz (200g) fresh Corn Masa (page 123, for homemade, or use *masa harina*), mixed with 1 cup/8 fl oz (250 ml) water

Heat the water in a pan with the sugar and cinnamon added. Bring to a boil, then lower the heat and simmer for about 10 minutes, or until the sugar is completely dissolved. Add the chocolate and stir continuously with a wooden spoon for 5 minutes, or until melted.
    Add the corn masa mixture to the pan and continue to whisk so there are no lumps. Increase the temperature to high and bring to a boil, then reduce the heat and let simmer for 15 minutes, stirring continuously, or until the mixture thickens.
    Serve hot.

Cocoa Drinks

According to Hernán Cortés, when Aztec emperor Moctezuma II ate, he only drank a frothy beverage made from cacao seeds (otherwise known as cocoa beans), that was flavored with vanilla and spices and poured in a golden goblet. "The divine drink, which builds up resistance and fights fatigue," said Cortes in 1519. "A cup of this precious drink permits a man to walk for a whole day without food."

The Olmecs fermented, roasted, and ground the bitter seeds for drinks and thin porridges as much as 3,500 years ago and there's evidence that the Mayo-Chinchipe culture in Ecuador had done so well before that. Later, the Maya ramped up production and learned to flavor it with herbs and spices. Cacao became a ritual food and a sign of prestige, and when the Spanish came along, they turned it into a confection, sweetening it with sugar to make chocolate.

Drinks made from cocoa beans remain widely prepared throughout Mesoamerica, many of them following recipes that date back centuries or more. They are thickened with nuts or corn masa, sweetened with honey or *piloncillo* (panela sugar), and spiced with vanilla, orange zest, and chiles. They are often whipped with a *molinillo*, a wooden whisk that is held between the palms and rotated by rubbing the palms together, giving them a pleasant froth, which can be done with *atoles* as well.

Sweetened Corn and Cocoa Drink

Pinolillo, pinol, tiste
Guatemala, Costa Rica, Nicaragua, Panama

Preparation time: 10 minutes
Cooking time: 30 minutes　　　　Serves: 4

In Nicaragua, consumption of the corn and cacao drink *pinolillo* is so widespread that they often refer to themselves as *Pinoleros*. The gritty drink is usually served in a *jícaro* gourd, and while most home recipes just use cocoa powder and corn flour, the real flavor comes from freshly grinding the corn and cocoa beans (and it will likely leave some sediment in the glass). *Tiste* is quite similar, though tends to use a greater amount of cocoa beans. In some preparations, such as those in Panama, *pinol* is made just with toasted corn and without cacao.

　　1 cup/6 oz (170 g) dried corn kernels
　　2 oz (60 g) cacao beans
　　¼ teaspoon ground allspice
　　¼ teaspoon ground cinnamon
　　1 clove
　　1 cup/8 fl oz (250 ml) milk, plus extra to taste
　　1 cup/8 fl oz (250 ml) water, plus extra to taste
　　3 tablespoons honey

Toast the corn kernels in a *comal* or cast-iron frying pan over medium heat for about 15–20 minutes, stirring continuously, until golden. Do the same with the cacao beans for about 7–10 minutes until they pop, then, when cool, remove the shells with your hands. Mix the cacao

nibs and the toasted corn with the allspice, cinnamon, and clove and then grind them into a powder, using a *metate*, hand mill, or coffee grinder. The mixture will still be quite coarse, so you should grind it a second or even a third time for a finer texture.

Pour the mixture into a pitcher (jug) and pour in the milk and water. Add the honey and stir with a wooden spoon or *molinillo* until mixed. Add more water and milk to taste, and serve.

Corn and Cocoa Drink

Tejate 🔲
Mexico

Preparation time: 45 minutes
Cooking time: 10 minutes　　　　Serves: 8

Every *tejatera* has her own recipe, though in Oaxaca it's almost always some blend of nixtamalized corn, cocoa, mamey seeds, and *rosita de cacao* (*Quararibea funebris*), the flower of the funeral tree. Everything gets ground together with water to a paste, in a community *molino*, or stone mill, then kneaded continuously until a foam forms on the top. It's served with some of the froth and a sweetener, such as simple syrup.

　　3 oz (85 g) cacao beans
　　1 mamey seed
　　2 oz (50 g) *rosita de cacao* (cacao flowers)
　　1 lb (450 g) fresh Corn Masa (page 123,
　　for homemade)
　　simple sugar syrup or sugar, to taste

Toast the cacao beans, mamey seed, and *rosita de cacao* in a *comal* or cast-iron frying pan over medium heat, stirring constantly, until the cacao seeds pop, about 7–10 minutes. When cool, remove the shells of the cacao seeds with your hands. Grind the toasted ingredients together on a *metate*, sprinkling with water as needed, until it forms a paste. Alternatively, use a food processor.

In a large bowl, add the cacao paste to the corn masa, and gradually add cold water, while kneading, until it is liquid, and a significant amount of white foam floats to the top. Add ice to keep cool, and sugar syrup or sugar to taste.

Note: to make a simple sugar syrup, heat 1 cup/ 8 fl oz (240 ml) water and 1 cup/7 oz (200 g) superfine (caster) sugar, over medium heat until all the sugar has dissolved.

Corn and Cocoa Drink

Rice and Cocoa Drink

Chilate, atol chilate
El Salvador, Guatemala, Honduras, Mexico

Preparation time: 30 minutes,
plus 40 minutes soaking
Cooking time: 10 minutes

Serves: 8

Most forms of *chilate* are a mixture of cacao with corn, such as among Ch'orti' and Lenca communities in El Salvador, Guatemala, and Honduras. In villages around the Costa Chica in the Mexican state of Guerrero, *chilate* made with rice is more common, though some variations will use *pataxte* (*Theobroma bicolor*) instead of cacao or toasted corn in place of rice. If desired, dried chiles can be added to the pan to soak with the rice.

    1 cup/6 oz (180 g) rice
    1 cinnamon stick
    4 oz (115 g) cacao beans
    4 cups/32 fl oz (950 ml) water
    ½ cup/3½ oz (100 g) panela sugar (or use light
    muscovado)

Place the rice and cinnamon in a small pan and add cold water to cover. Let soak for about 30 minutes.
    Meanwhile, toast the cacao beans in a *comal* or cast-iron frying pan over medium heat, stirring continuously until they pop, about 7–10 minutes. When cool, remove the shells with your hands.
    Add the cacao nibs to the pan with the soaking rice, stir, and let soak for a further 10 minutes. Drain, and grind the solids to a paste on a *metate* or in a food processor, adding a little water if needed.
    In a large bowl, combine the rice and cacao mixture with the water. Stir until smooth, then strain to remove some of the lumps. Stir in the sugar.
    Serve at room temperature or over ice.

Teas

In much of Latin America, teas are mostly infusions of local plants, usually with a medicinal connotation. Herbs, leaves, barks, roots, flowers, and seeds are infused in hot water to cure ailments of every sort. In parts of the Amazon, *guayusa* (*Ilex guayusa*), the caffeinated leaves of native holly trees, keep indigenous hunters awake at night. In the Andes, coca leaves help alleviate the effects of altitude sickness.

Hibiscus Tea

Agua de Jamaica, agua de saril
Belize, El Salvador, Costa Rica, Guatemala, Honduras, Mexico, Nicaragua, Panama

Preparation time: 5 minutes,
plus 10 minutes resting, and cooling
Cooking time: 5 minutes

Serves: 10

This tart tea made from hibiscus flowers (*Hibiscus sabdariffa*) has a taste similar to cranberries. It's one of the most common *aguas frescas* in Mexico and found throughout much of Central America. In Panama and parts of Costa Rica, where hibiscus tea is called *agua de saril*, it takes on more of an Afro-Antillean flavor, adding lime juice and sometimes ginger.

    6 cups/50 fl oz (1.5 liters) water
    ½ cup/¾ oz (20 g) dried hibiscus flowers
    ⅓ cup/2¼ oz (70 g) sugar

In a medium pan, bring the water to a boil. Add the flowers and let the water boil for a further 3 minutes. Remove from the heat, add the sugar and stir until dissolved. Let the infusion sit for 10 minutes, then strain into a pitcher (jug) and let cool.
    Serve cold.

Iced Yerba Maté

Tereré
Paraguay

Preparation time: 5 minutes

Serves: 1

While it's still common to drink hot *yerba maté* during the summertime, a cold infusion of *yerba maté* called *tereré* is far preferable to some. The national drink of Paraguay, *tereré* is of Guaraní origin and has an entire culture around it. Often, additional herbs can be added and there are names for particular mixes. For instance, *tereré tantano* or swamp *tereré*, is when medicinal herbs are added, adjusted for specific ailments. In northeastern Argentina and southwestern Brazil, *tereré ruso*, or Russian *tereré*, is so named when citrus juices are mixed in, a practice common among immigrant communities there. To drink *tereré*, you need a *guampa*, which is a vessel a bit larger than the typical gourd used for hot *yerba maté*. It's often a hollowed out bull's horn, though can also just be a glass. It is also necessary to have a *bombilla*, a metal straw, so you don't ingest the tea. Don't stir, just take a few sips until the water is gone then add more and pass it on.

    yerba maté, to taste

Fill your *guampa* about halfway with *yerba maté*, then add iced water and the *bombilla* (metal straw). Refill the water as needed until it loses its flavor.

Drinks

Iced Yerba Maté

Paraguayan Burnt Tea

Maté cocido
Paraguay

Preparation time: 5 minutes
plus 8 minutes resting
Cooking time: 10 minutes

Serves: 4

In rural Paraguay, this tea made from toasting *yerba maté* and sugar with hot charcoal is the typical breakfast drink. Often served with milk and, in some parts of Paraguay, ground peanuts, it has a peculiar, almost smoky taste.

    3 tablespoons sugar
    3 tablespoons *yerba maté*
    4 cups/32 fl oz (950 ml) water

Place the sugar on one side of a small heatproof dish, and the *maté* on the other side.
    Over a flame, heat small pieces of charcoal until bright red and place on top of the sugar and herbs. Let sit for 8 minutes, occasionally moving the charcoal so all the ingredients are toasted. Remove the excess charcoal and place the burnt herbs and sugar in a small pan with the water. Bring to a boil, strain and serve hot.

Andean Barley Herb Tea

Emoliente
Bolivia, Colombia, Ecuador, Peru

Preparation time: 5 minutes
Cooking time: 15 minutes

Serves: 10

On chilly mornings and nights in the Andes, there are few remedies as soul-stirring as a steaming hot cup of this barley herbal tea, often made by street vendors called *emolienteras*. Different regions adapt their *emoliente* to local ingredients, such as adding the seeds of the red cactus fruit airampo in the Cusco area, or a syrup called *algarrobina* from black carob trees in northern Peru. Others add maca, aloe vera, pollen, and any herbs, preferably wild ones, are fine to add to the pot.

    6 cups/50 fl oz (1.5 liters) water
    1¹/₄ cups/8 oz (230 g) pearl barley
    2 oz *cola de caballo* (horsetail herb)
    ¹/₂ cup/2¹/₄ oz (65 g) linseed
    ¹/₄ oz boldo leaves
    ¹/₂ cup/3¹/₂ oz (100 g) sugar
    juice of 2 limes

Place all the ingredients except the sugar and lime juice in a pan and bring to a boil. Simmer for 10 minutes. Remove from the heat, strain, then add the sugar and lime juice. Stir with a wooden spoon and serve warm.

Chichas and Fermented Drinks

During the time of the Incas, the ritual importance of *chicha*, a low-alcohol corn beer, grew significantly. Inca rulers are said to have drunk *chicha* from golden cups in tribute to the sun rising, while offerings of *chicha* were made to dead rulers to appease their spirits. Still today, under the *ayni* system, a concept of reciprocity in Andean communities, or *ayllus*, planting, harvesting, and construction is done with the help of others and during that work, there's always *chicha*. Always.

Throughout Latin America, fermentation is used in drinks as a means of preservation, as a means of adding flavor, and, of course, a means of making alcohol. The word *chicha* might mean something different based on geography. While in the Andes, it usually signifies *chicha de jora*, a low-alcohol corn beer, there's also *chicha morada*, made of purple corn, which is not fermented. In parts of Colombia, Venezuela, and Central America, *chicha* might refer to a drink made of fermented fruits or rice. In Mexico, *tepache* is made from fermented pineapple rinds, while *pulque* is made from fermented agave sap.

Corn Beer

Chicha de jora
Bolivia, Colombia, Ecuador, Peru

Preparation time: 10 minutes,
plus overnight soaking and
6 days drying and fermenting
Cooking time: 2 hours 5 minutes

Serves: 10

When a house in the Andes has *chicha de jora* for sale, a stick with a plastic bag, usually red or white depending on the location, is hung outside like a flag pole. Inside, the sour, low-alcohol corn beer is sold in ¹/₂-liter glasses, sometimes sweetened with fruits, such as strawberries, called a *frutillada*. Before the first sip, some of the foamy head is often poured out for *pachamanca*, or mother earth. *Chicha* has been a staple drink in the Andes for more than a thousand years and the significance to Andean culture should not be understated. Recipes for *chicha de jora* vary considerably from every *chichera*, or chicha maker. In its basic form it is a milky, pale orange color with a sour taste, a bit like cider, though its strength can vary. Forms of *chicha* are made by chewing the corn kernels, spitting them out and letting them ferment, rather than germinating the corn. *Chicha de jora* can also be used as a base for cooking, such as Andean stews like adobo.

    3 lb (1.4 kg) *jora* (dent) ears of corn
    2 lb (900 g) pearl barley
    21 cups/10¹/₂ pints (5 liters) water
    1 cup/7 oz (200 g) panela sugar (or light muscovado)

Cut the corn kernels off the cobs and soak in water overnight. The next day, drain and rinse the corn well. Place a clean tea towel in a fresh (cool) spot and spread the corn on it, then cover with another clean tea towel. Leave for 2 days to germinate.
    Once the corn kernels have sprouted, spread them on another clean tea towel in a sunny place to dry for 2–3 days. When dry, coarsely grind the corn.
    Toast the barley in a dry frying pan for 5 minutes over medium heat, moving it constantly.
    Bring 8¹/₂ cups/4¹/₄ pints (2 liters) of the water to a boil in a large pan. Tip the corn and barley into the water and simmer, uncovered, for 1 hour or until the water has reduced by half, stirring frequently so it doesn't thicken. Add the remaining water and simmer for a further 1 hour over low heat. Remove from the heat and let cool.
    Once cooled, stir in the sugar. Strain into a jar and cover with a clean tea towel or into an earthenware pot with a lid. Let the liquid ferment for a minimum of 3 days, stirring it once a day. When it starts foaming, it's ready.

Drinks

Corn Beer

Purple Corn Juice

Chicha morada
Peru

Preparation time: 15 minutes
Cooking time: 45 minutes,
plus cooling

Serves: 5–6

Chicha morada is a gateway *chicha*. It opens your mind to drinks made of corn. It's sweet, a bit fruity, and unfermented, so many kids in Peru grow up drinking it instead of soft drinks. The anthocyanin pigment is said to be rich in antioxidants and good for the blood.

    8 cups/64 fl oz (1.9 liters) water
    4 ears of purple corn, halved
    1/2 cinnamon stick
    2 cloves
    peel of 1/2 pineapple
    1 quince, cut into medium cubes
    juice of 2 limes
    chancaca (panela sugar), to taste
    1 red apple, cored and diced, to serve

Put the water, corn, cinnamon, cloves, pineapple peel, and quince in a large pan and bring to a boil. Simmer for 45 minutes, or until the corn softens. Strain the juice into a pitcher (jug) and let cool in the refrigerator. Once cold, add the lime juice and sweeten with the sugar.
    Serve cold with the apple.

Fermented Pineapple Drink

Chicha de piña, tepache, carato de piña
Ecuador, Mexico, Panama, Venezuela

Preparation time: 10 minutes,
plus 2 days fermenting
Cooking time: 10 minutes

Serves: 10

Commonly sold by street vendors around Mexico, the refreshing and lightly fermented pineapple drink ferments extremely fast without a starter. Similar preparations can be found elsewhere in the region under different names. It's a great drink to mix with beer or spirits.

    8 cups/64 fl oz (1.9 liters) water
    1 cup/7 oz (200 g) panela sugar (or use light muscovado)
    1 medium pineapple
    1 cinnamon stick
    3 cloves

In a large pan, bring the water to a boil, then add the sugar. Stir until it dissolves completely, about 5–7 minutes. Remove from the heat and let cool.
    Peel the pineapple and place the rind in a jar with the cinnamon and cloves. Slowly add the sweet water. Cover the jar with a clean tea towel and let ferment for at least 2 days in a dry, fresh (cool) place. Try the *tepache*, and add more sugar or water if desired.
    Strain and serve cold over ice.

Fermented Masa Drink

Tejuino
Mexico

Preparation time: 5 minutes,
plus 3 days fermenting
Cooking time: 10 minutes

Serves: 6

Typical of the Mexican states of Jalisco and Colima, *tejuino* is a lightly fermented corn drink served cold in plastic cups or bags by street vendors. Some serve it with *nieve de limón*, a scoop of lime sorbet.

    4 cups/32 fl oz (950 ml) water
    2 cups/14 oz (400 g) panela sugar (or use light muscovado)
    1 lb (450 g) fresh Corn Masa (page 123, for homemade)
    juice of 4 limes
    salt
    2 limes, 1 cut into wedges, 1 sliced
    crushed ice

Boil 3 cups/24 fl oz (710 ml) of the water in a large pan. Add the panela and stir for 3 minutes, or until dissolved.
    In a bowl, whisk the masa with the remaining 1 cup/8 fl oz (250 ml) of water. Then add the sweetened boiled water and stir until mixed. Remove from the heat and pour into a clay pot or crock. Let cool and add the lime juice. Cover with a clean tea towel or cheesecloth and let ferment for 3 days in a dry and fresh (cool) place.
    To serve, rub the rim of a glass with a lime wedge and dip in salt. Stir the *tejuino* then pour it in the glass over crushed ice with a slice of lime.

Fermented Peach Palm Juice

Chicha de pejibaye 🔲
Costa Rica, Panama

Preparation time: 5 minutes,
plus 2 days fermenting
Cooking time: 10 minutes

Makes: 4 1/2 cups/
34 fl oz (1 liter)

Called *pejibaye*, *chontaduro*, or *pupunha* in different parts of the region, the yellow to red colored fruit of the fast-growing peach palm (*Bactris gasipaes*) has a wide variety of uses. In indigenous communities like the Boruca in the mountainous regions of Costa Rica, as well as over the border in Panama, it's one of the favorite fruits to use for making *chichas*.

    3 lb (1.4 kg) ripe *pejibaye* (peach palm fruit)
    2 cups/16 fl oz (475 ml) water
    1/2 cup/3 1/2 oz (100 g) *dulce de tapa* (panela sugar)

Place the ripe and unpeeled *pejibayes* in a medium pan with the water. Bring to a boil, simmer for 10 minutes, then remove from the heat.
    While still warm, remove the seeds and mash the fruit, together with the skin. Strain the pulp, keeping as much liquid as you can without pushing the solids through. Add the panela to the liquid and pour into a glass or earthenware jar or crock covered with a clean tea towel or cheesecloth. Let it ferment for 2 days in a dry, fresh (cool) place.

Fermented Peach Palm Juice

Fermented Fruit Drink

Fresco de súchiles
Guatemala

Preparation time: 10 minutes,
plus 1 week fermenting
Cooking time: 15 minutes

꙳ ⌀ 🍯 ♡

Serves: 10

In Guatemala, *fresco de súchiles*, typically made during Semana Santa, is a cross between an *atole* and Central American-style *chichas*. Toasted corn and barley flavored with fruits are soaked in water before being fermented.

    2¹⁄₂ cups/12 oz (350 g) fresh yellow corn kernels
    2¹⁄₃ cups/15 oz (430 g) pearl barley
    4 tablespoons black peppercorns
    1 tablespoon anise seeds
    2 tablespoons cloves
    ¹⁄₂ cinnamon stick
    1 cup/7 oz (200 g) panela sugar (or light muscovado)
    3 cups/25 fl oz (750 ml) boiling water
    peel of 1 pineapple
    2 tablespoons chopped fresh ginger

Toast the corn kernels in a *comal or* cast-iron pan over medium heat for 10 minutes, stirring continuously. Repeat the process for 5 minutes with the barley, peppercorns, anise seeds, and cloves. Place in a clay pot or crock with the cinnamon and panela. Pour the boiling water over, stir, then add the pineapple peel and ginger. Cover with a clean, dry cloth and secure with twine. Let ferment for 1 week, stirring every 2 days. Strain before serving.

Fermented Rice Drink

Masato de arroz, chicha de arroz
Colombia, Venezuela

Preparation time: 10 minutes,
plus overnight soaking and
3–14 days fermenting
Cooking time: 20 minutes

꙳ ⌀ 🍯 ♡ ᵛᵛ

Serves: 10

This creamy, fermented rice drink is made primarily in the central Colombian departments of Cundinamarca, Santander, Tolima, and Boyacá. It's often eaten with *almojábanos con queso* (Chiriqui-Style Corn and Cheese Fritters, page 112) or cookies. In Venezuela, where it is called *chicha de arroz*, it is left unfermented.

    1 cup/6 oz (180 g) rice
    2 cinnamon sticks, plus ground cinnamon, to serve
    4 cloves
    ³⁄₄ cup/5 oz (150 g) sugar

Soak the rice in cold water overnight. Drain and rinse the rice a few times. Bring 12 cups/6 pints (2.8 liters) water to a boil in a pan over medium heat, then add the drained rice, cinnamon, and cloves. Stirring every 5 minutes so it doesn't stick, simmer for 15 minutes, or until the rice is cooked. Let cool to just warm. Remove the spices and blend in a mixer, for 2 minutes on high speed. Strain; you should have a thick liquid. Stir in the sugar.

If preferred, serve the drink chilled, though many prefer to let it ferment. To do this, after adding the sugar, let the *masato* sit in a clay pot for 3 days to 2 weeks, depending on the alcohol level preferred. Stir each day. Taste the sweetness, adding sugar, cinnamon, and cloves as preferred. Serve cold, sprinkled with ground cinnamon.

Witch's Brew

Chicha bruja
Nicaragua

Preparation time: 10 minutes,
plus overnight soaking and
4 days fermenting
Cooking time: 10 minutes

꙳ ⌀ 🍯 ♡ ᵛᵛ

Serves: 12

There's no exact recipe for *chicha bruja*, a fermented corn drink that is quickly disappearing in Nicaragua. Only a few brewers still make the drink in communities in the central part of the country, such as San Juan de Oriente.

    8 oz (225 g) dried corn kernels
    4 cups/32 fl oz (950 ml) water
    3 cups/1 lb 5 oz (600 g) panela sugar (or light muscovado)
    3 tablespoons vanilla extract

Wash the corn well, soak it overnight, then drain, and rinse thoroughly. Grind in a hand mill or food processor until quite coarse.

In a large pan, mix the ground corn with the measured water and bring to a boil. Remove from the heat, add the sugar and vanilla, then stir until dissolved. Pour into an earthenware pot, cover with a clean tea towel and let ferment for 4 days in a dry, fresh (cool) place.

Fermented Cassava Drink

Cauim, masato de yuca
Brazil, Ecuador, Peru

Preparation time: 15 minutes,
plus 5 days fermenting
Cooking time: 20 minutes

꙳ ⌀ 🍯 ♡ ᵛᵛ

Serves: 10

Indigenous communities in the Amazon rainforest make this drink much in the same way as Andean communities make *chicha de jora*. The starch is converted to sugar by chewing, though many opt for the less labor-intensive process of adding sugar directly before fermenting. The sour drink is generally low in alcohol, so large quantities are often consumed, especially during festivals. In some communities, only women are allowed to prepare this.

    6 lb (2.7 kg) cassava, peeled and cut into chunks
    2 cups/16 fl oz (475 ml) boiling water
    Option 1 only:
    2 cups/16 fl oz (475 ml) hot water
    2¹⁄₂ cups/14 oz (400 g) sugar
    1 tablespoon (3.5 g) active dry yeast, optional

Cook the cassava in boiling water for 20 minutes or until soft. Drain and place in a large bowl. Mash with a wooden spoon or pestle. From this point there are two options.

Option 1: Slowly add the hot water and sugar. If you want to accelerate the process of fermentation, add the yeast activated in warm water to the mashed cassava.

Option 2: Chew the cassava and spit into a separate container to break down the starch and turn it into sugar.

The final steps are the same. Let ferment in a dark place for 5–10 days, stirring each day. The longer it ferments, the more alcohol there is. On the last day, add the boiling water. Strain and keep just the liquid. To serve, boil the liquid one more time.

Serve hot.

Fermented Cassava Drink

Cocktails

Some of the world's finest spirits are produced in Latin American (rums, piscos, singanis, cachaça, mezcals), plus an immense assortment of tinctures and aguardientes. While margaritas are well-known globally, here are some other libations.

Chuflay, Chilcano

Chuflay, chilcano
Bolivia, Peru

Preparation time: 10 minutes

Serves: 1

These two variations of the same drink from grape distillates singani and pisco from Bolivia and Peru, the *chuflay* and *chilcano* are standard highballs for hot days. For best results, use the best ginger ale (or ginger beer) you can find.

 2 lime slices
 2–3 ice cubes
 1/4 cup/2 fl oz (60 ml) singani or pisco
 1/2 cup/4 fl oz ml (120 ml) ginger ale
 2 drops of Angostura bitters

Place one of the lime slices on the bottom of a highball glass and add the ice cubes. Pour in the singani or pisco, then the ginger ale, and stir. Add the Angostura bitters, garnish with the second slice of lime, and serve.

South American Sangria

Clericot
Argentina, Uruguay

Preparation time: 10 minutes

Serves: 10

Introduced by Brits living in Argentina and Uruguay, who called it the Claret Cup, this summertime drink is a favorite during New Year's Eve parties. Everyone has their own recipe, mixing in seasonal fruits with wine of choice, usually a dry white wine. Some will also add brandy, triple sec, or other liquors.

 2 bottles (3 cups/25 fl oz/750ml) chilled white wine
 4 peaches, cut into 1/2-inch (1-cm) cubes
 1 medium orange, cut into 1/2-inch (1-cm) cubes
 1 apple, peeled and cut into 1/2-inch (1-cm) cubes
 1 1/2 cups/5 oz (150 g) strawberries, quartered
 1 lime, cut into 8 pieces
 sugar, to taste, optional
 ice cubes, to serve

Mix all the ingredients in a pitcher (jug). If adding sugar, stir until it is dissolved. Add ice cubes and serve.

Caipirinha

Caipirinha
Brazil

Preparation time: 10 minutes

Serves: 1

If you ever go to Brazil, chances are that a caipirinha will end up in your hands somehow and you'll just have to accept your fate and drink it. Some call it a Brazilian mojito, but there's no mint in it, just the muddled lime and sugar, and the base spirit can be far funkier than rum. Cachaça is made from fermented sugar cane juices, unlike rum that's made from molasses, and it can taste earthy and vegetal. While technically caipirinha refers specifically to the drink being made with lime, variations with other fruits (such as cashew, passionfruit, or mango) are often called caipirinhas.

 1/2 lime, cut into wedges or slices, plus a wheel to serve
 2 teaspoons sugar
 crushed ice
 1/4 cup/2 fl oz (60 ml) cachaça

Place the lime on the bottom of an Old Fashioned glass. Add the sugar and muddle it with the lime using a pestle, squeezing out the juices. Cover both ingredients with crushed ice, add the cachaça and mix with a bar spoon. Garnish with a lime wheel and serve.

Earthquake

Terremoto 📷
Chile

Preparation time: 10 minutes

Serves: 5–6

The story goes that some German reporters covering a March 1985 earthquake came in to El Hoyo, a dive bar in Santiago, and asked the barman for something refreshing. So, he plopped a scoop of pineapple ice cream into a half-liter glass filled with *pipeño*, a rustic, young, usually red, wine common in Chile. "Esto sí que es un terremoto," (meaning "this really is an earthquake") one of the reporters exclaimed.

 3/4 cup/4 oz (115 g) pineapple ice cream, plus extra to serve
 3 cups/25 fl oz (750 ml) *pipeño* wine
 1/3 cup/2 1/2 fl oz (75 ml) grenadine syrup

In a pitcher (jug), mix all the ingredients together using a bar spoon until you have a uniform mix.
 Place some pineapple ice cream in each glass and pour the liquid on top. Serve with a straw.

Earthquake

Golden Liquor

Licor de oro
Chile

Preparation time: 20 minutes,
plus 1 week macerating
Makes: 3½ pints
(2 liters)

Centuries ago, the Huilliche people in Chile's Chiloé archipelago used to make liquors from fermented grains, such as quinoa, and color them with fruits. Towards the end of the sixteenth century, the idea that gold had medicinal properties was in full swing and a liquor was made with gold flakes floating inside. In the town of Chonchi, this strange and wonderful yellow liquor flavored with lemon peels and colored yellow saffron instead of expensive gold was created, using a base of whey and aguardiente. (Note: in Chile, aguardiente is made from distilling grape residue left over from winemaking, similar to Italian grappa.) The original recipe is said to be guarded by just a few heirs, though some small producers sell bottles of it, often using papaya juice to brighten the color.

    4 cups/32 fl oz (950 ml) boiling water
    5 cups/2 lb 3 oz (1 kg) sugar
    10 cloves
    pinch of saffron
    2 vanilla beans (pods)
    peels and juice of 2 lemons
    4½ cups/36 fl oz (1 liter) whole milk
    4 cups/32 fl oz (950 ml) aguardiente (90% alcohol)

In a large bowl, mix the boiling water with the sugar, cloves, and saffron. Stir with a whisk until the sugar dissolves. Cut open the vanilla beans (pods), scrape out the insides, and add them to the mix. Add the lemon zests and juice and continue stirring. Add the milk and aguardiente and mix until the milk curdles.
    Let macerate for 1 week somewhere fresh, stirring every 24 hours.
    Strain the mixture through a cheesecloth; it should take a couple of hours for all the liquid to strain. Transfer to bottles and keep chilled.
    Serve in small amounts.

Chiliguaro

Chiliguaro
Costa Rica

Preparation time: 5 minutes,
plus chilling the glasses
Serves: 6

Guaro is Costa Rica's national firewater, a cheap and potent spirit that leaves a nightmarish hangover. Every bar in Costa Rica knows how to prepare a *chiliguaro*, which can be used to help cure said hangover.

    juice of 2 limes, plus extra for the glasses
    2 teaspoons salt, plus extra for the glasses
    4 cups/32 fl oz (950 ml) tomato juice
    ¼ cup/2 fl oz (60 ml) *guaro* liquor
    1 tablespoon hot sauce
    1 teaspoon Worcestershire sauce
    1 teaspoon ground black pepper
    a few ice cubes

Chill the glasses you will use in the refrigerator. When cold, add a little lime juice to the rim of each, and salt the rims.
    Place all the ingredients in a blender and blend for 1 minute on high speed.
    Serve cold in the chilled and salted glasses.

Macuá

Macuá
Nicaragua

Preparation time: 5 minutes
Serves: 1

Named after a tropical bird, the *macuá* is the tropical beach drink that you always hoped existed. Declared the national cocktail of Nicaragua in 2006 after a country-wide competition, it was created by a pediatrician from Granada. White or aged rum, preferably Nicaraguan, can be used.

    3 tablespoons rum
    2 tablespoons orange juice
    2 tablespoons guava nectar
    1 tablespoon lime juice
    ½ tablespoon simple syrup
    3 ice cubes

    To garnish
    1 cherry
    1 orange slice

Place all the ingredients in a cocktail shaker, then shake well for 2 minutes. Strain into a highball glass over ice. Place the cherry and orange slice on a toothpick and use to garnish.

Pisco Sour

Pisco sour
Chile, Peru

Preparation time: 5 minutes
Serves: 1

In the 1920s, inspired by the Whiskey Sour, an American bar owner in Lima named Victor Morris experimented with a version using pisco. While there is evidence that pisco was being mixed with lime and egg whites in years prior, the version refined at Morris' Bar by Peruvian bartender Mario Bruiget as the years went on is the form that grew widespread popularity. Both Peru and Chile claim it as the national drink, though recipes differ between countries. In Chile, egg whites are left out of the mix, plus Chilean pisco—which follows different production methods—is used.

    6 tablespoons pisco
    2 tablespoons lime juice
    2 tablespoons simple syrup
    1 tablespoon egg white
    3 ice cubes
    3 drops of Angostura bitters

In a cocktail shaker, place all the ingredients except the Angostura bitters. Shake for less than 1 minute, then strain into an Old Fashioned glass. Drip the Angostura bitter into the foam.
    Serve cold.

Drinks

Pisco Sour

Salsas and Condiments

With few exceptions, Latin Americans take pride in bestowing every bit of sweet, sour, bitter, salty, and umami flavor they can drop, squeeze, pour, ladle, or sprinkle on a dish. They might be fermented slaws to add punch and texture to a tortilla, an oil-based marinade to flavor grilled meats, or seasoning blends that are passed down through generations and provide the backbone of a family recipe.

This is the land of the chile and spicy sauces are plentiful, with regional varieties of chile being chopped, toasted on a *comal*, mashed in a mortar, or fermented into table sauces that can electrify a simple bowl of rice. While many have already been included in recipes throughout this book, here are some additional sauces and condiments to help stock your pantry.

Roasted and Ground Coconut

Coconut choka
Guyana

Preparation time: 5 minutes
Cooking time: 5 minutes

Serves: 4

The term *choka* is a form of preparing foods brought to Guyana and the southern Caribbean from India. Ingredients, such as eggplant, salt fish, or, in this case coconut, are fire roasted and then finely ground, often with a *lorha* and *sil*, grinding stones sometimes referred to as a masala brick. Afterwards, the powder is mixed with onions, garlic, chiles, and spices. Typically, coconut choka are eaten over rice and dhal, or roti. It is best served fresh, though it can be kept in an airtight container in the refrigerator for a few days.

    1 coconut
    3 garlic cloves, chopped
    ½ white onion chopped
    2 *wiri wiri* chiles, cored
    salt

Crack open the coconut, remove the shell and retain only the flesh. On a hot grill, over an open flame, or in a frying pan, slowly char the flesh, moving occasionally, until it becomes golden brown on all sides. It should take a few minutes.
    Coarsely chop the coconut and place on a *lorha* and *sil* or in a spice grinder. Grind or blend with the garlic, onion, and chiles. Season with salt.

Chimichurri

Chimichurri
Argentina, Uruguay

Preparation time: 15 minutes

Makes: 1 cup/
8 fl oz (250 ml)

This preparation made primarily of parsley, garlic, and olive oil is generally used to brush on meats as they are being grilled, or as a condiment at the table. Chimichurri is most widely found in Argentina and Uruguay, though you can come across it at steakhouses or barbecues almost anywhere in the region. It will keep for about 1 week, or 2–3 weeks in the refrigerator.

    2 cups/3 oz (80 g) parsley leaves
    2 tablespoons fresh oregano
    3 garlic cloves, minced
    ½ cup/¾ oz (20 g) chopped chives
    1 red chile, seeded and finely chopped, optional
    2 tablespoons red wine vinegar
    1 tablespoon lime juice
    ½ cup/4 fl oz (120 ml) olive oil
    salt and ground pepper

Chop the parsley leaves as finely as possible. Place all the ingredients in a medium bowl and mix them well. Season with salt and pepper.

Brazilian Garlic Sauce

Molho de alho
Brazil

Preparation time: 5 minutes
Cooking time: 20 minutes

Makes: 1 cup/
8 fl oz (250 ml)

In Brazil, *molho* is the typical accompaniment to grilled meats, though it comes in different forms. *Molho à campanha*, similar to *pico de gallo*, is a chunky garnish of chopped tomatoes, onions, and bell peppers in olive oil. At many *churrascarias* you will also find *molho de alho*, a garlic sauce, to drizzle on meats and vegetables, or spread over bread.

    2 tablespoons butter
    5 garlic cloves, minced
    2 tablespoons all-purpose (plain) flour
    1 cup/8 fl oz (250 ml) milk
    ½ cup/4 oz (115 g) mayonnaise
    ¼ teaspoon fresh oregano
    salt and ground pepper

In a small pan, heat the butter over high heat. Add the garlic, lower the heat and cook, stirring, for 15 minutes, or until brown. Sprinkle in the flour and stir well for 3 minutes. Pour in the milk and whisk for 2 minutes, or until the ingredients are well mixed. Remove from the heat and add the mayonnaise and oregano. Season with salt and pepper and continue stirring for 5 minutes or until the sauce is smooth. Serve warm as a side for grilled fish or meat.

Colombian Sofrito

Hogao
Colombia

Preparation time: 10 minutes
Cooking time: 15 minutes

Makes: 1 cup/
8 fl oz (250 ml)

Hogao is the seasoning blend that's used as a base in countless Colombian dishes. Ingredients and proportions change from region to region and every cook has their own recipe. It's quite simple to make, though bottled forms are available.

    3 tablespoons vegetable oil
    2 scallions (spring onions), chopped
    1 garlic clove, minced
    5 tomatoes, peeled and chopped
    1 teaspoon ground cumin
    salt and ground pepper

In a pan, heat the vegetable oil over high heat. Add the scallions (spring onions), garlic, and tomatoes. Lower the heat, add the cumin and season with pepper, then stir for 10 minutes, or until the sauce thickens. Check the seasoning, adding salt, and remove from the heat.

Roasted and Ground Coconut

Chilean Green Sauce

Salsa verde chilena
Chile

Preparation time: 10 minutes

Makes: 1 cup/
8 fl oz (250 ml)

This simple green salsa is used on hot dogs, sandwiches, bread, seafood, meats, and in soups in Chile. When refrigerated, it will last for up to 1–2 weeks.

 ½ white onion
 4 cups/5½ oz (160 g) parsley leaves
 2 tablespoons olive oil
 1 tablespoon lime juice
 salt and ground pepper

Mince the onion as finely as possible and place in a bowl. Chop the parsley leaves as finely as possible and mix them with the onion. Add the olive oil and lime juice, and season with salt and pepper. Refrigerate and serve cold.

Banana Vinegar

Vinagre de plátano
Costa Rica

Preparation time: 10 minutes,
plus 1 week straining

Makes: 1 cup/
8 fl oz (250 ml)

In Costa Rica, as well as in other parts of Latin America where bananas are grown, banana vinegar is a staple item in pantries and often sold at farmers' markets. It's used as the base for *chilera*, the ever-present jars of pickled vegetables found on every Costa Rican table, where it's often made with starchy bananas, like the *guineo negro*. If the variety of banana is too sweet, the vinegar will be flat. It can be used immediately, though the flavors will become increasingly complex as the months (and years!) go by.

 5 very ripe bananas

Peel the bananas and mash them. Place the purée in a cheesecloth and tie it well with butcher's twine, leaving a long piece to hang.
 Use a clay pot or a plastic bucket, with a good lid. Hang the cheesecloth from the lid, making sure it doesn't touch the bottom of the pot or bucket. Let sit for 1 week, after which you will find a dark vinegar in the bottom of the container. The exact time will depend on the ripeness of the bananas. Strain the liquid into a jar.

Salvadoran Cabbage Relish

Curtido
El Salvador

Preparation time: 20 minutes,
plus at least 3 days resting

Serves: 10

This cabbage slaw is an essential accompaniment for *pupusas* (Salvadoran Corn Patties, page 126), though are also used on tamales and with other traditional Salvadoran dishes. It's usually made a few days before using, allowing it to ferment a little bit. When refrigerated, it will last at least 1 month.

 1 white cabbage, thinly sliced
 1 white onion, thinly sliced
 1 carrot, peeled and thinly sliced
 ¼ cauliflower, small florets only
 6 cups/50 fl oz (1.5 liters) boiling water
 1 cup/8 fl oz (250 ml) apple vinegar
 1 bay leaf
 3 tablespoons salt

Place all the vegetables in a pot. Pour the boiling water on them, place a lid on the pot and let rest for 15 minutes. Strain the vegetables and place them in a jar. Add the vinegar, bay leaf and salt. Mix well, close the jar with a lid and let rest for a minimum of 3 days.

Ground Squash Seed Seasoning

Alguashte
El Salvador

Preparation time: 10 minutes
Cooking time: 20 minutes

Makes: 1 cup/
8 fl oz (250 ml)

This seasoning blend, which is pre-Columbian in origin, is used on sweet or savory foods in El Salvador. It's often sprinkled on fruits and vegetables and sold by street vendors, though is also used to season soups, *atoles*, and sauces. When stored in an airtight container at room temperature, it will keep for up to 1 week.

 1 cup/4 oz (120 g) husk-on squash seeds (ideally *ayote* seeds)
 ¼ cup/1¼ oz (35 g) cooked corn kernels
 1 dried green chile, seeded and chopped, optional
 salt

Toast the squash seeds in a small frying pan over medium heat for 12 minutes, moving them around the pan constantly. Place the seeds in a blender with the corn kernels and chile, and grind into a flour. Season with salt to taste.
 Note: to make into a sauce, in a small pan, mix with ¼ cup/2 fl oz (60 ml) of water, some roasted onions and tomatoes and boil for 5 minutes, or until thick.

Salvadoran Cabbage Relish

Ground Corn and Peanuts

Salprieta ▣
Ecuador

Preparation time: 15 minutes

Makes: 2 cups/
16 fl oz (475 ml)

In Ecuador's Manabí province, *salprieta* is sprinkled on roasted plantains, rice, or fish dishes. There, they use a type of corn called *canguil blando*, which has small, pointy corn kernels that can also be popped for popcorn.

    1 lb (450 g) peanuts, toasted and chopped
    1 lb (450 g) toasted corn
    1 teaspoon ground cumin
    ½ teaspoon ground black pepper
    1 tablespoon annatto oil
    2 tablespoons chopped cilantro (coriander)
    salt

In a mortar, mash the peanuts and toasted corn into a powder. Place the powder in a bowl and add the cumin, black pepper, and annatto oil and mix well. Season with salt. Set aside in a fresh (cool) place until ready to use. Stir through the cilantro (coriander) just before serving.

Central American Tomato and Radish Salsa

Chimol
El Salvador, Honduras

Preparation time: 15 minutes, plus 10 minutes marinating

Makes: 1 cup/
8 oz (250 g)

In parts of Central America, radishes get added to what is essentially *pico de gallo*, for this condiment that gets paired with grilled meats.

    5 tomatoes, peeled and chopped
    2 radishes, cut into small cubes
    ½ red onion, finely chopped
    1 tablespoon chopped cilantro (coriander)
    1 teaspoon dried oregano
    2 tablespoons lime juice
    salt and ground pepper

Mix the tomatoes, radishes, and onion in a bowl and add the cilantro (coriander), oregano, and lime juice. Let rest for 10 minutes, then season with salt and pepper and refrigerate until ready to use.

Pico de Gallo

Pico de gallo
Mexico

Preparation time: 10 minutes, plus 15 minutes chilling

Makes: 2 cups/
16 oz (475 g)

At its worst, *pico de gallo* is a watery bowl of chopped tomatoes and onions. It doesn't have to be like that, however. In Mexico, *pico de gallo*, which translates as "beak of the rooster," can be quite wonderful, using heirloom tomatoes and spicy chiles to actually enrich the flavor of a dish. In some regions additional ingredients like *jicama*, cucumbers, avocados, tomatillos, and various fruits are often added. It will keep for about 3 days.

    4 tomatoes, diced
    ½ white onion, finely chopped
    2 serrano chiles, cored and chopped
    3 tablespoons lime juice
    2 tablespoons chopped cilantro (coriander)
    salt and ground pepper

Carefully mix everything together in a bowl, seasoning with salt and pepper. Cover the bowl with a lid or plastic wrap (clingfilm) and refrigerate for 15 minutes before serving.

Yucatecan Pumpkin Seed Dip

Sikil p'aak
Mexico

Preparation time: 15 minutes
Cooking time: 20 minutes

Makes: 2 cups/
16 fl oz (475 ml)

This thick dip is usually served with tortillas or tortilla chips in the Yucatán. The texture can vary, depending on how it is puréed and the exact ingredients. It's usually made with unhulled pumpkin seeds, which gives it a grittier texture, though hulled seeds, called *pepitas*, can also be used.

    8 oz (225 g) tomatoes, quartered
    1 white onion, peeled and quartered
    2 habanero chiles
    1 cup/4 oz (120 g) raw pumpkin seeds
    2 tablespoons chopped cilantro (coriander)
    1 tablespoon lime juice
    salt

Place the tomatoes, onion, and chiles in a frying pan over high heat. Toast well for 20 minutes, or until they are charred on all sides.
    Meanwhile, place the pumpkin seeds in a mortar and mash into a powder. Add the charred vegetables and cilantro (coriander) and grind into a paste. Add the lime juice and season with salt. Serve at room temperature.

Ground Corn and Peanuts

Spicy Tomatillo Salsa

Salsa verde
Mexico

Preparation time: 15 minutes
Cooking time: 15 minutes

Makes: 2 cups/
16 fl oz (475 ml)

In Mexico, tomatillo-based *salsa verde* is a general sauce slathered on eggs, enchiladas, and various *antojitos*. It will keep for about 3 days.

    8 green tomatillos
    2 garlic cloves, peeled
    2 serrano chiles
    1/2 white onion, chopped
    salt

Half fill a medium pan with water and bring to a boil. Add the tomatillos, garlic, chiles, and onion. Cook for 15 minutes, or until soft. Drain, reserving 1 cup/8 fl oz (250 ml) of the cooking water.
    Place the drained vegetables in a mortar and grind until smooth, if necessary adding the reserved cooking water. Alternatively, you can do this in a blender.
    Season with salt and reserve in the refrigerator until ready to use.

Annatto Paste

Recado rojo, pasta de achiote
Belize, Mexico

Preparation time: 15 minutes

Makes: 1 cup/
8 fl oz (250 ml)

Ground annatto, or achiote, seeds help give a reddish color and a nutty, peppery flavor to foods throughout Latin America. In paste form, it's mostly used as a marinade for meats or to color masa for tamales and empanadas. When refrigerated, it will keep for about 1 month in an airtight container.

    3 tablespoons annatto seeds
    1/2 tablespoon ground cumin
    1 teaspoon dried oregano
    12 black peppercorns
    2 allspice berries
    3 garlic cloves
    2 dried serrano chiles
    1/2 cup/4 fl oz (120 ml) bitter orange juice
    1/2 cup/4 fl oz (120 ml) water
    2 tablespoons white vinegar

Place all the ingredients in a mortar and grind into a paste. Alternatively, use a blender to mix the ingredients for 2 minutes on medium speed, or to a smooth paste. In either case, pass through a fine strainer (sieve).

Cassava Extract

Tucupí
Brazil, Colombia, Ecuador, Peru

Preparation time: 15 minutes,
plus 14 hours resting
Cooking time: 1 hour 30 minutes

Makes: 3 1/2 pints
(2 liters)

To make *tucupí*, the grated pulp of the bitter forms of cassava is squeezed through a woven, basket-like instrument called a *tipiti* and then left for hours or sometimes days for the liquid and starch to separate, as well as to remove the cyanide within. The resulting liquid is boiled, while the starch, as well as the leftover pulp, is used in the production of tapioca and cassava flour. In large swaths of the Amazon rainforest, it has been used as a base for soups like *tacacá* (Shrimp, Jambu, and Fermented Cassava Soup, page 104) and traditional dishes like *pato no tucupí* (Duck in Tucupí Sauce, page 314). While commercial forms are available, many cooks buy artisan versions that are sold in markets in plastic soda bottles. Additionally, *tucupí* can be further reduced and seasoned to make sauces like *tucupí preto*, also called *tucupí negro* or *ají negro*, or cassareep. It's best to use within 1 week.

    6 lb 8 oz (2.9 kg) bitter cassava (*M. esculenta*)
    4 garlic cloves, crushed
    4 chicory leaves
    salt and ground pepper

Peel and grate the cassava, then squeeze the yellow liquid from the pulp into a small bucket. Let rest for at least 12 hours, allowing the starch to separate from the liquid. Remove the starch that has settled on the bottom of the bucket and use for another preparation, then cover with a clean tea towel and let ferment for 1–2 hours.
    In a large pan, boil the liquid with the garlic, chicory, and salt for 1 hour 30 minutes. Let cool and store in bottles in the refrigerator.

Creole Sauce

Salsa criolla
Peru

Preparation time: 10 minutes,
plus 1 hour resting

Makes: 1 1/2 cups/
13 fl oz (375 ml)

This mildly spicy onion relish is used on everything in Peru, from ceviches to sandwiches.

    1 red onion, thinly sliced
    1 *ají amarillo*, seeded and cut into thin strips
    1 tablespoon chopped cilantro (coriander)
    2 tablespoons lime juice
    1 teaspoon olive oil
    salt and ground pepper

Place the sliced onion in a bowl with salted iced water and let rest for 30 minutes. Drain and pat dry the slices. Place the onions and the remaining ingredients in a bowl, adding salt and pepper to taste, and mix well. Cover the bowl with plastic wrap (clingfilm) and refrigerate for 30 minutes before serving.

Huacatay Sauce

Salsa ocopa
Peru

Preparation time: 10 minutes
Cooking time: 20 minutes

Makes: 2 cups/
16 fl oz (475 ml)

Used similarly to *huancaína* sauce in *papas a la huancaína* (Huancayo-Style Potatoes, page 89), *ocopa*, from Arequipa, is green from the addition of *huacatay* (*Tagetes minuta*), sometimes called black mint, which grows in much of the Andes.

> 2 tablespoons vegetable oil
> 1 white onion, chopped
> 2 garlic cloves, minced
> 6 *ají amarillo*, seeded and chopped
> 1 cup/1 oz (30 g) *huacatay* (Peruvian black mint) leaves
> 4 saltine (cream) crackers
> 10 oz (275 g) *queso fresco* (or use ricotta salata or paneer)
> 3 oz (80 g) roasted peanuts
> ¾ cup/6 fl oz (175 ml) heavy (double) cream
> salt

In a frying pan, heat 1 tablespoon of the oil over medium heat. Add the onion, garlic, and chiles. Sauté for 10 minutes, or until well browned. Add the *huacatay* leaves and cook for a further 10 minutes over low heat.
    Place the sautéed ingredients in a blender with the crackers, *queso fresco*, peanuts, and heavy cream. Blend for 2 minutes on medium speed and season with salt. The sauce should be thick. If necessary, add the remaining vegetable oil to emulsify and give the sauce a better texture.

Uruguayan Steak Sauce

Mojo
Uruguay

Preparation time: 10 minutes,
plus 4 days marinating

Makes: 1 cup/
8 fl oz (250 ml)

Similar to chimichurri, *mojo* is used as a marinade for grilled meats or as a condiment to serve with them. It will keep for about 1 week, or up to 2–3 weeks when stored in the refrigerator.

> 1 cup/8 fl oz (250 ml) olive oil
> 1 tablespoon red wine vinegar
> 1 tablespoon capers, coarsely chopped
> 3 garlic cloves, minced
> 2 green onions (salad onions), chopped
> salt and pepper

Place all the ingredients in a jar, adding salt and pepper to taste, mix well and close the jar. Let marinate for at least 4 days at room temperature.

Chilean Pepper Sauce

Ají pebre
Chile

Preparation time: 15 minutes,
plus 30 minutes marinating

Makes: 1 cup/
8 fl oz (250 ml)

Chilean food tends to be less spicy than elsewhere in the region, though this chunky sauce is the exception. It's a common table condiment, used on grilled meats, bread, empanadas, *humitas*, and sandwiches. The level of spice can vary considerably from one recipe to the next, depending on the amount of chile used. It will keep for about 3 days.

> 2 cups/3 oz (80 g) chopped parsley leaves
> 2 cups/3 oz (80 g) chopped cilantro (coriander) leaves
> 2 garlic cloves, minced
> 1 tomato, peeled and coarsely chopped
> ½ red onion, chopped
> 2 *ají cristal*, seeded and chopped
> 2 tablespoons olive oil
> 1 tablespoon *rocoto* paste
> salt and ground pepper

Place all the ingredients in a bowl, adding salt and pepper to taste, and mix well. Let rest for 30 minutes. Check the seasoning and serve at room temperature.

Bolivian Pepper Sauce

Llajua, llajwa 〔◯〕
Bolivia

Preparation time: 15 minutes

Makes: 1 cup/
8 fl oz (250 ml)

This chunky, uncooked chile sauce is used in the Bolivian Andes to add spice to empanadas and *salteñas*, to slather on bread, and garnish meats. It will keep for about 3 days.

    1 tomato, peeled and coarsely chopped
    2 *locoto* (*rocoto*) chiles
    2 teaspoons *quirquiña* (Bolivian coriander)
    2 teaspoons *huacatay* (Peruvian black mint)
    ½ white onion, chopped
    salt

Place all the ingredients in a mortar and grind until smooth. Season with salt and keep at room temperature until ready to use.

Peruvian Yellow Chile Paste

Pasta de ají amarillo
Peru

Preparation time: 10 minutes
Cooking time: 15 minutes

Makes: 1 cup/
8 fl oz (250 ml)

Ají amarillo paste is used routinely in Peruvian cooking, even when fresh chiles are available. If you have a batch of fresh *ají amarillo* in your garden, this is a good way to extend their shelf life without drying them. If you prefer the paste to be milder, blanch them three times, changing the water each time, before blending. When refrigerated, it will keep for up to 1 week. You can also freeze the paste in ice cube trays and cover in plastic and it will last for several months.

    6 cups/50 fl oz (1.5 liters) water
    2 tablespoons white vinegar
    1 teaspoon sugar
    5 *ají amarillo*, halved and seeded
    1 tablespoon vegetable oil

Put the water, vinegar and sugar in a large pan, and bring to a boil. Once the water is boiling, add the chiles and let cook for 10 minutes once it returns to a boil.
    Drain and rinse under cold water for 5 minutes, or until cool. Pat dry and place in a blender with the vegetable oil. Blend for 2 minutes on medium speed or until it forms a smooth paste. Pass through a strainer (sieve) and into an airtight container.

Andean Chile Sauce

Uchucuta
Peru

Preparation time: 15 minutes
Cooking time: 5 minutes

Makes: 1 cup/
8 fl oz (250 ml)

In the Andes, chunky chile sauce *uchucuta* is made by grinding the ingredients on a *batán*, a flat grinding stone, or in a mortar and pestle. In its basic form it is prepared with just chiles and herbs, sometimes with a vegetable and a little bit of liquid like *chicha de jora* mashed in for texture and flavor. It's served alongside tubers or grilled meats. When refrigerated, it will keep for about 3 days.

    1 tablespoon *chicha de jora* (Corn Beer, page 388, for homemade) or vegetable oil
    ½ red onion, chopped
    4 garlic cloves, minced
    2 *rocoto* chiles, seeded and chopped
    1 tablespoon chopped cilantro (coriander)
    1 cup/1 oz (30 g) chopped *huacatay* (Peruvian black mint)
    1 cup/1 oz (30 g) chopped *chincho* leaves (a local herb, also called *culantrillo*; or use 15 g *huacatay*)
    ½ cup/2 oz (50 g) *queso fresco*
    1 cup/5 oz (150 g) peanuts, coarsely chopped
    salt

In a frying pan, heat the oil over medium heat, add the onion, garlic, and chiles, and sauté for 5 minutes. Add all the herbs, season with salt and place all the ingredients in a mortar with the *queso fresco* and peanuts. Grind into a coarse sauce.

Oaxacan Smoked Chile Paste

Chintextle
Mexico

Preparation time: 10 minutes
Cooking time: 2 minutes

Makes: 1½ cups/
13 fl oz (375 ml)

This nutritious, smoky paste can be spread over *tlayudas* or used as a rub for grilled meats. It will keep for about 2–3 weeks at room temperature, or up to 3 months in the refrigerator.

    10 *pasilla* chiles, seeded
    3 garlic cloves, peeled
    2 avocado leaves
    8 oz (225 g) dried shrimp (prawns)
    ½ cup/4 fl oz (120 ml) apple cider vinegar
    salt

In a *comal* or a dry frying pan over medium heat, roast the chiles, garlic, and avocado leaves for 2 minutes, stirring occasionally and without letting them burn. Place in a mortar and grind them well with the dried shrimp (prawns). Gradually add the vinegar until it reaches the desired consistency. Season with salt.

Bolivian Pepper Sauce

Spicy Peanut Sauce

Ají de maní
Colombia

Preparation time: 15 minutes
Cooking time: 20 minutes

※ ⊘ 🍵 ♡

Makes: 1½ cups/
13 fl oz (375 ml)

Popular in Popayán and Cali in southwestern Colombia, this spicy peanut sauce is used in tamales and with *Empanadas de pipián* (Potato and Peanut Empanadas, page 46). When refrigerated, it will keep for about 1 week.

    2 tablespoons vegetable oil
    2 scallions (spring onions), coarsely chopped
    ¼ cup/⅓ oz (10 g) cilantro (coriander) leaves
    ¾ cup/3 oz (90 g) toasted peanuts
    1 garlic clove, minced
    ¼ teaspoon annatto paste
    ½ teaspoon ground cumin
    1 tabasco or habanero chile, seeded and minced
    2 cups/16 fl oz (475 ml) water
    salt and ground pepper

Heat the oil in a frying pan over high heat. Add the scallions (spring onions) and cilantro (coriander) and cook for 7 minutes, stirring constantly. Add the mixture to a blender with the remaining ingredients, adding salt and pepper to taste, and blend for 1 minute on medium speed, or until it forms a smooth paste. Place the blended paste in a frying pan over low heat and simmer for 10 minutes. Place in a bowl and let cool.
    Serve cold.

Drunk Sauce

Salsa borracha
Mexico

Preparation time: 5 minutes
Cooking time: 10 minutes

※ 🍵 ⚱

Makes: 1 cup/
8 fl oz (250 ml)

The low-alcohol, fermented maguey sap called *pulque*, a drink of pre-Columbian origins, serves as the base of this table sauce, though you can replace with beer if unavailable. Either way the alcohol gets burned off. It's often served alongside *Barbacoa de borrego* (Lamb Barbacoa, page 332). When refrigerated, it will keep for up to 3 days.

    1 cup/8 fl oz (250 ml) *pulque*
    ¼ cup/2 fl oz (60 ml) orange juice
    4 *pasilla* chiles, seeded and coarsely chopped
    ½ white onion, chopped
    2 garlic cloves, roasted and chopped
    ¼ cup/2 fl oz (60 ml) water
    3 oz (80 g) *queso añejo* or *cotija*, crumbled
    salt

Place a small pan over medium heat with the *pulque* and orange juice. Add the chiles and cook for 10 minutes. Let cool.
    Blend the chiles and their cooking liquid, the onion, garlic, and water for 2 minutes on medium speed, or until smooth. Season with salt. Sprinkle the *queso añejo* over before serving.

Spicy Fruit Sauce

Chamoy 🍲
Mexico

Preparation time: 5 minutes
Cooking time: 15 minutes

※ ⊘ 🍵 ♡ ⚱

Makes: 2 cups/
16 fl oz (475 ml)

It's believed Chinese immigrants brought forms of making salted and pickled or dried fruits to Mexico, but in recent decades the country added chiles and turned it into something all its own. Much of the *chamoy* sold today is mass-produced candy or sauce; however, when it's made with care its uses are infinite. Use it as a glaze, drizzle it on fresh fruit, stir it into cocktails, or pour over shaved ice. When refrigerated, it will keep for up to 2 months in an airtight container.

    1 cup/5 oz (150 g) dried, salted ume plums
    (or use apricots)
    1 cup/1½ oz (40 g) dried hibiscus flowers
    3 tablespoons sugar
    ¼ cup/1 oz (30 g) ground *chile de árbol*
    ¼ cup/2 fl oz (60 ml) orange juice
    ½ cup/4 fl oz (120 ml) lime juice

Put the plums (or apricots) and hibiscus flowers in a pan. Add enough water to three-quarters cover the ingredients and bring to a boil. Reduce the heat and simmer for 10 minutes.
    Drain and place in a blender with the sugar and ground chile and blend for 1 minute on medium speed, until a smooth and sticky paste is formed.
    Place the paste in the pan and heat for 3 minutes. Add the orange and lime juices and stir well. Check the seasoning, adding salt to taste. Remove from the heat and let cool.
    Serve at room temperature.

Spicy Fruit Sauce

LISTA DE PRECIOS

Causa Ferreñafana	S/. 10.00
Cabrito Arroz con Frijol	S/. 10.00
Pepián de Pava	S/. 14.00
Arroz con Pato	S/. 12.00
Pato Arvejado	S/. 12.00
Ceviche de Toyo o Mixto	S/. 10.00
Espesado Lunes	S/. 8.00
Carne Seca	S/. 10.00

NOTA: Los Precios Incluyen I.G.V

Atendemos todos los días.

Gracias por su Visita

Glossary

Annatto:
The red seeds of the annatto tree (*Bixa orellana*), which grows in tropical parts of Central and South America and is also called achiote or *urucum*, are used to give food a red-orange color, as well as a nutty, peppery flavor. The seeds are ground into a powder and can be used directly in food, or infused into an oil or paste (such as *recado rojo*).

Antojitos:
Antojitos translates to "little cravings." They are casual snacks, most often eaten on a whim at markets and from street stalls, particularly in Mexico. It's a loose term though, and entire meals can be made up of *antojitos*. Corn masa, in the form of tortillas, tamales, or masa cakes like *gorditas*, is a connecting feature.

Arracacha:
A gnarled-shaped root crop that originated in the Andes. Its distinctive yellow, white, or purple roots have a sweet, nutty flavor when roasted or boiled. It's found under many regional names such as *apio*, *mandioquinha*, or *zanahoria blanca*.

Bijao:
A common term for several types of tropical plants in Central and South America, usually the *Calathea lutea*. Its large, waxy green leaves are used in a similar way to banana leaves to wrap foods like *juanes* or *patarashca*.

Cassareep:
A flavoring and preservation agent, cassareep is widely used in Guyanese cooking, most famously in pepperpot. The thick black liquid is made by reducing the juice of bitter cassava and mixing it with other spices such as cinnamon and clove.

Cassava:
Also called manioc or yuca (but not to be confused with yucca), this tropical and semi-tropical shrub that hails from western Brazil is widely cultivated in much of Latin America for its starchy, edible root. Aside from roasting, frying, or boiling it, cassava can be fermented to make drinks or sauces, or ground into flour to make breads, among other preparations.

– **Cassava flour:** Called *farinha* in Portuguese, cassava flour has a powdery texture and is mostly used for baking. It is grain- and gluten-free and can often be swapped in recipes calling for wheat flours.

– **Farofa:** Toasted cassava flour, sometimes mixed with corn (maize) flour and/or other ingredients like smoked meats or vegetables.

– **Tapioca:** The starch extracted from cassava roots, it's used for puddings or to make *beiju*, a flatbread that is often filled like a crepe in parts of Brazil.

Cecina:
Cecina is a general term for dried or cured meats that changes its exact definition by region. In South America, *cecina* generally refers to pork, while in Mexico and Central America, cecina might be made of pork or beef.

Chancaca:
Similar to panela, *chancaca* often refers to the sweet syrup made from the unrefined cane sugar in Peru, Chile, and Bolivia. It is often flavored with cinnamon and orange peels and is most often drizzled over fried sweets like *picarones* or *sopaipillas*.

Charqui:
Also spelled *charque* or *ch'arki*, this is a Quechua term for dried meat. Traditional preparations use llama meat or game, though beef or lamb are now common. It can be eaten as is or rehydrated in soups or stews. The term jerky is derived from this.

Chaya:
The nutritious green leaves of this fast-growing shrub, also called *chicasquil* or tree spinach, are widely consumed in much of Mexico and Central America. The leaves contain hydrocyanic acid, so must be cooked before eating.

Chayote:
Also known as *güisquil*, *chuchu*, or the mirliton squash, chayote is a light green, pear-shaped fruit that belongs to the gourd family Cucurbitaceae. Its crisp, edible flesh and skin are mild in flavor. They are eaten raw, much like cucumber, but can also be baked, stir-fried, or added to stews.

Cheeses:

– **Queijo coalho:** A firm, rennet cheese with an elastic texture used for grilling, from northeastern Brazil.

– **Queijo minas/mineiro:** Produced in the Brazilian state of Minas Gerais, *minas* cheese comes in three forms: fresh (*frescal*), half-aged (*meia-cura*), and aged (*curado*). The aged variety is the one most used for cooking, including in *pão de queijo*.

– **Quesillo:** Quesillo is a term that takes on different meanings throughout the region. In most cases, it refers to a soft white cheese. In Venezuela, however, it is a dessert, similar to *flan*.

– **Queso añejo:** A firm, salty, aged cheese typically made from skimmed goat's milk, though skimmed cow's milk has become quite common.

– **Queso blanco:** A general name for a white cheese, though most commonly the name refers to a mild tasting cheese that can range in consistency from soft to firm.

– **Queso chaqueño:** A semi-hard cow's milk cheese produced in Bolivia, sometimes called *queso benianco*.

– **Queso colonia:** A yellow medium hard cheese typical of Uruguay's Colonia department. Introduced by Swiss immigrants in the 1850s, it is similar to Gruyère and Emmental.

– **Queso cotija:** From Michoacán, Mexico, *cotija* is an aged, strong-flavored, salty cow's milk cheese with a granular texture. It's often sprinkled on dishes as a garnish, such as *elote*.

– **Queso cuajada/queijo coalhada:** Found in Colombia, Central America, and rural areas of Brazil, *cuajada* is a type of milk curd introduced to the region from the Iberian Peninsula. It's fresh, creamy, and has a mild flavor.

– **Queso de mano:** A variation of queso fresco made from a combination of cow's and ewe's milk curd that is typical in Venezuela.

– Queso duro: Hard, salty, dry-aged cheese from El Salvador that's often sold in large blocks and used mostly for crumbling or grating.

– Queso en capas: A mild, mozzarella-like white cheese from Mompox, Colombia, that is laid out in thin strips and then rolled in small squares that are sold by street vendors.

– Queso fresco: A versatile fresh cheese with a mild flavor made from cow's, or sometimes goat's, milk. It is produced throughout the region with subtle variations in flavor and texture. It can be crumbled, eaten fresh, or used to thicken sauces. Good substitutes include farmer's cheese and paneer.

– Queso llanero: A hard, salty, and white cow's milk cheese often used to top arepas and cachapas in Venezuela.

– Queso mantecoso: Translating as "buttery cheese," mantecoso is a soft, pale yellow cheese made from cow's milk that is primarily produced in southern Chile.

– Queso Oaxaca: White, semi-hard cheese from Oaxaca made from cow's milk with a texture similar to mozzarella or string cheese. It's sometimes called quesillo or queso asadero. It's prized for its ability to melt quickly and is used for quesadillas, tacos, and enchiladas.

– Queso palmita: A fresh, white, salty cheese similar to Oaxacan cheese that is produced in Venezuela's Zulia state, as well as in Costa Rica.

– Queso Paraguay/kesú paraguai: Widely used in Paraguayan cuisine, this soft cow's milk cheese has a mildly acidic flavor.

– Queso ranchero: A generic term for Mexican soft, curd-style fresh cheeses made from cow's and/or goat's milk.

– Queso seco: A hard, salty, fresh cheese typical of Central America that can be crumbled, grated, or fried.

Chicha de jora:
This low-alcohol corn beer has been prepared since the time of the Inca and remains widely consumed in the Andes. It's made by germinating jora corn, extracting the sugars, and then boiling the wort and letting it ferment for days in earthenware vessels. It has a cloudy, pale yellow appearance and sour taste and is often flavored with different fruits or spices. In Peru, it's often used for cooking in some recipes like sudados and adobos.

Chicharrón:
Called torresmo in Portuguese, chicharrón means fried pork in the most general definition of the term. Sometimes it refers to fried pork skin, while in some South American countries it signifies fried chunks of pork, usually with the skin and fat attached. In Bolivia, it refers to pork ribs cooked in their own fat.

Chiles:

– Ají amarillo: An orange chile that's widely used throughout the Andean region, especially in Peruvian cuisine. It has a bright, fruity flavor and heat that's roughly equivalent to a tabasco chile. Many recipes call for it in the form of paste, which can be store-bought or homemade, and it's often used in sauces. They can also be used raw, ground into a powder, or fried. When dried, they're called ají mirasol.

– Ají charapita: A pea-sized yellow chile from the Peruvian Amazon with a lot of heat and a distinct citrusy flavor. When used in sauces or ceviches, it's often mixed with the cocona fruit.

– Ají chombo: A very hot, red or yellow chile that resembles a habanero. It's native to Panama, though sometimes found elsewhere in Central America as ají panameño.

– Ají dulce: A general term for several varieties of small, sweet chiles found throughout Latin America. As the name suggest, they have a sweet, mild flavor.

– Ají panca: A deep-red, dried chile with a smoky, berry-like flavor with mild spice. It's grown on the coast of Peru and is often found as a paste and used for marinades, stews, or sauces.

– Ají limo: A very spicy chile that comes in a variety of colors (red, orange, yellow, green, white, purple, etc), most famously used raw for ceviches.

– Ancho: The dried form of the poblano chile. It has moderate-to-mild heat and a smoky flavor.

– Cascabel: A round, smooth, dark red chile with a mild flavor used for stews and sauces in Mexican cooking. When dried, the seeds rattle around inside.

– Cheiro: Very hot and fruity, cheiro are Brazilian chiles with a purple hue. They make for good substitutes for habanero or Scotch bonnet chiles.

– Chilacate: Common in Western Mexico, chilacate chiles are used either fresh or dried. They have a slightly sweet flavor and the heat ranges from mild to hot.

– Chilcostle: An increasingly rare red chile that's integral to several dishes from the Mixteca region in Oaxaca, such as mole colorado and mole amarillo. It has a fruity, nutty flavor and medium heat.

– Chile de árbol: Small, thin Mexican chiles that are very hot and used mostly for sauces.

– Chilhuacle/Chilcahuatle negro: The robust flavored chilhuacle is an essential chile in making Oaxaca's mole negro, giving the dish its distinctive flavor and color.

– Cobanero: An earthy, smoky, and fruity red chile from the Guatemalan city of Cobán that is used for the dish kak'ik, as well as in sauces and rubs.

– Costeño: In red and yellow forms, these hot Mexican chiles are used mostly for stews and sauces, especially moles.

– Guajillo: A dried, red chile with mild-to-medium heat, commonly used for sauces in central and northern Mexico. In Guatemala, a version from the central highlands is sometimes referred to as guaque.

– Güero: A hot and mildly sweet pale yellow or green chile from northern Mexico and the southwestern United States. In southeastern Mexico, it is called the xcatic chile.

– Habanero: Growing primarily in southern Mexico and parts of Central America, the habanero is very hot with a fruity flavor and flowery aroma. Ranging in color from yellow-orange to bright red, habaneros have a wide variety of cultivars, produced through selective breeding.

- Jiquitaia: An ancestral blend of chile peppers made by the Baniwa people in Brazil's Alto Rio Negro region in the northwest of the country. Very hot, it's used to flavor meats, fish, or stews.

- Malagueta: Heavily used in stews and sauces in the Brazilian state of Bahia, the small, thin, and red *malagueta* chile is extremely hot.

- Morita: Made from smoked, red jalapeño chiles. They are similar to chipotle peppers, though smoked for less time and with a fruitier flavor.

- Mulato: A mild-to-medium, brownish-black dried chile made from a variety of poblano chile that turns a deep red when mature. They are often used for moles and stews.

- Pasilla: The dried form of the long, thin *chilaca* chile. It has a mild-to-hot amount of heat and is used primarily in sauces. In Guatemala, it's called the *pasa* chile.

- Rocoto/locoto: Found throughout the Andes, the *rocoto* resembles a bell pepper with its thick walls and juicy interior, though it packs in a surprising amount of heat. They are rather versatile and can be used raw, blended into paste, baked, fried, or added to stews.

- Sambo/zambo: An earthy, smoky red chile from Alto Verapaz, Guatemala, used primarily for sauces.

- Serrano: Originating in the Mexican states of Puebla and Hidalgo, a fresh, usually green chile that resembles a small jalapeño but is hotter.

- Wiri wiri: A tiny, very hot chile that turns from green to yellow to red when mature. It's widely used in Guyanese cuisine.

Chipilín:
Used primarily in El Salvador, Guatemala, and southern Mexico, this leafy green is most often found in *pupusas*, tamales, or soups.

Chuño:
Ayamara and Quechua communities in the southern Andes make these freeze-dried potatoes by leaving them outside in the frigid air or letting them soak in cold streams, drying them in the sun, and stomping on them to release the moisture. The potatoes retain their nutrients and gain a shelf life that can extend for a decade, while losing their weight and allowing easy transportation. They can be rehydrated and eaten as is or ground into flour and used as a thickener in soups and stews.

- Papas amarillas: A general term for several varieties of potatoes with a yellow interior and rich texture. They are a signature ingredient of Peruvian recipes like *causa* and *papas a la Huancaína*.

- Papas coloradas: Small, reddish skinned potatoes from southern Colombia, used for stews and ground with peanuts, annatto, and other seasonings to make *pipián*.

- Papas secas: Cooked, cut, and sun-dried pieces of potato, often used for the dish *carapulcra*.

Comal: Usually a flat griddle typically used in Mexico and Central America for heating tortillas or to toast chiles and spices. Some versions are concave and made of *barro*, or natural untreated clay. They are similar to a Venezuelan *budare*, which are used to heat arepas.

Corn (maize) flour
In its most rudimentary definition, corn flour is finely ground dried corn kernels, called *harina de maíz* in most of Latin America. In the UK it's known as maize flour, while in the US it is sometimes labeled cornmeal or maize flour. However, there are countless variations of corn flour in the region and they are not interchangeable in most cases. Each has a unique purpose.

- Masa harina: Dough flour made by nixtamalizing dried corn to remove the germ and outer lining of the kernels before being ground. For Mexican recipes like corn tortillas, *sopes*, *gorditas*, or tamales, when not being made from fresh masa, you will likely want *masa harina*.

- Masarepa: Corn dough that is dried and ground into a precooked corn flour, used most often for making arepas and *cachapas* in Colombia and Venezuela.

- Maseca: A commercial version of instant corn flour, which can just be mixed with water to make the dough, or masa, for tortillas, tamales, *pupusas*, or *atoles*.

Crema mexicana:
A rich, mildly tangy cream with the consistency of crème fraîche. While they have subtle differences, it can generally be used interchangeably with Central American versions such as *crema salvadoreña* or *crema hondureña*.

Culantro:
A green herb with long serrated leaves similar in flavor to cilantro, but stronger and more aromatic. It's widely used in cooking in and around the Caribbean region and it can also be found by names like shadow beni and Mexican coriander. In parts of Peru, where cilantro is called culantro, it goes by the name *sacha culantro*.

Curtido:
A lightly fermented relish from El Salvador made from cabbage and sometimes onions, carrots, oregano, and chiles.

Dendê oil:
A thick, red-orange, strong-flavored oil extracted from the pulp of the African oil palm. It's widely used in the state of Bahía in northern Brazil.

Dulce de leche:
A sweet confection made by heating sweetened milk until it has a consistency similar to caramel sauce. Regional names, which may have slight variations in preparation, include *doce de leite*, *manjar blanco*, *arequipe*, and *cajeta*.

Epazote:
Called *paico* in the Andes and found in much of Latin America, epazote is a strong, distinctly flavored herb that can be used fresh or dry. It is known for its anti-flatulence properties and is often cooked with beans.

Guineos:
Unripe yellow bananas, which must be cooked to eat. Not to be confused with plantains, which have more starch.

Huacatay:
A strong, aromatic herb from the marigold family, native to the Peruvian Andes. Sometimes called black mint, it's most often used to flavor stews and sauces.

Huitlacoche:
Corn smut, the Mexican truffle. Farmers around the world consider the blueish fungus a pest, but in Mexico it is considered a delicacy for its mushroomy, earthy flavor. It is commonly added to tacos, tamales, and quesadillas.

Jícama:
A starchy root vegetable from Mexico with a mildly sweet flavor.

Jitomate:
In Mexico, red tomatoes are called either *jitomates* or *tomates* depending on the region you are in.

Longaniza:
A long, thin sausage made from minced pork and seasoned with black pepper. There are dozens of regional variations. For example, in Argentina and Uruguay aniseeds are added, while chiles are added to Mexican versions.

Linguiça:
A long, smoked pork sausage flavored with garlic and paprika that's common in Brazil.

Loroco:
An edible flower used in the cooking of El Salvador and Guatemala.

Maíz chulpe:
A special variety of corn used primarily to make *cancha*, or toasted corn kernels, in parts of South America.

Mashua:
Found primarily in Peru and Bolivia, *mashua* have a flavor and texture reminiscent of a turnip when cooked. When eaten raw, they have a spicy flavor and crunchy texture.

Merkén/merquén:
A ground pepper blend made from the *cacho de cabra* chile. It's a traditional condiment of the Mapuche people in Chile.

Metate:
A traditional Mesoamerican grinding stone used to treat grains and seeds, especially for making corn masa. They are typically made of porous volcanic stone, such as basalt or andesite.

Mexican oregano:
A herb with an earthy, citrusy flavor used in Mexican and Central American dishes. Unlike common oregano, it comes from the verbena family and therefore they are not interchangeable in recipes.

Mote:
Also called Andean hominy, it is made from several varieties of large-kernel corn that undergo the process of nixtamalization. It's eaten in dozens of preparations from Ecuador to Argentina.

Nopales:
The pads of the prickly pear cactus, which can be eaten raw or cooked.

Oca:
A small tuber native to the Andes that comes in a rainbow of different colors. It has a waxy texture and mildly sweet flavor. It's the second most commonly cultivated tuber in the Andes after potatoes.

Olluco/ullucu/papa lisa/melloco:
Eaten raw or cooked, *olluco* tubers come in a variety of shapes and sizes and bright colors. They have been cultivated in the Andes for several thousand years and they remain a staple crop, as do their healthy green leaves.

Panela/piloncillo/rapadura:
Unrefined whole cane sugar made by the boiling and evaporation of sugarcane juice. It's found under dozens of names and forms in many parts of Latin America.

Pepitas:
Hull-less seeds, from certain varieties of squash, that don't require shelling.

Pepitoria:
A powder of Mayan origin made by roasting and grinding squash seeds, used mostly in Guatemala and neighboring countries. It's used to thicken sauces or more as a spice, sprinkled on foods.

Pipián squash:
A variety of cucurbit commonly grown in parts of southern Mexico and Central America that is harvested when immature. It's sometimes called the cushaw pumpkin and is often used for stews or as a filling for *pupusas*.

Plantains:
Sometimes called green bananas, plantains are generally larger and have a thicker skin than the sweeter, more common yellow bananas. Starchy, they need to be cooked and can be used ripe or unripe.

Tamarillos/tomate de árbol/ sacha tomate:
An oval-shaped, deep-orange or yellow fruit native to the Andes that's sometimes called a tree tomato. They have an intense, complex flavor, a little bit sweet, and are often eaten raw or used for juices or sauces.

Tomatillos:
These are small green tomatoes, or husk tomatoes, which are sometimes called *tomates* in some parts of Mexico.

Tucupí:
A bright yellow-orange, acidic liquid made by extracting the liquid from peeled and grated cassava and then boiling it. It's mostly used in Amazonian regions and is a signature ingredient in recipes like *tacacá* and *pato no tucupí*. It is sold in plastic soda bottles in markets, though commercial forms are also available. When further reduced, it makes a black sauce called *tucupí preto* or *tucupí negro*.

Index

Author Acknowledgments

A book of this scale, which extends across so many borders, both political and geographical, would not be possible without the help of an immeasurable number of friends and colleagues from every part of the region.

Aside from Nick's atmospheric images, there was our photographer and frequent collaborator, Jimena Agois, who brought the recipes to life visually in a way few ever could.

Our team at Central and Mater Iniciativa, coming from the furthest corners of Latin America, were integral to the creation, adaptation, and testing of these recipes. First and foremost, Camila Chávez Vinatea, who lead the team in Peru, which included Ken Motohasi Herrera, Nicanor Vieyra, Bernabé Simón-Padrós, Carlos Valderrama, Luis Valderrama, Camila Unzueta, Valentino Galán Cortés, Santiago Fernandez, Luis Escobedo, Lorena Serrudo, Gal Chacin, Cesar Del Rio, Pedro Trujillo, Ignacio Linian, Braian Graneros, Laura Tibaquirá, Gustavo Castañeda, Ines Castañeda, Francisco Castillo, Rodrigo Mejía, Sofía Tertzakian, Rodrigo Cabrera, Hibett Antiporta, Jefferson Garcia, and Daniela Herrera, not to mention the dozens of others who were indirectly involved with their hard work in the kitchens of Central and Kjolle. Many also brought tablecloths, dinnerware, and glassware for photos (sometimes borrowed from their mothers). Also, special thanks to Martha Mora for her help with the introduction.

Then there are the hundreds of people we relied on for support in trying to understand the recipes, cultures, and landscapes from where they originated. Cooks and anthropologists, writers and cheesemakers, restaurateurs, and biologists. They collaborated through emails, phone calls, texts, in person, and on the ground— supporting during research and testing, plus the laborious task of helping us source many unusual ingredients for us to work with. We would need an entire extra book to name everyone.

Lastly, we also express our gratitude to everyone at Phaidon, especially Emily Takoudes, who continues to take a chance on us.

The recipes would not be what they are without the relentless efforts of Lisa Pendreigh, Sally Somers, and Caroline Stearns, while the design is thanks to the incredible work of Christopher Lawson and Marcos Villalba. Hélène Gallois Montbrun, Pedro Martin, and Baptiste Roque-Genest were also essential in helping us get the translations of the book into a form that we could all appreciate.

About the Authors

After cooking in prestigious restaurants around the world, renowned chef Virgilio Martínez returned to Lima in 2009 and opened Central. Since 2013 the restaurant has appeared on the World's 50 Best list and was named the #1 restaurant in Latin America multiple times. He is the co-founder of Mater Iniciativa, which documents the indigenous foods of Peru, and continues to expand its work into far flung locales like Tokyo and Moscow. Aside from his restaurants in Lima, he operates Mil above the terraces of Moray, an interdisciplinary space for research regarding Andean traditions and the hundreds of cultivars in the surrounding landscape, alongside the farming communities of Kacllaraccay and Mullaka's Misminay.

Mater Iniciativa is an interdisciplinary organization based in Peru, directed by Malena Martínez, that promotes megadiversity without borders. Their mission is to articulate knowledge through research, interpretation, and cultural expressions.

Writer and photographer Nicholas Gill travels extensively throughout Latin America and is the co-author of the Phaidon books *Central*, also with Virgilio Martínez, and *Slippurinn: Recipes & Stories from Iceland*, with Gísli Matt.

Photography Notes

Page 6: Women selling fruit in the port city of Cartagena, Colombia.
Page 8: The Salar de Uyuni, the world's largest salt flat, in Bolivia.
Page 10: Laguna Colorada, a shallow lake that is red from algae and minerals, in southwestern Bolivia.
Page 11: The wild, high altitude landscape of near the border of Bolivia and Chile.
Page 12: A relaxing swim in Salvador de Bahia in northern Brazil.
Page 13: The extremely arid conditions of the Atacama Desert in northern Chile result in slow growing plants with unique flavors found nowhere else, like rica rica and rosa del año.
Page 14: Kaieteur Falls, on the Potaro River in Guyana, is the world's largest single drop waterfall.
Page 15: The Solar do Unhão, a sixteenth-century complex that was once a distribution center for sugar produced from Bahian plantations in Brazil.
Page 16: A Guyanese woman selling bora, or yard long beans, at Stabroek Market in Georgetown, Guyana.
Page 18: The baking of pan de fiesta is a 500-year-old tradition in San Juan Totolac, Mexico.
Page 48: After the 1940s, Salvadoran migration turned the pupusa, once an obscure regional corn masa disc, into an international street food.
Page 60: Rice harvested by hand from a field on Panama's Azuero Peninsula.
Page 82: A Quechua farmer gathers potatoes from field near the village of Huatata in the Peruvian Andes.
Page 106: The preservation of heirloom corn varieties, like these in Peru's Urubamba Valley, are essential for the survival of Latin America's ancestral cuisines.
Page 144: In São Paulo, Brazil, a farmer tends to an intercropped field as part of a project to revive the forgotten flora and fauna of the Vale do Paraíba.
Page 170: African slaves destined for Brazil's sugar plantations were once auctioned in the Pelourinho section of Salvador de Bahia, one of the largest slave markets of the New World. Page 182: A woman sorts just-harvested bananas on a small island on Lake Nicaragua near Granada.
Page 198: Paria, a soft Andean cheese produced in the Ocongate District, for sale in Cuzco, Peru's San Pedro Market.
Page 210: On the Amazon River in the port area of Manaus, Brazil,

artisanal fishermen lay out their morning catch.

Page 246: The parrilla is an open fire hearth where various cuts of meat are cooked for an asado, or barbecue.

Page 274: Cured ham legs hanging in Montevideo, Uruguay's Mercado del Puerto.

Page 292: A chicken balances on a bench on the remote Pacific Coast of Colombia in Coqui.

Page 316: Chapulines, grasshoppers of the genus Sphenarium, are collected during Mexico's rainy season and sold by the scoop in markets around the country.

Page 328: A whole lamb low roasting on an iron cross beside a fire in the Uco Valley in Mendoza, Argentina.

Page 338: Calavera, or sugar skulls, are used to decorate the ofrendas of the deceased for Día de los Muertos in Mexico.

Page 376: A cart full of pineapples strolls the beach in Trancoso in northern Brazil.

Page 398: Chiles, like these in northern Brazil, serve as the foundation of recipes in nearly every part of Latin America.

Page 412: A menu plastered to the door of a typical restaurant in the northern Peruvian town of Ferreñafe.

Page 417: Summer in full bloom in outside of Pucón in Chile's Lakes District.

Recipe Notes

Flour is all-purpose (plain) flour, unless specified otherwise.

Sugar is white granulated sugar, unless specified otherwise.

Butter is unsalted butter, unless specified otherwise.

Milk is whole (full-fat) milk, unless specified otherwise.

Cream is fresh heavy (whipping) cream, unless specified otherwise.

Eggs are assumed to be US size large (UK size medium) and preferably organic and/or free-range, unless specified otherwise.

Black pepper is freshly ground, unless specified otherwise.

Sea salt is unrefined, unless specified otherwise.

Chocolate is bittersweet (dark) chocolate and with a minimum of 70% cocoa solids, unless specified otherwise.

Breadcrumbs are fresh unless specified otherwise.

Individual fruits and vegetables are assumed to be of medium size, unless specified otherwise, and should be peeled and/or washed, unless specified otherwise.

When the zest of a citrus fruit is used, always use unwaxed organic fruit.

Herbs are fresh herbs, unless specified otherwise.

All herbs, shoots, flowers, and leaves should be picked fresh from a clean source. Exercise caution when foraging for ingredients; any foraged ingredients should only be eaten if an expert has deemed them safe to eat. Mushrooms should be wiped clean.

Fish and shellfish are cleaned and gutted (and fish are filleted) before recipe preparation, unless specified otherwise.

When no quantity is specified for an ingredient—for example, oils for frying, herb for garnishing finished dishes—then quantities are discretionary and flexible.

Cooking and preparation times given are for guidance only, as individual ovens vary. If using a convection (fan) oven, follow the manufacturer's instructions concerning oven temperatures.

Exercise a high level of caution when following recipes involving any potentially hazardous activity. This includes the use of slaked lime, high temperatures and open flames, such as using a cook's blowtorch. In particular, when deep frying, slowly and carefully lower the food into the hot oil to avoid splashes, wear long sleeves to protect your arms, and never leave the pan unattended.

When deep-frying, heat the oil to the temperature specified, or until a cube of bread browns in 30 seconds. After frying, drain the fried foods on paper towels.

Exercise caution when making fermented products, ensuring all equipment is spotlessly clean, and seek expert advice if in any doubt.

When sterilizing jars or bottles for preserves, wash them in clean, hot soapy water and rinse thoroughly. Heat the oven to 275°F/140°C/120°C Fan/Gas Mark 1. Place the jars or bottles on a baking sheet and place in the oven to dry. Fill the jars or bottles while they are still hot and seal immediately.

Imperial and metric measurements, as well as volumetric cup measurements, are given for each recipe. Follow only one set of measurements throughout a recipe, and not a mixture, as they are not interchangeable.

All volumetric cup measurements given are level. Flour cup measures are spooned and leveled. Brown sugar cup measures are packed, while other dry ingredient measures are loosely packed.

All tablespoon and teaspoon measurements given are level, not heaping, unless otherwise stated.

1 teaspoon = 5 ml

1 tablespoon = 15 ml

Australian standard tablespoons are 20 ml, so any Australian readers are advised to use 3 teaspoons in place of 1 tablespoon when measuring small quantities.

Some recipes include uncooked or very lightly cooked eggs, meat, or fish. These should be avoided by the elderly, infants, pregnant women, convalescents, and anyone with an impaired immune system.

Phaidon Press Limited
2 Cooperage Yard
London E15 2QR

Phaidon Press Inc.
65 Bleecker Street
New York, NY 10012

phaidon.com

First published 2021
© 2021 Phaidon Press Limited

ISBN 978 1 83866 312 4
ISBN 978 1 83866 385 8 (Signed Edition)

A CIP catalogue record for this book is available from the British Library and the Library of Congress.

Commissioning Editor:
Emily Takoudes
Project Editor: Lisa Pendreigh
Production Controllers: Jane Harman and Rebecca Price
Artworker: Ana Teodoro

Designed by Villalba Lawson

Photography by Jimena Agois, except pages 6, 8, 10, 11, 12, 13, 14, 15, 16, 18, 48, 60, 82, 106, 144, 170, 182, 198, 210, 246, 274, 292, 316, 338, 376, 398 by Nicholas Gill.

Printed in China

The publisher would like to thank Vanessa Bird, Julia Hastings, Jo Ireson, Sarah Kramer, João Mota, Ellie Smith, Tracey Smith, Sally Somers, Caroline Stearns, and Emilia Terragni for their contributions to this book.